Sensorimotor Foundations of Higher Cognition

Attention and Performance

Sensorimotor Foundations of Higher Cognition

Attention and Performance XXII

Edited by

Patrick Haggard
Institute of Cognitive Neuroscience
University College London
London
UK

Yves Rossetti
INSERM, U864
Université Claude Bernard – Lyon, Hospices Civils de Lyon
Bron Cedex
FRANCE

Mitsuo Kawato
ATR Computational Neuroscience Laboratories
Kyoto
JAPAN

OXFORD
UNIVERSITY PRESS

OXFORD
UNIVERSITY PRESS

Great Clarendon Street, Oxford OX2 6DP

Oxford University Press is a department of the University of Oxford.
It furthers the University's objective of excellence in research, scholarship,
and education by publishing worldwide in

Oxford New York

Auckland Cape Town Dar es Salaam Hong Kong Karachi
Kuala Lumpur Madrid Melbourne Mexico City Nairobi
New Delhi Shanghai Taipei Toronto

With offices in

Argentina Austria Brazil Chile Czech Republic France Greece
Guatemala Hungary Italy Japan Poland Portugal Singapore
South Korea Switzerland Thailand Turkey Ukraine Vietnam

Oxford is a registered trade mark of Oxford University Press
in the UK and in certain other countries

Published in the United States
by Oxford University Press Inc., New York

A catalogue record for this title is available from the British Library

Data available

Library of Congress Cataloging in Publication Data

ISSN 1047–0387 Data available

Typeset by Cepha Imaging Private Ltd., Bangalore, India
Printed in Great Britain
on acid-free paper by
Biddles Ltd., King's Lynn, Norfolk, UK

ISBN 978-0-19-923144-7

10 9 8 7 6 5 4 3 2 1

Preface

Since its origins in the nineteenth century, progress in psychology has involved a balance of two elements. On the one hand, it has relied strongly on studies of primary processes of sensory input and motor output. In these areas, the classic scientific method of systematically manipulating input variables, and describing resulting changes in mental states, has proved relatively easy and extremely successful. In addition, the measurement of all types of psychological function has been aided by Helmholtz's early appreciation that transmission of neural signals takes readily measurable lengths of time. On this basis, processing delays provide an important measure for exploring sensory and motor function.

On the other hand, psychology aspired to give a scientific account of *all* mental life. William James, in particular, aimed for a scientific account of 'higher' mental functions that seem very far removed from sensory input and motor output, yet are evidently important in normal human experience. These higher aspects of cognition range from attention, to conceptual reasoning, to moral judgement, and seem to lie at the heart of what it is to be human.

How should this apparent mismatch between the classical methods of scientific psychology and its greater ambitions be reconciled? There are two broad possibilities. One view emphasizes the continuity between the two domains. There are no qualitative differences between sensorimotor processing and higher cognition, though there may be quantitative ones. On this view, explaining higher cognitive functions may simply require extending the same kind of neural processing that yields primary sensory and motor representations. The generalization of the reflex model to all brain functions at the end of the nineteenth century forms one example. Similarly, concept formation might be an extension of feature extraction in perceptual systems; planning complex sequences of behaviour might simply be a precocious form of motor preparation; mentalizing might simply involve sensorimotor simulation; language might simply involve extended speech acts. This principle of continuity receives support from studies of hierarchical information in sensory cortex, and from concepts of developmental trajectories first formulated in a comprehensive way by Piaget. It also fits with the general principle of cognition involving cortical associations between simpler representations.

A second, alternative view sees a clear dichotomy between primary representations and 'true' higher cognition; a qualitative discontinuity between feedforward sensory and motor processes and such functions as language, reasoning, mentalizing and so on. This view captures the idea that human cognition and human intelligence have benefited from a dramatic evolutionary change in neural organization. This change has enabled levels of abstraction and flexibility of internal representation not previously possible, and only loosely related to the basic neural input and output functions that may originally have stimulated their evolution. On this view, psychologists studying these higher representations need not be much concerned with the detailed form of inputs and outputs upon which those representations operate or from which they may ultimately derive.

A balanced resolution between these two positions remains a fundamental theoretical challenge for both psychology and neuroscience. The continuity view may have the merit of Occam's razor, and the attraction of reducing complex cognitions to simpler ones. But can the continuity view successfully capture the characteristic forms of information processing involved in higher cognitive function? This question lies squarely within the tradition of the Attention and Performance (A&P) series. Since its beginning, A&P has had a special focus on bottom-up processing, and on insights into cognition that can be achieved with rigorous experimental methods. For these reasons, we proposed to the Attention and Performance Association to organize the 2006 meeting on the topic "Sensorimotor Foundations of Human Cognition". The overarching aim of this meeting was to generate a debate between continuity and dichotomy views of human cognition, exploring how much of higher cognitive function can be explained by reduction to simpler sensorimotor processes. As a symbol of both the interconnection and the discontinuity between low level sensorimotor processes and higher level cognition, an art exhibition by Eric Sanchez presented matrices of close-up pictures of the artist's neck (See Figure 1). With this aim in view, we invited 65 leading psychologists, physiologists, neuroimagers and computational modelers to a meeting at Chateau de Pizay, Beaujolais, France, for 5 days during July 2006. This volume presents the written-up papers from the presentations at that meeting.

We chose a series of specific cognitive domains to explore the sensorimotor bases of human cognition. The structure of the book largely follows the same plan, with some reallocation of speakers to themes as seemed appropriate. The first section deals with the common neural bases for primary and 'cognitive' processes. Recent studies in animals and humans show that even primary areas may be activated in highly context-dependent ways, consistent with quite abstract representations. This session examined the key neural systems and computational architectures at the interface between cognition, sensation and action. The chapters provide a range of views defining whether sensorimotor toolboxes are a valuable guide to higher cognition, and, if so, how?

The second session of the meeting dealt with specific themes in abstract cognition: the origins of action, and the conceptual aspects of sensory, particularly somatosensory, processing. Here, a series of speakers dealt with the mental and neural processes of abstraction that are vital to the cognitive–sensorimotor interface. The papers in this section, on topics such as tool-use, bodily awareness and executive organization of action patterns, probe the extent to which principles of sensorimotor information-processing extend to further representations at further levels in the hierarchy.

The next section of the book deals with the representation of the self and others. The questions of self-consciousness and of attribution to other minds have a fundamental place, and a long history in psychology. At first sight, few aspects of cognition could seem more abstract, more refined than these. But recent research suggests that sensorimotor systems are good 'social levellers': your sensory and motor apparatus is much like mine. Can people vicariously experience the sensory and motor events of other individuals?

What aspects of social representation are explained by sensorimotor sharing, and what are not? The chapters in this section offer strongly contrasting perspectives. Some place sensorimotor simulation at the heart of mental life and social interaction, while others adopt a strongly propositional account. This section of the book also houses the 2006 Attention and Performance Association lecture by Marc Jeannerod, in which he develops a novel approach to the self and social representation based on spatial sensorimotor transformation. This seems particularly appropriate, since his career in neuroscience has spanned a range of topics from object-oriented actions to social cognition.

The final section of the book deals with upper limits of cognition: the most abstract and conceptual levels of thought, including action syntax, language, and consciousness. Symbolic thought is often treated as a dramatic cognitive gear-change, and the heart of true intelligence. These papers investigate which aspects, if any, of such concepts as time, space, identity and number may be linked to representations of basic sensory and motor events.

Taken as a whole, we believe that the chapters in the book provide a strong overview and re-examination of the sensorimotor foundations of human cognition. While we do not feel able to draw a single overall conclusion on whether the continuity or the dichotomy view is most appropriate, we feel that the work presented here at least identifies the extent of the challenge for general psychological theories that start with input and output. We hope that our readers will appreciate both the generality and theoretical importance of the question.

This meeting and this book could not have happened without the help of many individuals and groups of people. We are grateful above all to the Attention and Performance Association for giving us the opportunity to organize the meeting, and particularly to Nancy Kanwisher for advice and support at several stages in the development of the project. The Attention and Performance Association, ATR, INSERM, Institut Fédératif des Neurosciences de Lyon, Région Rhône Alpes (Cluster programme Handicap, Vieillissement, Neurosciences), Lyon University, Pôle Rhône-Alpes de Sciences Cgnitives, Hospices Civils de Lyon and Elsevier NV all gave generous financial support. In addition to the invited papers forming this book, several younger researchers attended the meeting. Their participation, discussion and poster presentations were also much appreciated. We also thank Jody Culham, David Rosenbaum, Pierre Jacob, Marc Jeannerod and Wolfgang Prinz for chairing sessions at the meeting. We are grateful to Michelle Soulier for preparing the programme and the meeting, and to Rosalyn Lawrence for organizing the collection and reviewing of manuscripts. Finally, we would like to thank Oxford University Press, and Martin Baum in particular, for help with editing and production of the volume.

Patrick Haggard
Yves Rossetti
Mitsuo Kawato

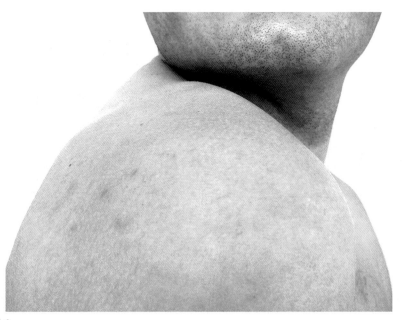

Figure 1

Figure 2: Garden of the Chateau de Pizay

Contents

Section 3 **Self and Other**

Section 4 **Conceptual and Symbolic Thought**

The Attention and Performance Symposia

Since the first was held in The Netherlands in 1966, the Attention and Performance Symposia have become an established and highly successful institution. They are now held every 2 years, in a different country. The original purpose remains: to promote communication among researchers in experimental cognitive psychology and cognate areas working at the frontiers of research on 'attention, performance and information processing'. The format is an invited workshop-style meeting, with plenty of time for papers and discussion, leading to the publication of an edited volume of the proceedings.

The International Association for the Study of Attention and Performance exists solely to run the meetings and publish the volume. Its Executive Committee selects the organizers of the next meeting, and develops the program in collaboration with them, with advice on potential participants from an Advisory Council of up to 100 members. Participation is by invitation only, and the Association's Constitution requires participation from a wide range of countries, a high proportion of young researchers, and a substantial injection of new participants from meeting to meeting.

Held usually in a relatively isolated location, each meeting has four and a half days of papers presented by a maximum of 26 speakers, plus an invited Association Lecture from a leading figure in the field. There is a maximum of 65 participants (including the current members of the executive committee and the organizers). There are no parallel sessions, and all participants commit themselves to attending all the sessions. There is thus time for substantial papers followed by extended discussion, both organized and informal, and opportunities for issues and ideas introduced at one point in the meeting to be returned to and developed later. Speakers are encouraged to be provocative and speculative, and participants who do not present formal papers are encouraged to contribute actively to discussion in various ways, for example as formal discussants, by presenting a poster, or as contributors to scheduled discussion sessions. This intensive workshop atmosphere has been one of the major strengths and attractions of these meetings. Manuscript versions of the papers are refereed anonymously by other participants and external referees and published in a high-quality volume edited by the organizers, with a publication lag similar to many journals. Unlike many edited volumes, the Attention and Performance series reaches a wide audience and has considerable prestige. Although not a journal, it is listed in journal citation indices with the top dozen journals in experimental psychology. According to the Constitution, 'Papers presented at meetings are expected to describe work not previously published, and to represent a substantial contribution ...' Over the years, contributors have been willing to publish original experimental and theoretical research of high quality in the volume, and this tradition continues.

A and P review papers have also been much cited. The series has attracted widespread praise in terms such as 'unfailingly presented the best work in the field' (S. Kosslyn, Harvard), 'most distinguished series in the field of cognitive psychology' (C. Bundesen, Copenhagen), 'held in high esteem throughout the field because of its attention to rigor, quality and scope . . . indispensable to anyone who is serious about understanding the current state of the science' (M. Jordan, MIT), 'the books are an up to the minute tutorial on topics fundamental to understanding mental processes' (M. Posner, Oregon).

In the early days of the Symposium, when the scientific analysis of attention and performance was in its infancy, thematic coherence could be generated merely by gathering together the most active researchers in the field. More recently, experimental psychology has ramified, 'cognitive science' has been born, and converging approaches to the issues we study have developed in neuroscience. Participation has therefore become interdisciplinary, with neuroscientists, neuropsychologists, and computational modelers joining the experimental psychologists. Each meeting now focuses on a restricted theme under the general heading of 'attention and performance'. Recent themes include: Synergies in Experimental Psychology: Artificial Intelligence and Cognitive Neuroscience (USA, 1990); Conscious and Unconscious Processes (Italy, 1992); Integration of Information (Japan, 1994); Cognitive Regulation of Performance: Interaction of Theory and Application (Israel, 1996); and Control of Cognitive Processes (UK, 1998); Common Processes in Perception and Actions (Germany, 2000); and Functional Brain Imaging of Visual Cognition (Italy, 2002).

Authors and Participants

Céline Amiez
Cognitive Neuroscience Unit
Montreal Neurological Institute
McGill University
Montreal
Quebec, Canada

Dominic J. Barraclough
Department of Brain and Cognitive
Sciences
Center for Visual Science
University of Rochester
Rochester, NY, USA

Paul M. Bays
Institute of Cognitive Neuroscience
University College London
London, UK

Harold Bekkering
Nijmegen Institute for Cognition and
Information
University of Nijmegen
Nijmegen, The Netherlands

Ariane Bazan
Department of Psychoanalysis
University of Ghent
Ghent, Belgium

Anna Berti
Psychology Department and
Neuropsychology Research Group
University of Turin
Turin, Italy

Geoffrey Bird
Department of Psychology
ESRC Centre for Economic Learning and
Social Evolution
University College London
London, UK

James W. Bisley
Center for Neurobiology and Behavior
Columbia University College of Physicians
and Surgeons and
New York State Psychiatric Institute
New York, NY
USA

Annabelle Blangero
Espace et Action
INSERM, U864
Université Claude Bernard-Lyon
Hospices Civils de Lyon
Bron, France

D. Boisson
Hôpital Henry Gabrielle
Hospices Civils de Lyon
Saint Genis Laval
France

Marcel Brass
Department of Experimental Psychology
Ghent University
Ghent, Belgium

Claudio Brozzoli
Espace et Action
INSERM, U864,
Université Claude Bernard-Lyon
Hospices Civils de Lyon
Bron, France

Sophie Courtois-Jacquin
Hôpital Henry Gabrielle
Hospices Civils de Lyon
Saint Genis Laval
INSERM, U864,
Université Claude, Bernard-Lyon
France

Laila Craighero
Department of Human Physiology
University of Ferrara
Ferrara, Italy

Gergely Csibra
Centre for Brain and Cognitive
Development
School of Psychology
Birkbeck, University of London
London, UK

James Danckert
Department of Psychology
University of Waterloo
Waterloo
Ontario, Canada

Stanislas Dehaene
INSERM, U562
Service Hospitalier Frédéric Joliot
Orsay, France

Jan Peter de Ruiter
Max Planck Institute for
Psycholinguistic
Nijmegen, The Netherlands

Luciano Fadiga
Department of Human Physiology
University of Ferrara
Ferrara, Italy

Alessandro Farnè
Espace et Action
INSERM, U864
Université Claude Bernard-Lyon
Hospices Civils de Lyon
Bron, France

Patrik Fazio
Department of Human Physiology
University of Ferrara
Ferrara, Italy

Valerie Gaveau
Espace et Action
INSERM, U534
Université Claude Bernard-Lyon
Hospice Civils de Lyon
Bron, France

Angela Gee
Center for Neurobiology and Behavior
Columbia University College of Physicians
and Surgeons and
New York State Psychiatric Institute
New York
NY, USA

Michael E. Goldberg
Center for Neurobiology & Behavior
Columbia University College of Physicians
and Surgeons and
New York State Psychiatric Institute
New York
NY, USA

Jacqueline Gottlieb
Center for Neurobiology and Behavior
Columbia University College of Physicians
and Surgeons and
New York State Psychiatric Institute
New York
NY, USA

Scott T. Grafton
Department of Psychology
University of California Santa Barbara
Santa Barbara, CA
USA

Patrick Haggard
Institute of Cognitive Neuroscience
University College London
London
UK

Peter Hagoort
F. C. Donders Centre for Cognitive
Neuroimaging
Radboud University Nijmegen
The Netherlands

Antonia F de C Hamilton
Department of Psychological
and Brain Sciences
Dartmouth College
Hanover, NH
USA

Cecilia Heyes
Department of Psychology
ESRC Centre for Economic
Learning and Social Evolution
University College London
London, UK

Nicholas P. Holmes
Espace et Action, INSERM, U864
Université Claude Bernard-Lyon
Hospices Civils de Lyon
Saint Genis Laval,
Bron, France

Anna Ipata
Center for Neurobiology and Behavior
Columbia University College of Physicians
and Surgeons and
New York State Psychiatric Institute
New York
NY, USA

Marc Jeannerod
Institut des Sciences Cognitives
Bron, France

Jean-Paul Joseph
INSERM, U846
Stem Cell and Brain Research Institute
Department of Integrative Neuroscience
Bron, France

Claudia Kalinich
Max Planck Institute for Human
Cognitive and Brain Sciences
Department of Cognitive Neurology
Leipzig Germany

Mitsuo Kawato
ATR Computational
Neuroscience Laboratories
Kyoto, Japan

Shigeru Kitazawa
Department of Neurophysiology
Juntendo University Graduate
School of Medicine
Tokyo, Japan

Thomas Klos
Zentrum für Neurologie und
neurologische Rehabilitation (ZNR)
Klinikum am Europakanal
Erlangen, Germany

Etienne Koechlin
INSERM
Université Pierre et Marie Curie
Paris, France

Elisabetta Làdavas
Dipartimento di Psicologia
Università degli Studi
di Bologna
Italy

Daeyeol Lee
Department of Neurobiology
Yale University School
of Medicine
New Haven, CT
USA

Dorothée Legrand
CREA, Centre de Rechercheen
Epistémologie Appliquée
Paris, France

Oliver Lindemann
Nijmegen Institute for Cognition and
Information
University of Nijmegen
Nijmegen, The Netherlands

Jacques Luauté
Hôpital Henry Gabrielle
Hospices Civils de Lyon
Espace et Action, INSERM, U864
Université Claude Bernard-Lyon
Saint Genis Laval, France

Shunjiro Moizumi
Department of Neurophysiology
Juntendo University Graduate School of
Medicine
Tokyo, Japan

Matthijs L. Noordzij
F. C. Donders Centre for
Cognitive Neuroimaging
Radboud University Nijmegen
The Netherlands

Sarah Newman-Norlund
F. C. Donders Centre for Cognitive
Neuroimaging
Radboud University Nijmegen
The Netherlands

Ayami Okuzumi
Department of Neurophysiology
Juntendo University Graduate
School of Medicine
Tokyo, Japan

Lorenzo Pia
Psychology Department and
Neuropsychology Research Group
University of Turin
Turin, Italy
and
Institute of Cognitive Neuroscience
University College London, London, UK

Laure Pisella
Espace et Action
INSERM, U846
Université Claude Bernard-Lyon
Hospices Civils de Lyon
Bron, France

Emmanuel Procyk
INSERM, U846
Stem Cell and Brain Research Institute
Department of Integrative
Neuroscience
Bron, France

Roméo Quilodran
INSERM, U846
Stem Cell and Brain Research Institute
Department of Integrative
Neuroscience
Bron, France

Marco Rabuffetti
Centro di Bioingegneria
Fondazione don Gnocchi IRLSS
Milan, Italy

Patrice Revol
Hôpital Henry Gabrielle
Hospices Civils de Lyon
Espace et Action
INSERM, U864
Université Claude Bernard-Lyon
Saint Genis Laval
France

Tony Ro
Psychology Department
Rice University
Houston
Texas, USA

Gilles Rode
Hôpital Henry Gabrielle
Hospices Civils de Lyon
Espace et Action
INSERM, U864
Université Claude Bernard-Lyon
Saint Genis Laval, France

Yves Rossetti
Espace et Action
INSERM, U864
Université Claude Bernard – Lyon,
Hospices Civils de Lyon
Bron, France

Alice Catherine Roy
Institut des Sciences Cognitives
Bron, France

Perrine Ruby
INSERM, U821
Brain Dynamics and Cognition
Bron Cedex, France

Raffaella I. Rumiati
Cognitive Neuroscience Sector
Scuola Internazionale Superiore di Studi
Avanzati
Trieste, Italy

Matthew F. S. Rushworth
Department of Experimental Psychology
University of Oxford
Oxford, UK

Fumine Saito
Department of Neurophysiology
Juntendo University Graduate School of
Medicine
Tokyo, Japan

Roméo Salemme
Espace et Action
INSERM, U864
Université Claude Bernard-Lyon
Hospices Civils de Lyon
Bron, France

Rebecca Saxe
Department of Brain and Cognitive Sciences
Massachusetts Institute of Technology
Cambridge, MA
USA

Ricarda I. Schubotz
Department of Cognitive Neurology
Max Planck Institute for Human
Cognitive and Brain Sciences
Leipzig, Germany

Natalie Sebanz
Psychology Department
Rutgers University
Newark, NJ
USA

Hyojung Seo
Department of Neurobiology
Yale University School of Medicine
New Haven, CT
USA

Satoshi Shibuya
Department of Integrative Physiology,
Kyorin University School of Medicine
Tokyo, Japan

Maggie Shiffrar
Psychology Department
Rutgers University
Newark, NJ
USA

Lucia Spinazzola
Dipartimento di Psicologia
Università di Torino
Torino, Italy

Christopher Striemer
Department of Psychology
University of Waterloo
Waterloo, Ontaro
Canada

Toshimitsu Takahashi
Department of Neurophysiology
Juntendo University Graduate School of
Medicine
Tokyo, Japan

Alessia Tessari
Department of Psychology
University of Bologna
Bologna, Italy

Ivan Toni
F. C. Donders Centre for Cognitive Imaging
Radboud University Nijmegen
Nijmegen, The Netherlands

Manos Tsakiris
Institute of Cognitive Neuroscience
University College London
London, UK

Michiel van Elk
Nijmegen Institute for Cognition and
Information
University of Nijmegen
Nijmegen, The Netherlands

Hein T. van Schie
Nijmegen Institute for Cognition and
Information
University of Nijmegen
Nijmegen, The Netherlands

D. Yves von Cramon
Max Planck Institute for Human
Cognitive and Brain Sciences
Department of Cognitive Neurology
Leipzig, Germany

Makoto Wada
Department of Neurophysiology
Juntendo University Graduate School of
Medicine
Tokyo, Japan

Mark E. Walton
Department of Experimental Psychology
University of Oxford
Oxford, UK

Daniel M. Wolpert
Department of Engineering
University of Cambridge
Cambridge, UK

Shinya Yamamoto
Neuroscience Research institute
National Institute of Advanced Industrial
Science and Technology
Tokyo, Japan

1. Mitsuo Kawato
2. Hiroshi Imamizu
3. Daeyeol Lee
4. Emmaneul Procyk
5. Yves Rossetti
6. Michael E. Goldberg
7. Anna Berti
8. Nancy Kanwisher
9. Raffaella I Rumiati
10. Rebecca Saxe
11. Daniel M. Wolpert
12. Silke Göbel
13. Annabelle Blangero
14. Jacinta O'shea
15. Shigeru Kitazawa
16. Manabu Honda
17. Marc Jeannerod
18. Claudio Brozzoli
19. Simone Bosbach
20. Jane Raymond

21. Frédérique De Vignemont
22. Gergely Csibra
23. Francesco Pavani
24. Antonia F. de C. Hamilton
25. Alessandro Farnè
26. Shbana Raham
27. Yann Coello
28. David Rosenbaum
29. Dorothée Legrand
30. Cecilia Heyes
31. Ivan Toni
32. Jody Culham
33. Ricarda I. Schubotz
34. Perrine Ruby
35. Marcel Brass
36. Berhard Hommel
37. Wolfgang Prinz
39. Patrick Haggard
40. Manos Tsakiris

41. Mariano Sigman
42. Luciano Fadiga
43. Harold Bekkering
44. Lorenzo Pia
45. Floris De Lange
46. Matthijs L. Noordzij
47. Nicholas P. Holmes
48. John Driver
49. Patric Bach
50. Søren Kyllingsbæk
51. Hein T. van Schie
52. Natalie Sebanz
53. Ariane Bazan
54. Geoffrey Bird
55. Claus Bundesen
56. Mark Johnson
57. Uta Wolfensteller
58. Pierre Jacob
59. Matthew Rushworth

Section 1

Sensorimotor Toolboxes

On the agnosticism of spikes: salience, saccades, and attention in the lateral intraparietal area of the monkey

Angela Gee, Anna Ipata, James W. Bisley,
Jacqueline Gottlieb and Michael E. Goldberg

Neural activity in the lateral intraparietal area (LIP) has been associated with attention to a location in visual space, and with the intention to make saccadic eye movement, and a debate has arisen as to whether the parietal cortex is predominantly involved in the generation of attention or intention. In the experiments described here we show first that the LIP predicts a monkey's attention on a millisecond-by-millisecond basis, and is absolutely independent from saccade planning when there is a conflict between the goal of a planned saccade and the locus of attention. We then show that the activity of LIP predicts the goal and latency of saccades in a free-viewing visual search task, but also contains information about the nature of the stimulus in the receptive field even when the monkey makes a saccade away from the receptive field. We suggest that the activity in LIP provides a salience map which is interpreted by the oculomotor system as a saccade goal when a saccade is appropriate, and simultaneously is used by the visual system to determine the locus of attention. This salience map is created by the summation of a number of different signals, but the genesis of the spikes is irrelevant to the recipient areas, which is why the saccadic system can use the abrupt onset of a visual stimulus to drive the eye, and the visual system can pin attention to the goal of a memory-guided saccade.

Key words: lateral intraparietal area, saccade, attention, contrast sensitivity and monkey

Introduction

The physiological role of posterior parietal cortex in the generation of behavior in the monkey has been the subject of controversy for decades. Early studies argued for the importance of parietal activity in motor commands (Hyvarinen and Poranen, 1974; Mountcastle *et al.*, 1975; Lynch *et al.*, 1977) and visual attention (Robinson *et al.*, 1978; Bushnell *et al.*, 1981). More recent studies have concentrated on one area, the lateral intraparietal area (LIP), which was defined on the basis of its connections to the lateral pulvinar and the superior colliculus (Asanuma *et al.*, 1985). Different studies have suggested that LIP has activity correlating with saccadic intention (Gnadt and Andersen, 1988;

Barash *et al.*, 1991a,b; Colby *et al.*, 1996; Snyder *et al.*, 1997), visual attention (Colby *et al.*, 1996; Gottlieb *et al.*, 1998; Bisley and Goldberg, 2003), expected value (Sugrue *et al.*, 2004), perceptual (Shadlen *et al.*, 2001; Roitman and Shadlen, 2002) or economic (Platt and Glimcher, 1999; Dorris and Glimcher, 2004) decision-making, perceived motion (Assad and Maunsell, 1995; Williams *et al.*, 2003), time representation (Leon and Shadlen, 2003; Janssen *et al.*, 2005) and stimulus shape (Sereno and Maunsell, 1998). LIP also has activity that seems uncorrelated with attention (Platt and Glimcher, 1997; Snyder *et al.*, 1997) and independent of saccadic eye movement (Powell and Goldberg, 2000; Bisley and Goldberg, 2003).

LIP is reciprocally connected to both the dorsal and ventral cortical visual streams (Seltzer and Pandya, 1984; Neal *et al.*, 1988) as well as to oculomotor areas such the frontal eye fields and superior colliculus (Asanuma *et al.*, 1985; Andersen *et al.*, 1990a; Schall *et al.*, 1995). Consistent with these connections, most neurons in LIP respond to visual stimuli, but many also give a burst around the time of an eye movement (Barash *et al.*, 1991b). In addition, many of the neurons are also active in the delay period of a memory-guided saccade. In this task the animals have to remember the location of a flashed target that indicates the goal of the upcoming eye movement. It is precisely because these neurons share these response characteristics that interpreting a unifying role has been difficult.

In this chapter we describe two sets of experiments. One demonstrates that neural activity in LIP correlates with a monkey's visual attention and can absolutely be separated from the planning or generation of saccades (Bisley and Goldberg, 2003, 2006). The other demonstrates that under conditions of free visual search, neural activity in LIP predicts not only the goal of a saccade but its latency (Ipata *et al.*, 2006a). We propose that LIP represents a salience map which can be used by both the oculomotor system to choose a saccade goal when a saccade is appropriate, and by the visual system to determine the locus of visual attention. Thus, rather than serving a dedicated function, the same signal can serve as an intention or attention signal, depending on the recipient area and the behavioral context. Furthermore, the genesis of the spikes is irrelevant to their interpretation. Spikes evoked by the abrupt onset of a visual stimulus can drive saccades, and spikes evoked by the plan for a memory-guided delayed saccade can drive visual attention.

LIP activity can be dissociated from saccade planning but not from attention

It is clear that neurons in LIP do not respond identically to all visual stimuli. Instead, the visual response of these neurons is modulated by the behavioral significance of the stimulus (Colby *et al.*, 1996). Thus when a monkey makes a saccade that brings a behaviorally irrelevant stable stimulus (e.g. a stimulus that has not recently appeared in the environment but instead, like the architectural features of the room in which the reader is reading this chapter, is stable and unchanging) onto the receptive of a neuron, the response of LIP neurons is weak. Conversely, when the monkey makes a saccade that brings a behaviorally relevant stimulus, for example a pending saccade target, or a recently flashed stimulus, onto the receptive field, the neurons discharge more intensely (Gottlieb *et al.*, 1998). If LIP were primarily to have a saccade-planning function, then in a similar way neurons in LIP should filter out irrelevant stimuli that are not the targets for saccades. Once the monkey was committed to a given saccade a stimulus appearing far away from the saccade goal should evoke a weaker response than a stimulus at the saccade goal. When we tested this hypothesis, we found the contrary result: neurons in LIP gave *enhanced* responses to task-irrelevant distractors that appeared away from the goal of a memory-guided saccade (Powell and Goldberg, 2000).

It is well known that in humans there is an attentional advantage at the goal of a saccade (Kowler *et al.*, 1995; Deubel and Schneider, 1996). There is also an attentional advantage at the site of an abruptly appearing stimulus (Yantis *et al.*, 1984). One logical way of interpreting our demonstration of an enhanced response to a stimulus that appears away from the goal of a planned memory-guided saccade is that the activity represents an attentionally salient object in the visual field.

We then designed an experiment in which we examined how a monkey's attention was affected by saccade planning and the abrupt onset of task-irrelevant stimuli (Bisley and Goldberg, 2003). Three methods have been used to describe the locus of attention: a post-hoc method which says that if a subject responds to a stimulus it must have attended to it (Goldberg and Wurtz, 1972); a reaction time method, defining the locus of spatial attention as the area of the visual field in which the response to a discriminandum has the lowest latency (Posner, 1980; Bowman *et al.*, 1993); and a contrast sensitivity method, which defines the spatial locus of attention as that area of the visual field with enhanced visual sensitivity (Bashinski and Bacharach, 1980). We chose to use the latter since it allows us to examine how attention changes over time and under different visual conditions. In addition, it allows us to rule out the possibility that any attentional advantage may be on the motor side of the response, a problem present when defining attention by changes in reaction time.

Our first problem was to establish that in the monkey, like in the human, attention is pinned at the goal of a saccade. Our task had two components: the monkeys had to plan a saccade to a remembered location and later had to discriminate the orientation of a probe stimulus (Figure 1.1). On any given day we used four possible saccade targets, which were symmetric across the horizontal and vertical meridians. The probe stimulus consisted of three circle distractors and a Landolt ring whose gap could be on the right or on the left. The orientation of the Landolt ring instructed the monkey either to cancel (gap on right) or to execute (gap on left) the planned saccade when the fixation spot disappeared. We used the contrast sensitivity of the probe to measure attention, by comparing the sensitivity at different spatial locations during the task. We measured the animal's GO/NOGO discrimination performance at a number of contrasts and calculated the contrast threshold, which we defined as the contrast at which the animal could correctly discriminate the probe in 75% of the trials. The animal's performance was better when the probe appeared at the saccade goal than when it appeared elsewhere (Figure 1.2).

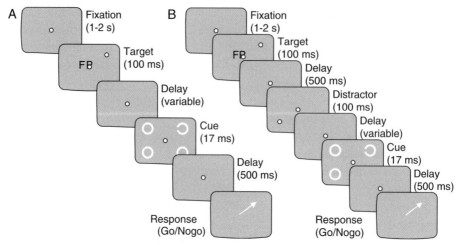

Figure 1.1 Psychophysical attention task. (**A**) The monkeys began the trial by fixating a small spot (FP), After a short delay a second spot (the target) appeared for 100 ms at one of four possible positions equidistant from the fovea and evenly distributed throughout the four visual quadrants. The exact target locations varied from day to day, to prevent long-term perceptual learning. This target specified the goal for the memory-guided saccade that the monkey would have to make unless the probe told it otherwise. At some time after the target disappeared, a Landolt ring (the probe) and three complete rings of identical luminance to the probe flashed for one video frame (~17 ms) at the four possible saccade target positions. Five hundred milliseconds after the probe the fixation point disappeared, and the animals had to indicate the orientation of the Landolt ring by either maintaining fixation for 1000 ms (when the gap was on the right—a NOGO trial) or making a saccade to the goal and remaining there for 1000 ms (when the gap was on the left—a GO trial). The Landolt ring could appear at any of the four positions. The luminance of the rings varied from trial to trial, changing the contrast between the probe and the background. (**B**) In half of the trials a task-irrelevant distractor, identical to the target, was flashed 500 ms after the target either at or opposite the saccade goal. Reproduced with permission from Bisley and Goldberg (2003).

To enable us to compare the thresholds and enhancements measured on different days, we normalized the data from each day, although all statistical comparisons were performed on the prenormalized data. The normalizing factor for each delay from each session was the threshold from trials in which the probe was not at the saccade goal (i.e. the threshold from the right-hand function in Figure 1.2A). The attentional advantage at the saccade goal, illustrated by the enhanced sensitivity, was significant throughout the task ($p < 0.05$ by paired t-test): we used stimulus onset asynchronies (SOAs) from the saccade target to probe of 800, 1300 and 1800 ms, and found enhanced performance in both animals for all SOAs that we studied. Figure 1.2B shows the normalized contrast thresholds for each monkey at each SOA. In keeping with the human studies we define the attentional advantage as this lowering of threshold at the saccade goal. We assume that the equally high thresholds for the probe at other locations represent the monkey's performance at loci to which attention has not been allocated by the endogenous process of the saccade plan.

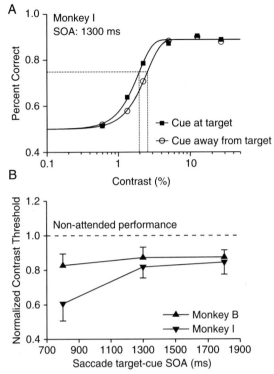

Figure 1.2 Effect of saccade planning on perceptual threshold. (**A**) Psychometric functions from monkey I from trials with a target-probe stimulus-onset asynchrony (SOA) of 1300 ms. The solid squares are from trials in which the probe was at the location of the target, the hollow circles are from trials in which the probe was not at the saccade goal. The data are pooled results from 22 sessions (~800 trials per point). The performance from the two conditions was significantly different on the slopes of the functions ($p < 0.01$, χ^2-test at each contrast). The solid lines were fitted to the data with a Weibull function, weighted by the number of trials at each point, using the maximum likelihood method programmed in Matlab. (**B**) Normalized contrast thresholds for the three SOAs from the two monkeys when the probe was at the location of the saccade goal (solid triangles). Data for each delay were normalized by the performance at that delay when the probe was not at the saccade goal (illustrated by the dashed line). Points significantly beneath the dashed line show attentional enhancement, and all points were significant when tested with paired t-test comparing the prenormalized performance when the probe was at the saccade goal with the prenormalized performance when the probe was away from the saccade goal. No distractor appeared in any of these trials. Reproduced with permission from Bisley and Goldberg (2003).

Attention also could be drawn to the spatial location of an abruptly appearing distractor. We flashed a task-irrelevant distractor during the delay to see if it could draw attention away from the goal of the planned saccade (Figure 1.1B). The distractor appeared on half of the trials and was either presented at the saccade goal or opposite the saccade goal (as in Figure 1.1B). The distractor was identical to the target in size, brightness and duration, but appeared 500 ms after the target. It remained on the screen for a duration of 100 ms.

When the distractor appeared in the opposite location of the target, and the probe appeared 200 ms after the distractor, the perceptual threshold went down to the attentionally advantaged level at the site of the distractor and rose to the baseline level at the saccade goal (Figure 1.3). However, 700 ms after the distractor had appeared, performance was once again enhanced at the saccade goal and not at the distractor location, and this was also the case with the 1200 ms SOA in monkey I, with a trend toward that result in monkey B. Thus as in humans the abrupt onset of a distractor in the visual field draws attention. In the monkey this occurs even while the animal is planning a saccade. The attentional effect of the distractor lasts for <700 ms, by which time attention has returned to the saccade goal. The distractor and the saccade plan had the same effect on the monkey's attention, lowering the contrast sensitivity threshold by the same amount.

Neuronal activity in LIP correlated with the monkey's attentional performance. We found that the activity of LIP neurons in the 100 ms interval before the appearance of the probe

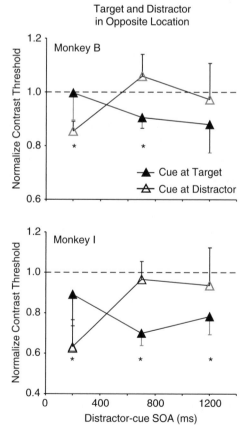

Figure 1.3 Effect of the distractor on perceptual threshold. Data for each delay were normalized by the performance at that delay when the probe was not placed at the saccade goal in trials without a distractor. In the trials shown here the distractor appeared opposite the saccade goal. Normalized contrast threshold was plotted against stimulus-onset asynchrony (SOA) for trials in which the probe appeared at the saccade goal (blue symbols) or at the distractor site (red symbols). Performance for both animals was recorded at SOAs of 200, 700 and 1200 ms. Points significantly beneath the dashed line show attentional enhancement (*$p < 0.05$, paired t-test on prenormalized data). Reproduced with permission from Bisley and Goldberg (2003).

predicted the monkeyís attention to the site of the probe (Bisley and Goldberg, 2003, 2006). We recorded the activity of 41 neurons in LIP with peripheral receptive fields in two hemispheres of the two monkeys from whom we gathered the psychophysical data. All neurons were visually responsive, and the majority had delay-period or perisaccadic activity as well.

The neurons responded both to the saccade goal and the distractor, but had maintained activity only at the saccade goal (Figure 1.4). Because the monkey could not predict the probe contrast, there was no difference in the activity evoked by the saccade plan or the distractor transient in threshold and suprathreshold trials. Rather than trying to relate the response of a single LIP neuron to the locus of attention, we normalized the responses of each neuron by the mean response throughout the duration of every trial, and then calculated the average normalized activity for each animal (Figure 4C and D). Presented like this, the data represent a population response to two different events: the appearance of the target and the subsequent generation of the memory-guided saccade; and the appearance of the distractor. Although we recorded the response of each of our neurons to those two events, one could as easily reinterpret the activity as that simultaneously seen in two different populations of neurons with the same overall properties, one with receptive fields at the saccade goal (the 'target population' in blue) and the other with receptive fields at the distractor site (the 'distractor population' in red).

The activity of the neuronal population in LIP parallels the attentional performance of the monkey. There was a consistent relationship between the activity in LIP (Figure 4E and F, lower plot) and the behavioral results from the three SOAs measured previously (Figure 4E and F, triangles). At any given time throughout the trial the attentionally advantaged part of the visual field was that which lay in the receptive fields of the most active neurons. For example, 200 ms after the appearance of the distractor the greatest activity in LIP was in the distractor population (red traces), and the attentional advantage lay at the distractor site. Five hundred milliseconds later the target population again had the greatest activity (blue traces), and attention had returned to the saccade goal.

The appearance of the distractor outside of the receptive field had no significant effect on the delay period activity in the target population. The distractor evoked a brief transient response, which decayed rapidly and soon crossed the level of activity in the target population. This crossing point had behavioral significance. We first determined the period in which there was no single significant preponderance of activity in LIP, by comparing the activity at the two sites in a 100 ms window that slid across the entire period in 5 ms steps (Figure 4E and F, black traces). For each monkey there was a window of neuronal ambiguity of 80–90 ms in which there was no significant difference between the activity evoked by the distractor and the activity related to the saccade plan ($p > 0.05$ by Wilcoxon sign rank test).

We returned to the psychophysics laboratory and measured the contrast sensitivities at the saccade goal and the distractor site at the crossing point in each monkey (455 ms for monkey B and 340 ms for monkey I) and 500 ms later. These times were the center of the window of neuronal ambiguity for each monkey. At the crossing point we found no spatial region of enhanced sensitivity in either monkey. However, within 500 ms attention had

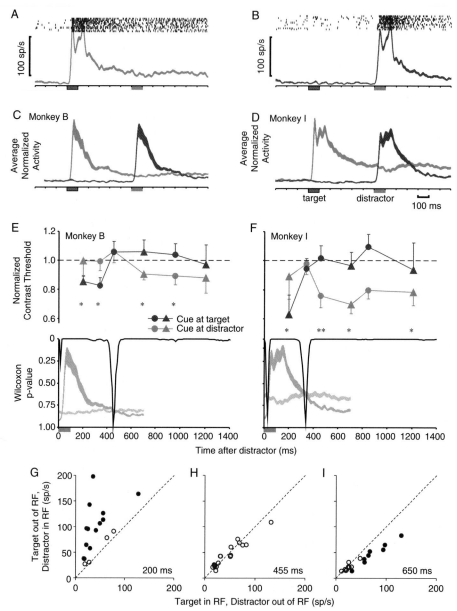

Figure 1.4 Neural activity and behavior in the attention task. (**A**) Raster diagram and spike density trace of response to the target appearing in the receptive field and to the distractor appearing outside of the receptive field. The thickness of the traces represents the standard error of the mean and the solid blue and red bars show the time and duration of the target and distractor respectively. These data were recorded while the monkey was performing the task on threshold. (**B**) Response of the same cell when the distractor is in the receptive field. (**C**) Averaged normalized spike density functions from 18 cells from monkey B. (**D**) Averaged normalized spike density functions from 23 cells from monkey I. (**E**) and (**F**) compare neural activity with behavior for each monkey. The top sections show the behavioral performance of the monkeys when the

shifted back to the site of the target in both monkeys, with normalized thresholds similar to those seen in the earlier experiment. This is in stark contrast to the effect of LIP activity on saccades: when there was equal activity in the two populations, even in the 50 ms epoch immediately before the saccade, there was no measurable effect on the latency, accuracy, or even early trajectory of the planned saccade (Powell and Powell, 2000). It is possible that there is a period of time following the distractor when attention is shifting, and this period just happens to coincide with the change in activity, while not being related to it. On the other hand, if the activity in LIP were related to attention, then we would expect the behavior to be different in the two animals, because the windows of neuronal ambiguity did not overlap between the two monkeys (see the troughs of the black traces in Figure 4E and F). We presented the probe to monkey I at the crossing point for monkey B (455 ms) and to monkey B at the crossing point for monkey I (340 ms). We found that the location of the attentional advantage in monkey I had already returned to the saccade goal at the crossing point for monkey B, and that for monkey B the attentional advantage was still at the location of the distractor at the crossing point for monkey I. These data support the hypothesis that there is indeed a correlation between activity in LIP and the locus of attention.

The absolute level of neural activity did not determine the locus of attention. Instead the locus of attention lay at the part of the visual field associated with the greatest neural activity in LIP. Thus the delay period activity, which determined the locus of attentional

◄───

probe was placed at the saccade goal (blue data) or at the location of the distractor (red data in trials in which the target and distractor were in opposite locations. The triangles are data collected before the recording, and the circles are from data collected after recording the activity of lateral intraparietal area (LIP) neurons in the same monkeys (red and blue traces in bottom section). The circle data were recorded at the crossing point in each monkey (455 ms for monkey B, 340 ms for monkey I) and 500 ms later. Data were also collected from both animals at the crossing point recorded in the other animal. Statistical significance was confirmed with a paired t-test on the prenormalized data (*$p < 0.05$). The black traces in the bottom section show the p-values from Wilcoxon paired sign-rank tests performed on the activity of all the neurons for a monkey over a 100 ms bin, measured every 5 ms. A low p-value (high on the axis) represents a significant difference in the activity from the two conditions. The normalized spike density functions from Figure 4C and D have been superimposed to show the time course of activity in LIP following the onset of the distractor for the two monkeys. The thickness of the traces represent the standard error of the mean. (**G–I**) A comparison of the activity when the distractor, but not the saccade goal, was in the receptive field to the activity when the saccade goal, but not the distractor, was in the receptive field from one monkey. Solid circles represent cells with significant differences in response (t-test, $p < 0.05$). (**G**) Mean activity 150–250 ms following the onset of the distractor for monkey B. The responses were different across the population ($p < 0.001$, Wilcoxon paired sign-rank test). (**H**) Mean activity during a 100 ms epoch centered at the crossing point for monkey B (455 ms after the onset of the distractor). The responses were not different across the population ($p > 0.95$). (**I**) Mean activity 600–700 ms following the onset of the distractor for monkey B. The responses were different across the population ($p < 0.01$). Modified from Bisley and Goldberg (2003).

advantage when it was the greatest activity in LIP, could not sustain that advantage when it was swamped by the huge transient response to the distractor. Although at times there was only a small difference in the normalized activity of neurons representing the attentionally advantaged and disadvantaged spatial locations, this difference was extraordinarily robust across the population. This is clear from the examples shown in Figures 4G–I. These plots compare the mean activity of each neuron measured in monkey B when the saccade goal was in the receptive field with the mean activity during the same 100 ms epoch when the distractor was in the receptive field, at three different times during the paradigm: 200 ms after the appearance of the distractor (Figure 1.4G); the crossing point (Figure 1.4H); and 650 ms after the appearance of the distractor (Figure 1.4I). In our analysis we included all classes of neurons that we encountered, since the major outputs from LIP contain all the classes of neurons found in LIP (Pare and Wurtz, 1997). We have separately illustrated those with (filled circles) and without (open circles) statistically significant differences in their responses ($p < 0.05$ by t-test). Generally those neurons without significant differences in delay activity during the task had no memory activity based on their responses to a regular memory guided saccade task.

The results we have discussed so far show that the activity present in LIP at the time that the probe appears predicts whether or not attention will be paid to a probe flashed for one video frame. This is in contradistinction to all previous studies of attentional modulation, which have suggested that the enhanced response evoked by the attended object itself is responsible for the attention to that object (Bushnell et al., 1981; Colby et al., 1996; Cook and Maunsell, 2002). We found, instead, that the responses evoked by the probe itself did not correlate with our measure of attention. When the probe was in the receptive field the initial on-responses were identical whether the cue dictated GO to the receptive field, GO elsewhere, or NOGO (Figure 1.5A shows the responses of a single cell; Figure 1.5B shows the mean responses for every cell in the sample). After 100 ms these responses diverge. When the probe signals GO elsewhere the response falls rapidly (dashed trace in Figure 1.5A). When the probe signals GO to the receptive field the response falls slightly more slowly, and resumes the preprobe delay period level (black trace in Figure 1.5A). When the probe signals NOGO and the monkey was planning a saccade to the receptive field, the response falls far less rapidly, as if the stimulus requiring a cancellation of a saccade plan evokes attention longer than one confirming the saccade plan (grey trace in Figure 1.5A). Across the sample the response to this cancellation of a saccade plan is significantly greater than the response to the continuation signal both when the saccade plan is to the receptive field (Figure 1.5C) and even more so when the saccade plan and its associated attentional advantage are directed away from the receptive field (Figure 1.5D). When the response finally falls, however, it falls to the level of the GO-elsewhere response. This enhanced response to a stimulus that cancels a saccade to the receptive field is the strongest evidence dissociating activity in LIP from an obligate relationship to motor intention, unless the first step in canceling a saccade is to plan it more.

Remember that on every trial there was either a probe (the Landolt ring) or a complete ring in the receptive field. We found no difference between the response to the GO probe or the ring in trials in which the saccade plan was directed to the receptive field

(Figure 1.5E), or away from it ($p > 0.2$, Wilcoxon paired sign-rank test), nor was there any difference in the responses to the probe in correct and incorrect trials. However, the enhanced cancellation response was only seen for the actual NOGO probe and not for a ring in the receptive field when the NOGO probe appeared outside of the receptive field (Figure 1.5F).

These results, which dissociate LIP from an obligate role in motor planning but confirm its importance in attentional processes, are in seeming contrast with the claim that LIP is predominantly concerned with the intention to generate a saccade (Andersen et al., 2002). This claim arises from the finding that, in LIP, neuronal activity during the delay period of a simultaneously planned memory-guided saccade and reach is greater when the saccade target is in the receptive field than it is when the reach target is in the receptive field (Snyder et al., 1997; Quian Quiroga et al., 2006). The authors asserted that the monkeys were attending to both the reach target and the saccade target throughout the delay, and, because LIP delay activity was greater when the monkey made a saccade to the receptive field, LIP activity was related to the saccade and not to attention. However, they did not measure attention directly, but only used the post hoc method to assert that the monkey's attention lay at both the saccade and reach goals throughout the delay period. This assertion is unlikely to be true. Deubel and Schneider (2003) showed that in a similar simultaneous reach and saccade task, attention, measured by perceptual threshold, leaves the reach goal within 300 ms after the goal's appearance, but remains at the saccade goal throughout the delay period. In fact, in the data reanalyzed by Qian Quiroga et al., the transient visual responses to the reach and saccade goals were identical (Snyder et al., 1997; Quian Quiroga et al., 2006), so in their conclusion the authors merely ignored the transient visual response. The equally enthusiastic responses to the saccade and reach goals occur at a time in which attention is likely to be at both places. LIP activity then declines when the reach goal is in the receptive field, but this is consistent with attention having actually left the reach goal. Thus faced with a binary choice between attention and intention, one must choose attention. However, such a binary choice is not necessary.

Under conditions of visual search, LIP predicts the goal and latency of saccades

The previous experiment, like the great bulk of studies using eye movements, rewarded the monkey at different times for making or not making an eye movement. In these experiments in which neurons were recorded in monkeys trained to make or not make a particular eye movement, the results inevitably reflect some bias of the experimental design. In the real world, however, primates make saccades to facilitate vision and there is no such thing as a wrong or incorrectly timed eye movement, except for the occasional social taboo. To see if we could garner a better idea of how parietal cortex acts in everyday behavior, we recorded the activity of neurons in LIP of monkeys trained on a visual search task in which they were free to move their eyes (Sheinberg et al., 2001; Mazer and Gallant, 2003; Bichot et al., 2005). In this task they reported their decision by a hand movement. There was no reward contingency linked to either fixation or saccade (Ipata et al., 2006a).

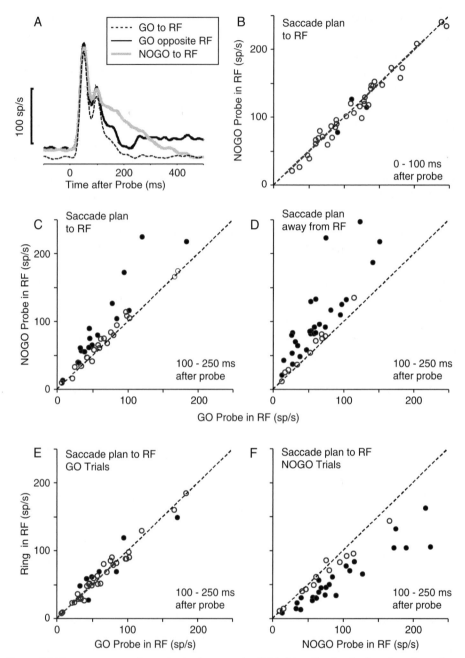

Figure 1.5 The response to the probe in the receptive field. (**A**) Spike density functions from the same neuron illustrated in Figure 4A and B. Data are from trials in which the monkey was instructed to plan a saccade into the receptive field and either the GO stimulus (black) or the NOGO stimulus (grey trace) appeared in the receptive field and from trials in which the saccade goal was opposite the receptive field and the GO probe appeared in the receptive field (dashed trace). The timing of the stimulus presentation is represented by the black bar starting at 0 ms. (**B**) The response to the NOGO stimulus plotted against the response to the GO stimulus in trials

The monkey initiated each trial by grabbing two bars, one with each hand (Figure 1.6A). Then a white spot appeared in the center of the screen, which the monkey had to fixate for 1–1.75 s. Subsequently, a search array appeared and the monkey was free to move its eyes. The array consisted of a target and seven distractors arranged in a radially symmetric circular pattern, so that one stimulus appeared in the center of the receptive field. On each trial, the relative position of the target among the distractors varied randomly. The target was a black, upright or inverted capital T and the monkeys had to signal the orientation of the target by releasing one of the two bars. On each trial the program randomly chose six distractors from a set of four different stimuli with horizontal and vertical components of the same color, luminance, width and height as the target, but which intercepted each other at different heights. The final distractor, the popout distractor, was bright green, but matched the shape of the other distractors. Eye movements were neither rewarded nor punished, so the animals' oculomotor behavior was completely unconstrained after the onset of the array. The monkeys had 3 s to respond and the responses were classified as incorrect only if monkeys released the wrong bar. Both monkeys performed the task correctly on 95–99% of the trials. On most trials, the monkeys fixated the target before responding. In a small proportion of trials (1–12%), one monkey gave the correct manual response but did not make a saccade to the target. The monkeys' performance in this paradigm resembled that of humans in a similar paradigm. When we were developing the paradigm we intermixed trials with 8, 12 and 16 member arrays, and blocks in which no stimulus popped out, in which the target popped out as well as blocks in which a distractor popped out. Like humans, there was

---

in which the monkey was instructed to plan a saccade to the receptive field. Data are from a 100 ms epoch starting at the onset of the probe. Solid circles are from cells in which the difference in activity was significant ($p < 0.05$, t-test), hollow circles are from cells in which there was no significant difference. Across the population there was no difference in response to the two stimuli ($p > 0.15$, Wilcoxon paired sign rank test). (C) The response to the NOGO stimulus plotted against the response to the GO stimulus in trials in which the monkey was instructed to plan a saccade to the receptive field. Data are from a 150 ms epoch starting 100 ms after the onset of the probe. Across the population there was a significant difference in responses to the GO and NOGO stimuli ($p < 0.001$). (D) The response to the NOGO stimulus plotted against the response to the GO stimulus in trials in which the monkey was instructed to plan a saccade away from the receptive field. Data are from a 150 ms epoch starting 100 ms after the onset of the probe. Across the population there was a significant difference in responses to the GO and NOGO stimuli ($p < 0.001$). (E) The response to the complete ring plotted against the response to the GO stimulus in trials in which the monkey was instructed to plan and execute a saccade to the receptive field. Data are from a 150 ms epoch starting 100 ms after the onset of the probe. Across the population there was no difference in the responses to the GO and ring stimuli ($p > 0.6$). (F) The response to the complete ring plotted against the response to the NOGO stimulus in trials in which the monkey was instructed to plan and then cancel a saccade to the receptive field. Data are from a 150 ms epoch starting 100 ms after the onset of the probe. Across the population there was a significant difference in the responses to the NOGO and circle stimuli ($p < 0.001$). Adapted from Bisley and Goldberg (2003).

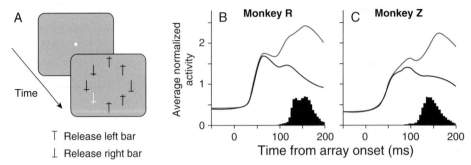

Figure 1.6 Search task and neuronal responses. The free-viewing visual search task and the response of the LIP population. (**A**) The free-viewing visual search task. After an initial fixation period (1–1.75 s), the search array appeared. One of the stimuli, either the target (an upright or inverted T) or a distractor, appeared in the center of the neuron's receptive field. Monkeys had 3 s to report the orientation of the target by releasing one of two bars. During the presentation of the search array, no constraints were imposed on the monkey's eye movements and they were not required to fixate the target before giving the response. (**B, C**) The average normalized activity from one- and two-saccade trials is plotted against time for monkeys R and Z. These represent 76 and 73% of all trials for monkeys R and Z respectively. Activity from trials in which the first saccade was made away from the receptive field is shown in blue. Activity from trials in which the first saccade was made toward the receptive field is shown in red. Trials in which the target was in the receptive field have been pooled with trials in which the distractor was in the receptive field. Histograms show the distribution of first saccade latencies relative to array onset. Reproduced with permission from Ipata *et al.* (2006a).

a set-size effect in manual reaction time when the target resembled the distractors (slopes of 15 and 5 ms/array object) in monkeys R and Z respectively) but not for trials in which the target popped out.

We recorded a total of 73 LIP neurons from two monkeys (42 from monkey R and 31 from monkey Z). Each neuron had significant visual activity and 71% of them responded significantly during the delay period of the memory-guided saccade task ($p < 0.05$, t-tests compared to background activity). The neurons began to discharge with short latency responses at around 35 ms. Until roughly 90 ms this visual response was unaffected by saccade direction or the nature of the stimulus in the receptive field. Activity in LIP began to distinguish the direction of the upcoming saccade roughly 90 ms after the array appeared (Figure 6B and C). The responses diverged so that the population was more active when the monkey was going to make a saccade to the receptive field (red trace) than when the monkey was going to make a saccade away from the receptive field (blue trace). To calculate the time at which the monkey's choice of saccade direction was clearly represented in LIP, we used a sliding window analysis (Ipata *et al.*, 2006a). Target selection occurred in the population 86 ms after the array appeared in monkey R, and 91 ms after array onset in monkey Z. In the interval from 70 to 120 ms after the appearance of the array, the average response of the majority of the neurons and that of the population as a whole ($p < 0.001$ by Wilcoxon sign rank) was greater when the monkey made a saccade to the receptive field than when the monkey made a saccade away from it). The difference was even more striking in the 50 ms epoch starting 25 ms before the saccade Almost all of the cells had more activity when the monkey made a saccade to the receptive field, producing a strong significant difference at the population level ($p < 0.0001$ by Wilcoxon signed rank). Thus, under conditions of free visual search, activity in LIP correlates with the monkey's selection of the saccade goal.

More strikingly, under conditions of free visual search, the time at which activity in LIP reflects the selection of the saccade target predicts the time at which the monkey will subsequently make the saccade. To show this relationship, we plotted the time to saccade goal selection against the mean saccadic latencies for groups of trials from single neurons, sorted by saccadic latency (Figure 1.7). Data are only shown for neurons that gave statistically significant selection times for all groups, and each solid black line connects the points from a single cell. The selection time of the group means changed as saccadic latency changed when calculated from array onset (analysis of variance: monkey R: $p < 0.001$, $F = 25$; df = 2; monkey Z: $p < 0.004$; $F = 10$; df = 1; Figure 7A and B), but not when calculated from saccade onset ($p > 0.5$ in both monkeys; Figure 7C and D). Selection times calculated relative to array onset, correlated with saccadic latency with a slope not different from 1 (Figure 7A and B), whereas selection times calculated relative to saccade beginning did not correlate all (Figure 7C and D). This means that the time at which the choice of saccade goal is reflected in LIP determines saccade latency, after which the actual time for generating the saccade is relatively constant, regardless of how long it takes for the goal to be selected.

Under conditions of visual search, LIP has information about the object in its receptive field independent of the saccade choice

The monkeys' response to the popout changed with experience. Initially, because we wanted to demonstrate the similarity between the monkey's search strategy and that of humans, we often made the popout stimulus serve as the target of the search. In one variation of this experiment, we alternated blocks of trials in which the popout was always the target, with blocks in which the popout was never the target. In the blocks in which the popout was the target, the monkeys made their first saccade to the popout in almost all of the trials (Figure 1.8) (Ipata et al., 2006b). In the blocks in which the popout was never the target, monkey R made the first saccade to the popout in 148/919 trials (16%), to the target in 520/919 trials (57 %) and to a non-popout distractor in 251/919 trials (27%). Monkey Z made the first saccade to the popout in 517/2438 trials (21%), to the target in 920/2438 trials (37%) and to a non-popout distractor in 1001/2438 trials (41%).

During the recording experiments, we were interested in trials in which the monkey made saccades away from the target, so we never made the target the popout. Under these circumstances the percentage of first saccades to the popout dropped to 4.0% in monkey R (1612/39 902) and to 0.2% in monkey Z (150/31 923). Monkey R made 22 427/39 902 (56%) first saccades to the target and 15 863/39 902 (40%) first saccades to

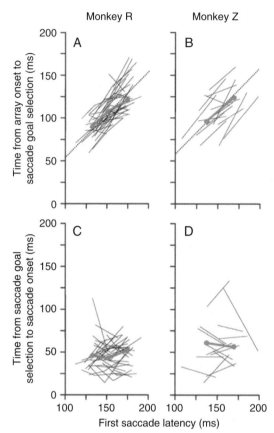

Figure 1.7 Relationship of saccade selection time to saccadic latency. Saccade latency correlates with saccade goal selection time in lateral intraparietal area (LIP). (**A, B**) The time from array onset to saccade goal selection is plotted against the mean first saccadic latency for each group for each cell. (**C, D**) The time from saccade goal selection to saccade onset is plotted against the mean first saccadic latency for each group for each cell. Lines connect points from the same cell. The solid red lines connect the population means. The dotted lines show example slopes of 1. (Reproduced with permission from Ipata et al., 2006a).

non-popout distractors; monkey Z made 14 066/31 923 (44%) first saccades to the target and 17 769/31 923 (55%) first saccades to non-popout distractors.

Neurons in LIP showed a suppressed response to the popout distractor, relative to either the response to the target or the response to the non-popout distractor (Figure 1.9). The initial visual responses to popout and non-popout distractors are identical, but after about 90 ms there is a marked suppression of the response to the popout distractor.

This distinction between popout and non-popout distractor was present across the sample of neurons, both in the population averages and the activity of the single neurons. We limited this analysis to cells which had at least five trials of each type (41 cells in monkey R, 29 in monkey Z). As in the single cell example, the responses to the two classes of distractor were initially similar, but diverged to give a consistently weaker response to the popout distractor.

The monkey's ability to suppress making saccades to the popout distractor varied from day to day, as did the neuronal suppression of the response to the popout distractor. On days in which the animals were unable to suppress saccades to the popout distractor, neuronal responses to the popout distractor were equal to, or stronger than, the responses

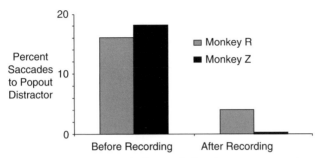

Figure 1.8 Monkeys' responses to popout before and after the target stopped popping out. In sessions before recording, blocks in which the popout was the target were occasionally presented. The data on the left show the proportion of saccades to the popout distractor from these sessions, but only from blocks in which the popout was always a distractor. The data on the right were taken from recording sessions in which the popout was never the target. Reproduced with permission from Ipata *et al.* (2006b).

to the non-popout distractors. For each cell we calculated the proportion of first saccades made to the popout distractor. We then plotted these data against the difference between the responses to the non-popout and popout distractors for the cell, in a 50 ms epoch starting at 80 ms after array onset (Figure 1.10). In monkey R, it is clear that whenever the differences were positive (i.e. the response to the popout was weaker), the monkey generally was able to inhibit saccades to the popout stimulus (Figure 1.10). However, in sessions in which the monkey was unable to suppress saccades toward the popout (i.e. those in which >5% of trials began with the monkey making a saccade to the popout), the responses to the popout stimulus were either equal to or greater than the responses to the non-popout stimuli. The results from monkey Z are less obvious (Figure 1.10), since this monkey almost always suppressed saccades to the popout. However, in line with this behavior, monkey Z had only three sessions in which the neuron being studied clearly responded more to the popout distractor than to the non-popout distractors. Furthermore, in the one session in which he was unable to suppress saccades to the popout, the response to the popout stimulus was not significantly lower than the response to the non-popout stimulus.

In a preliminary analysis (not shown here in detail) we have shown that LIP not only distinguishes between popout and non-popout distractor, but also between non-popout distractor and target. This distinction occurs both on trials in which the monkey makes a saccade to the receptive field, and on trials in which the monkey makes a saccade away from the receptive field. The distinction between distractor and target occurs roughly 25 ms after LIP reflects the choice of saccade, which may explain why the monkey makes so many saccades to the distractors.

How LIP can drive both attention and saccades

We have described two different experiments which illuminate the role of LIP in eye movements and visual attention. In the first we show that activity in LIP can be evoked

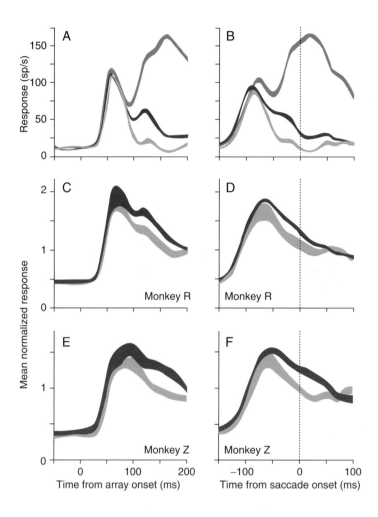

Figure 1.9 Suppression of response to the popout distractor. All data are from trials in which the monkey made the first saccade to the target and released the correct bar. (**a**) Responses of a single cell to the appearance of an array object in the receptive field are plotted against time from target onset. Red trace: response to the target in the receptive field when the monkey made a saccade to the target. Black trace: response to a non-popout distractor in the receptive field when the monkey made a saccade to the target elsewhere. Green trace: response to the popout distractor in the receptive field when the monkey made a saccade to the target elsewhere. (**b**) Same data as in (**a**), but aligned on saccade onset. (**c, d**) Population averages for monkey R aligned on array onset (**c**) or saccade onset (**d**). (**e, f**) Population averages for monkey Z aligned on array onset (**e**) or saccade onset (**f**). Reproduced with permission from Ipata *et al.* (2006b).

both by a saccade plan and by the appearance of a task-irrelevant distractor elsewhere |in the visual field. The monkey's attention, as measured by an independent perceptual measure, lies at the goal of the saccade except when it is involuntarily, but transiently, drawn to the site of the distractor. The activity of LIP tracks the monkey's attention on a millisecond-by-millisecond basis, and it predicts when attention will return from

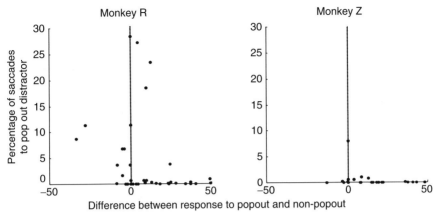

Figure 1.10 Relationship of popout suppression to the monkey's performance. Cell-by-cell correlation of response suppression with saccade suppression. The percentage of trials in which the first saccade went to the popout distractor for each session is plotted against the difference in the number of spikes between the responses (80–130 ms) to the non-popout and popout distractors for the cell recorded in that session from monkey R (**a**) and monkey Z (**b**). In monkey R there was a significant correlation between the proportion of saccades and the difference in activity ($p = 0.001$ from linear regression). Reproduced with permission from Ipata *et al.* (2006b).

the distractor to the saccade goal. Conversely, activity in LIP in this experiment does not indicate where, when, or if saccade will take place. In the second experiment, we show that activity in LIP not only predicts both the saccade goal and its latency, but also has information about the object in its receptive field which is independent of saccade direction.

These data are not consistent with LIP having a role exclusively dedicated to the planning of saccadic eye movements or to the placing of visual attention, but they are consistent with LIPs providing a representation of significant objects in the visual field—acting as a salience map. Of course, the goal of a saccade is usually the object of attention (Yantis *et al.*, 1984, 1996), and in fact Rizzolatti *et al.* (1987) have postulated that attention in the primate is merely a readout of a possible saccade plan. However, in our first experiment attention and the saccade plan were effectively dissociated, and LIP still predicted attention.

If, however, we consider that LIP describes a salience map of the visual field in an agnostic manner, without specifying how that salience map is used, the seemingly contradictory views described above can be reconciled. The salience map is constructed from a number of different and independent signals. The earliest signal is an undifferentiated visual signal which reports the abrupt onset of a visual stimulus in the receptive field without specifying either the nature of the stimulus or whether or not the monkey will attend or make a saccade to it (Bisley *et al.*, 2004). The second is a signal specifying the saccade, and the third is a signal dependent on the behavioral significance of the stimulus in the receptive field.

The actual function of the salience map depends on the area to which it projects. LIP has a strong projection to two oculomotor areas, the frontal eye field (Andersen *et al.*, 1990b) and the superior colliculus (Ferraina *et al.*, 2002). If a saccade is appropriate, the peak of the salience map in LIP can provide targeting information. If a saccade is inappropriate, for example during the delay period of a memory-guided delayed saccade task, the oculomotor system can ignore LIP. LIP also projects to inferior temporal cortex, the ventral visual stream areas involved in pattern recognition (Baizer *et al.*, 1991). Neurons here have large, bilateral receptive fields including the fovea, and could not be useful for targeting saccades—but attention is critical for visual perception, and neurons in inferior temporal cortex show attentional modulation (Moran *et al.*, 1985). The ventral stream can use the exact same salience map for attention that the oculomotor system uses for targeting—the salience map in LIP.

The use of the salience map does not depend on the genesis of the spikes. Bottom-up spikes from abrupt onset, top-down spikes from a saccade plan or a cognitive input about the stimulus all contribute to the salience map. LIP is agnostic to both the origin of the spikes and the use to which they will be put. Trying to determine if the spikes are 'sensory' or 'motor' is irrelevant. Thus the attentional system can be driven by a saccade plan, and the saccadic system by the abrupt onset of a visual stimulus.

This idea may have general implications for the interpretation of much neural data. Neurons in many areas of the brain have activity which physiologists divide into different visual or motor responses, just as many authors divide LIP activity during a delayed saccade task as visual, delay-period, and presaccadic components (Powell and Goldberg, 2000; Roitman and Shadlen, 2002; Quian Quiroga *et al.*, 2006). The physiologists have the advantage, unlike the postsynaptic neuron, of knowing when the stimulus appeared or the fixation point disappeared. They can relate neural activity to those externally determined events. The postsynaptic neurons cannot have information about when the external events occurred unless they have a second set of unambiguous inputs—sensory delay and presaccadic activity in the case of LIP—which would render the LIP signal superfluous. Instead, all the information the recipient neurons have is a spike count; any interpretation of the meaning of those spikes cannot invoke external knowledge of the stimulus. Just as a motor unit must interpret every action potential as a cue to contract, a recipient neuron must interpret the spikes it receives in a uniform manner. Clearly signals can be multiplexed in the waveform (Eskandar *et al.*, 1992), but even multiplexed signals must be interpreted without reference to other knowledge about the external world.

These experiments raise an important caveat: introspectively attention is both divisible and graded. Thus human subjects can attend to multiple objects at roughly the same time (Pylyshyn *et al.*, 1988; Sears and Pylyshyn, 2000) and a hallmark of parietal damage is the inability to do so (Bálint, 1995). Attention can also be graded; the more likely an object is to appear at a given location the better the performance it evokes (Ciaramitaro *et al.*, 2001). However, such distributed attentional processes only operate over relatively long periods of time. Over the time period in which we describe an attentional advantage, one video frame, there is evidence that attention may be indivisible and ungraded (Joseph *et al.*, 1996). However, the activity in LIP is graded, and so over a longer period of time the multiple peaks of the salience map in LIP may contribute to the divisibility and gradation of activity that is present in psychological studies.

Acknowledgements

This research was supported by grants from the U.S. National Eye Institute (to M.E. Goldberg), the U.S. National Science Foundation (to Angela Gee), the Dana, Whitehall, and Kavli Foundations, and the Human Frontiers Science Program.

References

Andersen, R. A. and Buneo, C. A. (2002) Intentional maps in posterior parietal cortex. *Annual Review of Neuroscience*, **25**, 189–220.

Andersen, R. A., Asanuma, C., Essick, G. and Siegel, R. M. (1990a) Corticocortical connections of anatomically and physiologically defined subdivisions within the inferior parietal lobule. *Journal of Comparative Neurology*, **296**, 65–113.

Andersen, R. A., Asanuma, C., Essick, G. and Siegel, R. M. (1990b) Corticocortical connections of anatomically and physiologically defined subdivisions within the inferior parietal lobule. *Journal of Comparative Neurology*, **296**, 65–113.

Asanuma, C., Andersen, R. A. and Cowan, W. M. (1985) The thalamic relations of the caudal inferior parietal lobule and the lateral prefrontal cortex in monkeys: divergent cortical projections from cell clusters in the medial pulvinar nucleus. *Journal of Comparative Neurology*, **241**, 357–381.

Assad, J. A. and Maunsell, J. H. R. (1995) Neuronal correlates of inferred motion in primate posterior parietal cortex. *Nature*, **373**, 518–521.

Baizer, J. S., Ungerleider, L. G. and Desimone, R. (1991) Organization of visual inputs to the inferior temporal and posterior parietal cortex in macaques. *Journal of Neuroscience*, **11**, 168–190.

Bàlint, R. (1995) Psychic paralysis of gaze, optic ataxia, and spatial disorder of attention. *Cognitive Neuropsychology*, **12**, 265–281. (Translated from *Monatschrift für Psychiatrie und Neurologie*, **25**, 51–81, 1909.)

Barash, S., Bracewell, R. M., Fogassi, L., Gnadt, J. W. and Andersen, R. A. (1991a) Saccade-related activity in the lateral intraparietal area. II. Spatial properties. *Journal of Neurophysiology*, **66**, 1109–1124.

Barash, S., Bracewell, R. M., Fogassi, L., Gnadt, J. W. and Andersen, R. A. (1991b) Saccade-related activity in the lateral intraparietal area. I. Temporal properties; comparison with area 7a. *Journal of Neurophysiology*, **66**, 1095–1108.

Bashinski, H. S. and Bacharach, V. R. (1980) Enhancement of perceptual sensitivity as the result of selectively attending to spatial locations. *Perception and Psychophysics*, **28**, 241–248.

Bichot, N. P., Rossi, A. F. and Desimone, R. (2005) Parallel and serial neural mechanisms for visual search in macaque area V4. *Science*, **308**, 529–34.

Bisley, J. W. and Goldberg, M. E. (2003) Neuronal activity in the lateral intraparietal area and spatial attention. *Science*, **299**, 81–86.

Bisley, J. W. and Goldberg, M. E. (2006) Neural correlates of attention and distractibility in the lateral intraparietal area. *Journal of Neurophysiol*, **95**, 1696–717.

Bisley, J. W., Krishna, B. S. and Goldberg, M. E. (2004) A rapid and precise on-response in posterior parietal cortex. *Journal of Neuroscience*, **24**, 1833–1838.

Bowman, E. M., Brown, V. J., Kertzman, C., Schwarz, U. and Robinson, D. L. (1993) Covert orienting of attention in macaques. I. Effects of behavioral context. *Journal of Neurophysiology*, **70**, 431–443.

Bushnell, M. C., Goldberg, M. E. and Robinson, D. L. (1981) Behavioral enhancement of visual responses in monkey cerebral cortex. I. Modulation in posterior parietal cortex related to selective visual attention. *Journal of Neurophysiology*, **46**, 755–772.

Ciaramitaro, V. M., Cameron, E. L. and Glimcher, P. W. (2001) Stimulus probability directs spatial attention: an enhancement of sensitivity in humans and monkeys. *Vision Research*, 41, 57–75.

Colby, C. L., Duhamel, J.-R. and Goldberg, M. E. (1996) Visual, presaccadic and cognitive activation of single neurons in monkey lateral intraparietal area. *Journal of Neurophysiology*, 76, 2841–2852.

Cook, E. P. and Maunsell, J. H. (2002) Attentional modulation of behavioral performance and neuronal responses in middle temporal and ventral intraparietal areas of macaque monkey. *Journal of Neuroscience*, 22, 1994–2004.

Deubel, H. and Schneider, W. X. (1996) Saccade target selection and object recognition: evidence for a common attentional mechanism. *Vision Research*, 36, 1827–1837.

Deubel, H. and Schneider, W. X. (2003) Delayed saccades, but not delayed manual aiming movements, require visual attention shifts. *Annals of the New York Academy of Sciences*, 1004, 289–296.

Dorris, M. C. and Glimcher, P. W. (2004) Activity in posterior parietal cortex is correlated with the relative subjective desirability of action. *Neuron*, 44, 365–378.

Eskandar, E. N., Richmond, B. J. and Optican, L. M. (1992) Role of inferior temporal neurons in visual memory. I. Temporal encoding of information about visual images, recalled images, and behavioral context. *Journal of Neurophysiology*, 68, 1277–1295.

Ferraina, S., Pare, M. and Wurtz, R. H. (2002) Comparison of cortico-cortical and cortico-collicular signals for the generation of saccadic eye movements. *Journal of Neurophysiology*, 87, 845–858.

Gnadt, J. W. and Andersen, R. A. (1988) Memory related motor planning activity in posterior parietal cortex of macaque. *Experimental Brain Research*, 70, 216–220.

Goldberg, M. E. and Wurtz, R. H. (1972) Activity of superior colliculus in behaving monkey. II. Effect of attention on neuronal responses. *Journal of Neurophysiology*, 35, 560–574.

Gottlieb, J. P., Kusunoki, M. and Goldberg, M. E. (1998) The representation of visual salience in monkey parietal cortex. *Nature*, 391, 481–484.

Hyvarinen, J. and Poranen, A. (1974) Function of the parietal associative area 7 as revealed from cellular discharges in alert monkeys. *Brain*, 97, 673–692.

Ipata, A. E., Gee, A. L., Goldberg, M. E. and Bisley, J. W. (2006a) Activity in the lateral intraparietal area predicts the goal and latency of saccades in a free-viewing visual search task. *Journal of Neuroscience*, 26, 3656–3661.

Ipata, A. E., Gee, A. L., Gottlieb, J., Bisley, J. W. and Goldberg, M. E. (2006b) LIP responses to a popout stimulus are reduced if it is overtly ignored. *Nature Neuroscience*, 9, 1071–1076.

Janssen, P. and Shadlen, M. N. (2005) A representation of the hazard rate of elapsed time in macaque area LIP. *Nature Neuroscience*, 8, 234–241.

Joseph, J. S. and Optican, L. M. (1996) Involuntary attentional shifts due to orientation differences. *Perception and Psychophysics*, 58, 651–665.

Kowler, E., Anderson, E., Dosher, B. and Blaser, E. (1995) The role of attention in the programming of saccades. *Vision Research*, 35, 1897–1916.

Leon, M. I. and Shadlen, M. N. (2003) Representation of time by neurons in the posterior parietal cortex of the macaque. *Neuron*, 38, 317–327.

Lynch, J. C., Mountcastle, V. B., Talbot, W. H. and Yin, T. C. T. (1977) Parietal lobe mechanisms for directed visual attention. *Journal of Neurophysiology*, 40, 362–389.

Mazer, J. A. and Gallant, J. L. (2003) Goal-related activity in V4 during free viewing visual search. Evidence for a ventral stream visual salience map. *Neuron*, 40, 1241–1250.

Moran, J. and Desimone, R. (1985) Selective attention gates visual processing in the extrastriate cortex. *Science*, 229, 782–784.

Mountcastle, V. B., Lynch, J. C., Georgopoulos, A., Sakata, H. and Acuña, C. (1975) Posterior parietal association cortex of the monkey: command functions for operations within extrapersonal space. *Journal of Neurophysiology*, 38, 871–908.

Neal, J. W., Pearson, R. C. A. and Powell, T. P. S. (1988) The organization of the cortico-cortical connections between the walls of the lower part of the superior temporal sulcus in the inferior parietal lobule in the monkey. *Brain Research*, **438**, 351–356.

Pare, M. and Wurtz, R. H. (1997) Monkey posterior parietal cortex neurons antidromically activated from superior colliculus. *Journal of Neurophysiology*, **78**, 3493–3497.

Platt, M. L. and Glimcher, P. W. (1997) Responses of intraparietal neurons to saccadic targets and visual distractors. *Journal of Neurophysiology*, **78**, 1574–1589.

Platt, M. L. and Glimcher, P. W. (1999) Neural correlates of decision variables in parietal cortex. *Nature*, **400**, 233–238.

Posner, M. I. (1980) Orienting of attention. *Quarterly Journal of Experimental Psychology*, **32**, 3–25.

Powell, K. D. and Goldberg, M. E. (2000) Response of neurons in the lateral intraparietal area to a distractor flashed during the delay period of a memory-guided saccade. *Journal of Neurophysiology*, **84**, 301–310.

Pylyshyn, Z. W. and Storm, R. W. (1988) Tracking multiple independent targets: evidence for a parallel tracking mechanism. *Spatial Vision*, **3**, 179–197.

Quian Quiroga, R., Snyder, L. H., Batista, A. P., Cui, H. and Andersen, R. A. (2006) Movement intention is better predicted than attention in the posterior parietal cortex. *Journal of Neuroscience*, **26**, 3615–3620.

Rizzolatti, G., Riggio, L., Dascola, I. and Umilta, C. (1987) Reorienting attention across the horizontal and vertical meridians: evidence in favor of a premotor theory of attention. *Neuropsychologia*, **25**, 31–40.

Robinson, D. L., Goldberg, M. E. and Stanton, G. B. (1978) Parietal association cortex in the primate: sensory mechanisms and behavioral modulations. *Journal of Neurophysiology*, **41**, 910–932.

Roitman, J. D. and Shadlen, M. N. (2002) Response of neurons in the lateral intraparietal area during a combined visual discrimination reaction time task. *Journal of Neuroscience*, **22**, 9475–9489.

Schall, J. D., Morel, A., King, D. J. and Bullier, J. (1995) Topography of visual cortex connections with frontal eye field in macaque: convergence and segregation of processing streams. *Journal of Neuroscience*, **15**, 4464–4487.

Sears, C. R. and Pylyshyn, Z. W. (2000) Multiple object tracking and attentional processing. *Canadian Journal of Experimental Psychology*, **54**, 1–14.

Seltzer, B. and Pandya, D. N. (1984) Further observations on parieto-temporal connections in the rhesus monkey. *Experimental Brain Research*, **55**, 301–312.

Sereno, A. B. and Maunsell, J. H. (1998) Shape selectivity in primate lateral intraparietal cortex. *Nature*, **395**, 500–503.

Shadlen, M. N. and Newsome, W. T. (2001) Neural basis of a perceptual decision in the parietal cortex (area LIP) of the rhesus monkey. *Journal of Neurophysiol*, **86**, 1916–1936.

Sheinberg, D. L. and Logothetis, N. K. (2001) Noticing familiar objects in real world scenes: the role of temporal cortical neurons in natural vision. *Journal of Neuroscience*, **21**, 1340–1350.

Snyder, L. H., Batista, A. P. and Andersen, R. A. (1997) Coding of intention in the posterior parietal cortex. *Nature*, **386**, 167–170.

Sugrue, L. P., Corrado, G. S. and Newsome, W. T. (2004) Matching behavior and the representation of value in the parietal cortex. *Science*, **304**, 1782–1787.

Williams, Z. M., Elfar, J. C., Eskandar, E. N., Toth, L. J. and Assad, J. A. (2003) Parietal activity and the perceived direction of ambiguous apparent motion. *Nature Neuroscience*, **6**, 616–623.

Yantis, S. and Jonides, J. (1984) Abrupt visual onsets and selective attention: evidence from visual search. *Journal of Experimental Psychology and Human Perception and Performance*, **10**, 601–621.

Yantis, S. and Jonides, J. (1996) Attentional capture by abrupt onsets: new perceptual objects or visual masking? *Journal of Experimental Psychology and Human Perception and Performance*, **22**, 1505–1513.

2

Modulations of prefrontal activity related to cognitive control and performance monitoring

Emmanuel Procyk, Céline Amiez, René Quilodran and Jean-Paul Joseph

Reacting to errors and adapting choices to achieve far-reaching goals are fundamental abilities allowing efficient reasoning and problem solving. These abilities require the proper operation of executive functions. These functions depend on the integrity of prefrontal networks and connections with other cortical and subcortical territories. This chapter focuses on the prefrontal correlates of cognitive control and performance monitoring, and tries to relate neurophysiological data to developments in computational modeling, without going into detailed descriptions of models.

Introduction

Executive functions and prefrontal cortex

Several theoretical models propose that executive functions consist of a superior cognitive control acting when routine actions need to be modified or reorganized (Shallice, 1988; Dehaene and Changeux, 1997; Robbins, 1998). It is possible to distinguish subcomponent processes such as selection of appropriate responses, active maintenance and the use of information for planning (working memory), inhibition, and performance monitoring (Miller and Cohen, 2001). In routine situations the selection of appropriate responses for particular stimulations (association through learning; habits) is based on fast and automatic selection processes, and particular instructions or unexpected events can initiate a 'supervised' control that overrides the automatic processing. In problematic situations, cognitive control can be triggered by unpredicted signals in order to avoid inefficient automatic responding and promote the selection of appropriate actions. The prefrontal cortex is central to these phenomena.

The prefrontal cortex includes several cytoarchitectonic areas that constitute the most anterior part of the frontal lobe. Its anatomical heterogeneity reveals a functional heterogeneity. These areas are highly interconnected and possibly interdependent but each contributes to specific aspects of prefrontal functions. Prefrontal areas are targets of monoaminergic afferences (especially on the medial wall: Williams and

Goldman-Rakic, 1993) the alteration of which results in psychiatric disorders character-ized by disorganized, inadequate, and poorly flexible cognitive performance.

The present paper focuses on the prefrontal correlates of the elaboration of, and transi-tions between, routine and nonroutine situations, or between exploitative and explor-ative behaviors. Computational modeling has been very helpful in building the current descriptions of the key cognitive processes and their differential contributions in time during adaptive behaviors. The estimation of value functions, the evaluation of current consequences of action, the triggering of increased cognitive control, and action selection are processes which participate in the overall regulation of adaptive behavior. They rely in part on the differential functions of prefrontal areas, on their interactions, and on their relationship with subcortical structures.

Models of control and performance monitoring

Critic, values, and prediction errors

Important insights into the structure and computational properties of adaptive systems come from reinforcement learning and models known as Actor–Critic (Sutton and Barto, 1998; Montague *et al.*, 2004). In such models the Critic learns to predict rewards from ongoing actions and information from the environment. The result is an estimation of value functions that allows predictions of future outcomes. Any unexpected discrepancy from outcome prediction results in phasic teaching signals (reflecting prediction errors) used by the Actor to optimize behavior and by the Critic to optimize prediction.

The interest in these models comes from the discovery that the firing pattern of mesen-cephalic dopaminergic neurons is very similar to the prediction error signal described in Actor–Critic models (Schultz, 1998). Actor–Critic models have been used to test whether specific brain structures and networks are differentially involved in Critic or Actor func-tions. We will show later that the attempts to directly assimilate prefrontal structures to Actors and Critic are still uncertain. These models are also at the source of many compu-tational developments (Dayan and Balleine, 2002). For instance, to account for some insufficiencies of these models (including fast adaptation to environmental changes), Daw *et al.* (2005) suggest the existence of two selection systems, one habit-related and one goal-based, that are relatively independent. For these authors, the Actor–Critic model (describing dopaminergic and basal ganglia function) is accompanied by a planning system (assimilated to the prefrontal cortex). The two-stage-like structure has been elab-orated in other forms for modeling the regulation of cognitive control.

Modulation of cognitive control

Norman and Shallice originally described a two-stage model composed of an automatic selector module (the contention scheduling system) and a control system (the supervi-sory attentional system) (Shallice, 1988). Whereas control had been associated with prefrontal function, contention scheduling was associated with striatal functions. While this model and others try to describe what is control and how it is performed, very few deal with how the system is engaged in controlling. In other words, how is the controller controlled? Botvinick *et al.* (2001) have proposed a solution to this problem while retaining the global features of the Norman–Shallice theory. They suggested that the lateral prefrontal cortex (LPFC) performs cognitive control (the maintenance of an adequate representation and inhibition of concurrent representations). Following recurrent correct responses, cognitive control decreases and automatic responses are more likely to occur. In complex situations, this supposedly leads to conflict between competing response representations, to behavioral errors, and finally to a need to re-engage cognitive control. In this context, Botvinick *et al.* proposed a conflict-monitoring hypothesis in which a system detects conflict in information processing (and therefore the need for control), and sends a signal that ultimately leads to an increase in cognitive control. Using data from functional magnetic resonance imaging (fMRI) and evoked related potentials (ERP) experiments, the authors hypothesize that a subdivision of dorsal anterior cingulate cortex (dACC) is the conflict detector. Indeed, dACC activation appears in situations where conflict is supposedly high (like the incongruent trials in the Stroop test) (Carter *et al.*, 1998; MacDonald *et al.*, 2000). dACC signals would be transferred to LPFC for adapting cognitive control. It implies that increased activity in ACC consecutive to conflict detection should be followed by increased activity in the LPFC. This effect has been studied with fMRI although the time scale of the method cannot precisely address the dynamics of the causal relationship between dACC and LPFC (Milham *et al.*, 2003; Kerns *et al.*, 2004).

Aston-Jones and Cohen (2005) propose that the noradrenergic system (locus coeruleus; LC) triggers changes in neuronal response modes of target structures like the LPFC. The authors argue that the output of computations performed within the orbitofrontal cortex (OFC) and the ACC (performance-monitoring and utility assessment) drives changes in the firing mode of LC neurons. This change is supposed to shift the dynamic of control on behavior between a mode facilitating optimization of task performance (exploitation of defined rewarding behaviors) and a mode facilitating disengagement from the current task to search for alternative behaviors (exploration). This hypothesis is supported by the existence of massive ACC projections to the locus coeruleus. Note that changes in LC activity would be the means by which a dACC/OFC output triggers changes in the LPFC. The noradrenergic system would be in close interaction or synergy with the mesencephalic dopaminergic system involved in reinforcement learning (Aston-Jones and Cohen, 2005; Bouret and Sara, 2005).

Dehaene *et al.* (1998) proposed a model based on two computational spaces. The first, the processing network, encloses functionally specialized subsystems ranging from primary sensory to heteromodal, or high-order categorical processors. The second computational space, the global workspace, consists of distributed neuronal populations connected to the processing network through long-range connections. Interestingly, the global workspace is not a group of fixed cardinal cortical areas but encompasses various sets of neurons, in different areas, that are engaged or configured at a particular time in a given task. In the primate brain, the LPFC, ACC and parietal cortex would be the core components of the global workspace. Processors are dynamically engaged by these particular subsets or workspace neurons. Among the five defined specialized processors, the evaluation circuit allows maintenance or change in workspace activity depending on its positive or negative value. The evaluation circuit theoretically includes the ACC.

The authors tested a minimal simulation of this architecture on the Stroop task at different stages of training. They show that the global workspace was fully activated during the initial search or learning period, then changed its mode of activation and refined the specificity of its top-down influence on processors during an effortful but efficient execution of the task. Moreover, routinization led to disengagement of the global workspace. Another interesting feature of the model is that repetitive correct performance during effortful execution leads to reduced vigilance and workspace activity and ends up with behavioral errors. The errors in turn induce reactivation of both the vigilance system and workspace activity. The effect is comparable to the reactivation of cognitive control in the Botvinick *et al.* model (see above).

Neurophysiological recordings in monkeys have not been able to support the proposed role of dACC in conflict monitoring. As we will show in the present paper, most data converge toward a role for dACC in building predictions and values and in computing prediction errors in collaboration with subcortical networks. However, we report data that strongly support the idea that dACC is the source of signals that trigger the increase in cognitive control performed by the LPFC.

Dorsolateral lateral prefrontal cortex (DLPFC), dorsal anterior cingulate cortex (dACC) and dopamine (DA)

Here we quickly review general anatomical and neurophysiological features of three main components used in computational models i.e. the DLPFC, the ACC, and the dopaminergic system.

The DLPFC includes areas 8A, 46, 9/46 and 9. Several theories are proposed regarding its functions (Goldman-Rakic, 1987; Fuster, 1997; Petrides, 1998; Miller and Cohen, 2001). Most of them are based on the fact that DLPFC neural activity participates in bridging cues and responses separated in time and space by actively representing task-relevant information, i.e. information relative to targets, responses and goals. Debates on functional dissociations within DLPFC are intense. However it is now admitted that active representation of information is a key feature of DLPFC neural activity. Although it is still under investigation, it is proposed that the maintenance and the control of information involve several mechanisms, somewhat dependent on dopaminergic input, and related to recurrent excitations within DLPFC and between DLPFC and distant areas like the parietal cortex (see Constantinidis and Procyk, 2004 for review).

Prefrontal areas and striatum are targets of dopaminergic neurons. The activity of mesencephalic dopaminergic neurons (DA neurons) seems to be related to the evaluation of prediction errors, i.e. the discrepancy between expected and actual outcomes. [Note that in computational terms the production and use of prediction errors is more sophisticated than a pure difference since it implies construction and adjustments of state value functions and of discounting factors (Montague *et al.*, 2004)]. Computing prediction errors is a powerful mechanism by which biological systems as well as artificial networks can learn and adapt their responses (Schultz and Dickinson, 2000). The origin of this signal and its consequences on information processing in DAergic target structures (cortex in particular) are poorly understood. The literature suggests that two defined cognitive processes, error detection and working memory, could depend on DA influences on prefrontal cortex (Williams and Goldman-Rakic, 1995; Holroyd and Coles, 2002). It has been shown using micro-iontophoresis that the activity of DLPF neurons is strongly modulated by DA antagonists (Williams and Goldman-Rakic, 1995; Wang *et al.*, 2004). These antagonists also alter behavioral performances in cognitive tasks. Recent theories and models postulate that DA afferences could serve as triggers to update goal representations maintained in DLPFC (Montague *et al.*, 2004). There is here a resemblance with the proposed role for DA afferences in error-related ACC activity.

The dACC (including in particular area 24c) has an intermediate position between limbic, prefrontal, and premotor systems (Paus, 2001; Amiez *et al.*, 2005b). Recordings in dACC reveal a role of the structure in planning reward-based voluntary movements (Shima and Tanji, 1998; Akkal *et al.*, 2002; Amiez *et al.*, 2005b), and show activity specific to trial and error (nonroutine) behavior (Procyk *et al.*, 2000). The role of the dACC in integrating reward in motor plans, and its apparently unique role in error detection, fit with recent ideas concerning the fundamental role of this structure in associating action and outcomes (Matsumoto *et al.*, 2003; Rushworth *et al.*, 2004; Amiez *et al.*, 2005a,b).

There are intense debates on the precise function of dACC in error detection. Event-related potentials recorded in humans and unit recordings in monkeys suggest that error-related negativity (ERN) in humans, and dACC error-related activity in monkeys, could be generated or modulated in response to the inhibition of DA inputs (negative prediction error) (Holroyd and Coles, 2002; Amiez *et al.*, 2005a). Holroyd and Coles (2002) proposed that the relationships between ACC and the mesocortical dopaminergic pathway are the source of the ERN. In their model, a negative prediction error signal (inhibition of dopaminergic neurons), which indicates a negative deviation to an expected reward, disinhibits ACC motor neurons, which then produce the cortical error signal. For correct trials, activation of dopaminergic neurons inhibits ACC motor neurons and thus no error signal is produced. However, this relation is currently challenged. The specificity of the ERN to errors is highly debated (Botvinick *et al.*, 2001; Vidal *et al.*, 2003; Allain *et al.*, 2004) and there is no direct evidence on the role of DA input on ACC error-related activity.

Pathways linking DLPFC and ACC have been described in animals and humans (Paus *et al.*, 2001). Brain-imaging studies concerning higher cognitive functions repeatedly show co-activation of DLPFC and ACC, in particular during tasks requiring active control of behavior. It has also been possible to show, using ERP in patients with DLPFC lesions, the role of a DLPFC–ACC interaction on the control and adaptation of behavior (Gehring and Knight, 2000). ERP studies of verbal fluency revealed an onset of ACC activity 50 ms before lateral prefrontal cortex activity (Posner and DiGirolamo, 1998). So far, however, both the dynamic and causal relationships between the activations of the two structures remain poorly understood.

Reviews of OFC functions suggest that in many cases OFC neurons represent the reinforcement association of visual stimuli (Rolls, 2004). The OFC would enable very rapid reversal by stimulus–reinforcement association relearning (Tremblay and Schultz, 2000a; Rolls, 2004). It has also been found that OFC neurons code for stimulus preference in terms of reward, i.e. for the motivational value of stimuli (Tremblay and Schultz, 1999).

From the set of data and theoretical propositions just reviewed, one can isolate constants and issues that need to be taken into account to better understand and study adaptive cognitive functions. First, it seems to be well accepted that signals issued when unexpected events or problems in information processing are detected trigger changes in LPFC activity. Such signals could be directly or indirectly transmitted to the LPFC. Second, these signals are related to outcome prediction and evaluation, and structures such as the ACC and OFC seem to participate in that function.

Based on this knowledge, the following questions emerge:

- Whether and how the OFC and the ACC differ in their contribution to the estimation of value functions and to the evaluation of outcomes?

- What is the specific role of dACC in outcome monitoring, and does it have a link to dopaminergic signals? Can we associate dACC function with the functions of Actor or Critic?

- What are the relationships between dACC and DLPFC activity, and what dynamic changes occur during behavioral adaptation?

Unit recordings in monkeys performing complex tasks requiring fast adaptation of behavior allow an essential access to the neural processing underlying cognitive functions.

Neurophysiology of cognitive control and performance monitoring

Evaluation of behavior, evaluation of outcomes

Adaptation of behavior is based on the ability to predict potential outcomes, compare those to actual outcomes, and decide whether there is a need to adapt responses. Because of its anatomical and functional position within networks devoted to reward processing and cognitive functions (Paus, 2001; Rushworth et al., 2004), the dACC might be a central structure for these processes. We studied the role of dACC in reward processing and behavioral evaluation by recording unit activity in the dorsal bank of the anterior cingulate sulcus (dACC, area 24c) in No-choice and Choice tasks (Amiez et al., 2003, 2006). The differential role of dACC and OFC in reward processing has been addressed in the same context.

Behavior

In the Choice task the monkey had to touch one of two visual stimuli, A and B, presented simultaneously on a touch screen. The task was one of probabilistic learning. New pairs of stimuli were presented in each block of trials, and in each block the monkey had to find the 'best', i.e. the best-rewarded one. Touching stimulus A yielded 1.2 ml of juice with a probability $p = 0.7$, and 0.4 ml with a probability $Q = 0.3$. The reinforcement ratio for stimulus B was the opposite: the touch stimulus B yielded 1.2 ml with a probability $p = 0.3$, and 0.4 ml with a probability $Q = 0.7$. These probabilities were implemented as follows: the animal performed successive blocks of 20 trials, in which the computer randomly selected trials without repetition. In this task, the systematic choice of stimulus A was the optimal strategy and was rewarded on the average in each trial by 0.96 ml ($0.7 \times 1.2 + 0.3 \times 0.4 = 0.96$). We refer to this average quantity as the task value. The task value represents the maximum average reward per trial offered in the task and is therefore different from the actual rewards received in single trials. Systematic choice of stimulus B was the worst strategy and was rewarded on the average per trial by 0.64 ml ($0.3 \times 1.2 + 0.7 \times 0.4 = 0.64$). The average reward of any intermediate strategy combining choices of A and B was between 0.64 ml and 0.96 ml, and was a linear function of the probability of choosing A.

The animals found the best stimulus in almost all blocks (Amiez et al., 2006). For each block we could identify a search period and a repetition period. A search period is the series of consecutive trials during which the animal searched for the good stimulus by touching either one of the two. We defined the repetition period as a series of five consecutive trials in which the same stimulus was selected followed by selection of the same stimulus in the next five trials, or in five of the next six trials. When the repetition period was terminated, two new stimuli were selected and another test was initialized.

As a control we trained monkeys on a No-choice task, which was identical to the Choice task, except that the two stimuli were fixed identical and well-learned and the quantity of reward delivered at the end of the trials was predictable. In this task, three kinds of trials were presented: 1.2, 0.4 and 0 ml trials, in which the stimuli were associated with the corresponding amount of reward. The task values in trials 1.2, 0.4 and 0 ml were respectively equal to 1.2, 0.4 and 0 ml. Thus, the task values in these trials are not different from the actual rewards obtained.

Recordings in ACC

Recordings in dACC that are reported here come from the same region located in the dorsal bank of the cingulate sulcus anterior to the level of the genu of the arcuate sulcus. Most recordings are likely to be within, and just anterior to, the rostral cingulate motor area (CMAr).

Analyses of 195 task-related unit activities revealed various ways in which ACC participates in behavioral evaluation (Amiez et al., 2006). For each unit we measured the average activity in several successive time epochs constituting trials.

Activity related to stimuli onset or to arm movement (sensorimotor activity) varied with expected reward size. In particular, during the No-choice task the average discharge rate in 25% of epochs was different when the monkey expected 1.2, 0.4 or 0 ml. Thus, during the No-choice task sensorimotor activity varied with the task value, i.e. with the actual expected reward.

We thus wondered whether ACC activity in the Choice task would still reveal reward expectation, knowing that in this task the animal could not predict the exact amount of reward delivered at the end of each trial. We normalized the activity measured in Choice trials according to activity measured in No-choice trials (1.2 ml = 100; 0.4 ml = 0) (Figure 2.1C). Remarkably the average activity during the repetition period appeared to

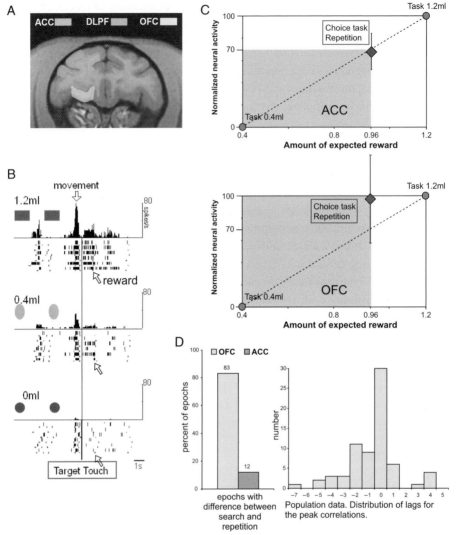

Figure 2.1 (A) Localization of areas of interest on a magnetic resonance imaging frontal section in a monkey. **(B)** Unit activity of one neuron recorded in the dorsal anterior cingulate cortex (dACC) in No-choice task. The firing rate of the neuron increases at the time of movement and is modulated by the expected reward signalled by the shape of stimuli (blue, green, and red) that are presented at the beginning of trials. Activity is aligned on the time of touch on a stimulus. **(C)** Normalized pre-reward activity in trials: 0, 0.4, 1.2 ml, and choice trials in ACC and orbitofrontal cortex (OFC). Population data. Task values are in abscissa. Data points in ordinates are the normalized average activities of epochs (mean ± SD). (There is no error bar for trial 1.2 ml and trial 0.4 ml, which following normalization are equal, in each epoch, to 100 and 0, respectively.) **(D)** Proportion of epochs with different activity in search and repetition in the Choice task for OFC and ACC (bar graph on the left). On the right: correlation analysis between performance and activity. Population data. Distribution of lags for the peak correlations. Negative lags indicate performance in advance of neural activity. When the cross-correlation was statistically significant at a time lag (trial), this lag—positive or negative—indicated a statistically significant time shift between the two curves and an advance of one curve over the other. When significant correlations were observed at different lags, we arbitrarily selected the time lag corresponding to the largest correlation. See color plate section.

be very close to 70 (68 ± 16.2 SD) on the normalized scale, which represents the average reward the monkey can get by choosing the best stimulus or 0.96 ml (1.2 ml × 0.7 + 0.4 ml × 0.3), the task value.

Surprisingly, this level of activity was stable during search and repetition periods, i.e. the task value was coded for on every choice even when the monkey did not know which stimulus was best. These data suggest that ACC neurons encode task values, i.e. the goal in terms of reward that the monkey can expect by using a particular course of action. This optimal value could be used as a reference (or goal) during search to find the correct target. The fact that there is no change in value encoding between search and repetition strongly supports a role for dACC in encoding the global task value, that is the optimal reward, which is fixed from one block to another and from one day to another, and that can be used to guide behavior toward the correct solution. Indeed muscimol injections in dACC induce strong deficits in finding the best stimulus (Amiez *et al.*, 2006). Recently, Kennerley *et al.* (2006) showed that dACC lesions induce failures in integrating reinforcement history to guide future choices. This work and our recordings converge toward describing a major role of ACC in integrating reward information over time. On the other hand, some cells showed error-related activity (when monkeys failed to maintain eye fixation or failed to hold the lever). Such activity was modulated by the expected reward size: the higher the expected size of reward the higher the error-related activity (Amiez *et al.*, 2005a). Thus, dACC might also have a particular role in monitoring feedback when expectations are not satisfied (see below).

Recordings in OFC

Here we analyzed 124 cells recorded in the OFC (area 11 and 13) in both Choice and No-choice tasks, or in Choice task only in two monkeys. As for dACC, in the No-choice task, expected reward had an influence on stimulus-related and movement-related OFC activity in about 37% of epochs (one-way ANOVA). Neuronal activity was modulated by the size of the expected rewards, or was different for unrewarded and rewarded trials. Reward size also had a major influence on activity recorded at the time of reward delivery (69% of epochs). Also comparable to the dACC, we observed cells which specifically reacted to free and unexpected rewards (as in Tremblay and Schultz, 2000b).

The probabilistic learning task (Choice task) revealed major differences between OFC and dACC. First, in contrast to the dACC, most OFC activity showed changes between search and repetition (for 86% of epochs). Second, the activity during the repetition period was equal to that observed in the 1.2 ml trials when the average reward values in the two situations were different (1.2 and 0.96 ml on average, respectively) (i.e. 97 ± 39.1 SD in the repetition trials versus 100 in trial 1.2 ml: $t = 1.42$, not significant at $p < 0.05$, unpaired t-test, see Figure 2.1C). Our data raise serious doubts regarding the capacity of OFC neurons to encode average reward values on a trial-by-trial basis.

To check whether changes in OFC activity had any relation with evolution of performance or choices, we compared the 'performance' curve (with the successive trials on the abscissa, and the choices on the ordinate: scored a 1 and 0 respectively to indicate choice of the better and the worse target) and the neural activity curve by a cross-correlation analysis

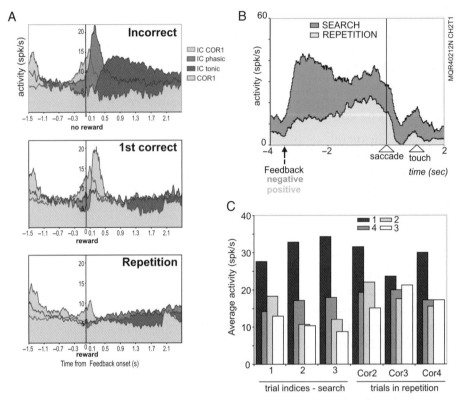

Figure 2.2 Dorsal anterior cingulate cortex (dACC) and dorsolateral lateral prefrontal cortex (DLPFC) activity during the PS task. (**A**) the three histograms present average activity of different neuronal population recorded in dACC. Activity is aligned on feedback for incorrect trials in search (upper histogram), first correct trials–reward (middle) and for correct trials during repetition—reward (bottom). Each population histogram is represented with a different colour: light orange: neurons with increased activity at the time of negative and positive feedback during search (incorrect + first correct; n = 20 neurons). Dark orange and red: neurons with increased discharge after errors. Phasic (in orange; n = 18 neurons) and tonic (in red; n = 39 neurons) activity are separated (see also Figure 2.3A). Blue: neurons that responded only after the first reward, i.e. the positive feedback terminating the search period (n = 13). (**B**) Average activity for one neuron recorded in the DLPFC. Activity is averaged separately for search trials and repetition trials, and aligned on the feedback (i.e. negative in search, positive in repetition). (**C**) Average activity for one neuron, measured in the delay before the saccade toward the target chosen during successive trials in search and repetition. The activity is measured for each target location (1 to 4). Note the change in firing amplitude and in selectivity (difference between the four locations) during search. See color plate section.

shifting one curve relative to the other in time (Mitz *et al.*, 1991; Amiez *et al.*, 2006). Negative lags indicate an advance of the performance over the activity. Figure 2.1D shows that for OFC, negative lags are more numerous than positive lags ($v^2 = 17.42$, $p < 0.001$, MacNemar's test). Thus, on average, OFC activity changed after the monkey decided to choose the best stimulus.

One interpretation is that OFC neurons become active only at the time of discovery of the best stimulus which then becomes the only target of behavior during further repetition trials. This supports the proposition that a major property of OFC activity is to encode stimulus preference (Tremblay and Schultz, 1999). We will discuss this point further below.

Modulation of cognitive control and performance monitoring

By definition, the contributions of cognitive control and performance monitoring vary rapidly during adaptation of behavior. To study their dynamic, we designed a task in which monkeys have to rapidly adapt and shift between exploration and exploitation according to current outcomes. The task was used to test activity changes in dACC and DLPFC.

Behavior

Monkeys were trained on a Problem-solving (PS) task (Procyk and Joseph, 1996; Procyk et al., 2000). The task consisted in finding by trial and error which of four simultaneously presented targets was rewarded. After initiating the first trial, and a 2.5 s delay, targets appeared and the animal had to make a saccade toward one of the targets, fixate it, and touch it. If incorrect, the animal was allowed to select another target in the following trial and so on until the correct target was selected (search period). Note that the first correct trial is included in the search period. The monkey was then allowed to repeat the correct response three times (repetition period). A juice reward followed each correct touch. One search period and the following repetition period defined a problem. After the fourth correct trial, a visual signal (a bright red circle surrounding the fixation point) indicated the beginning of a new problem, i.e. that another target was designated as correct. Eye movements were monitored and controlled. Breaking the eye fixation requirements (during the delay before target onset or during target fixation) stopped the trial (Break Fixation error). Feedback signals were defined as being either negative (after incorrect touch, or break of fixation: all targets switch off and the monkey is not rewarded) or positive (targets switch off and the monkey is rewarded).

Monkeys rarely repeated an 'incorrect' choice on the PS task before finding the correct target and rarely failed to repeat the correct response after discovering it. Analysis of problems revealed that the average number of trials to solution was 2.13 ± 1.06, 2.62 ± 1.19 and 2.29 ± 1.16 in the three monkeys respectively (see Procyk and Joseph, 1996 and methods for details on behavioral performance in PS tasks). The animals repeated the correct response almost perfectly. Although the animals' strategy for determining the correct target was highly efficient, the pattern of successive choices was not systematic. Analyses of series of choices during search periods revealed that monkeys could use clockwise, counterclockwise or crossing strategies without revealing clear stereotypic strategies. The animals could perform up to 120 problems per recording session.

As already observed in previous studies, behavioral parameters reflected important changes between search and repetition periods (Procyk and Joseph, 1996; Procyk et al., 2000). Both reaction time for arm movements and saccades varied between the two periods. The transition appeared after the first reward of a problem.

Recordings in dACC

We previously showed, using a similar PS task, that dACC activity observed before feedback onsets varies dramatically between search and repetition periods (Procyk *et al.*, 2000) (Figure 2.3A, left). This fits with the differential involvement of dACC in non-routine and routine behaviors. Using the PS task [used for DLPF experiments (Procyk and Goldman-Rakic, 2006)], we performed extensive recordings in dACC. Most neurons revealed changes in activity just before and after the feedback (positive or negative) but especially during the search period.

Global analysis of 384 neurons recorded in two monkeys revealed various types of feedback-related activity (Figure 2.2A). Three main types of feedback were defined: incorrect (incorrect touches—search), first correct (the first reward obtained in a problem—search), and repetition (all reward obtained in the repetition period). Note that the first reward could be obtained by chance on the first trial in search, or after several errors.

We discovered that a particular population was responsive to positive *and* negative feedback in the search period but showed very little activity after the rewards during repetition (Figure 2.2A; light orange). These contrasted with classic error-related activity that showed phasic or tonic increases after incorrect touches only (Figure 2.2A; dark orange and red). A third population showed phasic increased firing after the first reward only (Figure 2.2A; blue). These neural responses were not related to incorrect feedback, nor were they to reward delivery since no activity was found after rewards during the repetition period. These were very selective but other cells showed strong activation after the first reward and lower but significant activation for other rewards.

These data show that dACC is involved in positive and negative feedback processing when such feedback signals an event which is significant for the adaptation of behavior. Both signals are found in dACC, but overall the cells discriminate between the two events.

Recordings in DLPFC

Recordings in DLPFC (areas 8 and 46) also showed variations between search and repetition periods (Procyk and Goldman-Rakic, 2006). We focused our analyses on tonic activity that has been associated with a key role of DLPF in working memory, planning, or cognitive control (Goldman-Rakic, 1995; Miller and Cohen, 2001). We discovered that DLPFC tonic activity varied both in amplitude (average firing rate) and in selectivity (differential activation for the four targets). In search, the firing rate of delay cells increased sharply after negative feedback (Figure 2.2B). This was much less pronounced during repetition. The firing rate of delay activity was related to the position of the target that the animal was about to choose in the next trial, and defined what we called the spatial selectivity. Interestingly, the spatial selectivity of cells increased during the search periods while approaching the discovery of the correct—rewarded—target (Figure 2.2C). After the first reward delivery, levels of activity dropped and remained stable during the entire repetition period (Figure 2.3A, right). Thus, variation in delay activity could well reflect the varying level of cognitive control exerted by DLPFC during non-routine, exploratory, behavior.

The specific changes in spatial selectivity are good candidates for the top-down biasing effect that guides behavior (Miller and Cohen, 2001). Note that the changes do not follow reward probability since activity dropped in the repetition period when reward probability is maximal. Rather activity changes follow variation in uncertainty about reinforcement.

Potential interactions

Our recordings during the PS task allow investigation of important features of models invoking direct and/or indirect relationships between dACC and DLPFC.

Do activations of dACC and DLPFC neurons follow the same variations and depend on the current task requirement? Population data performed in two separate studies in dACC and DLPFC show that activity in the two structures varies similarly during PS tasks (Figure 2.3A). In particular, neurons in the two structures change their mode of discharge as soon as the animals discover the correct response, shifting rapidly from a search mode to a repetition mode. Although the precise type of modifications varies in the two structures (pure average response in dACC, average firing and spatial selectivity in DLPFC), the overall dynamic is similar.

Can we find evidence for sequential activation of dACC and DLPFC neurons after events that should trigger adaptation of cognitive control? Although we currently do not have enough strict simultaneous recordings in the two structures to precisely answer this question, population data of separate preliminary recordings are very suggestive. Figure 2.3B shows neural data obtained in one monkey in dACC and DLPFC during the PS task. The graph presents average discharge rates for three populations of neurons from dACC and DLPFC aligned on negative feedback. Phasic and tonic dACC error-related activities have been defined according to a statistically defined beginning and end of increase in firing rate relative to baseline (threshold at +2 SD of average activity measured within 200 ms before the feedback). These two populations respond only after negative feedback. Note that phasic error-related dACC activity starts and peaks before the time at which a significant change in DLPFC and tonic dACC error-related activity is revealed. Note also that tonic dACC activity exhibits a pattern similar to DLPF. These data support the idea of a transfer of information (directly or indirectly) from the ACC to DLPFC. More data are needed to investigate whether late tonic activations in both areas reveal a joint function and recurrent excitation between the two structures.

We look at the global picture of dACC and DLPFC activity during the PS task by averaging all task-related neurons recorded, without discriminating between types of responses, and aligned at the time of feedback: errors, first correct/first reward, and reward of repetitions (Figure 2.3C). Amazingly this indiscriminative average reveals the key features of the two areas. First the ACC codes for both negative feedback and first reward, and thus give a signal indicating either a need to shift or indicating a need to stay on the correct response. However, tonic activity after feedback detection is observable only for negative feedback. DLPFC shows strong activation after errors, later than ACC, with tonic activation. In contrast to the ACC, there is no DLPFC response to the first reward, suggesting that the ACC 'stay' signals did not trigger DLPFC activation.

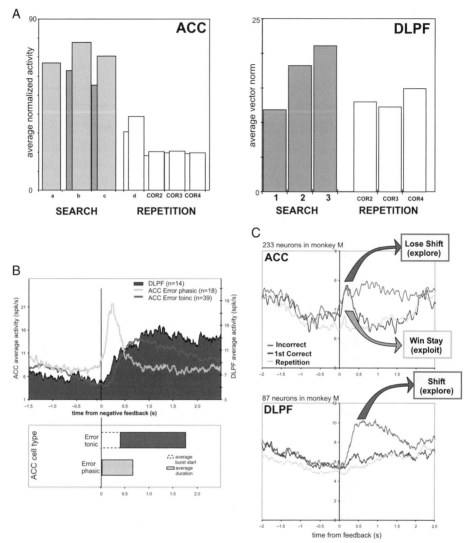

Figure 2.3 Dorsal anterior cingulate cortex (dACC) and dorsolateral lateral prefrontal cortex (DLPFC) activity during the Problem-solving (PS) task. (**A**) The two histograms present average measures on population activity recorded in ACC (left) and DLPFC (right) for the different trials of search and repetition periods of the PS task. ACC measures are based on normalized average activity at the around responses (from Procyk et al., 2000). For DLPFC activity the histogram shows average selectivity vector norm which amplitude reflects the spatial selectivity or discrimination between spatial positions (from Procyk and Goldman-Rakic, 2006). Note the clear transition on both areas between search and repetition, i.e. as soon as the animal discovers the correct response. (**B**) Average population activity for ACC error-related neurons (red and orange) and DLPFC delay (tonic) activity. PSTH are aligned on negative feedback (see text). Neurons are issued from separate recordings in the same monkey for both areas. The lower graph represents average start time and duration of significant firing for the two populations of error-related ACC neurons, i.e. phasic and tonic. Note that the two populations are overlapping in terms of duration. (**C**) Grand average of 233 ACC neurons and 87 DLPFC neurons that were task-related

These data are only correlations and clear understanding of the interplay between ACC and DLPFC will come from experiments interfering at different times and places within ACC, DLPFC and related structures.

Discussion and conclusions

About feedback detection

Since the 1990s a vast and fruitful literature has been devoted to the study of error detection and the major role of the ACC in this process (Holroyd and Coles, 2002; Ridderinkhof *et al.*, 2004). Observations of activity within or from the ACC during erroneous performances are numerous and highly reproducible. However, data about the involvement of ACC in more than negative feedback signaling are cumulating (Vidal *et al.*, 2003; Botvinick *et al.*, 2004; Rushworth *et al.*, 2004).

We showed, in our previous work and in the present paper, that the activity of dACC neurons suggest a major function of this cortex in representing expected reward values in simple, complex, and sequential behaviors, as well as in detecting and evaluating positive and negative feedback that is relevant for adapting such behaviors (Procyk *et al.*, 2000; Procyk and Joseph, 2001; Amiez *et al.*, 2005a, 2006). dACC unit activity reflects negative prediction errors (Amiez *et al.*, 2005a). We showed here that dACC monitors positive *and* negative feedback in relevant contexts and shows less activity to expected positive outcomes. This strongly supports an interaction between dACC and the dopaminergic system that itself encodes *both* positive and negative prediction errors. However, the direction of this interaction is far from being obvious and more experiments are needed to define relationships between DA neurons and dACC (for discussion of the origin of the DA signal, see Joel *et al.*, 2002).

We propose that the response of dACC to positive feedback is just a matter of context and predictability of outcome, which, in our PS task experiment, is disentangled by separating unexpected positive feedback with highly expected positive feedback. The bias of the literature toward a role of ACC in negative feedback processing only might come in part from experimental biases, i.e. nonequivalent status of positive and negative outcomes in terms of expectation during behavioral tasks.

The dACC detects unexpected positive outcomes. One hypothetical role for such detection is to label the just-executed action as correct (reinforced) and to shift behavior from an exploratory to an exploitative mode. It would be complementary to the detection of negative events. Thus, the dACC feedback-related signals could participate in the hypothesized driving of locus coeruleus activity toward phasic or tonic modes

---

but were not discriminated according to their specific event-related properties. Average discharge rates are aligned on negative feedback, first correct/reward, and repetition reward. Note that whereas ACC shows detection of negative feedback, it is positive when those are relevant for behavior adaptation. DLPFC neurons show a tonic activation only during exploration and in parallel with tonic ACC activation. See color plate section.

(Aston-Jones and Cohen, 2005), favoring either exploitative or explorative behaviors, themselves characterized by differential activity in dACC and DLPFC (see below). The role of noradrenergic cortical projections in adaptive behavior and its interaction with the ACC appears to be of major importance (Bouret and Sara, 2004, 2005).

The Actor, Critic and Values

dACC, OFC and Values

Only a few studies have been able to demonstrate a clear functional dissociation between ACC and OFC. Our data reveal complementary but differential roles of dACC and OFC in performance monitoring.

Our unit recordings during the Choice task suggest that *after* exploration/learning, the OFC (areas 13/11) might participate in biasing decisions and choice toward particular targets by tagging them as preferred (see similar conclusion in Tremblay and Schultz, 1999). OFC neurons encode preferences (motivational value), whether the competing items are experimentally contrasted in successive trials (in the No-choice trial) or in the same trials (in the Choice trial). Note that coding preferences amounts to another description of relative reward encoding.

By contrast, dACC represents expected values, at least in our experimental context. One hypothesis is that such values are used to internally drive behavior. dACC has particular activity in nonroutine situations which strongly call for internally based decisions. In agreement with these data, Walton *et al.* (2004) showed that whereas the ACC is particularly active when decisions are self-generated, the OFC appeared to be involved when decisions are based on external triggers (instructions, environment).

It might appear contradictory that, whereas dACC shows stable activity from search to repetition in the Choice task, it shows strong variations between search and repetition in the PS task. To reconcile these observations, one needs to consider the differences in goal and feedback status in both tasks. In the Choice task, one reward of one particular size does not have a particular significance in itself but must be integrated within the history of rewards, i.e. the relative proportions of rewards obtained after several trials. Here behavior must be directed toward a long-term abstract goal (the average maximum reward) that has been constructed during training. In the PS task, each feedback gives maximal information on a particular choice, and success (reward) matches exactly with the goal. In a probabilistic environment choices cannot be made in reaction to the actual feedback, whereas in trial and error reaction must be immediate, and decisions directly relate to feedback. Thus, in both tasks the dACC shows its main role in using the appropriate information (task value or feedback) to drive behavior.

Conflict

Overall, our data do not support a role for dACC in conflict monitoring. One could suggest that, in the choice task, conflict between stimuli or between responses are more likely to occur during the search period than during the repetition period. If the dACC is a conflict detector, its activity should be different in the two periods. Our data show that the activity is the same. Furthermore, reports of neural activity related to errors or to positive feedback are computationally easier to explain with the prediction error hypothesis (interactions between DA and dACC) than with the conflict-monitoring hypothesis. The hypothesis of a role for dACC in conflict monitoring does not account for our data. A similar conclusion has been reached previously using other protocols (Nakamura *et al.*, 2005).

Actor and Critic

Our data can be analysed in the context of attempts to attribute the functions of Actor and Critic to particular brain structures or networks (Suri, 2002; Dayan and Balleine, 2002; Montague *et al.*, 2004). Comparisons with brain structures suggest that the Critic may correspond to pathways from limbic cortex via limbic striatum to dopamine neurons, whereas the Actor may correspond to pathways from neocortex via sensorimotor striatum to basal ganglia output nuclei (Suri, 2002; Ullsperger and von Cramon, 2006).

Our work reveals that dACC shows many properties that we would attribute to a 'Critic' that is representing the expected value and generating prediction error signals, and not to an 'Actor'. However, lesion and neurophysiological studies in the monkey have suggested a role for ACC in building and selecting action–reward associations (Matsumoto *et al.*, 2003; Rushworth *et al.*, 2004). Central is the idea of a role for ACC in binding outcomes to action or events (see Chapter 6). Overall, the ACC may participate in Actor functions, i.e. in the selection of actions, and in Critic functions. We should also consider problems issuing from the functional heterogeneity of the ACC and recall that its posterior subdivisions are functionally closer to the premotor systems.

Also our data do not support the consensus about the OFC as being a major element of the Critic (Dayan and Balleine, 2002; O'Doherty *et al.*, 2003; Montague *et al.*, 2004). We show that the OFC does not represent average values, and apart from activities related to unexpected reward, we did not observe specific reinforcement-related activity during learning that would relate to prediction errors. Moreover, its role in preference encoding could be more related to the function of Actor (by participating in the selection process). Finally in our experiments, the OFC (areas 11 and 13) does not show the obvious properties that one associates with a Critic and that are displayed by the dACC. More experiments are needed since brain imaging in humans suggest correlation of OFC activity with prediction error (O'Doherty *et al.*, 2003).

We conclude that, in regards to our data, whether dACC and OFC should be associated with basic Actor or Critic functions is far from being obvious. Making parallels with other models describing interactions between Actor and Critic, or with a system devoted to goal-directed action-selection, might be more efficient (Joel *et al.*, 2002; Daw *et al.*, 2005).

Network activity during adaptation

fMRI and unit recordings reveal important interactions between dACC and DLPFC. However, the nature of these interactions remains unclear. Determining the relative contributions of indirect modulations through, for example, dopaminergic or noradrenergic systems (Cohen *et al.*, 2004; Aston-Jones and Cohen, 2005), or via direct transfer of information through cortico-cortical connections (Paus *et al.*, 2001), or as a result of a more complex transfer of information between fronto-striatal loops (Haber, 2003), is a key general issue for cognitive neuroscience. The system formed by dACC and DLPFC might be a good place to start to study the complex interplay between distant cortical areas, and between conceptually individualized cognitive processes.

It is noticeable that in the Dehaene *et al.* model, the differential involvement of the workspace is highly reminiscent of the DLPFC and dACC activity changes during nonroutine and routine situations in terms of dynamic, relation with performance etc. (Jueptner *et al.*, 1997; Dehaene *et al.*, 1998; Procyk *et al.*, 2000). This feature is also present in the models of Cohen and colleagues (Cohen *et al.*, 2004; Aston-Jones and Cohen, 2005). Our recordings in DLPFC fit with a role for this area in a top-down biasing process (Cohen *et al.*, 2004). More recently, Brown and Braver (2005) proposed that experienced negative signals could be used by the ACC to detect potentially negative environments and consequently to induce adaptation of control in advance. This model not only takes into account data showing ACC error signals but also the fact that ACC could be active in anticipation of outcomes even during correct performance. It also fits with our report of rapid changes in dACC activity between search and repetition periods.

Our data strongly suggest that very fast transfer of information occurs between dACC and DLPFC after behaviorally significant external events (e.g. negative feedback). But they also suggest that there might be quick changes in the types of relationships between the two areas once these key events have been integrated. More data are needed to understand these relationships and whether they rely on recurrent oscillatory activity or common neuromodulations.

General conclusion

Unit recordings in prefrontal cortex of monkeys during trial-and-error or probabilistic learning show the differential roles of DLPFC, dACC and OFC in detecting and evaluating outcomes, controlling and planning behavior, as well as in representing predictions about potential outcomes. These different processes are obviously interplaying during fast adaptation of behavior and when managing behavioral strategies adapted to current outcomes. The role of neuromodulatory systems appears to be important, although their complementary actions in fast adaptation of cortical processing during behavior are yet to be studied directly.

The collaboration between neurophysiology and computational modeling appears to be a complex but highly profitable path toward understanding the interplay between areas and describing the information processed in each area. Yet we think that real understanding of prefrontal functions will come from system neurophysiological studies devoted to cortico-cortical and cortico-subcortical interactions and their neuromodulation.

References

Akkal, D., Bioulac, B., Audin, J. and Burbaud, P. (2002) *European Journal of Neuroscience*, 15, 887–904.

Allain, S., Carbonnell, L., Falkenstein, M., Burle, B. and Vidal, F. (2004) *Neuroscience Letters*, 372, 161–166.

Amiez, C., Procyk, E., Honore, J., Sequeira, H. and Joseph, J. P. (2003) *Experimental Brain Research*, 149, 267–275.

Amiez, C., Joseph, J. P. and Procyk, E. (2005a) *European Journal of Neuroscience*, 21, 3447–3452.

Amiez, C., Joseph, J. P. and Procyk, E. (2005b) In Dehaene, S., Duhamel, J. R., Hauser, M. D. and Rizzolatti, G. (eds), *From Monkey Brain to Human Brain*. MIT Press, Cambridge, MA.

Amiez, C., Joseph, J. P. and Procyk, E. (2006) *Cerebral Cortex*, 16, 1040–1055.

Aston-Jones, G. and Cohen, J. D. (2005) *Annual Review of Neuroscience*, 28, 403–450.

Botvinick, M. M., Braver, T. S., Barch, D. M., Carter, C. S. and Cohen, J. D. (2001) *Psychological Review*, 108, 624–652.

Botvinick, M. M., Cohen, J. D. and Carter, C. S. (2004) *Trends Cognitive Science*, 8, 539–546.

Bouret, S. and Sara, S. J. (2004) *European Journal of Neuroscience*, 20, 791–802.

Bouret, S. and Sara, S. J. (2005) *Trends in Neuroscience*, 28, 574–582.

Brown, J. W. and Braver, T. S. (2005) *Science*, 307, 1118–1121.

Carter, C. S., Braver, T. S., Barch, D. M., Botvinick, M. M., Noll, D. and Cohen, J. D. (1998) *Science*, 280, 747–779.

Cohen, J. D., Aston-Jones, G. and Gilzenrat, M. S. (2004) In Posner, M. I. (ed.), *Cognitive Neuroscience of Attention*. Guilford, New York, pp. 71–90.

Constantinidis, C. and Procyk, E. (2004) *Cognitive and Affective Behavioral Neuroscience*, 4, 444–465.

Daw, N. D., Niv, Y. and Dayan, P. (2005) In Bezard, E. (ed.), *Recent Breakthroughs in Basal Ganglia Research*. Nova Science Publishers.

Dayan, P. and Balleine, B. W. (2002) *Neuron*, 36, 285–298.

Dehaene, S. and Changeux, J. P. (1997) *Proceedings of the National Academy of Sciences of the USA*, 94, 13293–13298.

Dehaene, S., Kerszberg, M. and Changeux, J. P. (1998) *Proceedings of the National Academy of Sciences of the USA*, 95, 14529–14534.

Fuster, J. M. (1997) *The Prefrontal Cortex. Anatomy, Physiology and Neuropsychology of the Frontal Lobe*. Lippincott–Raven.

Gehring, W. J. and Knight, R. T. (2000) *Nature Neuroscience*, 3, 516–520.

Goldman-Rakic, P. S. (1987) In Plum, F. (ed.), *Higher Functions of the Brain*, Vol. 5. American Physiological Society, Bethesda, MA, pp. 373–414.

Goldman-Rakic, P. S. (1995) *Neuron*, 14, 477–485.

Haber, S. N. (2003) *Journal of Chemical Neuroanatomy*, 26, 317–330.

Holroyd, C. B. and Coles, M. G. (2002) *Psychological Review*, 109, 679–709.

Joel, D., Niv, Y. and Ruppin, E. (2002) *Neural Networks*, 15, 535–547.

Jueptner, M., Frith, C. D., Brooks, D. J., Frackowiak, R. S. and Passingham, R. E. (1997) *Journal of Neurophysiology*, 77, 1325–1337.

Kennerley, S. W., Walton, M. E., Behrens, T. E., Buckley, M. J. and Rushworth, M. F. (2006) *Nature Neuroscience*, 9, 940–947.

Kerns, J. G., Cohen, J. D., MacDonald, A. W., 3rd, Cho, R. Y., Stenger, V. A. and Carter, C. S. (2004) *Science*, 303, 1023–1026.

MacDonald, A. W., 3rd, Cohen, J. D., Stenger, V. A. and Carter, C. S. (2000) *Science*, 288, 1835–1838.

Matsumoto, K., Suzuki, W. and Tanaka, K. (2003) *Science*, 301, 229–232.

Milham, M. P., Banich, M. T., Claus, E. D. and Cohen, N. J. (2003) *Neuroimage*, **18**, 483–493.

Miller, E. K. and Cohen, J. D. (2001) *Annual Review of Neuroscience*, **24**, 167–202.

Mitz, A. R., Godschalk, M. and Wise, S. P. (1991) *Journal of Neuroscience*, **11**, 1855–1872.

Montague, P. R., Hyman, S. E. and Cohen, J. D. (2004) *Nature*, **431**, 760–767.

O'Doherty, J. P., Dayan, P., Friston, K., Critchley, H. and Dolan, R. J. (2003) *Neuron*, **38**, 329–337.

Paus, T. (2001) *Nature Review of Neuroscience*, **2**, 417–424.

Paus, T., Castro-Alamancos, M. A. and Petrides, M. (2001) *European Journal of Neuroscience*, **14**, 1405–1411.

Petrides, M. (1998) In Roberts, A. C., Robbins, T. W. and Weiskrantz, L. (eds), *The Prefrontal Cortex. Executive and Cognitive Functions*. Oxford University press, Oxford, pp. 103–116.

Posner, M. I. and DiGirolamo, G. J. (1998) In Parasuraman, R. (ed.), *The Attentive Brain*, pp. 401–423. MIT Press, Cambridge, MA.

Procyk, E. and Goldman-Rakic, P. S. (2006) *Journal of Neuroscience*, **26**, 11313–11323.

Procyk, E. and Joseph, J. P. (1996) *Behavioural Brain Res*, **82**, 67–78.

Procyk, E. and Joseph, J. P. (2001) *European Journal of Neuroscience*, **14**, 1041–1046.

Procyk, E., Tanaka, Y. L. and Joseph, J. P. (2000) *Nature Neuroscience*, **3**, 502–508.

Ridderinkhof, K. R., Ullsperger, M., Crone, E. A. and Nieuwenhuis, S. (2004) *Science*, **306**, 443–447.

Robbins, T. W. (1998) In Roberts, A. C., Robbins, T. W. and Weiskrantz, L. (eds), *The Prefrontal Cortex. Executive and Cognitive Functions*, pp. 117–130. Oxford University Press, New York.

Rolls, E. T. (2004) *Brain Cognition*, **55**, 11–29.

Rushworth, M. F., Walton, M. E., Kennerley, S. W. and Bannerman, D. M. (2004) *Trends in Cognitive Science*, **8**, 410–417.

Schultz, W. (1998) *Journal of Neurophysiology*, **80**, 1–27.

Schultz, W. and Dickinson, A. (2000) *Annual Review of Neuroscience*, **23**, 473–500.

Shallice, T. (1988) *From Neuropsychology to Mental Structure*. Cambridge University Press, Cambridge, UK.

Shima, K. and Tanji, J. (1998) *Science*, **282**, 1335–1338.

Suri, R. E. (2002) *Neural Networks*, **15**, 523–533.

Sutton, R. S. and Barto, A. G. (1998) *Reinforcement Learning: An Introduction*. MIT Press, Cambridge, MA.

Tremblay, L. and Schultz, W. (1999) *Nature*, **398**, 704–708.

Tremblay, L. and Schultz, W. (2000a) *Journal of Neurophysiology*, **83**, 1877–1885.

Tremblay, L. and Schultz, W. (2000b) *Journal of Neurophysiology*, **83**, 1864–1876.

Ullsperger, M. and von Cramon, D. Y. (2006) *Journal of Cognitive Neuroscience*, **18**, 651–664.

Vidal, F., Burle, B., Bonnet, M., Grapperon, J. and Hasbroucq, T. (2003) *Biological Psychology*, **64**, 265–282.

Walton, M. E., Devlin, J. T. and Rushworth, M. F. (2004) *Nature Neuroscience*, **7**, 1259–1265.

Wang, M., Vijayraghavan, S. and Goldman-Rakic, P. S. (2004) *Science*, **303**, 853–856.

Williams, G. V. and Goldman-Rakic, P. S. (1995) *Nature*, **376**, 572–575.

Williams, S. M. and Goldman-Rakic, P. S. (1993) *Cerebral Cortex*, **3**, 199–222.

3

Perceptual deficits in optic ataxia?

Laure Pisella, Christopher Striemer,
Annabelle Blangero, Valerie Gaveau, Patrice Revol,
Roméo Salemme, James Danckert and Yves Rossetti

Lesions of the dorsal posterior parietal cortex (PPC) typically result in optic ataxia (OA)—a disorder in which patients have difficulty reaching toward and grasping objects presented in peripheral vision, in the absence of primary sensory or motor deficits. It is therefore considered as a human model of the PPC involvement in visuo-manual control. In the early twentieth century, OA was described as part of the Bálint–Holmes syndrome. The main aim of most analyses of OA in the second part of the twentieth century was then to isolate a pure visuo-motor symptomatology from the complex Bálint's syndrome (e.g. Garcin *et al.*, 1967; Rondot *et al.*, 1977). In addition, OA has been used over the last 15 years to argue in favor of dissociable functions within the dorsal ('How') and ventral ('What') streams of visual information processing and visuo-manual guidance (Jeannerod and Rossetti, 1993; Milner and Goodale, 1995; Rossetti and Pisella, 2002). In these contexts, research on OA has focused primarily on visuo-motor functions ('How') and has largely ignored visuo-spatial functions ('Where'). In this chapter, we will review recent accounts on the nature of the well-established visuo-motor deficits in OA and present original data revealing visuo-perceptual deficits in patients with OA. The possibility of a functional relationship between the visuo-motor deficits of OA patients and their perceptual deficits will be put forward and discussed.

History

OA is part of the Bálint syndrome

'Optische Ataxie'—a defect of visually guided hand movements—was initially defined by Bálint (1909) as one of the three components of a clinical entity comprised of a set of complex spatial behavior disorders following bilateral damage to the parieto-occipital junction (POJ), known as 'Bálint's syndrome'. The syndrome is a triad of spatial deficits including 'optische Ataxie', 'Seelenlähmung des Schauens'—often referred to as psychic paralysis of gaze (probably corresponding to simultanagnosia)—and 'räumlische Storung der Aufmerksamkeit'—lateralized spatial disorder of attention (probably corresponding to neglect) (Pisella *et al.*, 2007). A related 'visual disorientation' syndrome was described a few years later by Holmes (Smith and Holmes, 1916; Holmes, 1918) in soldiers who had sustained bilateral parietal damage. These patients exhibited a particular oculo-motor disorder: wandering of gaze during search for objects in the periphery and difficulty in maintaining visual fixation. This gaze ataxia or apraxia was also accompanied by a visual localization deficit in which patients had difficulty judging the location and distance of an object as well as difficulty determining the relative distance between two objects. Finally, there was a substantial impairment for visually guided reach-to-grasp movements, even when performed in central vision. This condition was interpreted by Holmes as a visual orientation disorder resulting from a retinal or an extraocular muscle position sense deficit. This condition was interpreted by Holmes as a visual orientation disorder resulting from a retinal or an extraocular muscle position sense deficit. Contrary to Holmes, Bálint clearly interpreted OA as being an autonomous symptom. Indeed, 'ataxie optique' was first empirically isolated from Bálint's syndrome by Garcin *et al.* (1967) who proposed a number of conditions necessary for diagnosing 'ataxie optique':

1. The visual field should be spared in the area of space in which visuo-motor deficits are evident. Objects presented in this region of the visual field must be seen, recognized and named by the patient, and no binocular stereopsis deficit should be present.

A

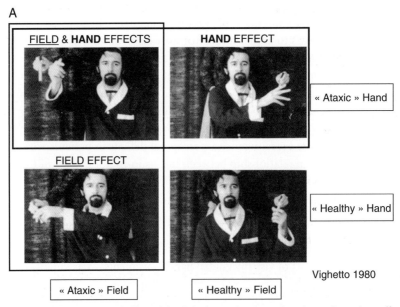

Figure 3.1 Field effect and hand effect. (**A**) Clinical examination of optic ataxia patients (from Vighetto, 1980). The clinician stands behind the patient and asks him to fixate straight ahead. Then he successively presents in the two fields target objects to be grasped with the two hands. This patient with right dorsal posterior parietal cortex (PPC) damage exhibits a gross deficit when reaching to left-sided objects (contralesional field effect) with his left hand (contralesional hand effect). Once the object has been missed, he exhibits exploratory movements comparable to blind subjects. This poor visuo-motor performance can be contrasted with the ability of the patient to describe the object and his normal ability to reach to central targets.

B

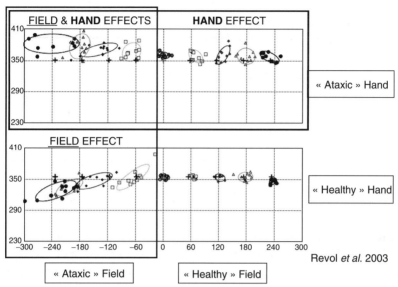

Figure 3.1 (*cont.*) (**B**) Movement endpoints and confidence ellipses obtained with the left hand (upper panels) or with the right hand (lower panels) in patient OK presenting right PPC damage (from Revol *et al.*, 2003). The horizontal and vertical axes correspond to the *x*- and *y*-coordinates (measured in millimeters) of the movement endpoints with respect to the starting position (i.e. close to the body and aligned with the patient's midsagittal plane). A different greyscale is used for the endpoints directed to each target. A confidence ellipse (95%) is drawn for the final pointing scatter corresponding to each target, with the use of the same grey. Black crosses match the eight target locations and the grey cross indicates the location of the fixation point. In the left visual field, irrespective of the hand used, pointing scatters were the largest. In contrast, pointing scatters in the right visual field were smaller and those with the right hand provide a control for unimpaired performances.

2. Proprioception should be spared.

3. There should be no intrinsic motor, oculo-motor or cerebellar deficit.

The term 'ataxie optique' has thus been initially used in French (Garcin *et al.*, 1967) to describe pure cases with unilateral lesions and deficits restricted to the peripheral visual field, whereas 'optische Ataxie' was used for patients with Bálint's syndrome resulting from bilateral damage, including visuo-motor problems in central vision, where praxic aspects are difficult to disentangle from ataxic symptoms. Unilateral OA is characterized by large errors produced when pointing to targets presented in the peripheral visual field contralateral to the lesion ('field effect'). These motor errors are larger when the action is to be performed with the contralesional hand ('hand effect') (Perenin and Vighetto, 1988; Figure 3.1).

Visuo-motor versus visuo-spatial interpretations

Eye–hand coordination is necessary for reaching to visual objects in order to interact with the environment. Whether this functional link between the eye and the hand

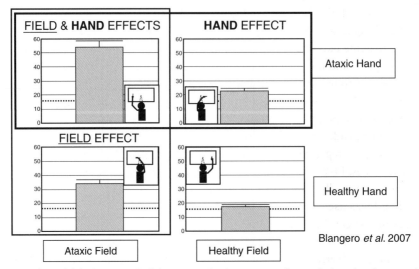

Figure 3.1 (*cont.*) (**C**) Histograms of the mean absolute errors when pointing visual targets in the dark (from Blangero *et al.*, 2007). Columns represent the means and standard deviations of the endpoint errors (in millimeters) for each four combinations of hemifield and pointing hand for the two patients Can and OK presenting unilateral optic ataxia. The dotted line shows the mean normal performance in the same condition.

(see Neggers and Bekkering, 2001) implies common neural substrates for saccades and reaching movements within the PPC remains a crucial question in the debate about whether the PPC is devoted to visuo-motor programming ('How') or visuo-spatial processing ('Where') and attention (Andersen and Buneo, 2002 and Colby and Goldberg, 1999, respectively). Historically, the parietal Bálint–Holmes syndrome described concomitant 'gaze' and reach impairments, which have been interpreted either in terms of a visuo-motor disconnection ('How'; Bálint, 1909) or a 'visual disorientation' ('Where'; Holmes, 1918). These two interpretations are reminiscent in the following literature on OA.

On the one hand it has been argued that OA cannot be explained exclusively in terms of a visual or motor deficit but rather involves the transformation of visual input into motor error ('How'; Bálint, 1909; Garcin *et al.*, 1967; Rondot *et al.*, 1977; Vighetto, 1980; Vighetto and Perenin, 1981; Perenin and Vighetto, 1988; Milner and Goodale, 1995; Battaglia-Mayer and Caminiti, 2002; Rossetti and Pisella, 2002). The 'How' interpretation has been heralded on the basis of studies (Garcin *et al.*, 1967; Vighetto, 1980; Vighetto and Perenin, 1981; Perenin and Vighetto, 1988) which have progressively demonstrated that visuo-motor deficits for peripheral targets can occur independently from perceptual disorders, supporting the initial view of Bálint (1909). A case described by Hecaen and De Ajuriaguerra (1954) provided evidence for a dissociation between OA and the oculo-motor deficits. Despite a massive deficit of ocular fixation over the whole visual space, their bilaterally lesioned patient exhibited OA only with his left hand. Rondot *et al.* (1977) also described cases in which OA was restricted to the contralesional hand, supporting the view that it cannot be attributed to a 'visual disorientation' deficit. Interpretation of OA as a specific visuo-motor disorder was further reinforced by the careful study of reaching behavior by Vighetto and colleagues (Vighetto, 1980, Vighetto and Perenin, 1981; Perenin and Vighetto, 1988). First, although verbal discrimination of dot position was impaired in some patients, a direct causal link between these subtle deficits in visual space perception and the gross misreaching errors was excluded by the authors. Second, patients demonstrated reaching errors related both to a visual field effect and to a hand effect (Figure 3.1A). This combination of visual and motor influences supported the idea of a specific deficit of the visuo-motor interface ('How').

On the other hand, other authors have argued that the basic deficit in OA lies at the level of the visual space representation ('Where'; Holmes, 1919; Godwin-Austen, 1965; Ratcliff and Davies-Jones, 1972; Kase *et al.*, 1977; Ratcliff, 1991). Specifically, Ratcliff (1991) emphasized that most visually guided reaching errors occur in contralesional space regardless of which hand was used and thus argued that visual mislocalization remains the best explanation for OA. Indeed, Ratcliff and Davies-Jones (1972) have observed that the errors produced by unilateral OA patients, regardless of the arm used, show a clear spatial pattern with error vectors converging toward the location of ocular fixation. Note, however, that most of their patients exhibited no pure visual deficit (most of them also presented with associated symptoms such as somatosensory defects, apraxia or unilateral neglect).

In summary, previous researchers have argued in favour of either the 'hand effect' (i.e. variants of the 'How' framework) or the 'field effect' (i.e. variants of the 'Where' framework) as the core deficit in OA. We will now argue that these two components of OA—and, further, these two lines of interpretations—are not mutually exclusive.

Recent accounts on the nature of the field and hand effects

The 'visual' ('Where') interpretation proposed by Ratcliff (1991)—that information derived from the contralesional visual field was systematically distorted as a result of a retinal or an extraocular muscle position sense deficit—was definitively ruled out by an experiment performed in two patients with unilateral OA (Khan *et al.*, 2005). This experiment allowed us to differentiate the location of the target with respect to the gaze axis at the time of target encoding and at the time of the manual response. Khan *et al.* (2005) compared the accuracy of manual pointing movements made to targets seen in peripheral vision or to targets initially seen in one visual field and then virtually projected into the opposite visual field. The projection of a given internalized target location into another position relative to gaze was achieved by an eye movement bringing the target location into the opposite field. Pointing errors were observed only in conditions when the target was represented in the contralesional visual field at pointing onset, independent of its position at the time of encoding. Thus, pointing errors can be said to be independent of visual input (Figure 3.2A).

Errors in an eye-centered reference frame

The first argument of Ratcliff (1991) in favour of a 'visual' interpretation of OA was the eye-centred pattern of pointing errors. In a recent group study (Ota *et al.*, 2003, submitted) involving seven patients with pure unilateral OA (four with right- and three with

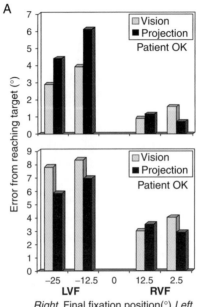

Figure 3.2 Eye-centered errors. (**A**) The ataxic field corresponds to the visual field when pointing and not the visual field when encoding (from Khan *et al.*, 2005). These graphs show absolute reaching errors [left panel: reaching target in the left visual field (LVF); right panel: reaching target in the right visual field (RVF)], for two patients with unilateral optic ataxia following damage to the right posterior parietal lobe (OK: upper panel; CF: lower panel), in two conditions of pointing: a Vision task (light grey) and a Projection task (dark grey). In both tasks, subjects foveated on a fixation position, while the target was illuminated. In the Vision task, after both light-emitting diodes (LEDs) (fixation and target) were extinguished, subjects reached toward the target location while keeping the eyes at the fixation position location. In the Projection task, after both LEDs were extinguished, subjects made a saccade to a second fixation position in the opposite visual field (left panel: second fixation toward the right—target in LVF relative to final gaze; right panel: second fixation toward the left—target in RVF). After this LED was also extinguished, subjects reached toward the target location while holding fixation at the final fixation position. Average errors are plotted as a function of target location relative to final gaze, e.g. the average error shown for 25° right means that subjects first viewed the target in their LVF, then made a saccade, and when they reached to it, the target was in their RVF. For both patients, errors were significant in the LVF in the two tasks, demonstrating that the 'ataxic field' is defined by the instantaneous eye position at pointing onset.

left-PPC damage), we confirmed the pattern of errors observed by Ratcliff and Davies-Jones (1972). As in Ratcliff and Davies-Jones (1972), we investigated the two-dimensional (2D) pointing behavior in order to explore the spatial pattern of error produced in peripheral vision. Targets were presented on a 24-dot virtual matrix comprising 12 points on each side of a central fixation point. The 2D direction and the amplitude of the error vectors were recorded for each patient in both visual fields and with both hands. Pointing errors consistently converged toward the fixation point, especially in the contralesional visual field, with both hands (Figure 3.2B). The single case studies of Khan *et al.* (2005) and

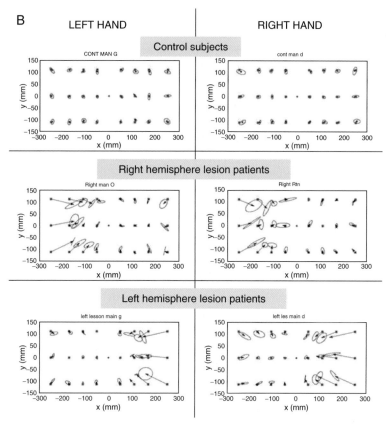

Figure 3.2 (*cont.*) (**B**) Group analysis of (2D) pointing in the frontal plane (from Ota *et al.*, 2002, submitted). The dots actually reached by the subjects constitute the arrows of the pointing error vectors. The first graph is for the control group, the next for the right hemisphere lesion patients and the last for the left hemisphere lesion patients. The control group shows an accurate pointing to all targets. The seven patients with pure unilateral optic ataxia all produced consistent pointing errors to peripheral visual targets for the two hands in their contralesional visual field. In the two optic ataxia groups, a clear undershooting was observed with error vectors clearly directed toward the fovea (fixation) and the magnitude of these errors increasing with target eccentricity. These results are compatible with the idea that optic ataxia is mainly expressed in an oculocentric reference frame.

Dijkerman *et al.* (2006) had definitively ruled out the hypothesis of a body midline reference and had rather put forward the hypothesis that reaching errors in optic ataxia were related to an eye-centered reference frame. The observations of Ota *et al.* (submitted) in seven patients with unilateral optic ataxia reinforced this hypothesis in favour of an eye-centered reference by demonstrating consistent error vectors directed towards fixation. Contrary to the idea put forward by Holmes, an eye-centered reference frame for pointing errors does not mean that OA is necessarily linked to a visual deficit ('Where'). The notion of an eye-centered reference frame can also be consistent with the visuo-motor hypothesis ('How'). Indeed, monkey electrophysiology has shown that the planning of reaching movements is based on an eye-centered representation of the target in the PPC (Batista *et al.*, 1999). In addition, functional brain-imaging studies have shown that the human PPC in each hemisphere represents contralateral space for pointing in oculocentric coordinates (Sereno *et al.*, 2001). Finally, Medendorp *et al.* (2003, 2005) have shown that information from both the target and the effector are integrated in the PPC in eye-centered coordinates for the planning of actions. A recent model suggests that an eye-centered reference frame is used to code target locations for direct visuo-manual transformations, as it could be compared with eye-centered hand location (Buneo *et al.*, 2002). Our own model for how visuo-manual transformations can use specific eye-centered coding of target location will be presented below in 'Dissociable Where and How components?'.

Effector independent pointing errors

The second argument of Ratcliff (1991) in favour of a 'visual' interpretation of OA was the observation in unilateral brain-damaged patients of the same pattern of pointing errors with either hand, suggesting that pointing errors were not dependent on the effector used, and further not 'visuo-motor' in nature. However, in Ratcliff and Davies-Jones (1972), no direct comparison in the same patient was provided between the reaching errors produced by the contralesional and the ipsilesional hands in the contralesional field. A recent group study (Ota *et al.*, submitted; Figure 3.2B) confirmed the observation that error vectors are qualitatively similar in the contralesional visual field with both hands. However, it also confirmed the observation of Perenin and Vighetto (1988) that errors are quantitatively larger when pointing is performed with the contralesional hand in the ipsilesional visual field (hand effect) and in the contralesional visual field (combination of hand and field effects), a finding which has also been observed in other studies of unilateral OA patients (Revol *et al.*, 2003; Blangero *et al.*, 2007; Figure 3.1B and 1C).

A recent study by Gaveau *et al.* (submitted) demonstrated the presence of similar deficits for saccade and reach movements in two patients (IG and AT) with bilateral OA. This suggests a common deficit for eye and hand effectors. This study investigated the saccadic behavior of bilateral OA patients using a double-step 'look and point' task in which the need for fast motor control was stressed by a target jump synchronized to primary saccade onset. The first aspect of the saccadic deficit described by Gaveau *et al.* (submitted) was a pathological increase of hypometry (undershoot errors) of primary saccades with increasing target eccentricity (Figure 3.3A). Pointing data from previous studies involving the same bilateral patients (IG and AT) also revealed hypometric reaching errors that drastically increased with target eccentricity (Milner *et al.*, 1999, 2003; Rossetti *et al.*, 2005). The second aspect of the saccadic deficit was impaired fast control of the saccadic sequence (see Figure 3.3B). Indeed, in control subjects, an update of the visual error takes place within about 150 ms, between the end of the primary saccade and the initiation of the corrective saccade (see Prablanc *et al.*, 1979; Becker and Jürgens, 1979; Gaveau *et al.*, submitted). In contrast, patient IG demonstrated an increased number of corrective saccades to achieve capture of the displaced visual target ('serial-saccade' behavior). Strikingly in these trials, her first corrective saccade was generated with no reaction time

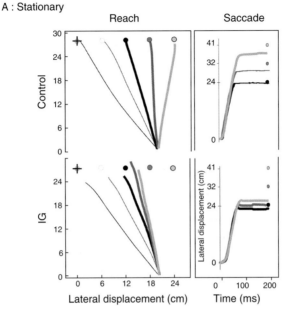

Figure 3.3 Similar pattern of errors for saccade and reach. (**A**) Comparison of the pattern of errors between pointing and reaching to stationary peripheral visual targets in bilateral optic ataxia (patient IG). Individual pointing (left panels) and saccadic (right panels) trajectories towards peripheral targets for one control subject (upper panels) and bilateral optic ataxia patient IG (lower panels). In the pointing task, subjects were asked to maintain their gaze fixed (black cross) while pointing to central (black dot) or peripheral targets (grey dots). Control subject reached accurately target positions estimated in peripheral vision whereas IG pointing behavior showed a pathological hand movement hypometry which increased with target eccentricity (from Milner *et al.*, 2003; Rossetti *et al.*, 2005). In the saccade task, subjects were instructed to move their eyes from a fixation point ('0') toward one of three peripheral targets (grey dots). Control subject presented a well-known undershoot (hypometry) of his primary saccade which increases with target eccentricity; it must be noted that following corrective saccade (not shown) will correct this hypometry; IG presented a pathological increase of hypometry of primary saccades with target eccentricity which appears similar to her pointing hypometry for peripheral targets. Note that this pathological hypometry of primary saccades is compensated by an increased number of corrective saccades (Gaveau *et al.*, submitted).

increase and was directed to the initial (extinguished) target location. Clearly, this observation indicates that the oculo-motor system does not have immediate access to the new retinal target location in patients with bilateral OA. Interestingly, the 'serial' saccadic behavior exhibited by patient IG is directly comparable to her reaching behavior described in Pisella *et al.* (2000) and Gréa *et al.* (2002), in which IG was unable to correct reaching movements 'on-line' following a target jump synchronized to the onset of hand movement but made a second 'corrective' movement to reach the targets (see Figure 3.3B). The similarity between saccadic and reaching deficits in OA also supports the notion of an oculocentric reference frame for both visuo-ocular and visuo-manual transformations.

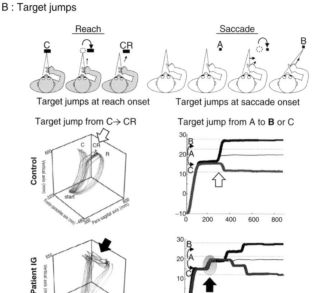

Figure 3.3 (*cont.*) (**B**) Comparison of hand and eye online visuo-motor control in bilateral optic ataxia (patient IG). This figure describes the performance of a control subject and a patient with bilateral optic ataxia (IG) in two experimental conditions. First, static objects were presented in central vision and all subjects were able to reach appropriately to gasp them in either position C or R. Second, when the object was quickly moved at the time of movement onset (C→R), controls were able to alter their ongoing trajectory and reach for the final location of the object (CR). The patient with bilateral optic ataxia was specifically impaired in this condition and produced a serial behavior. She performed a whole movement to the first location of the object (C), then followed by a secondary movement toward the second location (R). The time of target grasping was subsequently delayed with respect to stationary targets and control performance (from Gréa *et al.*, 2002; see also Pisella *et al.*, 2000). Similarly, her saccadic behavior (on the right: from Gaveau *et al.*, submitted) consisted of two corrective saccades, in addition to the primary saccade. The first 'corrective' saccade was directed to the initial target location (A) with no reaction time increase (i.e. as if the target had not been displaced), then a second late corrective saccade achieved visual capture of the target with a delay with respect to stationary targets and control performance. This pathological behavior (pointed by a black arrow, to be compared with the control performance pointed by an empty arrow) reveals a core deficit of on-line integration of visual target location.

Identifying the nature of the hand effect

It is often highlighted that the misreaching errors in unilateral OA are restricted to peripheral vision and to the contralesional visual field. However, the few experiments in which patients were tested for visual pointing in the absence of visual feedback of the hand have shown an increase in errors, and appearance of errors in central vision (Levine *et al.*, 1978; Vighetto, 1980; Brouchon *et al.*, 1986; Jeannerod, 1986). Blangero *et al.* (2007) assessed the nature of the hand effect by first demonstrating that this increase of pointing errors in the dark (with respect to a condition of visual pointing in the light, i.e. with visual feed-back of the hand) is specifically related to the use of the contralesional hand. In other words, pointing in the dark appeared mainly to increase the errors due to the hand effect. Searching for the underlying mechanisms of the hand effect would therefore consist in asking what is specific to visuo-manual reaching in the dark; specifically, the visuo-motor trans-formation has to rely on the felt position of the arm. Therefore, Blangero et al. (2006, 2007) designed a second task of pointing toward the ataxic hand in the dark. In this proprioceptive pointing task, the fingertip of the contralesional (ataxic) hand was the proprioceptive target (passively positioned by the experimenter on a vertical screen). This propriocep-tive pointing task specifically tested the subsequent hypothesis of a deficit in extracting the spatial location of the ataxic hand from multi-joint proprioceptive information accounting for the hand effect. Indeed, large absolute pointing errors (11 cm away from the target on average) were observed in the two unilateral OA patients of this study (Figure 3.4, lower panels). Since the patients have no primary proprioceptive deficit, this clearly revealed a deficit in localizing the felt position of the contralesional (ataxic) hand.

If the hand effect is due to proprioceptive mislocalization of the ataxic hand for aiming movements, then it appears logical that patients would exhibit this component of misreaching in the whole visual field (i.e. even in central vision: Brouchon et al., 1986) and for targets of other sensory modalities (Blangero et al., 2007; Figure 3.4, upper panels). That is, errors of this kind would be observed under any condition in which the hand effect cannot be compensated for via vision of the hand. Pointing errors linked to the hand effect should also be observed when pointing with their ataxic hand towards targets whose location is represented at a higher cognitive level, e.g. visuo-manual guid-ance through a mirror. Mirror ataxia is characterized by misreaching towards objects presented through a mirror following lesions localized in the anterior inferior parietal lobule and not in the superior parietal lobule (Binkofski et al., 1999). These patients therefore do not usually exhibit classical OA. However, the deficit of the less severely affected patients following a unilateral lesion only concerns the contralesional hand and at least one patient with mirror ataxia observed by Binkofski and Fink (2005) showed only the hand effect of OA (error with the contralesional hand in both visual fields and no error in the contralesional visual field with the ipsilesional hand) when pointing in peripheral vision was tested with left and right hands. Thus we suggested in Pisella et al. (2006) that mild mirror ataxia may correspond to OA with an isolated hand effect.

Dissociable Where and How components?

The demonstration of both field and hand effects in OA would require the co-existence of (1) a visuo-spatial 'updating' deficit common to eye and hand movements (Gaveau et al., submitted) which leads to the field effect and (2) a specific visuo-manual deficit correspon-ding to a mislocalization of the ataxic hand (Blangero et al., 2007) which corresponds to the hand effect. These deficits could correspond to the impairment of the two anatomical modules demonstrated in normal subjects by the imaging study of Prado et al. (2005): (1) an 'accessory' module located at the POJ and specifically activated in relation to reaching movements performed in peripheral vision and (2) a 'main' reach-related

Results for <u>proprioceptive</u> pointing

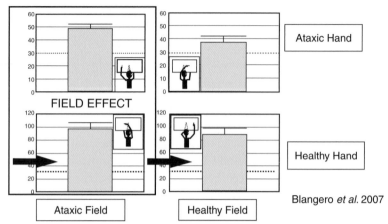

Blangero *et al.* 2007

Figure 3.4 Proprioceptive pointing reveals the nature of the hand effect. Histograms of the mean absolute errors when pointing toward proprioceptive targets in the dark (Blangero *et al.*, 2007). Columns represent the means and standard deviations of the endpoints errors (in mm) for the two patients presenting unilateral optic ataxia (Can and OK) when they pointed toward their ataxic hand (with their ipsilesional hand, upper panels) or toward their healthy hand (with their contralesional hand, lower panels), passively positioned at different locations in the two hemifields (left and right panels). The dotted line shows the mean normal performance in the same condition. Besides demonstrating a field effect for nonvisual targets, these results show unexpectedly large errors (11 cm in means) when pointing with the healthy hand toward the ataxic hand, in either hemispace. This latter result reveals a mislocalization of the ataxic hand from proprioceptive information (hence which can be compensated by vision of the hand), which accounts for the errors linked to the hand effect when pointing toward visual targets in the dark.

module located more anteriorly and always activated for reaching in central as well as in peripheral vision.

The POJ may also correspond to the posterior region lying within the parietal reach region that is correlated with saccades (Schluppeck *et al.*, 2005). We propose that the POJ region codes target location in oculocentric coordinates, and that the resulting visuo-spatial signal is directly used for saccade planning and also to 'update' manual reach plans that would be initially directed toward central vision. The observation of pointing errors in OA patients depending on the target location in an oculocentric reference frame (Ota *et al.*, 2003, submitted; Dijkerman *et al.*; 2006; Khan *et al.*, 2005; Figure 3.2) and the case of a parietal patient systematically pointing toward fixation ('magnetic misreaching': Carey *et al.*, 1997) are compatible with such a model of visuo-manual transformations. In addition, a model involving an updating of the reach plan based on the target–eye error may be particularly relevant for fast visuo-motor control. Accordingly, a deficit of fast visuo-motor control has been demonstrated in bilateral OA by means of 'target-jump' paradigms for reach-and-grasp movements (Pisella *et al.*, 2000; Milner *et al.*, 2001, 2003; Gréa *et al.*, 2002; review in Glover, 2003; Rossetti *et al.*, 2005) and for saccades in a look-and-point task (Gaveau *et al.*, submitted).

Attentional/perceptual ataxia?

Identification of a visuo-spatial deficit independent of effector (saccade and reach) could be seen as a novel argument in favour of the visuo-spatial ('Where') interpretation. It could also correspond to a deficient (eye-centered) coding of the target localization in peripheral vision which may be used specifically for visuo-motor transformation ('How') and not for perception ('Where' and 'What'). The latter was suggested by Perenin and Vighetto (1988) who reported that their unilateral OA patients performed relatively well (with respect to their reaching performance) in a location discrimination task in the visual periphery ('Where'). However, Michel and Hénaff (2004) have described a series of deficits of spatial vision ('Where') in patient AT who exhibits bilateral OA as a consequence of a large lesion. For example, patient AT had great difficulty deciding whether a point was inside or outside a simple shape. Nor could she navigate within a very simple maze to find the correct exit. She also completely failed to recognize biological movements (a man walking, throwing a ball, playing tennis, lifting a heavy weight) presented with simple dynamic patterns generated by displays of rigidly linked sets of points. Patient AT was only capable of tracking one slowly moving target disc, using foveal pursuit, when normal controls can track up to four target discs moving at the same time embedded among nine distractors (Intriligator and Cavanagh, 2001), a task which cannot be performed by pursuit eye movements but requires covert attention. Michel and Hénaff (2004) also tested visuo-spatial attention using the classical Posner paradigm. The results indicated that AT failed to demonstrate a significant effect of cueing (neither endogenously nor exogenously) for reaction times to detect peripheral targets in either visual field. The authors provided a complete and cogent examination of patient AT; they suggested that all deficits of spatial vision they described in AT require attention and interpret their results in terms of a concentric shrinkage of the attentional field. As a result of her large bilateral lesion, one can argue that this corresponds to simultanagnosia (or 'psychic paralysis of gaze' described by Bálint, 1909) and that patient AT is a case of Bálint syndrome rather than a pure bilateral OA patient. However, patient AT does not exhibit any sign of neglect neither in everyday life nor in neuropsychological tests of neglect such as line bisection. She could also identify easily different objects drawn and superimposed in a very restricted area of a sheet of paper, which is a classical test for dorsal simultanagnosia. In fact, simultanagnosia appears to be typically exhibited initially by bilateral OA patients who usually recover from it, but may still present with a more subtle deficit in terms of a concentric shrinkage of the attentional field. Further investigations will be described below, which have shown attentional/perceptual deficits in other OA patients, and especially in patients with unilateral OA who appear to show more pure visuo-motor symptoms independently from simultanagnosia.

A deficit in detection and anticipation of apparent motion

Rossetti et al. (2005) tested visuo-motor reactions to target changes in location in visual periphery occurring during a memory delay. Two patients with bilateral OA (IG and AT) and aged-matched controls were shown a visual target for 2 s in the peripheral visual field.

The target was then hidden for 5 s and was shown again at a congruent (80%) or an incongruent (differing by up to 20°) location. The subjects were instructed to point at it immediately after the second presentation. Results demonstrated that, contrary to healthy controls who initiated their reaches based only on the second target location, the pointing trajectory of the two patients were mostly influenced by the memorized information relating to initial target location rather than the present 'secondary' target location. Reactions to target changes in location were observed as mean trajectories between the memorized and the present locations or as late corrections of the trajectory in the direction of the present location (in nine of 16 trials for patient AT and in 13 trials for patient IG). This visuo-motor behavior extended the demonstration of a deficit in processing visual information for action in real time (Pisella *et al.*, 2000; Milner *et al.*, 2001; Gréa *et al.*, 2002) but also revealed a deficit of change detection in peripheral vision in the two patients (which was not present in central vision: same performance as healthy controls for a 'location-stop' response in Pisella *et al.*, 2000). Indeed, after this experiment, patient AT was questioned about her perception of the target jumps in the visual periphery: she reported that she never perceived that the target location sometimes changed during the delay. Patient IG, who spontaneously reported target changes in location during the experiment, was then asked systematically whether the target changed in location during the delay. Numerous false alarms were recorded on her verbal responses, as well as numerous trajectory corrections in the stationary trials carrying the hand further away from the true target location (also considered false alarms). Further analyses of the data compared the patient performance for visuo-motor and perceptual responses to target jumps (Figure 3.5).Whereas IG performed numerous (late) trajectory corrections for location-change trials with respect to no-change trials, her perceptual performance (d′ = 1.35) appeared to be even poorer than the visuo-motor performance (d′ = 3.9).

We have thus started to investigate the presence of visuo-perceptual deficits in OA patients. Since visuo-motor reactions to target jump (with an apparent motion) were impaired in these patients, we first postulated that perceptual anticipation of a moving object may also be impaired. Our subjects had to fixate the center of a large circular mask while a moving dot, following a linear oblique trajectory, was disappearing 'behind' the mask and reappearing at a proposed location (Figure 3.6). The subjects had to respond whether the proposed location was correct or incorrect. The mean performance of the three control subjects was a function of the amount of deviation (in mm) between location of reappearance and location that should have been anticipated. Deviations of 5 mm of the trajectory were well discriminated, suggesting a fine ability to mentally 'track' the trajectory of a moving object in controls. In contrast, the mean performance of the three patients remained low even for large trajectory deviations (15 mm). A temporal version of this test in which subjects will have to judge whether the timing of reappearance of the dot is true or false is currently being tested. We postulate that the perceptual judgment in these tests relies on the capacity to mentally simulate the spatial and temporal characteristics of the trajectory of a moving dot. It may be the case that not only a spatial but also a temporal deficit of perceptual anticipation of the trajectory of a moving dot may be revealed. These deficits could also be correlated to impaired performance in ocular and manual tracking in these patients.

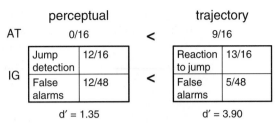

Figure 3.5 Impaired perception of large changes in location in visual periphery. Patients with optic ataxia were tested for their ability to process visual information in real time. They were shown a visual target for 2 s in the peripheral visual field. The target was then hidden for five seconds and was shown again. The patients were instructed to point at it immediately after the second presentation. Following a first block of trials during which the first and the second locations of the target were identical, a second block of trial included (20%) incongruent trials, in which the two locations differed by up to 20°. Healthy controls were not affected by the presence of the first target and reacted only to the second location. The two patients with bilateral optic ataxia (IG and AT) initiated their reaches on the basis of the memorized information rather than the present target location (Rossetti et al., 2005). Further analyses of the data aimed at comparing the patient performance for visuo-motor and perceptual responses to target jumps. Patient AT performed a limited number of trajectory updates but never perceived the target changes in location during the memory delay. Patient IG performed numerous trajectory corrections for incongruent trials with respect to congruent trials, but her perceptual performance (d′ = 1.35) appeared to be even poorer than the visuo-motor performance (d′ = 3.9).

Deficit in reflexive and voluntary covert attention in unilateral optic ataxia

The POJ may also correspond to the region described by Silver *et al.* (2005) correlated with saccades but also with covert attentional shifts. Saccade and reaching movements tend not to distinguish any more between target locations when target eccentricity increases (Figure 3.3A), as if spatial resolution were drastically decreasing, causing an apparent 'compression' of space. It has been shown that attention enhances spatial resolution ('Where', Yeshurun and Carrasco, 1998) and increases contrast sensitivity (Carrasco *et al.*, 2000). Impaired spatial attention in OA could explain the difficulty to report the occurrence of target changes in location (Figure 3.5) and may slow detection of a target in the visual periphery. We therefore asked whether a deficit of covert attention can be revealed in OA. Striemer *et al.* (2007) examined peripheral visual attention in two patients with left unilateral OA (right PPC lesion) with no clinical neglect and no clinical extinction (patients CF and ME). They utilized reflexive/exogenous (i.e. peripheral cue) and voluntary/endogenous (i.e. central arrow cue) versions of the covert orienting of visual attention task (COVAT) in which participants must fixate a central cross while attending to peripheral locations to the left and right (Posner, 1980). In a single trial, a cue (e.g. a brightening in the periphery, or a central arrow) directs the participant's attention to the left or right. On 'valid' trials, targets appear at the cued location. On 'invalid' trials, targets appear at the opposite, uncued location. The COVAT typically results in a response time (RT) advantage (i.e. faster RTs) for validly cued over invalidly cued targets

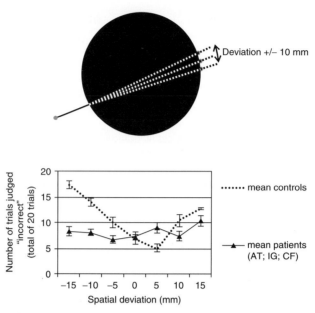

Figure 3.6 Impaired perceptual judgment of location based on 'mental tracking'. While subjects were instructed to fixate the center of a large circular mask of 140 mm diameter, a peripheral moving dot (constant velocity of 150/s, linear oblique trajectory) was disappearing 'behind' the mask and reappearing at a proposed location which could be correct (0 mm of deviation) or erroneous (5, 10 or 15 mm of deviation, plus means clockwise direction and minus means anticlockwise direction of deviation). Two main directions of trajectories were used: bottom-left toward top-right (subhorizontal trajectories, illustrated here) and bottom-right toward top-left (subvertical trajectories). The experiment tested response of whether the proposed location was correct or incorrect. The graph shows the performance (number of trials judged 'incorrect' among 20 trials) of three patients (IG, AT and CF) and three age-matched control subjects. The shift of the curve of the normal performance toward +5 mm results from the choice of two oblique orientations close to vertical and horizontal, revealing a bias of 'mental tracking' toward these well-known orientations. The impaired performance of the three patients, independent of the amount of deviation, reveals a deficit of 'mental tracking' preventing correct perceptual judgment of location.

(Posner, 1980). Faster RTs for valid trials reflect the fact that attention has already been directed to the cued location. On invalid trials participants must first disengage attention from the cued location, and then move and engage attention at the opposite, uncued location (Posner *et al.*, 1984). Previous studies examining covert attention in patients with parietal lesions without OA had demonstrated a characteristic deficit in 'disengaging' attention such that they are abnormally slow to detect targets in contralesional space when the preceding cue appears in ipsilesional space (Posner *et al.*, 1984; Losier and Klein, 2001). Results indicated that both unilateral OA patients were slower to respond to *all* targets in their (left) ataxic visual field (i.e. validly, invalidly, and no cue conditions), consistent with deficits in orienting *and* reorienting attention (Figure 3.7). The fact that both patients exhibited slower RTs for all targets occurring in contralesional space

EXOGENOUS POSNER TASK

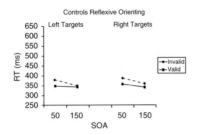

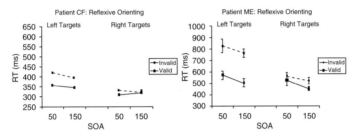

ENDOGENOUS POSNER TASK

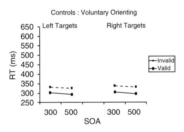

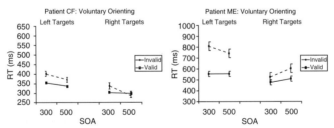

Figure 3.7 Impaired performance in the Posner task. These graphs show the mean reaction time to press a button in response to target onset in left or right peripheral visual field for healthy controls (upper panel) and two patients with unilateral optic ataxia (lower panels) and for two stimulus onset asynchrony (SOA) between the (exogenous or endogenous) cue and the target onsets. In this task initially designed by Posner (1980), healthy controls show a symmetrical pattern with a cost (increase of reaction times when the location of the cue was invalid to predict the location of the target (invalid trials). By contrast, the two patients exhibited an impaired detection in their (left) ataxic field revealed by higher reaction times to respond to left targets in valid and in invalid trials (Striemer et al., 2007).

(even when a cue was not presented) is consistent with an overall decrease in the salience of stimuli in the ataxic field.

The deficit of covert attention is associated with deficit of perception in the visual periphery

The model of Milner and Goodale (1995) postulated that OA was the typical deficit of the 'vision for action' dorsal pathway (i.e. 'How') with preservation of the 'vision for perception' ventral pathway (i.e. 'What'). The interesting question to ask is thus whether the deficits of covert attention demonstrated with the Posner paradigm in OA patients lead to feature-based perceptual problems ('What') in the visual periphery. Indeed, by boosting the strength and the quality of neural signals evoked by an object, attention may effectively provide a more fine-grained sample of the object's features. Impaired selective attention in the contralesional visual field may then lead to a perceptual deficit in a feature-based discrimination task ('What'). We thus designed a letter discrimination task in peripheral vision in a covert orienting context. This task is a 'covert' version of the paradigm of Deubel and Schneider (1996), in which five target locations are presented as '8' symbols on both sides of a central visual fixation (Figure 3.8). Then, a central cue appears as an arrow indicating to covertly shift attention toward the right green position. A letter (F or C) was presented at the cued location 100 ms later and remained present for 150 ms. Subjects had to perform a letter discrimination response in a forced choice via a button press. Perceptual performance was investigated in patient OK who presented with left OA following a right PPC lesion (see his pointing performance in Figure 3.1B, case report in Revol et al., 2003 and Khan et al., 2005). Results clearly demonstrated asymmetrical perceptual performance between the left and right visual fields (Pisella et al., unpublished data; Figure 3.8). That is, the percentage of correct letter discrimina- tion was at chance level (50%) in the left visual field (at $7.5°$ of eccentricity as well as at only $2°$) whereas in the right visual field patient OK's performance was equal to that of a group of healthy aged-matched subjects (80% accurate). Given the short time of presen- tation and the subsequent masking of the letter, the perceptual discrimination is possible only when the valid cue allows the subject to covertly shift selective attention to the specific location where the letter will be flashed. In addition, the normal performance is influenced by the visual eccentricity at which the letter is presented. That is, eyes remain- ing at fixation, selective attention does not compensate completely for the rapid loss of visual acuity in the visual periphery. His ability to covertly shift attention toward the contralesional visual field was not sufficient to allow patient OK to perform the percep- tual letter discrimination task even at $2°$ of visual eccentricity.

Conclusion: relationship between perception, attention and action in OA

In the present chapter we have reviewed and discussed experimental and theoretical accounts of OA, as well as presented new data arguing in favor of attentional and percep- tual deficits in patients with OA. Specifically, a direct perceptual impairment has been

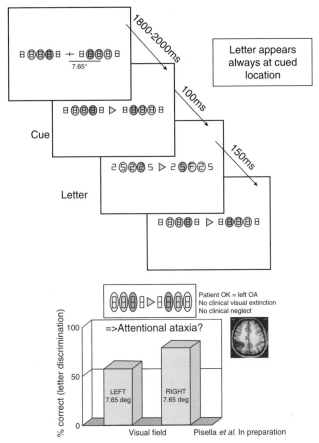

Figure 3.8 Impaired letter identification in peripheral vision. A central cue [green arrow (light grey in the figure) presented during 100 ms] indicates to covertly shift attention toward the corresponding green position, on the left or on the right. A target letter (F or C) is flashed at the cued location (in visual periphery, at 7.65° of visual angle) during 150 ms and then masked by the reappearance of the '8' symbols. Central fixation is required during the whole trial and checked by an eye-tracker. At the end of the trial, subjects have to respond by a button press whether the letter presented is C or F (forced choice). The performance of patient OK with left OA (right PPC lesion) is presented as a percentage of correct responses. The histogram indicates the percentage of correct identification of the letter when it was presented in the left or in the right visual field. The results clearly show an asymmetrical performance with a normal performance of 80% of correct perception in the right visual field and a perceptual deficit in the contralesional (left) visual field (chance level 50%). Note that this performance at chance level was also observed when the first target location in the left was cued and tested (at 2.5° of visual angle).

demonstrated in the visual periphery using a detection task (Striemer *et al.*, 2007, submitted) and a letter discrimination task (Pisella *et al.*, unpublished data), in single cases with unilateral OA. Further investigations will be needed to confirm this perceptual impairment on a larger sample of patients and to determine whether there is a functional relationship between the well-established visuo-motor deficits of OA patients and their perceptual deficits mentioned here. A functional link might be observed if attention is indeed 'yoked' to the endpoint of a pointing movement (e.g. Linnel *et al.*, 2005). One plausible alternative view is that OA corresponds to a dissociation between central and peripheral vision (Rossetti *et al.*, 2003). Along this line, Prado *et al.* (2005) have shown a specific module for reaching in peripheral vision (POJ) but no specific module for reaching in central vision. Similarly, in OA patients the 'field effect' component is by definition only present in the visual periphery in contrast to the 'hand effect'. We proposed that the POJ region codes target location in oculocentric coordinates, and that the resulting visuo-spatial signal is directly used to 'update' manual reach plans that would be initially directed toward central vision (Gaveau *et al.*, submitted). It is logical to assume that such an 'eye-centered' visuo-spatial updating signal would also be used for saccade control. We further postulate that such updating signals may also be used for perceptual and attentional processes (Pisella and Mattingley, 2004).

The qualitative similarity between the patterns of pointing and saccadic errors when target eccentricity increases (Figure 3.3A) has been used here as an additional argument for a core visuo-spatial deficit in OA that would affect both perception and action in the visual periphery. However, as Figure 3.3A demonstrates, errors for saccades and reaching movements become significant at different limits in the visual periphery (e.g. compare reach and saccade errors for a target presented horizontally at 24 cm from fixation). For the letter discrimination task (Figure 3.8), performance at chance level was observed even at $2°$ of visual eccentricity in the contralesional field. Current studies in our laboratory are further investigating the extent of perceptual/attentional deficits in OA, and whether or not these deficits are related to visuo-motor impairment. One ongoing study is examining the relationship between increases in target detection RT (button release) and pointing errors with eccentricity in the ataxic visual field. Preliminary results from this study suggest again a similar pattern, both RT to detect targets and pointing error increasing with target eccentricity. However, once again these two deficits do not appear to follow exactly the same linear trend with increasing target eccentricity in the periphery (Striemer *et al.*, unpublished data). Careful correlational analyses have thus far failed to mathematically establish a functional link between these deficits with respect to visual eccentricity and rather suggest that deficits in perception/attention and action may coexist in individual OA patients (as in the Bálint's syndrome) and result from damage to independent mechanisms. What would then explain the striking qualitative similarity of the error functions with visual eccentricity? Of course, pointing movements, saccades and button responses mainly involve independent mechanisms. Although they are all motor responses, they are generated from separate but interacting cognitive and motor neural systems that may still share a common spatial representation in the PPC (Silver *et al.*, 2005). Would the effects of the same deficient parietal module on these very different and complex circuits be expressed in such a way that a mathematical correlation could be established? Given that each of these separate complex systems relies only in part on common module, it may prove difficult to find a direct correlation between deficits in these systems in patients with PPC lesions. Therefore, we do not think that correlation is the best tool to determine the presence or absence of a functional link between these various deficits evident in the domains of action and perception in patients with OA.

We believe that the best way to investigate the functional link between different deficits remains the neuropsychological paradigm of dissociating impairments within individual patients. A possible confound is that many patients selected as 'pure' OA patients may initially present with mild neglect (in the case of unilateral lesions) or simultanagnosia (in the case of bilateral lesions), from which they have subsequently recovered. This can make interpreting attentional and perceptual disorders in OA somewhat difficult given that these deficits may be linked to the patients' previous pathology (e.g. neglect or simultanagnosia), and not to OA *per se*. The argument for such recovery of function in the case of hemorrhagic lesions centres on the reduction of the hematoma in the first few days following the vascular accident. Importantly, following watershed (ischemic) infarcts or hemorrhagic lesions, the positive and negative behavioral consequences of a given restricted lesion may be at least partially explained by the reorganization of surrounding intact brain tissue. A stronger case is provided by an anatomical 'double-dissociation', for which a lesion of structure X will specifically disrupt function A while sparing function B, and a lesion of structure Y will specifically affect function B while function A remains intact. Teuber (1955) termed this experimental tool 'double dissociation', and used it for both animal and human studies, arguing that it indicates some specificity of function. The separation of compound psychological functions into their primary elements has proved to be an important source of knowledge and theories about the organization of the human mind. In this context, dissociation is viewed as the demonstration that separate systems or structures are responsible for the two given variables (see Rossetti and Revonsuo, 2000). Single case studies have provided new directions for research and improved our understanding of the relationship between the brain and the functions. Their interpretation "has proved to be nothing less than revolutionary" (Code, 1996). It is still widely acknowledged that strong neuropsychological evidence for the existence of neurologically distinct functional systems depends on double dissociation of function (for a review, see also Rossetti and Revonsuo, 2000), although criticisms have been raised as to the validity and relevance of double-dissociations to anatomically localize cognitive processes (Passingham *et al.*, 2002). In some patients with OA, large portions of white matter are damaged and not only the neurons in the adjoining grey matter in the PPC (e.g. Karnath and Perenin, 2005). This makes it difficult to claim that only the lesioned area of the brain is correlated with the observed behavioral impairments. However, the classical neuropsychological 'dissociation' paradigm can nowadays been reinforced by detailed MRI scans and new techniques for imaging white matter such as diffusion tensor imaging (DTI). The use of these techniques will allow researchers to contrast the relationship between behavioral deficits and lesions, not simply in terms of their projection on the cortical surface (Thiebaut de Schotten *et al.*, 2005).

In conclusion, the research reviewed in this chapter challenges the long-held assumption that OA occurs independently from other perceptual or attentional deficits. However, it remains to be determined whether or not these deficits are in fact functionally related.

We suggest that the answer to this question may be obtained through future studies in which the performance of patients with OA in visuo-motor, attentional and perceptual tasks will be more systematically evaluated, compared across patients and correlated to anatomo-functional modules and their associated neural networks/circuits. The data reviewed in the present chapter definitively demonstrates that research on OA requires a fundamental reappraisal both regarding the specificity of visuo-motor deficits, and regarding the careful analysis of underlying lesions and disruptions to normal connectivity caused by those lesions which would benefit from DTI techniques.

References

Andersen, R. A. and Buneo, C. A. (2002) Intentional maps in posterior parietal cortex. *Annual Review of Neuroscience*, **25**, 189–220.

Bálint, R. (1909) Seelenlähmung des Schauens, optische Ataxie, raümliche Störung der Aufmerksamkeit. *Monatsschrift für Psychiatrie und Neurologie*, **25**, 51–81.

Batista, A. P., Bueno, C. A., Snyder, L. H. and Andersen, R. A. (1999) Reach plans in eye-centered coordinates. *Science*, **285**(5425), 257–260.

Battaglia-Mayer, A. and Caminiti, R. (2002) Optic ataxia as a result of the breakdown of the global tuning fields of parietal neurones. *Brain*, **125**, 225–237.

Becker, W. and Jürgens, R. (1979) An analysis of the saccadic system by means of double step stimuli. *Vision Research*, **19**, 967–983.

Binkofski, F. and Fink, G. (2005) [Apraxias.] *Nervenarzt*, **76**, 493–512.

Binkofski, F., Buccino, G., Dohle, C., Seitz, R. J. and Freund, H. J. (1999) Mirror agnosia and mirror ataxia constitute different parietal lobe disorders. *Annals of Neurology*, **46**, 51–61.

Blangero, A., Rossetti, Y. and Pisella, L. (2006) Saccade planning, pre-saccadic perceptive facilitation and covert attention: dissociated processes in posterior parietal patients. Abstract CNS, San Francisco.

Blangero, A., Delporte, L., Vindras, P., Ota, H., Revol, P., Boisson, D., Rode, G., Vighetto, A., Rossetti, Y. and Pisella, L. (2007) Optic ataxia is not only 'optic': impaired spatial integration of proprioceptive information. *Neuroimage*, **36**, 61–68.

Brouchon, M., Joanette, Y. and Samson, M. (1986) From movement to gesture: "Here" and "There" as determinants of visually guided pointing. In Nespoulos, J. L., Perron, A. and Lecours, R. A. (eds), *Biological Foundations of Gesture*, pp. 95–107. Erlbaum, Hillsdale, NJ.

Buneo, C. A., Jarvis, M. R., Batista, A. P. and Andersen, R. A. (2002) Direct visuomotor transformations for reaching. *Nature*, **416**, 632–636.

Carey, D. P., Coleman, R. J. and Della, S. S. (1997) Magnetic misreaching. *Cortex*, **33**, 639–652.

Carrasco, M., Penpeci-Talgar, C. and Eckstein, M. (2000) Spatial covert attention enhances contrast sensitivity across the CSF: support for signal enhancement. *Vision Research*, **40**, 1203–1215.

Code, C. (1996) Classic cases: ancient and modern milestones in the development of neuropsychological science. In Code, C., Wallesch, C.-W., Joanette, Y. and Roch, A. (eds), *Classic Cases in Neuropsychology*, pp. 1–10. Psychology Press, Hove.

Colby, C. L. and Goldberg, M. E. (1999) Space and attention in parietal cortex. *Annual Review of Neuroscience*, **22**, 319–349.

Deubel, H. and Schneider, W. X. (1996) Saccade target selection and object recognition: evidence for a common attentional mechanism. *Vision Research*, **36**, 1827–1837.

Dijkerman, H. C., McIntosh, R. D., Anema, H. A., de Haan, E. H., Kappelle, L. J. and Milner, A. D. (2006) Reaching errors in optic ataxia are linked to eye position rather than head or body position. *Neuropsychologia*, **44**, 2766–2773.

Garcin, R., Rondot, P. and De Recondo, J. (1967) Ataxie optique localisée aux deux hémichamps visuels homonymes gauches. *Revue Neurologique*, **116**, 707–714.

Gaveau, V., Pélisson, D., Blangero, A., Urquizar, C., Prablanc, C., Vighetto, A. and Pisella, L. A common parietal module for saccade and reach: eye-hand coordination and saccadic control in optic ataxia. Submitted.

Glover, S. (2003) Optic ataxia as a deficit specific to the on-line control of actions. *Neuroscience and Biobehavioural Reviews*, **27**, 447–456.

Godwin-Austen, R. B. (1965) A case of visual disorientation. *Journal of Neurology, Neurosurgery and Psychiatry*, **28**, 453–458.

Gréa, H., Pisella, L., Rossetti, Y., Desmurget, M., Tilikete, C., Grafton, S., Prablanc, C. and Vighetto, A. (2002) A lesion of the posterior parietal cortex disrupts on-line adjustments during aiming movements. *Neuropsychologia*, **40**, 2471–2480.

Hecaen, H. and De Ajuriaguerra, J. (1954) Bálint's syndrome (psychic paralysis of visual fixation) and its minor forms. *Brain*, **77**, 373–400.

Holmes, G. (1918) Disturbances of visual orientation. *British Journal of Ophthalmology*, **2**, 449–**468**, 506–518.

Jeannerod, M. (1986) Mechanisms of visuomotor coordination: a study in normal and brain-damaged subjects. *Neuropsychologia*, **24**, 41–78.

Jeannerod, M. and Rossetti, Y. (1993) Visuomotor coordination as a dissociable function: experimental and clinical evidence. In Kennard, C. (ed.), *Visual Perceptual Defects. Baillère's Clinical Neurology, International Practise and Research*, **2**, 439–460.

Karnath, H. O. and Perenin, M. T. (2005) Cortical control of visually guided reaching: evidence from patients with optic ataxia. *Cerebral Cortex*, **15**, 1561–1569.

Kase, C. S., Troncoso, J. F., Court, J. E., Tapia, J. F. and Mohr, J. P. (1977) Global spatial disorientation. Clinico-pathologic correlations. *Journal of Neurological Science*, **34**, 267–278.

Khan, A. Z., Pisella, L., Vighetto, A., Cotton, F., Luaute, J., Boisson, D., Salemme, R., Crawford, J. D. and Rossetti, Y. (2005) Optic ataxia errors depend on remapped, not viewed, target location. *Nature Neuroscience*, **8**, 418–420.

Levine, D. N., Kaufman, K. J. and Mohr, J. P. (1978) Inaccurate reaching associated with a superior parietal lobe tumor. *Neurology*, **28**, 555–561.

Linnel K. J., Humphreys G. W., McIntyre D. B., Laitinen S. and Wing A. M. (2005) Action modulates object-based attention. *Vision Research*, **45**, 2268–2286.

Losier, B. J. and Klein, R. M. (2001) A review of the evidence for a disengage deficit following parietal lobe damage. *Neuroscience and Biobehavioural Review*, **25**, 1–13.

Medendorp, W. P., Goltz, H. C., Vilis, T. and Crawford, J. D. (2003) Gaze-centered updating of visual space in human parietal cortex. *Journal of Neuroscience*, **23**, 6209–6214.

Medendorp, W. P., Goltz, H. C., Crawford, J. D. and Vilis, T. (2005) Integration of target and effector information in human posterior parietal cortex for the planning of action. *Journal of Neurophysiology*, **93**, 954–962.

Michel, F. and Hénaff, M. A. (2004) Seeing without the occipito-parietal cortex: simultagnosia as a shrinkage of the attentional visual field. *Behavioural Neurology*, **15**, 3–13.

Milner, A. D. and Goodale, M. A. (1995) *The Visual Brain in Action*. Oxford University Press, Oxford.

Milner, A. D., Paulignan, Y., Dijkerman, H. C., Michel, F. and Jeannerod, M. (1999) A paradoxical improvement of misreaching in optic ataxia: new evidence for two separate neural systems for visual localization. *Proceedings of the Royal Society of London B*, **266**, 2225–2229.

Milner, A. D., Dijkerman, H. C., Pisella, L., McIntosh, R. D., Tilikete, C., Vighetto, A. and Rossetti, Y. (2001) Grasping the past: delay can improve visuomotor performance. *Current Biology*, **11**, 1896–1901.

Milner, A. D., Dijkerman, H. C., McIntosh, R. D., Rossetti, Y. and Pisella, L. (2003) Delayed reaching and grasping in patients with optic ataxia. *Progress in Brain Research*, **142**, 225–242.

Neggers, S. F. and Bekkering, H. (2001) Gaze anchoring to a pointing target is present during the entire pointing movement and is driven by a non-visual signal. *Journal of Neurophysiology*, **86**, 961–970.

Ota, H., Pisella, L., Rode, G., Jacquin-Courtois, S., Luaute, J., Boisson, D., Vighetto, A. and Rossetti, Y. (2003) Spatial miscomputation in optic ataxia. Poster presented at TENNET XIV, June 23, 2003, Montreal.

Ota, H., Blangero, A., Fujii, T., Otake, H., Tabuchi, M., Vindras, P., Vighetto, A., Luauté, J., Boisson, D, Pisella, L. and Rossetti, Y. Visuo-motor fields show retinotopic error vectors in unilateral optic ataxia. Submitted.

Passingham, R. E., Stephan, K. E. and Kotter, R. (2002) The anatomical basis of functional localization in the cortex. *Nature Review Neuroscience*, **3**, 606–616.

Perenin, M. T. and Vighetto, A. (1988) Optic ataxia: a specific disruption in visuomotor mechanisms. I. Different aspects of the deficit in reaching for objects. *Brain*, **111**, 643–674.

Pisella, L. and Mattingley, J. B. (2004) The contribution of spatial remapping impairments to unilateral visual neglect. *Neuroscience and Biobehavioral Reviews*, **28**, 181–200.

Pisella, L., Gréa, H., Tilikete, C., Vighetto, A., Desmurget, M., Rode, G., Boisson, D. and Rossetti, Y. (2000) An 'automatic pilot' for the hand in human posterior parietal cortex: toward reinterpreting optic ataxia. *Nature Neuroscience*, **3**, 729–736.

Pisella, L., Binkofski, F., Lasek, K., Toni, I. and Rossetti, Y. (2006) No double-dissociation between optic ataxia and visual agnosia: multiple sub-streams for multiple visuo-manual integrations. *Neuropsychologia*, **44**, 2734–2748.

Pisella, L., Ota, H., Vighetto, A. and Rossetti, Y. (2007) Optic ataxia and the Bálint syndrome: Neurological and neurophysiological prospects. *Handbook of Clinical Neurology*, in press.

Posner, M. I. (1980) Orienting of attention. *Quarterly Journal of Experimental Psychology*, **32**, 3–25.

Posner, M. I., Walker, J. A., Friedrich, F. J. and Rafal, R. D. (1984) Effects of parietal injury on covert orienting of attention. *Journal of Neuroscience*, **4**, 1863–1874.

Prablanc, C., Echallier, J. F., Komilis, E. and Jeannerod, M. (1979) Optimal response of eye and hand motor systems in pointing at a visual target. I. Spatio-temporal characteristics of eye and hand movements and their relationship when varying the amount of visual information. *Biological Cybernetics*, **35**, 113–124.

Prado, J., Clavagnier, S., Otzenberger, H., Scheiber, C., Kennedy, H. and Perenin, M. T. (2005) Two cortical systems for reaching in central and peripheral vision. *Neuron*, **48**, 849–858.

Ratcliff, G. (1991) Brain and space: some deductions from the clinical evidence. In Paillard, J. (ed.), *Brain and Space*, pp. 237–250. Oxford University Press, Oxford.

Ratcliff, G. and Davies-Jones, G. A. (1972) Defective visual localization in focal brain wounds. *Brain*, **95**, 49–60.

Revol, P., Rossetti, Y., Vighetto, A. and Pisella, L. (2003) Pointing errors in immediate and delayed conditions in unilateral optic ataxia. *Spatial Vision*, **16**, 347–364.

Rondot, P., de Recondo J. and Ribadeau-Dumas J. L. (1977) Visuomotor ataxia. *Brain*, **100**, 355–376.

Rossetti, Y. and Revonsuo, A. (2000) Beyond dissociations: recomposing the mind-brain after all? In Rossetti, Y. and Revonsuo, A. (eds), *Beyond Dissociation: Interaction between Dissociated Implicit and Explicit Processing*, pp. 1–16. Benjamins, Amsterdam.

Rossetti, Y. and Pisella, L. (2002) Tutorial: Several 'vision for action' systems: a guide to dissociating and integrating dorsal and ventral functions. In Prinz, W. and Hommel, B. (eds), *Attention and Performance XIX; Common Mechanisms in Perception and Action*, pp. 62–119. Oxford University Press, Oxford.

Rossetti, Y., Pisella, L. and Vighetto, A. (2003) Optic ataxia revisited: visually guided action versus immediate visuomotor control. *Experimental Brain Research*, **153**, 171–179.

Rossetti, Y., Revol, P., McIntosh, R. *et al.* (2005) Visually guided reaching: bilateral posterior parietal lesions cause a switch from fast visuomotor to slow cognitive control. *Neuropsychologia*, **43**, 162–177.

Schluppeck, D., Glimcher, P. and Heeger, D. J. (2005) Topographic organization for delayed saccades in human posterior parietal cortex. *Journal of Neurophysiology*, **94**, 1372–1384.

Sereno, M. I., Pitzalis, S. and Martinez, A. (2001) Mapping of contralateral space in retinotopic coordinates by a parietal cortical area in humans. *Science*, **294**, 1350–1354.

Silver, M. A., Ress, D. and Heeger, D. J. (2005) Topographic maps of visual spatial attention in human parietal cortex. *Journal of Neurophysiology*, **94**, 1358–1371.

Smith, S. and Holmes, G. (1916) A case of bilateral motor apraxia with disturbance of visual orientation. *British Medical Journal*, **1**, 437–441.

Striemer, C., Blangero, A., Rossetti, Y., Boisson, D., Rode, G., Vighetto, A., Pisella, L. and Danckert, J. (2007) Deficits in peripheral visual attention in patients with optic ataxia. *Neuroreport*. in press.

Teuber, H. L. (1955) Physiological psychology. *Annual Review of Psychology*, **6**, 267–296.

Thiebaut de Schotten, M., Urbanski, M., Duffau, H. *et al.* (2005) Direct evidence for a parietal-frontal pathway subserving spatial awareness in humans. *Science*, **309**, 2226–2228.

Vighetto, A. (1980) Etude neuropsychologique et psychophysique de l'ataxie optique. PhD dissertation. Université Claude Bernard Lyon I.

Vighetto, A. and Perenin, M. T. (1981) Optic ataxia: analysis of eye and hand responses in pointing at visual targets. *Revue Neurologique*, **137**, 357–372.

Yeshurun, Y. and Carrasco, M. (1998) Attention improves or impairs visual performance by enhancing spatial resolution. *Nature*, **396**, 72–75.

4

Reversal of subjective temporal order due to sensory and motor integrations

Shigeru Kitazawa, Shunjiro Moizumi,
Ayami Okuzumi, Fumine Saito, Satoshi Shibuya,
Toshimitsu Takahashi, Makoto Wada
and Shinya Yamamoto

It is generally accepted that the brain can resolve the order of two stimuli that are separated in time by 20–50 ms. This applies to temporal order judgment of two tactile stimuli, delivered one to each hand, as long as the arms are uncrossed. However, crossing the arms caused misreporting (that is, inverting) of the temporal order. The reversal was not due to simple confusion of hands, because correct judgment was recovered at longer intervals (e.g. 1.5 s). When the stimuli were delivered to the tips of sticks held in each hand, the judgment was altered by crossing the sticks without changing the spatial locations of the hands. We recently found that temporal order judgments of tactile stimuli are sometimes reversed by visual distractors and by saccadic eye movements. The results suggest that tactile stimuli are ordered in time only after they are referred to relevant locations in space, where multisensory (visual, tactile and proprioceptive) and motor (saccade-related) signals converge. Results from functional imaging generally support this idea. Because performance of congenitally blind people in tactile temporal order judgment is much superior to the sighted and is never impaired by crossing the arms (Röder et al., 2004), we finally suggest that our integrity of multisensory signals in space is only achieved at the cost of continuity in time.

Introduction

Ordering sensory signals is a critical step for deciphering symbols, for instance in hearing speeches, reading books and reading Braille or sign language. In fact, poor readers are reported to be impaired in ordering sensory signals in multiple sensory modalities (May et al., 1988; Tallal et al., 1998; Habib, 2000; Laasonen et al., 2001). In this chapter we raise a question of how the brain orders successive events.

An ideal observer in physics is able to read his watch on the occurrence of each event no matter how small the interval of the events is. The brain is no way an ideal observer, but it is often assumed that there is a decision mechanism that plays a role much similar to the ideal observer in physics (Sternberg and Knoll, 1973). The decision mechanism was hypothesized to yield a judgment that a signal A preceded another signal B according to the temporal difference of their arrival times (T_A and T_B). The probability of the judgment that A preceded B was hypothesized to be determined by a monotonically increasing decision function G of the arrival-time difference ($T_B - T_A$). If there is such a decision mechanism in the brain, where is it located?

To maximize the temporal resolution in ordering the signals A and B, it is advantageous to locate such a decision mechanism as near as possible to the entrance of these signals, before the physical order of the two signals is obscured (Dennett and Kinsbourne, 1992). For example, timing in the 10 μs range is actually detected by the neurons in the medial superior olive that receives convergent inputs directly from the left and the right cochlear nuclei. However, we do not regard this as an example of the decision mechanism of temporal order, because these two successive sounds, delivered one to each ear, with an interval of 10 μs lead to perception of a single sound, not two successive sounds. The timing information in the medial superior olive is used for localizing a single sound source, rather than for ordering two successive sounds. In this chapter, we deal with the problem of how the brain orders two signals when they are subjectively perceived as two distinct events.

Interestingly, the threshold for detecting non-simultaneity of two sensory signals varies among sensory modalities, but the threshold for judging their temporal order seems to be independent of sensory modalities (Hirsh and Sherrick, 1961; Pöppel, 1997; although see Spence *et al.*, 2003). This suggests that there is a general decision mechanism that orders sensory events that originated from different sensory organs.

In the history of vision research, studies of illusions have much contributed to exploring the neural mechanisms of vision. Likewise, several anomalous experiences in time have provided us with insights on how conscious perceptions develop in time (Dennett and Kinsbourne, 1992). Here we focus on more recent illusions, reversals in subjective temporal order due to arm crossing (Yamamoto and Kitazawa, 2001a; Shore *et al.*, 2002) and during peri-saccadic periods (Morrone *et al.*, 2005) in the hope of shedding light on whether and where the hypothetical decision mechanism is located and how it orders sensory signals in time.

Reversal of temporal order due to crossings of the arms

We have been studying how the brain orders successive sensory signals that were delivered one to each hand (Yamamoto and Kitazawa, 2001a,b; Wada *et al.*, 2004; Yamamoto *et al.*, 2005). Signals A and B in Figure 4.1 correspond to those from the right hand and those from the left hand, respectively. Signals from each hand first reach the contralateral primary sensory cortex that is arranged somatotopically. If the signals from the two hands reach the decision mechanism while they are represented in the somatotopical coordinate but not in the spatial coordinate, the judgment would never be affected by the spatial position of the arms. To test which is the case, we examined temporal order

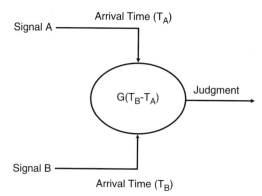

Figure 4.1 A decision mechanism of temporal order judgment. The probability of the judgment that a signal A preceded another signal B has been hypothesized to be a nondecreasing function (G) of the interval of the arrival times $(T_B - T_A)$ (e.g. Sternberg and Knoll, 1973).

judgment with the arms crossed and uncrossed. Seated subjects were asked to close their eyes and to judge the temporal order of successive mechanical stimuli, one delivered to the right hand and the other to the left hand, and to respond by extending the index finger of the hand that received the first (or, in half of the experiments, the second) stimulus. In the uncrossed condition, the order-judgment probability that the right hand was stimulated first was closely approximated by a monotonic sigmoid function (a cumulative density function of a Gaussian distribution) (Yamamoto and Kitazawa, 2001a; Wada *et al.*, 2004). This basically agrees with the decision model of (Sternberg and Knoll, 1973), and the temporal resolution that was defined as the standard deviation of the Gaussian function in our studies (approximately corresponds to the 84%-correct interval)[1] was 52 ms for the right-handed subjects (Wada *et al.*, 2004).

When the arms were crossed, to our surprise, many subjects reported inverted judgment at intervals of around 100–200 ms. In the most apparent case (Figure 4.2A), the subject's report was completely inverted when the stimulation interval was 100–200 ms. The correct judgment was restored as the interval approached 1500 ms, clearly indicating that the inverted judgment was not caused by a trivial confusion in distinguishing between the two hands. As a result, the response curve of the subject became N-shaped with a peak and a trough, which was clearly distinct from the conventional non-decreasing sigmoid function as hypothesized in the decision model (Sternberg and Knoll, 1973). Because the degree of reversal varied considerably across subjects, the response curve was no longer N-shaped after the data was pooled for all 20 subjects in our initial study (Yamamoto and Kitazawa, 2001a). However, we later found that left-over-right crossing caused more judgment reversal than right-over-left crossing (Wada *et al.*, 2002). N-shape was preserved after pooling data from eight newly recruited subjects when the left arm was crossed over the right arm (Figure 4.2B). The asymmetric effect was only found in right-handers but not in left-handers (Wada *et al.*, 2002). This suggests that the effect

---

[1] Our temporal resolution can be converted to the conventional, just noticeable, difference that yields 75% correct responses by multiplying by 0.68.

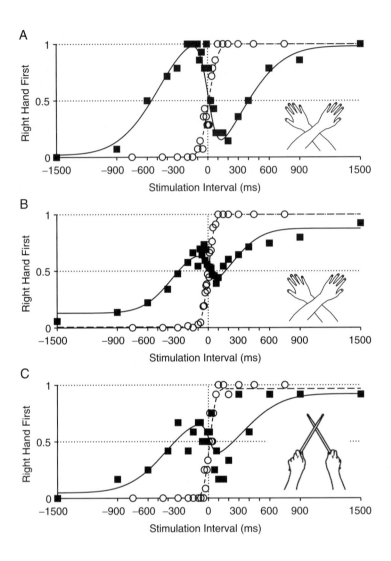

Figure 4.2 Reversal of subjective temporal order due to arm (**A**, **B**) and stick (**C**) crossing.
(**A**) The judgment probability that the right hand was stimulated earlier than the left hand is
plotted against the stimulation interval. A positive interval indicates that the right hand was
stimulated first. The response curve was a classical sigmoid when the arms were uncrossed
(open circles and broken curves), whereas it became N-shaped in the exemplified subject when the
arms were crossed (filled squares and solid curves). The results were basically similar when the
subject was required to respond by making saccadic eye movements to the right or left, rather
than by extending the corresponding index fingers. (**B**) Pooled data from eight naive subjects
who crossed the left hand over the right hand in the crossed-arm condition (filled squares). The
N-shape is still apparent. (**C**) Data from a subject with an apparent judgment reversal when the
sticks were crossed without crossing the arms (filled squares). Stimulation was delivered to the
tip of each stick, and the subject was required to judge which of the two tips was stimulated
first. Panel (**A**) was reproduced from Yamamoto and Kitazawa (2001a) by permission from
Nature Neuroscience, ©2005 Macmillan Publishers Ltd.

may be related with a kind of hemispheric lateralization that is generally more evident in right-handers than in left-handers.

Similar effects of arm crossing on tactile temporal order judgment was reported by another group (Shore *et al.*, 2002). Recently, Spence and colleagues showed that temporal resolution of the tactile temporal order judgment in the uncrossed condition depended on the distance of the two hands in the actual (Shore *et al.*, 2005) and virtual (mirror) space (Gallace and Spence, 2005). These studies clearly show that the hypothesized decision center (Figure 4.1A) does not receive tactile signals in a pure somatotopical coordinate, but only after proprioceptive signals converge on it. We suggest that the cutaneous signals from the respective hands are ordered in time only after the spatial locations of the hands are taken into account (Figure 4.3A).

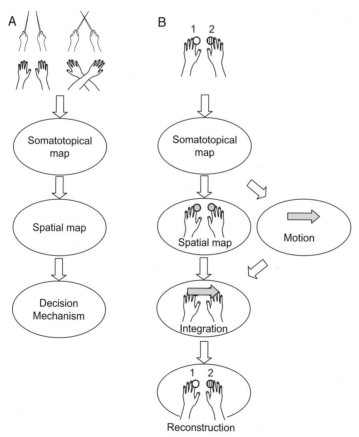

Figure 4.3 Models of tactile temporal order judgment. (**A**) A schema showing that signals from the skin mechanoreceptors of the right and the left hands are ordered in time after they are referred to a relevant location in space, whether it is the hand itself or the tip of the tool in the hand. (**B**) Motion projection hypothesis. Based on the results of a functional imaging study (Takahashi *et al.*, 2004), a motion signal was added to the model in (**A**). See text for further explanation.

Then we raise another question. Is the convergence of proprioceptive signals *per se* the determinant of whether the judgment was reversed or not? To address this issue, we examined temporal order judgments of mechanical stimuli that were delivered to the tips of sticks that were held one in each hand (Yamamoto and Kitazawa, 2001b). We found that the judgment was reversed just by crossing the sticks without crossing the arms, i.e. without much altering proprioceptive inputs. The tendency of judgment reversal was sufficiently strong in some subjects to yield an N-shaped response curve (Figure 4.2C). When the arms were crossed without crossing the sticks, there was a tendency of judgment reversal. Finally, when the sticks were crossed in addition to crossing the arms, the judgment curve returned to a normal sigmoid as when neither of the arms nor the sticks were crossed. We obtained similar results when subjects held L-shaped sticks instead of the straight ones (Yamamoto *et al.*, 2005) and when the subjects manipulated tools in virtual reality (Moizumi *et al.*, 2004). When the tip or the action point of each tool was located in the same hemispace as the hand that held the tool, response curves were ordinary sigmoid with temporal resolutions of about 60 ms. On the other hand, the curves showed a clear tendency of judgment reversal at moderately short intervals, when the tips were located in the contralateral hemispaces.

These results with real and virtual tools[2] show that temporal order judgment of tactile stimuli does not necessarily depend on the spatial positions of the hands *per se*. When the subjects were required to judge the order of mechanical stimuli that were delivered to the tips of tools in hands, judgments depended on the spatial positions of the tips of the tools irrespective of whether the arms were crossed or uncrossed. We suggest that signals from the skin mechanoreceptors of the right and the left hands are ordered in time after they are referred to a relevant location in space, whether it is the hand itself or the tip of the tool in the hand (Figure 4.3A).

It is well known in choice reaction-time tasks that response latencies to right-side stimuli are shorter when the responses are made with the right than with the left hand when the arms are uncrossed (Simon *et al.*, 1970; Riggio *et al.*, 1986). When the arms are crossed, in contrast, response latencies to right-side stimuli are shorter when the responses are made with the left hand that is now spatially compatible with the right-side stimuli. Riggio *et al.* (1986) used sticks to examine choice reaction time after crossing response goals without crossing the hands, and showed that reaction time is shorter when the location of the response goal, not that of the hand *per se*, is compatible with the side of stimulus. This phenomenon, known as stimulus–response compatibility, may seem to be closely related with the judgment reversal due to arm- or stick-crossing. However, this is not likely because stimulus–response compatibility is observed irrespective of whether the response goals are crossed or not. On the other hand, reaction latencies are generally longer when the response goals (or the hands) are crossed than when

---

2 In experiments with straight sticks and virtual tools, they were actually used for making responses, but L-shaped sticks were used as pure sensing tools and subjects used their foot for their response.

they are uncrossed (Riggio *et al.*, 1986; Yamamoto and Kitazawa, 2001a). We suggest that tactile signals of one hand are initially mapped to the response goal (the tip of a stick, or the hand itself) ipsilateral to the anatomical side of the hand, and that it takes time to remap the signals to the correct (contralateral) goal when the response goals are crossed. We later propose a hypothesis that explains judgment reversal by taking the process of remapping into account.

Studies of Iriki and colleagues give us some implications for neural mechanisms that underlie the referral of tactile signals to the hands or tips of tools. They showed in monkey that visual receptive fields of bimodal intraparietal neurons extended along a rake in hand (Iriki *et al.*, 1996) and were projected even to an action point in the video monitor (Iriki *et al.*, 2001). We infer that activation of such bimodal neurons in response to tactile stimuli would associate the tactile stimuli to the visual receptive fields of these neurons.

Motion projection hypothesis in temporal order judgments

The results so far strongly suggested that tactile temporal order judgment involves spatial representations in the brain. To test if this was the case, we examined which neural circuits are actually activated during the temporal order judgments (Takahashi *et al.*, 2004). Event-related functional magnetic resonance imaging (fMRI) was used while right-handed subjects ($n = 12$) judged the temporal order of two successive stimuli delivered one to each hand. Each subject was laid in a 3T magnetic resonance scanner (GE Medical Systems) with their eyes closed and with the index finger of each hand placed on a non-magnetic 8-pin braille stimulator (a 4×2 array with inter-pin intervals of 3 mm) fixed on the thigh. In each trial, right-then-left or left-then-right stimuli were delivered with a fixed stimulus onset asynchrony (SOA) by sticking out 1–7 pins from each stimulator. The subject was required to judge the temporal order of the stimuli in one condition (TOJ condition), and to compare the numerosity of the pins in the control condition. In both conditions, each stimulator served as a response button. The subject was required in a forced choice manner to push the 'second' button in the TOJ condition, and to push the button with the greater number of pins in the numerosity judgment condition. The SOA (50–100 ms) and the difference in the number of pins (2 or 3) were chosen for each subject so that correct response rate of approximately 80% was achieved in both tasks. Greater activation was elicited bilaterally during the temporal order judgment than during the numerosity judgment task in the following areas: bilateral posterior part of the middle temporal gyri (BA 37), bilateral premotor cortices (BA 6), bilateral inferior frontal gyri (BA 44), bilateral inferior parietal cortices (BA 40), and the left primary and secondary somatosensory cortices. The activation around the middle temporal gyri overlapped with the areas that were reported to respond to biological motion (Puce *et al.*, 1998; Puce and Perrett, 2003) and the most anterior part of the putative MT and MST (Dukelow *et al.*, 2001). From the results we propose that temporal order of tactile signals is ordered in time by combining representation of 'motion' in the temporal cortex with the spatial representation of the stimuli in the prefrontal and parietal cortices (motion projection hypothesis, Figure 4.3B). In the hypothesis, we assume that successive tactile stimuli evoke a kind of motion signal (such as tactile apparent motion) in the motion-related areas in the brain, and that they are also represented in spatial representations such as those in the parietal cortex. Then the order of two tactile events is reconstructed by integrating the motion signal with the two spatial locations of tactile stimuli.

Evidence of contribution of motion signals in tactile temporal order judgment

The motion projection hypothesis assumes that a motion signal, which is created from successive tactile stimuli, is critically important for reconstructing temporal order of the tactile stimuli. From the hypothesis we predict that tactile temporal order judgment would be affected by concurrent presentation of visual signals that elicit apparent motion and converge on the motion areas in the brain.

Experiment 1: Does visual apparent motion alter tactile temporal order judgment?

Methods

Subjects. Six naive subjects (two men and four women; 30 ± 10 years old, mean ± SD) participated in this experiment. They were all strongly right-handed according to the Edinburgh Inventory (Oldfield, 1971).

Apparatus and task procedures. Each subject sat in a chair and placed each hand on a tactile stimulator (Dot View DV-1; KGS, Saitama, Japan) that consisted of a matrix of 24 × 32 pins placed at 3 mm intervals with the arms uncrossed. Each pin (round head, 1.3 mm in diameter) could be raised by an independent piezoelectric actuator that produced 0.127 N within 5 ms from the onset of a command signal from a PC (Dimension 8200; Dell, Round Rock, TX, USA). A tilted (45°) 17 inch CRT monitor (CPD-G220; Sony, Tokyo, Japan) was used to present visual stimuli in a mirror (20 × 26 cm) placed above the tactile stimulator so that visual stimuli were presented on their fingers (Figure 4.4A, B). A masking board (30 × 43 cm) was positioned just below the mirror to occlude vision of the subject's hands and arms.

Two tactile stimuli were delivered to the third finger pad of the two hands, one to each hand. Each stimulus was delivered by simultaneously raising a 10 × 8 pin array under each finger pad. The distance between the third fingers was 18 cm. After the two 10 × 8 pin arrays had been raised one by one with an SOA that was randomly assigned for each trial from 24 values (−1500, −900, −600, −400, −300, −200, −150, −100, −80, −60, −30, −10, 10, 30, ..., 1500 ms), all 160 pins were lowered simultaneously at 1 s after the delivery of the second stimulus. Positive values indicate that the right hand was stimulated first and vice versa.

Simultaneously with the delivery of two tactile stimuli, visual stimuli appeared in two small squares (1.5 × 1.5 cm) placed at 18 cm intervals (center to center) so that they appeared in a randomized order on the tips of the third fingers (Figure 4.4B). The visual stimuli appeared in the order identical (congruent condition) or opposite (incongruent condition) to the order of tactile stimuli. Two lighted squares were turned off at 1 s after

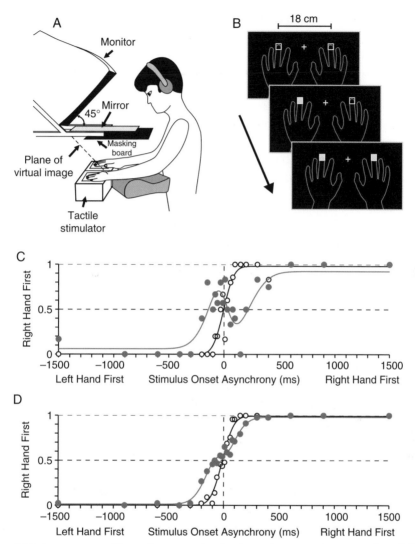

Figure 4.4 Judgment reversal in tactile temporal order due to incongruent presentation of visual stimuli (Experiment 1). (**A**) Apparatus. (**B**) Visual stimuli were presented in a mirror so that they appeared at the tips of the middle fingers to which tactile stimuli were delivered in succession. Each visual stimulus was presented simultaneously to each tactile stimulus, but the order was congruent or incongruent in a pseudorandom manner. (**C**) Data from a subject with the most apparent reversal. The response curve was sigmoid when the visual stimuli were congruent with the tactile stimuli (open circles), whereas it became N-shaped when they were incongruent (filled circles). (**D**) Data pooled from six subjects.

the delivery of the second visual and tactile stimuli. During the experiments, subjects were instructed to gaze at a fixation point at the middle of the two squares. Subjects were also required to ignore visual stimuli and make a forced choice between the two orders of tactile stimuli. White noise (80 dB) was played through headphones placed over the subjects' plugged ears to mask the sound of the stimulator, although the stimulator was basically silent. Thus, subjects could only feel the tactile stimulation and see the visual stimuli.

After the second stimulus was delivered, the subjects were required to report the order of tactile stimulation, by pressing a button under the index finger of the hand that was judged as stimulated later than the other. For each trial, subjects were forced to choose one of the two responses as soon as possible after the delivery of the second stimulus. All response data were recorded and stored on the personal computer for off-line analyses.

Each subject participated in one experiment that consisted of 384 trials in which two visual stimuli (congruent and incongruent) were assigned eight times each for 24 SOAs, in a pseudorandom order.

Data analysis. The response data were sorted by SOA to calculate the order–judgment probabilities that the right hand was stimulated earlier than the left hand under the congruent (p_{cong}) and the incongruent (p_{incong}) conditions. The order–judgment probability under the congruent condition (p_{cong}) was fitted by a cumulative density function of a Gaussian distribution:

$$p_{cong}(t) = (p_{max} - p_{min}) \int_{-\infty}^{t} \frac{1}{\sqrt{2\pi}\sigma_{cong}} \times \exp\left(\frac{-(\tau - d_{cong})^2}{2\sigma^2_{cong}}\right) d\tau + p_{min},$$

(4.1)

where t, d_{cong}, σ_{cong}, p_{max}, and p_{min} denote the SOA, the size of horizontal transition, the time constant, and the upper and lower asymptotes of the judgment probability, respectively. Matlab (optimization toolbox) was used for the fitting to minimize Pearson's χ^2 statistics (df = 19), which reflected the discrepancy between the sampled order–judgment probability (24 data points) and the prediction, using the four-parameter model. The time constant (σ_{cong}) is an effective measure of temporal order resolution.

The order–judgment probability under the incongruent condition (p_{incong}) was assumed to be flipped from the order–judgment probability under the congruent condition (p_{cong}) in a manner formulated as follows:

$$p_{incong}(t) = f_l(t)\left\{1 - p_{cong}(t)\right\} + \left\{1 - f_r(t)\right\}p_{cong}(t),$$

(4.2)

$$f_r(t) = A_r \exp\left(\frac{-(t - d)^2}{2\sigma^2_f}\right) + c,$$

(4.3)

$$f_l(t) = A_l \exp\left(\frac{-(t - d)^2}{2\sigma^2_f}\right) + c,$$

(4.4)

where f_r denotes the flip probability of judgment from right-hand-first to left-hand-first and f_l from left-hand-first to right-hand-first. We estimated five parameters in the flip probabilities that followed the Gaussian functions shown in Equations 4.3 and 4.4: the peak flip amplitude of the Gaussian functions (A_r and A_l), the size of the horizontal transition (d), the time window of the flip (σ_f), and a constant (c). Matlab (optimization toolbox) was used for the fitting to minimize Pearson's χ^2 statistics (df = 18).

Results

When the spatial direction of visual stimuli was congruent with that of visual stimuli, the order-judgment probability (p_{cong}) that the right hand was stimulated first (open circles, Figure 4.4C) was closely approximated by a monotonic sigmoid function (Equation 4.1, sigmoid curves in Figure 4.4C and D, $r^2 = 0.94$ and $r^2 = 0.91$, respectively). The temporal resolution (σ_{cong}) was 82 ms for the pooled data (Figure 4.4D) and comparable (mean $\pm$ S.E. = 71 ± 6 ms, $n = 6$) to those in our previous studies (Wada et al., 2004: mean $\pm$ SE = 52 ± 4 ms; Yamamoto and Kitazawa, 2001a: 71 ± 6 ms) in which there was no concurrent visual stimuli.

However, when the direction of visual stimuli was incongruent with that of tactile stimuli, many subjects reported inverted judgments at SOAs less than about 300 ms (filled dots in Figure 4.4C, D). In the most apparent case (Figure 4.4C), the response curve became N-shaped even though the arms were not crossed. The N-shaped response curve seems to be similar to those obtained when the arms were crossed (e.g. Figure 4.2A), though the reversal under the visual distraction peaked at ~100 ms in contrast to ~200 ms under the previous crossed-arm condition without any visual stimuli.

Discussion

The results clearly show that the subjects were unable to ignore visual stimuli when the visual stimuli were incongruent with tactile stimuli. This supports the prediction from the motion projection hypothesis that visual motion stimuli would interfere with the tactile temporal order judgment. However, it may be argued that the visual interference can be explained in terms of the 'ventriloquism effect', one-to-one mislocalization of a tactile stimulus to the location of visual stimulation, rather than the visual apparent motion. Although the effect was originally used to describe the mislocalization of a sound source to the location of visual stimulation (Howard and Templeton, 1966), tactile stimuli can also be referred to the location of concurrent visual stimuli (Botvinick and Cohen, 1998; Armel and Ramachandran, 2003; Spence et al., 2004). If such one-to-one mislocalization were the cause of judgment reversal, the cross-modal interaction should have been independent of the SOA, because each tactile stimulus was always accompanied with a simultaneous visual stimulus. However, the judgment reversal peaked at the SOA of ~100 ms, subsided as the SOA became longer and was no longer apparent when the SOA was longer than 400 ms. Thus, our findings do not support major involvement of the ventriloquism effect in the visuo-tactile interaction. On the other hand, a sensation of motion evoked by successive visual stimuli (apparent motion) has a peak at the interstimulus interval of ~100 ms or shorter and decays over several hundreds of milliseconds to disappear at ~1 s (Soto-Faraco *et al.*, 2004). This prediction was supported by the results that the reversal of judgment under the incongruent condition decayed and disappeared in a Gaussian manner with a standard deviation of ~150 ms (Figure 4.4). Thus the present results support the motion projection hypothesis that motion signals are integrated to the spatial representation of two events for ordering the two events in time.

Reversal of subjective temporal order due to saccades

Recently, Morrone *et al.* (2005) reported that subjective temporal order of two successive visual stimuli was reversed when the stimuli were delivered during perisaccadic periods. Subjects were required to make a 30° horizontal saccade from a left fixation point to a right target (Figure 4.5A), and judge the order of two green horizontal bands that were presented for a brief period (8 ms) in succession, one in the top and the other at the bottom of the red screen. When the bands were presented during a postsaccadic period (more than 100 ms after the saccade), the response curve was sigmoid (Figure 4.5B) and the exemplified subject responded correctly when the SOA was as small as 25 ms. However, when the visual stimuli were presented just prior to the saccade onset (within a time window between –70 and –30 ms), the response curve became N-shaped with complete reversal at stimulation intervals of –50 and +50 ms, and with recovery at longer intervals (Figure 4.5C). Although stimulus intervals that yielded the peak reversal was longer in the tactile temporal order judgment in the crossed-arm condition (100~200 ms) than in the judgment reversal prior to the saccade (~50 ms), this is clearly the second case of anomaly that cannot be explained in terms of the classic temporal order decision mechanism with a nondecreasing decision function (Figure 4.1).

Experiment 2: Replication of an experiment reported by Morrone *et al.*

As a control, we examined whether a saccade reverses subjective temporal order of visual stimuli, by replicating the experiments reported by Morrone *et al.* (2005).

Methods

Subjects. Six right-handed subjects participated in the experiments. Four were naive to the purpose of the experiment and the others were two of the co-authors.

Apparatus and task procedures. Each subject sat with their head rested on a chin rest, facing a 24 inch CRT monitor (HM204-DA, Iiyama, Tokyo, Japan) that was placed 45 cm apart from the eyes. The subject was required to fixate on a target in the left of the red monitor screen, and to make a visually guided saccade to another target that appeared 24° to the right of the fixation target. The fixation target was extinguished simultaneously to the appearance of the target for a saccade. Two visual stimuli, green horizontal bars at the top and at the bottom of the monitor, were briefly (10 ms) presented in succession with an SOA pseudorandomly chosen from 16 (–150, –100, –90, –75, –60, –50, –25, –15, 15, 25, 50, 60, 75, 90, 100 and 150 ms) in which positive SOA represented

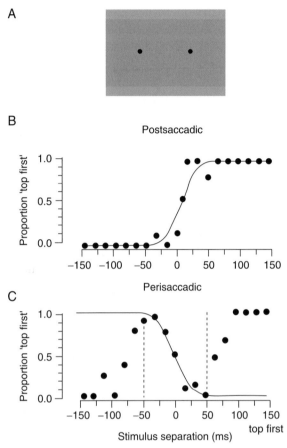

Figure 4.5 Temporal inversion during a perisaccadic period (Morrone *et al.*, 2005). (**A**) Two horizontal bars appeared in succession at the top and the bottom of the screen while a subject made saccade from a fixation point (left dot) to a target (right dot). (**B**) Judgment during a postsaccadic period. Stimuli were presented more than 100 ms after the saccade. Top-first judgment probability is plotted against the stimulus separation. The response yielded an ordinary sigmoid curve. (**C**) Temporal inversion during a presaccadic period (−70 ms to −30 ms). The response curve was N-shaped with the peak reversals at −50 and +50 ms. Data from a single subject. Adapted by permission from Morrone *et al.* (2005), *Nature Neuroscience*, ©2005 Macmillan Publishers Ltd.

top-first stimuli. The first visual stimulus was delivered after the target onset with an interval chosen from four (20, 50, 100 and 500 ms). The subject was required to judge the order of visual stimuli (top-first or bottom-first) and to respond by pressing one of two buttons in a forced-choice manner. During the task trials, gaze positions were measured at 500 Hz by an eye tracker (Eyelink2; SR Research, Ontario, Canada). The experiment was controlled by Experiment Builder (SR Research, Ontario, Canada). Each subject participated in one experiment that consisted of 128 trials in which 16 SOAs were assigned two times each for four visual delays, in a pseudorandom order.

Analysis. After each experiment, the onset of each saccadic eye movement, which was automatically detected by a built-in program of Eyelink2, was inspected one by one to be acknowledged, corrected or discarded. Based on the registered onsets of saccade, the delay of stimulus presentation was defined as the interval between the saccade onset and the middle of the timings of successive visual stimuli. Positive delays generally correspond to postsaccade presentation and vice versa, although in some conditions the first and the second stimulus could be presented before and after the saccade onset, respectively. Trials with presaccadic delays between −150 ms to 0 ms (presaccadic trials, $n = 52$), and those with postsaccadic delays larger than 100 ms (postsaccadic trials, $n = 178$) were used for further analysis. The response data were sorted by SOA to calculate the order–judgment probabilities that the top bar was presented earlier than the bottom bar in the pre- (p_{pre}) and post- (p_{post}) saccadic trials. The order–judgment probability in the postsaccadic trials (p_{post}) was fitted by a cumulative density function of a Gaussian distribution. The order–judgment probability in the presaccadic trials (p_{pre}) was assumed to be flipped from the order–judgment probability in the postsaccadic trials (p_{post}) in a manner similar to that formulated as Equations 4.3 and 4.4. The degree of judgment reversal was quantified by calculating the maximal discrepancy between the sigmoid fitting in the presaccadic trials and the flip model fitting in the postsaccadic trials.

Results and comments

The probability of top-first judgment in the postsaccadic trials (p_{post}) was well fitted by a sigmoid function with a temporal resolution of 46 ms (Figure 4.6A, open circles). On the other hand, subjects often made inverted judgments in the presaccadic trials at stimulation intervals of ~50 ms and the order–judgment probability in the presaccadic trials (p_{pre}) was N-shaped (Figure 4.6A, filled circles). The results generally agreed with those of Morrone *et al.* (2005), though the degree of judgment reversal (0.38) was not as strong as that (1.0) in the previous report. There are several factors that might explain the quantitative difference. First, we set a wider time window (−150 to 0 ms) than that (−70 to −30 ms) in Morrone *et al.* (2005) to increase the number of trials. The strongest reversal may be observed in the narrower time window. Second, the brightness of the green bar was not matched with the brightness of the red background so precisely in our experiment as in Morrone *et al.* (2005). Third, we presented pooled data from six subjects including four naive subjects, but those from a single expert subject were shown in Morrone *et al.* (2005).

Experiment 3: Does saccade reverse subjective temporal order of tactile stimuli?

If a temporal order judgment mechanism is shared by signals of different modalities, saccades would reverse temporal order judgments of not only visual stimuli but also those of other sensory modalities. We thus examined whether saccades reverse temporal order judgments of tactile stimuli.

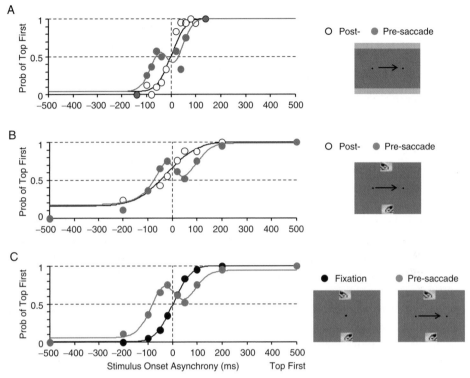

Figure 4.6 Perisaccadic reversal of subjective temporal order in visual (**A**) and tactile (**B**) temporal order judgments. (**A**) Visual temporal order judgments were often inverted during a presaccadic period within 150 ms prior to the saccade onset (filled circles and an N-shaped curve), but not in a postsaccadic period (open circles and a sigmoid curve) more than 100 ms after the saccade onset. Data from six subjects. (**B, C**) Tactile temporal order judgments during pre- (filled circles in **B** and **C**; within 100 ms prior to the onset) and postsaccadic (open circles in **B**; more than 100 ms after the onset) periods, and during fixation (open circles in **C**). Data from five subjects.

Methods

Subjects. Five right-handed subjects participated in the experiments. Four were naive to the purpose of the experiment and the other was one of the authors.

Apparatus and task procedures. All subjects sat with their head rested on a chin rest, facing a 24 inch CRT monitor (HM204DA; Iiyama, Tokyo, Japan). The subjects were required to make a visually guided saccade (24°) from a fixation target in the left to a target in the right, and to judge the order of successive tactile stimuli that were delivered one to each hand (finger pad of the index finger) at various timings. The second tactile stimulus was delivered after the target onset with an interval chosen from five (20, 50, 100, 200 and 500 ms). The left hand was placed 30 cm above the right hand on the midsagittal plane so that they were positioned at neutral positions relative to the saccades. In each trial, tactile stimuli were delivered with an SOA chosen from ten (−500, −200, −100, −50, −20,

20, 50, 100, 200 and 500 ms) in a pseudorandom manner. Positive SOAs represented top-first (left-hand-first) stimuli. The subjects were asked to judge which hand was stimulated second and to respond by pressing one of the two foot switches. During the task trials, gaze positions were measured at 500 Hz by an eye tracker (Eyelink2). One experiment consisted of 150 trials in which 10 SOAs were assigned three times each for five stimulus onset delays, in a pseudorandom order. Each subject participated in two experiments. As a control, the subjects were required to judge the temporal order of tactile stimuli while fixating on a fixation point at the middle of the two hands. Each subject participated in one fixation experiment that consisted of 100 trials in which 10 SOAs were assigned 10 times in a pseudorandom order.

Analysis. Data were analyzed in a manner similar to that in Experiment 2. After inspecting each eye movement, the delay of stimulus presentation was defined as the interval between the saccade onset and the middle of the timings of successive tactile stimuli. Trials with presaccadic delays between −100 ms to 0 ms (presaccadic trials, $n = 201$) and those with postsaccadic delays larger than 100 ms (postsaccadic trials, $n = 281$) were used for further analysis. Data under the fixation condition (500 trials) were also analyzed as a control. The response data were sorted by SOA to calculate the order–judgment probabilities that the top hand (left hand) was stimulated earlier than the bottom hand (right hand) in the presaccadic trials (p_{pre}), in the postsaccadic trials (p_{post}) and in the fixation control (p_{fix}). The order–judgment probability in the postsaccadic trials (p_{post}) and in the fixation control (p_{fix}) was fitted by a cumulative density function of a Gaussian distribution. The order–judgment probabilities in the presaccadic trials (p_{pre}) were assumed to be flipped from the order–judgment probability in the postsaccadic trials (p_{post}) and in the fixation control (p_{fix}) in a manner similar to that formulated as Equations 4.3 and 4.4. To evaluate whether the judgment in the test condition was reversed from the control condition, we tested the null hypothesis that the peak flip amplitudes in the flip model (A_l and A_r) were zero and that the remaining parameter is only c in the flip model (Equations 4.3 and 4.4). If the goodness-of-fit test using the Pearson's χ^2 statistic produced $p < 0.05$, we judged that the reversal was significant (Yamamoto et al., 2005).

Results and comments

The probability of top-first judgment in the postsaccadic trials (p_{post}) was well fitted by a sigmoid function with a temporal resolution of 97 ms (Figure 4.6B, sigmoid curve and open circles; $r^2 = 0.96$). When the stimuli were delivered just prior to the onset of the saccade (within 100 ms, filled circles in Figure 6B and C), the order–judgment probability in the presaccadic trials (p_{pre}) was N-shaped after averaging data from the five subjects. The judgment reversal as compared with the postsaccadic trials (~0.2 at SOAs of −50 and 50 ms) was significant [$\chi^2 (8) = 19.1; p = 0.0143$].

However, the lower asymptote of the sigmoid in the postsaccadic period was much larger than zero (Figure 4.6B) and the temporal resolution (97 ms) was worse than that obtained for visual temporal order judgment in the present study (46 ms) and those reported in the arms uncrossed condition in previous studies (Yamamoto and Kitazawa, 2001a; Wada et al., 2004). To see if this was due to the vertical arrangement of the hands, we examined responses when the subjects fixated on a fixation target (Figure 4.6C, inset). The order–judgment probability (p_{fix}) was closely fitted by the sigmoid function with asymptotes of zero and one, and the temporal resolution was 59 ms (Figure 4.6C, sigmoid curve), comparable to those reported in the previous studies (Yamamoto and Kitazawa, 2001a; Wada *et al.*, 2004). The results show that vertical arrangement of the hands does not interfere with the tactile temporal order judgments. When the order–judgment probability in the presaccadic period was compared with that in the fixation control (Figure 4.6C), the effect of judgment reversal was more prominent [$0.33, \chi^2 (8) = 36.9; p = 0.000012$].

The results show that the reversal effect in the presaccadic period extends to tactile temporal order judgments, and further support the idea that multimodal brain areas are involved in ordering sensory events in time. There was some additional effect in the postsaccadic period when tactile stimuli were used. The time course of recovery in the postsaccadic period remains to be elucidated.

Hypotheses for explaining judgment reversals

As shown, there have been two conditions that reverse subjective temporal order of successive stimuli delivered with a moderately short stimulation interval. One is the reversal due to arm crossing (Yamamoto and Kitazawa, 2001a) and the other is the reversal during perisaccadic periods (Morrone *et al.*, 2005). At present, it is not certain whether the underlying reversal mechanisms are common in these phenomena, but we present two hypotheses that would possibly explain both.

Hypothesis 1: Reversal occurs due to inverted motion signals

Assuming the motion projection hypothesis, subjective temporal order is reconstructed by integrating spatial representation of two signals with a motion signal created from successive stimuli. Thus the subjective temporal order can be reversed if the motion signal was erroneously inverted.

Is the inverted 'motion' generated by delivering tactile stimuli to the crossed hands?

Observations of saccadic eye movements to somatosensory targets (Groh and Sparks, 1996) provide a clue to answer this question. In their experiments, vibrotactile stimuli were delivered to the hands (somatosensory targets), which were concealed beneath a barrier. Interestingly, the trajectories of many saccades curved markedly when the arms were crossed. Many saccades began in the direction of the wrong target with an onset latency of ~200 ms, curved toward the correct one in midflight and reached the correct one ~400 ms after the delivery of tactile stimulus. Their results indicate that the spatial position of the stimulus delivered to the crossed hand (1 in Figure 4.7A, Physical events) was initially mapped to the wrong hand before the onset of the curved saccade (1' in Figure 4.7A) and is remapped to the correct hand before the end of the curved saccade (1″, ~400 ms after the touch). Thus, when two successive stimuli are delivered one to each crossed hand with an SOA of 100 ms (i.e. right hand then left hand, Physical events in Figure 4.7B), it is likely that the first right-hand stimulus is mapped to the left hand (1′, wrong hand) and the second left-hand stimulus (2) is mapped to the right hand (2′, wrong hand) before these inverted mappings are remapped to the correct hands. We suggest that a leftward motion signal (Motion area in the brain, Figure 4.7B), i.e. an inverted motion vector, is generated from the initial inverted mappings (1′ and 2′). It may be argued that another rightward (correct) motion signal can be generated by the signals after remapping. However, timing of remapping would not be so sharp as the initial wrong mapping after an additional processing time that the generated motion signal might be weaker if it were generated at all. Assuming the motion projection hypothesis, spatially represented two tactile stimuli represented in space are integrated with the inverted motion signal (integration), then the inverted experience (1″ then 2″, subjective experience) is reconstructed in a postdictive manner.

Is the 'motion' inverted during a perisaccade period?

It is generally accepted that saccadic suppression predominantly affects the magnocellular visual system (Burr *et al.*, 1994) and is particularly powerful in the motion domain (Burr *et al.*, 1982; Ilg and Hoffmann, 1993). The saccadic suppression thus leads to absence of motion signal that we hypothesized to be critically important in reconstructing the temporal order. This saccadic suppression of motion signal would explain why the proportion of correct judgment reduces during perisaccadic periods. Although it may seem difficult to explain the reversal, Thiele *et al.* (2002) reported that ~30–40% of neurons in the middle temporal and middle superior temporal cortical areas in monkeys reversed their direction tuning during saccadic eye movements (but see Price *et al.*, 2005). Because our results in functional imaging (Takahashi *et al.*, 2004) showed that motion areas in the temporal lobe are activated during the tactile temporal order judgment, reversal of preferred direction in these areas would result in the reversal of temporal order judgments not only in the visual (Morrone *et al.*, 2005) but also in the tactile temporal order judgments.

Hypothesis 2: Reversal occurs due to backward referral with a slowing neural clock (Morrone *et al.*, 2005)

In addition to the temporal inversion, Morrone *et al.* (2005) found that a physical 100 ms is perceived as ~50 ms during the perisaccadic period. Assuming that there is a neural clock that counts the subjective duration, this compression indicates that the frequency of the clock was halved, or in other words, the clock cycle was doubled. To explain the temporal inversion, Morrone *et al.* (2005) further assumed after Libet (Libet *et al.*, 1979; Libet, 2004) that any event is referred backward in time by a certain number of clock cycles. When the clock cycle is doubled, backward referral is doubled too. Thus, if the first stimulus is given during the normal cycle (S_1 in Figure 4.8A) and the second stimulus is given during the doubled cycle (S_2 in Figure 4.8A), the second stimulus is referred backward twice as large as the backward referral of the first stimulus (broken arrows in Figure 4.8B), resulting in the reversal of subjective temporal order ($S_{2′}$ and $S_{1′}$ in Figure 4.8B).

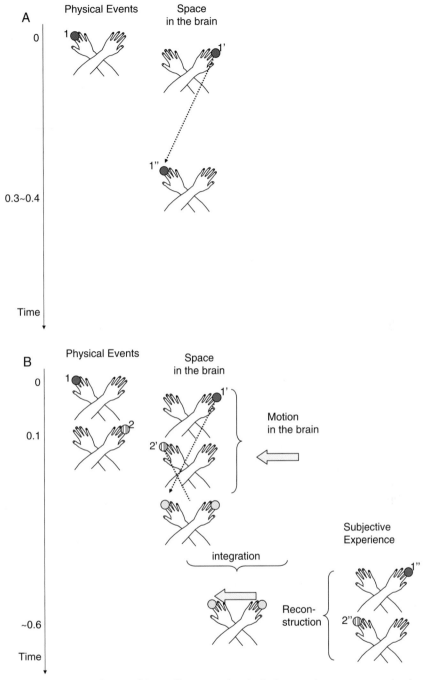

Figure 4.7 An account of reversal in tactile temporal order judgment due to arm crossing based on curved somatosensory saccades and the motion projection hypothesis. (**A**) A dynamic representation of a single tactile stimulus delivered to the right hand in the arm-crossed condition (1 in Physical events). From the data of curved somatosensory saccades (Groh and Sparks, 1996), we infer that the signal is initially mapped to the wrong hand (1′ in Space in the brain) and remapped to the correct hand (1″) in ~0.3–0.4 s after the stimulus. (**B**) An account of temporal reversal due to arm crossing when two stimuli are delivered in succession with an SOA of 0.1 s (Physical events). We infer that both stimuli are initially mapped to the wrong hands and an inverted motion signal is generated from these. In the spatial representation, the physical order of the two signals is obscured by remapping. The two events (tactile stimuli) in space are integrated with the inverted motion signal and an inverted experience is constructed therefrom.

Although the idea is intriguing, there occurs a contradiction. When a subjective time is plotted against the physical time to illustrate a subjective time-line (Figure 4.8B), the slope of the time-line should be inversely related with the cycle of the neural clock. When the slope is halved, subjective duration is halved with the clock cycle doubled. When the slope is zero, the neural clock stops with a cycle of infinity. Thus the clock cycle can be calculated as the inverse of the slope of subjective time-line as shown by the thin curve in Figure 4.8A. This is apparently different from the empirical data (solid curve) from which we started.

Before saccades, perception of space is compressed (Ross *et al.*, 1997) and visual receptive fields of neurons in the parietal cortex move dynamically (Duhamel *et al.*, 1992; Kusunoki and Goldberg, 2003). It is plausible that a neural clock is decelerated when there is such a massive computational load as mapping receptive fields to relevant locations upon each saccade. When successive stimuli are delivered to the crossed hands, mapping of the signals to the wrong hands and remapping to the correct hands would take a massive resource as in those associated with saccades and may decelerate the neural clock. Deceleration of the neural clock would lead to the temporal inversion, though causal relationship between the slowing and inversion remains elusive at present.

Support from the studies in the blind

Röder *et al.* (2004) examined temporal order judgments of successive taps to the hands in late-onset and congenitally blind people. They found that the temporal resolution of the congenitally blind people was much better than the control subjects: the 75% correct threshold was ~20 ms for the congenitally blind subjects compared with ~50 ms in the control subjects with normal vision. But the late-onset blind were no better than the control subjects. They further found that the congenitally blind people showed no trace of judgment reversal after crossing the arms, but temporal order judgments of the late-onset blind were impaired as in the control subjects. These results show that tactile signals are ordered in time without being referred to visuo-spatial representation in the congenitally blind who did not have any chance to associate tactile signals with visual inputs. On the other hand, the late-onset blind were no better than the control subjects, showing that such association of tactile signals with visual coordinates is maintained once it is achieved during infancy. The congenitally blind people should also be free from temporal inversion due to saccades, because they are not able to voluntarily initiate saccades or to track their outstretched thumb in a self-induced movement (Kompf and Piper, 1987).

More recently, Kobor *et al.* (2006) reported that subjects showed much-reduced deficits in tactile temporal order judgments when the arms were crossed behind their arms than when they were crossed in front. This shows that tactile signals are not referred to a spatial location where we cannot see, and the lack of visuo-tactile association is advantageous for ordering events in time.

These studies suggest that our brain achieves an integrated representation of space across sensory modalities at the cost of continuous flow of time in the brain. Subjective time

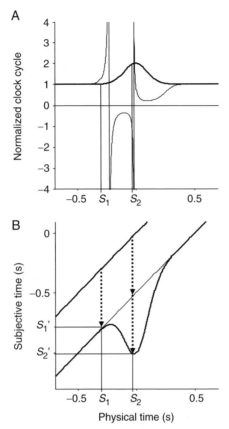

Figure 4.8 An account of perisaccadic temporal inversion based on slowing of a neural clock and backward referral of a conscious experience in time. The basic idea is adapted from Morrone *et al.* (2005). (**A**) An example of a change in the cycle time of a neural clock that measures subjective duration. In analogy with the time course of compression of subjective duration in a perisaccadic period (Morrone *et al.*, 2005), it is assumed that the cycle time increases from 1 to 2 and decreases back to 1 with a peak at time zero. The curve is borrowed from the density function of a normal distribution with a standard deviation of 0.1 s (thick curve). Thin curves show a time course of the clock cycle calculated from the slope of the subjective time-line in (**B**). Note a clear discrepancy between the two curves. (**B**) Reversal in the subjective temporal order due to backward referral of conscious experience. A hypothetical subjective time (*y*-axis) is plotted against the physical time (*x*-axis). A thick diagonal line shows $y = x$, representing a condition that the subjective time exactly matches the physical time without delay. We assumed, as an example, that a conscious experience is referred backward in time by 0.5 s (Libet *et al.*, 1979; Libet, 2004) when the cycle of the neural clock is one (a single dotted arrow at S_1). When the clock cycle is doubled, the backward referral should be as large as 1 s (two dotted arrows at S_2). This results in the reversal of temporal order in the subjective time-line (S_2' and S_1').

may go back and forth every time signals are integrated into a unified representation of space after each movement of the eyes and the arms. The discontinuity, or temporal reversal, may cause little trouble in our daily life, as long as it occurs during the short perisaccadic period in processing visual and tactile signals that are separated by 50 ms. Even the reversal in the 200 ms range would be left unnoticed, as long as it occurs with touches to both hands only when we cross our arms. However, the reversal would cause a more serious problem if it occurred in the auditory domain. Recent findings suggest that people with dyslexia, with learning deficits for reading, show evident deficits in phonological processing and have difficulty in detection of modulation at rather low rates (2–10 Hz) similar to those seen at the syllable level in speech (Goswami *et al.*, 2002; Demonet *et al.*, 2004). This suggests that temporal reversal with auditory signals would cause a serious problem, when it occurs in the range from 100 ms (10 Hz) to 500 ms (2 Hz), which is just longer than the 50 ms during the peri-saccadic period and coincides with the range of reversal due to arm crossing. Because dyslexics show diverse deficits in motion processing (Stein and Walsh, 1997; Eden *et al.*, 1996; Wilmer *et al.*, 2004) and in ocular saccades (Biscaldi *et al.*, 2000; Fischer and Hartnegg, 2000), we suggest from our motion projection hypothesis that temporal order would be disorganized beyond a physiological range in dyslexics (Habib, 2000). It remains to be tested in the future as to whether temporal reversal occurs with auditory signals during the perisaccadic period, and whether the degree of temporal reversal is greater in dyslexics.

Notes

Satoshi Shibuya, Toshimitsu Takahashi and Shigeru Kitazawa conducted Experiment 1. Toshimitsu Takahashi, Ayami Okuzumi, Fumine Saito, Shunjiro Moizumi and Shigeru Kitazawa conducted Experiments 2 and 3.

References

Armel, K. C. and Ramachandran, V. S. (2003) Projecting sensations to external objects: evidence from skin conductance response. *Progress in Biological Science*, **270**, 1499–1506.

Biscaldi, M., Fischer, B. and Hartnegg, K. (2000) Voluntary saccadic control in dyslexia. *Perception*, **29**, 509–521.

Botvinick, M. and Cohen, J. (1998) Rubber hands 'feel' touch that eyes see. *Nature*, **391**, 756.

Burr, D. C., Holt, J., Johnstone, J. R. and Ross, J. (1982) Selective depression of motion sensitivity during saccades. *Journal of Physiology*, **333**, 1–15.

Burr, D. C., Morrone, M. C. and Ross, J. (1994) Selective suppression of the magnocellular visual pathway during saccadic eye movements. *Nature*, **371**, 511–513.

Demonet, J. F., Taylor, M. J. and Chaix, Y. (2004) Developmental dyslexia. *Lancet*, **363**, 1451–1460.

Dennett, D. and Kinsbourne, M. (1992) Time and observer: the where and when of consciousness in the brain. *Behavioural Brain Research*, **15**, 183–247.

Duhamel, J. R., Colby, C. L. and Goldberg, M. E. (1992) The updating of the representation of visual space in parietal cortex by intended eye movements. *Science*, **255**, 90–92.

Dukelow, S. P., Desouza, J. F., Culham, J. C., Van Den Berg, A. V., Menon, R. S. and Vilis, T. (2001) Distinguishing subregions of the human MT+ complex using visual fields and pursuit eye movements. *Journal of Neurophysiology*, **86**, 1991–2000.

Eden, G. F., Vanmeter, J. W., Rumsey, J. M., Maisog, J. M., Woods, R. P. and Zeffiro, T. A. (1996) Abnormal processing of visual motion in dyslexia revealed by functional brain imaging. *Nature*, **382**, 66–69.

Fischer, B. and Hartnegg, K. (2000) Effects of visual training on saccade control in dyslexia. *Perception*, **29**, 531–542.

Gallace, A. and Spence, C. (2005) Visual capture of apparent limb position influences tactile temporal order judgments. *Neuroscience Letters*, **379**, 63–68.

Goswami, U., Thomson, J., Richardson, U., Stainthorp, R., Hughes, D., Rosen, S. and Scott, S. K. (2002) Amplitude envelope onsets and developmental dyslexia: a new hypothesis. *Proceedings of the National Academy of Sciences of the USA*, **99**, 10911–10916.

Groh, J. M. and Sparks, D. L. (1996) Saccades to somatosensory targets. I. Behavioral characteristics. *Journal of Neurophysiology*, **75**, 412–427.

Habib, M. (2000) The neurological basis of developmental dyslexia: an overview and working hypothesis. *Brain*, **123** Pt 12, 2373–2399.

Hirsh, I. J. and Sherrick, C. E., Jr. (1961) Perceived order in different sense modalities. *Journal of Experimental Psychology*, **62**, 423–432.

Howard, I. P. and Templeton, W. B. (1966) *Human Spatial Orientation*. Wiley, New York.

Ilg, U. J. and Hoffmann, K. P. (1993) Motion perception during saccades. *Vision Research*, **33**, 211–220.

Iriki, A., Tanaka, M. and Iwamura, Y. (1996) Coding of modified body schema during tool use by macaque postcentral neurones. *Neuroreport*, **7**, 2325–2330.

Iriki, A., Tanaka, M., Obayashi, S. and Iwamura, Y. (2001) Self-images in the video monitor coded by monkey intraparietal neurons. *Neuroscience Research*, **40**, 163–173.

Kobor, I., Furedi, L., Kovacs, G., Spence, C. and Vidnyanszky, Z. (2006) Back-to-front: improved tactile discrimination performance in the space you cannot see. *Neuroscience Letters*, **400**, 163–167.

Kompf, D. and Piper, H. F. (1987) Eye movements and vestibulo-ocular reflex in the blind. *Journal of Neurology*, **234**, 337–341.

Kusunoki, M. and Goldberg, M. E. (2003) The time course of perisaccadic receptive field shifts in the lateral intraparietal area of the monkey. *Journal of Neurophysiology*, **89**, 1519–1527.

Laasonen, M., Service, E. and Virsu, V. (2001) Temporal order and processing acuity of visual, auditory, and tactile perception in developmentally dyslexic young adults. *Cognitive and Affective Behavioural Neuroscience*, **1**, 394–410.

Libet, B. (2004) *Mind Time. The Temporal Factor in Consciousness*. Harvard University Press, London.

Libet, B., Wright, E. W., Jr., Feinstein, B. and Pearl, D. K. (1979) Subjective referral of the timing for a conscious sensory experience: a functional role for the somatosensory specific projection system in man. *Brain*, **102**, 193–224.

May, J. G., Williams, M. C. and Dunlap, W. P. (1988) Temporal order judgements in good and poor readers. *Neuropsychologia*, **26**, 917–924.

Moizumi, S., Yamamoto, S. and Kitazawa, S. (2004) Sensation at the tips of tools in the virtual reality. *Abstract Viewer/Itinerary Planner. Society for Neuroscience, 2004, Online*, Program No. 321.4.

Morrone, M. C., Ross, J. and Burr, D. (2005) Saccadic eye movements cause compression of time as well as space. *Nature Neuroscience*, **8**, 950–954.

Oldfield, R. C. (1971) The assessment and analysis of handedness: the Edinburgh inventory. *Neuropsychologia*, **9**, 97–113.

Pöppel, E. (1997) A hierarchical model of temporal perception. *Trends in Cognitive Science*, **1**, 56–61.

Price, N. S., Ibbotson, M. R., Ono, S. and Mustari, M. J. (2005) Rapid processing of retinal slip during saccades in macaque area MT. *Journal of Neurophysiology*, **94**, 235–246.

Puce, A. and Perrett, D. (2003) Electrophysiology and brain imaging of biological motion. *Philosophical Transactions of the Royal Society of London B*, **358**, 435–445.

Puce, A., Allison, T., Bentin, S., Gore, J. and McCarthy, G. (1998) Temporal cortex activation in humans viewing eye and mouth movements. *Journal of Neuroscience*, **18**, 2188–2199.

Riggio, L., Gawryszewski, L. and Umilta, C. (1986) What is crossed in crossed-hand effect? *Acta Psychologica*, **62**, 89–100.

Röder, B., Rosler, F. and Spence, C. (2004) Early vision impairs tactile perception in the blind. *Current Biology*, **14**, 121–124.

Ross, J., Morrone, M. C. and Burr, D. C. (1997) Compression of visual space before saccades. *Nature*, **386**, 598–601.

Shore, D. I., Spry, E. and Spence, C. (2002) Confusing the mind by crossing the hands. *Brain Res Cognitive Brain Research*, **14**, 153–163.

Shore, D. I., Gray, K., Spry, E. and Spence, C. (2005) Spatial modulation of tactile temporal-order judgments. *Perception*, **34**, 1251–1262.

Simon, J. R., Hinrichs, J. V. and Craft, J. L. (1970) Auditory S-R compatibility: reaction time as a function of ear-hand correspondence and ear-response-location correspondence. *Journal of Experimental Psychology*, **86**, 97–102.

Soto-Faraco, S., Spence, C. and Kingstone, A. (2004) Cross-modal dynamic capture: congruency effects in the perception of motion across sensory modalities. *Journal of Experimental Psychology, Human Perception and Performance*, **30**, 330–345.

Spence, C., Baddeley, R., Zampini, M., James, R. and Shore, D. I. (2003) Multisensory temporal order judgments: when two locations are better than one. *Perception and Psychophysics*, **65**, 318–328.

Spence, C., Pavani, F., Maravita, A. and Holmes, N. (2004) Multisensory contributions to the 3-D representation of visuotactile peripersonal space in humans: evidence from the crossmodal congruency task. *Journal of Physiology, Paris*, **98**, 171–189.

Stein, J. and Walsh, V. (1997) To see but not to read; the magnocellular theory of dyslexia. *Trends in Neuroscience*, **20**, 147–152.

Sternberg, S. and Knoll, R. (1973) The perception of temporal order: fundamental issues and a general model. In Kornblum, S. (ed.), *Attention and Performance*. Academic Press, New York.

Takahashi, T., Shibuya, S., Kowatari, Y., Yamamoto, M. and Kitazawa, S. (2004) Neural correlates of temporal order judgment—an fMRI study. *Society for Neuroscience, 2004, Online*. Abstract Viewer/Itinerary Planner, Program No. 321.2, Washington, DC.

Tallal, P., Merzenich, M. M., Miller, S. and Jenkins, W. (1998) Language learning impairments: integrating basic science, technology, and remediation. *Experimental Brain Research*, **123**, 210–219.

Thiele, A., Henning, P., Kubischik, M. and Hoffmann, K. P. (2002) Neural mechanisms of saccadic suppression. *Science*, **295**, 2460–2462.

Wada, M., Yamamoto, M. and Kitazawa, S. (2002) Effects of handedness on the temporal order judgment of successive hand stimuli. *Society for Neuroscience, 2002, Online*. Abstract Viewer/Itinerary Planner. Washington, DC, Program No. 673.19.

Wada, M., Yamamoto, S. and Kitazawa, S. (2004) Effects of handedness on tactile temporal order judgment. *Neuropsychologia*, **42**, 1887–1895.

Wilmer, J. B., Richardson, A. J., Chen, Y. and Stein, J. F. (2004) Two visual motion processing deficits in developmental dyslexia associated with different reading skills deficits. *Journal of Cognitive Neuroscience*, **16**, 528–540.

Yamamoto, S. and Kitazawa, S. (2001a) Reversal of subjective temporal order due to arm crossing. *Nature Neuroscience*, **4**, 759–765.

Yamamoto, S. and Kitazawa, S. (2001b) Sensation at the tips of invisible tools. *Nature Neuroscience*, **4**, 979–980.

Yamamoto, S., Moizumi, S. and Kitazawa, S. (2005) Referral of tactile sensation to the tips of L-shaped sticks. *Journal of Neurophysiology*, **93**, 2856–2863.

Section 2

Abstraction from Sensorimotor Foundations

5

How motor-related is cognitive control?

Marcel Brass and D. Yves von Cramon

In our daily life, we have to constantly adjust our behavior to changing environmental demands. This flexible adjustment requires motor and cognitive control processes. The relation between cognitive and motor control is still poorly understood. The aim of this chapter is to discuss how these two domains might be related. We report a functional magnetic resonance imaging (fMRI) study that investigates the relation between motor and cognitive control by testing whether frontolateral brain areas that are assumed to be related to cognitive control are sensitive to a manipulation of the response modality (whether participants responded with their hands or feet). In this study participants carried out a task-switching paradigm either with their hands or their feet. The behavioral data showed no interaction of response modality with cognitive-control-related manipulations, indicating that the response modality has no influence on cognitive control. This finding was further supported by the fMRI results. By directly contrasting the condition in which participants responded with their hands and feet, we showed that no frontal area was differentially activated for the implementation of cognitive control with different response modalities. Furthermore, we showed that the inferior frontal junction area, a region adjacent to the premotor cortex and which has been demonstrated to be related to cognitive control, is also response modality independent. Here we outline the implications of these findings and more general considerations for our understanding of the relation between cognitive and motor control.

Introduction

One crucial requirement of our daily life is to adjust our behavior to changing environmental demands. This flexible adjustment to a changing environment involves cognitive control processes. During the last decade, research on the neural basis of cognitive control has received much attention. With the help of a number of different experimental paradigms, it has been demonstrated that the prefrontal cortex plays a crucial role in cognitive control (Miller and Cohen, 2001). Furthermore, different regions within the frontal cortex have been functionally differentiated (Dreher et al., 2002; Koechlin et al., 2003; Brass et al., 2005a; Forstmann et al., 2005). In the posterior frontolateral cortex, a functional gradient from premotor to posterior frontolateral cortex has been proposed (Koechlin et al., 2003). Some of the regions found to be involved in cognitive control are very close to the premotor cortex. In particular, we showed that a region in the posterior part of the frontolateral cortex plays a crucial role in cognitive control (Brass *et al.*, 2005a). However, if the cortical regions which are related to higher order cognitive processes are very closely located to regions which are assumed to be involved in motor control, the question arises as to how motor control and cognitive control are related, both on the functional neuroanatomical level and on the cognitive level. In this chapter, we would like to shed some light on this relationship. First, we discuss the relationship of motor and cognitive control. Second, we outline some neuroscientific findings in both research areas. We report an experiment in which we have directly tested whether a manipulation on the motor level has an influence on activation in frontal areas which are related to cognitive control. Finally, we discuss more general ideas about the relationship of motor and cognitive control.

The relation between motor and cognitive control

The first question that we address is how to distinguish motor from cognitive control processes. In the present chapter, we will refer to motor control in a very narrow cognitive rather than 'motoric' sense. Here we define motor control as our ability to plan and select specific actions. While this includes planning and selection on the basis of external stimuli as well as on the basis of internal goals and intentions, we will focus on externally guided control. When we talk about motor control, we do not refer to the neural or functional mechanisms that are directly involved in motor coordination or motor implementation. Hence, the question we pursue does not concern which muscles are used to perform a specific motor program, but rather the selection of motor programs in general.

Like motor control, cognitive control refers to a number of heterogeneous concepts (Smith and Jonides, 1999). In this chapter the term cognitive control refers to the ability to coordinate sets of responses. The following example clarifies our distinction between motor and cognitive control. Imagine you are driving down a road and a traffic sign appears which signals that a traffic light will be present behind the bend. Control processes related to the traffic sign are cognitive control processes. Crucially, it is not efficient to prepare a specific response when seeing the traffic sign because one cannot predict whether the traffic light is going to be red or green. One can only use the contextual information to prepare a set of responses (apply the brakes when the light is red and accelerate when the light is green). However, when one reaches the traffic light one has to select a specific response depending on whether the traffic light is red or green. We refer to this process as motor control.

In the literature on motor control, different kinds of visuo-motor transformations have been distinguished (Petrides, 1985). On the one hand, there are so-called direct visuo-motor transformations. Grasping an object, for example, is such a direct visuo-motor transformation. In direct visuo-motor transformations, the object determines the adequate behavior in a given situation. On the other hand, we have so-called conditional or arbitrary visuo-motor transformations (Murray *et al.*, 2000; Wise and Murray, 2000). In this case the relation of stimulus and response is arbitrary, implying that the stimulus does not afford a specific response. In contrast to direct visuo-motor transformations, arbitrary visuo-motor transformations are based on abstract rules (e.g. apply the brakes when the traffic light is red). However, the application of abstract rules to guide behavior is something that is classically assumed to be related to cognitive control (see below). Hence, the distinction between cognitive control and motor control is sometimes difficult to draw.

The premotor cortex and the functional organization of motor control

The cortical area that is most closely related to motor control, in the sense we define it here, is the premotor cortex. Electrical stimulation of the premotor cortex elicits complex movements (Godschalk *et al.*, 1995). Furthermore, a number of imaging studies have shown that the premotor cortex is involved in movement preparation and the control of goal-directed actions (Adam *et al.*, 2003; see Picard and Strick, 2001 for a review). Interestingly, the premotor cortex is not only activated during motor execution, but also when observing action-related objects and complex stimulus sequences (e.g. Schubotz and von Cramon, 2003). Moreover, it was demonstrated that the premotor cortex is related to the observation of biological movements in a somatotopic manner (Buccino *et al.*, 2001; Sakreida *et al.*, 2005).

One of the guiding organizational principles of the motor system is its somatotopic organization. In the somatosensory cortex, the extremities are clearly separated so that each extremity occupies a specific location on the primary somotosensory cortex. In the primary motor cortex the somatotopic representation of the extremities is to some degree overlapping but still relatively distinguishable (Schieber, 2001). Finally, while a soma-totopic organization was also proposed for the premotor cortex (Godschalk *et al.*, 1995), it seems to be rather weak with overlapping representations for different extremities. Taken together, the somatotopic organization in the motor system seems to follow a posterior–anterior gradient with more anterior regions showing a looser somatotopy.

The posterior frontolateral cortex and cognitive control

For a long time it has been proposed on the basis of neuropsychological findings that the prefrontal cortex is the most crucial region for cognitive control (Milner, 1963). The last decade of brain imaging work on different cognitive control paradigms has supported this assumption (Duncan and Owen, 2000; Miller and Cohen, 2001). Conventionally, the lateral prefrontal cortex is divided into the dorsolateral prefrontal cortex and the ventrolateral prefrontal cortex (Owen *et al.*, 1998). These two areas are separated by the inferior frontal sulcus. The lateral prefrontal region on which most attention has been focused regarding cognitive control processes is the dorsolateral prefrontal cortex (MacDonald *et al.*, 2000). It was assumed that this region is involved in "implementing cognitive control" (MacDonald *et al.*, 2000). However, it has been shown that other fron-tolateral regions are also important for cognitive control (Koechlin *et al.*, 2003; Sakai and Passingham, 2003; Brass *et al.*, 2005a). In particular we found in a series of experiments that a region which is located in a more posterior region in the frontolateral cortex at the junction of the inferior precentral sulcus and the inferior frontal sulcus, the so-called inferior frontal junction area (IFJ), is very important in this respect (Brass *et al.*, 2005a). Interestingly, this region is closely located to the premotor cortex. This transitory position between premotor and prefrontal cortex is also supported by recent structural neuroanatomical findings (Amunts *et al.*, 2004). This cytoarchitectonic work suggests that the IFJ consists of dysgranular cortex and, therefore, constitutes a transition cortex between the agranular premotor cortex and the granular prefrontal cortex.

We have used the task-switching paradigm to investigate the role of the IFJ in cognitive control (Brass and von Cramon, 2002, 2004). In this paradigm participants have to alternate between two or more simple tasks. Since they have to switch between the tasks they are not able to adjust to only one task situation but instead have to continually update the relevant task set (Monsell, 2003). This updating process can be separated from task-related processing by introducing a cue in advance to the task. The cue corresponds to the traffic sign in the example we presented above. We have shown that this updating process is related to the IFJ (Brass and von Cramon, 2004). Furthermore, we were able to demonstrate that the IFJ is not only activated in the task-switching paradigm but also in other cognitive control paradigms which require the updating of task representations (Derrfuss *et al.*, 2004, 2005).

How motor-related is cognitive control?

If one assumes that the topographic organization of brain regions is not accidental but follows some functional organizational principle, our findings suggest that cognitive control and motor control might be closely related. This is further supported by the tight neuroanatomical connections between premotor cortex and adjacent prefrontal cortex (Dum and Strick, 2006). This raises the interesting possibility that the premotor cortex and the adjacent frontolateral cortex can be seen as a kind of functional continuation from concrete action rules to more abstract task rules. The idea that there is a functional continuum in the frontolateral cortex was recently put forward by Koechlin *et al.* (2003). He argues that there is a cascade of executive processes ranging from direct stimulus-driven control of behavior in the premotor cortex to the temporal episode-based control in the anterior prefrontal cortex. If the assumption of a functional continuum holds true, one reasonable prediction would be that the somatotopic organization of the motor system might extend into adjacent frontolateral cortex. That a cognitive-control-related brain area (the IFJ) is located just anterior to the premotor hand area seems to support such a prediction. To our knowledge, no brain-imaging study on cognitive control has ever investigated whether the response modality has an influence on the location of activations within the frontolateral cortex. Almost all experiments have used the hands as the response modality (the exceptions to this rule are studies that have used eye movements in antisaccade tasks and the Stroop interference task with verbal responses). This neglect of the issue of response modality in the cognitive control literature is surprising given that a number of authors have pointed to the crucial role of the frontolateral cortex in behavioral control and response selection (Rowe *et al.*, 2000; Miller and Cohen, 2001; Schumacher and D'Esposito, 2002).

The primary aim of the empirical work we present here was to investigate whether cognitive-control-related activation in the frontolateral cortex in general and the posterior dysgranular frontolateral cortex in particular is influenced by the body part with which participants respond. We used a cued task-switching paradigm that we have established previously to investigate the neural correlates of task-set updating (Brass and von Cramon, 2004; Brass *et al.*, 2005b). Here we were primarily interested in the manipulation of the response modality. In some experimental blocks participants had to respond with their right and left hands, and in other experimental blocks they had to respond with their right or left foot. By contrasting activation of hand and foot blocks, we can test whether cognitive-control-related regions in the frontolateral cortex are sensitive to the response modality. Another question is how participants anticipatorily prepare for hand and foot blocks. Some recent evidence indicates that participants prepare a specific task by preactivating the brain area which is involved in task processing (Wylie *et al.*, 2006; Yeung *et al.*, 2006). We therefore wanted also to investigate whether anticipatory preparation of hand and foot blocks involves a preactivation of the primary motor hand and foot areas.

Methods

Design

We used a task-switching paradigm (Figure 5.1), which we have recently developed to isolate the updating of task representations both with fMRI and electroencephalogram (EEG) (Brass and von Cramon, 2004; Brass *et al.*, 2005b). This paradigm was based on a modified version of a task-cueing paradigm introduced by Sudevan and Taylor (1987). Digits between 20 and 40 (except 30) were presented on the computer screen. Participants had to execute two tasks: judging whether a digit was smaller or greater than 30 (magnitude task) and judging whether the digit was odd or even (parity task). The response assignment was left response for numbers smaller than 30 and right response for number larger than 30 for the magnitude task and left response for even numbers and right response for odd numbers for the parity task. Which task they had to execute was signalled by a task-cue presented as a frame surrounding the digit. In the double-cue conditions, participants received two task-cues, before the actual task was presented. These task-cues could indicate the same or a different task. The trial length was 6 s. Trials started with a variable oversampling interval of 0, 500, 1000 or 1500 ms in order to obtain a temporal resolution of the BOLD signal of 500 ms. The experimental trial began with a fixation cross which was presented for 200 ms. The first task-cue was then presented for 100 ms. Before the presentation of the second cue, a fixed inter-cue interval of 700 ms was inserted. After the second cue, and a cue–target interval of 60 or 700 ms, the target was presented for 400 ms. Participants had 2000 ms time to respond to the target. After the response window a feedback was displayed for 200 ms. In single-cue trials, which have been inserted to ensure that participants use the first cue, the task was presented 60 or 700 ms after the first cue. Two different task-cues were assigned to each task (triangle and diamond to the

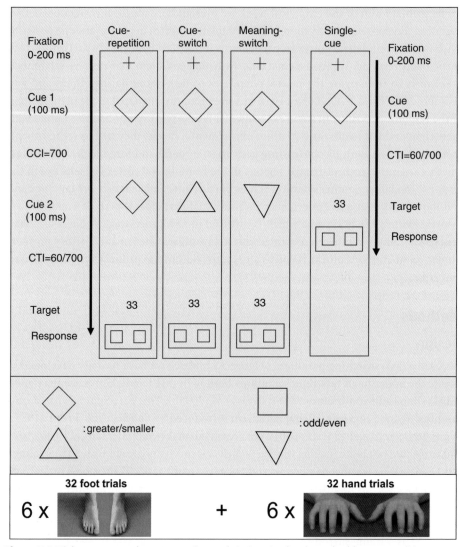

Figure 5.1 Trial structure and exact experimental timing. In the three double-cue conditions, two task-cues were presented before the target was displayed. In the single-cue condition, the target was presented after the first cue. The lower part of the figure displays the cue-task mappings. Two different cues were assigned to each task. In six experimental blocks participants responded with their right or left foot and six blocks with their right and left hand.

parity task and square and inverted triangle to the magnitude task). This resulted in three double-cue conditions: a condition in which both the cue and the cue meaning were repeated (cue-repetition condition), a condition in which the cue switched, but both cues indicated the same task (cue-switch condition) and a condition in which the cue switched to indicate the other task (meaning-switch condition). The experiment consisted of twelve blocks, with 32 trials each. Overall 192 double-cue trials (approximately

64 cue-repetition/64 cue-switch/64 meaning-switch), 128 single-cue trials and 64 null-events were presented.

The most crucial manipulation in the present experiment was the response modality was blocked. Before each experimental block, participants got a response modality cue which told them whether they had to respond with their hands or respond with their feet. They had to press a key with their right or left index finger in the hand condition and with their right or left foot in the foot condition. The response modality cue consisted of the German words for hand and foot ('Hand' and 'Fuss') which were presented for 12 s. Each block consisted of 32 experimental trials of both randomly inter-mixed tasks. Participants had to react with their feet in six blocks and with their hands in six blocks. Hand and foot blocks were alternated.

Participants

Fourteen participants (seven females and seven males) who gave informed consent participated in the present study. All participants (mean age: 26.5 years) were right-handed as assessed by a German adaptation of the Edinburgh Handedness Inventory (Oldfield, 1971) and had no neurological abnormalities.

Behavioral data analysis

The analysis of reaction-time data (RT) focused on double-cue trials, since single-cue trials were only included to ensure that participants used the first cue. For the RT analysis, erroneous trials were removed. With the remaining trials, we conducted an analysis of variance (ANOVA) with the factors cue–target interval (CTI, long, short), CONDITION (cue-repetition, cue-switch, meaning-switch) and response MODALITY (hand, foot). The same ANOVA was carried out with the error data.

fMRI acquisition and data analysis

The experiment was carried out on a 3T scanner (Siemens, Trio). Twenty axial slices (19.2 cm FOV, 64 × 64 matrix, 4 mm thickness, 1 mm spacing), parallel to the AC–PC plane, and covering the whole brain, were acquired using a single-shot, gradient-recalled EPI sequence (TR 2000 ms, TE 30 ms, 90 flip angle). Prior to the functional runs, 20 corresponding anatomical MDEFT slices and 20 EPI-T1 slices were acquired. Stimuli were presented using a headmounted display with a resolution of 1024 × 768 and a refresh rate of 60 Hz.

Analysis of fMRI data was performed using the LIPSIA software package (Lohmann et al., 2001). First, functional data were corrected for movement artifacts. The temporal offset between the slices acquired in one scan were then corrected using a sinc interpolation algorithm. Data were filtered using a spatial Gaussian filter with sigma = 1. A temporal highpass filter with a cutoff frequency of 1/100 Hz was used for baseline correction of the signal. In addition, a global scaling was carried out. All functional data sets were individually registered into three-dimensional (3D) space using the participants' individual high-resolution anatomical images. This 3D reference data set was acquired for each participant during a previous scanning session. The 2D anatomical MDEFT slices, geometrically aligned with the functional slices, were used to compute a transformation matrix containing rotational and translational parameters, that register the anatomical slices with the 3D reference T1-data set. These transformation matrices were normalized to the standard Talairach brain size by linear scaling, and finally applied to the individual functional data. The statistical evaluation was carried out using the General Linear Model for serially autocorrelated observations. The design matrix for event-related analysis was created using a model of the hemodynamic response with a variable delay. The model equation was convolved with a Gaussian kernel with a dispersion of 4 s FWHM. Contrast maps were generated for each participant. As the individual functional datasets were all aligned to the same stereotactic reference space, a group analysis was then performed. A one-sample t-test of contrast maps across participants (random-effects model) was computed to indicate whether observed differences between conditions were significantly different from zero. Subsequently, t-values were transformed into z-scores. To protect against false-positive activations, only regions with a z-score >3.1 and at least five adjacent voxels were reported.

Results

Behavioral results

The behavioral results replicated findings (Figure 5.2) from two previous studies with a similar paradigm (Brass and von Cramon, 2004). A main effect was found for the factor CTI, $F(1,13) = 246, p < 0.001$, with the short CTI resulting in longer reaction times than the long CTI. Furthermore, a main effect was found for CONDITION, $F(2, 26) = 13$, $p < 0.001$. Participants reacted significantly faster in the cue-repetition condition than in the cue-switch condition, which significantly differed from the meaning-switch condition. As in previous studies, the interaction of CTI and CONDITION was also significant, $F(2, 26) = 29, p < 0.001$. Finally, there was a main effect for MODALITY with slower reaction times when participants responded with their feet compared to their hands, $F(1,13) = 5, p < 0.05$. Most importantly, none of the interactions with MODALITY were significant or showed a statistical trend.

The error analysis revealed a main effect for CTI, $F(1,13) = 18, p < 0.01$, a main effect for CONDITION, $F(2, 26) = 6, p < 0.01$, but no two-way interactions. However, the three-way interaction of CONDITION × CTI × MODALITY was significant, $F(2, 26) = 5.5$, $p < 0.05$. This three-way interaction seems to indicate a modality-dependent speed–accuracy tradeoff in the meaning-switch condition of the short CTI.

fMRI results

We first computed a direct comparison of hand and foot trials (Figure 5.3). If cognitive control for the hand and foot modality recruits different frontal areas, this contrast should yield activation differences in the frontal cortex. However, while we found very focused activation in the primary motor hand and foot area, no other frontal activation difference was found, neither for the hand nor for the foot condition. Our second question was whether the IFJ, which was found to be activated in a number of cognitive

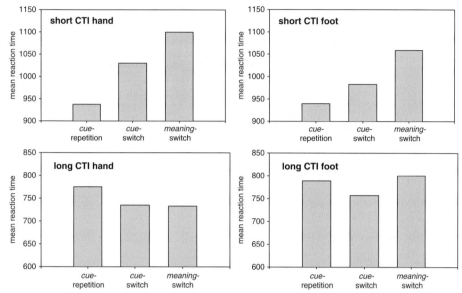

Figure 5.2 Upper part: Reaction time as a function of cue transition in the short cue–target interval (CTI) condition (double-cue conditions) for hand responses (left) and foot responses (right). Lower part: Reaction time as a function of cue-transition in the long CTI condition (double-cue conditions) for hand responses (left) and foot responses (right).

control experiments in which participants had to respond with their hands, is also active when participants respond with their feet. As outlined above, this region is very closely located to what is considered the hand area of the premotor cortex and might be sensitive to a manipulation of the response modality. To obtain the most reliable IFJ localization, we simply contrasted all trials from hand blocks with null events and all trials from foot blocks with the null events (Figure 5.4a and b). The location of the activation for the hand trials versus null events perfectly replicates the location we found in two previous fMRI experiments (Brass and von Cramon, 2002, 2004) indicating that the null event contrast provides a very good localizer for the IFJ. The IFJ activation in hand blocks (x: –40; y: 6; z: 32) was nearly identical to the activation in foot blocks (x: –37; y: 3; z: 32). The deviation was only 3 mm in the x-direction and 3 mm in the y-direction which corresponds to a displacement of approximately one voxel.

Finally, we wanted to investigate how participants prepared hand and foot blocks. The primary aim of this analysis was to establish whether participants activated their primary motor hand and foot area in preparation for the upcoming hand or foot blocks. Since a response modality cue was presented before each block, one can compare the preparation phase for hand and foot blocks. We used the coordinates of the primary motor hand and foot areas from the direct contrast of hand and foot trials and then carried out a region of interest analysis in these regions (Figure 5.5). An ANOVA of the factors *response modality* (hand and foot) and *area* (motor hand area and motor foot area)

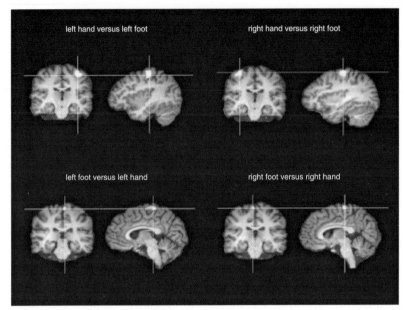

Figure 5.3 Cortical activation for the direct contrast of all left- and right-hand responses with all left- and right-foot responses (upper part). The lower part of the figure displays cortical activations for the direct contrast of all left- and right-foot trials with all left- and right-hand trials. The activation threshold was again set to $z > 3.1$. See color plate section.

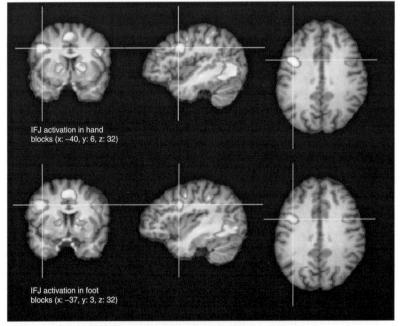

Figure 5.4 Cortical activation for the contrast of all experimental trials with null events for hand trials (upper part) and foot trials (lower part) with a z-value > 3.1. The peak Talairach coordinates for the inferior frontal junction area (IFJ) in hand and foot trials are plotted.

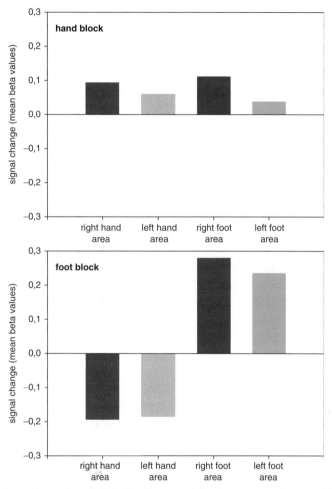

Figure 5.5 Region of interest analysis in the right and left primary motor hand and foot areas for the preparation phase of hand blocks (left part) and foot blocks (right part). The mean beta-values for each condition are plotted.

revealed a significant difference in the primary motor hand and primary motor foot area, $F(1, 13) = 14.8$, $p < 0.01$ with a stronger activation in the motor foot than in the motor hand area. Furthermore, the interaction of *response modality* and *area* was also significant, $F(1,13) = 16.5$, $p < 0.01$. Interestingly, when participants prepared for hand blocks, no significant activation was found, neither in the primary motor hand area, $t(13) = 1.5$, $p = 15$, nor in the primary motor foot area, $t(13) = 1.1$, $p = 0.27$. However, when participants prepared foot blocks a significant activation of the primary motor foot area was found, $t(13) = 5.4$, $p < 0.001$, and a relative deactivation of the primary motor hand area, $t(13) = -3.2$, $p < 0.01$ (Figure 5.5). These data suggest that hand responses are the default response modality that do not need to be specifically prepared, whereas foot responses require some additional preparatory effort.

Discussion

The aim of the present study was to investigate whether cognitive-control-related activation in the frontal cortex is sensitive to a manipulation of the response modality. More specifically, we wanted to know whether activation in the posterior frontolateral cortex is influenced by whether participants respond with their hands or feet. The behavioral data replicate findings from two previous studies with a similar design (Brass and von Cramon, 2004; Brass *et al.*, 2005b) and showed significant effects for task preparation and the cue manipulation as well as a reliable interaction. Most importantly, no interaction of these manipulations with response modality was found. When contrasting all trials in which participants responded with their hands with the identical trials in which participants responded with their feet, the only frontal activation difference was located in the primary motor hand and foot areas. Moreover, when we compared the location of the IFJ in hand and foot trials, the location was nearly identical. The second aim of the study was to investigate how participants anticipatorily prepare a specific response modality. Here we show that participants activated the primary motor foot area and inhibited the primary motor hand area when they prepared for a block in which they had to respond with their feet. In contrast, when they prepared hand blocks they neither activated their hand areas nor inhibited the foot areas.

We will discuss the implications of these findings from the point of view of the relation between motor and cognitive control. Furthermore, we discuss some broader theoretical accounts to integrate motor and cognitive control functions.

How motor-related is cognitive control?

The lack of a behavioral interaction of task preparation and the cue manipulation with response modality suggests that cognitive-control-related processes in the present paradigm do not rely on the response modality.

This point is further supported by a lack of cognitive-control-related frontal activation when hand and foot trials were directly contrasted. To our knowledge this is the first fMRI study which has directly addressed this question. Previous electrophysiological and fMRI studies have primarily focused on the question of whether different kinds of stimulus material are processed in different parts of the frontal cortex (McCarthy *et al.*, 1996; Ungerleider *et al.*, 1998) or whether different processes are implemented in different frontal areas (Owen *et al.*, 1998; Koechlin *et al.*, 2003; Koechlin and Jubault, 2006). While the finding of response modality independence seems to be more or less evident for areas located more anteriorly in the lateral prefrontal cortex (Sakai and Passingham, 2003), one could argue that cognitive-control-related regions close to the premotor cortex might differ in their location depending on whether participants respond with their hands or feet. This reasoning is further strengthened by a recent cortical connectivity study in non-human primates, suggesting that the ventral premotor cortex has strong connections to the adjacent ventral prefrontal cortex (Dum and Strick, 2005). In particular, it would be reasonable to assume that the somatotopic organization of the motor system extends into the adjacent frontolateral cortex. However, our data show that not even the IFJ, which is located in a transition zone between premotor and prefrontal cortex, is affected by the response modality. There are at least two possible interpretations of this finding. First, one could argue that processes that are implemented in the poster-ior frontolateral cortex are too abstract to show a response-modality dependency. Such a position would assume that the somatotopic organization, which is the guiding principle of the primary motor cortex and is less strict in the premotor cortex, completely dissolves in the posterior frontolateral cortex. We have previously argued that the IFJ is related to the updating of environmentally guided task representations (Brass von Cramon 2004; Brass *et al.*, 2005a). Task representations do not necessarily require the specification of a response or response modality and therefore might not be response modality dependent.

However, another interpretation for the lack of spatial variation in the posterior fron-tolateral cortex with different response modalities is the possibility that abstract task rules, as investigated in the current paradigm, are automatically mapped onto the hands. Rijntjes *et al.* (1999) showed, for example, that highly learned motor skills are automati-cally mapped on the extremity with which they are usually performed even when they are actually performed with another extremity. Indirect evidence for such a dominance of manual responses in the present context stems from the analysis of primary motor activation in the preparation phase before hand and foot blocks. While participants acti-vated the primary motor foot area before each foot block and inhibited the hand area, participants did not activate the hand motor area prior to hand blocks, suggesting that hand responses are the default mode of the system. One could speculate that the location of the IFJ anterior to the premotor hand area would reflect the fact that rule-guided behavior has evolved from tool use, which is primarily a manual skill. And in fact tool use involves cortical areas in the inferior frontal cortex that are very closely located to the IFJ (Johnson-Frey, 2004). From this perspective, such a rule-guided behavior would always activate the hand-related area in the posterior frontolateral cortex regardless of whether participants have to respond with their hands or feet. If participants are instructed to respond with their feet, a remapping to the relevant response modality would occur. A recent multisynaptic tracer study in the macaque monkey strongly supports such an interpretation of the data. Miyachi *et al.* (2005) showed that multisynaptic projections from the prefrontal cortex to the primary motor cortex are much stronger for the fore-limb motor areas compared with the hindlimb motor areas. This suggests that already in the macaque monkey the forelimbs seem to have a privileged connection to lateral prefrontal areas.

This interpretation leaves open the possibility that there are other abstract visuo-motor transformation systems which might map onto different response modalities. Two potential candidates are the language system and the spatial attentional system. Recently, Schubotz and von Cramon (2003) argued for such a trisection of the premotor cortex with spatial information mapped onto the dorsal premotor cortex, object information mapped onto the middle portion of the premotor cortex and auditory information mapped onto the ventral part of the premotor cortex.

Anticipatory preparation of the response modality

Another interesting finding of the present study is related to the involvement of primary motor regions when participants prepared the response modality. While a number of studies have investigated the preparation of specific responses (e.g. Toni *et al.*, 2001; Cunnington *et al.*, 2005), our data extend these findings to the response modality level. Furthermore, our data suggest that participants only prepare the nondominant response modality by activating the primary motor foot area. An interesting question is whether the relative deactivation in the primary motor hand area when participants prepared the foot responses reflects inhibitory processes on the neural level. There is some evidence that decreases in the BOLD response in primary motor areas can reflect inhibitory neural activity (Waldvogel *et al.*, 2000; Stefanovic *et al.*, 2004; Newton *et al.*, 2005). This point is further supported by the lack of a decrease in activation in the primary motor foot area when participants prepared hand responses.

In general, these results are consistent with recent task-switching findings showing that participants sometimes use the task preparation phase to preactivate the task-relevant areas (Wylie *et al.*, 2006; Yeung *et al.*, 2006). Wylie *et al.* (2006) showed that this strategy is only used for some tasks but not for others. Our study extends these findings from the task-set level to the response modality level. An interesting further question would be whether it is possible to produce behavioral switching effects by altering the response modality on a trial-by-trial basis. Furthermore, it would be interesting to investigate the frontal mechanisms involved in switching on the response modality level.

From stimulus-response (S-R) rules to task rules

In the Introduction, we argued that there might be a functional continuum from direct visuo-motor mappings through arbitrary visuo-motor mappings to cue-task mappings. Direct visuo-motor mappings differ from both arbitrary S-R mappings and cue-task mappings in their abstractness. While they directly relate a stimulus to a response, arbitrary S-R mappings and cue-task mappings require the application of an abstract rule. Interestingly, arbitrary S-R mappings and cue-task mappings seem also to be related on the functional neuroanatomical level. Recent research on arbitrary S-R mappings in humans (Boettiger and D'Esposito, 2005) revealed an activation for the acquisition of new arbitrary S-R mappings in the frontolateral cortex, which is very similar to the activation we found for the updating of cue-task mappings (Brass and von Cramon, 2004).

Recently, Diamond (2006) has developed an interesting interpretation for the role of the posterior frontolateral cortex in motor and cognitive control. She argued that this region comes into play whenever the information that guides behavior is not directly attached to the object on which participants act. She listed developmental evidence (Diamond *et al.*, 1999, 2003) and evidence from research in monkeys (Jarvik, 1956; Halsband and Passingham, 1982) in support of her position. Moreover, Rushworth *et al.* (2005) recently showed that separating the distance between the instructing stimulus and the stimulus on which monkeys had to act led to severe problems in animals with lesions to the ventral prefrontal cortex and the orbital prefrontal cortex (Rushworth *et al.*, 2005). From this perspective the specificity of task rules lies in the fact that the task information is presented spatially distant from the target. And, in fact, in almost all task-switching experiments the target does not carry the information which task to execute. If this assumption holds true, the crucial difference between task rules and response rules would not be the number of S-R associations which are related to a specific contextual cue, but rather the separation of the rule-guiding information and the stimulus on which the rule applies.

The role of the parietal cortex in cognitive and motor control

Interestingly, the tight relation between motor and cognitive control is not only reflected in the frontal cortex, but also in the parietal cortex. A number of cognitive control experiments revealed activation along the intraparietal sulcus (Kimberg *et al.*, 2000; Sohn *et al.*, 2000; Brass and von Cramon 2002, 2004). Regions along the intraparietal sulcus have also been reported to be crucially involved in motor control functions (Rizzolatti and Luppino, 2001). In particular, research in nonhuman primates revealed that the anterior intraparietal cortex plays a crucial role in visually guided hand actions (Sakata *et al.*, 1995, 1997). A homologue area has been identified in the human anterior intraparietal sulcus (Binkofski *et al.*, 1998). When comparing the location of cognitive-control-related activation in the anterior intraparietal sulcus (e.g. Brass and von Cramon, 2002) with the location of hand motor activation in the anterior intraparietal sulcus (e.g. see overview in Frey *et al.*, 2005), these locations are almost indistinguishable. Again, this functional neuroanatomical overlap of cognitive control and hand-motor control suggests that cognitive control can be understood as a kind of abstraction from hand-motor control.

Towards an integrated approach of motor and cognitive control

So far, cognitive control research and research on motor control has been kept mostly separate. This might be due to the fact that experimental approaches to investigate cognitive and motor control are difficult to compare. However, functional brain imaging research in humans and neurophysiological studies in nonhuman primates suggest that there are striking similarities between the brain circuits involved in cognitive and motor control. The frontoparietal network involved in externally guided actions is very similar to the network involved in contextually guided cognitive control. Moreover, from an evolutionary perspective it is highly reasonable that cognitive control processes evolved from motor control functions. To give considerations to this specific relation, future research needs to overcome the experimental borders between both research areas and needs more explicitly to address the similarities and differences between cognitive and motor control.

Conclusions

The aim of this chapter was to discuss the relationship between motor and cognitive control. Furthermore, we carried out an fMRI experiment to explicitly address the question whether the somatotopic organization of the motor system extends into the adjacent frontal cortex. Our study shows, for the first time, that cognitive-control-related activation in the frontal cortex in general and the posterior frontolateral cortex in particular does not depend on the response modality. When comparing a cognitive control paradigm in which participants responded with their hands with the same paradigm in which participants responded with their feet, the only activation difference in the frontal cortex was located in the primary motor areas. Moreover, the activation in the dysgranular posterior frontolateral cortex was not affected by the response modality. These data leave open two possible interpretations. On the one hand, one can argue that cognitive control is widely independent of motor control because cognitive-control-related activation in the posterior frontolateral cortex does not follow a somatotopic organization. On the other hand, one can argue that cognitive control functions evolved from hand-motor control and are therefore tied to the hand-motor system. Cortical connectivity data support this latter possibility. Furthermore, the close proximity of cognitive-control-related activation and hand-motor-control-related activation in the intraparietal sulcus is in accordance with this interpretation.

Acknowledgements

This work was supported by a grant from the German Research Foundation.

References

Adam, J. J., Backes, W., Rijcken, J., Hofman, P., Kuipers, H. and Jolles, J. (2003) Rapid visuomotor preparation in the human brain: a functional MRI study. *Cognitive Brain Research*, **16**, 1–10.

Amunts, K. *et al.* (2004) A receptor- and cytoarchitectonic correlate of the functionally defined inferior-frontal junction area. *Neuroimage*, **22** (Suppl.), 50.

Binkofski, F., Dohle, C., Posse, S., Stephan, K. M., Hefter, H., Seitz, R. J. and Freund, H. J. (1998) Human anterior intraparietal area subserves prehension: a combined lesion and functional MRI activation study. *Neurology*, **50**, 1253–1259.

Boettiger, C. A. and D'Esposito, M. (2005) Frontal networks for learning and executing arbitrary stimulus-response associations. *Journal of Neuroscience*, **25**, 2723–2732.

Brass, M. and von Cramon, D. Y. (2002) The role of the frontal cortex in task preparation. *Cerebral Cortex*, **12**, 908–914.

Brass, M. and von Cramon, D. Y. (2004) Decomposing components of task preparation with functional magnetic resonance imaging. *Journal of Cognitive Neuroscience*, **16**, 609–620.

Brass, M., Derrfuss, J., Forstmann, B. and von Cramon, D. Y. (2005a) The role of the inferior frontal junction area in cognitive control. *Trends in Cognitive Sciences*, **9**, 314–316.

Brass, M., Ullsperger, M., Knoesche, T. R., von Cramon, D. Y. and Phillips, N. A. (2005b) Who comes first? The role of the prefrontal and parietal cortex in cognitive control. *Journal of Cognitive Neuroscience*, **17**, 1367–1313.

Buccino, G., Binkofski, F., Fink, G. R. *et al.* (2001) Action observation activates premotor and parietal areas in a somatotopic manner: an fMRI study. *European Journal of Neuroscience*, **13**, 400–404.

Cunnington, R., Windischberger, C., Deecke, L. and Moser, E. (2003) The preparation and readiness for voluntary movement: a high-field event-related fMRI study of the Bereitschafts-BOLD response. *Neuroimage*, **20**, 404–412.

Derrfuss, J., Brass, M. and von Cramon, D. Y. (2004) Cognitive control in the posterior frontolateral cortex: evidence from common activations in task coordination, interference control, and working memory. *Neuroimage*, **23**, 604–612.

Derrfuss, J., Brass, M., Neumann, J. and von Cramon, D. Y. (2005) Involvement of the inferior frontal junction in cognitive control: meta-analyses of switching and Stroop studies. *Human Brain Mapping*, **25**, 22–34.

Diamond, A. (2006) Bootstrapping conceptual deduction using physical connection: rethinking frontal cortex. *Trends in Cognitive Sciences*, **10**, 212–218.

Diamond, A., Churchland, A., Cruess, L. and Kirkham, N. Z. (1999) Early developments in the ability to understand the relation between stimulus and reward. *Developmental Psychology*, **35**, 1507–1517.

Diamond, A., Lee, E. Y. and Hayden, M. (2003) Early success in using the relation between stimuli and rewards to deduce an abstract rule: perceived physical connection is key. *Developmental Psychology*, **39**, 825–847.

Dreher, J. C., Koechlin, E., Ali, S. O. and Grafman, J. (2002) The roles of timing and task order during task switching. *Neuroimage*, **17**, 95–109.

Dum, R. P. and Strick, P. L. (2005) Frontal lobe inputs to the digit representations of the motor areas on the lateral surface of the hemisphere. *Journal of Neuroscience*, **25**, 1375–1386.

Duncan, J., Owen, A. M. (2000) Common regions of the human frontal lobe recruited by diverse cognitive demands. Trends in *Neuroscience*, **23**, 475–483.

Forstmann, B. U., Brass, M., Koch, I. and von Cramon, D. Y. (2005) Internally generated and directly cued task sets: an investigation with fMRI. *Neuropsychologia*, **43**, 943–952.

Frey, S. H., Vinton, D., Norlund, R. and Grafton, S. T. (2005) Cortical topography of human anterior intraparietal cortex active during visually guided grasping. *Cognitive Brain Research*, **23**, 397–405.

Godschalk, M., Mitz, A. R., van Duin, B. and van der Burg, H. (1995) Somatotopy of monkey premotor cortex examined with microstimulation. *Neuroscience Research*, **23**, 269–279.

Halsband, U. and Passingham, R. (1982) The role of premotor and parietal cortex in the direction of action. *Brain Research*, **240**, 368–372.

Jarvik, M. E. (1956) Simple color discrimination in chimpanzees: effect of varying contiguity between cue and incentive. *Journal of Comparative and Physiological Psychology*, **49**, 492–495.

Johnson-Frey, S. H. (2004) The neural bases of complex tool use in humans. *Trends in Cognitive Sciences*, **8**, 71–78.

Kimberg, D. Y., Aguirre, G. K. and D'Esposito, M. (2000) Modulation of task-related neural activity in task-switching: an fMRI study. *Cognitive Brain Research*, **10**, 189–196.

Koechlin, E. and Jubault, T. (2006) Broca's area and the hierarchical organization of human behavior. *Neuron*, **50**, 963–974.

Koechlin, E., Ody, C. and Kouneiher, F. (2003) The architecture of cognitive control in the human prefrontal cortex. *Science*, **302**, 1181–1185.

Lohmann, G., Muller, K., Bosch, V. *et al.* (2001) LIPSIA—a new software system for the evaluation of functional magnetic resonance images of the human brain. *Computerized Medical Imaging and Graphics*, **25**, 449–457.

MacDonald, A. W. 3rd, Cohen, J. D., Stenger, V. A. and Carter, C. S. (2000) Dissociating the role of the dorsolateral prefrontal and anterior cingulate cortex in cognitive control. *Science*, **288**, 1835–1838.

McCarthy, G., Puce, A., Constable, R. T., Krystal, J. H., Gore, J. C. and Goldman-Rakic, P. (1996) Activation of human prefrontal cortex during spatial and nonspatial working memory tasks measured by functional MRI. *Cerebral Cortex*, **6**, 600–611.

Miller, E. K. and Cohen, J. D. (2001) An integrative theory of prefrontal cortex function. *Annual Review of Neuroscience*, **24**, 167–202.

Milner, B. (1963) Effects of different brain lesions on card sorting. *Archives of Neurology*, **9**, 90–100.

Miyachi, S., Lu, X., Inoue, S. *et al.* (2005) Organization of multisynaptic inputs from prefrontal cortex to primary motor cortex as revealed by retrograde transneuronal transport of rabies virus. *Journal of Neuroscience*, **25**, 2547–2556.

Monsell, S. (2003) Task switching. *Trends in Cognitive Sciences*, **7**, 134–140.

Murray, E. A., Bussey, T. J. and Wise, S. P. (2000) Role of prefrontal cortex in a network for arbitrary visuomotor mapping. *Experimental Brain Research*, **133**, 114–129.

Newton, J. M., Sunderland, A. and Gowland, P. A. (2005) fMRI signal decreases in ipsilateral primary motor cortex during unilateral hand movements are related to duration and side of movement. *Neuroimage*, **24**, 1080–1087.

Oldfield, R. C. (1971) The assessment and analysis of handedness: the Edinburgh inventory. *Neuropsychologia*, **9**, 97–113.

Owen, A. M., Stern, C. E., Look, R. B., Tracey, I., Rosen, B. R. and Petrides, M. (1998) Functional organization of spatial and nonspatial working memory processing within the human lateral frontal cortex. *Proceedings of the National Academy of Sciences of the USA*, **95**, 7721–7726.

Petrides, M. (1985) Deficits on conditional associative-learning tasks after frontal- and temporal-lobe lesions in man. *Neuropsychologia*, **23**, 601–614.

Picard, N. and Strick, P. L. (2001) Imaging the premotor areas. *Current Opinion in Neurobiology*, **11**, 663–672.

Rijntjes, M., Dettmers, C., Buchel, C., Kiebel, S., Frackowiak, R. S. and Weiller, C. (1999) A blueprint for movement: functional and anatomical representations in the human motor system. *Journal of Neuroscience*, **19**, 8043–8048.

Rizzolatti, G., Luppino, G. (2001) The cortical motor system. *Neuron*, **31**, 889–901.

Rowe, J. B., Toni, I., Josephs, O., Frackowiak, R. S. and Passingham, R. E. (2000) The prefrontal cortex: response selection or maintenance within working memory? *Science*, **288**, 1656–1660.

Rushworth, M. F. *et al.* (2005) Attentional selection and action selection in the ventral and orbital prefrontal cortex. *Journal of Neuroscience*, **25**, 11628–11636.

Sakai, K. and Passingham, R. E. (2003) Prefrontal interactions reflect future task operations. *Nature Neuroscience*, **6**, 75–81.

Sakata, H., Taira, M., Murata, A. and Mine, S. (1995) Neural mechanisms of visual guidance of hand action in the parietal cortex of the monkey. *Cerebral Cortex*, **5**, 429–438.

Sakata, H., Taira, M., Kusunoki, M., Murata, A. and Tanaka, Y. (1997) The TINS Lecture. The parietal association cortex in depth perception and visual control of hand action. *Trends in Neurosciences*, **20**, 350–357.

Sakreida, K., Schubotz, R. I., Wolfensteller, U. and von Cramon, D. Y. (2005) Motion class dependency in observers' motor areas revealed by functional magnetic resonance imaging. *Journal of Neuroscience*, **25**, 1335–1342.

Schieber, M. H. (2001) Constraints on somatotopic organization in the primary motor cortex. *Journal of Neurophysiology*, **86**, 2125–2143.

Schubotz, R. I. and von Cramon, D. Y. (2003) Functional-anatomical concepts of human premotor cortex: evidence from fMRI and PET studies. *Neuroimage*, **20** (Suppl. 1), 120–131.

Schumacher, E. H. and D'Esposito, M. (2002) Neural implementation of response selection in humans as revealed by localized effects of stimulus-response compatibility on brain activation. *Human Brain Mapping*, **17**, 193–201.

Smith, E. E. and Jonides, J. (1999) Storage and executive processes in the frontal lobes. *Science*, **283**, 1657–1661.

Sohn, M. H., Ursu, S., Anderson, J. R., Stenger, V. A. and Carter, C. S. (2000) Inaugural article: the role of prefrontal cortex and posterior parietal cortex in task switching. *Proceedings of the National Academy of Sciences of the USA*, **97**, 13448–13453.

Stefanovic, B., Warnking, J. M. and Pike, G. B. (2004) Hemodynamic and metabolic responses to neuronal inhibition. *Neuroimage*, **22**, 771–778.

Sudevan, P. and Taylor, D. A. (1987) The cuing and priming of cognitive operations. *Journal of Experimental Psychology: Human Perception and Performance*, **13**, 89–103.

Toni, I., Thoenissen, D. and Zilles, K. (2001) Movement preparation and motor intention. *Neuroimage*, **14**, 110–117.

Ungerleider, L. G., Courtney, S. M. and Haxby, J. V. (1998) A neural system for human visual working memory. *Proceedings of the National Academy of Sciences of the USA*, **95**, 883–890.

Waldvogel, D., van Gelderen, P., Muellbacher, W., Ziemann, U., Immisch, I. and Hallett, M. (2000) The relative metabolic demand of inhibition and excitation. *Nature*, **406**, 995–998.

Wise, S. P. and Murray, E. A. (2000) Arbitrary associations between antecedents and actions. *Trends in Neurosciences*, **23**, 271–276.

Wylie, G. R., Javitt, D. C. and Foxe, J. J. (2006) Jumping the gun: is effective preparation contingent upon anticipatory activation in task-relevant neural circuitry? *Cerebral Cortex*, **16**, 394–404.

Yeung, N., Nystrom, L. E., Aronson, J. A. and Cohen, J. D. (2006) Between-task competition and cognitive control in task switching. *Journal of Neuroscience*, **26**, 1429–1438.

6

The anterior cingulate cortex: reward-guided action selection and the value of actions

Matthew F. S. Rushworth and Mark E. Walton

Introduction

All of the choices we make are guided by an assessment of the expected value of the outcome we hope to obtain. As a general rule, whenever confronted by more than one possible course of action, our primary goal is to pursue the option which results in the greatest reward. Exactly what constitutes this ideal outcome in different circumstances is a complex and unresolved question. Nonetheless, over the past decades, great progress has been made in delineating the neural circuitry underlying such goal-directed behavior and reinforcement, and describing the way in which current motivation can influence the actions that are selected (Balleine, 2005; Schultz, 2006). There are also increasingly sophisticated theoretical models of how the brain achieves such valuations (Dayan and Balleine, 2002; Montague *et al.*, 2006).

Numerous studies in humans have demonstrated that parts of the frontal lobe are integral to the selection of actions and making optimal decisions. Patients with prefrontal lesions often perform poorly on many tasks where they have to implement a strategy to achieve a goal or weigh up the costs and benefits of different options (Rogers *et al.*, 1999; Bechara *et al.*, 2000; Burgess *et al.*, 2000; Manes *et al.*, 2002; Fellows and Farah, 2005). They are often described as demonstrating impulsive, irresponsible and risky behavior. Symptoms of apathy, indifference and motivational changes have also commonly been observed (van Reekum *et al.*, 2005; Levy and Dubois, 2006). However, the damage in these patients often spans several separate neuroanatomical areas and there remains a large degree of confusion over which regions are critical and what their exact contributions are.

One possible reason for the confusion over the roles of different frontal areas in reward- and rule-guided response selection is that research has largely failed to take into account that organisms do not just make decisions on the basis of an expected reward but also weigh up the potential costs of the different courses of action. In most circumstances, animals have to assess their internal states and particular mode of behavioral output to decide how to invest their time and energy in pursuit of a particular goal and how willing they are to take risks or explore the available options. Behavioral ecologists have emphasized that investing effort by travelling long distances to forage for nutrition, for example, may be preferable if the expected gain is greater than that from more proximal patches

(Charnov, 1976). Similarly, it can frequently be advantageous to resist the temptation of an immediately available reward and instead wait patiently for a more valuable future benefit (Kacelnik, 1997).

Here we discuss the contribution that ventral and medial prefrontal regions, in particular the anterior cingulate cortex (ACC) and orbitofrontal cortex (OFC), play in the optimal evaluation of cost-benefit decisions. In line with anatomical differences between these two regions, there appear to be dissociations in the way these regions integrate internally motivated or reinforcement-guided outcome information with different types of decision costs to guide choice behavior.

Action selection or action monitoring?

There is a large literature associating dorsomedial prefrontal cortex, including the ACC, with either monitoring for response conflict or detecting when erroneous responses are executed (Botvinick *et al.*, 2001; Holroyd and Coles, 2002). It is argued that the ACC does not itself exert control over response selection in such situations but that it signals to other regions a need to modify behavior. When single-neuron recording studies are conducted, however, it is clear that there is little evidence that the activity of ACC neurons is modulated by response conflict (Ito *et al.*, 2003; Nakamura *et al.*, 2005). On the other hand there is evidence that activity in adjacent areas in the superior frontal gyrus, such as the supplementary eye field, is modulated by conflict (Stuphorn *et al.*, 2000; Nakamura *et al.*, 2005). While it is currently unclear whether the activity of SEF neurons is actually compatible with their having a role in monitoring and detecting response conflict, there is evidence that the SEF may be important in resolving response conflict; microstimulation of the SEF affects response inhibition in conditions of high conflict (Stuphorn and Schall, 2006).

There are also a number of claims of ACC activation during task switching (Dosenbach *et al.*, 2006). One possibility is that, although the ACC may not be directly concerned with implementing the change in task set or monitoring the response conflict that occurs, it may be concerned with generating a novel response when it is not clear what the new conditions demand and monitoring whether or not the response is successful (Walton *et al.*, 2004).

While the evidence for an ACC role in monitoring response conflict is not clear there are data suggesting that it plays an active role in volitional action selection. Lesions of the superior frontal gyrus and the ACC in monkeys cause animals to be impaired at making self-paced movements but not when the response is paced by an auditory tone (Thaler *et al.*, 1995). Parts of the ACC sulcus, referred to as the cingulate motor areas, have been shown in monkeys to project directly both to primary motor cortex and to the ventral horn of the spinal cord (He *et al.*, 1995; Wang *et al.*, 2001) and electrical microstimulation of these regions can elicit multi-joint movements (Luppino *et al.*, 1991; Mattelli *et al.*, 1991). Similarly, stimulation of the ventral bank of the ACC sulcus in humans has been shown to evoke an urge to make spontaneous goal-directed movements (Kremer *et al.*, 2001) and this region is consistently activated in imaging tasks requiring self-generation of responses (Frith *et al.*, 1991; Jahanshahi *et al.*, 1995; Lau *et al.*, 2004).

One way of reconciling the response generation and the performance-monitoring roles is to consider these regions from a decision-making perspective where it is imperative to assess the value of the chosen course of action in the light of other possible options. Several lines of evidence suggest that the ACC and also the OFC play important roles in the selection and evaluation of actions based on their expected outcomes. These areas receive a rich innervation of dopamine fibres from the ventral tegmental area, a pathway that has been implicated in signalling discrepancies between predicted and received reward (Berger et al., 1988; Montague et al., 1996; Williams and Goldman-Rakic, 1998), as well as afferents from limbic structures such as the amygdala and parts of the parahippocampal cortical areas (Carmichael and Price, 1994). Neuroimaging studies of outcome monitoring and decision making frequently show activations in OFC and dorsal, supracallosal parts of ACC (Elliott et al., 2000; Berns et al., 2001; O'Doherty et al., 2003; Cohen et al., 2005; Coricelli et al., 2005). Both regions contain neurons that respond to the anticipation and delivery of reinforcement or recognition of errors (Tremblay and Schultz, 1999; Hikosaka and Watanabe, 2000; Procyk et al., 2000; Akkal et al., 2002; Wallis and Miller, 2003; Padoa-Schioppa and Assad, 2006) and lesions in either can cause difficulties in using reward information to guide action selection (Iversen and Mishkin, 1970; Jones and Mishkin, 1972; Hadland et al., 2003; Schoenbaum et al., 2003a).

Although correct and incorrect actions may be easily categorized in the laboratory by reference to the researchers' pre-programmed and fixed experimental contingencies, it can be more difficult to draw a defining line between the two types of outcome in more naturalistic settings. For many foraging animals the natural environment is more uncertain and variable than the laboratory and both positive and negative outcomes can be a source of information about the value of actions. If an outcome is only probabilistically associated with reward then what is important is not whether a given action on a given occasion failed to lead to reward, an occurrence normally referred to as an error, but whether the action is, on average, more profitable than an alternative. A given action and associated probability of reward may be the less preferred one if a more rewarding alternative is available but the more preferred option if the only alternative is even less rewarding. Hayden and Platt (2006) have drawn attention to the way monkeys in the wild will switch to foraging for a less-preferred food when a preferred food is no longer available. The next section reviews recent evidence that the ACC is part of a system for representing the recent history of reward and not just simply error outcomes (Amiez et al., 2006; Kennerley et al., 2006).

The net value of the action is, however, not just determined by its profitability but also by the costs that are associated with it. To take the example of the foraging animal once again, it is possible that the animal may learn that a certain course of action, such as climbing to the very top of a tree, is very likely to yield a food reward but the action may not be worth performing if only a small amount of food is expected and the action is very effortful. The subsequent section describes experiments that suggest that the ACC is also a critical locus for cost/benefit integration when choices are made (Walton et al., 2002, 2003).

Lesions of the ACC sulcus impair decision making and not simply error monitoring

To examine the role of the ACC sulcus (ACCs, Figure 6.1) in decision making and error monitoring, Kennerley *et al.* (2006) taught macaques a joystick reversal task. The animals learned to make two different joystick movements, pull or turn. One movement was deemed the correct one for 25 successive trials but subsequently further instances of the same action were not rewarded. The only way that the macaque could tell that the reward contingencies had changed was by monitoring the outcomes of the actions and changing to the alternative whenever a given action no longer yielded reward.

Error monitoring ability was indexed by performance on the trials that followed the programmed errors that occurred when the reward was reassigned from one action to another (Error + 1 trials, Figure 6.2, right). Animals with ACCs lesions were no worse than controls on these trials. Performance on Error + 1 trials was also compared with performance on trials that occurred after correct responses (Correct + 1, Figure 6.2, left). Although the animals with ACCs lesions performed the task worse than did the controls, there was no

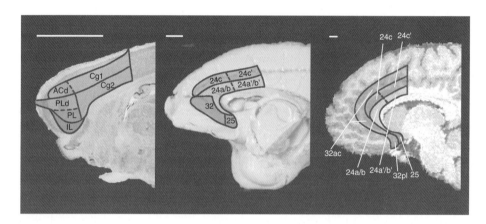

Figure 6.1 Comparative anatomy of the rodent (rat, left), and primate (macaque, centre and human, right) anterior cingulate cortex (ACC). In the macaque the ACC is divided into two broad regions: (i) ACC gyrus (blue) immediately dorsal and rostral to the corpus callosum and including area 24 (24a and 24b rostrally, 24a' and 24b' caudally), 32, and 25. (ii) ACC sulcus (red). A further cytoarchitectonic subdivision of area 24, 24c, occupies most of the sulcal ACC. Its caudal part, 24c', contains the rostral cingulate motor area (CMAr). Similarly, although further subdivision is possible, it is also useful to consider two broad subdivisions within the human ACC. Human ACC gyrus areas 32pl, 25, 24a and 24b resemble the macaque gyral areas 32, 25, 24a and 24b (Vogt *et al.*, 1995; Ongur *et al.*, 2003). Human areas 24c, 24c', and 32ac in the ACC sulcus and, when present, the second superior cingulate gyrus (CGs), bear similarities with the areas in the macaque ACC sulcus and include the cingulate motor areas (Vogt *et al.*, 1995; Ongur *et al.*, 2003). The identification of homologous structures in the rat is more controversial. There is a good case for thinking that parts of the rodent brain resemble the primate ACC gyrus [Cg1, posterior Cg1, infralimbic cortex (IL) and prelimbic cortex (PL)]. There is no equivalent of the primate ACC sulcus in the rat but it might tentatively be argued that rat rostral ACd bears some resemblance in its anatomical connexions. See color plate section.

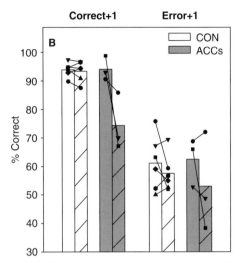

Figure 6.2 Performance on the trial immediately following a rewarded (Correct + 1) and non-rewarded (Error + 1) response. Control (CON) performance is shown in the white bars and performance by the anterior cingulate cortex sulcus (ACCs) lesion group is shown in the grey bars. For both groups performance on the first test, conducted in the preoperative period, is shown in unhatched bars while performance on the second test, conducted in the post-operative period, is shown in the hatched bars. The controls rarely correct an error on the very next trial (**B**, right) and this tendency was not reduced by the ACCs lesion.

evidence that the impairment was more prominent on the trials that followed errors as would be predicted by simple error-monitoring accounts of the ACC. In fact the reverse was true: the ACCs had a bigger impact on the Correct + 1 trials than it did on the Error + 1 trials.

In order to understand the impairment it is necessary to understand how the control animals responded to the occurrence of errors. Responding was guided by the recent history of reinforcement and not just by the most recent error. Control animals did not immediately switch to the alternative action on the very first trial that resulted in an error (E + 1 trials in Figure 6.3). Instead animals only gradually switched over to the alternative action. If a macaque switched to the correct action on the trial after an error then it was more likely to once again make the correct action on the next trial (EC + 1 trials in Figure 6.3). As the macaque accumulated more rewards by making the alternative action it became more and more likely to continue making the alternative response but the increase in the probability of the alternative action was gradual and occurred over the course of several trials (EC$_2$ + 1 trials and EC$_3$ + 1 trials, etc., Figure 6.3). Even after the experience of many thousands of trials of a task, macaques do not naturally treat reinforcement change as an unambiguous instruction to one action or another in quite the same way as they treat sensory cues which have been linked with actions through conditional associations. In other words, the animals were guided by a sense of the action's value which was based on its average reward history over the course of several trials and they were not simply guided by the most recent outcome that had followed the action. This is consistent with the prediction of learning theory that the value of an action should be dependent on the

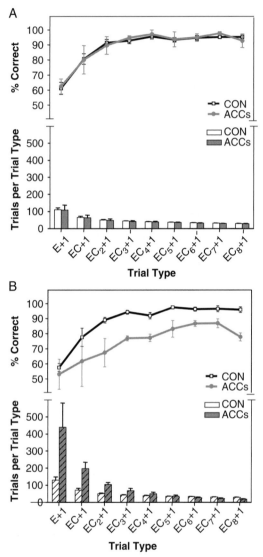

Figure 6.3 Pre- (**A**) and postoperative (**B**) performance for sustaining rewarded behavior following an error. The trial types are plotted across the x-axis and start on the left with the trial immediately following an error (E + 1). The next data point corresponds to the trial after one error and then a correct response (EC + 1), the after that corresponds to the trial after one error and then two correct responses (EC + 2), and so on. Moving from the left to the right of each panel corresponds to the animal acquiring more instances of positive reinforcement, after making the correct action, subsequent to an earlier error. Each graph shows the percentage of trials of each type that were correct. Control (CON) and anterior cingulate cortex sulcus (ACCs) lesion data are shown by the black and grey lines respectively. The histogram in the bottom part of each graph indicates the number of instances of each trial type. As in Figure 6.2, white and grey bars indicate the control and ACCs lesion data respectively while hatched bars indicate data from the postoperative session.

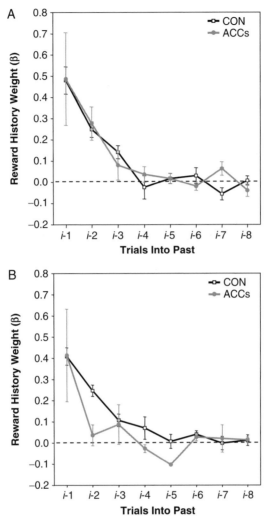

Figure 6.4 Estimates of the influence of previous reward history on current choice in the pre- (**A**) and postoperative (**B**) testing periods. Each point represents a regression coefficient value derived from the multiple logistic regression of choice on the current trial (i) against the outcomes (rewarded or unrewarded) on the previous eight trials. The influence of the previous trial (i-1) is shown on the left-hand side of each figure, the influence of the previous trial but one (i-2) is shown next, and so on up until the trial that occurred eight trials previously (i-8). Control (CON) and anterior cingulate cortex sulcus (ACCs) lesion data are shown by the black and grey lines respectively.

recent history of outcomes associated with that action and not just the most recent outcome (Sutton and Barto, 1998).

Even if the ACCs lesion did not impair error monitoring as indexed by performance on Error + 1 trials, it did affect the accumulation of a revised sense of the alternative action's value after the reward reassignment (Figure 6.3). The probability of making the alternative response did not increase as quickly as more rewards were received after the ACCs lesion.

The conclusion that average action values were disrupted after ACC lesion was supported by a logistic regression analysis which examined how well choices were predicted by the reward history associated with each action. Figure 6.4 plots the regression coefficients of choice on the current trial (i) against the outcomes (rewarded or unrewarded) on the previous eight trials (i-1, i-2, etc. up to i-8). The coefficients represent the weight of influence of the outcomes of previous choices on the current choice. The choices of controls were influenced even by outcomes that had occurred five trials before although the influence of the outcome of even earlier choices was negligible. The choices of animals with ACCs lesions, however, were only influenced by the outcome of the previous trial.

Outside of the laboratory in many foraging situations the value of an action will not be static but it will actually vary in a fashion that is dynamically dependent on which actions have already been made. To return to the example of the monkey foraging in the wild, the value of a course of action, such as foraging for fruit in a particular tree, will decrease if the course of action is repeated. Even if the tree is a very fruitful one the probability of finding fruit in any fixed time period decreases the more time the animal has already spent there. This happens because the fruit is depleted by the animal's previous actions and it is only renewed slowly as a result of further growth. When the animal first arrives at a copse of fruit-bearing trees it may be best first to forage in the tree that is likely to have the most fruit, but after some time, once the best tree's fruit is depleted, it may be better to move on to another type of tree even if it is a type associated with less fruit. According to the marginal value theorem (Charnov, 1976) the animal should switch when the rate of payoff falls below that associated with the alternative options.

It is possible to model this type of situation using matching tasks similar to those first devised by Herrnstein (1997) and used more recently with macaques by Sugrue *et al.* (2004). Kennerley *et al.* (2006) programmed the two joystick movements previously taught to the macaques to deliver reward with two different probabilities. Rewards were probabilistically and independently assigned to each response on each trial so that a reward could be assigned to either the pull response, the turn response, both responses, or neither response on any given trial. The monkey, however, had only one chance to make a response on each trial. If the monkey made a response with an allocated reward then it received that reward. If a reward was assigned to a response but the response was not made then the 'unharvested' reward was left assigned to the same response on the following trial. In such situations the optimal strategy is not simply to make the most profitable response on every trial but to switch between the more and less profitable responses. This is because the probability of the reward associated with the less profitable option gradually increases on every consecutive trial in which that response is not made; any unharvested reward that is allocated to the less profitable response when the more profitable response is selected will still be available on the next trial. After several trials the probability of reward associated with the normally less profitable response will exceed the average probability of reward associated with the pull response. As in the natural foraging situation, neither one action nor the other is categorically correct or incorrect although one is, on average, more likely to yield reward. Again, as in the natural setting, the probability of reward associated with each response is actually dependent on

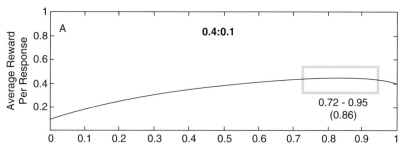

Figure 6.5 The average reward expected per response is plotted as a function of the proportion of the responses that are of the type associated with the higher probability of reinforcement (*H*) for one of the four action-reward pair ratios (0.4:0.1) tested in the matching experiment. As the proportion of *H* responses increases, the average reward income per response increases until the optimal response ratio is reached at the maximum point of the curve. Increasing the proportion of *H* responses beyond this ratio leads to a decrement in average reinforcement. A grey box indicates the criterion region that animals were required to reach. When animals respond within this region they are performing at a level of 97% of optimal performance and are expected to receive, on average, 97% of the maximum available rewards.

which responses the macaque has already made. Rewards are obtained at the highest rate if the fraction of responses of a given type is equal to the fraction of total rewards that can be earned by making that response (Figure 6.5).

The macaques were exposed to four sets of reward probabilities associated with each of the two actions (0.4:0.1; 0.5:0.2; 0.75:0.25; 1:0) and the number of trials taken before animals began to obtain rewards at 97% of the optimum rate was recorded. The grey rectangle in Figure 6.5 demarcates the range of response ratios at which rewards are being received at 97% of the optimum rate. Animals with ACCs lesions took significantly more trials to approach response ratios close to the optimum (Figure 6.6). The impairment was clear when the rewards were probabilistically associated with both responses (left-hand side of Figure 6.6b) but not when one response was always rewarded and the other response never rewarded (1:0 condition, right-hand side of Figure 6.6b). Such a pattern of results would be expected if the ACCs is not simply monitoring each action to see whether it leads to an error but if it is part of a system for representing the value of each action on the basis of its integrated reward history. In order to work out which action is the more profitable in the matching task it is necessary to integrate the outcomes received for each action over time and simply switching whenever there is an error that will not lead to the best allocation of responses.

The activity of some cells in the ACCs increases when errors occur but ACCs neurons also exhibit responses that are related to reward delivery and expectation (Procyk *et al.*, 2000; Amiez *et al.*, 2005). Importantly ACCs activity does not just reflect the most recent action outcome but it also represents the average reinforcement value of a response (Amiez *et al.*, 2006). The activity of posterior cingulate neurons has also been shown to reflect aspects of the reward history, such as variation in reward size with respect to the mean value (risk) (McCoy and Platt, 2005). It is clear, however, that the ACCs does not

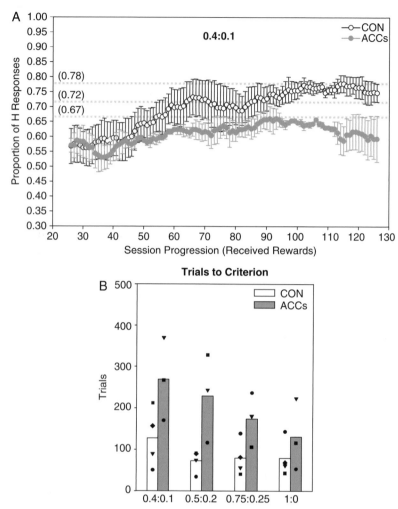

Figure 6.6 (a) Group response ratio plot for the action reward ratio 0.4:0.1. The ratio of responses with higher average reinforcement (*H*) as opposed to lower average reward (*L*) responses was calculated by smoothing behavioral performance across bins of 50 trials. To equate individual performance through the progression of a testing day, the data are plotted as a function of collected rewards, rather than as a function of trials, on the abscissa. Dashed grey lines denote 95%, 97%, and 99% optimum response thresholds for maximizing expected total reward income. **(b)** Summary of postoperative performance in the matching task in terms of the number of trials required to exceed the optimum response ratio threshold (Figure 6.5). Control (CON) and anterior cingulate cortex sulcus (ACCs) lesion data are shown by white and grey bars respectively.

encode which actions have been made and which rewards have been received in isolation; the activity of neurons in the dorsolateral prefrontal cortex and superior frontal gyrus also encode information not just about which action is currently being made and whether reward is being received but also information about which actions have recently been made and the reward that was received (Barraclough *et al.*, 2004; Genovesio *et al.*, 2005; Seo *et al.*, 2005).

Action values: costs and benefits in the ACC

An action's value is not just determined by its integrated reward history. An action may be associated with a very large reward but the action may not be selected if it is associated with costs as well as benefits. For example a bird may forage by walking or flying and each course of action may be associated with a different rate of reward encounter but the second model of action, flying, is more energetically demanding. Bautista *et al.* (2001) have shown that for starlings the choice between actions is based not just on the rate at which rewards are encountered but also on the metabolic costs of making each action. The optimal foraging theories devised by behavioral ecologists to explain animals' choices in naturalistic settings have, for some time, emphasized that the costs of obtaining and handling food are as important a consideration in prey choice as are the benefits to be derived from consuming the food (Stephens and Krebs, 1986).

Action costs can be manipulated in a direct and quantitative manner in the laboratory by increasing the number of times that a response must be repeated before a reward is delivered. Walton *et al.* (2006) taught rats to press one of two levers at different fixed ratios (FR) in order to obtain differing amounts of reward. The rats chose the lever associated with the higher reward (HR) as long as the FR associated with each action was the same. Two results indicated that the rats took the effort associated with the FR schedule into account when making a choice or initiating an action. First, rats chose the HR option significantly less as its associated FR increased and eventually, when the HR was associated with a very high FR, rats choose the lower reward (LR) option (Figure 6.7a). Second, on some trials rats were only able to respond on one option (Figure 6.7b). On such 'forced' trials the time the rats took to initiate the first response increased as the FR associated with the lever increased. The pattern of results suggested that the animals were disinclined to initiate the more effortful chains of response. Similar effects were seen when the impact of effort on choice and response initiation times was assessed in macaque monkeys (Walton *et al.*, 2006).

The amount of effort a rat is prepared to expend has also been assessed by measuring whether they are prepared to climb over barriers of different heights in order to obtain food rewards (Salamone *et al.*, 1994). The rats are placed in a T-maze and each arm of the maze is consistently associated with an HR or an LR. In order to obtain the HR, however, the rats had to climb over a barrier. In a series of experiments Walton *et al.* (2002, 2003, 2005) showed that the Cg1 and Cg2 fields of the rat ACC were critical for integrating the costs and benefits of each action when choices were made. After several days' experience climbing the 30 cm barrier in the preoperative period, most rats were fairly consistent in choosing the HR option even though it was associated with the expenditure of greater effort (Figure 6.8). After large medial frontal lesions, including Cg1 and Cg2 cortex, as well as prelimbic cortex, rats consistently chose the LR option (Walton *et al.*, 2002). Similar effects were seen after circumscribed lesions of Cg1 and Cg2 but not when the lesions were restricted to the prelimbic cortex (Walton *et al.*, 2003). The impairments could not be attributed to a simple loss of spatial or reward memory or an inability to climb because rats reverted to choosing the HR option when a second barrier was placed in the LR arm of the T-maze. When there is a barrier in each arm of the T-maze there is

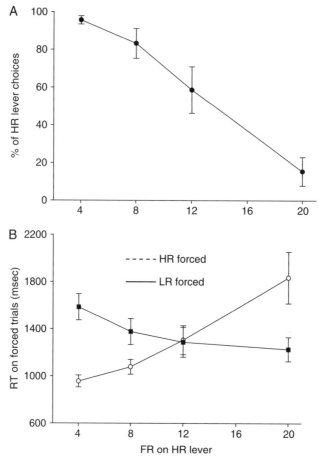

Figure 6.7 (A) Average percentage of high reward (HR) lever choices as a function of the fixed ratio (FR) schedule assigned to the HR (each averaged across three sessions at each FR). The LR was fixed as being FR4 for two rewards. **(B)** Latency to make an initial response on a forced trial, when only one of the two levers was presented, as a function of the LR schedule on the HR lever.

no need to integrate both the costs and the benefits associated with each option before coming to a decision because the costs of each option are equal and the choice is simply determined by reward size. Similar effects have been reported by Schweimer and Hauber (2005). In the case of large lesions that included the prelimbic cortex as well as the ACC the rats returned to choosing the LR option when the barrier was removed from that arm of the T-maze.

Because some of the experiments have been carried out in the macaque while others have been conducted with rats it is not clear if both aspects of action value estimation, both the integration of an action's reward history and the integration of its costs and benefits, are happening in the same or homologous parts of the ACC or if they are occurring in separate and specialized areas within the ACC. Similarities in cytoarchitecture and connexions mean that the Cg1 and Cg2 fields of the rodent ACC are thought to

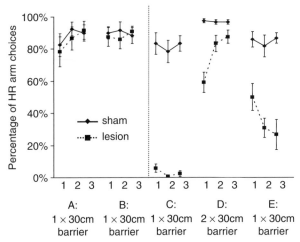

Figure 6.8 Performance on a T-maze cost-benefit task by groups of control rats and rats with lesions of medial frontal cortex including the anterior cingulate cortex. Performance is shown both before (sessions A and B) and after the making of the excitotoxic lesion or sham surgery (session C). Animals chose between climbing a 30 cm barrier to achieve a larger reward (HR) or selecting to obtain a smaller quantity of food from the vacant arm. Postoperatively the animals with lesions switched to make LR responses (C). (D) The deficit was no longer apparent when there was no longer a need to integrate both costs and benefits before making a choice; the animals with and without lesions performed similarly when the effort quotients of each goal arm were equated by placing barriers in each arm. (E) The deficit was re-established when both action costs and benefits had to be considered because the effort quotients associated with each action were distinct after the barrier was placed, once again, in just the HR arm.

correspond to relatively ventral tiers of the primate cingulate gyrus, areas 24a and 24b (Vogt and Peters, 1981; Sesack *et al.*, 1989; Conde *et al.*, 1995; Uylings *et al.*, 2003), rather than to the ACCs region investigated by Kennerley *et al.* (2006). The primate ACCs consists of areas 24c, and 24c′ (and in the human 32ac) and it is not clear if there is an obvious homologue of these areas in the rodent (Rushworth *et al.*, 2004). The best candidate in the rodent is probably the rostral ACd region because it has connexions with both sensorimotor cortex, possibly with oculomotor areas, and with other medial frontal areas (Sesack *et al.*, 1989; Conde *et al.*, 1995).

It is possible to describe the matching task as a cost/benefit task in which the cost that the monkey is attempting to reduce is the risk that the expected reward will not be delivered. Future experiments are needed to ascertain whether the ACCs and ACC gyrus are concerned with risk and effort costs respectively or whether the integration of all information pertaining to an action's value is handled by a single ACC region.

Perhaps the most difficult question to answer currently is whether the ACC's role in cost-benefit decision making is an evaluative one or an executive one. In other words, is its contribution related to the calculation of the cost-benefit ratio or is it more closely related to exerting control over behavior to ensure that the cost is paid? The fact that the ACC lesion only impairs performance when the costs associated with each option are unequal, and there is only one barrier, but not in the control condition, when there are two barriers, suggests that it has a role in evaluating and integrating the costs and benefits associated with the available options rather than in simply ensuring that there is sufficient motivation to overcome an option's cost. On the other hand, if the ACC had a straightforward evaluative role then it might be expected that the lesion would produce random responding rather than always a bias for the low cost option. At present it is difficult to distinguish clearly between these different interpretations. What is already clear, however, is that the ACC is only concerned with the representation and processing of certain types of decision costs, those that are closely related to the action, and this specialization sets it apart from other frontal areas such as the OFC.

The ACC and OFC have complementary specializations when choices are made about effort and delay costs

Although some researchers have considered the neural processing of effort costs (Salamone et al., 1994, 2003; Mingote et al., 2005) there has been far more interest in the neural mechanisms that underlie the ability to make decisions about the costs that are incurred when an animal must wait through a delay until a reward is received. Typically researchers have examined animals' choices when an LR and an HR are available immediately and after a delay respectively (Cardinal et al., 2001, 2004; Kheramin et al., 2002; Mobini et al., 2002; Winstanley et al., 2004; Cheung and Cardinal, 2005). In some cases animals refrain from the temptation of choosing an option that leads immediately to reward, albeit a small reward, and choose to wait for a longer delay until the HR is available. Choosing to wait through the delay is promoted by the presence of a conditioned stimulus that evokes the expectation of the large reward at the end of the delay period (Cardinal et al., 2002; Cardinal, 2006; Schoenbaum and Roesch, 2005).

There is evidence that decisions about effort and delay costs are quite different processes. Two species of monkey, cotton-top tamarins (*Saguinus oedipus*) and common marmosets (*Callithrix jacchus*) are, respectively, more inclined to tolerate high effort costs, incurred in travelling further to a larger food amount, or high delay costs in order to obtain larger food amounts (Stevens et al., 2005a, b; Long and Platt, 2005). The different predispositions of the two species may be due to their natural feeding ecology; while tamarins range over larger distances in pursuit of insects, marmosets wait patiently for tree exudates within a limited area.

If delay and effort-based decision making are subject to distinct evolutionary pressures then it is possible that they depend on separate brain mechanisms. In the case of delay-based decision making, interest has, within the frontal lobe, focused on the OFC but the evidence has been contradictory (Mobini et al., 2002; Kheramin et al., 2002, 2003; Winstanley et al., 2004).

Rudebeck et al. (2006b) directly contrasted effort- and delay-based decision making using similar procedures. They trained two sets of rats on two versions of the cost/benefit T-maze task. In one version of the task the cost was the effort entailed in climbing over the barrier to get to the HR. In the other version of the task the cost comprised waiting for 15 s in the HR arm before the HR was delivered. Either OFC or ACC lesions were made in separate groups of animals trained with each experiment and, in each case, performance was compared with a sham-operated control group trained on the task. After OFC lesions rats continued to choose the high effort/HR option but they became significantly more likely to choose the short delay/LR option in the delay-cost paradigm. Rats with ACC lesions still chose the delayed HR option but, as in previous experiments when response effort was a factor, they chose the low effort/LR option. While OFC lesions significantly affected performance on the delay task but not the effort task, ACC lesions caused the opposite pattern of disruption.

The results suggested that the ACC and OFC are involved in the integration of the costs and benefits associated with possible options when choices are made. Equation of the costs in either paradigm, by imposing a delay in both LR and HR arms of the T-maze in the delay-cost task or requiring barrier climbing in both HR and LR arms in the effort-cost task, meant that the better option in each task was simply determined by the greater size of its associated reward and there was no need to integrate both benefit and costs before making a decision. Such manipulations led to amelioration of both the ACC and OFC deficits.

Despite the superficial similarity of decisions about delay and effort, it is clear that overcoming the temptation to be impulsive or the temptation to be apathetic when choosing involves quite distinct processes. Contradictory tendencies towards impulsivity and apathy have been reported in patients with frontal lobe lesions (van Reekum et al., 2005; Levy and Dubois, 2006) and it is possible that the two types of decision bias are associated with dysfunction in two different circuits centered on the OFC and the ACC (Cummings, 1993). Beyond the frontal lobe other brain regions such as the nucleus accumbens (Salamone et al., 1994, 2003; Cardinal et al., 2001) and the basolateral amygdala (Winstanley et al., 2004; Floresco and Ghods-Sharifi, 2006) contribute to both effort- and delay-based decision making.

The OFC may be pre-eminent in delay-based decision making because of its importance in representing reward expectancies (Schoenbaum and Roesch, 2005). The rat will only choose the delayed HR option if it is able to maintain a representation of the expected reward at the end of the delay period, but such representations may be degraded after OFC lesions. Neurons encoding reward expectation are found not just in the OFC but also in the basolateral amygdala. The degree of activity in the basolateral amygdala related to reward expectation is, however, reduced after an OFC lesion (Schoenbaum et al., 2003b; Saddoris et al., 2005). The HR option may no longer seem the most valuable when the rat is weighing up the costs and benefits associated with each option after an OFC lesion.

The particular involvement of the ACC in effort-based decision making may be linked to its importance in representing arousal states which could provide a proximate indicator of energy expenditure and therefore be critical for making a decision about whether or not it is worth working hard for a given reward. ACC pyramidal neurons send projections to the hypothalamus and periaqueductal grey, both of which are associated with autonomic control (Floyd et al., 2000; Gabbott et al., 2005). A combined human imaging and lesion study has identified ACC activations related to changes in autonomic arousal during both effortful cognitive and motor behavior (Critchley *et al.*, 2003). Recording studies conducted in the macaque ACC have identified neurons that encode the number of actions still to be made, in other words the amount of remaining work, before a reward is expected (Shidara and Richmond, 2002). Although representations of work to be performed before reward are distributed across several brain areas, including the ventral striatum and the amygdala (Shidara *et al.*, 1998; Sugase-Miyamoto and Richmond, 2005), the special importance of the ACC is suggested by the fact that individual neurons encode a monkey's progression through the series of work steps towards reward. Lesions of the ACC may, therefore, have a particularly disruptive effect on the normal pattern of effort-based decision making.

Action value within a social context

Outside of the laboratory the value of choosing a particular action is also influenced by the choices made by other individuals. To return to the example of the monkey deciding in which tree to forage, the tree that is most likely to bear fruit might not be the best option to explore if there are several other individuals in the vicinity who are also likely to forage in that tree. A better option might be to forage in a less favoured tree if it is of less interest to competitors. Behavioral ecologists have shown that an animal's choices are influenced by its competitors' choices, and game theory approaches can be used to model these situations (Nash, 1950; Glimcher, 2002,). If the ACC is to represent the value of decisions then it must have access to information not just about the animal's own decisions but also about the decisions that are being made by competitors.

Several neuroimaging studies have reported signal changes in the ACC when human subjects perform tasks that involve consideration of other individuals or the playing of an interactive game where the possible decisions of an opponent influence one's own decisions (Frith and Frith, 1999; Rilling *et al.*, 2002, 2004; Singer *et al.*, 2004). Rudebeck *et al.* (2006a) examined the effect of ACCs lesions on the degree to which macaques valued the information that could be acquired from other individuals. Normally male macaques will sacrifice food to observe other macaques, particularly females and high status males (Deaner *et al.*, 2005). Rudebeck *et al.* (2006a) showed that if control macaques are shown an image of another macaque at the same time as they are given the opportunity to retrieve a small food item, then they will delay retrieving the food item if the image depicts a female or a dominant male. Neither ACCs lesions nor lesions incorporating the OFC altered the relative valuation of obtaining information about another individual as opposed to obtaining a small food item. However, lesions of an adjacent region in the ACC, the ACC gyrus, led to the relative devaluation of the social stimuli and a significant tendency to retrieve the food more quickly.

Conclusions

A number of lines of evidence suggest that the ACC is the cortical component of a distributed neural system that represents the values of actions. There is evidence that the ACC is active when errors are made but we have argued that this does not mean that its function is simply to detect errors. In other words, even though the ACC may register when actions lead to errors its function is not error detection *per se*. The ACC may be active when errors are made because the estimate of the value of the action that led to the error must be updated. The ACC, however, is critical for a representation of the average value of the reward that is based not just on the last trial but on the recent history of reinforcement associated with the action. In addition to being critical for integrating the recent reward history the ACC is also critical for integrating the benefits and effort costs associated with an action. Adjacent ACC regions are essential for the normal interest an individual takes in conspecifics. Such an interest in other individuals, and the choices they make, is a prerequisite for making the best choices oneself.

References

Akkal, D., Bioulac, B., Audin, J. and Burbaud, P. (2002) *European Journal of Neuroscience*, **15**, 887–904.

Amiez, C., Joseph, J. P. and Procyk, E. (2005) *European Journal of Neuroscience*, **21**, 3447–3452.

Amiez, C., Joseph, J. P. and Procyk, E. (2006) *Cerebral Cortex*, **16**, 1040–1055.

Balleine, B. W. (2005) *Physiology and Behavior*, **86**, 717–730.

Barraclough, D. J., Conroy, M. L. and Lee, D. (2004) *Nature Neuroscience*, **7**, 404–410.

Bautista, L. M. P., Tinbergen, J. and Kacelnik, A. (2001) *Proceedings of the National Academy of Sciences of the USA*, **98**, 1089–1094.

Bechara, A., Damasio, H. and Damasio, A. R. (2000) *Cerebral Cortex*, **10**, 295–307.

Berger, B., Trottier, S., Verney, C., Gaspar, P. and Alvarez, C. (1988) *Journal of Comparative Neurology*, **273**, 99–119.

Berns, G. S., McClure, S. M., Pagnoni, G. and Montague, P. R. (2001) *Journal of Neuroscience*, **21**, 2793–2798.

Botvinick, M. M., Braver, T. S., Barch, D. M., Carter, C. S. and Cohen, J. D. (2001) *Psychological Review*, **108**, 624–652.

Burgess, P. W., Veitch, E., de Lacy Costello, A. and Shallice, T. (2000) *Neuropsychologia*, **38**, 848–863.

Cardinal, R. N. (2006) *Neural Networks*, **19**, 1277–1301.

Cardinal, R. N., Pennicott, D. R., Sugathapala, C. L., Robbins, T. W. and Everitt, B. J. (2001) *Science*, **292**, 2499–2501.

Cardinal, R. N., Parkinson, J. A., Hall, J. and Everitt, B. J. (2002) *Neuroscience and Biobehavioral Reviews*, **26**, 321–352.

Cardinal, R. N., Winstanley, C. A., Robbins, T. W. and Everitt, B. J. (2004) *Annals of the New York Academy of Sciences*, **1021**, 33–50.

Carmichael, S. T. and Price, J. L. (1994) *Journal of Comparative Neurology*, **346**, 366–402.

Charnov, E. (1976) *Theoretical and Population Biology*, **9**, 129–136.

Cheung, T. H. and Cardinal, R. N. (2005) *BMC Neuroscience*, **6**, 36.

Cohen, M. X., Heller, A. S. and Ranganath, C. (2005) *Brain Research, Cognitive Brain Research*, **23**, 61–70.

Conde, F., Maire-Lepoivre, E., Audinat, E. and Crepel, F. (1995) *Journal of Comparative Neurology*, **352**, 567–593.

Coricelli, G., Critchley, H. D., Joffily, M., O'Doherty, J. P., Sirigu, A. and Dolan, R. J. (2005) *Nature Neuroscience*, **8**, 1255–1262.

Critchley, H. D., Mathias, C. J., Josephs, O., O'Doherty, J., Zanini, S., Dewar, B. K., Cipolotti, L., Shallice, T. and Dolan, R. J. (2003) *Brain*, **126**, 2139–2152.

Cummings, J. L. (1993) *Archives of Neurology*, **50**, 873–880.

Dayan, P. and Balleine, B. W. (2002) *Neuron*, **36**, 285–298.

Deaner, R. O., Khera, A. V. and Platt, M. L. (2005) *Current Biology*, **15**, 543–548.

Dosenbach, N. U., Visscher, K. M., Palmer, E. D., Miezin, F. M., Wenger, K. K., Kang, H. C., Burgund, E. D., Grimes, A. L., Schlaggar, B. L. and Petersen, S. E. (2006) *Neuron*, **50**, 799–812.

Elliott, R., Friston, K. J. and Dolan, R. J. (2000) *Journal of Neuroscience*, **20**, 6159–6165.

Fellows, L. K. and Farah, M. J. (2005) *Cerebral Cortex*, **15**, 58–63.

Floresco, S. B. and Ghods-Sharifi, S. (2007) *Cerebral Cortex*, **17**, 251–60

Floyd, N. S., Price, J. L., Ferry, A. T., Keay, K. A. and Bandler, R. (2000) *Journal of Comparative Neurology*, **422**, 556–578.

Frith, C. D., Friston, K., Liddle, P. F. and Frackowiak, R. S. (1991) *Proceedings of the Royal Society of London B*, **244**, 241–246.

Frith, C. D. and Frith, U. (1999) *Science*, **286**, 1692–1695.

Gabbott, P. L., Warner, T. A., Jays, P. R., Salway, P. and Busby, S. J. (2005) *Journal of Comparative Neurology*, **492**, 145–177.

Genovesio, A., Brasted, P. J., Mitz, A. R. and Wise, S. P. (2005) *Neuron*, **47**, 307–320.

Glimcher, P. (2002) *Neuron*, **36**, 323–332.

Hadland, K. A., Rushworth, M. F., Gaffan, D. and Passingham, R. E. (2003) *Journal of Neurophysiology*, **89**, 1161–1164.

He, S. Q., Dum, R. P. and Strick, P. L. (1995) *Journal of Neuroscience*, **15**, 3284–3306.

Herrnstein, R., Rachlin, H. and Laibson, D. (1997) *The Matchng Law: Papers in Psychology and Economics*. Harvard University Press, Cambridge, MA and London, UK.

Hikosaka, K. and Watanabe, M. (2000) *Cerebral Cortex*, **10**, 263–271.

Holroyd, C. B. and Coles, M. G. (2002) *Psychological Review*, **109**, 679–709.

Ito, S., Stuphorn, V., Brown, J. W. and Schall, J. D. (2003) *Science*, **302**, 120–122.

Iversen, S. D. and Mishkin, M. (1970) *Experimental Brain Research*, **11**, 376–386.

Jahanshahi, M., Jenkins, I. H., Brown, R. G., Marsden, C. D., Passingham, R. E. and Brooks, D. J. (1995) *Brain*, **118** (Pt 4), 913–933.

Jones, B. and Mishkin, M. (1972) *Experimental Neurology*, **36**, 362–377.

Kacelnik, A. (1997) *Ciba Foundation Symposium*, **208**, 51–67; discussion 67–70.

Kennerley, S. W., Walton, M. E., Behrens, T. E., Buckley, M. J. and Rushworth, M. F. (2006) *Nature Neuroscience*, **9**, 940–947.

Kheramin, S., Body, S., Mobini, S., Ho, M. Y., Velazquez-Martinez, D. N., Bradshaw, C. M., Szabadi, E., Deakin, J. F. and Anderson, I. M. (2002) *Psychopharmacology (Berlin)*, **165**, 9–17.

Kheramin, S., Body, S., Ho, M., Velazquez-Martinez, D. N., Bradshaw, C. M., Szabadi, E., Deakin, J. F. and Anderson, I. M. (2003) *Behavioral Processes*, **64**, 239–250.

Kremer, S., Chassagnon, S., Hoffmann, D., Benabid, A. L. and Kahane, P. (2001) *Journal of Neurology, Neurosurgery and Psychiatry*, **70**, 264–265.

Lau, H. C., Rogers, R. D., Ramnani, N. and Passingham, R. E. (2004) *Neuroimage*, **21**, 1407–1415.

Levy, R. and Dubois, B. (2006) *Cerebral Cortex*, **16**, 916–928.

Long, A. and Platt, M. (2005) *Current Biology*, **15**, R874–876.

Luppino, G., Matelli, M., Camarda, R. M., Gallese, V. and Rizzolatti, G. (1991) *Journal of Comparative Neurology*, **311**, 463–482.

Manes, F., Sahakian, B., Clark, L., Rogers, R., Antoun, N., Aitken, M. and Robbins, T. (2002) *Brain*, **125**, 624–639.

Mattelli, M., Luppino, G. and Rizzollatti, G. (1991) *Journal of Comparative Neurology*, **311**, 445–462.

McCoy, A. N. and Platt, M. L. (2005) *Nature Neuroscience*, **8**, 1220–1227.

Mingote, S., Weber, S. M., Ishiwari, K., Correa, M. and Salamone, J. D. (2005) *European Journal of Neuroscience*, **21**, 1749–1757.

Mobini, S., Body, S., Ho, M. Y., Bradshaw, C. M., Szabadi, E., Deakin, J. F. and Anderson, I. M. (2002) *Psychopharmacology (Berlin)*, **160**, 290–298.

Montague, P. R., Dayan, P. and Sejnowski, T. J. (1996) *Journal of Neuroscience*, **16**, 1936–1947.

Montague, P. R., King-Casas, B. and Cohen, J. D. (2006) *Annual Review of Neuroscience*, **29**, 417–48.

Nakamura, K., Roesch, M. R. and Olson, C. R. (2005) *Journal of Neurophysiology*, **93**, 884–908.

Nash, J. F. (1950) *Proceedings of the National Academy of Sciences of the USA*, **36**, 48–49.

O'Doherty, J., Critchley, H., Deichmann, R. and Dolan, R. J. (2003) *Journal of Neuroscience*, **23**, 7931–7939.

Ongur, D., Ferry, A. T. and Price, J. L. (2003) *Journal of Comparative Neurology*, **460**, 425–449.

Padoa-Schioppa, C. and Assad, J. A. (2006) *Nature*, **441**, 223–226.

Procyk, E., Tanaka, Y. L. and Joseph, J. P. (2000) *Nature Neuroscience*, **3**, 502–508.

Rilling, J., Gutman, D., Zeh, T., Pagnoni, G., Berns, G. and Kilts, C. (2002) *Neuron*, **35**, 395–405.

Rilling, J. K., Sanfey, A. G., Aronson, J. A., Nystrom, L. E. and Cohen, J. D. (2004) *Neuroimage*, **22**, 1694–703.

Rogers, R. D., Everitt, B. J., Baldacchino, A., Blackshaw, A. J., Swainson, R., Wynne, K. *et al.* (1999) *Neuropsychopharmacology*, **20**, 322–339.

Rudebeck, P. H., Buckley, M. J., Walton, M. E. and Rushworth, M. F. (2006a) *Science*, **313**, 1310–1312.

Rudebeck, P. H., Walton, M. E., Smyth, A. N., Bannerman, D. M. and Rushworth, M. F. (2006b) *Nature Neuroscience*, **9**, 1161–1168.

Rushworth, M. F. S., Walton, M. E., Kennerley, S. W. and Bannerman, D. M. (2004) *Trends in Cognitive Sciences*, **8**, 410–417.

Saddoris, M. P., Gallagher, M. and Schoenbaum, G. (2005) *Neuron*, **46**, 321–331.

Salamone, J. D., Cousins, M. S. and Bucher, S. (1994) *Behavioural Brain Research*, **65**, 221–229.

Salamone, J. D., Correa, M., Mingote, S. and Weber, S. M. (2003) *Journal of Pharmacology and Experimental Therapeutics*, **305**, 1–8.

Schoenbaum, G. and Roesch, M. (2005) *Neuron*, **47**, 633–636.

Schoenbaum, G., Setlow, B., Nugent, S. L., Saddoris, M. P. and Gallagher, M. (2003a) *Learning and Memory*, **10**, 129–140.

Schoenbaum, G., Setlow, B., Saddoris, M. P. and Gallagher, M. (2003b) *Neuron*, **39**, 855–867.

Schultz, W. (2006) *Annual Review of Psychology*, **57**, 87–115.

Schweimer, J. and Hauber, W. (2005) *Learning and Memory*, **12**, 334–342.

Seo, H., Barraclough, D. J. and Lee, D. (2005) Abstract Viewer/Itinerary planner, 891.11. Society for Neuroscience, Washington, DC.

Sesack, S. R., Deutch, A. Y., Roth, R. H. and Bunney, B. S. (1989) *Journal of Comparative Neurology*, **290**, 213–242.

Shidara, M. and Richmond, B. J. (2002) *Science*, **296**, 1709–1711.

Shidara, M., Aigner, T. G. and Richmond, B. J. (1998) *Journal of Neuroscience*, **18**, 2613–2625.

Singer, T., Seymour, B., O'Doherty, J., Kaube, H., Dolan, R. J. and Frith, C. D. (2004) *Science*, **303**, 1157–1162.

Stephens, D. W. and Krebs, J. R. (1986) *Foraging Theory*. Princeton University Press, Princeton, NJ.

Stevens, J. R., Hallinan, E. V. and Hauser, M. D. (2005a) *Biology Letters*, **1**, 223–226.

Stevens, J. R., Rosati, A. G., Ross, K. R. and Hauser, M. D. (2005b) *Current Biology*, **15**, 1855–1860.

Stuphorn, V. and Schall, J. D. (2006) *Nature Neuroscience*, **9**, 925–931.

Stuphorn, V., Taylor, T. L. and Schall, J. D. (2000) *Nature*, **408**, 857–860.

Sugase-Miyamoto, Y. and Richmond, B. J. (2005) *Journal of Neuroscience*, **25**, 11071–11083.

Sugrue, L. P., Corrado, G. S. and Newsome, W. T. (2004) *Science*, **304**, 1782–1787.

Sutton, R. and Barto, A. G. (1998) *Reinforcement Learning*. MIT Press, Cambridge, Massachusetts.

Thaler, D., Chen, Y. C., Nixon, P. D., Stern, C. E. and Passingham, R. E. (1995) *Experimental Brain Research*, **102**, 445–460.

Tremblay, L. and Schultz, W. (1999) *Nature*, **398**, 704–708.

Uylings, H. B., Groenewegen, H. J. and Kolb, B. (2003) *Behavioural Brain Research*, **146**, 3–17.

van Reekum, R., Stuss, D. T. and Ostrander, L. (2005) *Journal of Neuropsychiatry and Clinical Neuroscience*, **17**, 7–19.

Vogt, B. A. and Peters, A. (1981) *Journal of Comparative Neurology*, **195**, 603–625.

Vogt, B. A., Nimchinsky, E. A., Vogt, L. J. and Hof, P. R. (1995) *Journal of Comparative Neurology*, **359**, 490–506.

Wallis, J. D. and Miller, E. K. (2003) *European Journal of Neuroscience*, **18**, 2069–2081.

Walton, M. E., Bannerman, D. M. and Rushworth, M. F. S. (2002) *Journal of Neuroscience*, **22**, 10996–1003.

Walton, M. E., Bannerman, D. M., Alterescu, K. and Rushworth, M. F. S. (2003) *Journal of Neuroscience*, **23**, 6475–6479.

Walton, M. E., Devlin, J. T. and Rushworth, M. F. S. (2004) *Nat Neuroscience*, **7**, 1259–1265.

Walton, M. E., Croxson, P. L., Rushworth, M. F. S. and Bannerman, D. M. (2005) *Behavioral Neuroscience*, **119**, 323–328.

Walton, M. E., Kennerley, S. W., Bannerman, D. M., Phillips, P. E. and Rushworth, M. F. (2006) *Neural Networks*, **19**, 1302–1314.

Wang, Y., Shima, K., Sawamura, H. and Tanji, J. (2001) *Neuroscience Research*, **39**, 39–49.

Williams, S. M. and Goldman-Rakic, P. S. (1998) *Cerebral Cortex*, **8**, 321–345.

Winstanley, C. A., Theobald, D. E., Cardinal, R. N. and Robbins, T. W. (2004) *Journal of Neuroscience*, **24**, 4718–4722.

7

How anticipation recruits our motor system: the habitual pragmatic event map revisited

Ricarda I. Schubotz, Claudia Kalinich
and D. Yves von Cramon

The motor system, particularly the premotor cortex, is engaged not only in motor but also in a variety of purely attentional tasks, including perceptual prediction. The usage of motor strategies or the occurrence of a spontaneous motor resonance in the observing subject can in many cases account for these findings, but it fails for the processing of abstract stimuli which cannot be directly translated into bodily actions. The recently proposed 'habitual pragmatic event map' provides a general account for premotor activation in attentional tasks. It suggests that the prediction of perceptual events, no matter whether caused by our own actions or externally generated, recruits different subregions of the premotor cortex dependent on what stimulus property prediction is based on. In the present functional magnetic resonance imaging study we investigated if such systematic correspondence exists between premotor areas and stimulus *modality* as well. Subjects were asked to predict either rhythm or objects (= stimulus properties) in either visually or acoustically (= stimulus modalities) presented stimulus sequences. Results show that premotor areas which also control grasping are engaged not only in object but also in visual prediction, whereas premotor areas which also control vocalization are engaged in rhythmic and auditory prediction. These findings add strong evidence to the habitual pragmatic event map account and help to further understand how the motor system figures in attention and anticipation.

Introduction

When we are about to cross a road and think about waiting for the next car to pass or not, we have to coordinate two predictions in parallel. We anticipate both how things will change in our environment and how we will change things in our environment, i.e. the effects of our own actions. A large number of imaging studies demonstrate that even if we do not plan to cross the road—or plan any other action—we still activate brain areas for action planning, particularly the premotor cortex, when we try to predict ongoing perceptual events. Why is it that the prediction of perceptual events has to recruit a genuine 'motor' region of the brain?

One possible explanation for this phenomenon builds on the fact that an action is always event-like, i.e. it is extended in time or inherently dynamic. Motor control theories hence suggest that in order to generate and control action, we have to predict the sensory consequences of our actions (Wolpert and Flanagan, 2001). It is therefore principally possible to assume that areas involved in the forward modeling of self-generated actions may also be recruited for prediction of perceptual events that are externally generated. This assumption can be reconciled with recent versions of motor control theories which have suggested that the same computational mechanisms that were developed for sensorimotor prediction may have adapted for other cognitive functions as well (Wolpert and Flanagan, 2001; Grush, 2004).

The present paper addresses one application of forward modeling that has been the focus of a recent series of functional magnetic resonance imaging (fMRI) studies: perceptual prediction. When observing an ongoing action performed by someone else with the hand, for example, it was found that activity in the premotor cortex strongly resembles the activity found during the actual execution or the imagery of that hand action (Schubotz and von Cramon, 2004). There is now abundant literature on 'mirroring' observed action and other so-called 'resonance phenomena' (see e.g. Rizzolatti and Craighero, 2004, for a review). But which parts of the motor system are active when we are required to predict the course of a melody, a ball's trajectory, or a series of numbers presented consecutively on a computer screen? Brain imaging can be used to develop an idea about how different premotor fields figure in perceptual dynamics which are *not* directly or obviously related to our bodies and hence do not appear to be directly translatable into bodily (re)actions—they refuse, one could say, re-enactment. Functional MRI findings suggest that perceptual predictions of this kind are reflected by premotor modulations that follow two different and reciprocally independent anatomical organization principles, one which is related to the stimulus property which is attended to and another which is related to the sensory modality of that stimulus.

On the one hand, the locus of maximal activation in premotor cortex depends on the stimulus *property* that a prediction is based on. These can be spatial properties like rotation angle or location in space, or object properties like color and form, or properties concerning the stimulus duration or, in the case of auditory stimuli, the stimulus pitch. In particular, predictions based on spatial properties draw on the dorsal part of the premotor cortex, which is also involved in reaching movements, whereas predictions based on object properties engage the superior ventral premotor cortex, an area known to be involved in grasping and manipulation. Finally, rhythm- and pitch-related predictions cause enhanced metabolism in the most inferior part of the premotor cortex, the area for vocal and articulatory control (cf. Schubotz and von Cramon, 2003, for a meta-analysis).

These findings suggest some degree of significant isomorphism between the property-based categories of perception and the limb-based categories of action whose integration may be mediated (among other areas) in the lateral premotor cortex. This view was expressed by the *habitual pragmatic event map* account, which proposes that for each stimulus property there is a *default* pragmatic significance that becomes apparent during anticipatory attention to that property. For instance, predicting a stimulus sequence on the basis of object properties such as color or form engages the premotor area for grasping and manipulation because the hand is best adapted for object manipulation. The same default type of correspondence exists between spatial properties and the motor effectors for reaching (arm, eyes, neck) and between rhythmic and pitch properties and articulatory effectors (mouth, larynx) (Schubotz and von Cramon, 2003). Note that somatotopy in lateral premotor cortex is clearly restricted to rough between-limb differences and that multiple overlapping representations of body parts exist in dorsal and ventral premotor regions (for a literature review, see Schubotz, 2004). Hence, rather than containing one or several representations of body parts, it has been suggested that the premotor cortex houses a repertoire of action ideas (Fadiga *et al.*, 2000) or peripersonal-space-defined postures (Graziano *et al.*, 2002).

However, there seems to be a second relevant factor, and that is the sensory stimulus *modality* that prediction is based on (Schubotz, 2004). Such modality-driven modulations of the premotor cortex appear to be independent of those driven by the stimulus property. In particular, the inferior ventral premotor cortex responds both to all auditorily guided predictions and to pitch-or rhythm-based prediction independent of whether stimuli are presented acoustically or visually. Likewise, the superior ventral premotor cortex responds to all visually guided predictions and to all object-based predictions. How can this finding be integrated into the idea of an habitual pragmatic event map ruling the premotor correlates of perceptual prediction? There are two alternatives:

According to the *property-and-modality hypothesis*, the modulation of premotor activation reflects two neuronal populations that are tuned either (1) to certain stimulus properties such as spatial coordinates or object form, or (2) more generally to certain stimulus modalities such as auditory or visual stimuli. According to this view, the neuro-physiological effects of attending to stimulus property and stimulus modality coexist in lateral premotor cortex. In particular, the premotor area for objects is generally dominated by visual input, and the area for rhythm and pitch is generally dominated by auditory input.

According to the alternative view, the *property-only hypothesis*, visually guided predictions recruit the premotor 'object field' because visual dynamic properties typically are owed to (moving) objects. Likewise, auditorily guided predictions draw on the premotor 'rhythm and pitch field' because auditory dynamic properties typically are owed to signals defined by their acoustic spectrum and frequency. Accordingly, there are no areas in the premotor cortex that reflect attention to visual or auditory dynamics in addition to stimulus properties. Instead, they reflect insuppressible processing of object properties when predictions are visually guided, and pitch processing when predictions are acoustically guided. In short, property effects actually account for modality effects. Note that the immanent assumption of a reduction of modality onto property, and not that of property onto modality, is based on the finding that property effects are found throughout the entire lateral premotor cortex, but putative modality effects only within its ventral portion (Schubotz and von Cramon, 2003).

The present fMRI study aimed to test these alternative hypotheses. Subjects were presented with either visual or auditory stimulus sequences upon which predictions were to be made. Prediction in turn was based either on object properties or on rhythmic properties of the stimulus sequences.

If the property-and-modality hypothesis were correct, we should expect the superior ventral premotor cortex to show the strongest responses to visual object sequences, less strong responses for auditory object sequences and visual rhythm sequences, and the weakest effects for auditory rhythm sequences. Likewise, the inferior ventral premotor cortex should show strongest responses to auditory rhythm sequences, less strong responses for auditory object sequences and visual rhythm sequences, and the weakest effects for visual object sequences. If the property-only hypothesis were correct, however, the superior ventral premotor cortex should show comparable responses to visual object sequences, auditory object sequences, and visual rhythm sequences, but significantly weaker effects for auditory rhythm sequences. Likewise we expected the inferior ventral premotor cortex to show comparable responses to auditory rhythm sequences, auditory object sequences, and visual rhythm sequences, but weak responses to visual object sequences.

Methods

Participants

Twenty right-handed healthy volunteers (10 male; age range, 20–30; mean age, 25 years) participated in the study. All of them had normal or corrected-to-normal visual and auditory acuity. No participant was familiar with the semantic meaning of the Asian language symbols used in the present study. Subjects were informed about potential risks of the MRI procedure. After having been screened by a physician of the institution, subjects gave informed consent before participating. The experimental standards were approved by the local ethics committee of the University of Leipzig. Data were handled anonymously.

Stimuli

The stimulus material of the experiment consisted of 12 visual and 12 auditory stimuli. Visual and auditory stimuli were designed to be at a similar level of abstraction. The visual stimuli were composed of a 25 mm black circle (0.14 of visual angle), filled with a circular color transition from turquoise outside to white inside, or vice versa. Within each circle, a slightly smaller black Kanji character was placed. Twelve Kanji characters were selected on the basis of a pre-experimental testing in a different group of participants. This procedure aimed to identify those characters which were both particularly difficult to verbalize and easy to visually distinguish from each other. Visual stimuli were presented in the screen center. The 12 auditory stimuli were selected from a battery of sounds that had been used in a previous fMRI study (Schubotz *et al.*, 2003). These stimuli were generated from natural sounds, e.g. flowing water or opening a bottle, which were distorted artificially such that they could no longer be attributed to natural events. Participants reported that the stimuli sounded like odd machine noises. Sounds had a mean pitch of 8625 Hz (ranging from 6000 to 12 000 Hz), and each sound had a duration of 250 ms. Sounds were presented binaurally.

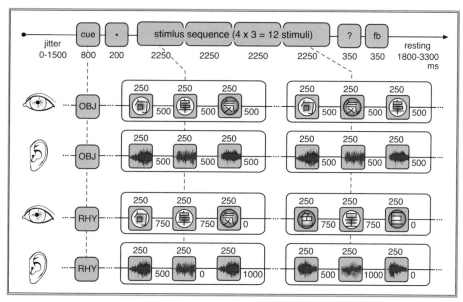

Figure 7.1 Experimental conditions. All trials followed the same temporal schema, shown at the the top of the panel. For each condition (Object Visual OV, Object Auditory OA, Rhythm Visual RV, and Rhythm Auditory RA), examples for the first three and the last three stimuli in a trial are shown. Participants were asked whether sequences followed a regular order or if the order was violated within the last two stimuli of a trial. In the examples given in the figure, conditions OV and RA show sequential violations. In object tasks (OV, OA), order was determined by what the subjects saw or heard, whereas in rhythm tasks (RV, RA), order was determined by how long the subjects saw or heard each stimulus. For further details, see Methods section.

Each visual or auditory stimulus was presented for a constant duration of 250 ms. The length of the inter-stimulus intervals varied from 0 to 1500 ms in equal steps of 250 ms. Thereby, different rhythms of presentation were generated. The presentation of three successive stimuli, including two inter-stimulus intervals and a pause following the third stimulus, always added up to 2250 ms (e.g. 250–500 ms; 250–750 ms; 250–250 ms; see also Figure 7.1). In the auditory conditions, inter-stimulus intervals were silent. In order to facilitate fixation, a fixation sign (black 25 mm square) was presented in the center of the screen whenever no visual stimulus was presented (i.e. during all inter-stimulus intervals of the visual conditions and during the entire stimulus presentation phase of the auditory conditions).

Tasks

Five experimental conditions, comprising four different serial prediction tasks (SPT: Schubotz 1999) (Object Auditory, Object Visual, Rhythm Auditory, Rhythm Visual; hereafter OA, OV, RA, and RV respectively) and one resting condition, were presented in a random trial design (Figure 7.1). Thirty-six trials were presented per condition, with an onset-to-onset trial interval of 14 s. Within each trial of each condition, visual or auditory stimulation lasted 9 s (four times 2250 ms) and was preceded by an 800 ms verbal cue and 200 ms fixation; stimulation was followed by a 350 ms question mark and a 350 ms feedback immediately following the subject's response. The next cue was presented after 3300 ms. To enhance the temporal resolution of the blood oxygenation level-dependent (BOLD) signal, variable jitter times of 0, 500, 1000 or 1500 ms were inserted preceding the first cue.

At the beginning of each experimental trial, a verbal cue instructed participants as to what property of the presented stimuli would be relevant for the upcoming trial (the order of stimulus durations, i.e. rhythm, or the order of objects). The same cue also announced the sensory modality of the upcoming stimuli (visual or auditory). The cue was followed by 12 stimuli presented successively. In the object conditions (OA and OV), the succession of the objects presented within each trial exposed a regular order such that three objects built up a sequence that was repeated four times. The inter-stimulus interval, i.e. the rhythm of presentation which was irrelevant to these conditions, was kept constant (750 ms). In half of all trials, the order of the last two objects was flipped, resulting in a sequential violation of the object order. In the rhythm conditions (RA and RV), 12 different objects were presented in random order, as object information was task-irrelevant in these conditions. In contrast, the succession of the presentation durations exposed a regular order such that three inter-stimulus intervals built up a sequence (e.g. 750–1000–500) that was repeated four times. In half of all trials, the order of the last two intervals was flipped, resulting in a sequential violation of the rhythm of presentation.

In all conditions OA, OV, RA and RV, participants were asked to attend to sequential order of the stimulus property announced by the instruction cue. Performance was tested by a forced-choice response. Participants had to indicate whether the object sequence (OA, OV) or the rhythm (RA, RV) was regular until the end of presentation (button yes, right middle finger) or not (button no, right index finger). The response could be delivered as soon as participants noticed a sequential violation, but at the latest after the end of the stimulus presentation when the question mark came up.

Data acquisition

Participants were instructed before the MRI experiment. In the MRI session, subjects were supine on the scanner bed with their right index and middle finger positioned on the response buttons. To prevent postural adjustments, the subject's arms and hands were carefully stabilized by form-fitting cushions. Participants were provided with earplugs to attenuate scanner noise. Imaging was performed at 3T on a Bruker Medspec 30/100 system equipped with the standard birdcage head coil. Sixteen axial slices (field of view 192 mm; 64 × 64 pixel matrix; thickness 4 mm; spacing 1mm) parallel to bicommissural line (AC-PC) were acquired using a single-shot gradient echo-planar imaging (EPI) sequence (echo time, 30 ms; flip angle, 90°; repetition time, 2000 ms) sensitive to BOLD contrast. A set of two-dimensional (2D) anatomical images was acquired for each subject immediately before the functional experiment, using a modified driven equilibrium Fourier transformation (MDEFT) sequence (256 × 256 pixel matrix). In a separate session, high-resolution whole-brain images were acquired from each subject to improve the localization of activation foci using a T1-weighted three-dimensional (3D) segmented MDEFT sequence.

Data analysis

The MRI data were processed using the software package LIPSIA (Lohmann *et al.*, 2001). Functional data were corrected for motion using a matching metric based on linear correlation. To correct for the temporal offset between the slices acquired in one scan, a sinc-interpolation based on the Nyquist Shannon theorem was applied. A temporal high-pass filter with a cutoff frequency of 1/160 Hz was used for baseline correction of the signal and a spatial Gaussian filter with 4.24 mm FWHM was applied. To align the functional data slices with a three-dimensional stereotactic coordinate reference system, a rigid linear registration with 6 df (3 rotational, 3 translational) was performed. The rotational and translational parameters were acquired on the basis of the MDEFT and EPI-T1 slices to achieve an optimal match between these slices and the individual three-dimensional reference data set. This three-dimensional reference data set was acquired for each subject during a previous scanning session. The MDEFT volume data set with 160 slices and 1 mm slice thickness was standardized to the Talairach stereotactic space (Talairach and Tournoux, 1988). The rotational and translational parameters were subsequently transformed by linear scaling to a standard size. The resulting parameters were then used to transform the functional slices using trilinear interpolation, so that the resulting functional slices were aligned with the stereotactic coordinate system. This linear normalization process was improved by a subsequent processing step that performed an additional nonlinear normalization (Thirion, 1998). Slice gaps were interpolated to generate output data with a spatial resolution of $3 \times 3 \times 3$ mm. The statistical evaluation was based on a least-squares estimation using the general linear model for serially autocorrelated observations (Friston, 1994; Friston *et al.*, 1995a,b; Worsley and Friston, 1995). The design matrix was generated with a box-car function, convolved with the hemodynamic response function. Brain activations were analyzed in an epoch-related design, time-locked to the first stimulus of the trial and comprising the presentation of three full-sequence repetitions (three by three stimuli), excluding the last repetition (three stimuli) which in 50% of the cases contained a sequential violation (see task description). Only correctly answered trials entered the analysis. The model equation, including the observation data, the design matrix, and the error term, was convolved with a Gaussian kernel of dispersion of 4 s full width at half maximum to deal with the temporal autocorrelation (Worsley and Friston, 1995). In the following, contrast images, i.e. estimates of the raw-score differences between specified conditions, were generated for each participant. The single-subject contrast images were entered into a second-level random-effects analysis for each of the contrasts. The group analysis consisted of a one-sample t-test across the contrast images of all subjects that indicated whether observed differences between conditions were significantly distinct from zero (Holmes and Friston, 1998). Subsequently, t-values were transformed into z-scores. To protect against false-positive activations, only regions with $z > 3.09$ ($p < 0.001$; uncorrected) and with a volume >324 mm^3 (12 contiguous voxels) were considered (Forman *et al.*, 1995). All reported activations survived a threshold corresponding to $p < 0.001$ at the cluster level. To validate the chosen thresholds we performed Monte Carlo simulations using AlphaSim. Using 1000 iterations it was confirmed that the true false-positive probability of clusters consisting of at least 12 contiguous voxels (324 mm^3) with an individual voxel threshold of $p = 0.001$ is smaller than $p = 0.001$. Local maxima (l.m.) within the same cluster were separated by at least 10 mm (see also Tables).

In addition, the underlying signal time courses of the brain areas significantly activated in the contrast O > R (and R > O) were analyzed. The percentage signal change was calculated in relation to the mean signal intensity across all time steps. To this end, the percentage signal change was averaged for each trial and condition (OA, OV, RA, RV, and NN) and collapsed over all participants.

Results

Behavioral performance

Performance was assessed by error rates. Mean error rates were 8.9% for OA, 8.1% for RA, 6.2% for OV and 11.4% for RV. A repeated-measures analysis of variance (ANOVA) with the two-level factor PROPERTY (O, R) and the two-level factor MODALITY (A, V) indicated no significant main effects [PROPERTY: $F(1,19) = 1.48$; $p = 0.2394$; MODALITY: $F(1,19) = 0.08$; $p = 0.7817$] but a significant interaction [$F(1,19) = 10.30$; $p = 0.0046$] indicating that rhythm sequences were more demanding than object sequences when presented in the visual modality.

fMRI data

Direct contrasts between R conditions and O conditions (main effect PROPERTY) revealed a direct replication of previous findings regarding property-specific activations of the lateral premotor cortex (overview in Schubotz and von Cramon, 2003) (Table 7.1, Figure 7.2). In contrast to the rhythm tasks, object-based sequence tasks engaged the left superior ventral premotor cortex, the left presupplementary motor area, the bilateral dorsal premotor cortex, left inferior frontal sulcus, right middle frontal gyrus, as well as several postcentral regions including the left fusiform gyrus, and intraparietal sulci within both hemispheres. Conversely, rhythm sequences yielded more significant activations within the bilateral inferior ventral premotor cortex (possibly primary motor regions in the left hemisphere), right inferior frontal gyrus (BA 45/47), right superior temporal gyrus and sulcus, as well as several mesial cortical regions. The direct contrast between visual and auditory conditions (main effect MODALITY) revealed typical activation patterns within primary and secondary sensory cortices (Table 7.2). Interestingly, within both hemispheres superior ventral premotor cortex as well as dorsal premotor cortex were found to be significantly activated for the V > A contrast.

In order to test for our specific hypotheses regarding an interaction between the factors MODALITY and PROPERTY, we analyzed the BOLD signal changes in the main regions of interest (Figure 7.2). Percentage signal changes were calculated within the voxels that

Table 7.1 Main effects of stimulus property: anatomical location, hemisphere (Hemi), Talairach coordinates, maximal z-scores (z_{max}) of activations, and cluster size in mm³ (Cluster)

Anatomy	Hemi	x	y	z	z_{max}	Cluster
Rhythm versus object						
inferior ventral premotor cortex	R	49	3	9	4.62	1323
inferior ventral (pre)motor cortex	L	−53	−6	9	3.79	378
inferior frontal gyrus	R	43	30	0	5.12	1350
superior temporal sulcus/gyrus	R	43	−27	−3	4.80	12 339
supramarginal gyrus	R	46	−60	30	4.21	702
mesial prefrontal cortex	R	16	39	39	4.09	1134
posterior cingulate	R	4	−45	24	4.25	4023
	R	1	−24	48	4.62	l.m.
precuneus	L	−11	−63	33	4.20	1269
Object versus rhythm						
superior ventral premotor cortex	L	−38	4	27	4.59	8127
inferior frontal sulcus	L	−42	27	22	4.40	l.m.
dorsal premotor cortex	L	−26	3	48	5.22	l.m.
	R	25	−6	45	4.10	810
presupplementary motor area	L	−2	18	42	5.29	3537
intraparietal sulcus	R	25	−69	42	4.06	1161
superior parietal lobule	L	−26	−72	39	5.12	16 821
fusiform gyrus	L	−41	−63	0	4.04	837
middle frontal gyrus	R	31	45	18	3.68	324
anterior dorsal insula	R	34	9	0	4.50	351
putamen	L	−32	−12	0	3.49	324

l.m. = local maxima, see Methods.

showed maximal activation in O > R (−38, 4, 27) and in R > O (−53, −6, 9 and 49, 3, 9) in the group average. Since dorsal premotor areas were found to be significantly activated for both V > A and O > R, we also analyzed signal changes within these. Corresponding voxels were selected from the direct contrast O > R (−26, 3, 48 and 25, −6, 45). Finally, presupplementary motor area (of contrast O > R) was included (−1, 18, 42). All BOLD signals in the areas more activated by O than by R (left superior ventrolateral premotor cortex, dorsal premotor cortex bilaterally and left presupplementary motor area) followed the pattern predicted from the property-and-modality hypotheses, with highest amplitude for OV, lower for OA and RV, and lowest for RA. Among the areas activated more by R than by O, signal changes followed the predicted pattern in the right inferior premotor activation (49, 3, 9) with highest amplitude for RA, lower for RV and OA, and lowest for OV. The same was also true for the left inferior ventrolateral premotor or primary motor cortex (−53, −6, 9), but BOLD responses for RV and OA differed considerably in that OA showed a higher amplitude as compared to RV. Thus, this area showed a strong bias towards auditory tasks. Signal changes in all of these areas showed main effects for both PROPERTY (O, R) as well as for MODALITY (A, V) [all $F(1,19) > 4.82$, all $p < 0.05$; calculated for the mean percentage signal change in a time

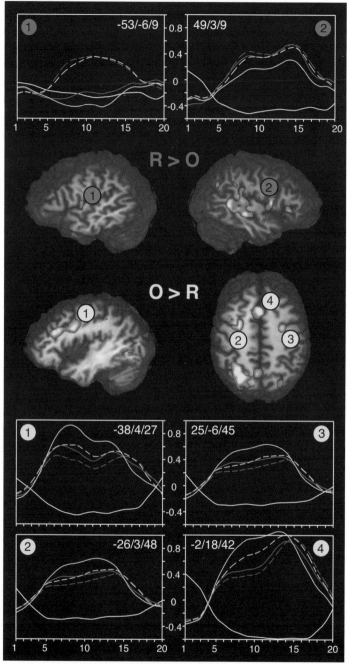

Figure 7.2 Middle panel shows group-averaged (*n* = 20) statistical maps of significantly activated areas for prediction based on objects as compared to rhythm (O > R) and vice versa (R > O), each collapsed across visually and acoustically presented stimulus sequences. *z*-Maps were thresholded at *z* = 3.09. Percentage signal changes are shown for all premotor activations (upper and lower panels) in order to demonstrate significant interactions of stimulus modality (visual = solid lines, auditory = dashed lines) and stimulus property (object = yellow lines, rhythm = red lines).

Table 7.2. Main effects of stimulus modality: anatomical location, hemisphere (Hemi), Talairach coordinates, maximal z-scores (z_{max}) of activations, and cluster size in mm³ (Cluster)

Anatomy	Hemi	x	y	z	z_{max}	Cluster
Auditory versus visual						
superior temporal sulcus/gyrus	L	−41	−21	6	4.13	26 406
	R	43	−12	−3	4.24	28 620
inferior frontal gyrus	R	46	18	3	3.53	1026
	L	−44	18	6	3.41	432
cuneus	R	1	−75	12	4.17	28 998
Visual versus auditory						
superior parietal lobule	L	−29	−93	9	−3.96	31 995
	R	25	−66	42	−3.97	30 591
dorsal premotor cortex	L	−26	−3	42	−3.47	1809
	R	28	−6	45	−3.50	3132
superior ventral premotor cortex	R	46	3	30	−3.40	810
	L	−38	−3	30	−3.39	1026
retrosplenial area	R	1	−27	33	−3.37	945
thalamus, pulvinar nucleus	R	16	−33	3	−3.91	1458
	L	−20	−33	6	−3.93	1998

window from 5 to 13 s after onset of the stimulus sequence]. Except the presupplementary motor area, all areas also showed significant PROPERTY by MODALITY interactions [$F(1,19) = 5.52, p = 0.0297$ (in −53, −6, 9); $F(1,19) = 5.99, p = 0.0243$ (in 49, 3, 9); $F(1,19) = 6.04, p = 0.0237$ (in −38, 4, 27); $F(1,19) = 6.09, p = 0.0233$ (in −26, 3, 48); and $F(1,19) = 4.50, p = 0.0473$ (in 25, −6, 45)]. Hence, overadditive effects were found in the expected (and further) regions, i.e. for vision and objects in left superior ventral premotor cortex and for audition and rhythm in the inferior ventral premotor cortex bilaterally. In none of these regions did signal changes follow the performance scores (error rates) of the corresponding conditions, hence ruling out that effects were due to general attentional load differences.

Discussion

The present study addressed the question of whether stimulus property (here: color–form combinations or stimulus duration) is the only perceptual factor modulating activation in premotor cortex in perceptual prediction. Previous experiments suggested stimulus

---

In particular, left and right inferior ventral premotor cortex (tagged by red numbers 1 and 2, respectively) showed highest signals for RA and lowest for OV, with RV and OA in between. Although it has to be considered that left inferior ventral premotor cortex exposed a considerable preference for auditory as compared to visual stimuli, interaction was significant in both inferior ventral premotor areas. Left superior ventral as well as left and right dorsal premotor cortex and left presupplementary motor area (tagged by yellow numbers 1, 2, 3 and 4, respectively) showed the opposite pattern. See color plate section.

modality (i.e. vision or audition) to be possibly an additional factor and, consequently, two competing hypotheses were tested. According to the property-only hypotheses, visually guided prediction triggers by default attention to objects, and acoustically guided prediction triggers attention to pitch and/or rhythm; i.e. putative modality effects can be actually explained by (and hence reduced to) property effects. According to the property-and-modality hypothesis, in contrast, premotor activation reflects two differently tuned neuronal populations: one which is tuned to stimulus properties and another one which is tuned to input modalities.

Present fMRI findings clearly speak in favor of the property-and-modality hypothesis. In particular, results demonstrate that activity in the superior ventrolateral ('hand') field of the premotor cortex during the prediction of visually presented rhythms is due to the visual modality of the task rather than due to the inability to suppress the processing of (task-irrelevant) object properties in the visual domain. Likewise, activity in the inferior ventrolateral ('vocal') field of the premotor cortex during the prediction of auditorily presented objects is caused by the auditory task modality rather than reflecting the inability to suppress the processing of (task-irrelevant) pitch or rhythm properties in the auditory domain. Thus, in perceptual prediction, BOLD responses in the lateral premotor cortex seem to reflect the summed activity of both property-tuned and modality-tuned neurons.

This interpretation is based on both the z-maps and signal change analyses. First, a main effect for stimulus property was observed, with enhanced activity in superior ventrolateral premotor cortex for object versus rhythm prediction, whereas the converse contrast showed enhanced activity in the inferior ventrolateral premotor cortex. These findings are a direct replication of previous studies and have been interpreted as reflecting an isomorphism between certain categories of stimulus properties and motor effectors (habitual pragmatic event map; Schubotz and von Cramon, 2001; Schubotz et al., 2003; Wolfensteller et al., in press). In order to test for stimulus modality effects over and above stimulus property effects, we analyzed modality-modulated signal changes in those premotor areas which showed a main effect for property. This analysis showed interaction effects in the expected manner: overadditive effects of vision and objects were seen in left superior ventral premotor cortex and overadditive effects of audition and rhythm in the inferior ventral premotor cortex bilaterally. The signal changes in both dorsal premotor areas and the presupplementary motor area which were not originally hypothesized to show an interaction (see Introduction), but which were also found to be more activated for both V-A and O-R, revealed the same pattern as that for the left superior ventral premotor cortex. Thus, the BOLD amplitude of visual object prediction was greatest and that of auditory rhythm prediction smallest in the left superior ventrolateral premotor 'hand' field, with visual rhythm and auditory objects in between, whereas precisely the opposite pattern was found for left and right inferior ventrolateral 'vocal' field. Hence, in predictive tasks, property and modality of the stimulus are reflected in subregions of the premotor stripe, with a coarse spatial overlap (in terms of spatial resolution of fMRI) for object and visual attention on the one hand and an overlap for rhythm and auditory attention on the other.

Premotor engagement in prediction: more than a 'motor strategy'?

What do we learn from these findings? The present and related preceding investigations were motivated by the question as to which parts of the motor system are active, and why they are active, when we are required to predict the course of a melody or a ball's trajectory. Previous fMRI studies suggested that these behaviors are reflected by modulations of our motor system, and that these modulations follow the input property: attention to pitch for the melody and attention to space for the ball's trajectory. However, present findings add further evidence that they at the same time also follow input modality: auditory attention for the melody and visual attention for the ball's trajectory. This point is particularly important for our understanding of how to characterize 'motor' or 'perceptual' premotor responses (cf. Fadiga *et al.*, 2000) and hence may change our current functional conceptions of the human motor system.

Premotor areas are seen to be activated in studies investigating attention. The standard (mostly *post hoc*) explanation that can be found in the literature for premotor engagement in various kinds of attentional tasks is the occurrence of some kind of *motor* or *action preparation*. This means that in these cases, premotor activation reflects a rather task-irrelevant co-activation, because the prepared action is not requested by the instructed task and, if actually existent, has to be suppressed for the real task to be performed. But in fact, patient studies (Schubotz *et al.*, 2004) and studies using transcranial magnetic stimulation (Aziz-Zadeh *et al.*, 2002; Brighina *et al.*, 2002; Tewes *et al.*, 2004) rule out that premotor engagement in attentional tasks is task irrelevant, showing that natural as well as virtual lesions cause severe impairments in different sorts of attentional tasks including serial prediction. These findings are in line with research in the macaque monkey which indicates that the premotor cortex serves as a sensorimotor platform for many types of tasks, of which action preparation is, though highly relevant, just one of many others (Rizzolatti and Luppino, 2001). Modifying the influential definition by Allport (1987), one could consider attention as selection for *potential* action, and the premotor cortex to be a crucial component for attention in this sense (cf. *premotor theory of attention*: Rizzolatti *et al.*, 1987). Attentional impairments which result from lesion studies rather urge an interpretation that leaves a causally (task) relevant subfunction to the premotor cortex.

Nevertheless, when following the traditional functional concept of the motor system further, it often cannot be ruled out that premotor engagement in perception and attention simply reflects the subjects' application of a *motor strategy* (i.e. motor imagery; possibly including even subvocal rehearsal). Explicitly used motor strategies may operate on the basis of precompiled action templates stored in the lateral premotor cortex (cf. Fadiga *et al.*, 2000). But there are also cases for an implicit use of such premotor 'action ideas'. For example, the perception of tools in contrast to the perception of animals for instance, leads to significant premotor activation and is taken to reflect action knowledge triggered by mere sight (Martin *et al.*, 1996; Grafton *et al.*, 1997; Handy *et al.*, 2003). Here, one would possibly like to avoid the term *strategy* but a similar premotor algorithm could underlie motor facilitation triggered by the sight of objects that bear a pragmatic meaning or affordance. Beyond that, even abstract stimuli like circles or triangles can be reminiscent of real objects which in turn are associated with a learned object-related action. The usage of such action ideas may hence also account for premotor engagement during the serial prediction of entirely abstract objects, as required in the present and preceding studies.

However, this explanation is not always convincing. For instance, when subjects are required to process a rapidly presented sequence of color transitions filling the entire presentation screen, it seems impossible to identify some kind of everyday action that those stimuli could be reminiscent of. Explanations along the lines of motor strategies, or, attenuating the assumption of explicit usage along the lines of bottom-up triggered action knowledge, both face the same problem for any 'unproducible' or 'inimitatable' stimulus material. Taking this problem into account, it appears to be more convincing to conceive of premotor algorithms as contributing to many different behaviors, including action preparation, explicit usage of motor strategies, or purely attentional processes which are indirectly referenced to the body as well. While the elaboration of this assumption remains an empirical question that goes beyond the present study, the current data suggest that some portion of premotor is driven merely by visual attention and auditory attention, without calling for action.

The combination of property-specific and modality-specific activations in premotor cortex makes clear predictions about which portions of this brain area should be engaged in certain types of attentional, particularly anticipatory, tasks such as in tracking external motion or other dynamic stimuli. Considering attention to auditory space, we would expect concurrent activation in two subregions of the premotor cortex: the dorsal portion, due to spatial attention, and the inferiormost ventral portion, due to the auditory attention. This view seems to explain reported findings very well (Griffiths and Green, 1999; Griffiths et al., 2000). More specifically, auditory and visual space processing should both engage dorsal premotor areas, but different inferior and superior ventral premotor areas respectively. This pattern of results has been reported in imaging studies (Bushara et al., 1999; Lewis et al., 2000). However, a systematic testing of the supposedly dual modulation of premotor cortex by stimulus property and input modality remains an issue for future studies.

Integrating the findings with monkey data

Imaging data in itself cannot provide any direct evidence about neural tuning. Single-cell recordings and projection (tracer) studies from the macaque monkey can help to gain better insights into the neurophysiological and anatomical characteristics of the considered brain region and hence to see whether the suggested interpretations of BOLD findings are plausible against this neurophysiological background. Considering single-cell recordings on the one hand, we know that macaque premotor neurons respond to tactile, visual, and auditory stimuli even when monkeys are trained not to react to these stimuli (Rizzolatti et al., 1981a,b; Kurata and Tanji, 1986; Gentilucci et al., 1988; Fogassi et al., 1996; Graziano et al., 1997, 1999). Most of these sensorimotor neurons are tactile, visual or visuo-tactile neurons referenced to a certain body part. Overall, tactile responses prevail in premotor cortex, followed by visuo-tactile and visual neurons. In contrast, auditory responses in lateral premotor cortex are relatively rare, or were less frequently investigated and reported. Authors reported auditory responses often in those premotor neurons which responded to visual and/or tactile stimuli as well, i.e. in bi- or trimodal neurons (Kurata and Tanji, 1986; Vaadia *et al.*, 1986; Graziano and Gandhi, 2000). Furthermore, while visual and tactile responses are broadly distributed along the entire lateral premotor cortex, auditory responses were reported to have a rather patchy distribution (Graziano and Gandhi, 2000). Recent findings have demonstrated audiomotor (mirror) neurons in macaque ventral premotor region F5 (Keysers *et al.*, 2003).

On the other hand, cortico-cortical afferents to premotor cortex have been reported from visual, auditory, and somatosensory association cortex. Tracking cortical degenerations after focal cortical lesions, Chavis and Pandya (1976) reported that auditory, visual, and somatosensory cortices project to the periarcuate zone, i.e. the border between lateral premotor and lateral prefrontal cortex in the macaque brain. In line with single-cell findings, authors state that somatosensory projections dominate the premotor cortex. According to their findings, primary and secondary auditory projections go to both pre- and postarcuate portions (prefrontal and premotor sites) in the arcuate concavity (middle portion) and the dorsal area, but remain clearly on the prearcuate (i.e. prefrontal) site for the ventral region. In line with these findings, Deacon (1992) showed in a tracer study that the ventral premotor (i.e. postarcuate) zone of the macaque brain exposed no significant connections with superior temporal gyrus whereas adjacent prearcuate (prefrontal) areas did extensively.

In contrast, Pandya and Kuypers (1969) reported projections from the superior temporal gyrus into both ventral and dorsal premotor areas. These authors state that projections from visual and auditory areas terminate primarily in the rostral part of the frontal motor areas, i.e. the premotor area and the rostral part of the precentral area. They suggest particularly that the premotor area "provides the route whereby at cortical levels visual and auditory information influence the activity of the precentral gyrus" (p. 31). Accordingly an interesting finding is that auditory discrimination is disrupted by lesions of the prefrontal inferior convexity or the ventral arcuate region (Gross and Weiskrantz, 1962; Iversen and Mishkin, 1970). Considering auditory input to the frontal lobes in general, superior temporal sulcus projects extensively to the ventral prefrontal region directly adjacent to the arcuate sulcus, whereas its premotor target region lies more dorsally in the arcuate concavity (Seltzer and Pandya, 1989; Romanski *et al.*, 1999). This is also supported by the finding that auditory responses were restricted to a so-called 'polysensory zone' in arcuate concavity (Graziano and Gandhi, 2000). However, since prearcuate cortex gains access to premotor cortex via projections to the arcuate region (Pandya *et al.*, 1971) auditory information probably reaches premotor cortex at least indirectly via prefrontal mediators.

At first sight, macaque data does not appear to help understand the specific modality-dependent modulations of the premotor cortex which were found in the present fMRI study, with auditory effects dominant in the inferiormost ventral portion and visual effects in the superior ventral and dorsal as well as mesial premotor cortex. Aside from the general visual dominance, which is in line with our findings, macaque findings do not seem to support a particular 'auditory area' in the inferior ventrolateral premotor cortex. However, there are several arguments or hypotheses to deal with this discrepancy.

First of all, it could turn out that the area we found to be activated by rhythm and pitch prediction as well as by auditory prediction in general is more comparable to what has been referred to as area 6bβ (Vogt and Vogt, 1919). Unfortunately, most single-cell studies as well as projection studies on premotor areas do not consider this inferiormost portion of the postarcuate region. Following Roberts and Akert (1963), Preuss and Goldman-Rakic (1989) described this dysgranular region as precentral opercular area (PrCO). The authors state that it is unclear which function this area has but that stimulation studies hint towards a role in laryngeal control (Hast *et al.*, 1974; but compare Sievert *et al.*, 1986). Like adjacent premotor areas for facial and intraoral muscle representation, this area hence appears to be closely connected with the cortical larynx area. This in turn, as a primary motor area, shows a very atypical cortico-cortical projection pattern; actually its projections look more like those of the premotor and peri-Sylvian cortex (Simonyan and Jürgens, 2005). Most interestingly for the present study, the larynx area holds direct and reciprocal connections to the temporal cortex (see Simonyan and Jürgens, 2002, for a discussion). Together, these findings indicate the inferior ventral premotor cortex to be densely connected to areas of auditory perception and acoustic production, but also to respiratory control. Against this background, activation in the inferiormost ventral premotor part during rhythm and pitch prediction and more generally in auditory prediction appears to be fairly plausible. It remains an open question, of course, whether the area we identified in the human motor system is functionally homologous to the monkey area 6V or rather area PrCO. Moreover, since activation was located more posteriorly in the left hemisphere, and this region also showed a slightly different pattern of activation from the right inferior ventral premotor area, we cannot rule out that this left area reflects the (primary motor) larynx area rather than a premotor field.

Secondly, it could be that in humans, the vast evolution in the domain of language and speech called for further development or quantitative increase of audiomotor neurons in the premotor area controlling speech and articulation as well. In this case, the macaque would not be a good functional model for the inferior ventral premotor cortex of the human, just because the macaque has not evolved a language capacity. Actually, activation during rhythm, pitch, or auditory prediction is typically found to lie exactly at/on the ventral end of the inferior precentral sulcus and hence encompasses both inferiormost BA6 and BA44. As mentioned before, Deacon (1992) reports a prefrontal region chiefly devoted to auditory connections within the ventral frontal cortex and discusses this finding in the context of its adjacency to areas associated with vocal muscle movement and its connections to midline cortical areas associated with vocal functions. He hypothesizes that it may provide "important clues to the organization of Broca's language area". Interestingly, Kohler *et al.* (2002) found 13% of investigated neurons in premotor area F5 to be audiovisual-motor (mirror) neurons. As such, they are considered part of the action vocabulary in area F5 which codes both how actions are executed and what goals they are directed at (Rizzolatti *et al.*, 2001).

Finally, attention plays a significant role for premotor engagement in humans—and perhaps also in macaque monkeys. Hence, studies investigating premotor responses to sensory stimulation in anaesthetized monkeys may fail to activate a large portion of sensorimotor, including audiomotor, neurons. Stressing the role of attention when comparing different auditory and visual spatial localization tasks, Vaadia *et al.* (1986) reported dorsal premotor cortex and frontal eye fields to respond predominantly during active localization behavior. The amount of audiomotor neurons may thus be underestimated simply by purely perceptual or even anesthetic experimental approaches. Moreover, previous fMRI investigations have shown that not attention *per se* but only anticipatory attention suffices to engage the premotor cortex when using abstract stimulus material (Schubotz and von Cramon, 2003). Comparable studies or experimental paradigms do not exist in the macaque monkey.

Implications for the habitual pragmatic event map account

The habitual pragmatic event map account (Schubotz and von Cramon, 2003) suggests that premotor activation during perceptual prediction reflects a process or representation which is also active and required in sensorimotor transformation: perception is referenced to the body. This reference is in the first instance an attentional process which precedes and escorts any voluntary action, but which not conversely necessitates a motor preparatory process. Possibly, attention to dynamics – anticipation – can be defined as that kind of attention that requires exactly this premotor-driven sensorimotor reference. Action is dynamic by nature and hence premotor cortex controlling action planning and execution may provide the best cerebral 'platform' we have for tracking of dynamics, no matter whether observed in the environment or produced by ourselves.

The habitual pragmatic event map account suggests that during prediction of a perceived event we activate that premotor area whose corresponding body part is habitually used to produce this very event as an action effect or to be guided by this very event. Present findings now specify this account in two important ways. First, prediction-related activation reflects activity of two different sets of neural populations, each of which codes either for stimulus property or for stimulus modality but not for both. Second, as we have found for different stimulus properties before, different fields of the lateral premotor cortex are also preferably activated by different sensory modalities. Taken together it seems that the premotor reaching area is addressed for space-based and visual tracking, the grasping/manipulation area for object-based and visual tracking, and the vocalization/articulation area for rhythm-based, pitch-based, and auditory tracking. This attribution is intuitively plausible, since everyday action effects of the hands are object-related *as well as* visually guided—I see my hands interacting with objects; of course I can also hear them (folding paper, writing, and other everyday routines make specific noise, cf. Keysers *et al.*, 2003), but this is typically less relevant for guiding my hand actions than vision. Likewise, effects of the vocal system are rhythm- and pitch-related *as well as* auditory-guided – I hear myself producing rhythm and pitch; I cannot see it. However, I see others producing rhythms with their mouth and lips while I hear them producing rhythm and pitch (cf. Keysers *et al.*, 2003), but this is less relevant for my understanding of what the others are saying than audition.

It has to be considered, finally, that of course the premotor cortex is enormously flexible when we observe its ability to support the acquisition of arbitrary sensorimotor mappings

(Wise and Murray, 2000). Thus it is essential that we learn for example to immediately step on the brake (or left) pedal if we become aware of a red traffic light when we are driving a car. What happens to the suggested default mapping of color (i.e. an object property) onto the premotor field for grasping/manipulation in this occasion? We recently showed that the default pragmatic significance of a stimulus property, as proposed by the habitual pragmatic event map, can be easily overridden by learning arbitrary sensorimotor mappings (Wolfensteller *et al.*, 2004). We trained groups of subjects to associate either object or spatial stimulus properties to different locations on a response plate, using either their right or their left hand. We found that after training, differential activation during object-based prediction and space-based prediction collapsed onto the dorsal premotor cortex. Thus, after acquisition of an arbitrary sensorimotor mapping, premotor activation no longer reflected the attended stimulus property, but rather the acquired associated action outcome, i.e. the spatial properties of the response plate that the stimulus now was indicative of. Interestingly, for premotor activation it did not matter whether action was performed with the right hand or the left hand—differential activation for the motor effector showed up only in the primary motor cortex. This clearly demonstrates that this area reflects the pragmatic meaning of perceptions rather than motor effectors.

Conclusion

Research in human and non-human primates has shown that, against classical functional concepts, the cortical motor system is also engaged in attention and perception. The present findings lend further support to this observation and particularly suggest that, even in the absence of action execution or planning, areas controlling reaching and grasping are engaged in object, space, and visual prediction whereas areas controlling vocalization and articulation are rather engaged in rhythm, pitch, and auditory prediction.

Acknowledgements

We would like to thank Shirley-Ann Rueschemeyer, Anna Abraham and Uta Wolfensteller for proof-reading and helpful suggestions about the manuscript.

References

Allport, A. (1987) Selection for action: some behavioral and neurophysiological considerations of attention and action. In Heuer, H. and Sanders, A. F. (eds), *Perspectives on Perception and Action*, pp. 395–419. Lawrence Erlbaum, NJ.

Aziz-Zadeh, L., Maeda, F., Zaidel, E., Mazziotta, J. and Iacoboni, M. (2002) Lateralization in motor facilitation during action observation: a TMS study. *Experimental Brain Research*, **144**, 127–131.

Brighina, F., Bisiach, E., Piazza, A. *et al.* (2002) Perceptual and response bias in visuospatial neglect due to frontal and parietal repetitive transcranial magnetic stimulation in normal subjects. *Neuroreport*, **13**, 2571–2575.

Bushara, K. O., Weeks, R. A., Ishii, K. *et al.* (1999) Modality-specific frontal and parietal areas for auditory and visual spatial localization in humans. *Nature Neuroscience*, **2**, 759–766.

Chavis, D. A. and Pandya, D. N. (1976) Further observations on corticofrontal connections in the rhesus monkey. *Brain Research*, **117**, 369–386.

Deacon, T. W. (1992) Cortical connections of the inferior arcuate sulcus cortex in the macaque brain. *Brain Research*, **573**, 8–26.

Fadiga, L., Fogassi, L., Gallese, V. and Rizzolatti, G. (2000) Visuomotor neurons: ambiguity of the discharge or 'motor' perception? *International Journal of Psychophysiology*, **35**, 165–177.

Fogassi, L., Gallese, V., Fadiga, L., Luppino, G., Matelli, M. and Rizzolatti, G. (1996) Coding of peripersonal space in inferior premotor cortex (area F4) *Journal of Neurophysiology*, **76**, 141–157.

Friston, K. J. (1994) Statistical parametric mapping. In RW Thatcher, M Hallet, T Zeffiro, ER John and Huerta, M. (eds), *Functional Neuroimaging: Technical Foundations*, pp. 79–93. Academic Press, San Diego.

Friston, K. J., Holmes, A. P., Poline, J. B. *et al.* (1995a) Analysis of fMRI time-series revisited. *Neuroimage*, **2**, 45–53.

Friston, K. J., Holmes, A. P., Worsley, K. J., Poline, J. P., Frith, C. D. and Frackowiak, R. S. (1995b) Statistical parametric maps in functional imaging: a general linear approach. *Human Brain Mapping*, **2**, 189–210.

Gentilucci, M., Fogassi, L., Luppino, G., Matelli, M., Camarda, R. and Rizzolatti, G. (1988) Functional organization of inferior area 6 in the macaque monkey. I. Somatotopy and the control of proximal movements. *Experimental Brain Research*, **71**, 475–490.

Grafton, S. T., Fadiga, L., Arbib, M. A. and Rizzolatti, G. (1997) Premotor cortex activation during observation and naming of familiar tools. *Neuroimage*, **6**, 231–236.

Graziano, M. and Gandhi, S. (2000) Location of the polysensory zone in the pre-central gyrus of anesthetized monkeys. *Experimental Brain Research*, **135**, 259–266.

Graziano, M., Hu, X. and Gross, C. (1997) Visuospatial properties of ventral premotor cortex. *Journal of Neurophysiology*, **77**, 2268–2292.

Graziano, M., Reiss, L. and Gross, C. (1999) A neuronal representation of the location of nearby sounds. *Nature*, **397**, 428–430.

Graziano, M., Taylor, C., Moore, T. and Cooke, D. (2002) The cortical control of movement revisited. *Neuron*, **36**, 349–362.

Griffiths, T. D. and Green, G. G. (1999) Cortical activation during perception of a rotating wide-field acoustic stimulus. *Neuroimage*, **10**, 84–90.

Griffiths, T. D., Green, G. G., Rees, A. and Rees, G. (2000) Human brain areas involved in the analysis of auditory movement. *Human Brain Mapping*, **9**, 72–80.

Gross, C. G. and Weiskrantz, L. (1962) Evidence for dissociation of impairment on auditory discrimination and delayed response following lateral frontal lesions in monkeys. *Experimental Neurology*, **5**, 453–476.

Grush, R. (2004) The emulation theory of representation: motor control, imagery, and perception. *Behavioral and Brain Science*, **27**, 377–442.

Handy, T. C., Grafton, S. T., Shroff, N. M., Ketay, S. and Gazzaniga, M. S. (2003) Graspable objects grab attention when the potential for action is recognized. *Nature Neuroscience*, **6**, 421–427.

Hast, M. H., Fischer, J. M., Wetzel, A. B. and Thompson, V. E. (1974) Cortical motor representation of the laryngeal muscles in Macaca mulatta. *Brain Research*, **73**, 229–240.

Iversen, S. D. and Mishkin, M. (1970) Perseverative interference in monkeys following selective lesions of the inferior prefrontal convexity. *Experimental Brain Research*, **11**, 376–386.

Keysers, C., Kohler, E., Umiltà, M. A., Nanetti, L., Fogassi, L. and Gallese, V. (2003) Audiovisual mirror neurons and action recognition. *Experimental Brain Research*, **153**, 628–636.

Kohler, E., Keysers, C., Umiltà, M. A., Fogassi, L., Gallese, V. and Rizzolatti, G. (2002) Hearing sounds, understanding actions: action representation in mirror neurons. *Science*, **297**, 846–848.

Kurata, K. and Tanji, J. (1986) Premotor cortex neurons in macaques: activity before distal and proximal forelimb movements. *Journal of Neuroscience*, **6**, 403–411.

Lewis, J. W., Beauchamp, M. S. and DeYoe, E. A. (2000) A comparison of visual and auditory motion processing in human cerebral cortex. *Cerebral Cortex*, **10**, 873–888.

Martin, A., Wiggs, C. L., Ungerleider, L. G. and Haxby, J. V. (1996) Neural correlates of category-specific knowledge. *Nature*, **379**, 649–652.

Pandya, D. N. and Kuypers, H. G. (1969) Cortico-cortical connections in the rhesus monkey. *Brain Research*, **13**, 13–36.

Pandya, D. N., Dye, P. and Butters, N. (1971) Efferent cortico-cortical projections of the prefrontal cortex in the rhesus monkey. *Brain Research*, **31**, 35–46.

Piazza, M., Mechelli, A., Price, C. J. and Butterworth, B. (2006) Exact and approximate judgements of visual and auditory numerosity: an fMRI study. *Brain Research*, **1106**, 177–188.

Preuss, T. M. and Goldman-Rakic, P. S. (1989) Connections of the ventral granular frontal cortex of macaques with perisylvian premotor and somatosensory areas: anatomical evidence for somatic representation in primate frontal association cortex. *Journal of Comparative Neurology*, **282**, 293–316.

Rizzolatti, G. and Craighero, L. (2004) The mirror-neuron system. *Annual Review of Neuroscience*, **27**, 169–192.

Rizzolatti, G. and Luppino, G. (2001) The cortical motor system. *Neuron*, **31**, 889–901.

Rizzolatti, G., Fogassi, L. and Gallese, V. (2001) Neurophysiological mechanisms underlying the understanding and imitation of action. *Nature Reviews Neuroscience*, **2**, 661–670.

Rizzolatti, G., Scandolara, C., Matelli, M. and Gentilucci, M. (1981a) Afferent properties of periarcuate neurons in macaque monkeys. I. Somatosensory responses. *Behavioural Brain Research*, **2**, 125–146.

Rizzolatti, G., Scandolara, C., Matelli, M. and Gentilucci, M. (1981b) Afferent properties of periarcuate neurons in macaque monkeys. II. Visual responses. *Behavioural Brain Research*, **2**, 147–163.

Rizzolatti, G., Riggio, L., Dascola, I. and Umiltà, C. (1987) Reorienting attention across the horizontal and vertical meridians: evidence in favor of a premotor theory of attention. *Neuropsychologia*, **25**, 31–40.

Roberts, T. S. and Akert, K. (1963) Insular and opercular cortex and its thalamic projection in Macaca mulatta. *Schweizer Archiv für Neurologie, Neurochirurgie und Psychiatrie*, **92**, 1–43.

Romanski, L. M., Tian, B., Fritz, J., Mishkin, M., Goldman-Rakic, P. S. and Rauschecker, J. P. (1999) Dual streams of auditory afferents target multiple domains in the primate prefrontal cortex. *Nature Neuroscience*, **2**, 1131–1136.

Schubotz, R. I. (2004) Human premotor cortex: beyond motor performance. *MPI Series in Human Cognitive and Brain Sciences*, vol. 50, Max Planck Institute of Human Cognitive and Brain Sciences, Leipzig.

Schubotz, R. I. and von Cramon, D. Y. (2001) Functional organization of the lateral premotor cortex: fMRI reveals different regions activated by anticipation of object properties, location and speed. *Cognitive Brain Research*, **11**, 97–112.

Schubotz, R. I. and von Cramon, D. Y. (2002) Predicting perceptual events activates corresponding motor schemes in lateral premotor cortex: an fMRI study. *Neuroimage*, **15**, 787–796.

Schubotz, R. I. and von Cramon, D. Y. (2003) Functional-anatomical concepts of human premotor cortex: evidence from fMRI and PET studies. *Neuroimage*, **20**, 120–131.

Schubotz, R. I. and von Cramon, D. Y. (2004) Sequences of abstract nonbiological stimuli share ventral premotor cortex with action observation and imagery. *Journal of Neuroscience*, **24**, 5467–5474.

Schubotz, R. I., von Cramon, D. Y. and Lohmann, G. (2003) Auditory what, where, and when: a sensory somatotopy in lateral premotor cortex. *Neuroimage*, **20**, 173–185.

Schubotz, R. I., Sakreida, K., Tittgemeyer, M. and von Cramon, D. Y. (2004) Abstract motor areas beyond motor performance: deficits in serial prediction following ventrolateral premotor lesions. *Neuropsychology*, **18**, 638–645.

Seltzer, B. and Pandya, D. N. (1989) Frontal lobe connections of the superior temporal sulcus in the rhesus monkey. *Journal of Comparative Neurology*, **281**, 97–113.

Sievert, C. F., Crammond, D. J., Abbs, J. H., Welt, C. and Gracco, V. L. (1986) Orofacial movements evoked by ICMS in a nonprimary motor area of monkey lateral precentral cortex. *Abstract of the Annual Meeting of the Society for Neuroscience*, **12**, 260.

Simonyan, K. and Jürgens, U. (2002) Cortico-cortical projections of the motorcortical larynx area in the rhesus monkey. *Brain Research*, **949**, 23–31.

Simonyan, K. and Jürgens, U. (2005) Afferent cortical connections of the motor cortical larynx area in the rhesus monkey. *Neuroscience*, **130**, 133–149.

Talairach, J. and Tournoux, P. (1988) *Co-planar Stereotaxic Atlas of the Human Brain*. Thieme, New York.

Tewes, A., Schubotz, R. I., Wolfensteller, U. and von Cramon, D. Y. (2004) Repetitive Transcranial Magnetic Stimulation (rTMS) over dorsal premotor areas interferes with visuospatial attention. In Kerzel, D., Franz V., and Gegenfurtner, K., (eds), *Beiträge zur 46. Tagung experimentell arbeitender Psychologen*, p. 261. Pabst Science Publishers, Lengerich.

Thirion, J. P. (1998) Image matching as a diffusion process: an analogy with Maxwell's demons. *Medical Image Analysis*, **2**, 243–260.

Vaadia, E., Benson, D. A., Hienz, R. D. and Goldstein, M. H. Jr. (1986) Unit study of monkey frontal cortex: active localization of auditory and of visual stimuli. *Journal of Neurophysiology*, **56**, 934–952.

Vogt, C. and Vogt, O. (1919) Allgemeine Ergebnisse unserer Hirnforschung [german; General results of our brain research]. *Journal für Psychologie und Neurologie*, **25**, 279–462.

Wise, S. P. and Murray, E. A. (2000) Arbitrary associations between antecedents and actions. *Trends in Neurosciences*, **23**, 271–276.

Wolfensteller, U., Schubotz, R. I. and von Cramon, D. Y. (2004) "What" becoming "where": functional magnetic resonance imaging evidence for pragmatic relevance driving premotor cortex. *Journal of Neuroscience*, **24**, 10431–10439.

Wolfensteller, U., Schubotz, R. I. and von Cramon, D. Y. (2007) Understanding non-biological dynamics with your own premotor system. *Neuroimage*, **36**(Suppl 2): T33–43.

Wolpert, D. M. and Flanagan, J. R. (2001) Motor prediction. *Current Biology*, **11**, 729–732.

Worsley, K. J. and Friston, K. J. (1995) Analysis of fMRI time-series revisited—again. *Neuroimage*, **2**, 173–181.

8

Motor awareness and motor intention in anosognosia for hemiplegia

Anna Berti, Lucia Spinazzola, Lorenzo Pia
and Marco Rabuffetti

In everyday life, a successful monitoring of behavior requires a continuous updating of the effect of motor acts. It is, therefore, crucial to know whether a programmed action has actually been performed. Some patients who, as consequence of right-brain damage, develop a paresis of the left side of the body, obstinately deny their motor deficit (motor denial or anosognosia), and when asked to move their paralysed limb they pretend having performed the action required by the examiner. Anosognosia has both clinical and theoretical implications. From a clinical point of view, anosognosia for hemiplegia can have a negative impact on motor rehabilitation. From a theoretical point of view, anosognosia can shed light on the neural structures that underlie conscious motor processes. We shall briefly review the clinical characteristics of anosognosia for hemiplegia, the false beliefs reported by the patients, the associations and dissociation with other neuropsychological symptoms and the anatomical correlation of the disorder. On the bases of anatomo-clinical data, it will be argued that anosognosia is due to the failure of a motor monitoring component that does not detect the mismatch between a desired action and the actual status of the sensorimotor system in face of an intact capacity of programming movements and forming sensorimotor predictions. This would imply that the brain activity leading to the construction of a conscious intention of action is normal. We shall present observational and electromyogram data strongly suggesting that motor intentional processes are still available in hemiplegic anosognosic patients.

Introduction

Clinical description

Anosognosia is a term that indicates the denial behavior for one's own disease or deficit. It can be observed in relation to many different kinds of pathological conditions, ranging from denial of mental disease, such as schizophrenia, to unawareness of neurological and cognitive deficits following focal brain damage. In these latter cases, patients may be unaware of their reading or language or memory disorder (Prigatano and Schacter, 1991) or may even resolutely deny the contralesional motor deficits developed after the stroke. The term anosognosia was, in fact, first used by Babinski (1914) to denote the puzzling behavior of right-brain-damaged patients, who, after a having developed contralesional hemiplegia, deny that there is anything wrong with their limbs (anosognosia for hemiplegia, AHP). For instance, if inquired about their potential capability of performing actions either with the right or with the left hand, or even bimanual action, they claim that they can perform any kind of movement equally well. Patients' false belief of being still able to move remains unchanged even when, having been requested to actually perform different kinds of actions, sensory and visual feedbacks from the affected motionless side should suggest that no movement has been performed. For instance, we described an anosognosic patient who, asked to clap the hands, lifted her right hand and put it in the position of clapping, perfectly aligned with the trunk midline, moving it as if it was clapped against the left hand. She appeared perfectly satisfied with her performance, never admitting that the left arm did not participate in the action. This despite the fact that the patient could see that the left hand did not clap against the right hand and that the typical noise of clapping was not heard. When the examiner pointed out that, in clapping hands, she did not make any noise, she claimed that she never made noise (Berti *et al.*, 1998).

Although anosognosia is evident in the hemiplegic patients' everyday behavior (they may for instance, try to get off the bed, because they are convinced of being able to walk), structured interviews are used for a clinical diagnosis of AHP. Usually the patients are first questioned about the reason why they are in the hospital and, if not openly acknowledging the motor deficit, more stringent questions about the affected limbs are asked (Bisiach *et al.*, 1986). Scores range from 0 (the patient readily acknowledges the left-side hemiplegia) to 3 (the patient resolutely denies any motor problem even when after the request of making an explicit motor act, no movement is actually executed). It is worth noting that for an unambiguous diagnosis of AHP the patient must be completely plegic on the affected side. If not, i.e. if the affected limb has some degrees of weakness but can still move, then the patient's claim of still being able to move cannot be considered absolutely wrong and a score of 3 would not, in this case, relate to a condition of real unawareness.

In search of an explanation

Anosognosia for hemiplegia is a specific cognitive disorder

In the last century, AHP was not studied as extensively as other neuropsychological deficits, often associated with it, such as spatial neglect. This disregard may be related to the fact that some authors ascribed AHP to a defensive adaptation against the stress caused by the illness (motivational theories, e.g. Weinstein and Kahn, 1955). Consequently, AHP was not considered a disturbance related to a direct effect of the brain damage, calling for a neuropsychological explanation, but instead a motivational reaction, possibly due to the functioning of mechanisms not directly involved in the brain damage. However, in a seminal paper on the neurological bases of AHP, Bisiach and Geminiani (1991) pointed out that many clinical observations, related to anosognosia, were not expected on the bases of a pure motivational account of AHP. For instance, a defense mechanism would predict the same frequency of anosognosia after right and left hemisphere stroke, and not only when the left part of the body is affected by motor disabilities (indeed, patients are expected to protect themselves against both left and right motor disorders). However,

AHP is far more frequent after right than after left hemisphere damage (e.g. Cutting, 1978; Gilmore *et al.*, 1992; Carpenter *et al.*, 1995; for a review see Pia *et al.*, 2004). Moreover, anosognosia is more frequent in the acute phase of the stroke than in the chronic phase (Berti *et al.*, 1996) and, during the amytal testing, when one hemisphere is functionally excluded, even after a few seconds from the amytal injection. A defense mechanism would also predict the opposite temporal pattern, insofar as time is needed for establishing a psychodynamic reaction. Furthermore, anosognosia can be temporally eliminated by vestibular stimulation. Cappa *et al.* (1987) found that the elicitation of the vestibular reflex by introducing cold water in the patient's left ear (thus provoking left-side nystagmus), can transitorily ameliorate AHP, whereas a psychodynamic reaction should not be influenced by physiological manipulation (for a review of the limits of the motivational theory of AHP see also Bisiach and Berti, 1995).

Once motivational explanations had been rejected, AHP was then considered a disorder directly related to the presence of a focal brain damage. However, most theories explained away anosognosia as due to the presence of other concomitant neurological and/or neuropsychological disorders. These accounts of anosognosia would receive support by findings that the denial behavior always coexists with somatosensory and cognitive problems. On the other hand, the presence of double dissociations between denial and neurological/neuropsychological disorder would falsify these accounts. Bisiach and Berti (1987) conceived anosognosia as part of a complex disorder of space representation (named dyschiria), associated with the manifestation of unilateral spatial neglect. However, AHP has been found to be double-dissociated from neglect phenomena (Bisiach *et al.*, 1986; Berti *et al.*, 1996, 2005; Dauriac-Le Masson *et al.*, 2002). Therefore, although we do not deny that there seem to be spatial constraints on the way in which anosognosia manifests itself, the unawareness of contralesional motor impairment cannot simply depend on patients ignoring the left part of either extrapersonal or personal space. Indeed, in dissociated cases, patients do not acknowledge their motor problems despite the fact that they are still able to direct attention to the left side of the body and that they are fully aware that the left side of the body belongs to them. Other authors pointed to the role of somatosensory disorders associated with intellectual deficits in determining the denial behavior. According to Levine *et al.* (1991), the coexistence of these disorders would preclude patients discovering their impairment. In addition, the possibility of memory problems, which may prevent the acquisition and fixation of new information, including those related to the disease, has been considered a possible cause of AHP (Berti *et al.*, 1996). However, it has been found that although most patients with anosognosia are also affected by left-side anesthesia, it is possible to observe anosognosic patients without sensory (tactile or proprioceptive) disorders, as tested at bedside examination. On the other hand there are patients with severe somatosensory problems without denial of hemiplegia (Bisiach *et al.*, 1986; Berti *et al.*, 1996; Small and Ellis, 1996; Marcel *et al.*, 2004). In addition, the possibility of ascribing anosognosia to a general intellectual impairment or to memory problems has been ruled out by the observation of double dissociations between these disorders (Berti *et al.*, 1996). These findings showed that, although anosognosia is often associated with other neurological/neuropsychological disorders, which may shape or even aggravate the manifestations of the denial behavior, cognitive and sensorimotor impairments seem to be neither necessary nor sufficient to cause AHP. Therefore, denial of hemiplegia in right-brain-damaged patients cannot be explained away by referring to other concomitant symptoms, but rather it has to be considered a specific neuropsychological disorder that calls for a proper explanation (Berti, 2000).

Anosognosia for hemiplegia as a selective disorder of monitoring

The impairment in detecting contralesional hemiplegia may depend on a disorder of self-monitoring. The damage to a general multipurpose control mechanism, responsible for the inspection of subjects' physical and cognitive capabilities, would cause a generalized impairment in detecting all possible concomitant disorders affecting, after the stroke, either personal or extrapersonal aspects of patients' behavior. On the contrary, a disorder of a selective self-monitoring mechanism would predict the possibility that normal awareness for some of the deficits would be observed together with an impaired monitoring capacity for other coexisting deficits. It has been found that patients with motor impairment of the left limbs may be aware of the paralysis of the upper limb but not of the paresis of the lower limb and vice versa (Von Hagen and Ives, 1937; Berti et al., 1996). We studied the presence of cognitive deficits related to hemispatial neglect in a group of left-hemiplegic patients (Berti et al., 1996). Some of these patients were found to have multiple concomitant disorders (i.e. hemiplegia, neglect in drawing and neglect dyslexia). Patients' awareness for all these deficits was investigated. We found that some patients were anosognosic for the motor problems, but admitted their cognitive deficits, whereas other patients did not admit their cognitive deficits but were well aware of their left hemiplegia. Awareness dissociated also within the cognitive deficits so that some patients were aware of the neglect dyslexia, but did not acknowledge neglect in drawing and vice versa. The existence of dissociations between different kinds of unawareness (see also Breier et al., 1995; Jehkonen et al., 2000) in the same patient indicates that denial, in general, can be considered a selective disorder of monitoring and that anosognosia for hemiplegia, in particular, can be conceived as a monitoring disorder that selectively affect motor awareness.

The feed-forward hypothesis of anosognosia for hemiplegia

Gold et al. (1994) explained the denial behavior by referring for the first time to a cognitive model of motor control (feedforward hypothesis of anosognosia). In this model, a comparator system has to match the congruity between the intended movement and the sensory consequences of the actually executed movement (see Figure 8.1). When an intended movement is not performed, the comparator should detect the mismatch between the movement/no-movement conditions.

According to the feed-forward hypothesis, for patients to diagnose themselves as hemiplegic, they should attempt to move, and therefore they should have the intention for action. However, Gold et al. (1994) proposed that hemiplegic patients affected by AHP have lost the intention to move with the plegic side. If they have no intention to move, they do not even attempt to move. The loss of motor intention prevents motor programming and

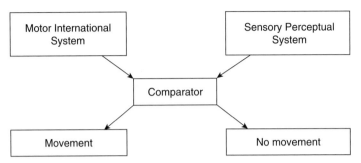

Figure 8.1 The feedforward hypothesis of anosognosia (modified from Gold et al., 1994). According to this hypothesis, anosognosia is due to loss of intention to move (see text).

removes anticipation of action. This loss renders defective the efferent input into the system that monitors movements. Because the comparator does not receive any information about movement planning, it cannot interpret the lack of movements as aberrant. In this view, patients do not discover the hemiplegia because the comparator is ill-fed, or not fed at all, and not because of direct damage to it. Gold et al. (1994) tested the feed-forward hypothesis by evaluating the activity of proximal/axial muscles through surface electromyogram (EMG) in one AHP patient and different control subjects on the following assumptions. Proximal limb and axial muscles receive bilateral corticospinal innervations. Therefore, when normal subjects move either the right or the left limb, the activation, in each case, comes from both contralateral and ipsilateral motor cortex. Moreover, the activation of the muscles of one side is often accompanied by activation of the contralateral agonist muscles. The consequence of this bilateral innervation is that if, after a unilateral stroke, patients are asked to attempt a movement with the paretic side, they should still be able to activate contralesional proximal muscles. However, anosognosic patients who have lost intention should not activate proximal muscles of the affected side, even if these muscles, contrary to the distal ones, are not completely plegic. On the contrary, anosognosic patients, as normal subjects, should show activation of proximal muscles when asked to move their unaffected limb. Gold et al. (1994) registered the activity of the pectoralis majoris muscle bilaterally. The results showed that the patient with AHP did not contract either of his pectoralis muscles when asked to squeeze a dynamometer with his contralesional hand, whereas normal subjects and hemiplegic patients without AHP did. Therefore, their interpretation was that the EMG data demonstrated loss of intention to move in anosognosic patients, and that the loss of intention is the cause of the denial behavior.

This approach to the study and interpretation of AHP was very innovative because, for the first time, anosognosia was not considered as a secondary disorder due to the presence of other neurological/neuropsychological symptoms, but instead as a specific and selective cognitive disturbance related to motor monitoring and motor awareness. However, we would like to indicate some points that need to be taken into account in relation to patients' selection. First, as we have already discussed, an unambiguous diagnosis of AHP can be reached only in patients with complete contralateral hemiplegia.

In the Gold *et al.* (1994) study the AHP patient was able to squeeze a dynamometer with the left contralesional hand and, therefore in this case the diagnosis of anosognosia is misleading. Although the patient might have underestimated the motor disorder, his condition cannot be taken as a definite example of unawareness of disease. The clinical description of the patient suggested, instead, the presence of motor neglect, a disturbance in which patients, who are not hemiplegic, do not spontaneously move the contralesional limb (Laplane and Degos, 1983). Therefore, the hypothesis that the behavior of the patient described by Gold *et al.* (1994) was due to loss of intention is plausible and the idea of ascribing motor neglect to a deficit of intentionality deserves further experimental verification. However, this condition is different from the denial of contralesional complete left hemiplegia.

Anosognosia as a disturbance of the comparator system of the feed-forward model of action generation

Anosognosic patients are not aware of being unable to move and their behavior is abnormally driven by the false belief of being capable to perform coherent actions. We have already mentioned that double dissociation between anosognosia and tactile–proprioceptive disorders suggested that somatosensory information is neither sufficient nor necessary for gaining a coherent view of motor behavior. Even in normal subjects the sensations associated with the actual execution of movements can be unnecessary for the construction of movement awareness (Fourneret and Jeannerod, 1998). In a seminal paper on motor consciousness, Libet *et al.* (1983) demonstrated that when subjects had to estimate the time at which they became aware of a voluntary movement (the so called 'M' judgment) they indicated a moment that precedes the actual initiation of the movement of 50–80 ms. These findings demonstrated that motor awareness is not simply constructed on sensory feedbacks coming from the moving muscles, but instead emerges before the afference of any sensory proprioceptive input. It is worth noting that in anosognosic patients even visual feedbacks are not sufficient for the patients to achieve a veridical motor awareness. Indeed, in many instances, when the patient's attention is drawn on the left plegic side, the direct view of the motionless limb does not change their false belief of being able to move. On the other hand, hemiplegic non-anosognosic patients are fully aware of their motor impairment even when the plegic limb is out of sight. Therefore, although proprioception and vision are fundamental aspects of our capacity of judging the course, and the consequences, of a motor event, its full appreciation is somehow independent from their operations. Based on these observations, it has been suggested (Blakemore and Frith, 2003) that motor awareness is related to some signal that precedes the movement and that is formed prior to the processing of sensory feedbacks. Referring to the forward model of the motor systems (Wolpert *et al.*, 1995; Haggard, 2005), they proposed that, once that the appropriate motor commands are selected and sent to muscles for the execution of the desired movement, a prediction of the sensory consequences of the movement is formed and would be successively compared with the feedback associated with the actual execution of the intended movement. According to

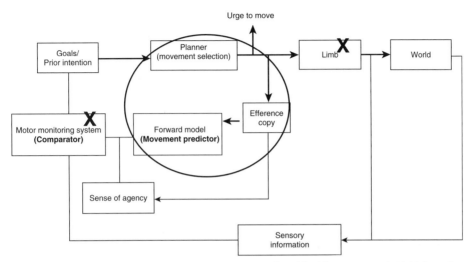

Figure 8.2 The feedforward model of action generation (modified from Haggard, 2005; see also Berti and Pia, 2006). **X**: the parts of the model damaged by the lesion in patient CR. The circle indicates the part of the model that still functions. In the hemiplegic patient SF, who was not affected by anosognosia, the lesion should be localized only in limb.

Blakemore *et al.* (2002), this prediction, based on the efference copy of the programmed motor act, constitutes the signal on which motor awareness is constructed (the one responsible for Libet's 'M' judgment) (see Figure 8.2).

It is worth noting that such a model would imply that whenever the system makes sensory predictions about certain programmed movement we may construct the belief that this movement is actually performed (see Berti and Pia, 2006). The comparator would then match the congruency between the belief of the intended movement and the representation of the actual status of the system. When the motor act corresponds to the representation of the intended movement, motor awareness is veridically constructed. When the peripheral event does not correspond to the prediction, the comparator should detect the discrepancy. On the bases of this model, we proposed that in hemiplegic patients without anosognosia the comparator, still able to detect the mismatch between the prediction and the actual condition, allows the normal construction of veridical motor awareness. Consequently, when hemiplegic patients without anosognosia are asked to move their affected limb, they can acknowledge their motor failure (Berti and Pia, 2006). On the contrary, hemiplegic–anosognosic patients may have damage to the comparator component of the forward model of the motor system. Because of this damage, the comparator cannot detect the mismatch between the predictions and the feedback and the patients are not able to distinguish between a purely intended action and the real movement execution. This leads to the construction of a nonveridical motor awareness and therefore to the false beliefs of being able to move. We found (Berti *et al.*, 2005) that denial is related to lesions mainly involving the frontal premotor cortex, particularly areas 6 and 44, known to be fundamental components of circuits related to motor control (Rizzolatti *et al.*, 1998). Less frequently other regions such as the insula (a brain area involved in sensorimotor control; see also Karnath *et al.*, 2005) can be affected. It is worth noting that Haggard and Magno (1999), with different experimental design and technique, obtained significant evidence that motor awareness arises somewhere between primary motor and premotor cortex. Therefore, we proposed that these areas constitute the neural bases of the comparator operations of the forward model of action generation, which is lesioned in AHP patients (see Figure 8.2). This hypothesis can also account for the transient amelioration of anosognosia that can sometimes be observed during vestibular stimulation (Cappa *et al.*, 1987; Rode *et al.*, 1992) when the injection of cold water into the patient's left ear may cause a short-lasting awareness of contralesional hemiplegia. As shown by Bottini *et al.* (1995), vestibular signals project to the putamen, supramarginal gyrus, somatosensory area II, insula and premotor cortex. Therefore, considering that the insula and the premotor cortex are part of the proposed circuit for motor awareness, it is reasonable to assume that when, in an anosognosic patient, a subset of these areas is not completely destroyed by the lesion, the vestibular stimulation may maximally activate the spared nodes of the comparator network, momentarily restoring the motor monitoring capacity. Rode *et al.* described a patient who, during the effect of vestibular stimulation, was even able to report what happened when he had first had the stroke. The activation of some sort of implicit memory during the effect of caloric stimulation is more puzzling and might be due to spreading of activation outside the areas described by Bottini *et al.* (1995).

Note that, in the view proposed here, anosognosia is considered to be the consequence of direct damage to the comparator component of the model and not, as in Gold *et al.*'s (1994) proposal, of a malfunctioning of the comparator due to the loss of intentionality. Therefore, while Gold *et al.*'s assumption was that anosognosic patients have lost the intention to move, our hypothesis is exactly the opposite. Anosognosic patients, with strong beliefs of movements, should still have intention for voluntary actions and their motor system should still form predictions about the intended movement. The activity of the areas related to the emergence of motor intention can be considered the neural bases of anosognosic patients' false belief of moving and should be preserved in anosognosic patients.

Anosognosia for hemiplegia and conscious intention

In the seminal paper quoted above, Libet *et al.* (1983) asked their subjects to signal not only when they became aware of the movement (the 'M' judgment), but also when they first felt the intention to move (or urge to move, the 'W' judgment). They found that the conscious judgment about the intention to move preceded the actual movement of about 200 ms and that the 'W' judgment followed (instead of proceeding) the electrophysiological preparatory activity related to movement, usually registered over the supplementary motor area (SMA) of hundreds of milliseconds. Haggard and Magno (1999) found that awareness of intention to move was correlated to a brain potential considered to be an indicator of action selection (called 'lateralized readiness potential'), responsible for the specification of the characteristics of the movement. This potential is subsequent to the very earliest neural preparation of action that may represent the initial decision to move (prior intention in Figure 8.2). In an fMRI study, Lau *et al.* (2004) were able to identify the brain areas where intention for action arises. They asked normal subjects to perform voluntary movements and to report either the time of the conscious intention of starting the movement (W judgment), or the time of movement awareness itself (M judgment). The results showed that the judgment of conscious intention was related to greater activation in the presupplementary motor area (preSMA) and in the intraparietal sulcus. Interestingly, Berti *et al.* (2005) found that SMA and preSMA are usually spared in anosognosic patients. These data further suggest that the activity of the areas involved in the construction of conscious intention of action should be accessible to anosognosic patients and may contribute to the emergence of the delusional belief of being able to perform motor acts, despite the complete left hemiplegia.

An experimental demonstration of the presence of intention for action in anosognosic patients

The aim of the present experiment was to demonstrate the presence of intention for voluntary action in anosognosia for hemiplegia, using EMG recording of proximal muscle activity.

Methods

Muscle electrical activity (EMG) was continuously recorded using surface electrodes, placed over the upper trapetius bilaterally. Data were recorded using a DEM EMG apparatus [cut-off frequency (low pass): 500 Hz; sampling rate: 2 kHz; A/D resolution: 12 bit]. The peak value in microvolts of the EMG-rectified signal was taken as a parameter of muscle activity in each trial. Seated at a table, subjects were instructed to reach either with the right or with the left hand for the examiner's hand, to keep the position for a few seconds and then to relax. The examiner's hand was placed, in front of the subjects, aligned with their body midline, at a distance of about 40 cm. Each trial lasted 5–10 s. The inter-trial interval lasted approximately 30 s. Subjects were also instructed to relax the limb not being tested as much as they could. In the inter-trial period, the subjects were requested to relax both limbs. In summary, there were three conditions: reaching with the left limb (plegic in brain-damaged patients), reaching with the right limb and resting. Under all conditions, the activity of both the right and the left upper trapetius was recorded. Therefore, six conditions were tested: (1) the activity of the left upper trapetius during left arm reaching movement; (2) the activity of the left upper trapetius during the right arm reaching movement; (3) the activity of the upper right trapetius during the left arm reaching movements; (4) the activity of the right upper trapetius during the right arm reaching movements;(5) the baseline activity of the left upper trapetius during the inter-trial resting period; (6) the baseline activity of the right upper trapetius during the inter-trial resting period. There were ten trials for each condition.

Subjects

Two right-brain-damaged patients affected by contralesional hemiplegia and one neurologically intact subject (Control) were studied. Of the two patients, one was severely

Table 8.1. Clinical data of the two brain-damaged patients

Patient	Lesion site	Age	Education	Hemiplegia	Hemianesthesia	N	PN	AHP
CR	Cortico-subcortical FTPO	74	5	+	+	+	−	+
SF	Subcortical rIC and LN	73	5	+	−	−	−	−

N, extrapersonal neglect; PN, personal neglect; AHP, anosognosia for hemiplegia; F, frontal; P, parietal; T, temporal; O, occipital; rIC, right internal capsule; LN, lenticular nucleus.

anosognosic for the motor impairment (AHP), whereas the other one was completely aware of the motor deficit (NonAHP). Clinical data are reported in Table 8.1.

Case reports

Patient CR

CR is a 74-year-old right-handed woman, with 5 years of formal education, who after a right-hemisphere stroke developed a complete contralesional left hemiplegia, left hemianesthesia and severe personal and extrapersonal left-sided neglect. A neuropsychological examination carried out 32 days after the stroke showed that she was fully oriented and cooperative. She had no global reasoning or language problems. Her spontaneous speech was well organized with good intentional contour, grammatical and logical structure and rich in information content. She could readily understand and follow test instructions. She still showed extrapersonal neglect in many daily activities and on conventional clinical testing such as cancellation bisection and drawing test. Her reading abilities were affected by neglect dyslexia. There were signs of left personal neglect for the left upper limb (Bisiach *et al.*, 1986). The reconstruction of her brain damage is shown in Figure 8.3.

CR presented severe and persistent anosognosia for her left hemiplegia (score 3, following Bisiach *et al.*, 1986). She never spontaneously reported her motor problems. Questioned about her left arm, she always claimed that it could move without any problem. When asked to actually perform movements, she attempted to perform the action, and after a few seconds she appeared to be satisfied with her performance. On the day of the EMG experimental testing (39 days after the stroke), her personal neglect was

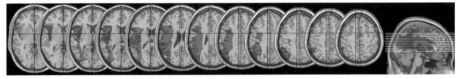

Figure 8.3 Reconstruction of patient CR lesion. The brain-damage-affected cortico-subcortical areas in frontal, parietal, temporal and occipital regions, involving areas related to motor awareness (Berti *et al.*, 2005; Karnath *et al.*, 2005) but leaving intact the mesial areas related to intention to action (Lau *et al.*, 2004).

resolved and her extrapersonal neglect was much improved both in formal cancellation tasks and in daily activities. A conversation that we had with her is reported below.

E: Where are we?

P: In the Hospital

E: Which hospital?

P: Somma Lombardo.

E: Why are you in the hospital?

P: Because I had a stroke.

E: What is a stroke?

P: I do not know.

E: How is your left arm?

P: Fine.

E: Can you move it?

P: Yes.

E: Would you be able to raise your left arm up in the air?

P: Yes, I would.

E: Would you be able to lift the telephone receiver with your left hand?

P: Yes, I would.

E: Would you be able to open a bottle, using both your hands?

P: Yes, I would.

E: Would you be able to brush your hair handling the hairbrush with your left hand?

P: Yes, I would.

E: Would you be able to wash your face using both your hands?

P: Yes, I would.

(The patient was then asked to actually perform some movements.)

E: Could you touch my hand with your right hand?

P: (The patient does it without any problem.)

E: Could you touch my hand with your left hand?

P: (Although she seems to try the movements, she cannot raise the arm and reach the examiner's hand. Nonetheless, after a while she says 'Done.')

E: Have you done it?

P: Yes, I think so.

E: Could you touch your left hand with your right hand?

P: (She does it without problem, thus showing that the left personal neglect has vanished.)

E: Could you open this bottle for me, please?

P: (The patient attempts to do it using only the right hand.)

E: Can you manage?

P: No.

E: Why?

P: Because it does not open.

E: How do you open a bottle?

P: With one hand I hold the bottle, with the other I unscrew the cap.

E: Are you doing it?

P: Yes.

E: Can you put your left hand on your left shoulder?

P: Yes, I can.

E: Then please do it.

P: (the patient seems to try the movement: she also overtly looks at the left motionless arm and at the shoulder. After that, she looks at the examiner, as if she had finished performing the requested action).

E: Have you done it?

P: Yes, I think so.

(The patient, on the wheelchair, is taken to the bathroom and placed in front of the basin.)

E: Could you wash your face using both hands, please?

P: (The patient takes the bottle of the liquid soap with the right hand and attempts to soap her left hand as if the left hand was actually over the basin, near the midline. However, the left hand was not there because it was lying on her lap. After having soaped the 'ghostly' hand, she started to move the right arm/hand forward and backward as if she was washing the two hands, one against the other. Finally, she washed the face using the right hand.)

E: Are you washing both your hands?

P: Yes, I am.

E: Are you washing your face?

P: Yes, I am.

E: With both hands?

P: Yes, I think so.

(Then the patient was asked to brush her hair handling the hairbrush with the left hand. The hairbrush was on the table and the left hand was lying motionless on the table as well. She took the hairbrush with the right hand and forced it below the left hand. While 'holding' the hairbrush with the left hand she moved the head as if she was actually brushing the hair. After a while, she looked at the examiner and seemed satisfied with her performance.)

E: Have you done it?

P: Yes, I have, but only on the left side (!).

Patient SF

SF is a 73-year-old right-handed woman, with 5 years of formal education, who showed hemiplegia following an ischemic stroke. A computed tomography scan revealed an ischemic lesion affecting the right internal capsule and the lenticular nucleus. The damage in the right hemisphere caused severe left hemiplegia without hemianaesthesia. No other neurological/neuropsychological disorders were found.

Predictions

Patient CR was an ideal candidate for verifying the hypothesis put forward by Berti *et al.* (2005), according to which anosognosia for hemiplegia is a circumscribed disorder of motor awareness where the strong false belief of being able to move relies on the normal functioning of part of the chain of events leading to movement production and movement control. Indeed, she was affected by severe anosognosia for hemiplegia, which was stable and persisting even when the patient voluntarily and directly looked towards the motionless left arm. Moreover, the clinical impression just observing her behavior was that she attempted the movement requested by the examiner. If so, the activation of proximal muscles should be observed and it would be the evidence of normal activation of intentional processes.

Therefore, the predictions are as follows:

1. In the neurologically intact subject, the request of reaching either with the right or with the left arm should cause activation of proximal muscles.

2. In the NonAHP the request of reaching with the right arm should normally activate right-side proximal muscles. Similarly, the request of attempting to move the left arm should activate the left-side proximal muscles. Indeed, the patient should not have any intentional problem, and although aware of being hemiplegic she should try, under request, to move the affected side.

3. In the brain-damaged patient with anosognosia for hemiplegia, two potential predictions can be advanced:

    (a) The patient has no intention to move; in this case, she should show activation of proximal muscles of the unaffected side when requested to move the right arm, whereas she should not show any activation of the left-side proximal muscles when requested to reach with the hemiplegic arm.

    (b) The patient still has intention to move: in this case, she should show activation of proximal muscles on both sides for reaching movement with either arm.

Results

Data (peak values of the EMG-rectified signal) were analysed by means of repeated measures ANOVA with Subject (three levels: Normal, NonAHP patient, AHP patient) as between-subject factor and Movement (three levels: Right reaching; Left reaching, Resting) and Muscle [two levels: Left upper trapetius (LUT); Right upper trapetius (RUP)] as within-subjects factor. All factors and interactions were significant at $p < 0.00001$. In particular, the interaction Muscles × Subjects [$F(2, 27) = 98\,785$, $p = 00000$] showed that the activation of proximal muscles was in general higher in the two hemiplegic patients than in the control subject (see Figure 8.4). A *post hoc* test (Newman–Keuls) showed that the difference was significant for all comparisons, that is both the LUT and RUT were more active in the NonAHP patient than in the Normal control ($p < 0.05$ for both comparisons) and in the AHP patient than in the Normal control ($p < 0.001$ for both comparison). Moreover the interaction Muscles × Subjects showed that while in the Normal subject and in the NonAHP patient the activation of the LUT did not differ from the activation the RUT, in the AHP patient the activation of the RUT significantly differed from that of the LUT (Newman–Keuls, $p < 0.001$).

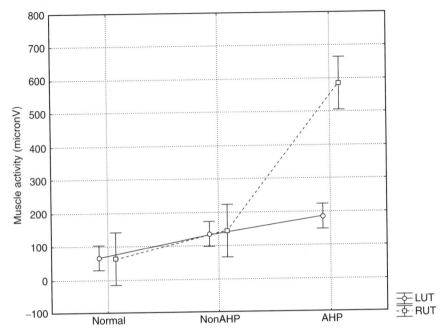

Figure 8.4 The activity of both the right upper trapetius and left upper trapetius, independently of the reaching conditions. Normal, neurologically intact subject; NonAHP, hemiplegic patient without anosognosia; AHP, hemiplegic patient with anosognosia.

The Movement $\times$ Muscles $\times$ Subjects significant interaction [$F(4, 54) = 6{,}3345$, $p = 0.0003$] confirmed that in all subjects the LUT is activated during Left-side reaching (the difference with the resting condition is significant, in Normal $p < 0.05$, in NonAHP $p < 0.005$, in AHP $p < 0.05$) and the RUT is activated during Right-side reaching (the difference with the resting condition was significant, in the Normal $p < 0.05$, in NonAHP $p < 0.001$, in AHP $p < 0.001$), thus demonstrating that also in the anosognosic patient proximal muscles activate even during left-side attempt to reach (see Figure 8.5).

It is worth noting that in the anosognosic patient the resting condition of the RUT significantly differs from the resting condition of the RUT in the other two subjects ($p < 0.001$), suggesting for the anosognosic patient a great difficulty in relaxing the ipsilesional muscles. This causes the activation of the RUT in the anosognosic patient, being evident also during Left-side reaching (difference with resting condition $p < 0.001$). Finally, during Right-side reaching the RUT is hyperactive (see Figure 8.5). Hyperkinetic motor behavior contralateral to hemiplegia in acute stroke has already been described and related to active processes induced by disinhibition, in order to establish new compensatory pathways (e.g. Ghika *et al.*, 1995). Alternatively, and more speculatively, it might be argued that the ipsilesional hyperactivity observed in a right-brain-damaged patient affected by neglect might be a motor counterpart of the hyperattention sometimes observed in the perceptual domain.

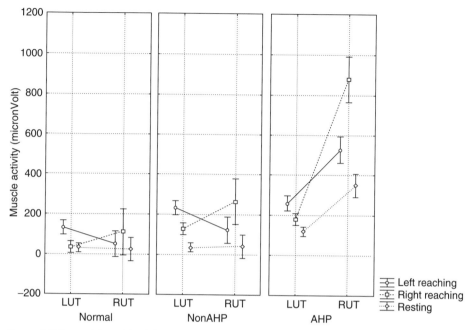

Figure 8.5 The activity of the left upper trapetius (LUT) and the right upper trapetius (RUP) as function of the side of the reaching movement and resting condition. Normal, neurologically intact subject; NonAHP, hemiplegic patient without anosognosia; AHP, hemiplegic patient with anosognosia.

Discussion

The aim of the present study was to investigate the presence of intention to move in anosognosia for left-side hemiplegia by means of an EMG study of the activity of proximal muscles. The assumption was that, when subjects are requested to perform reaching with the upper limbs, the presence of intention would manifest itself in the activation of proximal, bilaterally innervated, muscles, and this should be also the case in anosognosic patients showing strong beliefs of being capable of moving. Remember that our hypothesis is that anosognosic patients, presenting with the kind of behavior described in CR, should retain their intentions to move, but not be aware of the somatic reality of their body failure to respond to them. Our results, although obtained on a single case study, confirmed this prediction. The pattern of muscle activation was similar in all three subjects we tested (a neurologically intact control, a right-brain-damaged patient without anosognosia and a right-brain-damaged patient with anosognosia), and for both arms. All subjects, including the anosognosic patients, when requested to perform reaching movements with either arm, activated the corresponding proximal muscles with respect to the resting condition. In other words, right-side reaching movements activated right-side proximal muscles. The right side was the unaffected side in the two brain-damaged patients. Crucially, left-side reaching movement activated left-side proximal muscles even when, as in the two right-brain-damaged patients, action could not be performed because of the presence of left hemiplegia. From this pattern of activation, we may infer that in right-brain-damaged patients normal intentional attitudes trigger, as in neurologically intact subjects, the chain of neural events that would lead to action execution. While in patient SF, with intact comparator system, the discrepancy between the intended action and the absence of movement could be normally detected, giving raise to 'veridical' motor awareness, in patient CR the damage to the comparator system, coupled with the normal functioning of the intention/prediction system, caused the generation of 'nonveridical' motor awareness and the consequent emergence of false belief. In fact, with this paradigm we did not explicitly ask the patients whether they were 'aware' of their intention to move (as in the Libet paradigm). However, the assumption is that if a patient has intention to move then she/he should be aware of this intention. This may be experimentally tested in future research by applying the Libet paradigm to the study of anosognosic patients.

Finally, this model can also account for observations reported in deafferented patients. These patients are clinically different from anosognosic patients insofar as they can still make movements, in absence of any sensory feedback. However, although the absence of tactile/proprioceptive input may alter the functioning of the comparator system, an intact capacity of making predictions should *per se* be sufficient for constructing a normal veridical motor awareness. Interestingly, this prediction has received support from a deafferented patient, GL, who suffered a total loss of body sensation after subsequent attacks of polyneuropathy. GL performed self-paced index finger flexion nearly as well as the controls without any afferent sensory input to the cortex, documented by the absence of MEP (movement-evoked potential, related to the afferent sensory feedback (Kristeva *et al.*, 2006). Despite the absence of any sensory feedback, she was aware (1) of being able to make movements and (2) of giving the commands for executing the movements. In other words, she had a normal/veridical motor awareness. However, the absence of any sensory feedback to the comparator system and, therefore, the impossibility of confronting the predictions with the actual motor activity, prevented her from perceptually feeling the movements. Indeed, although she was able to assess and scale the muscle force, she did not perceive any fatigue or effort of applying force throughout the experiment (Lafargue *et al.*, 2003). Note that the peripheral damage, as opposed to the comparator damage, allowed the patient to monitor correctly the reality of her motor condition with a full acknowledgment of the impairment in perceptual awareness. These results clearly demonstrate that motor awareness is still possible in the absence of 'perceptual awareness' and that motor control can rely only on an internal model for giving the subject the normal belief of making appropriate voluntary movements.

General conclusions

Everyday interaction with other individuals and, more in general, with the environment is mediated by motor actions, through which we convey our beliefs and desires and try to achieve our goals and purposes. Action generation and execution requires a continuous updating of the effectiveness of motor acts through a motor monitoring process that is crucial for becoming aware of the movements we are performing. The study of the consequence of brain damage on motor control may represent a fundamental step for trying to establish the neurobiological events underlying the processes of motor awareness. In this chapter we have discussed how the observation of the counterintuitive behavior of brain-damaged patients, together with neuroanatomical and neurophysiological evidence underpinning the areas involved in the construction of veridical beliefs about our own actions, can shed light on the processes that are more generally involved in the construction of a coherent sense of self (Jeannerod, 2004).

Acknowledgments

This paper has been supported by a MIUR-PRIN grant and a Regione Piemonte and C.I.P.E. grant to A.B.

References

Babinski, J. (1914) Contribution à l'étude des troubles mentaux dans l'hémiplégie organique cérébrale (anosognosie). *Revue Neurologique*, 27, 845–848.

Berti, A. (2000) Neuropsychological syndromes and the structure of conscious processes. *International Symposium: The Emergence of the Mind*. Fondazione Carlo Erba, Milano.

Berti, A. and Pia, L. (2006) Understanding motor awareness through normal and pathological behavior. *Current Directions in Psychological Science*, 15, 245–250.

Berti, A., Làdavas, E. and Della Corte, M. (1996) Anosognosia for hemiplegia, neglect dyslexia, and drawing neglect: clinical findings and theoretical considerations. *Journal of the International Neuropsychological Society*, 2, 426–440.

Berti, A., Làdavas, E., Stracciari, A., Giannarelli, C. and Ossola, A. (1998) Anosognosia for motor impairment and dissociations with patient's evaluation of the disorders: theoretical considerations. *Cognitive Neuropsychiatry*, 3, 21–44.

Berti, A., Bottini, G., Gandola, M., Pia, L., Smania, N., Stracciari, A., Castiglioni, I., Vallar, G. and Paulesu, E. (2005) Shared cortical anatomy for motor awareness and motor control. *Science*, 309, 488–491.

Bisiach, E. and Berti, A. (1987) Dyschiria: and attempts at its systemic explanation. In Jeannerod, M. (ed.), *Neurophysiological and Neuropsychological Aspects of Spatial Neglect*. North-Holland, Amsterdam.

Bisiach, E. and Berti, A. (1995) Consciousness in dyschiria. In Gazzaniga, M. S. (ed.), *The Cognitive Neurosciences*. MIT Press, Cambridge, MA.

Bisiach, E. and Geminiani, G. (1991) Anosognosia related to hemiplegia and hemianopia. In Prigatano, G. P. and Schacter, D. L. (eds), *Awareness of Deficit after Brain Injury*. Oxford University Press, New York.

Bisiach, E., Vallar, G., Perani, D., Papagno, C. and Berti, A. (1986) Unawareness of disease following lesions of the right hemisphere: anosognosia for hemiplegia and anosognosia for hemianopia. *Neuropsychologia*, 24, 471–482.

Blakemore, S. J. and Frith, C. (2003) Self-awareness and action. *Current Opinion in Neurobiology*, 13, 219–224.

Blakemore, S. J., Wolpert, D. M. and Frith, C. D. (2002) Abnormalities in the awareness of action. *Trends in Cognitive Sciences*, 6, 237–242.

Bottini, G., Paulesu, E., Sterzi, R., Warburton, E., Wise, R. J., Vallar, G., Frackowiak, R. S. and Frith, C. D. (1995) Modulation of conscious experience by peripheral sensory stimuli. *Nature*, 376, 778–781.

Breier, J. I., Adair, J. C., Gold, M., Fennell, E. B., Gilmore, R. L. and Heilman, K. M. (1995) Dissociation of anosognosia for hemiplegia and aphasia during left-hemisphere anesthesia. *Neurology*, 45, 65–67.

Cappa, S., Sterzi, R., Vallar, G. and Bisiach, E. (1987) Remission of hemineglect and anosognosia during vestibular stimulation. *Neuropsychologia*, **25**, 775–782.

Carpenter, K., Berti, A., Oxbury, S., Molyneux, A. J., Bisiach, E. and Oxbury, J. M. (1995) Awareness of and memory for arm weakness during intracarotid sodium amytal testing. *Brain*, **118**, 243–251.

Cutting, J. (1978) Study of anosognosia. *Journal of Neurology, Neurosurgery and Psychiatry*, **41**, 548–555.

Dauriac-le Masson, V., Mailhan, L., Louis-Dreyfus, A., De Montety, G., Denys, P., Bussel, B. and Azouvi, P. (2002) Double dissociation between unilateral neglect and anosognosia. *Revue Neurologique*, **158**, 427–430.

Fourneret, P. and Jeannerod, M. (1998) Limited conscious monitoring of motor performance in normal subjects. *Neuropsychologia*, **36**, 1133–1140.

Ghika, J., Bogousslavsky, J., Van Melle, G. and Regli, F. (1995) Hyperkinetic motor behaviors contralateral to hemiplegia in acute stroke. *European Neurology*, **35**, 27–32.

Gilmore, R. L., Heilman, K. M., Schmidt, R. P., Fennell, E. M. and Quisling, R. (1992) Anosognosia during Wada testing. *Neurology*, **42**, 925–927.

Gold, M., Adair, J. C., Jacobs, D. H. and Heilman, K. M. (1994) Anosognosia for hemiplegia: an electrophysiologic investigation of the feed-forward hypothesis. *Neurology*, **44**, 1804–1808.

Haggard, P. (2005) Conscious intention and motor cognition. *Trends in Cognitive Sciences*, **9**, 290–295.

Haggard, P. and Magno, E. (1999) Localising awareness of action with transcranial magnetic stimulation. *Experimental Brain Research*, **127**, 102–107.

Jehkonen, M., Ahonen, J. P., Dastidar, P., Laippala, P. and Vilkki, J. (2000) Unawareness of deficits after right hemisphere stroke: double-dissociations of anosognosias. *Acta Neurologica Scandinavica*, **102**, 378–284.

Karnath, H. O., Baier, B. and Nagele, T. (2005) Awareness of the functioning of one's own limbs mediated by the insular cortex? *Journal of Neuroscience*, **25**, 7134–7138.

Kristeva, R., Chakarov, V., Wagner, M., Schulte-Monting, J. and Hepp-Reymond, M. C. (2006) Is the movement-evoked potential mandatory for movement execution? A high-resolution EEG study in a deafferented patient. *Neuroimage*, **31**, 677–685.

Lafargue, G., Paillard, J., Lamarre, Y. and Sirigu, A. (2003) Production and perception of grip force without proprioception: is there a sense of effort in deafferented subjects? *European Journal of Neuroscience*, **17**, 2741–2749.

Laplane, D. and Degos, J. D. (1983) Motor neglect. *Journal of Neurology, Neurosurgery and Psychiatry*, **46**, 152–158.

Lau, H. C., Rogers, R. D., Haggard, P. and Passingham, R. E. (2004) Attention to intention. *Science*, **303**, 1208–1210.

Levine, D. N., Calvanio, R. and Rinn, W. E. (1991) The pathogenesis of anosognosia for hemiplegia. *Neurology*, **41**, 1770–1781.

Libet, B., Gleason, C. A., Wright, E. W. and Pearl, D. K. (1983) Time of conscious intention to act in relation to onset of cerebral activity (readiness-potential). The unconscious initiation of a freely voluntary act. *Brain*, **106**, 623–642.

Marcel, A. J., Tegnèr, R. and Nimmo-Smith, I. (2004) Anosognosia for plegia: specificity, extension, partiality and disunity of bodily unawareness. *Cortex*, **40**, 19–40.

Pia, L., Neppi-Mòdona, M., Ricci, R. and Berti, A. (2004) The anatomy of anosognosia for hemiplegia: a meta-analysis. *Cortex*, **40**, 367–377.

Prigatano, G. P. and Schacter, D. L. (1991) Awareness of deficit after brain injury. In Prigatano, G. P. and Schacter, D. L. (eds), *Awareness of Deficit after Brain Injury*. Oxford University Press, New York.

Rizzolatti, G., Luppino, G. and Matelli, M. (1998) The organization of the cortical motor system: new concepts. *Electroencephalography and Clinical Neurophysiology*, **106**, 283–296.

Rode, G., Charles, N., Perenin, M. T., Vighetto, A., Trillet, M. and Aimard, G. (1992) Partial remission of hemiplegia and somatoparaphrenia through vestibular stimulation in a case of unilateral neglect. *Cortex*, **28**, 203–208.

Small, M. and Ellis, S. (1996) Denial of hemiplegia: an investigation into the theories of causation. *European Neurology*, **36**, 353–363.

Von Hagen, K. O. and Ives, E. R. (1937) Anosognosia (Babinski), imperception of hemiplegia. Report of six cases, one with autopsy. *Bulletin of Los Angeles Neurological Society*, **2**, 95–103.

Weinstein, E. A. and Kahn, R. L. (1955) *Denial of Illness: Symbolic and Physiological Aspects*. Charles C. Thomas, Springfield, IL.

Wolpert, D. M., Ghahramani, Z. and Jordan, M. I. (1995) An internal model for sensorimotor integration. *Science*, **269**, 1880–1882.

9

Investigating multisensory spatial cognition through the phenomenon of extinction

Alessandro Farnè, Claudio Brozzoli,
Elisabetta Làdavas and Tony Ro

The study of pathologic behavioral phenomena following damage to the central nervous system has substantially contributed to our understanding of the normal organization of cognitive brain functions. The investigation of clinical extinction in neurological patients, for example, revealed that events occurring in the immediate proximity to the body (i.e. in near peripersonal space) undergo a high degree of multisensory processing. Indeed, visual–tactile extinction is most severe near a given body part: tactile stimuli on the contralesional hand are more severely extinguished by visual stimuli presented near, as compared to far, from the ipsilesional hand. Here, extinction-based evidence will first be reported to illustrate the peculiar nature of multisensory processing occurring in peri-corporeal space. Second, the plastic features of such processing following tool-use will be presented. Our findings in patients with visual–tactile extinction show that the use of a tool as an extension of reachable space may dynamically modulate the multisensory processing of farther, non-reachable sectors of space. Finally, a normal model of the clin-ical phenomenon of tactile extinction is proposed and demonstrated. We show that, despite accurate and comparable perception of single stimulation to the right or left hand, somatosensory performance is lower when reporting double simultaneous stimuli in neurologically healthy participants, thus replicating the typical extinction patient's behavior. This intrinsic limitation of the somatosensory perceptual system was exploited to further investigate multisensory interactions between proprioceptive–kinesthetic and tactile inputs in normal subjects. In this respect, we demonstrate that experiencing the functional property of a tool may selectively modulate the tactile extinction-like phenomenon in healthy subjects. These findings, in addition to validating the normal model of tactile extinction, may open new perspectives for investigating the pervasive aspects of multisensory processing in humans and their neurophysiological bases.

Introduction: from pathology to normal brain functions

"[Extinction is] a process in which a sensation disappears ... when another sensation is evoked by simultaneous stimulation elsewhere in the sensory field"

Morris B. Bender, *Disorders in Perception* (1952)

The neuropsychological phenomena termed 'neglect' and 'extinction' represent two models that provide considerable insight into the behavioral characteristics of multisensory spatial representation in humans (Ladavas and Farnè, 2004). Unilateral spatial neglect is a relatively common deficit that most frequently arises after right-brain damage (RBD). Its main characteristic is a lack of awareness for sensory events located in the contralesional side of space (towards the left-side space following a right lesion) and a loss of exploratory search and other actions normally directed toward that side. Some of the classic presentation symptoms of neglect patients include behaviors as if the left half of their world no longer existed, so that in daily life they may only eat from one side of their plate, shave or make-up only one side of their face (Driver and Vuilleumier, 2001), or draw or verbally describe only the right side of a remembered image or place (Bisiach and Luzzatti, 1978).

To some extent, neglect is similar to the phenomenon of extinction (Critchley, 1949), a pathological sign following brain damage whereby patients fail to report a stimulus, presented to the contralesional side, only when accompanied by a concurrent stimulus on the ipsilesional side (Bender, 1952), that is, under conditions of double simultaneous stimulation (DSS). Otherwise, extinction patients are able to detect (almost always) the presence of the very same contralesional stimulus when delivered singly to the affected side, that is, under conditions of single stimulation (SS). Extinction is less associated with right unilateral brain lesions than neglect (Rafal, 2000) and the lateralization may relate to handedness (Meador et al., 1998). It can be easily revealed by means of the 'confrontation' method, which consists of having the examiner sitting in front of the patient and wiggling the left, the right, or both index fingers simultaneously, while the patient is asked to verbally report which side(s) has been stimulated. When the patient's right or left visual fields (or hands for the tactile modality) are alternatively or simultaneously stimulated, extinction can be readily detected and quantified. An impaired ability to report contralesional stimuli under DSS, as compared to unilateral stimulation, is the hallmark of extinction. This technique is similarly used to assess extinction in the auditory modality.

Extinction is eminently a competitive phenomenon (Ward et al., 1994; di Pellegrino and De Renzi, 1995) that has been proposed to emerge because of the unbalanced competition between affected and unaffected spatial representations, with the ipsilesional events being provided with stronger competitive weights as compared to the contralesional ones (Duncan, 1996; Driver et al., 1997; Driver, 1998; Berti et al., 1999). Owing to the imbalance in competition, contralesional events will be suppressed, as if they were 'extinguished' by the ipsilesional events. Both neglect and extinction can occur despite relatively intact primary sensory pathways. Although extinction has long been considered as a residual form of spatial neglect, these two neuropsychological manifestations differ in some respects and double dissociations have been documented (Geeraerts et al., 2005), suggesting a distinct underlying neural mechanism for extinction and neglect (Vallar et al., 1994).

In what follows, we outline how the phenomenon of extinction can be used as a fruitful model for the study of multisensory coding of space in the human brain. In particular, we first review how extinction can be assessed to reveal the peculiar features of multisensory coding occurring in proximal space, as well as its plastic changes induced by using a tool as a functional modification of body-reachable space. We then turn to presenting a model of tactile extinction in neurologically healthy subjects, and validate it by showing that this model can similarly be exploited to further investigate the intrinsic multisensory nature of our normal perception.

The multisensory space around us

Despite the conscious experience of a unitary space surrounding the body, this unified percept is the integrated outcome of distinct neuronal systems providing a considerable amount of fusion among the senses (Calvert *et al.*, 2004; Spence and Driver, 2004). The notion of a modular organization for spatial representation is now widely accepted, and exemplified by the occurrence of neglect restricted to peripersonal (within reaching distance) or extrapersonal (beyond reaching distance) space (Coslett *et al.*, 1993; Vuilleumier *et al.*, 1998; Berti and Frassinetti, 2000; Halligan *et al.*, 2003). This double dissociation supports the existence of separate spatial representations for peripersonal and extrapersonal space, complementing the previously documented dissociation between personal and peripersonal neglect (Bisiach *et al.*, 1986). The space representation taxonomy thus includes three main sectors: personal, peripersonal and extrapersonal.

While no definitive answer has yet been given regarding the anatomical counterpart of these behavioral dissociations in humans, neuroanatomical evidence has been provided for the correlates of peripersonal and extrapersonal space in monkeys. Rizzolatti *et al.* (1981, 1983, 1997) coined the term 'peripersonal' to refer to a limited sector of space around the animal's body, the spatial boundaries of which are operationally defined by variations in the neuronal firing rates as a function of proximity between a three-dimensional (3D) visual object and a given body part. They found neurons in the premotor cortex (area 6) that respond to somatosensory and visual stimuli, provided that they are presented within the monkey's peripersonal space. In contrast, FEF neurons (area 8) respond when the same visual stimuli are located farther away in the extrapersonal space. Accordingly, unilateral ablation of area 6 or 8 provoked contralesional visual neglect for objects located, respectively, in the monkey's peripersonal or extrapersonal space (Rizzolatti *et al.*, 1981, 1983).

Today, several areas of the monkey brain, including the putamen, parietal areas 7b and VIP, as well as premotor areas, are thought to be crucially involved in representing near pericorporeal space. A relatively high proportion of multisensory neurons responding to tactile and visual and/or auditory stimuli have been reported in these structures. Their visual receptive fields (RF) are variably limited in depth, projecting from a few to several centimeters outward from the tactile RF, and they are in rough spatial register (i.e. they overlap) with the location of the somatosensory RF. These neurons respond best to both tactile and visual (or auditory) stimuli provided that visual (or auditory) stimuli are presented immediately adjacent to a particular body part (e.g. head or hand). Most notably, the visually evoked firing rate of bimodal neurons decreases as the distance between the visual stimulus and the animal body part where the tactile RF is located increases. For example, in the case of multisensory neurons with small visual RFs (~30 cm), a differential rate of firing occurs for stimuli within the animal's reach (Graziano and

Gross, 1995; Fogassi *et al.*, 1996; Duhamel *et al.*, 1998), thus coding for the limited portion of space immediately surrounding the body (i.e. near peripersonal space; for review, see Rizzolatti *et al.*, 2002).

In addition to animal evidence, recent functional neuroimaging studies in humans provide evidence in support of the existence of similar multisensory integrative structures in the human brain (Bremmer *et al.*, 2001). Most notably, however, converging behavioral evidence comes from neuropsychological studies on brain-damaged patients affected by the phenomenon of extinction, which show that peripersonal space in humans is also composed of a proximal and a distal sector (i.e. near and far peripersonal space).

Extinction as a tool for studying multisensory spatial representations

" ... in some cases it seemed as if visual or auditory stimuli produced extinction of cutaneous sensation"

Morris B. Bender, *Disorders in Perception* (1952)

How did the study of extinction contribute to our understanding of the multisensory coding of space? Contralesional extinction has long been known to occur within different sensory modalities (unisensory extinction), including visual (di Pellegrino and De Renzi, 1995), auditory (De Renzi, 1984), olfactory (Bellas *et al.*, 1988), and tactile (Gainotti *et al.*, 1989). However, the phenomenon of cross-modal extinction (i.e. extinction 'between' modalities) has been more elusive (e.g. see Inhoff *et al.*, 1992) and documented only more recently in studies on RBD patients affected by left unisensory tactile extinction. In particular, it has been demonstrated that the presentation of a visual stimulus in the right ipsilesional field can extinguish a tactile stimulus presented on the contralesional hand, which is otherwise well detected by patients when presented alone (Bender, 1952; di Pellegrino *et al.*, 1997; Mattingley *et al.*, 1997).

Since these initial observations, we have conducted several studies that have systematically shown that cross-modal extinction can be modulated by the spatial arrangement of the stimuli with respect to the patient's body (for review, see Ladavas and Farnè, 2004). In RBD patients with tactile extinction, for example, visual stimulation on the ipsilesional side produces contralesional tactile extinction, whereby the presentation of visual and tactile stimuli on the same contralesional side can reduce the deficit (Ladavas *et al.*, 1998a). Moreover, the modulation described is most consistently manifest when the visual–tactile interaction occurs in the space close to the patient's body, as compared to when the space far from the body is visually stimulated. For example, presenting a visual stimulus near (~5 cm) the patient's ipsilesional hand (i.e. in near peripersonal space) strongly extinguishes a tactile stimulus concurrently delivered on the contralesional hand. In contrast, much weaker extinction is observed when the same visual stimulus is presented farther away (~35 cm) from the patient's ipsilesional hand (i.e. in far peripersonal space). The finding that multisensory integration may occur in a privileged manner within near peripersonal space has been taken as evidence of the existence, in humans, of an integrated visual–tactile system coding near peripersonal space in a similar way to that described in monkeys (Ladavas, 2002).

Visual and tactile information is integrated in a similar way in other peripersonal space regions, such as around the face (Ladavas *et al.*, 1998b; Farnè *et al.*, 2005a). In these studies, extinction patients were presented with unilateral and bilateral tactile stimulation on both cheeks and visual stimuli were concurrently presented on the contralesional or ipsilesional side. As with the hand, high levels of extinction was found in the ipsilesional visual condition, whereas the visual stimulus enhanced tactile detection when delivered on the contralesional side. The modulation, again, was more evident when the visual stimulus was presented in a near body region of space rather than in a farther region, thus implying that multisensory integration only within proximal space regulates whether the tactile input will reach awareness.

Similar modulations of tactile extinction have been reported in the interaction between audition and touch (Ladavas *et al.*, 2001). When sounds are concurrently presented with single touches delivered to the neck in tactile extinction patients, their contralesional tactile detection is most likely to be hampered by proximal, as compared to distant, loud-speakers. Interestingly, such a multisensory effect is even stronger when cross-modal auditory–tactile extinction is assessed in the patients' back space (where vision is not available), suggesting that different degrees of multisensory integration may occur depending upon the functional relevance of a given modality for that particular sector of space (Farnè and Ladavas, 2002).

These findings support the notion of a multisensory coding of near peripersonal space in humans, akin to that described in animal studies. In monkeys, a strong multisensory integration in peripersonal space occurs at the single neuron level: the same neurons activated by tactile stimuli delivered on a given body part are also activated by visual or auditory stimuli delivered in space near that body part. In this respect, the selectivity of human visual–tactile extinction for the proximal sector of space is reminiscent of the spatial bias observed in visual neglect, which may selectively arise in near peripersonal space (Halligan and Mashall, 1991).

Altogether, these results show that the manifestations of cross-modal interactions can be selectively modulated by the relationship between the stimulus and the body, including distance and spatial location (but also auditory complexity, see Farnè and Ladavas, 2002). These findings are in good agreement with a modular organization of space, in which several neuronal structures are devoted to the processing of different space sectors across different sensory modalities, most likely for different behavioral purposes. Among these structures, the functional representations of near and far peripersonal space in humans parallels the circuit of multisensory areas that has been well documented in monkeys.

Plastic multisensory modulations induced by tool-use

An interesting characteristic of the multisensory representations of the region surround-ing the body is its plasticity. Through tool-use, for example, it is possible to functionally remap the space so that "far becomes near" (Berti and Frassinetti, 2000). Berti and Frassinetti showed that, when asked to use a long stick to bisect distant horizontal lines, the neglect patients' selective bias, formerly present only in near space, was trans-ferred to far space. Similar results have been described in neurologically healthy subjects

(Maravita and Iriki, 2004) and in extinction patients who, after tool-use, showed changes in cross-modal extinction that were compatible with a tool-use-dependent remapping of action space (Farnè *et al.*, 2005b). Most of these studies were inspired by the seminal paper by Iriki *et al.* (1996), which propelled several investigations of the physiological and behavioral effects exerted by the use of tools upon the multisensory representation of near peripersonal space. Iriki *et al.* reported that the visual receptive fields (RF) of a monkey's parietal visual–tactile neurons enlarged along the axis of a rake soon after its use for retrieving distant food pellets. The same visual RF shrunk following passive tool-wielding, recorded immediately after tool-use, thus showing a tool-use-dependent extension of the visual–tactile space immediately surrounding the hand (Iriki *et al.*, 1996).

In this context, the successful use of a tool, as an extension of the corporeal boundary, requires integration of (at least) visual, tactile, proprioceptive and motor aspects (Napier, 1956). Under normal circumstances, such a polymodal merging of sensorimotor information from different locations (hand and tool) ensures that the appropriate action (e.g. retrieval) is performed with an appropriately oriented tool (e.g. a rake), in the position where the target object is located (Beck, 1980; Farnè and Ladavas, 2000; Johnson-Frey, 2003). Accordingly, several studies have reported evidence that various types of tool-related experience may modify the spatial extent of the peri-hand area within which visual–tactile integration occurs. For example, adapting the task originally introduced for monkeys to humans (Iriki *et al.*, 1996), we showed that the weak visual–tactile integration usually observed far from the subject's hand can be significantly increased following tool-use (retrieving far objects with the rake for 5 min). By investigating left cross-modal extinction in right brain-damaged (RBD) patients, we found that ipsilesional visual stimuli presented at the distal edge of a 38-cm-long rake induced more left tactile extinction immediately after tool-use than before tool-use. Moreover, when tool-use was impeded, the severity of cross-modal extinction decreased to pre-tool-use levels. The increase in cross-modal extinction found after tool-use has been taken as evidence for an extension of peri-hand space along the tool axis, whereas its reduction following tool-inactivity has been considered as the behavioural counterpart of the contraction of the formerly extended peri-hand space (Farnè and Ladavas, 2000). In a similar vein, Maravita *et al.* (2001) also found stronger visual–tactile extinction at the tip of a stick wielded by a patient, as compared to when the stick was absent, or present but not connected to the patient's hand. Further evidence of tool-related far/near space re-mapping has been documented in neglect patients (Berti and Frassinetti, 2000; Humprheys *et al.*, 2004). Convergent evidence also comes from healthy participants investigated in tasks involving different types of tool-use (Riggio *et al.*, 1986; Yamamoto and Kitazawa, 2001; see also Chapter X). Maravita and colleagues, for example, reported significant changes in the spatial distribution of cross-modal effects after subjects repeatedly crossed-over two hand-held tools, with the phenomenon developing with increased practice in crossing the tools (Maravita *et al.*, 2002a).

By assessing visual–tactile extinction in RBD patients, we investigated the crucial determinants of such plastic changes. We tested the role played by passive versus active experience with tools in re-sizing peri-hand space (Farnè *et al.*, 2005c). In particular, we investigated whether a prolonged passive experience with a rake (60 cm long) was sufficient to elongate peri-hand space, or whether active tool-use was necessary. The results showed that the severity of visual–tactile extinction, as assessed at the distal edge of the tool (60 cm away from the patient's hand) after a prolonged passive exposure to the proprioceptive and visual experience of wielding a rake, did not differ from that obtained when the tool was absent. In contrast, cross-modal extinction was significantly increased in far space following an equally long period of active use of the same tool. Therefore, in agreement with both neurophysiological and neuropsychological findings (Iriki *et al.*, 1996; Maravita *et al.*, 2002b) these results suggest that plastic modifications of the body schema (Head and Holmes, 1911–1912) require the tool to be actively involved in a task.

In another study (Farnè *et al.*, 2005b) we investigated the relationships between the physical and functional properties of active tool-use and the spatial extent of the subsequent peri-hand space elongation. In particular, by assessing visual–tactile extinction far from the patients' hand (60 cm) after use of a 60- or 30-cm-long rake, we found that peri-hand space elongation varied according to the tool length. When assessed at the same 60 cm far location, cross-modal extinction was stronger after use of a long tool (60 cm) as compared to the use of a short tool (30 cm). Remarkably, even the use of the short tool (30 cm) produced a significant increase in cross-modal extinction at the same far location (60 cm), although weaker than that induced by the use of the long tool (60 cm).

This indicates that the area of peripersonal space that is subject to the tool-use-induced re-weighting of multisensory coding is not sharply limited to the tool tip, but extends beyond it to include a peri-tool space, where the strength of visual–tactile integration seems to fade. In the same study we also showed that the extent of tool embodiment tightly depends upon the functional, not the physical, length of the used tool. These properties were dissociated through a hybrid rake that was physically long (60 cm), but operationally short (30 cm). Indeed, the severity of cross-modal extinction observed at the same far location (60 cm) after the use of the hybrid tool was significantly less severe than that found after the use of the 60-cm-long tool. In contrast, comparable cross-modal extinction was observed after use of the short tool (30 cm) and the hybrid tool, whose absolute length was the same as the 60-cm-long tool, but whose functional length was the same of the 30-cm-long tool. These findings show that the functional distance made available by the tool is the crucial determinant of the change in the strength of multisensory processing (Farnè *et al.*, 2005b).

But is this a real elongation of the visual–tactile integrative area along the tool axis? The metaphor of peripersonal spatial elongation to explain the changes in the strength of multisensory coding occurring at a far distance after tool use has been recently addressed by Holmes *et al.*, (2004) in normal subjects. They assessed visual–tactile congruency effects (Spence *et al.*, 2004) in three positions along a tool (handle, middle, tip) while subjects completed interleaved series of tool-use trials. Tool-use involved having the subjects use the tip, the shaft or the handle of one of the two hand-held tools to push a button located at different distances from the subject's body. Their results were more compatible with selective incorporation of the tool-tip, rather than with peri-hand space elongation encompassing the whole tool. To shed further light on this issue, we investigated a group of extinction patients in a similar study (Bonifazi *et al.*, 2007).

We found that the tool-use-dependent increase in visual–tactile extinction was present both at the middle and distal location along the tool axis, whereas no change intervened at the hand proximity. These findings support the view that the tool-use dependent re-mapping of multisensory space in humans may affect the entire functional distance between the hand and the tool tip.

Summing up, using a tool to retrieve distant objects increases the strength of visual–tactile integrative effects in a region of space far from the patients' body. Such a transient size-change of peri-hand multisensory space has been ascribed to a change in the multisensory integrative strength that is strictly tool-use dependent and associated with the functional metric of the used tool (Farnè *et al.*, 2005b).

Tactile extinction in the normal brain

"Because the pattern ... was so consistent it was reasoned that similar patterns in function might also be found in the normal subject, provided the necessary conditions for testing were introduced"

Morris B. Bender, *Disorders in Perception* (1952)

As described in the previous sections, the pathological model of extinction has deeply contributed to the understanding of how the human brain represents near peripersonal space, as well as the plastic properties of such a multisensory coding that emerge following tool-use. Nonetheless, a normal model of extinction might represent an even better instrument for deepening our knowledge about the clinical phenomenon of extinction itself, as well as the way in which different sensory inputs are synthesized in the human brain. By allowing more flexibility and finer control of the experimental setting, in comparison to patient studies, the investigation of extinction in neurologically healthy subjects would also provide an opportunity to investigate several fundamental questions with neurophysiological and neuroimaging techniques. For example, such studies might shed light on how, where and when competing inputs interact in the normal brain, within as well as between sensory modalities (for a review on uni- and multisensory extinction, see Brozzoli *et al.*, 2006). Although these questions can certainly be investigated in patients, and Sarri *et al.* (2006) have recently provided a valuable single-case-based contribution in this direction by using functional magnetic resonance imaging (fMRI) and functional connectivity approaches, these types of studies are better-suited for investigations with a normal population (Fink *et al.*, 2000).

In this respect, some hints of normal extinction-like phenomena have been anecdotally reported by Bender (1952) in the tactile modality. He reported that the first of a series of DSS could be missed if subjects were not informed about the body parts that could be stimulated (e.g. the hand and the face). More recent experimental investigations have confirmed the possibility of revealing some competitive effects in the visual (Duncan *et al.*, 1996; Gorea and Sagi, 2002) and in the tactile modality (Meador *et al.*, 2001; Marcel *et al.*, 2004). However, to observe extinction-like effects in normals requires the use of complex displays, discriminative tasks, or masking procedures that are clearly distinguishable from the dramatic omitting of simple-feature stimuli in extinction patients. Alternatively, repetitive or single-pulse transcranial magnetic stimulation

(TMS) needs to be applied to obtain neglect and extinction-like effects in the normal brain (Seyal *et al.*, 1995; Oliveri *et al.*, 1999; Fierro *et al.*, 2000; Hilgetag *et al.*, 2001). By creating temporary and reversible lesions of the parietal cortex using TMS, transient deficits in sensory processing can be induced in otherwise neurologically normal subjects.

TMS-induced motor-sensory extinction

In a recent study attempting to use TMS to further examine tactile perception, we found that a robust tactile extinction-like phenomenon could also be induced in neurologically normal subjects solely by stimulating the nerves and muscles of the face (i.e. not the brain). Note that TMS, especially with larger stimulating coils, produces tap-like sensations directly underneath the coil and, when applied over certain regions of the scalp, induces muscle twitches in the face, neck, and/or shoulders. All of these sensations are readily felt by the participant and may sometimes cause some discomfort. We found during the course of one study that tactile extinction of a stimulus on the hand could be induced by this TMS activation of the muscles of the face.

This tactile extinction-like effect induced by facial nerve and muscle activation from the TMS coil was most readily observed in a case in which fMRI-guided TMS was used to target the secondary somatosensory cortex (SII) in the parietal operculum. Because of the relatively ventral location of SII, attempts to stimulate SII with TMS will almost always also activate the facial nerve and/or temporalis muscle, thereby causing large-scaled twitches of the face. The tactile stimuli in these experiments were 5 ms onsets of piezoelectric stimulators that were attached to the left and right hands. In one control block in which TMS pulses were never administered, the participant detected 80% of the tactile stimuli delivered to the left hand. After localizing the fMRI-activated SII in this participant, a single TMS pulse was administered at this site in one of the experimental blocks 150 ms after the tactile stimulus. When TMS was applied over the right SII at 110% of motor threshold, detection of these same unilateral left tactile stimuli dropped to 25%.

While at first this effect on tactile processing seemed like a direct effect of SII disruption, further sessions with TMS only affecting the facial nerve and muscles or with ipsilateral tactile stimulation proved otherwise. In one session with TMS intensities too low to simulate cortex but high enough to activate the facial nerve/temporalis muscle, detection of the same tactile stimulus delivered to the left hand dropped from 70% in the interleaved no TMS trials to 7.5% when the facial nerve was stimulated. Furthermore, TMS over the right SII at 110% motor threshold decreased tactile detection on the ipsilateral right hand from 45 to 10%. Thus, these results demonstrate a large effect on tactile detection from activation of muscles in the face, nicely paralleling the face–hand tactile extinction previously documented following recovery from peripheral hand deafferentation (Farnè *et al.*, 2002). In addition to replicating tactile extinction in normal participants under a vastly different set of conditions, these results illustrate some of the difficulties associated with, and considerations necessary for, conducting TMS studies of tactile perception. The use of control sites and different timings for TMS, as well as the delivery of tactile stimulation to different body parts, are essential for disentangling any cortical influences of TMS on tactile perception from the somatosensory artifacts produced by the technique.

Behavioral approach to tactile extinction

Recently we investigated neurologically healthy subjects with the twofold aim of (1) testing whether extinction-like phenomena exist for the tactile modality in healthy participants, and (2) verifying whether such a phenomenon would show some of the basic features of pathological extinction, thereby providing a normal model of this clinical deficit. In particular, the question we addressed was whether normal performance of the somatosensory perceptual system may be intrinsically limited when there is competition between simultaneous bilateral stimuli. In other words, tactile extinction-like symptoms may be a consequence of a normal physiological limit of the human's brain-processing abilities. Moreover, since our final aim was to provide a normal model of clinical extinction, we attempted to obtain extinction-like phenomena under testing circumstances that were the closest as possible to those routinely employed in the neurological testing of brain-damaged patients.

To this end, a group of neurologically healthy subjects underwent a standard assessment of tactile extinction whereby they were required to say "left", "right", "both", or "none", as fast as possible according to what they felt. The task simply required the localizing and reporting of single or double touches delivered to either hand alone, or to both hands simultaneously. Moreover, since some aspects of tactile perception have been shown to be modulated by the spatial separation between the hands, such as the discrimination of bilateral hand-vibrating stimuli (Driver and Grossenbacher, 1996), the distance between the hands was varied using two different postures to assess for distance-dependent modulations of any tactile extinction-like effect.

Subjects

Fifteen neurologically healthy subjects (eight females, seven males, mean age 26 years, age range 20–37 years) participated in this study, which was approved by the local ethics committee, after giving informed consent. All subjects were right-handed and had normal or corrected-to-normal vision and normal touch perception by self-report.

Material and apparatus

Participants were seated in a dimly illuminated, sound-attenuated room with their arms stretched out on a tabletop in front of them. Vision of their hands and forearms was impeded by a wooden panel (30 cm high × 60 cm long) that was placed in front of them and mounted on a wooden box that was positioned over the subject's arms. A central fixation cross was marked on the panel. Inside the box, the volar surface of the subjects' forearms faced upwards, with the wrist and hand resting on anatomically shaped foam supports (14 cm long). The hands were positioned such that each palm was oriented upwards and medially towards the fixation point. The position of the foam supports was adjusted for each subject to maintain a distance between the index fingers of either 7 or 90 cm (see conditions below); the two foam supports were placed symmetrically with respect to the subject's midline. A black fabric stretched from the proximal edge of the wooden box up to the subject's shoulders to cover subject's arms completely.

Tactile stimuli consisted of brief electro-tactile stimulations (100 μs duration) delivered on the distal phalanxes of the index finger of either or both hands via four self-adhesive disposable electrodes (Neuroline 700-K, Ambu). The electrodes were connected to two separate constant current stimulators (DS7A, Digitimer Ltd, UK), which were controlled via PC using Xgen software (.887 version, by C. Rorden). The onset of the subject's verbal response was detected by a microphone via a voice-key detector, which was connected to the same PC controlling the stimulus sequence. Response accuracy and latency were recorded.

Procedure

Before the experimental investigation, participants were familiarized with the task in a preliminary session, where tactile stimulation intensity was titrated for each subject according to a behaviorally defined criterion. Specifically, the current intensity was progressively increased until each subject was able to verbally report approximately 90% of single stimulations in a block of randomized trials constituted by 10 single left, 10 single right, and 10 double simultaneous stimulations. If the subject's performance on single stimulus trials was too high or too low, the current intensity was adjusted accordingly and the entire block was repeated. Once this intensity had been established, the experimental session followed. On each trial, an auditory cue (50 ms duration, 1500 Hz, 60 dB SPL, as measured at the subject's head position) was emitted by a loudspeaker located centrally in front of the subject and preceded the electro-tactile stimulation by 500 ms. Tactile stimuli could be either single (left or right) or double simultaneous pulses. Each experimental block consisted of 50 randomized trials: 10 single left, 10 single right, 20 double simultaneous stimulations, and 10 catch trials. The order of presentation within a block was randomized. Subjects were instructed to maintain central fixation and the experimenter checked compliance with the instructions. To assess for possible distance-dependent modulations of tactile perception, subjects underwent the same task in two different blocks whereby the distance between the hands was varied (Near = 7 cm, Far = 90 cm).

Results

The mean accuracy rates for detecting left, right, both or no stimulation was calculated for each subject. Participants' made very few errors on the catch trials (5% of errors). The mean accuracy rate for each participant was submitted to a two-way analysis of variance (ANOVA) with Distance (Near, Far) and Stimulus Type (Left, Right, Both) as within-subject factors, and revealed a highly significant effect of Stimulus Type [$F(2,28) = 23,5; p < 0.00001$)]. *Post hoc* comparisons confirmed that subjects were comparably accurate when reporting stimuli singly delivered to either the left or the right hand (91 and 92% of detection accuracy, respectively). However, accuracy was significantly lower for the double hand simultaneous stimulation conditions as compared to either single hand stimulation condition; participants were able to correctly report only 78% of the DSS trials (see Figure 9.1). Such a drop in accuracy in DSS versus SS was present irrespective of whether the subjects' hands were close together, or far apart, as confirmed by the lack of a significant difference for the main effect of Distance. The interaction between these factors was also not significant.

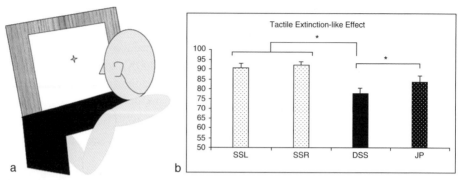

Figure 9.1 (a) Schematic of the experimental apparatus used in both experiments. **(b)** Mean percentage accuracy in reporting single stimulations to the left (SSL) and right (SSR) hand, double simultaneous (DSS), as well as the joint probability (JP). Asterisks indicate significant differences (see text for details).

The subjects' performance in single stimulation conditions was highly consistent across subjects, at ~91% correct. This was expected based on the titration procedure that immediately preceded the experimental testing. This performance level indicates that the electro-tactile stimuli, although clearly supra-threshold, were not strong enough to produce ceiling effects. To test whether the significant drop in DSS performance genuinely reflected an extinction-like phenomenon, and not the mere differential probability related to the detection of two stimuli versus one, we calculated for each subject the joint probability for correctly perceiving DSS on the basis of his/her probability of detecting SS. The joint probability (JP) was then contrasted using one-tailed t-tests with the actual performance of the same subject on DSS. This comparison confirmed the presence of an extinction-like phenomenon, in that performance was significantly less accurate both in the Near (76%, $p < 0.02$) and in the Far (80%, $p < 0.03$) conditions.

The mean correct response times (RT) were also calculated for each subject and submitted to a similar two-way ANOVA (with the same factors). The main effect of Distance was marginally significant [$F(1,14) = 4,4; p = 0.055$)], due to a tendency for subjects to be faster in reporting tactile stimuli when the hands were far apart (640 ms) as compared to when they were closer in space (665 ms). The analysis also revealed a significant effect of Stimulus Type that was due to the use of the different verbal labels used to respond rather than the extinction effect. The interaction between these factors was not significant.

Further, a laterality index {[(R − L)/(R + L)]} was calculated on the incorrect DSS trials for each subject to assess whether any bias was present when a subject failed to correctly perceive the presence of two simultaneous stimulations. t-Tests against zero were not significant for either condition [Near: $t(13) = 0,3; p = 0.7$; Far: $t(13) = 1,4; p = 0.2$]. A one-way ANOVA on this index, with Distance (Near, Far) as within-subject factor, also did not reveal any significant difference.

Discussion: tactile extinction in the normal brain

These results are the first formal demonstration of the presence of a tactile extinction-like phenomenon in neurologically healthy subjects. They reveal a significant and consistent lowering in performance that is selective for DSS. Despite accurate and comparable performance in single right and left stimulation conditions, performance in DSS was lower in accuracy, by about 14% on average. After correcting for the differential probability of detecting two versus one stimulus, the healthy subjects' accuracy was still significantly lower on the DSS trials, by about 6% on average, such that the single versus double pattern replicated the typical clinical extinction patients' behavior.

Moreover, the significant reduction of DSS accuracy was obtained by using a task that was in many ways similar to the confrontation method that is typically employed for assessing brain-damaged patients. The main differences were that (1) stimulus intensity was behaviorally defined to be comparable between the hands and, although not at ceiling, supra-threshold, and (2) speeded responses were required. With respect to the former difference, extinction patients should, by definition, present with well-preserved unilateral somatosensory perception on the affected hand, and, of course, normal tactile capability on the nonaffected hand. However, tactile stimuli of equal intensity would almost invariably be subjectively perceived as being different. When attempts have been made to equate for this difference, the extinction pattern has been reported to change considerably, at least in the visual domain (Geeraerts et al., 2005). We are currently investigating whether differences in the behaviorally defined intensity would produce any spatial bias in the extinction-like pattern of normal participants (see Meador et al., 1998; Gorea and Sagi, 2002). Concerning the second difference, preliminary findings from our laboratory suggest that the extinction-like phenomenon might not depend upon time-pressure, a similar pattern of results being observed when speeded responses are not required.

However, when considering the latency of speeded responses, subjects tended to be slower in reporting touches in the Near as compared to the Far condition. This effect, although marginally significant, is in agreement with behavioral and electrophysiological findings showing that the perception of touch is consistently modulated by the physical distance separating the hands (Driver and Grossenbacher, 1996; Eimer et al., 2002; Haggard et al., 2006). Since hand separation did not interact with the type of stimulus (SS or DSS), this tendency might reflect a basic aspect of tactile perception, suggesting that not only high-order (Aglioti et al., 1999), but also relatively low-level aspects of tactile perception may be modulated by body-parts posture in non-somatotopic coordinates.

Interestingly, no spatial bias was present on extinguished trials when considering the error distribution; subjects were equally likely to extinguish the left or the right touch. In the light of our proposed model of normal tactile extinction, this finding was expected on the basis of results coming from the visual modality. In particular, the lack of spatial bias is consistent with the few former instances of visual extinction-like effects in normals (Duncan et al., 1996; Fink et al., 2000; Peers et al., 2005) and could in principle be readily attributed to the lack of a hemispheric lesion. The predicted absence of any spatial bias may be the most important qualitative difference between normal and clinical extinction, suggesting that clinical extinction may be a pathological exacerbation of a normal limit of the tactile perceptual system.

Multisensory effects on tactile extinction in the normal brain

Now that a normal model of tactile extinction has been established, we can assess whether the somatosensory perceptual system can be modulated by inputs coming from different sensory modalities. This would validate the model not only as a replica of the pathological deficit in the healthy subject, but also as a useful tool to further investigate multisensory interactions in the normal brain. Several recent studies in our laboratory have started to address the interactions between vision, audition and touch using this extinction-like paradigm. In what follows we report a new attempt to investigate multisensory modulations within the somatosensory modality. Namely, we tested whether providing subjects with differential proprioceptive and kinesthetic information about the functional properties of an object they were grasping could affect the tactile extinction-like phenomenon. We reasoned that if proprioceptive and kinesthetic inputs are merged with touch perception, altering the former should affect the latter, as measured in terms of the tactile extinction-like phenomenon.

To test this hypothesis, a group of neurologically healthy subjects underwent a tactile extinction-like protocol similar to that described above, but under different experimental conditions. The common feature of all conditions was that each participant was tested while passively holding the same object in each hand (i.e. a portion of a real steering wheel). The main manipulation across conditions was that subjects could either grasp in each hand a portion of a solid steering wheel, or a broken version of the wheel, with single pieces kept together with strings. Note, however, that the two grasped pieces of wheel were otherwise identical (see Figure 9.2). Before the tactile extinction task, subjects were required to experience the properties of the grasped objects, and in particular how they moved when 'turning' the steering wheel with both hands for a short time interval. We hypothesized that experiencing the coherent movement properties of the solid steering wheel versus the independently moving properties of the broken steering wheel might differentially affect tactile extinction.

In particular, two possible outcomes could be expected. The (previously jointly moved) solid wheel might act as a tactile grouping factor, as compared to the (previously independently moved) broken wheel, which might yield weaker tactile extinction (Ward et al., 1994). In contrast, proprioceptive–kinesthetic inputs derived from moving the solid or broken wheel might not merge with touch, or our normal model of tactile extinction might be not sensitive enough to reveal any difference, yielding comparable tactile extinction levels across the two conditions.

Further, to test the possible influence of task-irrelevant visual information about the wheel on this tactile extinction-like phenomenon, in separate conditions the subjects could see life-sized images of the solid (or broken) wheel while grasping the solid (congruent visual and somatosensory condition) or the broken (incongruent condition) wheel (see Figure 9.3). On the basis of our previous studies on the effect of seeing or not

Figure 9.2 The solid (upper panel) and broken (lower panel) steering wheel on their own supports, as they were located behind the apparatus depicted in Figure 9.1a. Note that the solid wheel could only be rotated whereas the broken wheel pieces were independently fixed with strings that allowed each to be moved independently.

seeing the hands on multisensory processing in extinction patients (Ladavas *et al.*, 2000), as well as several findings showing the profound effects of task-irrelevant vision of the stimulated body part on touch perception (Press *et al.*, 2004; Ro *et al.*, 2004; Fiorio and Haggard, 2005; Johnson *et al.*, 2006) it was expected that adding congruent or incongruent visual information could further modulate the tactile extinction-like phenomenon.

Subjects

Eighteen neurologically healthy subjects (nine males and nine females, mean age 23 years, range 20–27 years) participated in this study, approved by the local ethics committee, after giving informed consent. All subjects were right-handed and had normal or corrected-to-normal vision and touch perception by self-report.

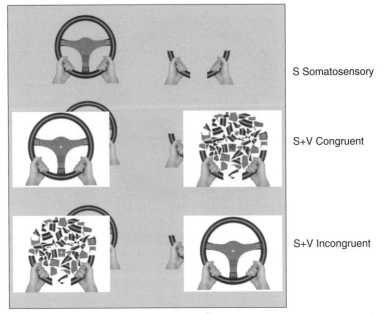

S Somatosensory

S+V Congruent

S+V Incongruent

Figure 9.3 Schematic representation of the six experimental conditions. Each type of wheel that was grasped by the subject (Solid on the left column, Broken on the right column) could be presented alone (Somatosensory, S), or with additional visual information (S+V) that could be either congruent or incongruent.

Material and apparatus

The setup and procedures were the same as that described in the previous experiment, except for the following. The position of the foam supports was adjusted for each subject to maintain a distance of 20 cm between their index fingers; the foam supports were symmetrically located with respect to their midline. The objects were two identical sport-car steering wheels (33 cm diameter; 9 cm section circumference). One wheel was kept functional, while the second one was sawed to obtain two identical portions of the same wheel (corresponding to the portion grasped by each hand), so that contact surface and texture were identical for each hand while passively grasping the solid or the broken wheel. Both were attached to a wooden support, at the same height from the table-top. While the solid wheel could rotate on its axis, the separate portions of the broken wheel were fixed separately, at the same distance and slope of the solid wheel, so that they could be moved independently (see Figure 9.2).

Task-irrelevant visual images of a (solid or broken) wheel (grasped by hands) could be added on the panel in front of the subject (see Figure 9.2, upper panel) in separate counterbalanced conditions that could be congruent or incongruent with the wheel actually grasped by the subject. Visual images were two high-definition, digitally edited pictures printed on A3 paper format (Figure 9.3), each depicting the central fixation point (yellow cross) that was also marked on a white A3 page in the condition whereby no visual information was added.

Procedure

Subjects were asked to experience the moving properties of the grasped object(s) by moving both hands for about 30 s before the beginning of each block of trials. Foam supports were then positioned by the experimenter so that the subject's hand gently and passively grasped the respective portion of either the solid or broken wheel. In this passive upward posture, the distal phalanxes of the index fingers, where the electrodes were located to deliver the tactile stimulation, were not in contact with the wheel. Subjects were instructed to maintain central fixation, to refrain from moving the hands and to report verbally what they felt, as described in the previous experiment. Tactile extinction-like effects were separately assessed for each grasping situation (solid versus broken) in three sensory contexts: somatosensory only (S), congruent somatosensory and vision (CSV), and incongruent somatosensory and vision (ISV), for a total of six separate blocks (three sensory contexts × two wheel characteristics) (Figure 9.3). The order of blocks was counterbalanced across subjects and, as in the previous experiment, each block contained 50 trials (10 left, 10 right SS, 20 DSS and 10 CT).

Results

Participants made almost no false alarms throughout the experiment. The mean percentage accuracy in reporting single and double stimulations was calculated for each subject and submitted to a three-way ANOVA with Wheel (Solid, Broken), Sensory Condition (S, CSV, ISV) and Stimulus Type (SS, DSS) as within-subject factors. The Wheel × Stimulus Type interaction was significant [$F(1,17) = 7,6$; $p < 0.02$]. *Post hoc* comparisons confirmed that subjects were comparably accurate when reporting singly delivered stimuli (SS = 89% of detection accuracy both in the solid and broken wheel condition). However, their performance when reporting bilateral simultaneous stimulations differed as a function of the wheel they were holding. As can be seen in Figure 9.4, subjects' accuracy in the solid wheel condition was markedly lower (67% correct detection) as compared to that obtained in the broken wheel condition (76% correct detection).

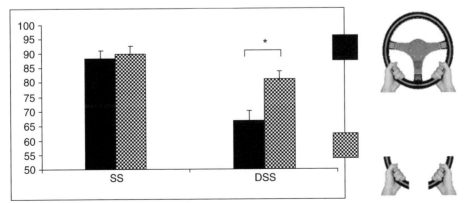

Figure 9.4 Mean percentage accuracy in reporting single (SS, left and right hand collapsed) and double simultaneous stimulations (DSS), as a function of the grasped wheel.

Such a selective drop in accuracy for DSS with the solid versus the broken wheel was present irrespective of whether the subjects were or were not additionally provided with visual contextual information. Indeed, the Wheel × Sensory Condition × Stimulus Type interaction was not significant.

To estimate whether any spatial bias was present when subjects failed to correctly perceive the presence of two simultaneous stimulations, a laterality index $\{[(R-L)/(R+L)]\}$ was calculated on the incorrect DSS trials for each subject in each condition. As in the previous experiment, the laterality index did not reveal any significant difference. t-Tests were not significantly different for either of the two wheel conditions [Solid: $t(17) = 0,3$; $p = 0.9$; Broken: $t(17) = 1,2$; $p = 0.3$]. A one-way ANOVA on this index, with Wheel (Solid, Broken) as the within-subject factor, did not reveal any significant difference.

Discussion: multisensory effects on normal tactile extinction

Two main findings emerged from this study. First, the tactile extinction-like aspect of subjects' tactile perception was selectively modulated by the type of preceding experience they had in manipulating the grasped objects. Second, this modulation did not introduce any bias in the subjects' response.

Critically, the former finding provides strong evidence supporting our proposal that the normal model of tactile extinction that has been presented and tested in the previous experiment can be used efficiently to investigate how the normal brain integrates multisensory inputs. The selective modulation of tactile perception under the two different DSS conditions is clearly in favor of our hypothesis that proprioceptive–kinesthetic inputs do affect tactile perception. In addition, it reveals that this occurs at a relatively high level of the tactile processing, because only accuracy in the DSS conditions was modified. Indeed, it is noteworthy that subjects' accuracy was equivalent when their hands were singly touched while grasping a piece of a solid or broken wheel. The latter finding also rules out any possible explanation of the increase in extinction due to a differential sensorimotor gating effect between the solid and the broken wheel. Moreover, these findings suggest that the proprioceptively induced modulation of the tactile extinction-like effect was relatively long-lasting, as subjects briefly experienced the functional properties of the wheel (solid or broken) only before starting each block (see Ro et al., 2004, for results demonstrating long-lasting effects of visual experience on touch perception).

Contrary to what was expected on the basis of the grouping hypothesis, however, the modulation of tactile extinction was manifest as a significant worsening of the subjects' performance rather than the improvement predicted based on the literature (Mattingley et al., 1997). Two alternative accounts of this unexpected result can be considered. First, it is possible that experiencing the moving properties of the solid wheel did actually produce a grouping phenomenon, but that this induced opposite effects in touch as compared to vision. In the somatosensory domain it is possible that grouping hands in a whole makes two simultaneously delivered touches less distinguishable (i.e. reduces 'two-ness'), thus increasing the tactile extinction-like effect. To the best of our knowledge, no grouping effect has been reported thus far in the tactile modality; therefore this possibility needs to be empirically addressed. Second, it is possible that two-ness was reduced by shortening the spatial separation of the sources of the tactile events, as has been reported in the auditory modality (Driver, 1996); however, no significant difference was found between the Near (76% of accuracy) and the Far conditions (80% of accuracy). If physical distance in external space does not alter tactile extinction, it is alternatively possible that the functional distance between them is reduced. This is precisely what should be expected in the case of the funneling illusion, whereby subjects perceive only one of two simultaneously delivered touches (Chen *et al.*, 2003), or in the case of use-dependent tool embodiment (see 'Plastic multisensory modulations induced by tool-use' above); yet, subjects were not asked to functionally use the tool in the present case, so further studies are necessary to disambiguate these alternatives. Concerning the second finding (i.e. that no spatial bias was introduced by the worsening of the tactile extinction effect), this confirms and extends the results reported in the previous study, and indicates that the lack of response bias is a stable feature of the tactile extinction-like effect. Indeed, response biases were absent even when subjects were grasping objects, showing a resistance to the addition of the static tactile stimulation provided by passive contact with the two wheel portions (Kakigi *et al.*, 1996).

Overall, the critical finding is that tactile extinction-like effects were selectively modulated by the proprioceptive and kinesthetic inputs, thus validating the proposed model as a suitable way to investigate multisensory interactions in the normal brain.

Conclusions and implications for clinical extinction

From both the patient and healthy subject investigations presented here, it should be apparent that the study of a relatively simple pathological sign, such as extinction, is useful for understanding the functional organization of normal brain processes. In particular, we provided evidence that studying cross-modal extinction can shed light into the functioning of multisensory brain mechanisms coding near peripersonal space in humans. The plastic properties of such mechanisms have also been inferred from this altered perceptual behaviour in neurological patients, allowing for a documentation of the transient multisensory effects produced by using functionally effective tools that widen the space made reachable by the hand. Moreover, the newly reported findings demonstrate that clinical tactile extinction might be a pathological exaggeration of a physiologically limited capacity of the somatosensory system, which limits multiple simultaneous stimuli from accessing awareness.

This finding has potential implications for the interpretation of clinical tactile extinction. Extinction is considered to be an attentional competition problem, as unilateral contralesional somatosensory processing is often largely spared, and when affected, does not explain the selectivity of the deficit following DSS; moreover, orienting patients' attention contralesionally reduces extinction severity. However, the presence of subtle sensory dysfunctions has been recently consistently reported in visual, tactile, and auditory studies of neglect and extinction (for review, see Brozzoli *et al.*, 2006). In a single RBD patient study, for example, the somatosensory neural activity recorded via ERP in the right hemisphere was reduced in amplitude when compared to the one elicited by right-hand stimulation on the left hemisphere (Eimer *et al.*, 2002). This suggests that, although tactile extinction is not a pure sensory deficit, there nonetheless may be an underlying pathology for the processing of contralesional unilateral stimuli. This is in agreement with what has been observed for visual extinction, whereby the early components of visual processing may be abnormal for contralesional stimuli (Remy *et al.*, 1999; Marzi *et al.*, 2000). Although still unclear, the role possibly played by early sensory deficits can no longer be excluded, as degradation or slowing of sensory inputs may contribute to the difficulty in perceiving contralesional events. In this respect, a recent study by Peers *et al.* (2005) has made clear that, quite paradoxically, the lesion volume regardless of lesion location is actually correlated with the presence and severity of the spatial response bias typical of neglect and extinction patients. In light of this latter finding and the existence of non-lateralized tactile extinction-like phenomena in the normal brain, it is possible to suggest that the hemispheric lesion is what makes clinical extinction qualitatively different from extinction in healthy subjects. Moreover, fronto-parietal and subcortical lesions, most frequently associated with extinction (Vallar *et al.*, 1994), reduce attentional resources. Therefore, a combination of a non-lateralized physiological limit (as described here), a lesion-induced spatial bias and reduced attentional capacity might be at the origin of pathological tactile extinction, n hypothesis currently under investigation in our laboratory using TMS.

Finally, the tactile extinction-like phenomenon has been shown to be selectively modulated by providing differential proprioceptive–kinesthetic input concerning the dynamic properties of an object. We think that these findings, by validating the normal model of tactile extinction, will open new perspectives for investigating the pervasive aspects of multisensory processing of human spatial cognition and their neurophysiological bases.

Acknowledgments

We thank all who consented to participate in our studies. We thank F. Frassinetti, N. Holmes, F. Pavani, Y. Rossetti and A. C. Roy for stimulating and insightful discussions, R. Salemme for engineering solutions and N. Laverdure for helping in data collection. We also thank C. Rorden for making his Xgen software freely available. This work was funded by MIUR (E.L., A.F.), the AVENIR grant #R05265CS (A.F., T.R.), and the European Mobility Fellowship (C.B.).

References

Aglioti, S., Smania, N. and Peru, A. (1999) Frames of reference for mapping tactile stimuli in brain-damage patients. *Journal of Cognitive Neuroscience*, 11, 67–79.

Beck, B. B. (1980) *Animal Tool Behavior: The Use and Manufacture of Tools by Animals*. Garland, New York.

Bellas, D. N., Novelly, R. A., Eskenazi, B. and Wasserstein, J. (1988) The nature of unilateral neglect in the olfactory sensory system, *Neuropsychologia*, 26, 45–52.

Bender, M. B. (1952) *Disorders in Perception*. Charles C. Thomas, Springfield, IL.

Berti, A. and Frassinetti, F. (2000) When far becomes near: remapping of space by tool use. *Journal of Cognitive Neuroscience*, 12, 415–420.

Berti, A., Oxbury, S., Oxbury, J., Affanni, P., Umiltà, C. and Orlandi, L. (1999) Somatosensory extinction for meaningful objects in a patient with right hemispheric stroke. *Neuropsychologia*, 37, 333–343.

Bisiach, E. and Luzzatti, C. (1978) Unilateral neglect of representational space. *Cortex*, **14**, 129–133.

Bisiach, E., Perani, D., Vallar, G. and Berti, A. (1986) Unilateral neglect: personal and extra-personal. *Neuropsychologia*, **24**, 759–767.

Bonifazi, S., Farnè, A., Rinaldesi and Ladavas, E. (2007) Dynamic size-change of peri-hand space through tool-use: spatial extension or shift of the multisensory area? *Journal of Neuropsychology*, **1**, 101–104.

Bremmer, F., Schlack, A., Shah, N. J. *et al.* (2001) Polymodal motion processing in posterior parietal and premotor cortex: a human fMRI study strongly implies equivalencies between humans and monkeys. *Neuron*, **29**, 287–296.

Brozzoli, C., Dematte, M. L., Pavani, F., Frassinetti, F. and Farne, A. (2006) Neglect and extinction: within and between sensory modalities. *Restorative Neurology and Neuroscience*, **24**, 217–232.

Calvert, G., Spence, C. and Stein, B. (eds) (2004) *The Handbook of Multisensory Processes*. MIT Press, Cambridge, MA.

Chen, L. M., Friedman, R. M. and Roe, A. W. (2003) Optical imaging of a tactile illusion in area 3b of the primary somatosensory cortex. *Science*, **302**, 881–885.

Coslett, H. B., Schwartz, M. F., Goldberg, G., Haas, D. and Perkins, J. (1993) Multi-modal hemispatial deficits after left hemisphere stroke. *Brain*, **116**, 527–554.

Critchley, M. (1949) The phenomenon of tactile inattention with special reference to parietal lesions. *Brain*, **72**, 538–561.

de Renzi, E., Gentilini, M. and Pattacini, F. (1984) Auditory extinction following hemisphere damage. *Neuropsychologia*, **22**, 733–744.

di Pellegrino, G. and De Renzi, E. (1995) An experimental investigation on the nature of extinction. *Neuropsychologia*, **33**, 153–170.

di Pellegrino, G., Làdavas, E. and Farnè, A. (1997) Seeing where your hands are. *Nature*, **338**, 730.

Driver, J. and Grossenbacher, P. G. (1996) Multimodal contraints on tactile spatial attention. In Innui, T. and McClelland, J. L. (eds), *Attention and Performance XVI*, pp. 209–236. MIT Press, Cambridge, MA.

Driver, J. and Vuilleumier, P. (2001) Perceptual awareness and its loss in unilateral neglect and extinction. *Cognition*, **79**, 39–88.

Driver, J., Mattingley, J. B., Rorden, C. and Davis, G. (1997) Extinction as a paradigm measure of attentional bias and restricted capacity following brain injury. In Thier, P. and Karnath, H. O. (eds), *Parietal Lobe Contribution to Orientation in 3D Space*, pp. 401–429. Springer-Verlag, Heidelberg.

Duhamel, J. R., Colby, C. L. and Goldberg, M. E. (1998) Ventral intraparietal area of the macaque: congruent visual and somatic response properties. *Journal of Neurophysiology*, **79**, 126–136.

Duncan, J. (1996) Coordinated brain systems in selective perception and action. In Innui, T. and McClelland, J. L. (eds), *Attention and Performance XVI*, pp. 549–578. MIT Press, Cambridge, MA.

Eimer, M., Maravita, A., Van Velzen, J., Husain, M. and Driver, J. (2002) The electrophysiology of tactile extinction: ERP correlates of unconscious somatosensory processing. *Neuropsychologia*, **40**, 2438–2447.

Farnè, A., Demattè, M. L. and Ladavas, E. (2005a) Neuropsychological evidence of modular organization of the near peripersonal space. *Neurology*, **65**, 1754–1758.

Farnè, A., Iriki, A. and Ladavas, E. (2005b) Shaping multisensory action-space with tools: evidence from patients with cross-modal extinction. *Neuropsychologia*, **43**, 238–248.

Farnè, A. and Ladavas, E. (2000) Dynamic size-change of hand peripersonal space following tool use. *Neuroreport*, **85**, 1645–1649.

Farnè, A. and Ladavas, E. (2002) Auditory peripersonal space in humans. *Journal of Cognitive Neuroscience*, **14**, 1030–1043.

Farnè, A., Serino, A. and Làdavas, E. (2007) Dynamic size-change of peri-hand space following tool-use: determinants and spatial characteristics revealed through cross-modal extinction. *Cortex*, **3**, 436–443.

Fierro, B., Brighina, F., Oliveri, M., Piazza, A., La Bua, V., Buffa, D. and Bisiach, E. (2000) Contralateral neglect induced by right posterior parietal rTMS in healthy subjects, *Neuroreport*, **11**, 1519–1521.

Fiorio, M. and Haggard, P. (2005) Viewing the body prepares the brain for touch: effects of TMS over somatosensory cortex. *European Journal of Neuroscience*, **22**, 773–777.

Fogassi, L., Gallese, V., Fadiga, L., Luppino, G., Matelli, M. and Rizzolatti, G. (1996) Coding of peripersonal space in inferior premotor cortex (area F4). *Journal of Neurophysiology*, **76**,141–157.

Gainotti, G., De Bonis, C., Daniele, A. and Caltagirone, C. (1989) Contralateral and ipsilateral tactile extinction in patients with right and left focal brain damage. *International Journal of Neuroscience*, **45**, 81–89.

Geeraerts, S., Michiels, K., Lafosse, C., Vandenbussche, E. and Verfaillie, K. (2005) The relationship of visual extinction to luminance-contrast imbalances between left and right hemifield stimuli. *Neuropsychologia*, **43**, 542–553.

Gorea, A. and Sagi, D. (2002) Natural extinction: a criterion shift phenomenon. *Visual Cognition*, **9**, 913–936.

Graziano, M. S. A. and Gross, C. G. (1995) The representation of extrapersonal space: a possible role for bimodal, visuo-tactile neurons. In Gazzaniga, M. S. (ed.), *Cognitive Neuroscience*, pp. 1021–1034. MIT Press, Cambridge.

Halligan, P. W. and Marshall, J. C. (1991) Left neglect for near but not far space in man. *Nature*, **350**, 498–500.

Halligan, P. W., Fink, G. R., Marshall, J. C., Vallar, G. (2003) Spatial cognition: evidence from visual neglect. *Trends In Cognitive Science*, **7**, 125–133.

Head, H. and Holmes, H. G. (1911–1912) Sensory disturbances from cerebral lesions. *Brain*, **34**, 102–254.

Hilgetag, C. C., Théoret, H. and Pascual-Leone, A. (2001) Enhanced visual spatial attention ipsilateral to rTMS-induced 'virtual lesions' of human parietal cortex. *Nature Neuroscience*, **4**, 953–957.

Holmes, N. P., Calvert, G. A. and Spence, C. (2004) Extending or projecting space with tools? Multisensory interactions highlight only the distal and proximal ends of tools. *Neuroscience Letters*, **372**, 62–67.

Humphreys, G. W., Riddoch, M. J., Forti, S. and Ackroyd, K. (2004) Action influences spatial perception: neuropsychological evidence. *Visual Cognition*, **11**, 401–427.

Iriki, A., Tanaka, M. and Iwamura, Y. (1996) Coding of modified body schema during tool use by macaque postcentral neurones, *Neuroreport*, **7**, 2325–2330.

Johnson, R., Burton, P. and Ro, T. (2006) Visually induced feelings of touch. *Brain Research,* **1073–4**, 398–406.

Johnson-Frey, S. H. (2003) What's so special about human tool use? *Neuron*, **39**, 201–204.

Kakigi, R., Koyama, S., Hoshiyama, M., Kitamura, Y., Shimojo, M., Watanabe, S. and Nakamura, A. (1996) Effects of a tactile interference stimulation on somatosensory evoked magnetic fields. *Neuroreport*, **7**, 405–408.

Ladavas, E. (2002) Functional and dynamic properties of visual peripersonal space in humans. *Trends in Cognitive Science*, **6**, 17–22.

Ladavas, E. and Farnè, A. (2004) Neuropsychological evidence on integrated multisensory representation of space in humans. In Calvert, G., Spence, C. and Stein, B. (eds), *The Handbook of Multisensory Processes*, pp. 799–818. MIT Press, Cambridge, MA.

Ladavas, E., di Pellegrino, G., Farnè, A. and Zeloni, G. (1998a) Neuropsychological evidence of an integrated visuo-tactile representation of peripersonal space in humans. *Journal of Cognitive Neuroscience*, **10**, 581–589.

Ladavas, E., Zeloni, G. and Farne, A. (1998b) Visual peripersonal space centred on the face in humans. *Brain*, **121**, 2317–2326.

Ladavas, E., Farne, A., Zeloni, G. and di Pellegrino, G. (2000) Seeing or not seeing where your hands are. *Experimental Brain Research*, **131**, 458–467.

Ladavas, E., Pavani, F. and Farnè, A. (2001) Feel the noise! A case of auditory-tactile extinction. *Neurocase*, 7, 97–103.

Maravita, A. and Iriki, A. (2004) Tools for the body (schema). *Trends in Cognitive Sciences*, 8, 79–85.

Maravita, A., Husain, M., Clarke, K. and Driver, J. (2001) Reaching with the tool extends visual-tactile interactions into far space: evidence from cross-modal extinction. *Neuropsychologia*, 39, 580–585.

Maravita, A., Spence, C., Kennett, S. and Driver, J. (2002a) Tool-use changes multimodal spatial interactions between vision and touch in normal humans. *Cognition*, 8, B25–B34.

Maravita, A., Clarke, K., Husain, M. and Driver, J. (2002b) Active tool use with the contralesional hand can reduce cross-modal extinction of touch on that hand. *Neurocase*, 8, 411–416.

Marcel, A., Postma, P., Gillmeister, H., Cox, S., Rorden, C., Nimmo-Smith, I. and Mackintosh, B. (2004) Migration and fusion of tactile sensation—premorbid susceptibility to allochiria, neglect and extinction? *Neuropsychologia*, 42, 1749–1767.

Marzi, C. A., Girelli, M., Miniussi, C., Smania, N. and Maravita, A. (2000) Elecrophysiological correlates of conscious vision: evidence from unilateral extinction. *Journal of Cognitive Neuroscience*, 12, 869–877.

Mattingley, J. B., Driver, J., Beschin, N. and Robertson, I. H. (1997) Attentional competition between modalities: extinction between touch and vision after right hemisphere damage. *Neuropsychologia*, 35, 867–880.

Meador, K. J., Ray, P. G., Day, L., Ghelani, H. and Loring, D. W. (1998) Physiology of somatosensory perception: cerebral lateralization and extinction. *Neurology*, 51, 721–727.

Meador, K. J., Ray, P. G., Day, L. J. and Loring, D. W. (2001) Relationship of extinction to perceptual thresholds for single stimuli. *Neurology*, 56, 1044–1047.

Napier, J. R. (1956) The prehensile movements of the human hand. *Journal of Bone and Joint Surgery*, 38, 902–913.

Oliveri, M., Rossini, P. M., Traversa, R., Cicinelli, P., Filippi, M. M., Pasqualetti, P., Tomaiuolo, F. and Caltagirone, C. (1999) Left frontal transcranial magnetic stimulation reduces contralesional extinction in patients with unilateral right brain damage. *Brain*, 122, 1731–1739.

Peers, P.V., Ludwig C.J., Rorden, C., Cusack, R., Bonfiglioli, C., Bundesen, C., Driver, J., Antoun, N. and Duncan J. (2005) Attentional functions of parietal and frontal cortex. *Cereb Cortex*, 15, 1469–84

Press, C., Taylor-Clarke, M., Kennett, S. and Haggard, P. (2004) Visual enhancement of touch in spatial body representation. *Experimental Brain Research*, 154, 238–245.

Rafal, R. D. (2000) Neglect II: Cognitive neuropsychological issues. In Martha, E., Farah, J., Todd E., Feinberg, E. *et al.* (eds), *Patient-Based Approaches to Cognitive Neuroscience*, pp. 125–141. MIT Press, Cambridge, MA.

Remy, P., Zilbovicius, M., Degos, J. D., Bachoud-Levy, A. C., Rancurel, G., Cesaro, P. and Samson, Y. (1999) Somatosensory cortical activations are suppressed in patients with tactile extinction: a PET study. *Neurology*, 52, 571–577.

Riggio, L., Gawryszewski, L. D. G. and Umiltà, C. (1986) What is crossed in crossed-hand effects? *Acta Psychologica*, 62, 89–100.

Rizzolatti, G., Scandolara, C., Matelli, M. and Gentilucci, M. (1981) Afferent properties of periarcuate neurons in macaque monkeys. II. Visual responses. *Behavioural Brain Research*, 2, 147–163.

Rizzolatti, G., Matelli, M. and Pavesi, G. (1983) Deficits in attention and movement following the removal of postarcuate (area 6) and prearcuate (area 8) cortex in macaque monkeys. *Brain*, 106, 655–673.

Rizzolatti, G., Fadiga, L., Fogassi, L. and Gallese, V. (1997) The space around us. *Science*, 277, 190–191.

Rizzolatti, G., Fogassi, L. and Gallese, V. (2002) Motor and cognitive functions of the ventral premotor cortex. *Current Opinion in Neurobiology*, 12, 149–154.

Ro, T., Wallace, R., Hagedorn, J., Farnè, A. and Pienkos, E. (2004) Visual enhancing of tactile perception in the posterior parietal cortex. *Journal of Cognitive Neuroscience*, 16, 24–30.

Seyal, M., Ro, T. and Rafal, R. (1995) Increased sensitivity to ipsilateral cutaneous stimuli following transcranial magnetic stimulation of the parietal lobe. *Annals of Neurology*, **38**, 264–267.

Spence, C. and Driver, J. (eds) (2004) *Crossmodal Space and Crossmodal Attention*. Oxford University Press, Oxford.

Spence, C., Pavani, F. and Driver, J. (2004) Spatial constraints on visual-tactile cross-modal distractor congruency effects. *Cognitive Affective and Behavioral Neuroscience*, **4**, 148–169.

Vallar, G., Rusconi, M. L., Bignamini, L., Geminiani, G. and Perani, D. (1994) Anatomical correlates of visual and tactile extinction in humans: a clinical CT scan study. *Journal of Neurology, Neurosurgery and Psychiatry*, **57**, 464–470.

Vuilleumier, P., Valenza, N., Mayer, E., Reverdin, A. and Landis, T. (1998) Near and far visual space in unilateral neglect. *Annals of Neurology*, **43**, 406–410.

Ward, R., Goodrich, S. and Driver, J. (1994) Grouping reduces visual extinction: neuropsychological evidence for weight-linkage in visual selection. *Visual Cognition*, **1**, 101–129.

Yamamoto, S. and Kitazawa, S. (2001) Sensation at the tips of invisible tools. *Nature Neuroscience*, **4**, 979–980.

10

Bottom-up visuo-manual adaptation: consequences for spatial cognition

Gilles Rode, Jacques Luauté, Thomas Klos, Sophie Courtois-Jacquin, Patrice Revol, Laure Pisella, Nicholas P. Holmes, D. Boisson and Yves Rossetti

A large proportion of right-hemisphere stroke patients exhibit unilateral neglect, a neurological condition characterized by deficits for perceiving, attending, representing, and/or performing actions within their left-sided space. Unilateral neglect is responsible for many debilitating effects on everyday life, for poor functional recovery, and for decreased ability to benefit from treatment. Prism adaptation (PA) to a right lateral displacement of the visual field (induced by a simple target-pointing task with base-left wedge prisms) is known to directionally bias visuo-motor and sensorimotor correspondences and has recently been found to improve various symptoms of neglect. For example, performance on classical pen-and-pencil visuo-motor tests could be improved for at least 2 h after adaptation. Effects of PA have also been described for nonmotor and nonvisual tasks, such as for somatosensory extinction, for deficits in mental imagery of geographic maps and in number bisection, and even for visuo-constructive disorders. These cognitive effects are been shown to result from indirect bottom-up effects of the adaptive realignment component of the reaction to prisms. Lesion studies and functional imaging data point to a cerebello-cortical network in which each structure plays a specific role, though not necessarily one that is crucial for adaptation. The variety of cognitive effects induced by PA suggests that this treatment acts not only specifically on the ipsilesional bias characteristic of unilateral neglect, but also rehabilitates more generally the visuo-spatial functions attributed to the right hemisphere. One could speculate that PA permits an enlargement of the visual-motor mapping of space. These results further support the idea that PA may activate brain functions related not only to multisensory integration, but to higher spatial representations as well, and hence may produce a generalization at a functional level. PA therefore appears as a powerful new therapeutic tool for spatial cognition disorders, producing central effects via a bottom-up activation process.

Neglect, a spatial cognition disorder

A behavioral disorder

Unilateral neglect is defined as the patient's failure to report, respond to, or orient toward novel and/or meaningful stimuli presented to the side opposite to the brain lesion

(Brain, 1941; Heilman *et al.*, 1985). This condition is most frequently found in right-brain-damaged patients, often in association with contralesional hemiplegia, hemianesthesia, and hemianopia. Neglect thus constitutes a space-oriented behavioral disorder with an ispilesional bias, typically toward the right side. The subject with neglect spontaneously displays a tonic ocular and cephalic deviation towards the right side. This behavioral bias will also be evidenced in many clinical tests, such as in bisecting a line (Schenkenberg *et al.*, 1980), searching for an object, or pointing to a straight-ahead position in darkness (Jeannerod and Biguer, 1987). The core phenomenon of neglect is that this behavioral ipsilesional bias is associated with unawareness of contralesional space (Bisiach, 1999; Kerkhoff, 2001; Halligan *et al.*, 2003). The subject with neglect is thus unable to compensate his or her illness by a voluntary orientation of attention—a situation quite unlike the patient with hemianopia who can nevertheless orient his or her gaze toward the blind hemi-field.

A spatial deficit

The deficit can be centered on the body axis, i.e. with respect to an egocentric reference frame and/or on external objects, according to an allocentric reference frame (Halligan *et al.*, 2003). The former may be illustrated, for example, by the performance of neglect patients in bisection (Schenkenberg *et al.*, 1980) or cancellation tasks (Albert, 1973), in which omission of targets on the left side of the sheet, and perseveration on the rightmost part, are common (Figure 10.1A). An object-centered neglect may in turn be evidenced in a task of drawing from memory or of copying simple items. These tasks may reveal an omission of the left part of the individual objects (Figure 10.1B and D). They may also bring to light other symptoms such as ipsilesional perseverations (Rusconi *et al.*, 2002), particularly in patients with lesions extending to the frontal region (Figure 10.1C), or completion phenomena (Figure 10.1E) (Meador *et al.*, 1991). Finally, subjects with unilateral neglect may exhibit representational neglect: a failure to report details from the left side of mentally visualized images (Figure 10.1F). This particular aspect of neglect was interpreted as a failure to generate or maintain a normal representation of the contralesional side of mental images, or else might reflect a failure to explore the left side of an otherwise normally generated mental image (Bisiach and Luzzatti, 1978; Bisiach *et al.*, 1979; Rode *et al.*, 2007).

A complex anatomo-clinic syndrome

Unilateral neglect is regarded as a complex neurological syndrome. This is dramatically illustrated by the apple tart made by a subject with a left neglect (Figure 10.1G): evidently, this patient not only forgot to put apple slices on the left part of the tart, but he was also unable correctly to organize these on the right side. It is the same part of space that is neglected in this task, both in drawing from memory (Figure 10.1B, C and D) and during mental evocation of space (Figure 10.1F), i.e. the part on the side opposite to the lesion.

Severe and persistent unilateral neglect is predominantly consecutive to lesions of the right hemisphere (Vallar, 2001; Halligan *et al.*, 2003). The first damaged cortical area evidenced was the inferior parietal lobule (Brodmann areas 39 and 40) (Hecaen *et al.*, 1956;

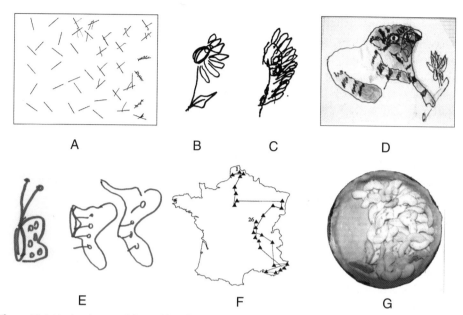

Figure 10.1 Neglect is a spatial cognition disorder. Left space-centered neglect assessed by a cancellation task (Albert, 1973) (**A**). Left object-centered neglect assessed by drawing from memory of a daisy or a tiger with three examples of performance: omission of left-sided petals (**B**). Ipsilateral perseverations (**C**). Lack of colour on the left part of the drawing (**D**). Left object-centered neglect with an 'allochiria' phenomenon: patients were asked to copy a butterfly. They were unable to draw a symmetrical object but the whole object was located on the right part of the drawing superimposed in one case, juxtaposed in another one (**E**). Left representational neglect evidenced by mental evocation of the map of France in a right-brain-damaged patient (**F**). An ecological consequence of neglect and visuo-spatial disorders, illustrated by an apple-tart made by a right-brain-damaged patient (**G**). See color plate section.

Heilman *et al.*, 1983; Vallar and Perani, 1986). Damage to other areas, such as Brodmann areas 6, 8 and 44 and to the superior temporal sulcus could also produce neglect, along with damage to subcortical structures and white matter fibres (Karnath *et al.*, 2001, 2002; Mort *et al.*, 2003; Doricchi and Tomaiuolo, 2003; Thiebaut de Schotten *et al.*, 2005). Given the variety and widespread nature of the lesions, both cortical and subcortical, which have been implicated in neglect, many component deficits have been proposed to underlie neglect, especially concerning the behavioral bias (see review: Parton *et al.*, 2003; Husain and Rorden, 2003): a disorder of directing attention to the left (Kinsbourne, 1993; Smania *et al.*, 1998; Posner *et al.*, 1984; Gainotti *et al.*, 1991); an impaired representation of space, which can be in multiple frames of reference (for example, retinotopic, head-centered, trunk-centered) (Bisiach and Berti, 1987; Karnath, 1997) and a directional motor impairment affecting the programming and initiation of contralesional eye or limb movements (Heilman *et al.*, 1985; Mattingley *et al.*, 1992). These proposed lateralized component deficits are not mutually exclusive, and several may coexist within the same neglect patient, having both parietal and frontal lesions (Husain *et al.*, 2000). In addition to these directional deficits, many nonspatially lateralized component deficits may also contribute to neglect: impairments in sustained attention (Robertson *et al.*, 1997), selective attention at central fixation (Husain *et al.*, 1997), or in both visual fields (Batelli *et al.*, 2001), a bias to local features in the visual scene (Doricchi and Incoccia, 1998), as well as a deficit in spatial working memory (Husain *et al.*, 2001) or in spatial remapping (Pisella and Mattingley, 2004). None of these deficits has been considered to be specific to neglect. However, such nonspatially lateralized deficits could exacerbate any directional deficit and have a significant impact on the neglect syndrome, reducing the potential for recovery (Robertson, 2001; Husain and Rorden, 2003).

Two approaches in neglect rehabilitation

Unilateral neglect induces many debilitating effects on everyday life and has been shown to be responsible for poor functional recovery and reduced ability to benefit from treatment of the impaired motor functions (Denes *et al.*, 1982; Fullerton *et al.*, 1986; Jehkonen *et al.*, 2000). Numerous attempts to rehabilitate neglect have thus been made over the last 40 years. The principal question which continues to be debated is how one can reduce the behavioral bias of neglect and, as a corollary, improve the consciousness of left peripersonal and personal spaces (for reviews, see Luauté *et al.*, 2006a,b). Two theoretical trends may be distinguished in the rehabilitation of neglect: a 'top-down' and a 'bottom-up' approach.

A 'top-down' approach

The first trend is a pragmatic clinical approach which is aimed at improving the perceptual and behavioral biases by acting on the patient's awareness of the deficit, i.e. at the highest cognitive levels, including training in visual scanning, cueing, or sustained attention (Diller and Weinberg, 1977; Robertson *et al.*, 1998). The visual scanning training consists of correcting the ipsilesional deviation of behavior (and gaze) by enclosing repetitive eye movement scanning exercises, in order to restore automatic scanning on the affected side. These training procedures produced substantial improvement in neglect patients with an additional generalization of improvement to a variety of everyday living situations involving spatial exploration. This generalization applied only when training lasted for between 4 consecutive weeks in the study of Diller and Weinberg (1977), and 8 weeks in other studies (Pizzamiglio *et al.*, 1992; Antonucci *et al.*, 1995; Paolucci *et al.*, 1996).

A 'bottom-up' approach

The second rehabilitative trend is a physiological approach aimed at modifying the sensorimotor level by passive sensory manipulations or by visuo-motor adaptation which bypasses the central awareness deficit and directly influences the highest levels of space and action representation (Rubens, 1985; Vallar *et al.*, 1997; Kerkhoff, 2003; Rossetti and Rode, 2002). Numerous manifestations of neglect have been shown to be alleviated by sensory stimulation (vestibular, optokinetic, transcutaneous electrical, transcutaneous mechanical vibratory and auditory). This bottom-up improvement has been reported mainly for extrapersonal neglect (for reviews, see Vallar, 1997; Rossetti and Rode, 2002; Kerkhoff, 2003). Improvement of many other aspects of the syndrome has also been reported, including for personal neglect, sensory and motor deficits of the left hemibody, and even for anosognosia and somatoparaphrenia (Cappa *et al.*, 1987; Rode *et al.*, 1992).

The reversibility of various symptoms of neglect suggests that a specific functional component is associated with damage to the right hemisphere. This may be explained by the fact that neglect follows damage of multimodal areas related to the orientation of spatial behaviors, and not to primary sensory or motor cortical areas. These associative areas can be activated by stimulation of various sensory modalities (Bottini *et al.*, 1994, 2001), and may be organized in parallel with other central nervous system structures which receive convergent multisensory inputs thereby modulating the functional deficits. Despite their selectivity, however, the effects of such passive bottom-up interventions remain highly transient (Rode *et al.*, 2002), at least unless repeated sessions are applied (Schindler *et al.*, 2002).

In summary, the two approaches to neglect rehabilitation are endowed with distinct clinical effects: specific training produces generalization restricted to situations involving spatial exploration, but the improvement on the learned tasks lasts a relatively long time after the learning process. By contrast, the sensory stimulation techniques produce a massive generalization, but the positive effects may last only about 10–15 min. It is therefore a challenge to develop a strategy to combine the advantages of these two approaches, and to propose a technique that, bypassing the level of conscious awareness in the patient, could also promote long-lasting effects. PA could combine both benefits, since it is characterized intrinsically by an aspect of learning, and it results from low-level, automatic modifications of visuo-motor correspondences.

Prism adaptation: an original bottom-up approach

Shift of proprioception in healthy subjects after PA

As we have argued, neglect is a space-oriented pattern of behavior characterized by a bias toward the ipsilesional side. In normal subjects, a behavioral bias may be experimentally induced by a simple PA procedure (Jeannerod and Rossetti, 1993; Rossetti *et al.*, 1993; Redding *et al.*, 2005). The relevant point for unilateral neglect rehabilitation is that after a rightward optical deviation of the visual field, subjects show a systematic leftward deviation of visuo-motor and proprioceptive responses with the adapted limb. The innovation proposed by Rossetti *et al.* (1998) was to use this after-effect as a method to help neglect patients re-orient their behavior towards the neglected side. This reorientation is such that it may be produced without requiring the patient's voluntary attention, i.e. according to a bottom-up process that bypasses awareness and intentional control. Two interesting and additional questions are to specify whether (1) lower-order visuo-motor action may induce changes in higher-level spatial representation, and (2) adaptation may produce longer-lasting effects compared to sensory stimulation, due to the fact that adaptation produces residual effects on neurological substrates (Clower *et al.*, 1996).

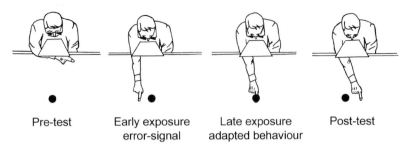

| Pre-test | Early exposure error-signal | Late exposure adapted behaviour | Post-test |

Figure 10.2 The four phases of the prismatic adaptation procedure. The pre-test (**A**); the perception of visual error signal (**B**); the adaptation (**C**); and the post-test (**D**).

The PA procedure

Three successive phases can be described in the prismatic adaptation procedure (see Figure 10.2).

The pre-test

The subject wears a pair of goggles fitted with wide-field point-to-point prismatic lenses creating a rightward optical shift of 10°. A shelf is placed under the patient's chin to prevent viewing of the hand at its starting position, while allowing an unobstructed view of the visual targets, two-thirds of the hand trajectory, and the terminal pointing errors (Figure 10.2A).

The exposure to the visual shift

When the classical procedure is used, two phases can be distinguished in the error reduction curves. The subject initially misreaches to one side of the target (towards the virtual image of the target), a systematic error referred to as the direct effect (Figure 10.2B). Most of the initial pointing error is resolved within a few trials (Weiner *et al.*, 1983; Rossetti *et al.*, 1993) as result of the strategic perceptual-motor control. Then the error decreases more progressively and tends to disappear as the participant is further exposed to the pointing task (Figure 10.2C), reflecting the slow development of the adaptation.

The post-test

The post-test is aimed at assessing after-effects: after removal of the prisms, the subject misreaches, in the direction opposite to the visual shift, producing an error which is referred to as the compensatory or negative after-effect. When pointing straight-ahead, this after-effect corresponds to a shift of proprioceptive representations and constitutes the major compensatory effect of short-term wedge-prism exposure as result of the adaptive spatial realignment (Figure 10.2D) (Redding and Wallace, 1996). When pointing to a visual target, the total shift obtained reflects the combination of proprioceptive shift along with a compensatory visual shift (see Redding *et al.*, 2005).

Two forms of learning

Investigations of PA in healthy subjects indicate that two forms of reactions to prisms can be distinguished: a *strategic perceptual-motor control* and an *adaptative spatial* (re)alignment. The strategic shift in motor responses occurs immediately, producing a rapid reduction in pointing errors made when the prisms are worn. The adaptive spatial alignment is developed after a more prolonged prism exposure, and is revealed when the prisms are subsequently removed. For Redding and Wallace (1996), this negative after-effect is held to be characteristic of longer-term plastic changes in visuo-motor mapping. These two components of PA depend on the integrity of distinct neuroanatomical substrates: the strategic component relies mainly on the parietal cortex (Clower *et al.*, 1996; Pisella *et al.*, 2004) whereas the adaptive realignment component relies on the cerebellum (Weiner *et al.*, 1983; Pisella *et al.*, 2005; Luauté *et al.*, 2006c). Testing patients with cerebellar atrophy, Weiner *et al.* (1983) showed that after PA exposure, patients showed reduced pointing errors, reflecting sparing of the strategic component of adaptation, in the absence of any after-effects (see Pisella *et al.*, 2006).

Improvement of visual neglect symptoms after PA

In the first prism rehabilitation study, Rossetti *et al.* (1998) demonstrated that a short period of pointing (50 movements over 2–5 min) toward targets viewed under a 10° rightward displacement, resulted in a shift in manual straight-ahead pointing toward the left side. Prior to prism exposure, six patients pointed, on average, about 9° to the right of center (towards the ispilesional side), reflecting an ipsilesional shift of the egocentric reference (Jeannerod and Biguer, 1987). After exposure, the neglect patients produced an average pointing bias of just 2° rightward, i.e. showing an after-effect of about 7° (or 80% compensation for the 10° optical displacement). This after-effect was much larger than the average 40% shift exhibited by healthy control participants, showing that neglect patients, in spite of their brain damage, could adapt more efficiently than the healthy controls.

Could this shift of proprioceptive representations toward the neglected side induced by PA in patients be associated with an improvement of the classical symptoms of visual neglect? In the initial study, a reduction of the rightward bias was observed in visuo-manual tasks, such as line cancellation (Albert, 1973), line bisection (Schenkenberg *et al.*, 1980), and drawing a daisy from memory, in each case when compared to control patients who performed identical procedures but wearing neutral, sham goggles with no optical displacement (Rossetti *et al.*, 1998). In a copying test of five items (Gainotti *et al.*, 1972), the mean number of items drawn, and the mean number of items drawn *symmetrically* were improved in the same way in the 'prism' group, showing that aspects of both object-based neglect and space-based neglect were improved equally by the adaptation procedure (Rossetti *et al.*, 1998). This improvement has also been obtained in patients with chronic neglect of 9 months, 5 years, and even of 19 years duration (McIntosh *et al.*, 2002; Rode *et al.*, 2003; Humphreys *et al.*, 2006). These clinical findings therefore suggest that low-level, automatic modifications of visuo-motor correspondences induced by prism exposure may influence visuo-spatial awareness even after a long post-stroke delay in right-brain-damaged patients.

Table 10.1 Review of relevant papers studying the generalization and the duration of prism adaptation effects in right-brain-damaged patients with unilateral neglect

Studies	Cases	After-effect	Generalization	Duration
			Single session	
Rossetti et al., 1998	6	8°	Visuo-motor tasks (bisection, cancellation, drawing, reading)	≥2 h
Rode et al., 2001	2	9°	Mental imagery task	Immediate
Tilikete et al., 2001	5	Not assessed	Postural imbalance	Immediate
Farnè et al., 2002	6	3°	Visuo-verbal tasks (object description; objects, words and no-words naming)	24 h
Pisella et al., 2002	2	9°	Visuo-motor tasks (bisection, cancellation, straight-ahead pointing)	96 h
Ferber et al., 2003	1	14.3°	Visual exploration bias	Immediate
Maravita et al., 2003	4	8°	Tactile extinction	Immediate
Dijkerman et al., 2003	3	Not given	Visual exploration bias	Immediate
Klos et al., 2004	10	Not assessed	Visuo-motor tasks (bisection, cancellation, drawing, reading)	5 h
Berberovic et al., 2004	4	4.33°	Attentional task (judgment of temporal order)	Immediate
Angeli et al., 2004	8	4.12°	Neglect dyslexia, visual exploration bias	Immediate
Rossetti et al., 2004	2	4.8° and 9.4°	Mental number bisection task	Immediate
Dijkerman et al., 2004	1	Not given	Somatosensory deficit	Immediate
Morris et al., 2004	4	7°	Visuo-motor tasks (bisection)	Immediate
Rousseaux et al., 2006	10	4.8°	Visuo-motor tasks (bisection, cancellation, drawing), reading	Not significant
Jacquin-Courtois et al., 2006	1	6.72°	Wheelchair driving	96 h
Rode et al., 2006	1	14.8°	Spatial dysgraphia	72 h
Saari et al., 2006	3	3.9°	Chimeric objects task	Immediate
Datié et al., 2006	20	Not given	Visual exploration bias in seven patients without improved verbal description	Immediate
			Repeated session	
Frassinetti et al., 2002[a]	6	2.7°	Visuo-motor tasks (bisection, cancellation, drawing), behavioral measures	5 weeks
MacIntosh et al., 2002[b]	1	Not given	Tactile spatial task	3 weeks

Serino et al., 2005[c]	16	3.6°	Visuo-motor tasks (BIT), reading task, visual exploration bias	3 months
Humphreys et al., 2006[d]	1	2°	Visuo-motor tasks (bisection, cancellation, drawing, reading)	1 year
Keane et al., 2006[e]	4	9.6°	Visuo-motor tasks, behavioral measures	6 days

[a] Twice-daily sessions over a period of 2 weeks; [b] three sessions, one a day over a period of 1 week; [c] 10 sessions, one a day over a period of 2 weeks; [d] 18 sessions, two per week over a period of 9 weeks; [e] five sessions over a period of 5 days.

BIT, behavioral inattention task.

Various effects of PA

Since Rossetti et al.'s initial publication, 24 papers have subsequently been published about the effects of PA on symptoms of neglect and possible underlying mechanisms (see Table 10.1). One hundred and eleven right-brain-damaged patients have benefited from this treatment, with varying results in terms of after-effects, clinical effects, and the duration of improvement. In these studies, the average size of the after-effect varied from 2.7 to 14° (the latter value should be interpreted with caution, since the procedure involved only a 10° shift), with a mean value of 7.1°, along with varying generalization to different tasks. The question concerning the quantitative relationship between the amplitude of the after-effect and any improvement of neglect remains open. Although some studies have reported that some patients did *not* exhibit significant benefits from the PA treatment, only one study concluded that the PA treatment was ineffective on the whole (Rousseaux et al., 2006). So far, only one randomized controlled clinical trial was performed in a sample of 10 right-brain-damaged patients with neglect (Geggus, 2002; Klos et al., 2004; see Rode et al., 2006a). The authors extended the study by Rossetti et al. (1998), using similar procedures. Post-tests were measured at 2 and 5 h post adaptation and a wider range of testing was employed. Patients showing neglect for more than 3 months were randomly sampled from different stages of rehabilitation. The experimental group was compared to a control group of patients exposed to goggles made of window glasses with no optical displacement. The results showed a clear difference between the experimental and the control groups, in favour of a selective effect of PA on unilateral neglect. For example, 6/10 patients were ameliorated by at least 25% in a reading task, whereas none reached this level of improvement in the control group (Geggus, 2002; Klos et al., 2004).

Duration of effects

The study of Rossetti et al. (1998) showed that improvement of neglect after a single session of adaptation was sustained over at least the 2 h follow-up period. Improvements have also extended to about 1–4 days in single cases of neglect (Pisella et al., 2002;

Rode *et al.*, 2006b; Jacquin-Courtois *et al.*, in press), and to 1 day in a group of five neglect patients (Farnè *et al.*, 2002), showing that the effects produced by a single 5 min session of adaptation may last for much longer than any other rehabilitation method.

Using repeated sessions (including twice-daily sessions over a period of 2 weeks) in a group of seven neglect patients, and compared to a control group of six patients, Frassinetti *et al.* (2002) demonstrated an improvement in the experimental patient's performance after PA, which was maintained over a 5 week post-treatment period. This long-term improvement of neglect symptoms was found both in standard as well as in non-standard behavioral tests. However, one minor caveat is that the control group was selected from a different hospital. Using repeated sessions (18 sessions of PA training; two per week over 9 weeks), Humphreys *et al.* (2006) reported finding a long-lasting beneficial effect in one chronic patient, which was maintained up to a year following the PA training. The improvement was evidenced in certain tasks, including line bisection, star-, and letter cancellation tasks. On the other hand, no modification of performance was noted in control tasks such as reading, mathematical cognition or chimeric face perception tasks.

Cognitive effects of PA

Visuo-verbal tasks

In most previous studies, the main tests used to assess the effects of prism training required a visuo-manual response, that is, the use of a physiological system that is directly involved in the adaptation procedure. One interesting question was whether the improvement observed after PA would also affect aspects of unilateral neglect, which are free from manual responses. Farnè *et al.* (2002) studied five right-brain-damaged patients with neglect. Neglect was assessed in both visuo-manual and visuo-verbal tasks following exposure to a single session of PA. Patients displayed similar levels of improvement/after-effect in both tasks, suggesting a generalization effect independent of the adapted hand.

Sensory neglect and extinction (tactile and auditory)

McIntosh *et al.* (2002) have shown an improvement in certain visual components of neglect as well as a reduction of haptic neglect as assessed by exploration of a circle. In the tactile domain, Maravita *et al.* (2003) showed an improvement of contralesional tactile extinction in four neglect patients. Tactile stimuli were delivered unilaterally either to the right, the left, or to both hands simultaneously. Detection of contralesional tactile stimuli during bilateral stimulation improved after PA in all patients. Tactile detection thresholds were also shown to improve in a single case study (Dijkerman *et al.*, 2004). Similar results have been obtained in the auditory domain. Following right-brain damage, unilateral omissions of auditory targets frequently occur in the situation where two auditory stimuli are presented simultaneously from the right and the left sides, while no omissions are observed when presenting one single stimulus (De Renzi *et al.*, 1989). Courtois-Jacquin *et al.* (2001) have studied the effects of PA on left auditory extinction in two groups of six right-brain-damaged patients with neglect, in which the experimental group received a classical PA treatment. The control group performed the same pointing procedure, but wore sham (neutral) glasses creating no optical shift. Effects of PA were assessed in conventional visuo-motor tasks and in a dichotic listening test, performed both immediately upon prism removal and 2 h later. The results showed a long-lasting improvement of both the visuo-spatial deficit, and of auditory extinction, but only in those patients exposed to the prism training. These results show that the beneficial effects of PA are not restricted merely to visuo-motor tasks, but can also affect perception in non-visual modalities. This suggests that the recalibration of visuo-motor transformations induced by prism exposure may influence the attentional or representational bias in other sensory modalities.

Representational neglect

A further group of findings in the cognitive domain concerns the effect of PA on representational neglect as assessed by an imagery task, free from manual responses and overt visual scanning. Representational neglect was explored in two patients asked to imagine a geographic space (the map of France) and to name as many towns as possible that they could 'see' on the imagined map within 2 min. The left representational deficit displayed by the two patients before adaptation was reduced immediately after prism exposure with an increase both of the total number of towns named, and the number of named towns located on the left half of the map (Rode et al., 1998, 2001), suggesting that the stimulation of active processes involved in the plasticity of sensorimotor correspondence can also influence cognitive functions at the level of mental representation.

However, this mental imagery task was explicitly spatial and the question was still open concerning whether similar cognitive effects could be obtained in an explicitly nonspatial or implicitly spatial task. This type of task was described by Zorzi et al. (2002), who reported that the mental bisection of the interval between two numbers was systematically shifted to the 'right' (i.e. towards bigger numbers) in neglect patients as compared to healthy subjects and brain-damaged patients without neglect. Using this mental number-bisection task, the effects of PA were assessed on bisection bias in physical and representational spaces in two neglect patients. Both patients displayed a stable 'rightwards' number-bisection bias both in two pre-test sessions and after a series of manual pointing while wearing neutral goggles (see Figure 10.3B). Surprisingly, after a period of visuo-motor adaptation with prismatic lenses, the two patient's reliable biases were greatly improved (Rossetti et al., 2004). These results suggest that PA may reduce representational neglect in both explicitly and implicitly spatial imagery tasks.

A last argument in favor of the wide generalization of PA concerns the positive influence of PA on the postural system. Left-hemiparetic patients following damage of the right hemisphere show a predominant imbalance as compared to right-hemiparetic patients (Rode et al., 1997). This postural imbalance can be evidenced in posturographic measures, which show a lateral displacement of the center of downwards pressure exerted by the

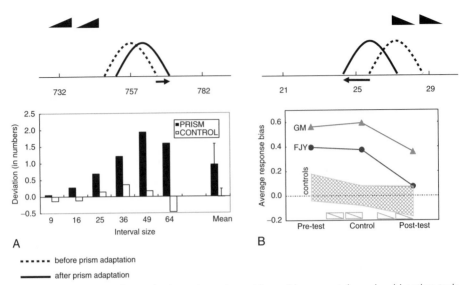

Figure 10.3 Cognitive effects of prism adaptation evidenced by a mental number bisection task in seven healthy subjects (**A**); and in two right-brain-damaged patients (**B**).

two feet towards the ipsilesional side. This ipsilesional postural imbalance can be observed in patients with associated neglect, but also independently of neglect (Perennou, 2006). This postural shift may be interpreted as reflecting a distortion of an internal postural map, and may even be influenced positively by sensory stimulation. We therefore investigated the effect of a PA procedure on postural imbalance in three groups of five right-brain-damaged patients (with no neglect at the time of the test): one group was adapted to a prism deviating the visual field to the right, one group to the left, and the third group was exposed to neutral prisms. All groups wore the goggles while performing reaching movements with the right arm. Postural imbalance was reduced only in the group of patients exposed to the rightwards optical shift. These results show that the effect of exposure to prisms that horizontally shift the visual field to the right during a reaching task generalizes to the postural frames of reference (Tilikete *et al.*, 2001). In sum, these beneficial effects suggest that PA may influence the higher-level supramodal representations associated with spatial attention.

Visuo-constructive disorders

Cognitive effects produced by PA have been reported in healthy subjects (Colent *et al.*, 2000; Michel, 2006). For example, M. Calabria *et al.* (unpublished data) have investigated the influence of PA on a number-bisection task. Pairs of numbers were presented orally (e.g. 717 and 753) and subjects were asked to bisect the interval between them without making an explicit calculation. As previously shown for line bisection (Colent *et al.*, 2000), only subjects exposed to a leftward prism deviation presented a right spatial bias after adaptation (see Figure 10.3A). The effects of PA in both healthy subjects and in subjects with perceptual and representational neglect therefore suggest that this procedure may influence more generally visuo-spatial functions which have been attributed to the right hemisphere. One could therefore speculate that PA might improve both neglect and certain associated visuo-constructive disorders consecutive to right-brain damage. Indeed, recent findings argue in favour of this hypothesis.

We reported a right-brain-damaged patient who showed a marked left-sided neglect and a remarkable spatial dysgraphia. Spatial dysgraphia is "a disturbance of graphic expression due to an impairment of visuospatial perception resulting from a lesion in the non language-dominant hemisphere" (Hécaen et al., 1963). Four main features define the clinical picture: (1) "right-page' preference: writing is crowded onto the right side of the page leaving an excessively wide "margin" on the left side; (2) sloping lines (inclination): patients fail to write horizontally and produce oblique or wavy lines; (3) broken lines: patients leave abnormally large spaces between words, thus leading to the fragmentation of the line into small segments; and (4) graphic errors: production of an incorrect number of strokes for a given letter or of letters for a given word (Hécaen and Marcie, 1974). The first feature reflects the left-sided neglect, i.e. the visual attentional bias, while the second and third ones reflect visuo-constructive disorders.

The performance of a neglect patient with spatial dysgraphia was evaluated before and after PA within a time period of 4 consecutive days. In this case, the improvement of attentional bias was clearly demonstrated by the reduction of the ipsilesional shift in the line bisection task, in drawing from memory, and by a decrease in the neglected surface in the writing task (Figure 10.4, patient A). The results also revealed a reduction of inclination of the lines, and of the number of broken lines, which was also maintained 48 h later. These beneficial effects suggest an improvement of both attentional bias and visuo-constructive disorders (Rode et al., 2006b).

Similar findings were obtained in two right-brain-damaged patients exhibiting a left unilateral neglect and a constructional apraxia. Before adaptation, geometric figure copying performance displayed a neglect of the left part of the model and constructional deficits showing a lack of proportions and incorrect orientation of component lines. After adaptation, an improvement of the drawing was observed for both patients, with a reduction of the left neglected area, and an improvement of line inclination and proportions (Figure 10.4, patients B and C).

Interestingly, the beneficial effect on visuo-spatial abilities assessed by the drawing concerned not only the left part of the model or the text, but also the ipsilesional right part. This data further supports the idea that PA might improve spatial-cognition deficits in neglect as well as in pathologies such as in constructional deficits and other pathological manifestations affecting spatial and bodily representations (e.g. Complex Regional Pain Syndrome; Sumitani et al., 2006, in press). One could therefore speculate that PA permits an enlargement of this visual-motor mapping of space, not only on the left side but also on the right side.

Negative effects

Finally, in order to better delineate the action of PA, it is also of prime interest to consider behavioral parameters that are *not* affected by this treatment. Dijkerman et al. (2003)

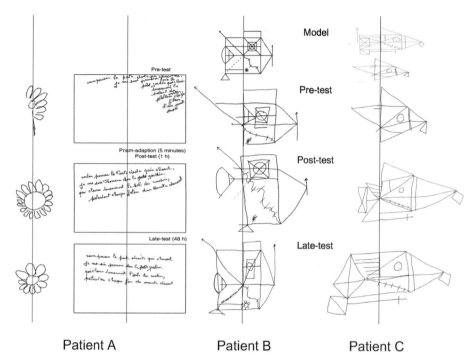

Patient A   **Patient B**   **Patient C**

Figure 10.4 Left object-centered neglect, spatial dysgraphia, and visuo-constructive disorders shown by three right-brain-damaged patients before prism adaptation (pre-test), immediately upon removal of the 10° prisms (post-test), and 2–4 h later (late-test): drawing from memory and writing under dictation (patient A); neglect and constructional apraxia assessed by the Taylor's figure (patient B), and the Rey's figure (patient C). Scores on the Rey's figure: 9.5/36 in the pre-test, 16/36 in the post-test and 19.5/36 in the late-test. Scores on the Taylor's figure: 26/36 in the pre- and post-tests (percentile 0), and 30/36 in the late-test (percentile 20).

have shown that PA can reduce ocular exploration asymmetries without affecting size underestimation in a neglect patient. Similarly, Ferber *et al.* (2003) reported, in a neglect patient exposed to a prismatic deviation, a shift of exploratory eye movements toward the left but a persistent deficit in awareness of the left side, as assessed by the patient's ability to judge the happiness of vertically arranged pairs of chimeric faces composed of half-smiling and half-neutral faces. The same negative effect of PA was recently replicated in a chimeric face task in a single case (Humphreys *et al.*, 2006), and a free visual exploration imagery task in a group of 20 right-brain-damaged patients (Datié *et al.*, 2006). However, the discordance between the effects of PA on different symptoms of neglect, particularly the ability to influence or not the awareness of the deficit, might be explained by the nature of the tasks used. This question was recently investigated by Saari *et al.* (2006), who tested, in three neglect patients, the impact of prism exposure on visual awareness of the side of chimeric objects as well as of chimeric faces. The authors replicated Ferber's earlier findings and showed that PA improved awareness only for the identity of the left side of the chimeric objects.

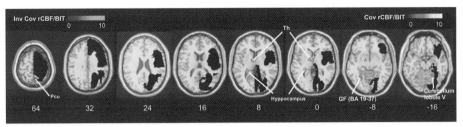

Figure 10.5 Functional imaging positron emission spectroscopy study: covariation analysis between modification of regional cerebral blood flow (rCBF) and behavioral inattention test (BIT) after prism. The overlay lesion mask of five patients with left neglect (in black), with activations mapped onto the horizontal slices corresponding to z-coordinates −16, −8; 0, 8, 16, 24, 32 and 64 in Talairach and Tournoux space, constructed by using the identical or the closest-matching horizontal slices of each individual. In red (Cov): areas of significant increase in neural activity (cluster level $p < 0.05$, corrected according to Gaussian random field theory) associated with the analysis of covariation between the increase of rCBF and the improvement of BIT after prism adaptation (PA). In blue (Inv Cov): areas of significant decrease in neural activity (cluster level probability, $p < 0.05$, corrected) associated with the analysis of covariation between the decrease of rCBF and the improvement of BIT after PA (from Luauté et al., 2006c). PCU, precuneus; Th, thalamus; GF, gyrus fusiform; BA, Brodmann area. See color plate section.

An anatomo-functional hypothesis

An additional intriguing question is whether PA favours the spontaneous recovery of neglect or facilitates the occurrence of selective compensation mechanisms. This question refers either to the cerebral plasticity naturally evoked after the cerebral damage, or to the cerebral plasticity specifically activated by the visuo-motor adaptation task. The fact that immediate effects can be produced, and even in chronic patients, suggests that PA does not simply enhance spontaneous recovery and that specific mechanisms are at work. There has been quite some controversy in the literature concerning the neural structures involved in PA. On the one hand, neuropsychological evidence historically suggested that only cerebellar patients were impaired in PA (e.g. Weiner et al., 1983; for review, see Jeannerod and Rossetti, 1993). On the other hand, recent imaging data (Clower et al., 1996) have suggested that the human posterior parietal cortex contralateral to the adapted arm is the only area activated during prism exposure.

More recently, Pisella et al. (2004) established that a bilateral lesion of the superior parietal lobule, although frequently leading to an impairment of visuo-manual guidance (optic ataxia), is not crucially involved in visuo-manual PA. The clinical effect of PA on visual neglect also precludes the possibility that the inferior parietal lobule, at least in the right hemisphere, might be crucial for adaptation to rightward prisms. Rather, neglect patients exhibit 'hyper-adaptation' characterized by more robust and durable sensorimotor after-effects (for reviews, see Pisella et al., 2006; Rode et al., 2006a). A patient with optic ataxia following a bilateral lesion also demonstrated a large inter-manual transfer, which suggests that the cerebellum remains likely to be the main substrate of true adaptation, although the posterior parietal cortex may also contribute to the strategic component of PA (Pisella et al., 2004).

A simple model was therefore proposed in which the cerebellum and the posterior parietal cortex are respectively specialized for the adaptive and strategic components of PA (Rossetti *et al.*, 2000; Pisella *et al.*, 2004). If lesions of the posterior parietal cortex reduce the strategic component, adaptation would consequently be achieved mostly by realignment processes (the true adaptive component), hence would more likely be stronger, longer-lasting, and have a greater potential to generalize to other tasks. Accordingly, neglect patients do not notice the visuo-spatial alteration resulting direcly from the optical deviation (Calabria and Rossetti, 2005), and normal subjects also exhibit larger adaptive after-effects when the prismatic deviation is not noticeable (Jakobson *et al.*, 1989; Michel *et al.*, 2007).

In a patient with a cerebellar lesion (including the superior part of the dentate nucleus and the anterior lobe of the left cerebellar hemisphere), Pisella *et al.* (2005) found that adaptation was limited to a rightward (not leftward) prism deviation, independently of the hand used during exposure. This observation confirmed the crucial involvement of the cerebellum in PA, and led Pisella and her collaborators propose a lateralized model for PA and its beneficial effect on spatial cognition. The pattern of impairments in this patient suggested a visual lateralization within the cerebellum, with the involvement of the cerebellar hemisphere ipsilateral to the prismatic deviation in the processing of visual errors, in addition to the well-known motor lateralization that primarily involves the cerebellar hemisphere contralateral to the hand in the modification of visuo-motor correspondences (Martin *et al.*, 1996).

To our knowledge, only one other anatomo-functional study has compared adaptation to right and left prismatic deviations (Kurata and Hoshi, 1999). In this study, deficit in adaptation was observed after inactivation of the ventral premotor cortical area (PMv) in monkeys only when vision was shifted contralaterally to the inactivated PMv. Since connections between the cerebellum and the cerebral cortex are crossed (Schmahmann and Pandya, 1997), this makes a consistent cerebro-cerebellar lateralized network for the computation and integration of directional visual error in PA. The implication of such a lateralized cerebello-cerebral network in the functional anatomy of the therapeutic effects of PA on neglect has been recently confirmed by a neuroimaging study in neglect patients (Luauté *et al.*, 2006c) showing that regional cerebral blood flow (rCBF) in the right cerebellar hemisphere and the right dentate nucleus covaried significantly with improvement in neglect (assessed by the Behavioral Inattention Test). Activation of the left temporal cortex also appeared to covary positively with the improvement in left spatial neglect (Luauté *et al.*, 2006c).

Altogether, anatomical and behavioral data suggest that the clinical effect of PA on neglect relies on a network of brain areas where visual error-signals generated by right prisms are initially processed in the left occipital cortex. The information is then transferred to the right cerebellum where the visuo-motor realignment (i.e. 'true adaptation') takes place in congruence with the rightward deviation of the prisms. The clinical effect could therefore be mediated through the modulation of cerebral areas in the left hemisphere via a bottom-up signal generated by the cerebellum (Michel *et al.*, 2003; Rode *et al.*, 2003; Pisella *et al.*, 2005). Notably, the temporal cortex, the frontal cortex, and the posterior parietal cortex have been shown to be targets of output from the cerebellum via a neuronal loop also implicating the dentate nucleus and certain sub-cortical structures such as the thalamus and the globus pallidus (Middleton and Strick, 2000; Clower *et al.*, 2001). The clinical effect might therefore be mediated by the recruitment of pathways in the left hemisphere that are functionally homologous to those acknowledged to be involved in spatial cognition in the damaged hemisphere.

Reciprocally, the cognitive effects of PA found in healthy subjects (Berberovic and Mattingley, 2003; Girardi *et al.*, 2004; Goebel *et al.*, 2006), evidenced by an asymmetrical pattern of performance on several spatial tasks, are strictly dependent upon the direction of the prismatic shift (Michel *et al.*, 2003). On the basis of the latter studies, and considering that the right parietal cortex seems to be specifically involved in line bisection judgment tasks (Fierro *et al.*, 2000; Fink *et al.*, 2000), we hypothesized that the function of the right parietal lobe would be inhibited by inputs from the left cerebellar cortex, coherent with the use of the leftward prismatic deviation, and generate "neglect-like" symptoms (Michel, 2006).

In principle, the proposed model is compatible with the involvement of the PA-induced realignment of the oculomotor system that, by reducing the rightward scanning bias, may facilitate exploration of the left, neglected side of space (Angeli *et al.*, 2004; Datié *et al.*, 2006; Serino *et al.*, 2006; Malhotra *et al.*, 2006). However, several dissociations have been documented between oculomotor change and the amelioration of visuospatial behavioral performances (Dijkerman *et al.*, 2003; Ferber *et al.*, 2003). Another proposal is that adaptation acts through plastic modification of the integration of proprioceptive and visual information, which would be particularly beneficial in neglect patients, whose symptoms result in part from an impaired visual–motor mapping of space (see Pisella and Mattingley, 2004). One could speculate that PA also induces an enlargement of this visual-motor mapping of space, not only on the left side, but also on the right side, as suggested by the improvement of constructional apraxia (Rode *et al.*, 2006a) and spatial dysgraphia (Rode *et al.*, 2006b) following PA. Recent findings mainly point to the need for appropriately applying prism exposure conditions and quantification (Redding and Wallace, 2005), for evaluating the role played by the type of PA (strategic versus realignment; Angeli *et al.*, 2004; Serino *et al.*, 2006), as well as the sufficient amount of adaptation (as measured in terms of after-effect) required to produce consistent neglect improvement (Rousseaux *et al.*, 2006).

Conclusions

The sensorimotor modifications induced by PA can improve different manifestations of the unilateral neglect syndrome. Most demonstrations of this improvement appear to affect spatial manifestations in an egocentric frame of reference, as suggested by the reduction of neglect in bisection and cancellation tasks, i.e. in tasks involving a visuomotor response. Cognitive effects are also evidenced in tasks involving neither visuomanual response, nor oculomotor scanning, suggesting that this recalibration may also influence higher-level space representation, particularly in other sensory modalities, though a cross-modal effect. These positive effects of PA on neglect are due not only to a reduction of the rightward attentional bias, but also consecutive to the improvement of visuo-spatial functions. These abilities affect the whole surrounding space of the subject, and it is now possible to argue that PA could be a tool for rehabilitation of neglect and other spatial cognition deficits due to damage of the right hemisphere.

Acknowledgments

This work was supported by the INSERM AVENIR grant to Y.R., Hospices Civils de Lyon and Université Claude Bernard.

References

Albert, M. L. (1973) A simple test of neglect. *Neurology*, **23**, 658–664.

Angeli, V., Benassi, M. G., Ladavas, E. (2004) Recovery of oculo-motor bias in neglect patients after prism adaptation. *Neuropsychologia*, **42**, 1223–1234.

Antonucci, G., Guariglia, C., Judica, A. *et al.* (1995) Effectiveness of neglect rehabilitation in a randomized group study. *Journal of Clinical Experimental Neuropsychology*, **17**, 383–389.

Batelli, L., Cavanagh, P., Intriligator, J. *et al.* (2001) Unilateral right parietal damage leads to bilateral deficits for high-level motion. *Neuron*, **32**, 985–995.

Berberovic, N. and Mattingley, J. B. (2003) Effects of prismatic adaptation on judgements of spatial extent in peripersonal and extrapersonal space. *Neuropsychologia*, **41**, 493–503.

Berberovic, N., Pisella, L., Morris, A. P. and Mattingley, J. B. (2004) Prismatic adaptation reduces biased temporal order judgements in spatial neglect. *Neuroreport*, **15**, 1199–1204.

Bisiach, E. (1999) Unilateral neglect and related disorders. In Denes, F. and Pizzamiglio, L. (eds), *Handbook of Clinical and Experimental Neuropsychology*. Psychology Press, Hove, UK.

Bisiach, E. and Berti, A. (1987) Dyschiria. An attempt at its systemic explanation. In Jeannerod, M. (ed.), *Neurophysiological and Neuropsychological Aspects of Spatial Neglect*, pp. 183–201. North-Holland, Amsterdam.

Bisiach, E. and Luzzatti, C. (1978) Unilateral neglect of representational space. *Cortex*, **14**, 129–133.

Bisiach, E., Luzzatti, C., Perani, D. (1979) Unilateral neglect, representational schema and consciousness. *Brain*, **102**, 609–618.

Bottini, G., Sterzi, R., Paulesu, E. *et al.* (1994) Identification of the central vestibular projections in man: a positron emission tomography activation study. *Experimental Brain Research*, **99**, 164–169.

Bottini, G., Karnath, H. O., Vallar, G. *et al.* (2001) Cerebral representations for egocentric space. Functional–anatomical evidence from caloric vestibular stimulation and neck vibration. *Brain*, **124**, 1182–1196.

Brain, W. R. (1941) Visual disorientation with special reference to lesions of the right cerebral hemisphere. *Brain*, **64**, 244–271.

Calabria, M. and Rossetti, Y. (2005) Interference between number processing and line bisection: a methodology. *Neuropsychologia*, **43**, 779–783.

Calabria, M., Michel, C., Courtois-Jacquin, S., Goebel, S. and Rossetti, Y. Prism adaptation distorts the mental number line: simulating spatial neglect in healthy individuals. In preparation.

Cappa, S., Sterzi, R., Vallar, G. and Bisiach, E. (1987) Remission of hemineglect and anosognosia during vestibular stimulation. *Neuropsychologia*, **25**, 775–782.

Clower, D. M., Hoffman, J. M., Votaw, J. R., Fabert, T. L., Woods, R. and Alexander, G. E. (1996) Role of posterior parietal cortex in the recalibration of visually guide reaching. *Nature*, **383**, 618–621.

Clower, D. M., West, R. A., Lynch, J. C. and Strick, P. L. (2001) The inferior parietal lobule is the target of output from the superior colliculus, hippocampus, and cerebellum. *Journal of Neuroscience*, **21**, 6283–91.

Colent, C., Pisella, L., Bernieri, C., Rode, G. and Rossetti, Y. (2000) Cognitive bias induced by visuo-motor adaptation to prisms: a simulation of unilateral neglect in normal individuals? *Neuroreport*, **26**, 1899–902.

Courtois-Jacquin, S., Rossetti, Y., Rode, G. *et al.* (2001) Effect of prism adaptation on auditory extinction: an attentional effect? International Symposium on neural control of space coding and action production. INSERM. Lyon Mars poster.

Datié, A. M., Paysant, J., Destainville, S., Sagez, A., Beis, J. M., André, J. M. (2006) Eye movements and visuoverbal descriptions exhibit heterogeneous and dissociated patterns before and after prismatic adaptation in unilateral spatial neglect. *European Journal of Neurology*, **13**, 772–79.

De Renzi, E., Gentilini, M. and Barbieri, C. (1989) Auditory neglect. *Journal of Neurology, Neurosurgery and Psychiatry*, **52**, 613–617.

Denes, G., Semenza, C., Stoppa, E. and Lis, A. (1982) Unilateral spatial neglect and recovery from hemiplegia: a follow-up study. *Brain*, **105**, 543–552.

Dijkerman, H. C., McIntosh, R. D., Rossetti, Y., Tilikete, C., Roberts, R. C. and Milner, A. D. (2003) Ocular scanning and perceptual size distortion in hemispatial neglect: effects of prism adaptation and sequential stimulus presentation. *Experimental Brain Research*, **153**, 220–230.

Dijkerman, H. C., Webeling, M., Walter, J. M., Groet, E. and van Zandvoort, M. J. (2004) A long-lasting improvement of somatosensory function after prism adaptation, a case study. *Neuropsychologia*, **42**, 1697–1702.

Diller, L. and Weinberg, J. (1997) Hemi-inattention in rehabilitation: the evolution of a rational remediation program. *Advances in Neurology*, **18**, 63–82.

Doricchi, F. and Incoccia, C. (1998) Seeing only the right half of the forest but cutting down all the trees? *Nature*, **394**, 75–78.

Doricchi, F. and Tomaiuolo, F. (2003) The anatomy of neglect without hemianopia: a key role for parietal–frontal disconnection? *Neuroreport*, **14**, 2239–2243.

Farnè, A., Rossetti, Y., Toniolo, S. and Ladavas, E. (2002) Ameliorating neglect with prism adaptation: visuo-manual and visuo-verbal measures. *Neuropsychologia*, **40**, 718–729.

Ferber, S., Danckert, J., Joanisse, M., Goltz, H. C. and Goodale, M. A. (2003) Eye movements tell only half the story. *Neurology*, **60**, 1826–1829.

Fierro, B., Brighina, F., Oliveri, M. *et al.* (2000) Contralateral neglect induced by right posterior parietal rTMS in healthy subjects. *Neuroreport*, **10**, 1519–1521.

Fink, G.R, Marshall, J. C., Shah, N. J. *et al.* (2000) Line bisection judgments implicate right parietal cortex and cerebellum as assessed by fMRI. *Neurology*, **54**, 1324–1331.

Frassinetti, F., Angeli, V., Meneghello, F., Avanzi, S. and Ladavas, E. (2002) Long-lasting amelioration of visuospatial neglect by prism adaptation. *Brain*, **125**, 608–623.

Fullerton, K. J., McSherry, D. and Stout, R. W. (1986) Albert's test: a neglected test of perceptual neglect. *Lancet*, **327**, 430–432.

Gainotti, G., Messerli, P. and Tissot, R. (1972) Qualitative analysis of unilateral spatial neglect in relation to laterality of cerebral lesions. *Journal of Neurology, Neurosurgery and Psychiatry*, **35**, 545–550.

Gainotti, G., D'Erme, P. and Bartolomeo, P. (1991) Early orientation of attention toward the half space ipsilateral to the lesion in patients with unilateral brain damage. *Journal of Neurology, Neurosurgery and Psychiatry*, **54**, 1082–1089.

Geggus, S. (2002) Effektivität von Prismenadaptation bei der Therapie von hemispatialem Neglect. Unpublished Medical Diploma-Thesis, University of Würzburg.

Girardi, M., McIntosh, R. D., Michel, C., Vallar, G. and Rossetti, Y. (2004) Sensorimotor effects on central space representation: prism adaptation influences haptic and visual representations in normal subjects. *Neuropsychologia*, **42**, 1477–1487.

Goebel, S., Calabria, M., Farnè, A. and Rossetti, Y. (2006) Parietal rTMS distorts the mental number line: simulating 'spatial' neglect in healthy subjects. *Neuropsychologia*, **44**, 860–868.

Halligan, P. W., Fink, G. R., Marshall, J. C. and Vallar, G. (2003) Spatial cognition: evidence from visual neglect. *Trends in Cognitive Sciences*, 7, 125–133.

Hécaen, H. and Marcie, P. (1974) Disorders of written language following right hemisphere lesions: spatial dysgraphia. In Diamond, S. S.J. and Beaumont, J. G. (eds), *Hemisphere Function in the Human Brain*, pp. 345–66. Elek, London.

Hécaen, H., Penfield, W., Bertrand, C. and Malmo, R. (1956) The syndrome of apractognosia due to lesions of the minor cerebral hemisphere. *Archives of Neurology and Psychiatry*, 57, 400–434.

Hécaen, H., Angelergues, R. and Douzenis, J. A. (1963) Les agraphies. *Neuropsychologia*, 1, 179–208.

Heilman, K. M., Bowers, D., Valenstein, E. and Watson, R. T. (1983) Localization of lesion in neglect. In Kertesz, A. (ed.), *Localization in Neuropsychology*, pp. 471–492. Academic Press, New York.

Heilman, K. M., Watson, R. T. and Valenstein, E. (1985) Neglect and related disorders. In Heilman, K. M. and Valenstein, E. (eds) *Clinical Neuropsychology*, pp. 243–293. Oxford University Press, New York.

Humphreys, G. W., Watelet, A. and Riddoch, M. J. (2006) Long-term effects of prism adaptation in chronic visual neglect: a single case study. *Cognitive Neuropsychology*, 23, 463–478.

Husain, M. and Rorden, C. (2003) Non-spatially lateralized mechanisms in hemispatial neglect. *Nature Neuroscience*, 4, 26–36.

Husain, M., Shapiro, K., Martin, J. *et al.* (1997) Abnormal temporal dynamics of visual attention in spatial neglect patients. *Nature*, 385, 154–156.

Husain, M., Mattingley, J. B., Driver, J. *et al.* (2000) Dissociation of sensory and motor impairments in parietal and frontal neglect. *Brain*, 123,1643–1659.

Husain, M., Mannan, S., Hodgson, T. *et al.* (2001) Impaired spatial working memory across saccades contributes to abnormal search in parietal neglect. *Brain*, 124, 942–952.

Jacquin-Courtois, S., Rode, G., Boisson, D. and Rossetti, Y. Wheel-chair driving improvement following visuo-manual prism adaptation. *Cortex*, in press.

Jakobson, L. S. and Goodale, M. A. (1989) Trajectories of reaches to prismatically-displaced targets: evidence for "automatic" visuomotor recalibration. *Experimental Brain Research*, 78, 575–87.

Jeannerod, M. and Biguer, B. (1987) The directional coding of reaching movements. A visuomotor conception of spatial neglect. In Jeannerod, M. (ed.), *Neurophysiological and Neuropsychological Aspects of Neglect*, pp. 87–113. Elsevier, Amsterdam.

Jeannerod, M. and Rossetti, Y. (1993) Visuomotor coordination as a dissociable visual function: experimental and clinical evidence. In Kennard, C. C. (ed.), *Visual Perceptual Defect*, pp. 439–460. I. P.R. Baillère Tindall, London.

Jehkonen, M., Ahonen, J. P., Dastidar, P. *et al.* (2000) Visual neglect as a predictor of functional outcome one year after stroke. *Acta Neurologica Scandinavica*, 101, 195–201.

Karnath, H. O. (1997) Spatial orientation and the representation of space with parietal lobe lesions. *Philosophical Transactions of the Royal Society London B*, 352, 1411–1419.

Karnath, H. O., Ferber, S. and Himmelbach, M. (2001) Spatial awareness is a function of the temporal not the posterior parietal lobe. *Nature*, 411, 950–953.

Karnath, H. O., Himmelbach, M. and Rorden, C. (2002) The subcortical anatomy of human spatial neglect: putamen, caudate nucleus and pulvinar. *Brain*, 125, 350–360.

Keane, S., Turner, C., Sherrington, C. and Beard, J. R. (2006) Use of Fresnel prism glasses to treat stroke patients with hemispatial neglect. *Archives of Physical Medicine and Rehabilitation*, 87, 1668–1672.

Kerkhoff, G. (2001) Spatial hemineglect in humans. *Progress in Neurobiology*, 63, 1–27.

Kerkhoff, G. (2003) Modulation and rehabilitation of spatial neglect by sensory stimulation. *Progress in Brain Research*, 142, 257–271.

Kinsbourne, M. (1993) Orientational bias model of unilateral neglect: evidence from attentional gradients with hemispace. In Robertson, I. H. and Marshall, J. C. (eds), *Unilateral Neglect: Clinical and Experimental Studies*, pp. 63–86. Erlbaum, Hillsdale, NJ.

Klos, T., Geggus, S. and Pauli, P. (2004) Improvement of visuospatial neglect by PA. Paper presented at the annual meeting of the German society of neuropsychology (GNP), Munich, September 2 to 5, 2004.

Kurata, K. and Hoshi, E. (1999) Reacquisition deficits in prism adaptation after muscimol microinjection into the ventral premotor cortex of monkeys. *Journal of Neurophysiology*, **81**, 1927–1938.

Luauté, J., Halligan, P., Rossetti, Y., Rode, G. and Boisson, D. (2006a) Visuo-spatial neglect; a systematic review of current interventions and their effectiveness. *Neuroscience and Biobehavioral Reviews*, **30**, 961–982.

Luauté, J., Halligan, P., Rode, G., Jacquin-Courtois, S. and Boisson, D. (2006b) Prism adaptation first among equals in alleviating left neglect. A review. *Restorative Neurology and Neuroscience*, **24**, 409–418.

Luauté, J., Michel, C., Rode, G. *et al.* (2006c) Functional anatomy of the therapeutic effects of prism adaptation on left neglect. *Neurology*, **66**, 1859–1867.

Malhotra, P., Coulthard, E. and Husain, M. (2006) Hemispatial neglect, balance and eye-movement control. *Current Opinion in Neurology*, **19**, 14–20.

Maravita, A., McNeil, J., Malhotra, P., Greenwood, R., Husain, M. and Driver, J. (2003) Prism adaptation can improve contralesional tactile perception in neglect. *Neurology*, **60**, 1829–1831.

Martin, T. A., Keating, J. G., Goodkin, H. P., Bastian, A. J. and Thatch, W. T. (1996) Throwing while looking through prisms. I. Focal olivocerebellar lesions impair adaptation. *Brain*, **119**, 1183–1198.

Mattingley, J. B., Bradshaw, J. L. and Phillips, J. G. (1992) Impairments of movement initiation and execution in unilateral neglect. Directional hypokinesia and bradykinesia. *Brain*, **115**, 1849–1874.

McIntosh, R. M., Rossetti, Y. and Milner, A. D. (2002), Prism adaptation improves chronic visual and haptic neglect. *Cortex*, **38**, 309–320.

Meador, K. J., Allen, M. E., Adams, R. J. and Loring, D. W. (1991) Allochiria vs allesthesia. Is there a misperception? *Archives of Neurology*, **48**, 546–549.

Michel, C. (2006) Simulating unilateral neglect in normals: myth or reality? *Restorative Neurology and Neuroscience*, **24**, 419–430.

Michel, C., Pisella, L., Halligan, P. W. *et al.* (2003) Simulating unilateral neglect in normals using prism adaptation: implications for theory. *Neuropsychologia*, **41**, 25–39.

Michel, C., Pisella, L., Prablanc, C. *et al.* (2007) Enhancing visuo-motor adaptation by reducing error signals: single-step (aware) versus multiple-step (unaware) exposure to wedge prisms. *Journal of Cognitive Neuroscience*, **19**, 1–10.

Middleton, F. A. and Strick, P. L. (2000) Basal ganglia and cerebellar loops: motor and cognitive circuits. *Brain Research, Brain Research Reviews*, **31**, 236–250.

Morris, A. P., Kritikos, A., Berberovic, N., Pisella, L., Chambers, C. D. and Mattingley, J. (2004) Prism adaptation and spatial attention: a study of visual search in normals and patients with unilateral neglect. *Cortex*, **40**, 703–721.

Mort, D., Malhorta, P., Mannan, S., Rorden, C. *et al.* (2003) The anatomy of visual neglect. *Brain*, **126**, 1986–1997.

Paolucci, S., Antonucci, G., Guariglia, C., Magnotti, L., Pizzamiglio, L. and Zoccolotti, P. (1996) Facilitatory effect of neglect rehabilitation on the recovery of left hemiplegic stroke patients: a cross-over study. *Journal of Neurology* **243**, 308–314.

Parton, A., Malhorta, P. and Husain, M. (2003) Hemispatial neglect. *Journal of Neurology, Neurosurgery and Psychiatry*, **75**, 13–21.

Perennou, D. (2006) Postural disorders and spatial neglect in stroke patients: a strong association. *Restorative Neurology and Neuroscience*, **24**, 319–334.

Pisella, L. and Mattingley, J. B. (2004) The contribution of spatial remapping impairments to unilateral visual neglect. *Neuroscience and Biobeahvioral Reviews*, **28**, 181–200.

Pisella, L., Rode, G., Farne, A., Boisson, D. and Rossetti, Y. (2002) Dissociated long lasting improvements of straight-ahead pointing and line bisection tasks in two unilateral neglect patients. *Neuropsychologia*, **40**, 327–334.

Pisella, L., Michel, C., Grea, H., Tilikete, C., Vighetto, A. and Rossetti, Y. (2004) Preserved prism adaptation in bilateral optic ataxia: strategic versus adaptive reaction to prisms. *Experimental Brain Research*, **156**, 399–408.

Pisella, L., Rossetti, Y., Michel, C. *et al.* (2005) Ipsidirectional impairment of prism adaptation after unilateral lesion of anterior cerebellum. *Neurology*, **65**, 150–152.

Pisella, L., Rode, G., Farnè, A., Tilikete, C. and Rossetti, Y. (2006) Prism adaptation in the rehabilitation of patients with visuo-spatial cognitive disorders. *Current Opinion in Neurology*, **19**, 534–542.

Pizzamiglio, L., Antonucci, G., Judica, A., Montenero, P., Razzano, C. and Zoccolotti, P. (1992) Cognitive rehabilitation of the hemineglect disorder in chronic patients with unilateral right brain damage. *Journal of Clinical Experimental Neuropsychology*, **14**, 901–923.

Posner, M. I., Walker, J. A., Friedrich, F. J. *et al.* (1984) Effects of parietal injury on covert orienting of attention. *Journal of Neuroscience*, **4**, 1863–1874.

Redding, G. M. and Wallace, B. (1996) Adaptive spatial alignment and strategic perceptual-motor control. *Journal of Experimental Psychology, Human Perception and Performance*, **22**, 379–394.

Redding, G. M. and Wallace, B. (2005) Prism adaptation and unilateral neglect: review and analysis. *Neuropsychologia*, **44**, 1–20.

Redding, G. M., Rossetti, Y. and Wallace, B. (2005) Applications of prism adaptation: a tutorial in theory and method. *Neuroscience and Biobehavioral Reviews*, **29**, 431–444.

Robertson, I. H. (2001) Do we need the "lateral" in unilateral neglect? Spatially nonselective attention deficits in unilateral neglect and their implications for rehabilitation. *Neuroimage*, **14**, 585–590.

Robertson, I. H., Manly, T., Beschin, N. *et al.* (1997) Auditory sustained attention is a marker of unilateral spatial neglect. *Neuropsychologia*, **35**, 1527–1532.

Robertson, I. H., Mattingley, J. B., Rorden, C. and Driver, J. (1998) Phasic alerting of neglect patients overcomes their spatial deficit in visual awareness. *Nature*, **395**, 169–170.

Rode, G., Charles, N., Perenin, M. T., Vighetto, A., Trillet, M. and Aimard, G. (1992) Partial remission of hemiplegia and somatoparaphrenia through vestibular stimulation in a case of unilateral neglect. *Cortex*, **28**, 203–208.

Rode, G., Tilikete, C. and Boisson, D. (1997) Predominance of postural imbalance in left hemiparetic patients. *Scandinavian Journal of Rehabilitation Medicine*, **29**, 11–16.

Rode, G., Rossetti, Y., Li, L. and Boisson, D. (1998) The effect of prism adaptation on neglect for visual imagery. *Behavioural Neurology*, **11**, 251–258.

Rode, G., Rossetti, Y. and Boisson, D. (2001) Prism adaptation improves representational neglect. *Neuropsychologia*, **39**, 1250–1254.

Rode, G., Tilikete, C., Luaute, J., Rossetti, Y., Vighetto, A. and Boisson, D. (2002) Bilateral vestibular stimulation does not improve visual hemineglect. *Neuropsychologia*, **40**, 1104–1106.

Rode, G., Pisella, L., Rossetti, Y., Farne, A. and Boisson, D. (2003) Bottom-up transfer of sensory-motor plasticity to recovery of spatial cognition: visuomotor adaptation and spatial neglect. *Progress in Brain Research*, **142**, 273–287.

Rode, G., Klos, T., Courtois-Jacquin, S. and Rossetti, Y. (2006a) Neglect and prism adaptation. A new therapeutic tool for spatial cognition disorders. *Restorative Neurology and Neuroscience*, **24**, 347–356.

Rode, G., Pisella, L., Marsal, L., Mercier, S., Rossetti, Y. and Boisson, D. (2006b) Prism adaptation improves spatial dysgraphia following right brain damage. *Neuropsychologia*, **44**, 2487–2493.

Rode, G., Revol, P., Rossetti, Y., Boisson, D. and Bartolomeo, P. (2007) Looking while imagining: the influence of visual imput on representational neglect. *Neurology*, **68**, 432–7.

Rossetti, Y. and Rode, G. (2002) Reducing spatial neglect by visual and other sensory manipulations: non-cognitive (physiological) routes to the rehabilitation of a cognitive disorder. In Karnath, H. O., Milner, A. D. and Vallar, G. (eds), *The Cognitive and Neural Bases of Spatial Neglect*, pp. 375–396, Oxford University Press, New York.

Rossetti, Y., Koga, K. and Mano, T. (1993) Prismatic displacement of vision induces transient changes in the timing of eye-hand coordination. *Perception and Psychophysics*, **54**, 355–364.

Rossetti, Y., Rode, G., Pisella, L. *et al*. (1998) Prism adaptation to a rightward optical deviation rehabilitates left hemispatial neglect. *Nature*, **395**, 166–169.

Rossetti, Y., Pisella, L., Colent, C. *et al*. (2000) A cerebellar therapy for a parietal deficit? (abstract) In Weiss, P. H. H. (ed.), *Action and Visuo-spatial Attention. Neurobiological Bases and Disorders*, p. 21. Life Sciences, Reihe Lebenswissenschaften, Forschungszentrum Jülich GmbH, Germany.

Rossetti, Y., Jacquin-Courtois, S., Rode, G., Ota, H., Michel, C. and Boisson, D. (2004) Does action make the link between number and space representation? Visuo-manual adaptation improves number bisection in unilateral neglect. *Psychological Science*, **15**, 426–430.

Rousseaux, M., Bernati, T., Saj, A. and Kozlowski, O. (2006) Ineffectiveness of prism adaptation on spatial neglect signs. *Stroke*, **37**, 542–543.

Rubens, A. B. (1985) Caloric stimulation and unilateral visual neglect. *Neurology*, **35**, 1019–1024.

Rusconi, M.L., Maravita, A. Bottini, G. and Vallar, G. (2002) Is the intact side really intact? Perseverative responses in patients with unilateral neglect: a productive manifestation. *Neuropsychologia*, **40**, 594–604.

Saari, M., Kalra, L., Greenwood, R. and Driver, J. (2006) Prism adaptation changes perceptual awareness for chimeric visual objects but not for chimeric faces in spatial neglect after right-hemisphere stroke. *Neurocase*, **12**, 127–135.

Schenkenberg, T., Bradford, D. C. and Ajax, E. T. (1980) Line bisection with neurologic impairment. *Neurology*, **30**, 509–517.

Schindler, I., Kerkhoff, G., Karnath, H. O., Keller, I. and Goldenberg, G. (2002) Neck muscle vibration induces lasting recovery in spatial neglect. *Journal of Neurology, Neurosurgery and Psychiatry*, **73**, 412–419.

Schmaahmann, J. D. (1998) Dysmetria of thought: clinical consequences of cerebellar dysfunction on cognition and affect. *Trends in Cognitive Science*, **2**, 362–371.

Serino, A., Angeli, V., Frassinetti, F. and Ladavas, E. (2006) Mechanisms underlying neglect recovery after prism adaptation. *Neuropsychologia*, **44**, 1068–1078.

Smania, N., Martini, M. C., Gambina, G. *et al*. (1998) The spatial distribution of visual attention in hemineglect and extinction patients. *Brain*, **121**, 1759–1770.

Sumitani, M., Shibata, M., Yagisawa, M. *et al*. (2006) Prism adaptation to optical deviation alleviates complex regional pain syndrome: longitudinal single case study. *Neurorehabilitation and Neural Repair*, **20**, 141–142.

Sumitani, M., Rossetti, Y., Shibata, M. *et al*. (2007) Prism adaptation to optical deviation alleviates pathological pain. *Neurology*, **68**, 128–133.

Thiebaut de Schotten, M., Urbanski, M., Duffau, H. *et al*. (2005) Direct evidence for a parietal–frontal pathway subserving spatial awareness in humans. *Science*, **309**, 2226–2228.

Tilikete, C., Rode, G., Rossetti, Y., Li, L., Pichon, J. and Boisson, D. (2001) Prism adaptation to rightward optical deviation improves postural imbalance in left hemiparetic patients. *Current Biology*, **11**, 524–528.

Vallar, G. (2001) Extrapersonal visual unilateral spatial neglect and its neuroanatomy. *Neuroimage*, **14**, 552–558.

Vallar, G. and Perani, D. (1986) The anatomy of unilateral neglect after right-hemsiphere stroke lesions. A clinical/CT-scan correlation study. *Neuropsychologia*, **24**, 609–622.

Vallar, G., Guariglia, C. and Rusconi, M. L. (1997) Modulation of the neglect syndrome by sensory stimulation. In *Parietal Lobe Contributions to Orientation in 3D Space*, pp. 555–578. Springer, Berlin.

Weiner, M. J., Hallett, M. and Funkenstein, H. H. (1983) Adaptation to lateral displacement of vision in patients with lesions of the central nervous system. *Neurology*, **33**, 766–772.

Zorzi, M., Priftis, K. and Umilta, C. (2002) Brain damage: neglect disrupts the mental number line. *Nature*, **417**, 198–199.

Section 3

Self and Other

11

From my self to other selves: a revised framework for the self/other differentiation*

Marc Jeannerod

This paper discusses the difference between self-identification and the self/other differentiation. Self-identification relies on the congruence of self-generated movements and their expected consequences, i.e. on the temporal correlation between the set of signals (command signals, sensory reafferences) that are related to that movement. Only the *origin* of the movement (i.e. whether it originates from the self or not), not its destination or its goal, is relevant for self-identification. Self/other differentiation requires both that one can understand the actions others perform, and that one can attribute these actions to them. Understanding implies that a complete description of the actions of other agents, from their origin to their end, can be available in the brain of the observer. Attributing implies that the agent can be clearly differentiated from the self. The model for the self/other differentiation proposed here can therefore be described as a 'rotate/simulate' model: I first rotate myself at the location of the person I observe in order to specify her location in space. Then, I simulate the action I observe from that person in order to understand what she is doing. Assuming that the two operations are more or less synchronous, the action I simulate is automatically attributed to the person I observe, not to myself. The simulation network in the observer's brain overlaps with the execution network in the agent's brain; by contrast, the rotation network is specific to the observer's brain.

Introduction

The general problem I will address in this paper is twofold. First, I will ask the question of how the self builds up as an independent entity. Second, I will try to understand how we differentiate ourselves from other selves. These two questions are the main objectives of the recently expanding field of 'motor cognition' (Jeannerod, 2006). As I will argue, motor cognition offers different possibilities for approaching the problem of the self, whether one considers the self from its own perspective (the 'selfish' side of motor cognition), or from the perspective of the interaction between two or more selves (the 'interactive' side of motor cognition).

---

* This paper was read as the Association Lecture at the XXII Attention and Performance Meeting, at Château de Pizay, France, July 2006.

A note of caution is needed before entering the core of the study. The self is a psychological concept, and the description of its mechanisms must obey the usual constraints inherent to psychological studies. By this, I mean that the basic mechanisms which underlie the self can only be inferred from the explicit content of corresponding mental states, as expressed by the conscious subject. Therefore, although I will stand here at the subpersonal level of description of the self, what other authors refer to as the 'minimal self' (e.g. Gallagher, 2000), or the 'embodied self' (e.g. Gallese *et al.*, 2004), I will base my conclusions on experiments where the results are acquired through subjective responses. In other words, my attempt will be to describe the physiological building blocks which represent the underpinnings of the more elaborate aspects of the self, those which allow the self to have a sense of itself. In order to achieve this task, I will use this sense of self as a source of information for demonstrating the existence of the physiological mechanisms, in experiments where they can be manipulated or in pathological conditions where they are altered. In addition, as it is now becoming customary, I will decompose the sense of self into the 'sense of ownership' and the 'sense of agency'. The sense of ownership corresponds to the ability to recognize oneself as the owner of a body which makes the self have an appearance and boundaries. The sense of agency corresponds to the ability to recognize oneself as the agent of a motor behavior which can influence the course of external events and the behavior of other selves.

The next section deals with the construction of the self as an independent entity, a process to which I refer as self-identification. The subsequent sections deal with the self/other differentiation. The point is that self-identification and the self/other differentiation, although they capitalize on similar mechanisms, are two distinct processes: identifying oneself is a first-person experience, whereas perceiving another self is a third-person experience. I will propose that the main difference between the two processes relies on the type of spatial transformation that takes place during the perception of one's own actions and during the perception of the actions of other selves, respectively.

Self-identification and the primacy of self-generated action

It is essential for a moving animal to individualize itself from the surroundings and particularly to disentangle the effects that its own movements produce on the external world from those produced by external events. The external world comprises other moving objects (or selves). Even the 'background' to these objects is rarely stationary: clouds move in the sky, tree branches are agitated by the wind, water flows, etc. The basic function of self-identification has been clearly described in many animal species, including insects, fishes, reptiles and mammals (see review in Jeannerod *et al.*, 1979). Since the 1950s, several authors have proposed plausible physiological models for achieving this task (Sperry, 1950; von Holst and Mittelstaedt, 1950; Wolpert *et al.*, 1995).

Monitoring the degree of congruence between the internal cues arising at the time of a self-generated movement and the sensory cues arising as the outcome of this movement is therefore a relatively safe means for determining the authorship of a movement and, by way of consequence, for eliminating confusion regarding possible external sources for this movement. In this section, I will report two experiments from our laboratory in which this congruence was experimentally manipulated in normal subjects and the effects of these manipulations on the sense of self were examined.

The first experiment tested the effect of manipulating the degree of congruence between a self-generated movement and its corresponding visual consequences (Franck *et al.*, 2001). The subjects were instructed to hold a joystick with their right hand. The hand and the joystick were hidden from their view. Instead, they saw the electronically reconstructed image of a hand holding a joystick appearing at the precise location of their own hand (Figure 11.1).

When they moved their actual hand, the electronic hand also moved by the same amount and in the same direction: subjects rapidly became acquainted with this situation and felt

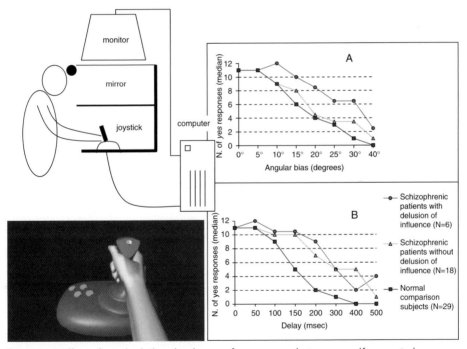

Figure 11.1 Effect of manipulating the degree of congruence between a self-generated movement and its visual consequences. (Upper left) Experimental display. The subject sits in front of a mirror hiding his hand and reflecting a computer-generated image of a hand holding a joystick. (Lower left) Subject's view of the computer-generated image. The movements of the electronic hand faithfully reproduce the movements the subject performs with his own hand. (Right) (**A**) Effect of imposing an angular bias on the movements of the electronic hand. The dark squares represent the 'yes' responses from of 29 normal subjects. Note decrease of 'yes' responses as a function of the increase of the angular bias. The triangle and circle symbols refer to groups of schizophrenic patients performing the same task. (**B**) Effect of imposing a delay on the movements of the electronic hand. Note decay of 'yes' responses as the delay increases. Data from Franck *et al.* (2001).

the movements of the electronic hand as their own. Each trial consisted in executing, with the joystick, reaching movements to briefly presented visual targets. On some trials the movement of the electronic hand was rotated with respect to that of the real hand. Rotations went in either direction by up to 40°, by steps of 5°. At the end of each trial, the subjects had to answer the question of whether the movement they saw on the screen corresponded to the movement they had made with their hand. Verbal ('Yes' or 'No') responses were collected for the neutral trials (no rotation) and for the rotated trials. In the neutral trials, the subjects gave 99% 'Yes' responses. In the rotated trials, the proportion of 'Yes' responses progressively decreased as the degree of rotation increased, up to the point (when the rotation exceeded 15°) where the 'No' responses predominated (Figure 11.1). This experiment demonstrates that the actual sensory consequences of a movement have to match its expected consequences in order for this movement to be identified as self-generated. The system that compares the expected and the actual sensory consequences of a movement has a relatively broad tolerance, as shown by the fact that, in the present experiment, discrepancies up to 10° were only poorly detected.

In this experiment, however, self-identification cues were limited to a relatively crude representation of the movement, and did not allow exploring the factors involved in self-attribution. This was the objective of a second experiment, which tested the respective roles of body and movement cues for self-identification. A situation which combined uncertainty about the ownership of the subject's hand and the authorship of the movements performed with that hand was created. This situation (van den Bos and Jeannerod, 2002; see also Knoblich, 2002), involved simultaneous presentation of two hands, one of which was the subject's hand, the other being an 'alien' hand. The subject and the experimenter sat at the opposite sides of a table. The subject was facing a screen. Both the subject and the experimenter placed their right gloved hand below the screen. A mirror attached to the back of the screen reflected the image of the two hands to a video camera connected to a computer. A program processed the digitized video image in real time (within 20 ms) and sent an image of the hands onto the screen (Figure 11.2). The program allowed rotating the image displayed on the screen. So, the subject could see his or her own hand at the bottom of the screen, where it would be in reality (0° rotation), at the top of the screen (180° rotation), at the left of the screen (90° rotation) or at the right of the screen (−90° rotation), while the experimenter's hand was always in the opposite direction. Different angles of rotation were combined across trials with different movements. At the beginning of each trial, the subject was instructed either to extend the index finger or the thumb, or to make no movement. During the trials where the subject was instructed to make a movement, the experimenter would either make the same or the alternative movement (Figure 11.2). Once the movements were performed, the screen returned dark within about 1 s. Then a pointer was placed at the position where one of the two hands had been. Subjects had to determine whether the hand indicated by the pointer was theirs or that of the experimenter.

This experiment first allowed us to study the role of the apparent positions of the hands on self-identification. When the two hands visually appeared on the screen at positions

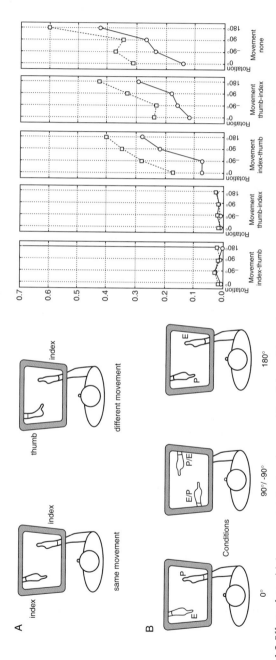

Figure 11.2 Effect of combining uncertainty about ownership of the subject's hand and authorship of the movements performed with that hand. (Left) Experimental situation. (**A**) Subject's hand and experimenter's hand appear in concordance with their real position. The two participants may perform the same or a different finger movement, or no movement. (Courtesy of G. Knoblisch) (**B**) Subject's hand and experimenter's hand can appear rotated with respect to their real position. Conditions of movement and hand rotation are combined across successive trials. (Right) Mean error in a group of normal subjects in attributing one of the two hands to themselves (open squares) or to the experimenter (open circles). Each box shows the results for each movement condition according to the apparent position of the hands. Note absence of errors when the two hands made different movements (first two boxes). From van den Bos and Jeannerod (2002).

corresponding to their real positions, subjects showed relatively little difficulty in recognizing their own hand. However, when the apparent locations of the hands were changed with respect to reality, they made attribution errors. This confirms that the congruence between visual and proprioceptive signals (kinesthesia and position sense) arising from a body part plays a role in self-attributing this body part. Although visual signals can have several possible origins, proprioceptive signals unambiguously pertain to the moving limb and can indeed be considered as first-person signals par excellence.

However, the most critical factor for correct attribution was the presence of finger movements. When finger movements were present and these movements were clearly attributable to the self (i.e. they differed from those of the experimenter), no attribution errors were found. The most surprising finding was that accurate self-identification was possible for all orientations of the display, including the 180° rotation (Figure 11.2). This result stands in apparent contradiction with what was said previously about the importance of the congruence of visual and proprioceptive signals as a cue for self-attributing a hand. In fact, it shows that movement cues are so prominent that they can override sensory signals. In other words, when distinctive movements are available, subjects tend to recognize movements, not just hands: referring to the definitions made in the introduction, the sense of agency tends to dominate the sense of ownership for providing a sense of self.

The main conclusion to be drawn from these data is that self-identification primarily relies on the congruence of self-generated movements and their expected consequences, i.e. on the temporal correlation between the set of signals (command signals, sensory reafferences) that are related to that movement (Blakemore *et al.*, 1998; Farrer *et al.*, 2003). Thus, the critical condition for self-identification is that the self-generated movement is unambiguously self-attributed. Note that, although there were two hands in the display shown to the subjects of the second experiment, the alien hand was not formally attributed to another person. It was a disembodied hand with no specific intention, performing movements devoid of goal and content. Indeed, a critical point in the present discussion is that only the *origin* of the movement (i.e. whether it originates from the self or not), not its destination or its goal, is relevant for self-identification. This mode of identification is a clearly 'selfish' mechanism, in the sense that it fulfills the limited function of disentangling self-produced events from events in the external world, but ignores the content of these events (Jeannerod and Pacherie, 2004). As we shall see in the next section, this content-independent mode of 'tagging' a self-produced movement contrasts with the full description of an action which is required for the self/other differentiation.

The same action as seen from different perspectives

I now turn to the 'interactive' level of motor cognition, which describes the interaction between subjects and which implies the existence of a specific process for self/other differentiation. In keeping with the framework I used for the process of self-identification, I will assume that self-generated actions also play a critical role for differentiating selves from one another. Thus, the problem will be how one can recognize that others are both agents *like* us, i.e. that they self-generate movements and meaningful actions, and agents *distinct from* us, i.e. that the actions we see them perform are theirs, not ours. In other words, I will assume that the process of the self/other differentiation requires both that we can understand the actions others perform, and that we can attribute these actions to them. Understanding implies that a complete description of the actions of other agents, from their origin to their end, can be available in the brain of the observer. Attributing implies that the agent can be clearly differentiated from the self.

A given action can be seen from different perspectives. It can be seen from the perspective of the agent who performs it, the first-person perspective; but it can also be seen from the perspective of an observer who watches the agent acting, i.e. from a third-person perspective. The capacity to recognize an action as the same from the agent's and the observer's different perspectives is far from trivial. Our first task is thus to determine the main parameters which have to be taken into account for identifying an action from different perspectives. To this end, I will devote the next section to a brief description of the familiar visuo-motor action of reaching toward an object and grasping it, which I will subsequently use as a prototypical example for understanding this process of action recognition.

Grasping an object and the degrees of freedom problem

The action of grasping an object placed in front of the agent can be typically decomposed into two components: the reaching component which projects the hand at the object location, and the grasping component which ensures a stable grasp of the object (Jeannerod, 1981). This apparently simple motor coordination involves a number of physiological constraints, which relate to the agent himself (the biomechanical limitations of his arm), to the object (its size, shape and orientation) and to the relative positions of the agent and the object. A successful reach requires that the spatial position of the object has been encoded in a set of coordinates which has its origin on the agent's body (a set of egocentric coordinates), and that the arm movement is planned according to this same set of coordinates. A successful grasp requires that the fingers are placed at the appropriate position on the object surface or, more specifically, that the opposition axis is properly oriented (Figure 11.3). Things are more complex, however, because it turns out that the orientation of the opposition axis is in fact the controlled parameter, not only of the grasping component itself, but of the reach-and-grasp action as a whole. In other words, the two components have to be coordinated with one another in order to ensure the efficiency of the final grasp (Weiss and Jeannerod, 1998).

Consider for example an object which imposes a specific placement of the fingers on its surface: different orientations of the opposition axis will have to be used for each position of the object relative to the body; and, by way of consequence, the configuration of the whole limb will be different for each of these orientations. As illustrated in Figure 11.3, different degrees of freedom of the upper limb (e.g. dorsal or ventral flexion of the wrist, abduction or adduction of the shoulder, hyperpronation or supination of the forearm) have to be engaged for different orientations of the object (Stelmach *et al.*, 1994). Even with so many degrees of freedom, the number of possible configurations of the arm compatible with a stable grasp is limited by biomechanics. Indeed, there is a tendency of

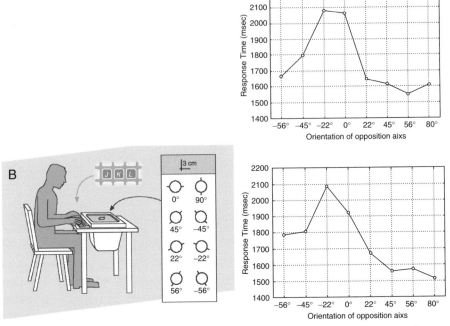

Figure 11.3 Time to perform and to mentally simulate reach and grasp movements with different degrees of difficulty. (Upper right) Time to reach and grasp a cylinder with different orientation of the opposition axis. Zero degrees represents the orientation of the opposition axis parallel to the subject's frontal plane. Note longer time to perform awkward grasps. (Lower left) Experimental situation for the mental simulation of the same movements. Subjects press key J, K or L according to whether grasping the object with a given angle of the opposition axis will be easy, difficult or impossible, respectively. (Lower right) Time to give the response. Note longer response time for awkward orientations of the opposition axis, as for performing the actual movement. Data from Frak *et al.* (1997).

the visuo-motor system, whenever possible, to shift to the arm configuration which involves the minimum number of degrees of freedom (Paulignan *et al.*, 1997). This spontaneous behavior of spatial adjustment for restoring 'natural' or 'easy' movements reflects the fact that engaging additional degrees of freedom has a cost (Rosenbaum *et al.*, 2004). The cost is reflected in an increase in the time taken to prepare more 'difficult' movements. With Victor Frak, we demonstrated this effect by comparing the time to perform reach-and-grasp movements with an easy orientation of the opposition axis and movements with a difficult orientation (Frak *et al.*, 2001) (see Figure 11.3).

A final important point is that these physiological constraints on movement execution are already taken into account at the planning stage of the movement. This can be demonstrated by using the paradigm of motor mental imagery. In this condition, where the movements are purely represented, not executed, the preparation time for imagining the movement also increases with the 'difficulty' of the grasp, as it does for overt movements (Parsons, 1994; Johnson, 2000; Frak *et al.*, 2001). This result is in agreement with the notion of a functional equivalence of overt and covert movements, which assumes that covert movements involve many of the constraints that are met by overtly executed movements (for review, see Jeannerod, 2006). Thus, the choice of the coordinate system for executing a movement (e.g. in egocentric coordinates or in object-centered coordinates) has to be done prior to execution, at the level of the central representation of the action.

Taking the perspective of the observer. The third-person perspective as a rotated first-person perspective

Using both the reach-and-grasp movement and the motor imagery paradigm, we can now describe how the same action looks from different perspectives. In a recent experiment with T. Anquetil, we instructed subjects to imagine the same action of reaching and grasping an upright cylinder with different orientations of the opposition axis, as in the experiment by Frak *et al.* (2001). In addition, the subjects were instructed to adopt different perspectives in simulating the grasping action: they had either to imagine themselves performing the action from their own first-person perspective or to imagine another person facing them performing the same action, i.e. from the third-person perspective (Figure 11.4). We measured the response time for two orientations of the opposition axis (easy and difficult) performed from the two different perspectives to probe the strategy of the subjects when they imagined themselves or another person facing them performing the task (Anquetil and Jeannerod, 2007).

As expected, we confirmed that it takes longer to actually grasp the cylinders with a difficult orientation of the opposition axis than with an easy one. The important finding was that the same constraint on mental movement time equally applied, whether the subject simulated the grasping action as an agent in the first person perspective, or simulated that same action as performed by another agent facing him. No significant difference could be detected between response times in the two conditions of simulation: the mean response times were similar during simulation in the first-person and in the third-person perspective, as was the difference in response time between the two orientations of the grasp (Figure 11.4).

This result is better understood if one assumes that the subjects in fact simulated the action in the same way for both first- and third-person perspective conditions. They could do this by mentally rotating themselves so as to superimpose with the virtual subject facing them. In so doing, the spatial relationship between the acting body and the object was preserved: then, they simply had to use the same set of egocentric coordinates from their new perspective for obtaining the same movement (see also Sebanz *et al.*, 2003; Wohlschläger *et al.*, 2003). Note that it is critical that the system of coordinates used by the observer corresponds to that of the agent he/she observes, in order to preserve the laterality of the body parts involved in the observed action. As I will point out below, this is what distinguishes observing an action made by another agent from viewing the mirror image of a self-generated action.

This finding has further implications: if the observer simulates the agent's action in the same system of coordinates he/she would use for executing it, so that the action can obey the same constraints in the same reference frame transposed to the agent's spatial position,

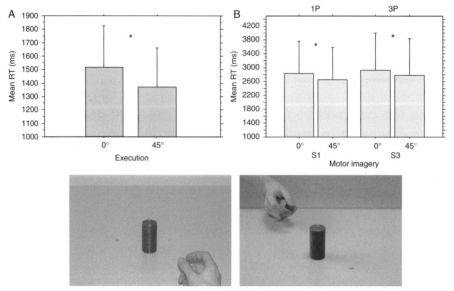

Figure 11.4 Mental simulation of a reach-and-grasp movement in the first- and third-person perspectives. The lower part of the figure shows the subject's view of the image presented during simulation in the first-person perspective (left) and in the third-person perspective (right). (**B**) Response times (RT) for mental simulation of the movements with two different orientations of the opposition axis: 0° awkward grasp; 45° easy grasp. 1P, first-person perspective; 3P, third-person perspective. Note similar longer duration of response time for the awkward grasp in the two perspectives. (**A**) Execution condition with the same subjects. From Anquetil and Jeannerod (2007).

it follows that the motor simulation network of the observer should match the motor execution network of the agent. The same neural structures should be activated in the brains of the two subjects. Indeed, this hypothesis of a similarity of the neural networks for self-generating an action and for understanding it (e.g. Rizzolatti *et al.*, 1995; see Jeannerod, 2001) is supported by numerous experimental data. Take for example interference experiments. If executing and observing an action share the same network, mere observation of the action should facilitate its execution because the same network will be activated both by execution and by observation; but the reverse should occur if the observed and the executed actions differ from one another, because of the interference between two concurrent networks. Stürmer *et al.* (2000), Brass *et al.* (2001) and Kilner *et al.* (2003) found that, when the movements performed by the observer were congruent with those performed by the other person, they were clearly facilitated (their reaction time was shorter and their accuracy was better). Conversely, the non-congruence of the movements of the observer with those of the other person yielded degraded performance. These results demonstrating the existence of an interference between executed and observed incongruent movements clearly supports our view that the actions one observes from other agents are coded by the same neural network and within the same coordinates as those one would use for executing these actions.

The degree of similarity of the neural network for executing and understanding an action can also be tested by recording the changes in cortico-spinal excitability during action observation. If an observer watches an agent performing, say, a thumb abduction/adduction movement, a large motor potential will be evoked in his thumb abductor muscle by transcranial stimulation of his motor cortex. Conversely, if the observer watches an index finger flexion/extension movement, the motor-evoked potential will be larger in his index flexor muscle. Importantly, these changes are recorded on the side corresponding to the laterality of the movements one observes, i.e. the excitability of the left motor cortex is increased while observing the movements of a right hand (Fadiga et al., 1995; Strafella and Paus, 2000; Clark et al., 2004). Maeda et al. (2002) found that the excitability of the left motor cortex during watching a moving right hand was greater when the hand was presented in a direction pointing away from the body, than in a direction pointing towards the body. In the away condition, it was as if the observer had transposed himself to the position of an agent sitting on his left; in the toward condition, it was as if the observer had rotated himself at the position of an agent facing him. Both spatial transformations are compatible with using the same system of egocentric coordinates, in the sense that they both provide a picture of the action as it is seen when executed by another agent.

The situation created by rotated or displaced egocentric coordinates radically differs from the mirror situation. Mirrors show us images of ourselves, not of others (see Ramachandran and Rogers-Ramachandran, 1996). When I see myself in a mirror and move my right arm, what I expect to see is that my mirror image will move the arm facing my right arm. This is because my mirror image is a mere reflection of myself. But the way we see ourselves in a mirror is not the way other people see us. Remember the famous scene in one of the Marx Bothers' films, *Duck Soup*: a mirror breaks, and Harpo imitates Groucho, move for move, to postpone the discovery of the broken mirror. If the mirror breaker wants to give the illusion that he is the mirror image of the person facing him (and in fact that the two are one single person), he must replicate the moves of the other not only move to move, but also in a set of coordinates opposite to that of the movements of the other. This is so unnatural that the match between the two rapidly falls apart. Conversely, if you were seeing an image of yourself moving in egocentric coordinates rather than in mirror coordinates, you would tend to disregard the possibility that it could be you, and you would attribute this image to an alien person. This is indeed what happens when people unknowingly see an on-line television display of themselves: they frequently tend to believe that the image is that of somebody else, because they see it moving as they would see another person. Facing oneself as another person is a biologically implausible situation.

The attribution problem. If we see the others as rotated versions of ourselves, why do we attribute the actions we observe to the others and not to ourselves?

The fact that a reach-and-grasp action looks the same from the agent's perspective and from the observer's perspective suggests that the motor simulation mechanism in itself is neutral with respect to where the action is seen and who performs it. The mirror system provides the observer with a copy of the observed action irrespective of the agent's position in space (Rizzolatti *et al.*, 1996). The hard question now is: why does the observer attribute the observed action to the agent and not to him/herself? The tentative answer that I will propose is that it is the encoding of the spatial transformation made by the observer to match the agent's perspective which provides the cues for the self/other differentiation and for the correct attribution.

At the beginning of this paper, I stressed the role of action cues for identifying an action as self-generated, and ultimately for identifying oneself as the agent of that action (the sense of agency). Can these same cues be used for attributing the action to another agent? If the motor simulation is so realistic as to exactly match the observed action, then, in theory, there would be no possibility for differentiating the two agents from one another by using the action cues. Identifying an agent as a self independent from oneself first requires that this agent is localized at a specific position in space, different from one's own position. The popular expression of putting oneself in the other's shoes or skin expresses the need for taking the perspective of the other on the external world and on external objects for understanding or feeling what she experiences. By translating (or rotating) oneself to the location of the other, one sees things as she would see them. Thus, the possibility for identifying the other must rely on the mechanism that operates the translation of the egocentric coordinates at a different spatial location. This mechanism, distinct from the motor simulation network, is needed for encoding the spatial transformation and differentiating the spatial positions of the two selves.

Although little is known about the mechanism for this spatial transformation, many data in the literature point to the role of the inferior parietal lobule, in the posterior part of the parietal lobe, as the main constituent of a spatial transformation network. In monkeys, the inferior parietal lobule, in addition to receiving its visual input through the 'classical' dorsal visual stream, also receives dense connections from the ventral stream. Areas located in the superior temporal sulcus and in other regions of the inferotemporal cortex do project to the inferior parietal lobule (Rizzolatti and Matelli, 2003). Particularly relevant to the present discussion is the specialization of several of these areas in processing representations of the body. A cortical zone selective for visual processing of the human body (the extrastriate body area, EBA) has been identified in humans at the occipito-temporal junction, (Downing *et al.*, 2001, 2006). EBA is activated by moving body parts as well, and this activation is selective for body movements produced by other persons, rather than for self-produced movements (Astafiev *et al.*, 2004; see Jeannerod, 2004b). This selectivity is also retained in the STS (Hietanen and Perrett, 1993). The inferior parietal lobule, which receives these visual signals, would therefore be well suited for disentangling actions performed by external bodies from those arising from one's own body.

This view is supported by experimental and clinical data. Experimentally, the posterior parietal cortex is associated with body-in-space operations. Imagining an action in the third-person perspective (as in the above experiment), and not from one's own perspective, activates the inferior parietal lobule on the right side (Ruby and Decety, 2001). Likewise, direct electrical stimulation of this region elicits illusory perceptions of one's own body, such as out-of-body experiences (Blanke *et al.*, 2002). Clinically, posterior parietal lesions produce various sorts of visuo-spatial disorders, including right–left disorientation and disorientation in spatial exploration. Similar lesions also affect the representation of the body image (Berlucchi and Agliotti, 1997). One specific disorder in this regard is the so-called mirror agnosia after right-sided parietal lesion (Ramachandran et al., 1997). This role of posterior parietal cortex in the topographical representation of the body is well illustrated by a single case of 'heterotopagnosia' reported by Félician et al. (2003). One patient (AP) with a left-sided atrophic lesion of the inferior parietal lobule (areas 39–40) was impaired when she had to point on command at the examiner's body parts, although she was unimpaired in pointing at her own body parts. When asked to point at the examiner's body parts, AP frequently tended to point at the corresponding body part on her own body. This inability to point to the body of another person contrasted with the preserved ability to point at objects on the examiner's body. She could also correctly point at body parts on drawings. In the context of this chapter, heterotopagnosia can be interpreted as a difficulty in transferring one's own body coordinates to another body.

Conclusion

We see others as rotated or displaced ourselves, so that we are able to see things as they would see them. And indeed, from their perspective they see us as we would be if they rotated or displaced themselves by the same amount. The same action, whether it is executed by us or by the other, is merely transposed at another location with keeping the same system of coordinates. The mechanism which underlies this transformation tells the observer that the other he/she sees stands at a distinct spatial location. The model for the self/other differentiation which I have proposed here can therefore be described as a 'rotate/simulate' model: I first rotate myself at the location of the person I observe in order to specify her location in space. Then, I simulate the action I observe from that person in order to understand what she is doing. Assuming that the two operations are more or less synchronous, the action I simulate is automatically attributed to the person I observe, not to myself. The simulation network in the observer's brain overlaps with the execution network in the agent's brain (Georgieff and Jeannerod, 1998; Jeannerod, 2001); by contrast, the rotation network is specific to the observer's brain. Note, however, that there are situations where the two persons are both the agent and the observer at the same time, when they are involved in a joint action, for example. Not surprisingly this type of situation frequently causes the agents/observers to misattribute to themselves actions they have not performed (Daprati et al., 1997).

'Rotate' and 'simulate' are two distinct operations, in the sense that they rely on two distinct neural networks for attributing and understanding, respectively. On the other hand, they can hardly be conceived as separate, in the sense that they both contribute to the same function, the self/other differentiation. Rotation alone, i.e. taking the perspective of another person without interacting with her, would correspond to a differentiation without content, as it may be the case in autistic patients. Simulation alone, without being able to attribute the action one observes to another agent, would lead to false attributions, and ultimately to the impossibility of differentiating oneself from other persons, as this may occur in schizophrenia. Thus, the rotate/simulate model accounts for the possibility of the two selves preserving their individuality. The self/other differentiation is the gateway to social communication, because communication between two selves requires that they both understand each other and remain distinct from one another. The purpose of communication is precisely to avoid fusion of the two selves which interact and to keep a clear separation between them (Jacob and Jeannerod, 2005).

Acknowledgments

I thank Prof. Patrick Haggard for his thoughtful suggestions on an earlier draft of this chapter. My work received constant support from Université Claude Bernard, Lyon.

References

Anquetil, T. and Jeannerod, M. (2007) Simulated actions in the first and the third person perspectives share common representations. *Brain Research*, **1130**, 125–129.

Astafiev, S.V., Stanley, C.M., Shulman, G.L. and Corbetta, M. (2004) Extrastriate body area in human occipital cortex responds to the performance of motor actions. *Nature Neuroscience*, **7**, 542–548.

Blakemore, S. J., Wolpert, D. and Frith, C. D. (1998) Central cancellation of self-produced tickle sensation. *Nature Neuroscience*, **1**, 635–640.

Berlucchi, G. and Agliotti, S. (1997) The body in the brain: neural bases of corporeal awareness. *Trends in Neuroscience*, **20**, 560–564.

Blanke, O., Ortigue, S., Landis, T. and Seeck, M. (2002) Stimulating illusory own-body perceptions. The part of the brain that can induce out-of-body experiences has been located. *Nature*, **419**, 269.

Brass, M., Bekkering, H. and Prinz, W. (2001) Movement observation affects movement execution in a simple response task. *Acta Psychologica*, **106**, 3–22.

Clark, S., Tremblay, F. and Ste-Marie, D. (2004) Differential modulation of corticospinal excitability dutring observation, mental imagery and imitation of hand actions. *Neuropsychologia*, **42**, 105–112.

Daprati, E., Franck, N., Georgieff, N., Proust, J., Pacherie, E., Dalery, J. and Jeannerod, M. (1997) Looking for the agent. An investigation into consciousness of action and self-consciousness in schizophrenic patients. *Cognition*, **65**, 71–86.

Downing, P.E., Jiang, Y., Shuman, M. and Kanwisher, N. (2001) A cortical area selective for visual processing of the human body. *Science*, **293**, 2470–2473.

Downing, P.E., Peelen, M.V., Wiggett, A.J. and Tew, B.D. (2006) The role of the extrastriate body area in action perception. *Social Neuroscience*, **1**, 52–62.

Fadiga, L., Fogassi, L., Pavesi, G. and Rizzolatti, G. (1995) Motor facilitation during action observation. A magnetic stimulation study. *Journal of Neurophysiology*, **73**, 2608–2611.

Farrer, C., Franck, N., Georgieff, N., Frith, C. D., Decety, J. and Jeannerod, M. (2003) Modulating the experience of agency: a PET study. *Neuroimage*, **18**, 324–333.

Félician, O., Ceccaldi, M., Didic, M., Thinus-Blanc, C. and Poncet, M. (2003) Pointing to body parts: a double dissociation study. *Neuropsychologia*, **41**, 1307–1316.

Frak, V. G., Paulignan, Y., and Jeannerod, M. (2001) Orientation of the opposition axis in mentally simulated grasping. *Experimental Brain Research*, **136**, 120–127.

Franck, N. Farrer, C., Georgieff, N., Marie-Cardine, M., Daléry, J. D'Amato, T. and Jeannerod, M. (2001) Defective recognition of one's own actions in schizophrenic patients. *American Journal of Psychiatry*, **158**, 454–459.

Gallagher, S. (2000) Philosophical conceptions of the self: implications for cognitive science. *Trends in Cognitive Science*, 4, 14–21.

Gallese, V., Keysers, C. and Rizzolatti, G. (2004) A unifying view of the basis of social cognition. *Trends in Cognitive Science*, 8, 396–403.

Georgieff, N. and Jeannerod, M. (1998) Beyond consciousness of external reality. A "Who" system for consciousness of action and self-consciousness. *Consciousness and Cognition*, 7, 465–477.

Hietanen, J. K. and Perrett, D. I. (1993) Motion sensitive cells in the macaque superior temporal polysensory area. I. Lack of response to the sight of the monkey's own hand. *Experimental Brain Research*, 93, 117–128.

Jacob, P. and Jeannerod, M. (2005) The motor theory of social cognition: a critique. *Trends in Cognitive Science*, 9, 21–25.

Jeannerod, M. (1981) Intersegmental coordination during reaching at natural visual objects. In Long, J. and Baddeley, A. (eds), *Attention and Performance IX*, pp. 153–168. Erlbaum, Hillsdale, NJ.

Jeannerod, M. (2001) Neural simulation of action: a unifying mechanism for motor cognition. *Neuroimage*, 14, 103–109.

Jeannerod, M. (2004a) Actions from within. *International Journal of Sport and Exercise Psychology*, 2, 376–402.

Jeannerod, M. (2004b) Visual and action cues both contribute to the self-other distinction. *Nature Neuroscience*, 7, 422–423.

Jeannerod, M. (2006) *Motor Cognition. What Actions Tell the Self.* Oxford University Press, Oxford.

Jeannerod, M. and Pacherie, E. (2004) Agency, simulation and self-identification. *Mind and Language*, 19, 113–146.

Jeannerod, M., Kennedy, H. and Magnin, M. (1979) Corollary discharge. Its possible implications in visual and oculomotor interactions. *Neuropsychologia*, 17, 241–258.

Johnson, S.H. (2000) Thinking ahead: the case for motor imagery in propspective judgements of prehension. *Cognition*, 74, 33–70.

Kilner, J. M., Paulignan, Y. and Blakemore, S. J. (2003) An interference effect of observed biological movement on action. *Current Biology*, 13, 522–525.

Knoblich, G. (2002) Self recognition: body and action. *Trends in Cognitive Science*, 6, 447–449.

Maeda, F., Kleiner-Fisman, G. and Pascual-Leone, A. (2002) Motor facilitation while observing hand actions: specificity of the effect and role of observer's orientation. *Journal of Neurophysiology*, 87, 1329–1335.

Parsons, L. M. (1994) Temporal and kinematic properties of motor behavior reflected in mentally simulated action. *Journal of Experimental Psychology, Human Perception and Performance*, 20, 709–730.

Paulignan, Y., Frak, V. G., Toni, I. and Jeannerod, M. (1997) Influence of object position and size on human prehension movements. *Experimental Brain Research*, 114, 226–234.

Ramachandran, V. S. and Rogers-Ramachandran (1996) Synaesthesia in phantom limbs induced with mirrors. *Proceedings of the Royal Society of London, B*, 263, 377–386.

Ramachandran, V. S., Altschuler, E. L. and Hillyer, S. (1997) Mirror agnosia. *Proceedings of the Royal Society of London, B*, 264, 645–647.

Rizzolatti, G. and Matelli, M. (2003) Two different streams for the dorsal visual system: anatomy and functions. *Experimental Brain Research*, 153, 146–157.

Rizzolatti, G., Fadiga, L., Gallese, V. and Fogassi, L. (1995) Premotor cortex and the recognition of motor actions. *Cognitive Brain Research*, 3, 131–141.

Rosenbaum, D. A., Meulenbroek, R. G. J. and Vaughan, J. (2004) What is the point of motor planning? *International Journal of Sport and Exercise Psychology*, 2, 439–469.

Ruby, P. and Decety J. (2001) Effect of subjective perspective taking during simulation of action: a PET investigation of agency. *Nature Neurosciences*, 4, 546–550.

Sebanz, N., Knoblich, G. and Prinz, W. (2003) Representing other's actions: just like one's own? *Cognition*, **88**, B11–B21.

Sperry, R.W. (1950) Neural basis of the spontaneous optokinetic response produced by visual inversion. *Journal of Comparative and Physiological Psychology*, **43**, 482–489.

Stelmach, G. E., Castiello, U. and Jeannerod, M. (1994) Orienting the finger opposition space during prehension movements. *Journal of Motor Behavior*, **26**, 178–186.

Strafella, A.P. and Paus, T. (2000) Modulation of cortical excitability during action observation. A transcranial magnetic stimulation study. *Neuroreport*, **11**, 2289–2292.

Stürmer, B., Aschersleben, G. and Prinz, W. (2000) Correspondence effects with manual gestures and postures: a study of imitation. *Journal of Experimental Psychology: Human Perception and Performance*, **26**, 1746–1759.

Van den Bos, E. and Jeannerod, M. (2002) Sense of body and sense of action both contribute to self-recognition. *Cognition*, **85**, 177–187.

Von Holst, E. and Mittelstaedt, H. (1950) Das Reafferenzprinzip. Wechselwirkungen zwischen Zentralnervensystem und Peripherie. *Naturwissenschaften*, **37**, 464–476.

Weiss, P. and Jeannerod, M. (1998) Getting a grasp on coordination. *News in Physiological Science*, **13**, 70–75.

Wohlschläger, A., Haggard, P., Gesierich, B. and Prinz, W. (2003) The perceived onset time of self- and other-generated actions. *Psychological Science*, **14**, 586–591.

Wolpert, D. M., Ghahramani, Z. and Jordan, M. I. (1995) An internal model for sensorimotor integration. *Science*, **269**, 1880–1882.

12

Neural basis of social interactions in primates

Daeyeol Lee, Dominic J. Barraclough and Hyojung Seo

Compared to decisions made by socially isolated individuals, the problem of making decisions in a socially interactive group is fundamentally more complex. Although game theory provides optimal solutions to social decision making, assumptions of formal game theory are often violated, and human and animal behaviors in various social contexts are largely shaped by the dynamics of learning and heuristic routines. To gain insights into the neural basis of socially interactive decision making in primates, monkeys were trained to perform free-choice tasks modeled after binary (matching pennies) and tertiary (rock-paper-scissors) competitive zero-sum games. Choice behaviors during both games were consistent with the predictions of reinforcement learning models, suggesting that the animal's decision-making strategies were revised mostly based on the outcomes of previous choices. However, predictions about the animal's choices during the rock-paper-scissors game improved somewhat when the hypothetical outcomes expected from unchosen actions were taken into account. Single-neuron recordings from the dorsolateral prefrontal cortex showed that signals related to the past choices of the animals and their outcomes are encoded in this brain area, suggesting a key role of the prefrontal cortex in dynamically updating the animal's decision-making strategies.

Introduction

Decisions are made constantly whenever a particular action is emitted and even when potential actions are suppressed. However, decisions vary greatly in their complexity. For example, the rapid escape response of a cockroach triggered by air-puff relies on a relatively simple and well-defined neural circuitry (Ritzmann and Eaton, 1997). In contrast, many of our daily decisions, even simple ones such as choosing a dessert, rely on multiple factors, and the corresponding neural mechanisms are still poorly understood (Lee, 2006). Regardless of their complexity, theoretical and empirical studies of decision making often share the following features (von Neumann and Morgenstern, 1944; Camerer, 2003). First, the problem of decision making is posed as that of choosing a particular action from a set of alternative actions. In the experimental studies of decision making, this is enforced by providing the subject with a small number of available choices.

Second, the outcome of each action is usually determined by a probability density function over alternative outcomes. Third, each possible outcome is associated with a numerical value, often referred to as its utility, which specifies the subjective desirability of each outcome. Accordingly, actions that maximize utility are considered optimal.

The problems of decision making are greatly simplified when the number of available actions is small and each action maps deterministically to a particular outcome. In such cases, an optimal action can be easily discovered through an exhaustive search that compares the outcomes of all available actions. If the choice outcomes are uncertain, an action that maximizes the expected utility would be optimal. Regardless of outcome uncertainty, if the relationship between actions and outcomes were fixed during evolution, the animal's nervous system could be genetically programmed to produce specific patterns of innate behaviors or reflexes that correspond to optimal actions. By contrast, when the likely outcomes of behaviors change frequently and unpredictably, the animals must adjust their behaviors and decision-making strategies through experience. The problem of learning an optimal decision-making strategy becomes particularly challenging when the outcomes of an animal's behavior depend on the actions of other animals. Social interactions can be infinitely diverse, so in general, it may not be possible to compute optimal solutions to the problem of decision making. Thus, humans and animals often use heuristic algorithms in order to approximate optimal solutions (Simon, 1957; Gigerenzer et al., 1999). Similarly, actual choice behaviors observed in humans and animals during social interactions often display systematic deviations from the predictions of game theory (Camerer, 2003).

In game theory, a game is defined by a set of players, a set of actions available to each player, and a rule that maps each possible combination of actions taken by all players to the outcome for each player. When the same game is played repeatedly, players may adjust their decision-making strategies according to the outcomes of their previous choices, similar to Thorndike's law of effect (Thorndike, 1911). For example, according to reinforcement learning theory, decision-making strategies are updated based on the discrepancies between the predicted reward and the actual reward received by the player. Human and animal behaviors during social interactions as well as during individual decision making are largely consistent with the predictions of reinforcement learning theory (Erev and Roth, 1998; Barraclough et al., 2004; Haruno et al., 2004; Tanaka et al., 2004; Samejima et al., 2005; Daw et al., 2006). For decision making in a social group, however, more complex learning rules may apply. One possibility is that a player may choose a particular action based on his or her belief about the behaviors of other players. Beliefs or internal models about the strategies of other players are often referred to as theory of mind, and may play an important role in social cognition (Wolpert et al., 2003; Lee, 2006; Saxe, 2006). In belief learning, each player updates his or her belief about the behaviors of other players based on their previous choices and uses this belief to determine the likelihood of taking a particular action (Robinson, 1951). This implies that decision-making strategies are adjusted not only based on the actual outcome from the player's choice, as in reinforcement learning algorithms, but also on the hypothetical outcomes that would have resulted from unchosen actions (Camerer, 2003). It is also possible that strategies are adjusted according to a hybrid model combining the features of reinforcement learning and belief learning models (Camerer and Ho, 1999).

To understand how decision-making strategies are adjusted during social interactions in nonhuman primates, we examined the choice behaviors of rhesus monkeys during two different computerized competitive games. In both of these games, the computer simulated the behavior of an intelligent opponent by exploiting statistical biases present in the animal's previous behavior. In the first behavioral experiment, the animal played a so-called matching pennies game, was required to choose one of the two peripheral targets, and received its reward only when it selected the same target as the computer (Lee et al., 2004). The computer was programmed to predict the animal's choice and choose the opposite target. In the second behavioral experiment, the animal played a rock-paper-scissors game, was required to choose among three peripheral targets, and received its reward according to the payoff matrix of a rock-paper-scissors game (Lee et al., 2005). We also recorded neural activity in the dorsolateral prefrontal cortex (DLPFC) during the matching pennies game. The results suggest that this brain area may play an important role in representing and processing multiple types of information necessary to update the animal's behavioral strategy.

Choice behavior during a matching pennies game

Behavioral task

During this experiment, the animal began each trial by fixating a yellow square presented at the center of a computer screen (Figure 12.1A). After a 0.5 s fore-period, two green disks were presented 5° away from the fixation target along the horizontal meridian. When the central square was extinguished after a 0.5 s delay period, the animal was required to shift its gaze towards one of the targets within 1 s and maintain its fixation for a 0.5 s hold period. At the end of the hold period, a red ring was displayed around the target chosen by the computer opponent for 0.2 or 0.5 s (133 and 189 neurons, respectively). The animal was rewarded with a drop of fruit juice if it selected the same target as the computer.

In algorithm 1, the computer stored the entire sequence of choices made by the animal in a given daily session. In each trial, the computer then used this information to estimate the probability that the animal would choose the leftward or rightward target, as well as the conditional probability that the animal would choose each target given its previous N choices ($N = 1$ to 4). When none of these probabilities deviated significantly from the probability of 0.5, the computer made its choice randomly between the two targets with equal probabilities. Otherwise, the computer biased its target selection using the probability that deviated maximally and significantly from 0.5. This was achieved by selecting, with the probability of $1 - p$, the target that the animal had selected with the probability of p. In algorithm 1, therefore, the animal was required to select the two targets with equal probabilities and independently from its previous choices, in order to maximize its total reward.

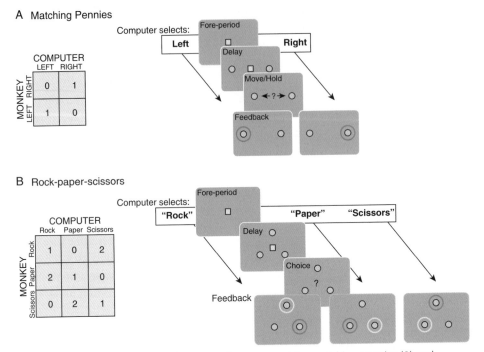

Figure 12.1 Payoff matrix and spatio-temporal sequence of the matching pennies (**A**) and rock-paper-scissors (**B**) games.

In algorithm 2, the computer used the entire choice and reward history of the animal in a given session to predict the animal's choice in the next trial. In addition to the probabilities used in algorithm 1, the conditional probabilities that the animal would choose each target, given the animal's choices in the preceding N trials ($N = 1$ to 4) and their payoffs, were also estimated. When any of these probabilities deviated significantly from 0.5, the computer biased its target selection according to the same rule used in algorithm 1. In algorithm 2, therefore, the animal was required to select its targets not only with equal probabilities and independently from its previous choices, but also independently from the combination of its previous choices and their outcomes, or, equivalently, from the choices of both players.

Reinforcement learning model for decision making in the matching pennies game

Three monkeys (C, E and F) were tested for both algorithms 1 and 2. Each of these animals displayed a significant bias to choose the same target if it was rewarded in the previous trial, and to switch to the other target otherwise. The probability that this so-called win-stay-lose-switch (WSLS) strategy was used by each animal was 0.65, 0.76 and 0.64 for algorithm 1, and it decreased to 0.55, 0.54 and 0.58 for algorithm 2. The difference in the probability of WSLS strategy was significant for all animals ($p < 0.0001$).

This is not surprising, since the frequent use of WSLS strategy was exploited by the computer opponent only in algorithm 2. Nevertheless, the probability of WSLS strategy was still significantly greater than 0.5 even in algorithm 2.

The possibility that the outcomes in several previous trials might influence the animal's subsequent choice behavior was tested by applying a reinforcement learning model. In reinforcement learning algorithms, an estimate for a weighted sum of future rewards is referred to as a value function (Sutton and Barto, 1998). In the present application, the value function at trial t for a given target x ($x = L$ for the leftward target, R for rightward target), $V_t(x)$, was updated after each trial according to the following.

$$V_{t+1}(x) = \alpha\, V_t(x) + \Delta_t(x),$$

where α is a decay factor, and $\Delta_t(x)$ reflects a change in the value function that depends on the outcome of a choice. It was assumed that $V_1(R) = V_1(L) = 0$. In the current model, $\Delta_t(x) = \Delta_{rew}$ if the animal selects the target x and is rewarded, $\Delta_t(x) = \Delta_{unrew}$ if the animal selects the target x and is not rewarded, and $\Delta_t(x) = 0$ if the animal does not select the target x. The probability that the animal would select the rightward target is then determined by the following softmax rule.

$$p_t(R) = \exp V_t(R) / \{\exp V_t(R) + \exp V_t(L)\}.$$

Previously, we have estimated the parameters of this model for each algorithm using the entire data set obtained from each animal, using a maximum likelihood procedure (Lee et al., 2004). In contrast, in the present study, the parameters of this reinforcement learning model were estimated separately for each daily session to investigate the variability in the animal's behavior across different sessions.

The reinforcement learning accounted for the animal's choice behavior in algorithm 1 relatively well, as indicated by the fact that in approximately 90% of the sessions, the decay factor remained between zero and one (Table 12.1). The signs of Δ_{rew} and Δ_{unrew} also indicated that the animal's behavior in algorithm 1 was well described by the model,

Table 12.1 Parameters of reinforcement learning model for the matching pennies game

Algorithm	Monkey	Days	α	Δ_{rew}	Δ_{unrew}	Correct (%)
1	C	36 (36)	0.17	0.71	−0.63	65.5*
	E	53 (63)	0.22	1.22	−1.32	77.8
	F	24 (26)	0.33	0.56	−0.56	63.5
2	C	21 (33)	0.51	0.26	−0.05	58.8**
	E	27 (41)	0.83	0.17	−0.23	58.4**
	F	21 (23)	0.44	0.18	−0.32	58.3*

Days indicate the number of sessions in which the decay factor (α) was between zero and one, and the values within the parentheses indicate the total number of sessions. The median for each model parameter is also shown. The value in the last column (Correct) shows the percentage of trials in which the model predicted the animal's choice correctly. Symbols indicate that this was significantly more accurate than the prediction of win-stay-lose-switch strategy (*$p < 0.05$; **$p < 0.001$).

since in more than 95% of the sessions, $\Delta_1 > 0$ and $\Delta_2 < 0$. However, the reinforcement learning model predicted the animal's choice significantly better than the WSLS strategy only in one animal (monkey C). Overall, the percentages of trials in which the WSLS strategy and the reinforcement learning model predicted the animal's choice correctly were 71 and 72%, respectively.

When the computer exploited the relationship between the animal's choices and their outcomes using algorithm 2, the animal's choice behavior changed qualitatively. First, the decay factor was sometimes negative, indicating that the reinforcement learning did not always successfully provide a reasonable account for the animal's behavior. Second, even when the decay factor was positive, the decay factor estimated for the choice behavior in algorithm 2 tended to be larger than in algorithm 1, suggesting that the outcomes of multiple trials in the past might have influenced the animal's choice. This was supported by the fact that compared to the predictions of WSLS strategy, the reinforcement learning model frequently provided more accurate predictions for the animal's behavior. Considering only the choice behavior in sessions where the decay factor was positive in algorithm 2, the percentages of trials in which the WSLS strategy and the reinforcement learning model predicted the animal's choice correctly were 55.4 and 58.5%, respectively. This difference was statistically significant in all animals. Finally, the magnitude of changes made in the value functions in algorithm 2 was smaller than in algorithm 1 (Table 12.1). Thus, compared to the results obtained in algorithm 1, changes made in the value functions after each choice in algorithm 2 were relatively small, but these changes decayed more slowly. As a result, the choice behavior in algorithm 2 was more stochastic and more difficult to predict than in algorithm 1.

Choice behavior of monkeys during a rock-paper-scissors game

Behavioral task

The rock-paper-scissors game used in this study was similar to the matching pennies game except that it included three different choices (Figure 12.1B). Three peripheral visual targets were arbitrarily designated as rock, paper, and scissors, respectively. At the beginning of each trial, the computer opponent selected its target according to one of the algorithms described below, and the outcome of the animal's choice was classified as loss, tie, and win, according to the following rule: rock beats scissors, scissors beat paper, and paper beats rock. At the end of each completed trial, the animal was rewarded with one or two drops of juice for tie and win, respectively. No reward was given for a trial with a loss.

The animals began each trial by fixating a yellow square presented at the center of a computer screen (Figure 12.1B). After a 0.5 s fore-period, three identical green disks were presented equidistant from the fixation target at the vertices of an imaginary equilateral triangle. The animal maintained its fixation on the central square during the following 0.5 s delay period. At the end of this delay period, the central square was extinguished, and the animal was required to shift its gaze towards one of the targets and maintain its fixation for a 0.5 s hold period. At the end of the hold period, a yellow ring was displayed for 100 ms around the target that was selected by the computer. Simultaneously, a red ring was also displayed around the target that would beat the computer's choice.

In each trial of algorithm 1, the computer analyzed the animal's choices in all previous trials in a given session to estimate the probability that the animal would choose each target, and the conditional probability that the animal would choose each target given the animal's choices in the preceding N trials ($N = 1$ to 4). Then the computer selected the probability that deviated maximally and significantly from 1/3. Denoting a set of probabilities for rock, paper, and scissors as p, q, and $1 - (p + q)$, that includes the probability that satisfies the above criteria, the computer selected each of these three targets with the probabilities of $1 - (p + q)$, p, and q. For example, if the animal tended to choose rock more frequently, the computer chose paper more frequently. If none of the tested probabilities deviated significantly from 1/3, then the computer chose each target randomly with a 1/3 probability. In algorithm 2, the computer used the entire choice and reward history of the animal in a given session to predict the animal's choice in the next trial. Thus, in addition to the probabilities tested in algorithm 1, the computer also tested the conditional probability that the animal would choose each target given the animal's choices and their outcomes in the preceding N trials ($N = 1$ to 4). If none of these probabilities deviated significantly from 1/3, then the computer selected each target randomly with the probability of 1/3. Otherwise, the computer biased its target selection according to the same rule used in algorithm 1. In algorithm 2, therefore, the animal was required to select its targets not only with equal probabilities and independently from its previous choices, but also independently from the combination of its previous choices and their outcomes.

Comparison of learning models for decision making in the rock-paper-scissors game

Two rhesus monkeys (E and F) were tested for algorithms 1 and 2, and three different learning models were fitted to the animal's choice behavior during the rock-paper-scissors game. A feature common to all three models is that the preference for each target is numerically represented by a value function. Thus, for all models, the value function at trial t for a given target x ($x = $ R, P, or S, for rock, paper, scissors, respectively), $V_t(x)$, was updated after each trial according to the following:

$$V_{t+1}(x) = \alpha\, V_t(x) + \Delta_t(x),$$

where α is a decay factor, and $\Delta_t(x)$ reflects a change in the value function for target x determined by the outcome of the animal's choice or the choice of the computer (see below). The probability that the animal would select each target in a given trial was then determined according to the softmax transformation. In other words,

$$p_t(x) = \frac{\exp V_t(x)}{\displaystyle\sum_{u \in \{R,P,S\}} \exp V_t(u)}$$

In the reinforcement learning model, the value function for each target was adjusted strictly according to the outcome of the animal's choice. Thus, $\Delta_t(x) = \Delta_L$ if the animal selects the target x and loses (i.e. no reward), $\Delta_t(x) = \Delta_T$ if the animal selects the target x and ties with the computer (i.e. small reward), and $\Delta_t(x) = \Delta_W$ if the animal selects the target x and wins (i.e. large reward). In addition, $\Delta_t(x)$ is set to 0, if the animal does not select the target x. By contrast, in the belief learning model, the value function for each target was adjusted strictly according to the choices of the computer opponent, regardless of the choice of the animal. Therefore, $\Delta_t(x) = \Delta_{BL}$ for the target that would have been beaten by the computer's choice, $\Delta_t(x) = \Delta_{BT}$ for the target that would have resulted in a tie, and $\Delta_t(x) = \Delta_{BW}$ for the target that would have beaten the computer's choice. In the belief learning model, therefore, value functions are adjusted for all targets after each trial, regardless of the animal's choice. This model is over-determined, however, when it is combined with the softmax transformation, since adding a constant offset to the value function of each target does not change the probability of choosing a given target. Therefore, Δ_{BL} was arbitrarily set to 0.

The reinforcement learning and belief learning models correspond to the two extreme cases in a spectrum (Camerer and Ho, 1999), since it is possible to update the value functions based on the choices of other players as well as on the outcomes of one's own choices. In this hybrid model, two different value functions were estimated for each target using the procedures described above for the reinforcement learning and belief learning models. Denoting these two value functions for target x at trial t as $V_t^R(x)$ and $V_t^B(x)$, the value function for target x in the hybrid model was defined as

$$V_t(x) = (1-\delta)V_t^R(x) + \delta V_t^B(x).$$

Therefore, the reinforcement learning and belief learning models are nested in this hybrid model. The reinforcement learning model corresponds to $\delta = 0$, whereas the belief learning model corresponds to $\delta = 1$. The parameters of all models were estimated according to the maximum likelihood procedure.

In general, the performance of a model, as evaluated by such measures as the sum of squared errors, improves with an increasing number of free parameters used to estimate the model. Therefore, in order to compare the performance of multiple models with different numbers of parameters, it is necessary to correct for the improvement in the model fit expected from the difference in the number of free parameters. Two different methods, both based on the log likelihood, were utilized in the present study. First, Akaike's information criterion (AIC), was computed by the following,

$$\text{AIC} = -2 \log L + 2k,$$

where L is the likelihood of the data given the model, and k is the number of free parameters used in a given model (Hastie *et al.*, 2001). Second, Bayesian information criterion (BIC) was obtained according to the following,

$$\text{BIC} = -2 \log L + k \log N,$$

where N denotes the number of data points. BIC penalizes complex models more than AIC (Hastie *et al.*, 2001).

Overall, the reinforcement learning model accounted for the animal's choice behavior better than the belief learning model or the hybrid model. Compared to the reinforcement learning model, there was only weak evidence for the belief learning model. This was true for both algorithms in both animals. For algorithm 1, the reinforcement learning model performed better than the belief learning model in 80 and 90% of the sessions for monkeys E and F, respectively. For algorithm 2, the reinforcement learning model performed better in 100 and 95% of the sessions for the two animals. The results were the same, regardless of whether the model performance was evaluated with AIC or BIC.

The results for the hybrid model differed somewhat for the two algorithms. If the hybrid model provided a genuine improvement over the reinforcement learning or belief learning model, the value of δ should lie between zero and one. This was the case in the majority of the sessions in algorithm 1, especially for monkey E (Table 12.2). In contrast, this parameter frequently became negative when the hybrid model was applied to the data obtained with algorithm 2. In addition, when the value of δ fell between zero and one, the hybrid model accounted for the results obtained for monkey E in algorithm 1 better than the other models, regardless of whether the models were evaluated using AIC or BIC. For the results obtained from monkey F in algorithm 1, the reinforcement learning model and the hybrid model performed similarly according to AIC, whereas BIC always favored the reinforcement learning model. This is not surprising, since BIC penalizes complex models more severely. For the choice behavior in algorithm 2, the hybrid model was seldom favored (Table 12.2). Among the sessions in which δ was positive, the

Table 12.2 Performance of different learning models for the animal's choice behavior during the rock-paper-scissors game

Algorithms	Monkey	RL	BL	Hybrid	Days
AIC					
1	E	0	0	19	19 (20)
	F	7	2	7	16 (31)
2	E	4	0	1	5 (19)
	F	3	0	1	4 (19)
BIC					
1	E	0	0	19	19 (20)
	F	14	2	0	16 (31)
2	E	5	0	0	5 (19)
	F	4	0	0	4 (19)

The numbers of sessions in which reinforcement learning (RL), belief learning (BL), and hybrid models provided the best fit to the data according to Akaike's information criterion (AIC) or the Bayesian information criterion (BIC) are shown. Only the sessions in which the weight for the belief learning model (δ) stayed between zero and one were included in this comparison. The values in parentheses indicate the total number of daily sessions tested.

median value of δ in algorithm 1 was 0.247 and 0.155 for monkeys E and F, respectively. For algorithm 2, the corresponding values were 0.101 and 0.192. These results showed that the contribution of belief learning was relatively small, even when it was considered within the hybrid model in combination with the reinforcement learning.

Neural activity in the prefrontal cortex during a matching pennies game

Neurophysiological recording

Single-unit activity was recorded from the neurons in the dorsolateral prefrontal cortex of five rhesus monkeys while the animals were performing the matching pennies game against the computer opponent that exploited the bias in the animal's choice and reward history (algorithm 2). The detailed methods were described previously (Barraclough *et al.*, 2004).

Regression analysis

Activity of each neuron was analyzed by first counting its spikes in a series of 500 ms bins starting 1000 ms before the animal fixated the central target. The spike counts in each bin were then subjected to a linear regression analysis, to determine whether they were significantly influenced by the animal's choice, computer's choice, and reward in the same trial and by the same variables in the previous trials. These three behavioral events in a given trial were not statistically independent, since the reward was determined by the choices of the two players. Nevertheless, they were linearly independent, so their effects could be evaluated separately in a regression model. In addition, the animal's choice behavior in algorithm 2 was only weakly related to its previous choices and their outcomes (Lee *et al.*, 2004), and this made it possible to evaluate how neural activity was influenced by these different behavioral events in multiple trials. The regression model tested in this study included the animal's choice, computer's choice, and reward in the same trial from which neural activity was taken as well as the same variables in the four preceding trials. Cortical neurons often display slow drift in their excitability (Lee and Quessy, 2003), and this could be mistaken for the effect of certain behavioral events in previous trials. To control for such confounding, the regression model also included the spike counts in the same bin from the last four previous trials as autoregressive terms (Ljung, 1999).

Activity related to choice and reward history

Many neurons in the dorsolateral prefrontal cortex modulated their activity according to the animal's choice, computer's choice, and reward not only in the same trial but also in previous trials. However, individual DLPFC neurons varied substantially in terms of which of these three variables affected their activity and the time course in which their effects were revealed. For example, the neuron shown in Figure 12.2 modulated its activity according to each of these three behavioral events. This neuron increased its activity at

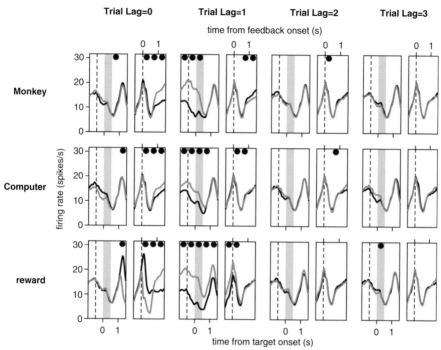

Figure 12.2 An example neuron in the dorsolateral prefrontal cortex that modulated its activity according to the animal's choice, computer's choice and reward in the previous trial (Trial Lag = 1). Spike density functions are aligned either at the target onset (left graph in each panel) or at the onset of the feedback ring (right graph), and are estimated separately for two sets of trials sorted by each of the three behavioral events (monkey's choice, computer's choice, and reward) in the current trial (Trial Lag = 0) or previous trials (Trial Lag = 1 to 3). In the top two rows, the black and grey lines correspond to the leftward and rightward choices, whereas in the bottom row, they correspond to the unrewarded and rewarded trials, respectively. Dotted vertical lines correspond to the time when the animal fixated the central target or the onset of the feedback ring, and shaded area corresponds to the delay period. Black dots at the top of each panel indicate that the spike counts in the corresponding 500 ms bin were significantly different for the two conditions.

the end of a trial when the animal selected the rightward target, and maintained this differential activity until the end of the delay period in the next trial. In addition, the activity during the inter-trial interval between trials $N + 1$ and $N + 2$ was weakly but significantly influenced by the animal's choice in trial N (Figure 12.2, top, Trial Lag = 1, right). The same neuron also modulated its activity according to the computer's choice in the previous trial during the inter-trial interval and during the fore-period and delay period in the following trial (Figure 12.2, middle). Finally, this neuron also changed its activity depending on whether the choice in a given trial was rewarded or not, and maintained its differential activity throughout the next trial (Figure 12.2, bottom).

Among 322 neurons recorded in the DLPFC, 37 and 39% modulated their activity significantly according to the animal's choice in the previous trial during the fore-period and delay period, respectively (Figure 12.3). The percentage of neurons in which the activity was significantly affected by the computer's choice in the previous trial was 20 and 19% for fore-period and delay period, respectively. Whether the animal was rewarded or not in the previous trial affected the activity in 39 and 35% of the neurons during the fore-period and delay period, respectively. In addition, a small but still significant number of neurons in the DLPFC modulated their activity according to the animal's choice and reward received by the animal two trials before the current trial. The percentage of neurons that showed such different activity was approximately 11 and 9% for fore-period and delay period, respectively. The percentage of neurons that modulated their activity according to the reward received by the animal two trials before the current trial was 9 and 10% for the fore-period and delay period, respectively. In contrast, the

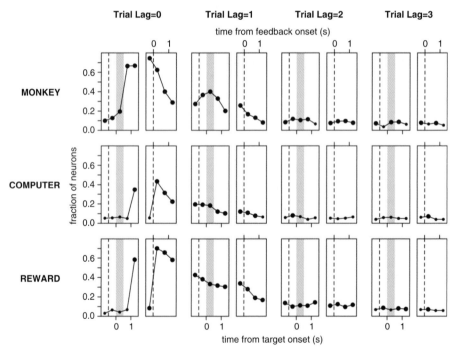

Figure 12.3 Fraction of neurons that significantly modulated their activity according to the animal's choice (top), computer's choice (middle), and reward (bottom) in the current and three previous trials. Time bins used to estimate neural activity were aligned either at the target onset (left graph in each panel) or at the onset of the feedback ring (right). Dotted vertical lines correspond to the time when the animal fixated the central target or the onset of the feedback ring. Shaded area corresponds to the delay period. Large dots indicate that the observed fraction is significantly higher than the significance level used in the regression analysis ($p = 0.05$).

computer's choice two trials before the trial did not have any significant effect on the activity of neurons in the DLPFC. These results show that the animal's previous choices and their outcomes influenced the activity of neurons in the DLPFC more frequently and their effects were more sustained than the computer's choice.

Discussion

Social decision making and learning

Compared to physical properties of inanimate objects and plants, animal behavior is much more difficult to predict, since animals can adapt their behaviors according to the changes in their surroundings. This makes it harder to predict the outcomes of one's own actions in a social context, and decision making in an environment that includes other animals is much more challenging and can become computationally intractable. It is therefore not surprising that decision-making strategies in a social setting undergo adaptive changes. By providing a mathematically rigorous framework to define and solve the problem of decision making in social settings, game theory plays a central role in understanding how such strategies adapt dynamically through learning or evolution. In the present study, monkeys were trained to perform free-choice tasks modeled after two simple competitive games, matching pennies and rock-paper-scissors, and their choice behaviors were analyzed using quantitative models to understand the nature of the learning process. It is difficult to know whether the animals in these tasks treated the computer as an intentional being, and whether they will apply the same learning algorithms to a more complex social environment. Nevertheless, the tasks used in our study capture a fundamental feature of social interaction in that the outcome of the animal's choice changed as an intelligent opponent exploited the statistical biases of the animal's behavior. Therefore, the learning algorithms identified in this study and the corresponding neural mechanisms are also likely to play an important role during more complex social interactions.

In both matching pennies and rock-paper-scissors, the animal's behavior was well accounted for by a relatively simple reinforcement learning model. This is consistent with the results from previous studies in human subjects (Mookherjee and Sopher, 1994; Erev and Roth, 1998; Feltovich, 2000), and suggests that the outcomes of previous choices may directly modify the decision maker's preference towards each choice. This learning algorithm may be relatively easy to implement. First, only the value functions for available actions need to be stored, and second, after each action, only the value function for the chosen action needs to be updated. In contrast, belief learning algorithms rely on the information about the actions that other decision makers are likely to take. In the present study, the reinforcement learning algorithm accounted for the animal's behavior better than the belief learning algorithm. However, in some cases, the animal's choice behavior was more consistent with the hybrid model that incorporated the features of both models. The lack of evidence for belief learning might be due to the relatively simple nature of the competitive games used in the present study, and therefore, the abilities of humans and other primates to use information about the intentions of other decision makers require further studies.

Belief learning can be implemented in at least two different ways, depending on the type of information maintained across different trials. One possibility is to remember the intentions of other decision makers, and at the time of decision making, the expected payoff from each action can be calculated from the expected actions of other players. Another possibility is to update the value functions of alternative actions after each action according to the hypothetical payoffs that could have been earned. Hypothetical payoffs can be calculated through simulations in which each unchosen action is evaluated in the context of the most recent actions of other decision makers in the group. Once value functions are adjusted according to the hypothetical payoffs, then the problem of action selection is simplified, since this can now be achieved simply by choosing the action with the maximum value function, as in the reinforcement learning algorithms. In this second scenario, the expected actions of other players are not explicitly stored, but instead they are incorporated into the value functions of alternative actions. In the hybrid model considered in the present study, the reinforcement learning and belief learning models were merged using actual and hypothetical payoffs. However, it is also possible that the actions favored by the belief learning model are determined based on the expected actions of other players and then compared with the actions chosen by the reinforcement learning algorithm. It would be difficult to distinguish between these two different versions of learning algorithms only on the basis of behavioral evidence. Neurobiological data might provide the information necessary to do so.

Role of prefrontal cortex in social decision making

In our neurophysiological experiment, the activity of individual neurons in the DLPFC was examined while the animal played against the computer opponent in a matching pennies game. The results showed that the DLPFC neurons encode at least three different types of information related to the animal's previous experience. First, many neurons encoded signals related to the animal's own choices in the previous trials. Second, some neurons changed their activity according to the choice of the computer opponent in the previous trial. Finally, many neurons modulated their activity according to whether the animal was rewarded or not in previous trials. These signals in the dorsolateral prefrontal cortex provide some clues regarding its function during decision making in a competitive game.

A common feature of many goal-directed behaviors is that the outcome of a given behavior may not be revealed immediately. In order to associate a particular outcome with the action that was responsible for that outcome, the animal has to maintain a memory of the previously chosen actions. In reinforcement learning theory, this is referred to as eligibility trace. DLPFC neurons with signals related to the animal's previous choices, therefore, may provide eligibility trace necessary to update the value functions of various actions appropriately.

When making decisions in a social group, any information about the behaviors of other players plays a fundamental role, since optimal choices can be determined relatively easily when the behaviors of other players are completely known. The actions taken by other players during the recent interaction with them could potentially provide such information, especially when they tend to repeat the same choices. Neurons in the DLPFC that modulated their activity according to the choice of the computer opponent in the previous trial, therefore, may be involved in choosing an optimal action according to the predicted behaviors of other players in a social setting. During the matching pennies game, the animal's choice was rewarded only when it matched the choice of the opponent. Accordingly, signals related to the computer's choice might be used directly to estimate the value functions of two alternative choices. The relationship between the information about the expected choices of other players and the value functions of alternative actions would become more complex as the number of players and alternative actions increases. Currently, the precise role of the DLPFC during games more complex than the matching pennies remains unknown.

Finally, many neurons in the DLPFC also modulated their activity according to whether the animal was rewarded for its choices in recent trials. These neurons may be involved in computing and representing the expected average rate of reward. Such signals can be important, because a sudden change in the average rate of reward may indicate potentially important changes in the environment that require the animal to adjust its decision-making strategy (Aston-Jones and Cohen, 2005; Soltani et al., 2006). For example, such a change may occur when other decisions makers in a social group change their strategies. In fact, in some reinforcement learning algorithms, learning is driven by the deviation of actual reward from the average reward rate (Putterman, 1994). Such learning algorithms are also consistent with the finding that the animal's motivation level is more strongly related to the changes in the reward rate, rather than the absolute amount of reward (Flaherty, 1982).

In summary, activity of individual neurons in the DLPFC reflected various signals that could be useful for improving strategies for interactive decision making in a social group. Nevertheless, the precise role of DLPFC during socially interactive decision making is still largely unknown. For example, the present study focused on how neural activity was influenced by the choice of the animal, the choice of the opponent, and reward. These three behavioral events are, however, not independent. This implies that in theory, one of these variables can be computed from the other two variables. It remains to be determined whether the DLPFC receives information about all three variables from other brain areas, or whether it plays any role in computing one of these variables from the other two variables. In addition, signals related to the previous choices and their outcomes must be used to improve the animal's decision-making strategies. This process may be distributed in multiple brain regions including the lateral and medial prefrontal cortex as well as the basal ganglia (Lee, 2006; Daw and Doya, 2006). It remains as an important topic for future studies to investigate the nature of interaction and communication among these multiple brain areas.

References

Aston-Jones, G. and Cohen, J. D. (2005) An integrative theory of locus coeruleus-norepinephrine function: adaptive gain and optimal performance. *Annual Review of Neuroscience*, **28**, 403–450.

Barraclough, D. J., Conroy, M. L. and Lee, D. (2004) Prefrontal cortex and decision making in a mixed-strategy game. *Nature Neuroscience*, 7, 404–410.

Camerer, C. F. (2003) *Behavioral Game Theory: Experiments in Strategic Interaction*. Princeton University Press, Princeton.

Camerer, C. F. and Ho, T.-H. (1999) Experience-weighted attraction learning in normal form games. *Econometrica*, **67**, 827–784.

Daw, N. D. and Doya, K. (2006) The computational neurobiology of learning and reward. *Current Opinion in Neurobiology*, **16**, 199–204.

Daw, N. D., O'Doherty, J. P., Dayan, P., Seymour, B. and Dolan, R. J. (2006) Cortical substrates for exploratory decisions in humans. *Nature*, **441**, 876–879.

Erev, I. and Roth, A. E. (1998) Predicting how people play games: reinforcement learning in experimental games with unique, mixed strategy equilibria. *American Economic Review*, **88**, 848–881.

Feltovich, N. (2000) Reinforcement-based vs. belief-based learning models in experimental asymmetric-information games. *Econometrica*, **68**, 605–641.

Flaherty, C. F. (1982) Incentive contrast: a review of behavioral changes following shifts in reward. *Animal Learning Behavior*, **10**, 409–440.

Gigerenzer, G., Todd, P. M. and the ABC Research Group (1999) *Simple Heuristics that Make Us Smart*. Oxford University Press, New York.

Haruno, M., Kuroda, T., Doya, K., Toyama, K., Kimura, M., Samejima, K., Imamizu, H. and Kawato, M. (2004) A neural correlate of reward-based behavioral learning in caudate nucleus: a functional magnetic resonance imaging study of a stochastic decision task. *Journal of Neuroscience*, **24**, 1660–1665.

Hastie, T., Tibshirani, R. and Friedman, J. (2001) *The Elements of Statistical Learning: Data Mining, Inference, and Prediction*. Springer, New York.

Lee, D. (2006) Neural basis of quasi-rational decision making. *Current Opinion in Neurobiology*, **16**, 191–198.

Lee, D. and Quessy, S. (2003) Activity in the supplementary motor area related to learning and performance during a sequential visuomotor task. *Journal of Neurophysiology*, **89**, 1039–1056.

Lee, D., Conroy, M. L., McGreevy, B. P. and Barraclough, D. J. (2004) Reinforcement learning and decision making in monkeys during a competitive game. *Cognitive Brain Research*, **22**, 45–58.

Lee, D., McGreevy, B. P. and Barraclough, D. J. (2005) Learning and decision making in monkeys during a rock-paper-scissors game. *Cognitive Brain Research*, **25**, 416–430.

Ljung, L. (1999) *System Identification: Theory for the User*. Prentice-Hall, Upper Saddle River, NJ.

Mookherjee, D. and Sopher, B. (1994) Learning behavior in an experimental matching pennies game. *Games and Economics Behavior*, 7, 62–91.

Putterman, M. L. (1994) *Markov Decision Processes: Discrete Stochastic Dynamic Programming*. Wiley, New York.

Ritzmann, R. E. and Eatson, R. C. (1997) Neural substrates for initiation of startle responses. In Stein, P. S. G., Grillner, S., Selverston, A. I. and Stuart, D. G. (eds), *Neurons, Networks, and Motor Behavior*, pp. 33–44. MIT Press, Cambridge, MA.

Robinson, J. (1951) An iterative method of solving a game. *Annals of Mathematics*, **54**, 296–301.

Samejima, K., Ueda, Y., Doya, K. and Kimura, M. (2005) Representation of action-specific reward values in the striatum. *Science*, **310**, 1337–1340.

Saxe, R. (2006) Uniquely human social cognition. *Current Opinion in Neurobiology*, **16**, 234–239.

Simon, H. A. (1957) *Models of Man*. Wiley, New York.

Soltani, A., Lee, D. and Wang, X.-J. (2006) Neural mechanism for stochastic behaviour during a competitive game. *Neural Networks*, **19**, 1075–1090.

Sutton, R. S. and Barto, A. G. (1998) *Reinforcement Learning: An Introduction*. MIT Press, Cambridge, MA.

Tanaka, S. C., Doya, K., Okada, G., Ueda, K., Okamoto, Y. and Yamawaki, S. (2004) Prediction of immediate and future rewards differentially recruits cortico-basal ganglia loops. *Nature Neuroscience*, 7, 887–893.

Thorndike, E. L. (1911) *Animal Intelligence: Experimental Studies*. Macmillan, New York.

von Neumann, J. and Morgenstern, O. (1944) *Theory of Games and Economic Behavior*. Princeton University Press, Princeton.

Wolpert, D. M., Doya, K. and Kawato, M. (2003) A unifying computational framework for motor control and social interaction. *Philosophical Transactions of the Royal Society of London, B*, **358**, 593–602.

13

Bodily bonds: effects of social context on ideomotor movements

Natalie Sebanz and Maggie Shiffrar

Introduction

In David Mitchell's latest novel, 13-year-old Jason Taylor observes a fight among some of his rather brutal classmates. As he later reports, seeing one of the bullies leashing out at a weaker kid, "my own body flinched under the punches, automatically, like how your leg hoists itself when you're watching a high jumper on TV" (2006, p. 75). This captures an experience we have quite frequently when observing others' actions: There seems to be a mysterious bodily bond between ourselves and others that makes us draw back in our seat when a movie character is heading towards an abyss, has us kick our legs when we watch our favorite soccer player trying to score a goal, and makes us bounce our knees when we see a kid jumping up and down on the trampoline. Such movements occurring in response to observed actions are referred to as 'ideomotor movements' (Knuf et al., 2001). They are of interest to researchers studying perception–action links because they can provide insights as to how one's own body is involved in the perception of others' actions.

Two different kinds of ideomotor movements have been identified in previous studies (De Maeght and Prinz, 2004). On the one hand, observers sometimes re-enact or mimic an actor's movements, acting as if they were the observed rather than the observer. Such 'perceptually induced' ideomotor movements may be explained by the fact that when we observe someone performing an action, corresponding representations in our own action system are activated (for recent reviews, see Viviani, 2002; Buccino et al., 2004; Rizzolatti and Craighero, 2004; Wilson and Knoblich, 2005). This phenomenon will be referred to as 'motor resonance'.

On the other hand, compensatory rather than imitative movements occur when observers watch someone who is experiencing difficulties achieving a goal or who is about to fail in some way, such as when someone is close to falling off a cliff. Such compensatory movements are of particular interest because they suggest that the assumption that action perception always triggers a tendency to execute the same action may be oversimplified. Rather, compensatory ideomotor movements are also known as 'intentionally induced' movements, because they seem to reflect the observer's awareness of the actor's intention. By this interpretation, intentionally induced ideomotor movements reflect the interaction of sensorimotor processes with mental states.

To date, only a few studies have investigated ideomotor movements, and very little is known about the factors that determine whether people produce imitative or compensatory movements while watching other people's actions. As will be discussed below, possible factors that could modulate the degree to which motor resonance takes place include the psychological relationship between actor and observer, the nature of their interaction, and the spatial relation of their bodies. A closer understanding of the factors modulating motor resonance is critical for understanding the social functions of perception–action links (Knoblich and Sebanz, 2006). In the following, we will provide a short overview of ideomotor theory, which provides a foundation for the empirical study of ideomotor movements. In a next step, we will review studies that speak to the question of how social context modulates motor resonance. We then report two experiments that investigated the role of shared orientation on ideomotor movements.

From magic to ideomotor theory

The notion of a close link between perception and action has received considerable attention in recent years, spurred by the discovery of mirror neurons in macaque premotor (Gallese *et al.*, 1996) and parietal (Fogassi *et al.*, 2005) cortex. These much-discussed neurons fire both when a monkey performs an action and when the monkey observes someone performing the same action (Rizzolatti and Craighero, 2004). However, theoretical roots supporting the notion of a close link between perception, imagination, and execution of action can be traced back to the work of Carpenter (1874) and James (1890), who developed ideomotor theory (for a historical overview, see Knuf *et al.*, 2001). Carpenter was concerned with the question of how ideas guide movements without or against the actor's voluntary control. He referred to all action that is produced involuntarily, through a strong idea or image, as 'ideomotor action'. By assuming that ideas or mental images can directly trigger movements, he was able to account for a range of phenomena that seemed magic at the time, including the swinging of a hand-held pendulum despite instructions to hold it still.

Based on Lotze's work, James (1890) developed a theory of voluntary action based on the idea that "… every representation of a movement awakens in some degree the actual movement which is its object" (Vol. 2, p. 526). Simply put, thinking about a particular action effect creates a tendency to perform this action, as long as no conflicting thoughts are present. For example, thinking about a light turning on may trigger the action of operating the light switch. According to ideomotor theory, such regularities between movements and their more or less distant perceivable consequences are represented through learned associations (Knoblich and Prinz, 2005).

Greenwald (1970, 1972) realized that the ideomotor principle can be extended from imagination to the perception of action. If thinking of perceivable events triggers the movements that produce them, then perceiving the same events in the environment, e.g. as the result of somebody else's action, should also create a tendency to perform the movements that produce the observed events. For example, seeing a light turn on (rather than thinking about this effect) may activate a representation of the action of operating the light switch. Through this extension, ideomotor theory not only provides a functional principle for understanding voluntary action, but also offers a theoretical framework for understanding links between action perception and action production. A basic interpersonal link is provided by the assumption that perceived actions (performed by others) and planned actions (performed by oneself) are coded in a common representational domain (Prinz, 1997; Hommel *et al.*, 2001).

Constraints on motor resonance

Behavioral (e.g. Brass *et al.*, 2001), brain imaging (e.g. Stevens *et al.*, 2000; Calvo-Merino *et al.*, 2005), and neurophysiological studies (e.g. Fogassi *et al.*, 2005) have confirmed that when we observe someone performing an action, corresponding representations in our own action system are activated, creating a tendency to perform the observed action. For example, behavioral studies have shown that the execution of an action is facilitated when one concurrently observes someone making a similar movement, while it is impaired when one observes someone making an opposite movement (Stuermer *et al.*, 2000; Brass *et al.*, 2001; Kilner *et al.*, 2003). Interestingly, the findings by Kilner *et al.* suggest that these effects might be restricted to the observation of human motion and do not apply to the same extent when humans observe robot movements that have different kinematics.

A compelling demonstration of our tendency to covertly simulate observed actions was recently provided by Flanagan and colleagues (Flanagan and Johansson, 2003; Rotman *et al.*, 2006) who measured the gaze patterns of people performing a block-stacking task while observing another person performing the same task. They found highly similar gaze patterns for action perception and execution, suggesting that as people were watching the other's hand movements, corresponding action plans were activated. Flanagan *et al.* concluded that these action plans entail eye motor programs directed by motor representations of the manual actions. In other words, participants covertly simulated the observed hand actions, which led them to perform eye movements they would normally make when performing the observed actions themselves. Thus, the eyes provided a rare window into the mind, as action observation usually does not lead to overt action execution.

The relationship between self and other

While covert simulation may be the default (Wilson and Knoblich, 2005), there are instances where action representations are activated so strongly by observation that one finds oneself doing what one's interaction partner just did. For example, when talking to each other, people often engage in nonconscious mimicry, unwittingly imitating the postures, mannerisms or facial expressions of their interaction partner (for an overview, see Chartrand and Bargh, 1999). For example, Chartrand and Bargh (1999) showed that participants performing a task together with a confederate who shook her foot were also more likely to shake their foot, whereas participants paired with a confederate who rubbed her face rubbed their face more often. How can action observation lead to overt simulation given that the observer has no intention to imitate the other? One possible explanation is that nonconscious mimicry occurs when inhibitory processes that normally keep us from executing observed actions (Wilson, 2003; Brass *et al.*, 2005) are overridden. Evidence for this assumption is provided by the study of patients with frontal lobe lesions, who show a tendency to imitate observed actions as a consequence of impaired inhibitory control (Lhermitte *et al.*, 1968; Luria, 1980; De Renzi *et al.*, 1996; Brass *et al.*, 2003).

Although several studies have provided evidence for a link between nonconscious mimicry and rapport (e.g. La France, 1982; Tickle-Degnen and Rosenthal, 1987; Bernieri and Rosenthal, 1991), Chartrand and Bargh (1999) were the first to show a causal relationship: Naive participants whose actions had been mimicked by a confederate during an interaction reported liking the confederate better than participants whose actions had not been mimicked. Furthermore, they also felt that the interaction had gone more smoothly. In a further experiment, the authors showed that high-perspective takers— people who have a strong tendency to take others' perspective—engaged more in nonconscious mimicry. This finding suggests that the degree to which motor resonance occurs depends on cognitive style and personality variables of the observer (see also van Baaren *et al.*, 2003, 2004). In line with this finding, a recent functional magnetic resonance imaging study by Gazzola *et al.* (2006) showed a correlation between activation in brain areas pertaining to the auditory mirror system, and perspective taking. Listening to action-related sounds, like a paper being torn apart, high-perspective takers showed more activation in premotor and parietal areas that are also active during action execution than low-perspective takers.

Further studies suggest that motivational factors also play an important role. In a study by Lakin and Chartrand (2003), participants whose goal it was to connect with another person (affiliation goal) engaged more in nonconscious mimicry, independently of whether the goal was conscious or had been activated through a priming procedure without the participants' awareness. Furthermore, participants who failed to affiliate in an interaction were subsequently more likely to mimic the behavior of a new interaction partner than those who had not failed in the previous interaction. How can one account for these findings? One possibility is that people who wish to be liked and hope to have a successful interaction pay closer attention to the other's behavior, thus increasing the likelihood of 'motor contagion'. An alternative explanation is that having an affiliation goal decreases action inhibition, thus facilitating the execution of pre-activated actions. This would imply that the threshold for inhibition can be re-set in a top-down fashion through social goals.

While nonconscious mimicry seems to play a role in enhancing mutual liking and improving the quality of interactions (Lakin *et al.*, 2003; Chartrand *et al.*, 2005), research on ideomotor movements has shown that people also mimic movements when the observed person cannot see them. This is the case when "your leg hoists itself when you're watching a high jumper on TV". Although the term 'ideomotor movement' goes back to Carpenter (1874) (see Prinz, 1987; Knuf *et al.*, 2001; Prinz *et al.*, 2005, for a historical account), the empirical investigation of ideomotor movements has only recently started to gain momentum. Importantly, studies on ideomotor movements have shown that observers' actions do not always match the perceived actions.

Knuf *et al.* (2001) used a task where people watched the outcome of their own preceding actions, much like when one has set a bowling ball in motion and watches on as it rolls toward the pins. Participants saw a ball moving towards a target on a computer screen. The trajectory of the ball was always initially defined so that the ball would miss the target. However, during the initial phase of each trial, participants could correct the ball's trajectory by moving a joystick. Once the joystick was no longer effective (second phase of each trial), participants merely watched the ball approach the target. Unbeknownst to them, during this phase, their hand movements were measured. Analysis of the movements revealed that participants unwittingly performed compensatory movements when it looked like the ball was going to miss the target (e.g. moving the hand to the left when the ball was too far to the right). Thus, movements were clearly 'intentionally induced' in that they were driven by what one would like to see happen.

The next question was, of course, whether people would also make compensatory movements when observing another's actions. De Maeght and Prinz (2004, Experiment 3) showed participants the performance of another player and asked them to track the vertical position of the ball during the second phase of the trial as it was approaching the target. This allowed them to investigate subtle horizontal movements of the joystick that participants were not aware of making. Again, they found evidence for intentional induction: when participants saw that the ball would miss the target, they performed compensatory movements, although neither they themselves nor the player whose performance they saw could affect the ball's trajectory in any way. Thus, participants performed movements that were in line with the player's intention and *should* be performed. These results suggest that action observation does not always lead to a tendency to perform the observed actions, as is generally assumed. Rather, a representation of the actor's intention can override the tendency to imitate the observed movements and lead one to perform what the other should be doing.

The current study

The studies reviewed above demonstrate that sometimes observers spontaneously imitate the actions they observe while at other times they spontaneouly produce movements that compensate for the actions they observe. What factors determine whether imitative or compensatory movements are produced during action observation? The studies above seem to suggest that compensatory actions are associated with the observation of moving objects while imitative actions are associated with the observation of moving people. Given this trend, the aim of the present study was to extend our understanding of perception–action links in social context. In two experiments, we surreptitiously measured participants' body sway as they watched short movies of an actor balancing on a wobbly foam roller and judged whether the actor would be able to walk to the end of the roller or would fall off before reaching the end (see Figure 13.1).

Experiment 1

We sought to extend the study of ideomotor movements (De Maeght and Prinz, 2004) in four ways. First, in previous ideomotor experiments, participants' movements were

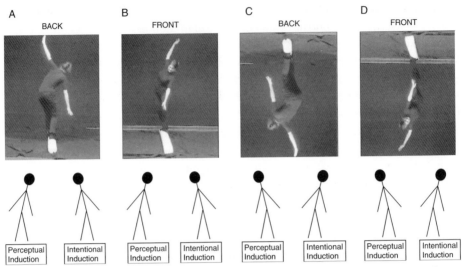

Figure 13.1 Illustration of perceptual induction and intentional induction in the upright and inverted conditions.

measured while observed actions could not be affected in any way. We think that more typically, one observes a person trying to achieve a particular action goal, rather than just observing the consequences of earlier actions. Second, in the study by De Maeght and Prinz, the task rules created a strong interest in the outcome of the observed actions because participants' score went up when the observed actor scored a goal. Here, we wanted to investigate to what extent ideomotor movements also occur in the absence of a reward associated with the action outcome. Third, it is well known that the body is a special object of perception (Knoblich *et al.*, 2006). While in previous studies only the consequences of bodily movements were shown as stimuli, we presented life-size displays of the actor's body to investigate how ideomotor movements are shaped by the perception of human motion. Finally, to investigate the role of the spatial relation between actor and observer, we included orientation as an independent variable and showed the actor from the front (different orientation) and from the back (shared orientation) in upright and inverted displays.

Predictions

There are three possible outcomes for the upright views. First, participants could show perceptual induction, moving the same way as they see the actor moving. For example, if the actor leans slightly or dangerously far to the right, the participants should also lean to the right, even when that means mimicking a potential fall. This would suggest that the perception of bodily movements triggers imitative tendencies, regardless of the known intention of the actor to avoid falling. Second, participants could show intentional induction, performing compensatory movements by leaning in the direction opposite of the actor's lean so as to 'maintain balance'. This would provide evidence for the assumption that a representation of the actor's intention, in this case, the intention to avoid falling, modulates perception–action links.

Finally, the extent to which perceptual or intentional induction occurs could be modulated by orientation. When participants see the actor from the back, thus sharing the same body orientation, perceptual induction occurs when participants lean to the same side as the actor (see Figure 13.1a). For example, when the actor tilts to the right, participants should also tilt to the right. Intentional induction occurs when participants see the actor leaning to one side and lean to the other side. For example, when the actor tilts to the right, they should tilt to the left. Thus, they would be compensating for the actor and perform the kind of action she should be performing.

When participants see the front of the actor's body, perceptual induction can be defined in more than one way, because 'left' and 'right' can be coded from the observer's point of view or from the actor's point of view. We here define perceptual induction in terms of spatial direction from the observer's point of view, based on the assumption that people do not perform a mental self-rotation to imagine sharing the same viewpoint with the actor (cf. Zacks *et al.*, 1999). Thus, perceptual induction occurs for example when the actor moves to the right from the point of view of the observer (actor's upper body moves to the right side of the screen) and the observer also moves right. Intentional induction occurs when actor and observer tilt in opposite directions. For example, when the actor tilts to the observer's right, the observer leans to the left (see Figure 13.1b).

Two opposing predictions can be made for the role of orientation (front versus back). If one assumes that a shared orientation leads to greater motor resonance, participants should be more likely to perform ideomotor movements when they see the actor from the back than when they see the actor from the front. Greater motor resonance could lead to more perceptually induced movement, but could also lead to more intentionally induced movement. For example, it could be that participants are better able to simulate the observed actions when they see the actor from the back, and thus, are able to anticipate when the actor is about to fall off. This could trigger stronger intentionally induced movements. If one assumes that an actor seen from the front is usually socially more relevant than an actor seen from the back, it could also be that motor resonance is stronger when the observer sees the actor from the front. Again, this could both lead to increased perceptually induced or intentionally induced movements.

The inverted view (see Figure 13.1c and 1d) served as a control condition. Perceptual and intentional induction were again defined in terms of the participant's point of view and were based on the assumption that participants would not imagine a self-rotation to share the same orientation with the actor. From studies on the perception of biological motion, it is known that point-light-defined movements of upright bodies tend to be processed globally, while point-light-defined movements of inverted bodies tend to be processed locally (Loula *et al.*, 2005). If participants simply moved in accordance with the shifts in spatial information in the displays, the pattern of ideomotor movements should be the same for the upright and inverted displays. In contrast, if the perception of a moving body induces ideomotor movements, participants should move systematically only in the upright condition.

Method

Participants. Seventeen participants (four male, 10 female) aged between 19 and 40 years took part in the experiment as part of a course requirement. All were right-handed and had normal or corrected-to-normal vision.

Material and apparatus. Participants were presented with movies of a person balancing on a foam roller (see Figures 13.1 and 13.2). To create the movies, a female actor was videotaped (recording rate 30 frames/s) while balancing and walking along a foam roller of about 2.5 m in total length. The actor was filmed from the front and back on separate balancing attempts. From this material, 30 movies were cut using the Apple software iMovie. Half of the movies showed the actor from the front, the other half showed her from the back. The movies lasted between 5 and 10 s, with a mean duration of 7.6 s. Each movie ended once the actor had passed about half the length of the foam roller. For both the front and back view, one-third of the movies ended with the actor leaning strongly to the left, one-third ended with the actor leaning strongly to the right, and one-third ended with the actor assuming a straight position. Each movie was presented in an upright and inverted view. The inverted view was created rotating the movies by 180° using QuickTime Pro.

The movies were rear-projected onto a large screen (12 ft × 8 ft) with a Sony VPC-PX40 projector with a refresh rate of 60 Hz and a 1024 × 768 pixel resolution. The actor in the movies was displayed approximately life-sized. Picture size from the participants' position was approximately 30 × 11 visual degree horizontally and vertically. The experiment was programmed in Microsoft Visual Basic 6.0, and stimulus presentation was controlled by a Dell Pentium computer. Participants' movements were recorded using a ReActor motion capture system from Ascension Technology. The recording rate was 30 frames/s. The motion capture recording and the movie presentation were started simultaneously via remote control.

Procedure. At the beginning of the experiment, participants were asked to wear a suit specially designed for the motion capture system (see Figure 13.2). We attached motion sensors to the suit at the head, chest, upper back, and all major body joints (total of 20). Participants were told that the purpose of the experiment was to investigate how well they could make predictions about observed actions, and that the suit served to measure "how your body reacts to the movies". They were led to believe that the system captured physiological measures akin to heart rate and were not told that their movements were being recorded. Participants stood on a 1-inch-thick foam sheet that was positioned in front of the projection screen at a distance of about 3 m. They were told to keep their feet no more than hip distance apart and to assume a relaxed posture without putting all their weight on just one leg.

Each trial started with the presentation of a fixation cross presented for 1 s, followed by presentation of a movie. After each movie, participants judged on a 5-point scale whether the actor would be able to maintain her balance and continue to walk to the end of the foam roller without falling off. They were presented with the following options: "I predict that the person (1) will definitely reach the end, (2) will probably reach the end, (3) has a 50/50 chance to reach the end, (4) will probably not reach the end, (5) will definitely not reach the end." They gave their judgment by saying out loud the respective number, which the experimenter entered into the computer. The purpose of this task was to make

Figure 13.2 Illustration of the experimental set-up. For illustration purposes, the participant in this picture is standing slightly to the side. In the actual experiment, participants stood in one line with the actor in the movie.

participants look at the movies without drawing their attention to their own movements. Judgment accuracy was not evaluated because, during stimulus construction, the video-taped actor tilted her body from side to side, often dramatically while she walked along the roller, but she very rarely actually fell off. Participants watched 60 movies and were allowed to take a break after the first 30 movies. The experiment lasted about 30 min. After the experiment, participants were asked about their beliefs regarding the purpose of the experiment and were debriefed. Participants who reported being aware that their movements had been recorded ($n = 3$) were excluded from the analyses.

Design. The movies were shown in an upright and inverted view, and the actor could be seen from the front or from the back (2 × 2 design). Presentation of upright and inverted movies was blocked, so that half of the participants saw the inverted movies first, and half saw the upright movies first. Orientation was also blocked. Half of the upright movies started with the front perspective of the walker's body, and half with the back perspective of her body. The same was true for the inverted movies. Altogether, there were 60 trials (15 upright front, 15 upright back, 15 inverted front, 15 inverted back).

Results

The data analysis started with the specification of the direction of tilt of the observed actor's body at each point during each movie. Actor tilt was categorized as leftward whenever the actor was moving from right to left, regardless of position of the upper body relative to gravitational axis. Similarly, actor tilt was categorized as rightward whenever the actor was moving towards the right, regardless of position of the upper body from the mid line. The direction of tilt was determined through frame-by-frame visual inspection of the movies in iMovie.

To analyze participants' movements, we calculated the movement of their upper body across time, in degrees per second. The logic behind choosing a discrete measure to express the actor's movements, and a continuous measure to express the participants' movements, was as follows. First, we assumed that the respective end state of each of the actor's tilts would be critical in inducing participants' movements. Thus, the actor's movements were coded as 'leaning towards the left' and 'leaning towards the right'. Second, we chose to express the participants' movements through a spatial–temporal measure, because given the small amplitude of participants' movements, absolute values did not seem meaningful.

To calculate participants' lateral upper body movements in degrees per second, we extracted the spatial coordinates for the hips and shoulders on each frame. Specifically, we calculated the tilt of the upper body relative to the hips with a formula used to calculate the angle in a right-angled triangle where the hypotenuse and the opposite leg are known [tilt in degrees = arc-sine of (amplitude/hypotenuse)*180/P]. Amplitude was defined as the mean value of the shoulder coordinates minus the mean value of the hip coordinates on a horizontal axis, respectively. The hypotenuse was calculated as the square root of the quadrated sum of the difference between the mean value of the shoulder coordinates and the mean value of the hip coordinates (on a vertical axis, respectively) and the amplitude. Angular velocity was calculated based on the difference between subsequent frames.

Movements. Figure 13.3 shows mean angular velocity of observer body tilt in the upright (A) and in the inverted (A) condition while the actor was tilting towards the

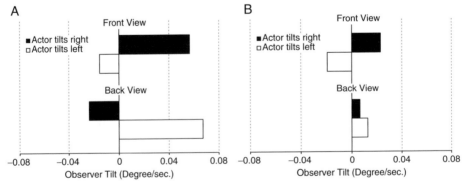

Figure 13.3 Results of Experiment 1. (**A**) Upright movies, (**B**) inverted movies. The participants' mean angular velocity (in degrees per second) is plotted across all frames in which the actor tilted rightward (black bars) and all frames in which the actor tilted leftward (white bars). Top: front view condition. Bottom: back view condition.

right or towards the left. For this analysis, we compared participants' mean angular velocity while the actor tilted leftwards or rightwards across all movies, and independent of the degree of the actor's tilt. To test for significant differences in the upright condition, a 2×2 within-subjects analysis of variance (ANOVA) with the factors Actor Body Tilt (left, right) and Actor Body Orientation (front versus back) was conducted. There were no significant main effects, all $p > 0.05$. Thus, whether participants saw the actor tilting towards the right or left, and whether they saw the actor from the front or from the back did not affect how much they moved overall. However, there was a significant interaction between Actor Tilt and Actor Orientation [$F(1, 13) = 9.22, p < 0.01$], indicating that participants' movements differed depending on whether they saw the actor from the front or from the back. When the actor was seen from the front, there was a tendency to mimic the observed movements, according to our definition of perceptual induction. Participants tilted more to the left when the actor tilted leftwards, and to the right when the actor tilted rightwards (see Figure 13.3A, upper half, and Figure 13.4A). A two-sided t-test confirmed that angular velocity was significantly different when the actor tilted left compared to when the actor tilted right [$t(1, 13) = 2.36, p < 0.05$]. In contrast, when the actor was seen from the back, compensatory movements occurred (intentional induction). Participants seemed to tilt more to the left when the actor tilted towards the right, and vice versa (see Figure 13.3A, lower half, and Figure 13.4B). This difference was not statistically significant, but showed a tendency [$t(1, 13) = 1.79, p = 0.09$]. Figure 13.4 provides an illustration of participants' tendency to mimic the actor's movements in the front condition and to perform compensatory movements in the back condition.

To test for differences in angular velocity in the inverted condition (see Figure 13.3b), a 2×2 within-subjects ANOVA with the factors Actor Tilt (left, right) and Orientation (front versus back) was conducted. No significant effects were observed, all p-values > 0.05. t-Tests showed that unlike in the upright condition, whether the actor was seen tilting leftwards or rightwards did not affect angular velocity [$t(1, 13) = 0.92, p = 0.37$ in the front view condition; $t(1, 13) = 0.11, p = 0.91$ in the back view condition].

Judgments. The mean judgment, along the 5-point scale, of the likelihood that the actor would fall off the roller was 3.05, SD = 0.2. t-Tests showed that the frequencies with which participants chose Judgment 2 (will probably reach the end), 3 (50/50 chance) and 4 (will probably not reach the end) were not significantly different. Judgment 1 (will definitely reach the end) and Judgment 5 (will definitely not reach the end) were chosen less frequently, all $p < 0.05$. To test for interactions between judgments, the orientation of the movies, and the perspective from which the actor was seen, a $2 \times 2 \times 5$ ANOVA with the factors Movie Inversion (upright versus inverted), Actor Orientation (front versus back), and Judgment (1, 2, 3, 4, 5) was performed. It showed a significant interaction between Actor Orientation and Judgment [$F(4, 48) = 7.48, p < 0.001$], but no significant interaction between Movie Inversion and Judgment, $F(4, 48) = 1.08, p = 0.38$. The 'definitive' judgments (Judgments 1 and 5) were made more frequently in the front view condition compared to the back view condition, as confirmed by Newman–Keuls *post hoc* tests, all $p < 0.05$. This suggests that when participants viewed the front of the walking actor's body, they felt more certain about their judgments.

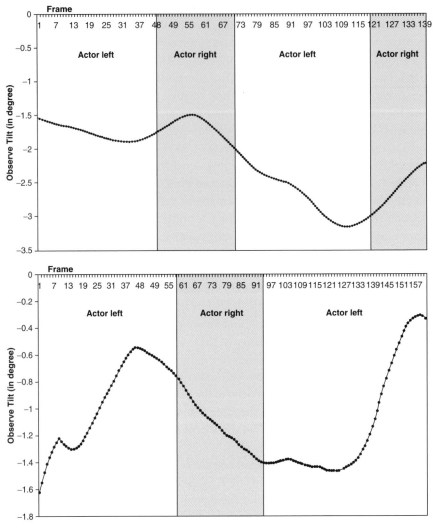

Figure 13.4 Data of one typical participant in Experiment 1. This graph shows one participant's tilt during one movie. The data were smoothed by averaging across ten frames. Higher values on the y-axis indicate that the participant tilted to the right, lower values indicate that the participant tilted to the left. A white background indicates the time window(s) during which the actor tilted leftward. A grey background indicates the time window(s) during which the actor tilted rightward. (**A**) Front view condition. (**B**) Back view condition.

To determine which information participants based their judgments on, we computed individual correlations between judgments and the mean tilt of the actor in each movie, as well as individual correlations between judgments and the actor's tilt at the end of each movie. The actor's tilt at the end of each movie was determined using a still frame and measuring the angle (in degrees). The mean tilt was calculated by averaging across the angles at all turning points (all maximal tilts to the left and right). If the correlation between mean tilt and judgment were stronger than the correlation between final tilt and judgment, it would mean that participants integrated information across the movies. If the correlation between judgments and the final position in the movie were equally strong or stronger, it would mean that judgments were based mainly on the final information about the actor's position.

Only participants who had given judgments from the whole range (1–5) were included in the analyses ($n = 12$). There was a significant positive correlation between mean tilt and judgments both in the upright condition ($r = 0.39$), and in the inverted condition ($r = 0.37$). There was also a positive correlation between last tilt and judgments in the upright ($r = 0.42$), and in the inverted condition ($r = 0.41$). Given that the actor's final tilt explains just as much of the variance as the mean tilt, these results suggest that both in the upright and inverted view condition, judgments were mostly based on the actor's position at the end of the movie, when the actor was closest to the end of the roller.

Discussion

The results of Experiment 1 provide evidence that ideomotor movements occur not only when the consequences of earlier performed actions are observed (De Maeght and Prinz, 2004), but are also induced by the online observation of body movements. While participants focused on making judgments about an actor's success in a balancing task, their bodies actually re-enacted and counter-acted the movements they observed. The difference between the upright and the inverted condition suggests that participants did not merely react to shifts in the spatial information in the displays, but that their movements were related to the perception of a human body moving in biologically possible ways.

Interestingly, we found a systematic relationship between the actor's and the observers' movements despite the fact that the actor's performance did not have any direct consequences for the observers. In previous studies, the experimental situation was such that observers were rewarded given particular action outcomes. Thus, it has been difficult to say whether ideomotor movements reflect the observer's hope for particular action outcomes, or whether they are of a more general nature. The present findings suggest that ideomotor movements occur in response to the perception of goal-directed actions and are not restricted to situations where the observer has a personal stake in particular action outcomes. It falls to future studies to investigate systematically the relationship between the observer's intentions and the induction of ideomotor movements. It seems likely that the tendency to perform ideomotor movements will be stronger when the outcome of observed actions has consequences for the observer or is of emotional significance.

The orientation from which the actor was seen determined the way ideomotor movements were induced. When the actor was seen from the front, perceptual induction seemed to occur: Participants moved to the side in space to which the actor's body moved. When the actor was seen from the back, intentional induction occurred. Participants leaned to the opposite side of space as the actor, thus moving in a way that was consistent with the actor's goal, but did not match the observed movements.

The results for the front view condition are consistent with findings from studies on nonconscious mimicry, which have shown that people facing each other tend to mimic each other's movements. It seems possible that a similar mechanism underlies noncon-scious mimicry and the induction of ideomotor movements in face-to-face encounters. It has been claimed that the tendency to mimic others occurs because observing others' movements activates corresponding motor programs in the observer. While this tendency may remain covert most of the time, the activation of the motor system can become strong enough to override inhibitory mechanisms that normally keep us from mimick-ing observed actions (Wilson, 2003; Brass *et al.*, 2005). Studies on nonconscious mimicry suggest that it acts as 'social glue', increasing feelings of liking and unity. Face-to-face interactions are likely one of the standard situations where nonconscious mimicry occurs (Grammer *et al.*, 1998). It seems possible that tuning in to the other in a face-to-face interaction is so deeply ingrained that we cannot help mimicking others even when they are just actors in a movie.

One could object that the imitative movements in the front condition were due to task demands. After all, it might be easier to judge how likely the actor is to fall off when one puts oneself in her shoes and imitates her movements. Two pieces of evidence argue against such an interpretation. First, the observed movements were very small, and most participants were not aware that they had moved in response to the actor's movements. Second, if participants strategically moved in accordance with the actor, imitative move-ments should have been observed in the back view condition as well.

A more serious objection to the present interpretation of the results is that we cannot exclude the possibility that participants performed a mental rotation to imagine sharing the same orientation with the actor in the front view condition, or were able to map the actor's movements onto their body as if they shared the same orientation. This implies that what we consider to be imitative movements would actually be compensatory move-ments. This interpretation is quite appealing given its parsimonious nature. Participants clearly performed compensatory movements in the back view condition, making it tempting to speculate that intentional induction may have occurred in the front view condition as well. We cannot rule out this possibility. However, we would like to point out that previous studies suggest that participants asked to imagine the perspective from a different viewpoint have difficulties performing this imagined self-rotation and thus might not do so unasked (Wapner and Cirillo, 1968; Ishikura and Inomata, 1995; Sambrook, 1998; Zacks *et al.*, 1999; for a different perspective, see Wraga, 2003). Further studies are needed to determine whether participants do perform a mental rotation or are able to map the other's actions onto their own body when they do not share the same orientation.

The results from the back view condition are unambiguous and provide evidence for intentional induction. Participants moved the way in which the actor should move to avoid falling off. This finding is in line with previous studies of ideomotor movements, where participants always saw events unfolding from an egocentric perspective (Knuf *et al.*, 2001; De Maeght and Prinz, 2004). In these studies, participants also showed a tendency to move in the direction that corresponded to the desired outcome rather than to the observed event. But is the mechanism behind intentional induction in the present experiment the same as in these previous studies?

The compensatory movements that occur when participants observe the trajectory of a ball about to miss a target can be explained by the assumption that observers' movements are guided by an idea of what they would like to see happening. This is precisely what William James's ideomotor principle refers to. He proposed that the idea or image of a particular action will trigger the execution of this action when no conflicting mental images are present: "Every representation of a movement awakens in some degree the actual movement which is its object; and awakens it in a maximum degree whenever it is not kept from doing so by an antagonistic representation present simultaneously in the mind" (James, 1890, p. 526). In the case of intentionally induced ideomotor movements, there is actually conflicting information in the form of the events that unfold. However, it seems that the representation of imagined actions dominates and can override the visual input.

In the present experiment, observers' movements could also have been guided by an image of what the actor should be doing. However, what the actor should be doing changed from moment to moment and was not easily predictable. Although it is possible that participants put themselves in the actor's shoes and tried to imagine what she should be doing, we think it is more likely that they simply felt as if they were in the actor's place. We would like to speculate that sharing the same orientation with the actor increased the degree to which observers identified with the actor's movements. Instead of projecting themselves onto the other, the other was mapped onto the self. While this distinction may seem subtle at first, it actually points towards two different mechanisms of intentional induction.

On the one hand, observers might make compensatory movements because they want someone or something to x. For example, when watching a bowling ball set in motion by a team player one might move in the direction one wants the ball to roll. Thus, in this case, observers project themselves *onto* a person or object. This projection is driven by a particular goal one anxiously hopes for. Thus, in the paradigmatic situation one wishes that one was able to exert control over observed actions or events. Importantly, compensatory movements that occur as a result of wanting x do not necessarily rely on simulation in the observer's action system.

On the other hand, observers might make compensatory movements when they start feeling to some extent as if they were the observed. One could say that, in this case, the other gets mapped onto the self, rather than the other way round. Examples include watching someone awkwardly learning to ice-skate or trying to climb a precipice. In such cases, compensatory movements might occur because the observer's motor system has been brought to resonate with the observed movements. Sharing the same orientation and being in similar surroundings could contribute to this resonance. Importantly, according to this view, compensatory movements would occur only because the actor appears to be struggling or failing. Otherwise, imitative movements are expected. The compensatory movements would arise directly out of a simulation in the observer's motor system that indicates that the performed movements do not lead to the intended goal. Future studies are needed to validate this distinction. In the meanwhile, it is tempting to speculate that the compensatory movements observed by Prinz and colleagues are of the first kind, whereas the compensatory movements observed in the present study pertain to the latter.

Experiment 2

In Experiment 2, we aimed to replicate the finding that actor orientation modulates ideomotor movements. Furthermore, by collecting continuous movement data not only from observers, but also from the actor, we hoped to be able to further specify the nature of ideomotor movements. As a new set of balancing movies was made, the actor's movements were recorded by the same motion capture system that was used to record the observers' movements. This allowed us to investigate to what extent movement characteristics of the actor can be found in the observer's motor 'echo'.

Method

Participants. Fourteen participants (three male, 11 female) aged between 19 and 41 years took part in the experiment as part of a course requirement. All were right-handed and had normal or corrected-to-normal vision.

Material and apparatus. A new set of movies was created in exactly the same way as in Experiment 1. The only difference was that this time, the actor wore the suit with sensors for movement recording. Actor movements were recorded using the same motion capture system that was used to record participants' movements in Experiment 1. The recording rate was 30 frames/s. As in Experiment 1, the actor was filmed from the front and back on separate balancing attempts. From this material, 30 movies were cut using the Apple software iMovie. Half of the movies showed the actor from the front, the other half showed her from the back. The motion capture data were edited so that the movement recordings started and ended at the same time as the movies. The movies lasted between 5 and 8 s, with a mean duration of 6.6 s. All other characteristics of the movies were the same as in Experiment 1. The apparatus used during the experiment was identical to that in Experiment 1.

Procedure. The procedure was exactly the same as in Experiment 1, except that only upright movies were shown. The experiment lasted about 30 min. After the experiment, participants were asked about their beliefs regarding the purpose of the experiment and were debriefed. Participants who reported being aware that their movements had been recorded ($n = 2$) were excluded from the analyses.

Design. Half of the movies showed the actor from the front perspective, and half from the back perspective. Presentation of front and back view movies was blocked, and the order of blocks was counter-balanced across participants. There were 30 trials (15 front, 15 back).

Results

The data of two participants had to be discarded due to problems with the movement recording, so the data of 10 participants were analyzed. One of the movies showing the actor from the front had to be excluded from the analysis because it turned out that there had been problems with the movement recording of the actor.

In a first step, we analyzed the results in exactly the same way as in Experiment 1. Thus, we classified whether the actor moved towards the left or towards the right and averaged the participants' movements across all instances where the actor moved leftwards or rightwards. We used the actor's motion capture data (tilt calculated in the same way as in Experiment 1) to classify movements as leftwards and rightwards. As can be seen in Figure 13.5, the pattern of results looks similar to the results observed in the upright condition in Experiment 1. To test for differences between the two experiments, a $2 \times 2 \times 2$ ANOVA with Experiment as a between-subject variable and Actor Orientation (back, front) and Actor Tilt (left, right) as within-subject variables was conducted. There was a significant main effect of Experiment [$F(1, 22) = 10.79, p < 0.01$]. Participants' movements were more pronounced in Experiment 2 than in Experiment 1. Again, participants had a general tendency to move to the right. Importantly, the interaction between Actor Orientation and Actor Tilt was significant [$F(1, 22) = 6.45, p < 0.05$]. No further significant effects were observed, suggesting that overall, a similar pattern was found in both experiments (see also Figure 13.6).

There were some differences between the front and back condition in the two experiments, however. Unlike in Experiment 1, a two-sided t-test comparing angular velocity when the actor tilted leftwards compared to when the actor tilted rightwards in the front view condition was not significant, $p > 0.05$. However, there was clear evidence for compensatory movements when the actor was seen from the back. Participants tilted more to the left when the actor tilted rightwards, and vice versa [$t(1, 9) = 4.06, p < 0.01$].

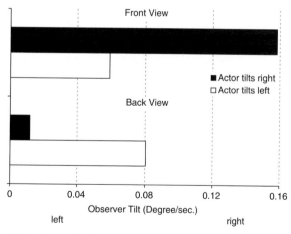

Figure 13.5 Results of Experiment 2. The participants' mean angular velocity (in degrees per second) is plotted across all frames in which the actor tilted rightward (black bars) and all frames in which the actor tilted leftward (white bars). Top: front view condition. Bottom: back view condition. Note that the x-axis label was kept the same as in Figure 13.3, but participants on average did not move to the left of the mid line.

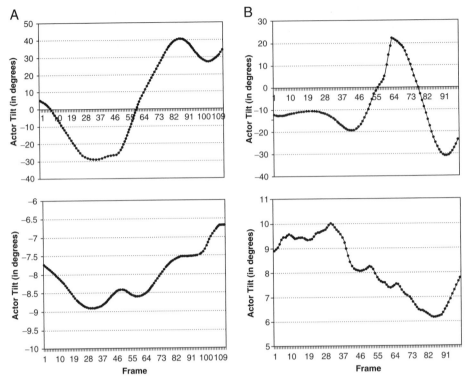

Figure 13.6 Data of the actor and one typical participant from Experiment 2. (**A**) Front view condition. (**B**) Back view condition. Upper panels: Actor. Lower panels: Participant. The actor's and the participant's data were smoothed by averaging across ten frames. Higher values on the y-axis indicate rightward movements and lower values indicate leftward movements.

To address the question of whether the amplitude of the actor's movements (how much the actor tilted to the side) had an impact on ideomotor movements, we calculated the mean standard deviation of the actor's tilt (in degrees) per movie and correlated this with the mean standard deviation of each observer's tilt during presentation of each movie. The actor's tilt was calculated in the same way as the participants' tilt (see Experiment 1 for details). In the front view condition, the average correlation coefficient was close to zero ($r = 0.07$), in the back condition it was slightly higher ($r = 0.21$). However, this difference was not significant [$t (1, 9) = 1.23, p = 0.25$].

Discussion

Experiment 2 replicated the finding that actor orientation modulates ideomotor movements. Participants seemed to mimic the actor's movements when the actor was seen from the front, and performed compensatory movements when the actor was seen from the back. Contrary to Experiment 1, the compensatory movements in the back view condition were more pronounced, while the tendency to imitate the observed movements was weaker. Overall, participants tended to move more to the right. Analyses of the movies in Experiments 1 and 2 showed that in both experiments, the actor moved approximately an equal amount of time to the left and to the right, so it seems unlikely that participants' general tendency to lean to the right was due to the observed movements. However, there could be a connection between participants' right-handedness and their tendency to move to the right.

Analysis of the movement amplitudes did not show a correlation between the amount to which actor and observer tilted sideways. It seems possible that ideomotor movements do not reflect the extent to which observed actions 'go wrong', but rather occur whenever the success of performed actions is perceived as questionable. Previous studies have not analyzed ideomotor movements in such a fine-grained way. It could be a promising endeavour for future studies to investigate the relation between observers' intention and the similarity of movement characteristics of observed and performed movements.

General discussion

The study of ideomotor movements is a challenging endeavour, because in everyday life, ideomotor movements usually occur as single instances in response to highly specific situations. With the present paradigm, we were able to induce consistent ideomotor movements. Orientation modulated the way in which observers unwittingly moved: when the actor was seen from the front, participants seemed to mimic the observed movements, whereas when the actor was seen from the back, they performed compensatory movements.

One could argue that it was not orientation alone that modulated observers' movements, but also the movement direction of the actor. In Experiments 1 and 2, orientation and movement direction were confounded such that in the front view condition, the actor always moved closer to the observer, whereas in the back view condition, the actor moved away from the observer. It seems unlikely that movement direction alone would induce different patterns of ideomotor movements, but on the basis of the present study, we cannot rule out the possibility that direction also played a role. This could be investigated in future studies by manipulating orientation and movement direction independently of one another. For now, we would just like to note that the change in distance between actor and observer was not very pronounced in our experiments, because actors only moved a short way along the balancing beam.

In the following, we will discuss in more detail which mechanisms might give rise to ideomotor movements. As we suggested earlier, an important dimension along which ideomotor movements could be characterized is intentionality. Prinz and colleagues distinguished between perceptually induced and intentionally induced ideomotor movements. This distinction implies that people move in response to observed actions or events either because they hope for a particular outcome (intentional induction) or simply because, due to close links between action perception and action execution, the observation of an action creates a tendency to perform this action (perceptual induction). However, movements one would typically interpret as intentionally induced could still result from different processes. They could either reflect an urge to exert control over the observed event (such as when one wishes one could give the soccer ball a little spin to push it into the goal), or they could reflect a kind of 'over-identification' whereby one feels as if one were in the place of the observed rather than the observer and thus start moving accordingly. Meyer and Hobson (2005) have also described this phenomenon as a process of assuming another's stance, whereby "actions and attitudes anchored in the other person's bodily located orientation towards the world become assimilated to the individual's own bodily located orientation" (p. 225).

One important difference between these two mechanisms is the contribution of the observer's action system. While the 'control urge' type of intentional induction does not imply resonance in the observer's motor system, the 'projection' kind of induction is assumed to occur because similar motor programs are activated in the actor and in the observer. Thus, it seems likely that ideomotor movements of the first kind will occur primarily in response to objects, while ideomotor movements due to motor resonance might be primarily associated with the perception of human action. One could assume that due to motor resonance, visual information about the other's movements is treated as feedback about one's own actions.

According to the internal model theory of control, we normally guide and control our actions by comparing predicted with actual sensorimotor consequences of our actions (Wolpert and Kawato, 1998; Frith et al., 2000). It could be that due to a tight coupling between perception and action, the prediction of sensorimotor consequences is no longer based on one's own actions, but based on the observed actions. By running simulations of the other's movements in one's own action system, the sensory consequences of moving in the observed way are predicted (Wilson and Knoblich, 2005). When a monitoring process signals that the planned movements will not lead to the desired outcome, this will automatically result in adjustments, reflected in compensatory movements.

If the account described above is correct, it follows that anything that will increase motor resonance and thereby simulation processes in the observer will lead to a stronger tendency to perform ideomotor movements. Sharing the same orientation as another person is a good candidate for increasing motor resonance, because it it easier to map someone's movements onto one's own body when the orientation is the same. Another interesting prediction that follows is that experts in a particular action domain might have a stronger tendency to perform ideomotor movements than novices. It has been shown that the greater one's expertise in a particular action domain, the greater the neural activation in the motor system (Calvo-Merino et al., 2005; Cross et al., in press). In a study by Calvo-Merino et al. (2005), ballet dancers showed more activation in areas of the human mirror system when watching movies of someone dancing ballet compared to movies of someone dancing capoeira, whereas the opposite pattern was observed for capoeira dancers. Accordingly, one could predict that gymnasts observing someone engaged in a tricky balancing task might show more ideomotor movements than novices, because motor resonance is increased.

Another interesting question is whether the ability to put oneself in someone else's shoes to predict their feelings, beliefs, and intentions—known as theory of mind (ToM)—bears any relation to these highly automatic phenomena of resonance. Many authors have speculated that the mirror system might be a precursor to, or even provide aspects of, theory of mind (e.g. Gallese and Goldman, 1998; Gallese et al., 2004). It has also been claimed that the mentalizing difficulties observed in people with autism might be connected to a mirror system deficit (e.g. Williams *et al.*, 2001; Gallese, 2003). While some studies have provided evidence for this claim (Nishitani *et al.*, 2004; Oberman *et al.*, 2005; Théoret *et al.*, 2005), it still remains to be determined whether the mirror system deficit observed in autism is a primary dysfunction or a result of dysfunction in other brain areas (Oberman *et al.*, 2005), and whether there is a causal relationship between the mirror system deficit and impairments in theory of mind. Nevertheless, it is worth considering how a mirror system deficit would affect the production of ideomotor movements.

If one assumes that individuals with autism have a mirror system deficit, they should show less ideomotor movements than healthy controls in our balancing paradigm. Based on findings by Théoret *et al.* (2005), one could even speculate that they would move less in particular when the orientation is shared with the actor. In the study by Théoret *et al.*, muscle-specific facilitation during action observation was absent in individuals with autism specifically when the actions were seen from an egocentric perspective. Thus, in our paradigm, fewer ideomotor movements would be expected especially in the back view condition. In contrast, when individuals with autism observe objects rather than human agents and want the object to *x*, 'control-urge' type of ideomotor movements should still be observed. Thus, one should see the following dissociation: People with autism should move less when they see someone balancing, but just as much as healthy controls when they see a ball missing a goal. This prediction remains to be tested in future studies. Note that similar predictions also follow from the more general view that individuals with autism have a deficit relating self to other (Barresi and Moore, 1996; for an overview, see Meyer and Hobson, 2005).

We would like to conclude this paper with some more general remarks on the nature of bodily bonds between self and other. While some may be sceptical about the 'mirror neuron hype' that cognitive neuroscience has seen in past years, it seems obvious that now that there is extensive behavioral, neurophysiological, and brain-imaging evidence for a close link between action observation and action execution, we must go on to find out what functions these close perception–action links have. Much points towards social functions (Knoblich and Sebanz, 2006), ranging from action understanding (Rizzolatti and Craighero, 2004) and the predictions of other's actions (Wilson and Knoblich, 2005) to establishing feelings of rapport and liking (Lakin and Chartrand, 2003). It might be useful to distinguish between convert and overt imitation phenomena and ask whether these have similar or different purposes.

One could speculate that while covert simulation is related to action understanding and action prediction, overt simulation is related to the establishing of interpersonal bonds. Nonconscious mimicry has been shown to enhance mutual liking, and is even used as a tool to overcome ostracism and create bonds with others. While research on nonconscious mimicry has focused on postural similarities between people, one should not lose sight of other perception–action coupling processes that might contribute to social interactions. A range of studies has shown that people have a tendency to entrain, be it swinging pendulums in synchrony despite the instruction to keep one's own pace

(Richardson *et al.*, 2005) or sitting next to each other in rocking chairs and moving in synchrony despite different eigenfrequencies of the chairs (Goodman *et al.*, 2005). Interestingly, coupling of body sway was found even between people who could not see each other but were engaged in a conversation (Shockley *et al.*, 2003), and there is evidence for close couplings between speakers' and listeners' eye movements (Richardson and Dale, 2005). It remains to be seen whether common mechanisms can be postulated for these different kinds of perception–action links, and how they contribute to so-called 'higher' cognitive functions. So far, we can conclude that people have a strong tendency to use their bodies to create social bonds, and that social context creates different affordances for this bodily bonding. Ideomotor movements may reflect a spill-over of the motor resonance that contributes to action understanding, prediction, and bonding in social interactions.

Acknowledgments

This research was funded by NIH grant EY12300. We would like to thank Mischa Kozhevnikov for his help in programming the experiment, and Ana Radonjic for starring in the balancing movies. Many thanks to Guenther Knoblich for his help with the data analysis. This article was prepared during a stay at the Center for Interdisciplinary Research (ZIF) of Bielefeld University. We would like to thank Ipke Wachsmuth and Guenther Knoblich, the organizers of the research year on 'Embodied Communication' at ZIF, for enabling us to participate in this project.

References

Barresi, J. and Moore, C. (1996) Intentional relations and social understanding. *Behavioral and Brain Sciences*, **19**, 107–154.

Bernieri, F. and Rosenthal, R. (1991) Interpersonal coordination, behavior matching, and interpersonal synchrony. In Feldman, R. and Rime, B. (eds), *Fundamentals of Nonverbal Behavior*, pp. 401–433. Cambridge University Press, Cambridge.

Carpenter, W. B. (1874) Principles of mental physiology, with their applications to the training and discipline of the mind and the study of its morbid conditions. Appleton, New York.

Brass, M., Bekkering, H. and Prinz, W. (2001) Movement observation affects movement execution in a simple response task. *Acta Psychologica*, **106**, 3–22.

Brass, M., Derrfuss, J., Matthes-von Cramon, G. and von Cramon, D. Y. (2003) Imitative response tendencies in patients with frontal lesions. *Neuropsychology*, **17**, 265–271.

Brass, M., Derrfuss, J. and von Cramon, D. Y. (2005) The inhibition of imitative and overlearned responses: a functional double dissociation. *Neuropsychologia*, **43**, 89–98.

Buccino, G., Binkofski, F. and Riggio, L. (2004) The mirror neuron system and action recognition. *Brain and Language*, **89**, 370–376.

Calvo-Merino, B., Glaser, D. E., Grezes, J., Passingham, R. E. and Haggard, P. (2005) Action observation and acquired motor skills: an fMRI study with expert dancers. *Cerebral Cortex*, **15**, 1243–1249.

Chartrand, T. and Bargh, J. (1999) The chameleon effect: the perception-behavior link and social interaction. *Journal of Personality and Social Psychology*, **76**, 893–910.

Chartrand, T. L., Maddux, W. and Lakin, J. (2005) Beyond the perception–behavior link: The ubiquitous utility and motivational moderators of nonconscious mimicry. In Hassin, R., Uleman, J. and Bargh, J. A. (eds), Unintended thought II: The new unconscious. Oxford University Press, New York.

Cross, E., Hamilton, A. and Grafton, S. (2006) Building a motor simulation de novo: Observation of dance by dancers. *Neuroimage*, **31**, 1257–1267.

De Maeght, S. and Prinz, W. (2004) Action induction through action observation. *Psychological Research*, **68**, 97–114.

De Renzi, E., Cavalleri, F. and Facchini, S. (1996) Imitation and utilisation behavior. *Journal of Neurology, Neurosurgery, and Psychiatry*, **61**, 396–400.

Flanagan, J. R. and Johansson, R.S. (2003) Action plans used in action observation. *Nature*, **424**, 769–771.

Fogassi, L., Ferrari, P. F., Gesierich, B., Rozzi, S., Chersi, F. and Rizzolatti, G. (2005) Parietal lobe: from action organization to intention understanding. *Science*, **308**, 662–667.

Frith, C. D., Blakemore, S.-J. and Wolpert, D. M. (2000) Abnormalities in the awareness and control of actions. *Philosophical Transactions of the Royal Society of London, B*, **355**, 1771–1788.

Gallese, V. (2003) The roots of empathy: the shared manifold hypothesis and the neural basis of intersubjectivity. *Psychopathology*, **36**, 171–180.

Gallese, V. and Goldman, A. (1998) Mirror neurons and the simulation theory of mind-reading. *Trends in Cognitive Sciences*, **2**, 493–501.

Gallese, V., Keysers, C. and Rizzolatti, G. (2004) A unifying view of the basis of social cognition. *Trends in Cognitive Sciences*, **8**, 396–403.

Gazzola, V., Aziz-Zadeh, L. and Keysers, C. (2006) I hear what you are doing—an fMRI study of the auditory mirror system in humans. *Journal of Neuroscience*, **26**, 2964–2970.

Goodman, J. R. L., Isenhower, R. W., Marsh, K. L., Schmidt, R. C. and Richardson, M. J. (2005) The interpersonal phase entrainment of rocking chair movements. In Heft, H. and Marsh, K. L. (eds), *Studies in Perception and Action VIII*, pp. 49–53. Erlbaum, Mahwah, NJ.

Grammer, K., Kruck, K. B. and Magnusson, M. S. (1998) The courtship dance: patterns of nonverbal synchronization in opposite-sex encounters. *Journal of Nonverbal Behavior*, **22**, 3–29.

Ishikura, T. and Inomata, K. (1995) Effects of angle of model-demonstration on learning of motor skill. *Perceptual and Motor Skills*, **80**, 651–658.

James, W. (1890) *The Principles of Psychology* (2 vols). Holt, New York.

Keller, P., Knoblich, G. and Repp, B. (2007) Pianists duet better when they play with themselves: on the possible role of action simulation in synchronization. *Consciousness and Cognition*, **16**, 102–111.

Knoblich, G. and Prinz, W. (2005) Linking perception and action: an ideomotor approach. In Freund, H.-J., Jeannerod, M., Hallett, M. and Leiguarda, R. C. (eds), *Higher-order Motor Disorders*, pp. 79–104. Oxford University Press, Oxford, UK.

Knoblich, G. and Sebanz, N. (2006) The social nature of perception and action. *Current Directions in Psychological Science*, **15**, 99–104.

Knoblich, G., Thornton, I., Grosjean, M. and Shiffrar, M. (eds) (2006) *Perception of the Human Body*. Oxford University Press, New York.

Knuf, L., Aschersleben, G. and Prinz, W. (2001) An analysis of idemotor action. *Journal of Experimental Psychology: General*, **130**, 779–798.

La France, M. (1982) Posture mirroring and rapport. In Davis, M. (ed.), *Interaction Rhythms. Periodicity in Communicative Behavior*, pp. 279–298. Human Sciences Press, New York.

Lakin, J. and Chartrand, T. L. (2003) Using nonconscious behavioral mimicry to create affiliation and rapport. *Psychological Science*, **14**, 334–339.

Lakin, J. L., Jefferis, V. E., Cheng, C. M. and Chartrand, T. L. (2003) The Chameleon Effect as social glue: evidence for the evolutionary significance of nonconscious mimicry. *Journal of Nonverbal Behavior*, **27**, 145–162.

Lhermitte, F., Pillon, B. and Serdaru, M. D. (1986) Human autonomy and the frontal lobes: I. Imitation and utilization behavior. A neuropsychological study of 75 patients. *Annals of Neurology*, **19**, 326–334.

Loula, F., Prasad, S., Harber, K. and Shiffrar, M. (2005) Recognizing people from their movements. *Journal of Experimental Psychology: Human Perception and Performance*, **31**, 210–220.

Luria, A. R. (1980) *Higher Cortical Functions in Man*. Consultants Bureau, New York.

Meyer, J. A. and Hobson, R. P. (2004) Orientation in relation to self and other. The case of autism. *Interaction Studies*, **5**, 221–244.

Mitchell, D. (2006) *Black Swan Green*. Random House, New York.

Nishitani, N., Avikainen, S. and Hari, R. (2004) Abnormal imitation-related cortical activation sequences in Asperger's syndrome. *Annals of Neurology*, **55**, 558–562.

Oberman, L. M., Hubbard, E. M., McCleery, J. P., Altschuler E. L., Ramachandran, V. S. Pineda, J. A. (2005) EEG evidence for mirror neuron dysfunction in autism spectrum disorders. *Cognitive Brain Research*, **24**, 190–198.

Prinz, W., De Maeght, S. and Knuf, L. (2005) Intention in action. In Humphreys, G. and Riddoch, J. (eds), *Attention in Action: Advances from Cognitive Neuroscience*. Psychology Press, Hove, UK.

Repp, B. H. and Knoblich, G. (2004) Perceiving action identity: how pianists recognize their own performances. *Psychological Science*, **15**, 604–609.

Richardson, D.C. and Dale, R. (2005) Looking to understand: the coupling between speakers' and listeners' eye movements and its relationship to discourse comprehension. *Cognitive Science*, **29**, 39–54.

Richardson, M. J., Marsh, K. L. and Schmidt, R. C. (2005) Effects of visual and verbal interaction on unintentional interpersonal coordination. *Journal of Experimental Psychology: Human Perception and Performance*, **31**, 62–79.

Rizzolatti, G. and Craighero, L. (2004) The mirror-neuron system. *Annual Review of Neuoscience*, **27**, 169–192.

Rotman G., Troje, N. F., Johansson, R. S. and Flanagan, J. R. (2006) Eye movements when observing predictable and unpredictable actions. *Journal of Neurophysiology*, **96**, 1358–1369.

Sambrook, T. (1998) Does visual perspective matter in imitation? *Perception*, **27**, 1461–1473.

Shockley, K., Santana, M. V. and Fowler, C. A. (2003) Mutual interpersonal postural constraints are involved in cooperative conversation. *Journal of Experimental Psychology: Human Perception and Performance*, **29**, 326–332.

Stevens, J.A., Fonlupt, P., Shiffrar, M. and Decety, J. (2000) New aspects of motion perception: selective neural encoding of apparent human movements. *Neuroreport*, **11**, 109–115.

Théoret, H., Halligan, E., Kobayashi, M., Fregni, F., Tager-Flusberg, H. and Pascual-Leone, A. (2005) Impaired motor facilitation during action observation in individuals with autism spectrum disorder. *Current Biology*, **15**, R84–85.

Tickle-Degnen, L. and Rosenthal, R. (1987) Group rapport and nonverbal behavior. *Review of Personality and Social Psychology*, **9**, 113–136.

Van Baaren, R., Maddux, W. W., Chartrand, T.L., de Bouter, C. and van Knippenberg, A. (2003) It takes two to mimic: behavioral consequences of self-construals. *Journal of Personality and Social Psychology*, **84**, 1093–1102.

Van Baaren, R. B., Horgan, T. G., Chartrand, T. L. and Dijkmans, M. (2004) The forest, the trees, and the chameleon: context dependency and mimicry. *Journal of Personality and Social Psychology*, **86**, 453–459.

Viviani, P. (2002) Motor competence in the perception of dynamic events: a tutorial. In Prinz, W. and Hommel, B. (eds), *Common Mechanisms in Perception and Action. Attention and Performance XIX*, pp. 406–442. Oxford University Press, New York.

Wapner, S. and Cirillo, L. (1968) Imitation of a model's hand movements: age changes in transpositions of left–right movements. *Child Development*, **39**, 887–894.

Williams, J. H. G., Whiten, A., Suddendorf, T. and Perrett D. I. (2001) Imitation, mirror neurons and autism. *Neuroscience and Biobehavioral Reviews*, **25**, 287–295.

Wilson, M. (2003) Imagined movements that leak out. *Trends in Cognitive Sciences*, **7**, 53–55.

Wilson, M. and Knoblich, G. (2005) The case for motor involvement in perceiving conspecifics. *Psychological Bulletin*, **131**, 460–473.

Wolpert, D. M. and Kawato, M. (1998) Multiple paired forward and inverse models for motor control. *Neural Networks*, **11**, 1317–1329.

Wraga, M. (2003) Thinking outside the body: an advantage for spatial updating during imagined versus physical self-rotation. *Journal of Experimental Psychology: Learning, Memory, and Cognition*, **29**, 993–1005.

Zacks, J., Rypma, B., Gabrieli, J. D. E., Tversky, B. and Glover, G. H. (1999) Imagined transformations of bodies: an fMRI investigation. *Neuropsychologia*, **37**, 1029–1040.

14

Neuro imaging the self ?

Perrine Ruby and Dorothée Legrand

Introduction

The concept of self lacks clear definition and boundaries and is still widely debated in the philosophical community. Positions oscillate between an elimination of the notion of self and the extension of the list of different forms of self. Following Strawson, one can easily quote up to 25 forms of self: "it is difficult to know where to begin, because there are many different notions of the self. Among those I have recently come across are the cognitive self, the conceptual self, the contextualized self, the core self, the dialogic self, the ecological self, the embodied self, the emergent self, the empirical self, the existential self, the extended self, the fictional self, the full-grown self, the interpersonal self, the material self, the narrative self, the philosophical self, the physical self, the private self, the representational self, the rock bottom essential self, the semiotic self, the social self, the transparent self, and the verbal self" (Strawson, 2000, p. 39).

It is important to note that whether 'the self'is eliminated or multiplied, it remains under-specified since the following questions remain unanswered: What is it that has to be eliminated? Or what is it that is common to all phenomena referred to as 'self', despite their diversity? In either case, one needs a criterion to determine what a 'self' is, to justify its elimination or the categorization of different phenomena as a form of 'self'(Legrand, 2004). Therefore, the question is to determine such a criterion. It is the reason why the question we will tackle in this paper is the following: what is self-specific? Answering this question is a prerequisite to understand what the self is.

In order to answer this question, we will start with a review of neuroimaging studies which investigated the cerebral correlates of 'self', 'other' representation, the resting state, reasoning and memory recall. This merging of results from these various domains of research will lead to a reinterpretion of the brain activations found in studies which investigated the self in cognitive neuroscience. On the basis of the conclusions of this review, we will then elaborate a theoretical framework allowing the understanding of self-specificity as a self-specifying sensorimotor process. We will conclude by considering the consequence of our approach for the very possibility of 'neuroimaging the self'.

The neuroimage of the 'self' is not self-specific

The 'self'cerebral network

Even if it is an ill-defined notion, numerous studies experimentally investigate the self and base their research on a rather intuitive notion of 'self'. This is the case of research in cognitive science which now extensively studies the self with neuroimaging techniques. In this discipline, the 'self' is investigated by opposition to 'nonself' using self-related stimuli versus non self-related stimuli of various types. Hence, studies using positron emission tomography (PET) and functional magnetic resonance imaging technique (fMRI), informed us of the cerebral correlates of recognizing one's own face (Kircher *et al.*, 2000, 2001; Platek *et al.*, 2004), detecting one's own first name (Perrin *et al.*, 2005; Sugiura *et al.*, 2006), attributing an action to oneself (Farrer *et al.*, 2003), recalling personally relevant information (Maguire and Mummery, 1999; Vinogradov *et al.*, 2006) or assessing one's own personality, physical appearance, attitudes or feelings (Craik *et al.*, 1999; Gusnard *et al.*, 2001; Kircher *et al.*, 2000, 2002; Kelley *et al.*, 2002; Johnson *et al.*, 2002; Kjaer *et al.*, 2002; Fossati *et al.*, 2003; Schmitz *et al.*, 2004; Lou *et al.*, 2004; Ochsner *et al.*, 2005).

This list illustrates that even if these studies are considered as investigating a common and unique 'self', they in fact involve a large variety of cognitive tasks and stimuli. The result is that brain regions reported to be activated when subjects are involved in such 'self'-related tasks are as many as in the following list: medial prefrontal cortex, precuneus/posterior cingulate gyrus, temporal pole, temporo-parietal junction, insula, postcentral gyrus, superior parietal cortex, precentral gyrus, lateral prefrontal cortex, hippocampus, parahippocampal gyrus, fusiform gyrus, occipital cortex (see Table 14.1).[1]

However, some regions of this long list turn out to be repeatedly activated in self versus nonself contrast. The following are particularly represented: medial prefrontal cortex, precuneus/posterior cingulate gyrus, the temporo-parietal junction and to a lesser degree the temporal pole. As such, these regions were considered (especially the medial prefrontal cortex) as 'self' specific (Kelley *et al.*, 2002; Northoff *et al.*, 2004, 2006). But which self are we talking about here? What may be finally common to all these studies? Let's have a closer look at the literature to get a better understanding of what this network may underlie.

The 'other' cerebral network

The very striking result to note is the undeniable resemblance of the cerebral network involved in the representation of 'self-referential' contents and in the representation of others. The commonly reported active brain regions during others' mind reading comprise medial prefrontal cortex, precuneus/posterior cingulate gyrus, the temporo-parietal junction and the temporal pole (see Table 14.1). Studies which directly tested common brain activation for self and other mind representation reported also regions of this network (see Table 14.1). So the aforementioned list appears to be the same, and

---

[1] Table 14.1 reports the results of most major studies which investigated the self with neuroimaging techniques. In order to guide interpretation of the results of the review, Table 14.1 also reports nonself-related conditions of activation of the brain areas in which main self-related activations were reported. Note that for this review we chose to use large brain regions as units. This choice was guided by a failure to find in the literature any unanimous subdivisions of the main regions of interest (medial prefrontal, precuneus, temporo-parietal junction and temporal pole) according to a pertinent functional criterion [see Northoff *et al.* (2006) for the medial prefrontal cortex; this review reveals that activations for self versus nonself contrast were found all along the medial prefrontal cortex].

representing oneself and others minds seems to rely on the activation of importantly overlapping cerebral regions (see Calder *et al.*, 2002; Wicker *et al.*, 2003b for reviews). It is important to note that according to studies, regions of the mentioned network are over-activated either for the self or for others, which lead the authors to interpret them as either self or other specific.

At this point the question is: What would explain the fact that representation of oneself and others involves the same wide cerebral network and also that some regions of the network are sometimes more activated for the self and sometimes more activated for others?

The 'baseline' cerebral network

Interestingly, the aforementioned brain areas, medial prefrontal cortex, precuneus/posterior cingulate gyrus, temporo-parietal junction and temporal pole also constitute the active network of the resting state, 'the default mode' of the brain (Gusnard and Raichle, 2001), whose only objective characteristic is to be deprived of external stimulation. In this state, the subject has no cognitive constraints so that he is free to think whatever he wants (and nothing in particular). Therefore, it turns out that a similar cerebral network is active for the representation of self-referential content, for the representation of others' mind, and for the operational processing going on in the solitary and undisturbed brain at rest. From these observations, it now seems that these brain areas are not activated in relation to a specific content (self versus others) since they are also activated when no specific content is processed by the subject, i.e. during resting states. Rather, what would be common to all these heterogeneous tasks would be a type of processing such as a general ability to compute, i.e. to run an ongoing evaluative process.

A 'reasoning' cerebral network

What may clarify what type of computation is systematically involved in the diverse tasks activating the aforementioned network (medial prefrontal cortex, precuneus/posterior cingulate gyrus, temporo-parietal junction and temporal pole) is the consideration that most of the time the attribution of some characteristic features to the self or to others does not rely on the knowledge of a unique verifiable answer. Rather, such tasks and the resting state (most probably) typically require evaluative processing and answers (Self: Are you shy? How would you react if someone break you car? Other: Is your friend ingenious? How would you describe the personality and appearance of the Danish Queen? Resting state: Which kind of food should I cook tonight? Perhaps I could spend my holidays in Russia?) i.e. recall and integration of representations to extract a general property, or creation of new representations from previous ones recalled from memory. This type of computation has to be differentiated from recall and statement of factual knowledge and typically defines reasoning in general and inductive reasoning in particular. The latter requires 'evaluating arguments', where prior propositions (the premises) provide some grounds for generating a conclusion. An important characteristic of inductive reasoning is that it is open-ended and takes one beyond the information contained in the premises (as opposed to deduction which requires making implicit information explicit, in a closed system). Unlike deduction, induction is a function of the content of the premise and our knowledge of the world. It is usually a matter of knowing which properties generalize in the required manner and which do not (Goel *et al.*, 1997). Interestingly, and as recalled by Goel and Dolan (2000): "Induction is an ubiquitous, often effortless, process involved in many cognitive tasks, from perception, categorization, to explicit reasoning in problem-solving and decision-making. Cognitive/computational models of induction typically view it as a form of hypothesis generation and selection, where one must search a large database and determine which items of information are relevant and how they are to be mapped onto the present situation (Carbonell *et al.*, 1983; Russell, 1986)."

Interestingly the neuroimaging literature reveals that the aforementioned cerebral network (medial prefrontal cortex, precuneus/posterior cingulate gyrus, temporo-parietal junction and temporal pole) comprises regions involved both in reasoning and in memory recall.

A number of results suggest that medial prefrontal cortex would run computations such as hypothesis generation/selection. Several studies showed that inductive and deductive reasoning involved medial prefrontal cortex. Goel *et al.* (1997) showed that inductive reasoning whatever the content of the premises (object, or subjects) recruited the dorsomedial prefrontal cortex. A recent fMRI experiment further showed that medial prefrontal cortex comes on the scene precisely during the so-called 'premise integration phase' of the deductive reasoning process. It defines the period during which the second premise is presented. At this point, the two premises are integrated into one unified representation and a putative conclusion is drawn. This study used no human-related stimuli, but arrays of single letters as premise (Fangmeier *et al.*, 2006). Even more striking, Fonlupt demonstrated that medial prefrontal cortex was involved at a very simple level of logical reasoning. The stimulus was two balls rolling, and blood flow increased in the medial prefrontal cortex when the subject had to answer whether a ball caused the movement of the other versus when he had to decide the direction of the movement of the balls (Fonlupt, 2003). Importantly, meta-analysis of results from different teams clearly demonstrated that focus of activation for self-referential information processing, theory of mind and reasoning were all conflated in the medial prefrontal cortex (Calder *et al.*, 2002; Wicker *et al.*, 2003b; see Table 14.1). In other studies, both the medial prefrontal cortex and the posterior cingulated/precuneus were involved in evaluative processing (Vogt *et al.*, 1992; Zysset *et al.*, 2002; Cavanna and Trimble 2006). Finally, Geake and Hansen (2005) explored the ability to make fluid and creative analogical relationships between distantly related concepts or pieces of information, using the fluid analogy-making task. Subjects chose their own 'best' completions from four plausible response choices to 55 fluid letter string analogies across a range of analogical depths. Interestingly, while doing this task which typically requires creating new representations, subjects activated a large brain network comprising medial prefrontal, precuneus and temporo-parietal junction.

On the other hand, medial parietal cortex, temporo-parietal junction and the temporal pole would provide the large database necessary for hypothesis production, recalling information from memory. Indeed, all of these last three regions have been repeatedly reported to be involved in memory recall (Maguire and Mummery, 1999; Dolan *et al.*, 2000; Piefke *et al.*, 2003; Graham *et al.*, 2003; Lundstrom *et al.*, 2005; Wagner *et al.*, 2005; Cavanna and Trimble, 2006; see Table 14.1).

A nonspecific cerebral network

In conclusion, this review of neuroimaging results demonstrates that 'self' information processing, 'others' mind reading, resting during a 'baseline' condition and 'reasoning' in many contexts induce activations in widely overlapping brain areas. From this observation, it may be suggested that what has been considered as a 'self' network is in fact a nonspecific network. On the basis of many results of the neuroimaging literature, it can be argued that this network is rather involved in a reasoning process of hypothesis generation and selection using information available in the context and recalled from memory. The benefit of this interpretation is that it fits the putative cognitive profile of all the aforementioned tasks which involve this temporo-parieto-frontal network.

Understanding the modulation of the activation of the nonspecific cerebral network by self- and non self-related tasks

The proposition to explain the non content-specific network activity by a reasoning process using information recalled from memory is broadly congruent with results of neuroimaging studies on inductive/deductive reasoning and on memory recall, as demonstrated above. Let us now see how the proposed framework explains why regions of the 'reasoning network' are sometimes more activated for the self and sometimes more activated for the other.

The issue here would be that according to the paradigms and/or group of subjects a large variability is induced by the (uncontrolled) variable strategy used by the subject to answer the question, i.e. a variable balance between inductive reasoning and memory recall. Going back to the literature will help to show how this proposition may apply to experimental results of 'self' studies. In the study of Johnson *et al.* (2002), for example, subjects were asked to make decisions about themselves on specific statements requiring self-evaluation in the domains of mood, social interactions, cognitive and physical abilities (i.e. "I forget important things", "I'm a good friend", "I have a quick temper") versus truthfulness, assessment of statements of factual knowledge such as "Ten seconds is more than a minute" and "you need water to live". This study thus contrasts questions with no absolute answers with questions with known absolute answer. Our proposition well explains that in this case the medial prefrontal, posterior cingulate, and bilateral temporal pole lighted up for the self condition since it required more evaluative judgment and episodic memory recall than the factual knowledge condition, i.e. that the dichotomy self/non-self is concomitant with the dichotomy complex evaluative reasoning/simple reasoning. In another study (Sugiura *et al.*, 2006), one may explain the increased activity in the memory-related regions (both temporal pole, both temporo-parietal junction and precuneus) for self versus other because the self-related first names are related to many autobiographical memories (and then triggers it consciously or not) whereas unfamiliar first names may be associated with less episodic or semantic events especially if the subject does not know anybody with this name. In another study, however, this effect may be reversed and the 'other' condition would trigger more autobiographic recall than the self condition. Specifically, the role of the temporal pole in autobiographical memory (Fink *et al.*, 1996; Graham *et al.*, 2003; Piefke *et al.*, 2003) may explain why this region is less detected in self versus other than in other versus self contrast. Lou *et al.* (2004) demonstrated that the left temporal pole was recruited both for self and other personality trait representation but to a greater extent for the other. This result may be explained by an increased need (or more effortful recall) for autobiographical (memories of situations involving the self and the other in interaction) recall for the other (less well known than the self) versus the self in order to create a general representation of his personality.

Summary

In sum, the different observations cited here demonstrate that (1) not only the medial prefrontal cortex but also precuneus/posterior cingulate, temporo-parietal junction and temporal pole were repeatedly reported to be activated in neuroimaging studies of the 'self'; (2) the usually reported overlap between cerebral correlates of self and others minds representation have been underestimated and involve medial prefrontal cortex, precuneus/posterior cingulated, temporo-parietal junction and temporal poles; and suggest that (3) the activation of these regions can be explained by evaluative processes of reasoning using information recalled from memory; (4) hence it cannot be argued that a network specific to the self shares its resources with representations of others, nor that this brain network is specifically common to only self and others; rather (5) this network activated in both tasks is not specific, i.e. the labelled 'self' or 'mind representation' network is specific neither to 'self' nor to 'mind representation' but is activated (be it about cars, philosophy, or sweets).

What is self-specific?

We began our investigation of self-specificity by asking the following question: do neuroimaging techniques tell us a lot about what characterizes the self? Do the tasks involving the identification of specific features and their attribution to the self have anything to do with self specificity? Are these tasks tackling the self? Considering the review and the reinterpretation of the results of the literature that we propose here, we can now justifiably propose that, at the level of the cognitive tasks involved in the aforementioned experiments, the process to reflect upon a subject is not different for self and others. A critical point to note here is that the difference between self and other in the aforementioned experiments is the content of the representation, not the process required to form such a representation. Subjects were required to do the same task (perception, recognition) with different stimuli, i.e. self-related or other-related (my face/someone's else face; my first name/another first name …).

Reviewing the results of neuroimaging studies which investigated the processing of such stimuli, Gillihan and Farah (2005) showed how difficult it is to convincingly isolate any specific self-related brain activation from the neuroimaging literature. It is no surprise from our point of view since it cannot be argued nowadays that neuroimaging techniques can differentiate such kinds of content of representation. The scanner will show the same image whatever the precise episode I recall from memory, e.g. my grandmother cooking, my cat purring on the bed or the day I received my first doll. The neuroimage of the 'self' cannot be seen through the manipulation of contents (names, personality traits, etc ...) because different contents cannot be distinguished with neuroimaging techniques such as PET and fMRI. Neither, we claim, can general processes of representation (i.e. identification and attribution) reveal anything about the self because they are not topic specific. So at this point of the discussion, one may question whether neuroimaging techniques did in fact tell us much about the cerebral correlates of the 'self', and conclude that self-specificity remains mysterious.

These two failures are related to each other and should be tackled together: clarifying what self-specificity corresponds to, will have consequences for its investigation with neuroimaging techniques. Gillihan and Farah (2005) emphasized that the concept of 'self' is difficult to define in an explicit and noncircular way. Contrary to their opinion, we believe that such a lack of specific definition is an obstacle to progress. To overcome this obstacle, let us attempt to clarify what self-specificity may require.

A self-specific content?

The first intuitive type of self-specific content is the feeling of one's body: we don't feel others' body (science-fictional stories apart). Therefore, it is relevant to recall that somatosensory-related cortices represent any kind of physical event taking place on the skin which is intuitively the physical boundary between self and the rest of the world. In that sense, somatosensory-related cortices might be good candidates for some self-signature. Any somatosensory signal indicates the boundaries between me and the rest of the world, and crossing this line is dangerous for Me. In that sense, it could be considered that activation of this cerebral region may play a role in grounding a sense of the physical boundaries of the self.

Likewise, proprioception, in itself or in conjunction with other sensory information, is often considered as "the modality of the self 'par excellence'" (Rochat and Striano, 2000, pp. 516–517). Further, and according to these authors, the crucial factor would be the redundancy of different sets of sensorial information whose integration would be specific to one's own body. For example, visual information about one's body part would be systematically correlated to proprioceptive information about this same body part. This invariant correlation of different sets of sensory information with proprioception would provide a reliable signature of the self.

Interestingly, the somatosensory or multisensory criterion for the self seems crucial to account for our intuitive sense of being ourselves located where the body is felt and represented. Somatosensory contents would indeed be necessary to support a conception of the self as physically separated from the rest of the world by its skin boundary. However, we also want to point out that these special contents are not sufficient to ensure self-specificity. Three arguments may be cited in support.

First, let us recall that the somatosensory cortex is hosted by the postcentral gyrus and that the insula is closely related to somesthesia as reavealed by several functional neuroimaging studies which showed activation of insular cortex in response to painful and nonpainful somesthetic stimuli (Peyron *et al.*, 2000). It is thus relevant to underline first that activation of postcentral gyrus and of the insula were reported both for the self-feeling of touch or disgust and for the perception of another one being touched or disgusted (Wicker *et al.*, 2003a; Keysers *et al.*, 2004). The somatosensory cortex was even reported to be activated when the subject sees an object being touched (Keysers *et al.*, 2004). If one considered that we know all about the somatosensory activity by registering the amount of blood irrigating it during the task, these results would argue against the self-specificity of somatosensory cortex and we may conclude that the processing of somatosensory stimuli, even if necessary, is not enough to ensure self-specificity. Whether this interpretation is correct or not, it remains that these results cast some doubt and call for further clarification.

Second, the *source* of a signal, in this case in-skin or on-skin sensory receptors, cannot provide any specific signature of the self since a same receptor can provide information not only about the self but also about the external world. More in detail, in discussing the somatosensory criterion, it is important to recall that sensorial information about one's own body comes from diverse sources, among which are neuromuscular, vestibular, cutaneous, tactile receptors. In fact, the important point is not merely to provide an exhaustive list. Rather, what is at stake here is to determine whether these sets of information are self-specific. Eilan *et al.* (1995, p. 13) differentiate three types of proprioceptive systems: some process information about one's body only (homeostatic processes, for example), others process information about the body relative to the external environment (the vestibular system, for example), and still others process information that can either be about the world or about one's body (touch, for example). The authors conclude: "it is neither true that internal proprioceptive systems can provide information only about the body, nor is it true that information about the body comes only via the internal proprioceptive systems" (1995, p. 14). In other words, it would not be enough to have proprioceptive information to ensure self-specificity. If this is the case, can the integration of several of these contents be specific? It seems hard to constitute self-specificity by merely integrating together contents that are not intrinsically self-specific. To be relevant here, the integrative process itself should be self-specifying. We return to this point below.

Third, it is important to underline that the reason why we consider somatosensory content as insufficient to ensure self-specificity is not merely because it lacks systematic self-specific brain activation. Rather, from a theoretical perspective, there is no way to define a content as *intrinsically* self-specific. Let us develop this point in slightly more detail. Neither proprioceptive information that happens to be about one's body only, nor the conjunction of multiple sets of sensory information—and in fact no perceptual content—is self-specific in itself. By analogy, no neuronal activation is intrinsically afferent or intrinsically efferent. Rather, a signal is only functionally afferent or efferent. In other words, a signal is afferent versus efferent because of the way it is processed, not because it is architecturally linked to a sensory receptor, i.e. not because some kind of mechanism would be able to compute the fact that this signal has been generated by the activation of a sensory receptor. Rather, being generated by the activation of a sensory receptor normally implies being processed in a way that makes a signal afferent: it is the processing not the source that specifies a signal as afferent versus efferent. Likewise, there is no particular information that is *intrinsically* labelled 'self', even when it happens to be architecturally about the self, i.e. even if the source happens to be one's body: a perceptual content is not intrinsically but *functionally* self-specific.

A self-specific perspective?

To recap, self-specificity might be importantly rooted in somatosensory information and multisensory integration but these special contents remain insufficient. In addition, such signals have to be processed in a self-specifying manner, i.e. from the perspective specifically held by the subject. Being a self is not only being a particular object, physically situated in space, where the body is (represented). Rather, and fundamentally, the self is also characterized by the perspective specifically held by the subject, the first-person perspective. Crucially, one and the same self is both the body as differentiated from the world by self-specific contents and the body as a point of departure of the first-person perspective, characterized by self-specifying processes.

As we are here pointing to a process (holding a perspective) as opposed to a content of information, we can expect to gain further information about the physiological mechanisms underlying self-specificity by manipulating perspective taking in neuroimaging studies (Ruby and Decety, 2001, 2003, 2004; Vogeley *et al.*, 2001, 2004; Farrer and Frith, 2002; Ochsner *et al.*, 2004, 2005; Seger *et al.*, 2004; see Table 14.1). The critical issue characterizing these studies in comparison to the previously quoted ones is that they used the same stimuli (same content) in the self and other condition. The difference between conditions relied on the processing of information, i.e. the perspective taken by the subject to answer the question (What can you see? versus What can he see? How would you react? versus How would he react?).

Authors of these studies reported activity for first- versus third-person perspective taking, in all the regions mentioned earlier and corresponding to the "reasoning network" (see Table 14.1). However, contrary to the results obtained in the aforementioned "self-content" studies, regions out of this non-specific network came on the scene, among which the postcentral gyrus and the insula were reported several times in self versus other but not in other versus self contrast (see Table 14.1). In nearly all studies contrasting first- and third-person perspective taking, greater activity in somatosensory-related corticies (postcentral gyrus or insula) was reported for the first-person perspective, whatever the context (motor, visual, conceptual, emotional), the target person to take the perspective of (Avatar, lay person, a friend, the mother of the subject …) and the predictions of the authors. Interestingly, Neggers *et al.* (2006) detected greater activity just behind the postcentral gyrus (superior parietal cortex, Brodman area 5) for egocentric versus allocentric representation of space, egocentricity being a fundamental characteristic of first-person perspective. Another argument for a putative role of the somatosensory-related cortices in self-representation/specification is that these regions were activated in self versus other's perspective outside any sensorimotor context (stimuli presenting conceptual facts: Ruby and Decety, 2003, 2004;

stories: Vogeley *et al.*, 2001; personality trait: Kircher *et al.*, 2001). In these studies, the post-central activity cannot be explained by some kind of somatosensory imagery triggered by action/senses related stimuli. According to these results one may conclude that somatosensory-related cortices code for some abstract and global representation of the boundary between the self and the external world.

Thus, it turns out that sensorimotor cortices were reported to be activated both for the representation of self-relevant *contents* (self-personality assessment: Kircher *et al.*, 2000, 2001; self-action attribution: Farrer *et al.*, 2003; self-feeling assessment: Gusnard *et al.*, 2001) and for self-specific *processes* like first-person perspective-taking. Hence, according to these results one may conclude that the somatosensory cortex plays a crucial role in the signature of the self.

However, merely pointing to common brain activation (in the somatosensory-related corticies for specific content and process) does not provide any explanation and the remaining question here is: how is the signature of the self made possible?

Self-specifying processes?

To answer this question, we now need to specify what it involves to be a self not only as a special object (content) but also, and crucially, as a subject holding a specific perspective on the world. To put it differently, we are now specifically looking for a self-specific way of processing information.

At the experiential level: "the question of self-awareness is not primarily a question of a specific *what*, but of a unique *how*." (Zahavi, 2005, p. 204). To clarify this point, let us consider the simple experience of biting a lemon. The latter is characterized by a specific content (e.g. lemon versus chocolate), a specific mode of presentation (e.g. tasting versus seeing a lemon) and a quality of mineness (e.g. *my* experience of tasting a lemon). The latter is what makes the experience/representation of the lemon *my own* experience/representation. This same quality of mineness is also what characterizes one's experience of one's (psychological or physical) features, e.g. the experience of one's action. In what follows, we will thus tackle this self-specific feature and propose a mechanism that would underlie subjective experience, be it tasting a lemon or experiencing one's action, i.e. a model of subjectivity applying both to self-related and non self-related contents.

The question we are now asking is the following: what are the processes allowing for the quality of mineness, i.e. for the self-specific subjectivity of experience? Here, we propose that the subjectivity of experience corresponds to the aspects of perceptual experience that are not determined by states of the external world, but specifically by states of the experiencing subject. In other words, experiencing oneself as subject corresponds to experiencing the world from a subjective perspective. This constitutive dimension of experience is (notably) supported by processes of modulations of perceptual experience that are specifically due to states of the subject. Some experimental protocols manipulate this modulation (that is operational continuously and most of the time silently), thereby making it salient.

For example, it has been shown (Haggard *et al.*, 2002; Tsakiris and Haggard, 2003, 2005) that when a subject's action causes a perceptual event, the subject perceives his action and its consequence as closer together in time than when he has to judge the timing of these two events separately (hence the term '*binding*'). Moreover, this effect is specific of intentional action, by contrast with passive movement (hence the term '*intentional* binding'). The self-relative modulation of perception also concerns its spatial structure. For example, it has been shown that the active use of a tool modifies the representation of peri-personal space, where objects are within reach. This has been measured at the neuronal (Iriki *et al.*, 1996; Maravita and Iriki, 2004) and the behavioural (Farnè *et al.*, 2005) levels. In all these cases, there is a modulation of the subject's perceptual experience that is not relative to a state of the world but to a state of the perceiving subject himself.

Proposition of a functional description of a self-specifying process at the sensorimotor level

A functional way to describe such self-relative modulation of perception, and to differentiate them from world-relative modulation of perception, is by distinguishing between ex-afference and re-afference. The former corresponds to afferent signals coming from the external world while the latter corresponds to afferent signals issuing from the perceiving subject's own action. To put it differently, re-afferent perception is specifically processed by being related to one's own action. A given perceptual content will be processed differently whether it is re-afferent or ex-afferent, i.e. whether or not it is directly related to oneself as a perceiving agent/active perceiver. The interesting fact here is that there is no way to define what a re-afference is without mentioning the fact that it is related to the perceiving subject's own action. In other words, there is nothing like a non self-related re-afference. By definition, a re-afference is a perception (partly) caused by one's own action. In other words, this proposal implies a functional mechanism allowing the comparison of the incoming sensory information with the relevant characteristics of efference, i.e. allowing the distinction between re-afference and ex-afference.[2]

For example, when I bite a lemon, afferent information (muscular contractions, somatosensory feeling of the lemon in my mouth …) is not a mere ex-afference but a re-afference, i.e. it is linked to my biting action. The proposal here is that being related to one's own action, the perceptual experience is related to oneself, hence perceived subjectively: the experience is characterized not only by a given content (the acidity of the lemon) but also by a self-specific quality of mineness (I am the one experiencing the acidity of the lemon juice).

If this hypothesis is correct, then experiencing one's experience as one's own would (notably) rely on the functional coherence self-specifically characterizing the integration of one's perceptual and one's motor processes. Thus, one's action (and not another agent's action) has specific perceptual consequences. Processing the latter as such leads the subject to perceive the world from his own perspective (it is important to note here that, given that action/movement never totally stops, re-afferences are always available to be integrated with efferent information). In these general cases, one's experience of the external world is self-specific. In some particular cases, what is perceived is oneself, and actions

---

[2] This is further discussed in Legrand (2006).

are consciously attributed to oneself. Here again, these situations are characterized by a self-specific coherence. For example, when one visually observes one's action, and not when one visually observes another action, there is a specific match between the content of one's perception and the content of one's action.

To put it differently, the difference between you perceiving Mary's hand and me perceiving Mary's hand is notably that my actions towards Mary's hand (from automatic saccades to deliberate actions like grasping it), and not your action towards it, specifically and directly modulates my perception of Mary's hand, and not your perception of it. In other words, only one's own action has such action-specific perceptual consequences. This thus determines a self-specific way to process non self-specific contents. Now, the difference between me perceiving your hand and me perceiving my hand is that the actions of my hand and not the actions of your hand modulate at the same time both motor content (the action I execute) and perceptual content (the action I observe visually). It is only in the case of the perception of one's own action that action-specific perceptual consequences are also self-specific contents, or to put it the other way around, it is only in the case of the perception of one's own action that self-specific contents are processed as action-specific perceptual consequences. This self-specific coherence is not merely multisensory, but sensorimotor, since it implies some coherence between what one does and what one perceives (note that this position is coherent with the results obtained by Rochat et al., even though their interpretation mentions only multisensory integration). To rephrase our proposal in the terms used in the framework of the internal model of action (Wolpert, Frith), the self would be limited neither to the initiator of action, active before the action takes place, nor to the agent as observed after the action is executed. Self-specificity would thus rely neither only on the desired and predicted states, nor only on the actual state of the forward model. Both of these conceptions of the self and self-specificity are problematic (Legrand, 2006). Rather, we argue here that self-specificity is not a state but a process of integration of efferent and re-afferent processes. Importantly, this sensorimotor conception of self-specificity coheres with the appeal of an hypothesis of a role of the somatosensory-related cortices in such specification.

Our approach intended to clarify what the self is (not a mere object but also a subject) and what self-specificity involves (not merely contents but also low level processes). According to this framework, the subjective perspective is anchored to the sensorimotor processing of re-afferences that are received in a continuous manner (the action–perception loop never totally stops). Processing re-afference would thus allow the arising of the first-person perspective anchoring each moment of experience, and would also make possible the identification of oneself (versus others) as the source of an action.

Matching this new framework to neuroimaging results

Given what we just proposed, let us consider studies that have investigated the self in a sensorimotor context, manipulating the strength of the link between one's action and its re-afference, and exploring the effect of this experimental manipulation on the attribution of an action to oneself. In the Daprati et al. (1997) study, the subject was asked to perform a simple action (e.g. lift his finger) and to report whether the action he saw was his own action or not. The visual feedback was manipulated so that the subject saw either his own gloved hand doing the action, or the experimenter's gloved hand doing either the same action or a different action. In such experimental conditions, healthy subjects were able to correctly attribute the action to its agent when they were observing their own hand or the experimenter's hand performing a different action. However, they made 30% of erroneous attributions of the experimenter's hand to themselves when the actions performed by the two hands were similar. Results also showed that hallucinating and deluded schizophrenic patients were more impaired in discriminating their own hand from the alien one than control subjects, and tended to misattribute the alien hand to themselves.

Using such an empirical set-up, Farrer et al. (2003) manipulated visual feedback and reported that in healthy subjects, activity in the right posterior insula increased as a function of the degree of concordance between the executed and the seen movements. In the framework we propose here, these results can be understood in the following way: the less the visual feedback is distorted, the more the subject tends to relate his action to the visual stimulus he sees, which means that the more the visual stimulus is processed as a re-afference, i.e. the more the condition goes towards self-specificity (i.e. increase of the number of answers "it is my hand"), the more the insula is activated. In other words, a possible interpretation could be that activation of the insula is related to matching one's action to its visual consequence leading to the conclusion "it is me". No correlation between activation of the insula and the sense of control of one's movement was found in schizophrenic patients (Farrer et al., 2004). Given that these patients may confuse between 'self' and 'other' origin of an action during delusional symptoms, one can hypothesize that the integration of re-afference and efference is impaired. This result appears as a supplementary argument to support a role of the somatosensory-related cortices in self-specifying processes.

However, these studies cannot be taken as providing any decisive result to support our hypothesis since the paradigm implies both low level processes (efference copy/re-afference comparison) and higher level processes of self-attribution to answer the question "is it your hand?" Further experiments will be needed to isolate the cerebral correlates of each phenomenon separately.

Conclusion

This critical review of neuroimaging results revealed that processing self-related contents, reading others' mind and resting state recruit a wide common cortical network (medial prefrontal cortex, precuneus, temporal poles, temporo-parietal junction). On this basis, we conclude that such a network cannot be considered as self-specific. Rather we argue that reasoning using information recalled from memory is enough to account for activation of this network. We propose that the self is primarily characterized by its first-person perspective and functionally determined by self-specifying processes. We further elaborate that such a process involves sensorimotor integration, i.e. the distinction between ex-afference and re-afference, only the latter issuing from the action of the subject.

Table 14.1 Results of neuroimaging studies (positron emission tomography and functional magnetic resonance imaging) investigating cerebral correlates of Self and Other processing, Resting state, Reasoning and Memory recall.

References	Contrast reported	PM	P	AT	TPJ	I	Post	SP	Pre	PL	H	PH	FG	O
Self														
Kircher et al. (2001)	Self–Other face recognition	a¹	1	R	L	R					R		L	
	Common to Self face recognition and Self personality trait assessment	a	1	R		R							L	R
Platek et al. (2004)	Self–Other face recognition	a								R				
Perrin et al. (2005)	Brain area varying with the amplitude of P300 to one's own first name	a¹	1		R									
Sugiura et al. (2006)	Self-related—Unfamiliar first names recognition	a	1	LR	LR									
	Self–Famous name recognition	a	1		LR									
Maguire et al. (1999)	Personally relevant time*-specific memories recall	a¹		L										
Vinogradov et al. (2006)	Memory for words (Self-generated—Presented by the experimenter)	a¹												
Farrer et al. (2003)	Self–Other action attribution	a				R								
Gusnard et al. (2001)	Self feeling—In/out judgment [IAPS pictures]	a¹				LR	LR							
	Self feeling judgment seeing IAPS pictures—Fixation cross	a¹												
Kjaer et al. (2002)	Self–Other reflection about physical appearance	a¹							L					
	Self–Other reflection about personality	a¹			LR									
Kircher et al. (2000)	Fitting judgment of personality trait (Self descriptive–Nonself descriptive)	a				L	L	L					L	
Kircher et al. (2002)	Overlap between Incidental and Intentional Self personality trait processing	a					L	L					L	

Study	Task						
Johnson et al. (2002)	Reflection and Self trait-General knowledge condition	a1		LR			LR
Lou et al. (2004)	Self–Queen fitting judgment of personality trait	a		R			
	Self fitting judgment of personality trait—Lexical task	a1	L	LR			LR
Fossati et al. (2003)	Self–Other fitting judgment of emotional personality traits	a1	1				
Kelley et al. (2002)	Self–Other fitting judgment of personality traits	a1	1				
Schmitz et al. (2004)	Self–Other fitting judgment of personality traits	a1				R	
Craik et al. (1999)	Self–Other fitting judgment of personality traits	a		No significant increase			
Ochsner et al. (2005)	Self–Close Other fitting judgment of personality traits	a		No significant increase			
	1PP on Self-1PP on Friend personality [personality traits]	a1					
	1PP on Self-1PP on Other personality [personality traits]	a1		R			
	1PP–3PP on Self personality assessment [personality traits]	b	1				
Seger et al. (2004)	1PP–3PP in food preference assessment [written words]	b	1	LR			
Farrer and Frith (2002)	I(1PP)–He (3PP) cause the movement of the dot [moving dot during action]	b		LR			
Vogeley et al. (2001)	Main effect of 1PP [written stories]	b1	1	R	R	R	
	1PP–3PP [written stories]	b	1	LR	R	R	
	Interaction 1PP and 3PP = (1PP when also 3PP) –(1PP without 3PP)	b			R	R	

Table 14.1 (continued) Results of neuroimaging studies (positron emission tomography and functional magnetic resonance imaging) investigating cerebral correlates of Self and Other processing, Resting state, Reasoning and Memory recall.

References	Contrast reported	PM	P	AT	TPJ	I	Post	SP	Pre	PL	H	PH	FG	O
Self														
Vogeley et al. (2004)	1PP–3PP in visual field assessment [pictures]	b↑	↑	L	L	R	R							
Ruby and Decety (2001)	1PP–3PP in action imagination [pictures of objects and spoken sentences]	b			L	L	L							LR
Ruby and Decety (2003)	1PP–3PP in conceptual knowledge assessment [written sentences]	b	↑	R	R		LR						R	
Ruby and Decety (2004)	1PP–3PP in socio-emotional reaction assessment [written sentences]	b					R							
Ochsner et al. (2004)	1PP–3PP in emotion assessment [IAPS pictures]	b↑		↑										
Other														
Gusnard et al. (2001)	In/out judgment seeing IAPS pictures—Fixation cross	↑												
Farrer et al. (2003)	Other–Self action attribution	↑			LR					R				
Fletcher et al. (1995)	TOM–Physical task [written stories]	↑	↑		R									
Goel et al. (1995)	TOM–Visual task [pictures of objects]	↑	↑	L	L									
Brunet et al. (2000)	TOM–Physical causality with character [drawings]	↑	↑	LR	LR				L	LR				L
Gallagher et al. (2000)	TOM–NonTOM stories	↑		LR	LR									
	TOM–NonTOM drawings	↑	↑	R	R					R		R		
	TOM–NonTOM stories and drawings	↑	↑	L	LR					R				
Castelli et al. (2000)	TOM mvt–Random mvt [videos of simple shapes]	↑		LR	LR									LR

Study	Contrast / task							
Calarge et al. (2003)	Create a TOM story–Read a NonTOM story	↑					L	
Lou et al. (2004)	Queen fitting judgment of personality trait–Lexical task	↑	LR					LR
	Queen–Self fiting judgment of personality trait		L				L	
Sugiura et al. (2006)	Famous–Unfamiliar first names recognition		LR				L	
Craik et al. (1999)	Other–Self fitting judgment of personality traits	No significant increase						
Ochsner et al. (2005)	1PP on Friend–1PP on Self personality [personality traits]	↑		R	LR	LR		LR
	1PP on Other–1PP on Self personality [personality traits]		R				L	
	3PP [Friend]–1PP on Self personality assessment [written words]	↑		R	L		L	L
	3PP [Other]–1PP on Self personality assessment [written words]		LR					
Seger et al. (2004)	3PP–1PP in food preference assessment [written words]	↑					L	
Farrer and Frith (2002)	He [3PP]–I [1PP] cause the movement of the dot [moving dot during action]		LR				L	
Vogeley et al. (2001)	Main effect of 3PP [written stories]	↑	L		L			
Vogeley et al. (2004)	3PP–1PP in visual field assessment [pictures]	↑	L				LR	L
Ruby and Decety (2001)	3PP–1PP in action imagination [pictures of objects and spoken sentences]	↑	R				R	R
Ruby and Decety (2003)	3PP–1PP in conceptual knowledge assessment [written sentences]	↑	LR	LR			L	

Table 14.1 (continued) Results of neuroimaging studies (positron emission tomography and functional magnetic resonance imaging) investigating cerebral correlates of Self and Other processing, Resting state, Reasoning and Memory recall.

References	Contrast reported	PM	P	AT	TPJ	I	Post	SP	Pre	PL	H	PH	FG	O
Self														
Ruby and Decety (2004)	3PP–1PP in socio-emotional reaction assessment [written sentences]	↑	↑	L	LR									
Ochsner et al. (2004)	3PP–1PP in emotion assessment [IAPS pictures]									L				LR
Common to self and other														
Fossati et al. (2003)	(Self condition–Lexical task) and (Other condition–Lexical task)	↑	↑											
Sugiura et al. (2006)	(Self condition–Unfamiliar condition) and (Famous condition–Unfamiliar condition)			LR	L									
Lawrence et al. (2006)	Brain activation correlated with 'self overlap' in the trait task	↑	↑		L									
Ochsner et al. (2005)	(Self condition–Lexical task) and (Other condition–Lexical task)	↑												
Ochsner et al. (2004)	(Self–In/out judgment) and (Other–In/out judgment) [IAPS pictures]	↑	↑		LR					L				
Resting State														
Gusnard and Raichle (2001)	Most active regions during the Resting state	↑		LR	LR									
Wicker et al. (2003b)	Internally vs Externally guided task	↑												
D'argembeau et al. (2005)	Brain activation common to ('Self'–'Other') and (Resting state–'Society')	↑												

Inductive and deductive reasoning

Study	Task					
Goel et al. (1995)	Simple inference—Visual task		↑			
	TOM—Memory retrieval	↑			L	
	TOM—Simple inference	↑	L		L	
Goel et al. (1997)	Deduction—Sentence comprehension	↑			L	L
	Induction—Sentence comprehension	↑	L		L	L
	Induction—Deduction	↑				
Goel et al. (2000)	Difficult inductive reasoning				R	R
Fangmeier et al. (2006)	Integration phase of Deductive reasoning	↑				
Geake and Hansen (2005)	Fluid analogies	↑			LR	LR
Zysset et al. (2002)	Evaluative judgment—Semantic memory tasks	↑			L	L
	Evaluative judgment—Episodic memory tasks	↑				L
Fonlupt (2003)	(Judgment–Neglect) of causality [movies of balls rolling]	↑				

Memory recall

Study	Task					
Cavanna and Trimble (2006)	Episodic memory retrieval (review)	↑				
Wagner et al. (2005)	Episodic memory retrieval (review)	↑			LR	
Lundstrom et al. (2005)	Correct source memory retrieval—New item	↑	R	L		L
	Incorrect source memory retrieval—New item	↑			L	L

Table 14.1 (continued) Results of neuroimaging studies (positron emission tomography and functional magnetic resonance imaging) investigating cerebral correlates of Self and Other processing, Resting state, Reasoning and Memory recall.

References	Contrast reported	PM	P	AT	TPJ	I	Post	SP	Pre	PL	H	PH	FG	O
Self														
Graham et al. (2003)	Autobiographic–Semantic recall	1		LR	LR									
	Semantic–Autobiographic recall			L	L					LR				
Dolan et al. (2000)	Emotional – Neutral memory conditions [IAPS pictures]			LR										
	Pictures Recognition-related activation [IAPS pictures]		1		R									
Maguire et al. (1999)	All memory task (+/- personally relevant and +/- precise in time)—Lexical task	1	1	L	LR						L	L		
	Memory-related activations (no difference according to the different tasks)	1		L								L		
	Personally relevant memories irrespective of temporal context				LR									
	Personally relevant time-specific memories	1		L							L			

Study	Contrast												
Fink et al. (1996)	Autobiographical episodic memory retrieval—Rest	1	1	LR									
	Autobiographical—Nonautobiographical episodic memory retrieval	1	R	R	R	R							
Piefke et al. (2003)	Autobiographical memory—Baseline	1	1	LR	L	R	L	L	L	LR	LR		
Goel et al. (1995)	Memory retrieval—Visual task		1										
Zysset et al. (2002)	Episodic—Semantic memory tasks	1	1										

Contrast reported: the type of stimuli used in the study is indicated in square brackets; TOM, theory of mind; IAPS, International Affective Picture System; 1PP and 3PP, first- and third-person perspective respectively; 'self-overlap' in Lawrence et al. (2006) refers to the percentage of Self traits that were attributed to the Other.

Brain regions: PM, medial prefrontal cortex from $x = 0$ to the superior frontal sulcus (BA 6, 8, 9, 10, 11, 24, 32); P, precuneus/posterior cingulate cortex (BA 23, 31, 7); AT, anterior temporal cortex (BA 38 and anterior part of BA 20, 21 and 22); TPJ, temporo-parieto-occipital junction (BA 39 and posterior part of BA 40 and 22); I, insula; Post, post-central gyrus; SP, superior parietal cortex; Pre, precentral gyrus; PL, lateral prefrontal cortex; H, hippocampus; PH, parahippocampal gyrus; FG, fusiform gyrus; O, occipital cortex. Activation is indicated with an '1'in medial regions, with a 'L' when it was located in the left hemisphere and with a 'R' when it was located in the right hemisphere. We stressed two types of approach in experiments which investigated the Self.

[a] Studies which manipulated stimuli (my face/your face, my name/your name, my personality/your personality) with a constant type of processing (recognition, reflection, assessment) and

[b] Studies which manipulated process (first- and third-person perspective) with constant stimuli (pictures of object, written sentences describing social situations, IAPS pictures).

This proposition is compatible with many results of neuroimaging studies of perspective taking which showed increased cerebral blood flow in the somatosensory cortex for first- versus third-person perspective.

At the end of this investigation, we cannot offer any clear-cut "yes" or "no" answer to the question: Can we neuroimage the self? However, we hope we can make progress by outlining the methodological implications of the proposed approach. On the one hand, even if, for the multiple reasons suggested in this chapter, we did not yet manage to neuroimage the self, it remains that we can make some cognitive neurosciences of the self, for example by conceiving experiments on the basis of the functional description of subjectivity proposed above. On the other hand, even if we can (and/or will be able to) neuroimage the self, neuroimaging cannot be self-sufficient. Specifically, the cognitive neurosciences of the self would involve four steps: (1) an experiential description of the self in such a detailed way that allows for (2) an operationalization of this description in functional terms, allowing for (3) the identification of the types of neurophysiological processes involved in (2), and then (4) the design of neuroimaging studies allowing the correlation between neuronal activation and (3). The point here is that it is illusory to investigate the self without a detailed description of the self at the experiential level, just as it would be methodologically flawed to extrapolate directly from such experiential considerations to a neuroimage of the 'self'.

References

Blakemore, S.-J., Wolpert, D. M. and Frith, C. D. (1998) Central cancellation of self-produced tickle sensation. *Nature Neuroscience*, 1, 635–640.

Blakemore, S.-J., Wolpert, D. M. and Frith, C. D. (2000) Why can't you tickle yourself? *Neuroreport*, 11, R11–R16.

Brunet, E., Sarfati, Y., Hardy-Bayle, M. C. and Decety, J. (2000) PET investigation of the attribution of intentions with a nonverbal task. *Neuroimage*, 11, 157–166.

Calarge, C., Andreasen, N. C. and O'Leary, D. S. (2003) Visualizing how one brain understands another: a PET study of theory of mind. *American Journal of Psychiatry*, 160, 1954–1964.

Calder, A. J., Lawrence, A. D., Keane, J. *et al.* (2002) Reading the mind from eye gaze. *Neuropsychologia*, 40, 1129–1138.

Castelli, F., Happe, F., Frith, U. and Frith, C. (2000) Movement and mind: a functional imaging study of perception and interpretation of complex intentional movement patterns. *Neuroimage*, 12, 314–325.

Cavanna, A. E. and Trimble, M. R. (2006) The precuneus: a review of its functional anatomy and behavioural correlates. *Brain*, 129, 564–583.

Craik, F. I. M., Moroz, T. M., Moscovitch, M. *et al.* (1999) In search of the self: a positron emission tomography study. *Psychological Science*, 10, 26–34.

Daprati, E., Franck, N., Georgieff, N. *et al.* (1997) Looking for the agent: an investigation into consciousness of action and self-consciousness in schizophrenic patients. *Cognition*, 65, 71–86.

D'Argembeau, A., Collette, F., Van der Linden, M. *et al.* (2005) Self-referential reflective activity and its relationship with rest: a PET study. *Neuroimage*, 25, 616–624.

Dolan, R. J., Lane, R., Chua, P. and Fletcher, P. (2000) Dissociable temporal lobe activations during emotional episodic memory retrieval. *Neuroimage*, 11, 203–209.

Eilan, N., Marcel, A. and Bermudez, J. L. (1995) Self-consciousness and the body: an interdisciplinary introduction. In Bermudez, J. L., Marcel, A. and Eilan, N. (eds), *The Body and the Self*, pp. 1–28. MIT Press, Cambridge, MA.

Fangmeier, T., Knauff, M., Ruff, C. C. and Sloutsky, V. (2006) fMRI evidence for a three-stage model of deductive reasoning. *Journal of Cognitive Neuroscience*, **18**, 320–334.

Farnè, A., Iriki, A. and Làdavas, E. (2005) Shaping multisensory action-space with tools: evidence from patients with cross-modal extinction. *Neuropsychologia*, **43**, 238–248.

Farrer, C. and Frith, C. D. (2002) Experiencing oneself vs another person as being the cause of an action: the neural correlates of the experience of agency. *Neuroimage*, **15**, 596–603.

Farrer, C., Franck, N., Georgieff, N., Frith, C. D., Decety, J. and Jeannerod, M. (2003) Modulating the experience of agency: a positron emission tomography study. *Neuroimage*, **18**, 324–333.

Farrer, C., Franck, N., Frith, C. D. *et al.* (2004) Neural correlates of action attribution in schizophrenia. *Psychiatry Research Neuroimaging*, **131**, 31–44.

Fink, G. R., Markowitsch, H. J., Reinkemeier, M., Bruckbauer, T., Kessler, J. and Heiss, W. D. (1996) Cerebral representation of one's own past: neural networks involved in autobiographical memory. *Journal of Neuroscience*, **16**, 4275–4282.

Fletcher, P. C., Happe, F., Frith, U. *et al.* (1995) Other minds in the brain: a functional imaging study of "theory of mind" in story comprehension. *Cognition*, **57**, 109–128.

Fonlupt, P. (2003) Perception and judgement of physical causality involve different brain structures. *Cognitive Brain Research*, **17**, 248–254.

Fossati, P., Hevenor, S. J., Graham, S. J. *et al.* (2003) In search of the emotional self: an fMRI study using positive and negative emotional words. *American Journal of Psychiatry*, **160**, 1938–1945.

Gallagher, H. L., Happe, F., Brunswick, N., Fletcher, P.C., Frith, U. and Frith, C.D. (2000) Reading the mind in cartoons and stories: an fMRI study of 'theory of mind' in verbal and nonverbal tasks. *Neuropsychologia*, **38**, 11–21.

Geake, J. G. and Hansen, P. C. (2005) Neural correlates of intelligence as revealed by fMRI of fluid analogies. *Neuroimage*, **26**, 555–564.

Gillihan, S. J. and Farah, M. J. (2005) Is self special? A critical review of evidence from experimental psychology and cognitive neuroscience. *Psychological Bulletin*, **131**, 76–97.

Goel, V. and Dolan, R. J. (2000) Anatomical segregation of component processes in an inductive inference task. *Journal of Cognitive Neuroscience*, **12**, 110–119.

Goel, V., Grafman, J., Sadato, N. and Hallett, M. (1995) Modeling other minds. *Neuroreport*, **6**, 1741–1746.

Goel, V., Gold, B., Kapur, S. and Houle, S. (1997) The seats of reason? An imaging study of deductive and inductive reasoning. *Neuroreport*, **8**, 1305–1310.

Graham, K. S., Lee, A. C., Brett, M. and Patterson, K. (2003) The neural basis of autobiographical and semantic memory: new evidence from three PET studies. *Cognitive, Affective, and Behavioral Neuroscience*, **3**, 234–254.

Gusnard, D. A. and Raichle, M. E. (2001) Searching for a baseline: functional imaging and the resting human brain. *Nature Reviews Neuroscience*, **2**, 685–694.

Gusnard, D. A., Akbudak, E., Shulman, G. L. and Raichle, M. E. (2001) Medial prefrontal cortex and self-referential mental activity: relation to a default mode of brain function. *Proceedings of the National Academy of Sciences of the USA*, **98**, 4259–4264.

Haggard, P., Clark, S. and Kalogeras, J. (2002) Voluntary action and conscious awareness. *Nature Neuroscience*, **5**, 382–385.

Iriki, A., Tanaka, M. and Iwamura, Y. (1996) Coding of modified body schema during tool use by macaque postcentral neurones. *Neuroreport*, **7**, 2325–2330.

Johnson, S. C., Baxter, L. C., Wilder, L.S., Pipe, J. G., Heiserman, J. E. and Prigatano, G. P. (2002) Neural correlates of self-reflection. *Brain*, **125**, 1808–1814.

Kelley, W. M., Macrae, C. N., Wyland, C. L., Caglar, S., Inati, S. and Heatherton, T. F. (2002) Finding the self?: An event-related fMRI study. *Journal of Cognitive Neuroscience*, **14**, 785–794.

Keysers, C., Wicker, B., Gazzola, V., Anton, J. L., Fogassi, L. and Gallese, V. (2004) A touching sight: SII/PV activation during the observation and experience of touch. *Neuron*, **42**, 335–346.

Kircher, T. T., Senior, C., Phillips, M. L. *et al.* (2000) Towards a functional neuroanatomy of self processing: effects of faces and words. *Cognitive Brain Research*, **10**, 133–144.

Kircher, T. T., Senior, C., Phillips, M. L. *et al.* (2001) Recognizing one's own face. *Cognition*, **78**, B1–B15.

Kircher, T. T., Brammer, M., Bullmore, E., Simmons, A., Bartels, M. and David, A. S. (2002) The neural correlates of intentional and incidental self processing. *Neuropsychologia*, **40**, 683–692. [Erratum in: *Neuropsychologia*, 2003;41(9), 1279.]

Kjaer, T. W., Nowak, M. and Lou, H. C. (2002) Reflective self-awareness and conscious states: PET evidence for a common midline parietofrontal core. *Neuroimage*, **17**, 1080–1086.

Lawrence, E. J., Shaw, P., Giampietro, V. P., Surguladze, S., Brammer, M. J. and David, A. S. (2006) The role of 'shared representations' in social perception and empathy: an fMRI study. *Neuroimage*, **29**, 1173–1184.

Legrand, D. (2004) Problèmes de la constitution du soi. Thèse de philosophie de l'université de provence.

Legrand, D. (2006) The bodily self. The sensori-motor roots of pre-reflexive self-consciousness. *Phenomenology and the Cognitive Sciences*, **5**, 89–118.

Lou, H. C., Luber, B., Crupain, M. *et al.* (2004) Parietal cortex and representation of the mental Self. *Proceedings of the National Academy of Sciences of the USA*, **101**, 68227–68232.

Lundstrom, B. N., Ingvar, M. and Petersson, K. M. (2005) The role of precuneus and left inferior frontal cortex during source memory episodic retrieval. *Neuroimage*, **27**, 824–834.

Maguire, E. A. and Mummery, C. J. (1999) Differential modulation of a common memory retrieval network revealed by positron emission tomography. *Hippocampus*, **9**, 54–61.

Maravita, A. and Iriki, A. (2004) Tools for the body (schema). *Trends in Cognitive Sciences*, **8**, 79–85.

Neggers, S. F., Van der Lubbe, R. H., Ramsey, N. F. and Postma, A. (2006) Interactions between ego- and allocentric neuronal representations of space. *Neuroimage*, **31**, 320–331.

Northoff, G. and Bermpohl, F. (2004) Cortical midline structures and the self. *Trends in Cognitive Sciences*, **8**, 102–107.

Northoff, G., Heinzel, A., de Greck, M., Bermpohl, F., Dobrowolny, H. and Panksepp, J. (2006) Self-referential processing in our brain—a meta-analysis of imaging studies on the self. *Neuroimage*, **31**, 440–457.

Ochsner, K. N., Knierim, K., Ludlow, D. H. *et al.* (2004) Reflecting upon feelings: an fMRI study of neural systems supporting the attribution of emotion to self and other. *Journal of Cognitive Neuroscience*, **16**, 1746–1772.

Ochsner, K. N., Beer, J. S., Robertson, E. R. *et al.* (2005) The neural correlates of direct and reflected self-knowledge. *Neuroimage*, **28**, 797–814.

Perrin, F., Maquet, P., Peigneux, P. *et al.* (2005) Neural mechanisms involved in the detection of our first name: a combined ERPs and PET study. *Neuropsychologia*, **43**, 12–19.

Peyron, R., Laurent, B. and Garcia-Larrea, L. (2000) Functional imaging of brain responses to pain. A review and meta-analysis. *Clinical Neurophysiology*, **30**, 263–288.

Piefke, M., Weiss, P. H., Zilles, K., Markowitsch, H. J. and Fink, G. R. (2003) Differential remoteness and emotional tone modulate the neural correlates of autobiographical memory. *Brain*, **126**, 650–668.

Platek, S. M., Keenan, J. P., Gallup, G. G. Jr and Mohamed, F. B. (2004) Where am I? The neurological correlates of self and other. *Cognitive Brain Research*, **19**, 114–122.

Rochat, P. and Striano, T. (2000) Perceived self in infancy. *Infant Behavior and Development*, **23**, 513–530.

Ruby, P. and Decety, J. (2001) Effect of subjective perspective taking during simulation of action: a PET investigation of agency. *Nature Neuroscience*, **4**, 546–550.

Ruby, P. and Decety, J. (2003) What you believe versus what you think they believe: a neuroimaging study of conceptual perspective-taking. *European Journal of Neuroscience*, **17**, 2475–2480.

Ruby, P. and Decety, J. (2004) How would you feel versus how do you think she would feel? A neuroimaging study of perspective-taking with social emotions. *Journal of Cognitive Neuroscience*, **16**, 988–999.

Schmitz, T.W., Kawahara-Baccus, T.N. and Johnson, S.C. (2004) Metacognitive evaluation, self-relevance, and the right prefrontal cortex. *Neuroimage*, **22**, 941–947.

Seger, C. A., Stone, M. and Keenan, J. P. (2004) Cortical activations during judgments about the self and an other person. *Neuropsychologia*, **42**, 1168–1177.

Sugiura, M., Sassa, Y., Watanabe, J. *et al.* (2006) Cortical mechanisms of person representation: recognition of famous and personally familiar names. *Neuroimage*, **31**, 853–860.

Strawson, G. (2000) The phenomenology and ontology of the self. In Zahavi, D. (ed.), *Exploring the Self: Philosophical and Psychological Perspectives on Self-experience. Advances in Consciousness Research*, Vol. 23, pp. 39–54. John Benjamins, Amsterdam/Philadelphia.

Tsakiris, M. and Haggard, P. (2003) Awareness of somatic events following a voluntary action. *Experimental Brain Research*, **149**, 439–446.

Tsakiris, M. and Haggard, P. (2005) Experimenting with the acting self. *Cognitive Neuropsychology*, **22**, 387–407.

Vinogradov, S., Luks, T. L., Simpson, G. V., Schulman, B. J., Glenn, S. and Wong, A. E. (2006) Brain activation patterns during memory of cognitive agency. *Neuroimage*, **31**, 896–905.

Vogeley, K., Bussfeld, P., Newen, A. *et al.* (2001) Mind reading: neural mechanisms of theory of mind and self-perspective. *Neuroimage*, **14**, 170–181.

Vogeley, K., May, M., Ritzl, A., Falkai, P., Zilles, K. and Fink, G. R. (2004) Neural correlates of first-person perspective as one constituent of human self-consciousness. *Journal of Cognitive Neuroscience*, **16**, 817–827.

Vogt, B. A., Finch, D. M. and Olson, C. R. (1992) Functional heterogeneity in cingulate cortex: the anterior executive and posterior evaluative regions. *Cerebral Cortex*, **2**, 435–443.

Wagner, A. D., Shannon, B. J., Kahn, I. and Buckner, R. L. (2005) Parietal lobe contributions to episodic memory retrieval. *Trends in Cognitive Sciences*, **9**, 445–453.

Wicker, B., Keysers, C., Plailly, J., Royet, J. P., Gallese, V. and Rizzolatti, G. (2003a) Both of us disgusted in My insula: the common neural basis of seeing and feeling disgust. *Neuron*, **40**, 655–664.

Wicker, B., Ruby, P., Royet, J. P. and Fonlupt, P. (2003b) A relation between rest and the self in the brain? *Brain Research Reviews*, **43**, 224–230.

Zahavi, D. (2005) *Subjectivity and Selfhood: Investigating the First-person Perspective.* MIT Press, Cambridge, MA.

Zysset, S., Huber, O., Ferstl, E. and von Cramon, D. Y. (2002) The anterior frontomedian cortex and evaluative judgment: an fMRI study. *Neuroimage*, **15**, 983–991.

15

An attempt towards an integrative comparison of psychoanalytical and sensorimotor control theories of action

Ariane Bazan

In his 'Project for a scientific psychology', Freud (1895) distinguishes two fundamental modes of mental functioning: primary processes, which aim at releasing received activations by the shortest pathways possible, and secondary processes, which aim at producing adequate actions in order to realize specific alterations in the external world. In the modern neurosciences of the last 30 years numerous studies also resulted in the converging conclusion that two visual pathways could be differentiated in the brain, a dorsal pathway hosting vision for action and a ventral pathway hosting vision for identification (e.g. Ungerleider and Mishkin, 1982; Milner and Goodale, 1995). In this paper these psychodynamic and sensorimotor models are compared. This analysis starts with the observation that Freud, who adhered to the school of physiology of Helmholtz, used a concept, called 'indication of reality', to characterize the function of the secondary process. It is proposed that this concept parallels the modern notion of 'efference copy'. On the basis of this parallel it is then proposed that the secondary process is carried by the dorsal pathway which hosts a comparison mechanism involving the efference copies. In Freud's model secondary process functioning has an inhibiting effect on primary processes. For this and other reasons, parallels are then proposed between the primary process and ventral pathway functioning, which is constrained by interferences from the dorsal pathway. In final, a brief case description of a psychotic patient is commented from both sensorimotor and psychodynamic perspectives.

Introduction

With the publication of his seminal work 'The interpretation of dreams' in 1900, Freud moves from a predominantly private address for his theoretical elaborations to his friend Wilhelm Fliess to a large public address. This can be seen as coinciding with the elaboration of a psychoanalytic theory as a discipline with its proper framework and instruments. His publications prior to the 'The interpretation of dreams' are therefore sometimes called 'preanalytic' writings, of which the two most important are 'On aphasia, a critical study' (short: 'On aphasia', 1891) and 'The project for a scientific psychology' (short: 'The project', 1895). 'The project' is actually a manuscript which was originally destined only for Fliess and was first published after Freud's death in 1950. While the preanalytic writings are explicitly grounded in the neurology of his time, from 1900 Freud seemingly abandons this terminology and starts to use a framework specific to psychoanalysis. Some have therefore considered that Freud's preanalytic writings should be read as a metaphor and that psychoanalysis starts with the rejection or neglect of neurological models (but see e.g. Van de Vijver and Geerardyn, 2002). However, in particular in his metapsychological writings, Freud explicitly uses his 'preanalytic' models to develop his theory. In 'The unconscious' (1915), for example, he not only refers to his linguistic model of 'On aphasia' (1891), but he adds these pages as an appendix to the paper. For these reasons, it might also be defended that Freud always worked with a physiological framework while writing his psychoanalytical oeuvre. The fact that Freud continuously worked with different frameworks, including a philosophical one, might be one of the reasons for his intellectual rigour, which now enables a productive dialogue between psychoanalysis and neurosciences (e.g. Panksepp, 1999; Shevrin, 2001; Solms, 2004; Bazan and Van Bunder, 2005).

In his 'Project for a scientific psychology' Freud (1895) starts with a fundamental distinction between two modes of mental functioning, called primary and secondary processes. It is remarkable that in the modern neurosciences of the last 30 years numerous studies issuing from different domains (electrophysiology, neuropsychology, functional neuroimaging) also resulted in the converging conclusion that two visual pathways could be differentiated in the brain, a dorsal pathway hosting vision for action and a ventral pathway hosting vision for identification (e.g. Ungerleider and Mishkin, 1982; Jeannerod, 1994; Milner and Goodale, 1995; Rossetti and Pisella, 2002). It is important to understand that Freud wrote 'The project' by inferring from his clinical experience with unlesioned patients the constraints to which the nervous system should be submitted. Modern neuroscientists, in contrast, have described their model on the basis of clinical findings almost exclusively originating from brain-lesioned people. In this paper it will be my aim to underscore possible parallels between these different models. The interest of this comparison is predominantly of a heuristic kind that goes both ways. On the one hand, it might enlarge the physiological understanding of Freud's mental model. This might be a benefit for psychoanalysis, for example because it might reintroduce an intellectual strictness in the use of a terminology and a theoretical framework by the fact that some of its concepts might be shown to be common to both fields and should therefore be used in agreement with these fields. On the other hand, it might also enlarge the psychological understanding of the neuroscientific models. The psychoanalytical clinic allows a unique perspective on the human mind. Indeed, this clinic, embedded in its elaborate theoretical framework, has yielded insights which enable us to make sense of a broad range of apparently nonsensical human behaviors in patients with both everyday or more serious psychopathology. In this sense, psychoanalysis may have a privileged status for informing neurophysiological models of the mind.

Freud's model of 'The project'

Primary and secondary processes

The distinction between inside and outside

Freud (1895) considers the nervous system as the inheritor of the ancient protoplasm, characterized by an irritable external surface interrupted by considerable stretches of non-irritable surface. Unspecified quantities are received at the level of the surface of the protoplasm. The primary function of this nervous system is the discharge of received quantities of activation. An increase in energy threatens to destabilize the system and therefore has to be released as soon as possible. This is the principle of inertia. Since release is the priority, it follows that "among the paths of discharge those are preferred and retained which involve a cessation of the stimulus" (Freud 1895, p. 296); this is what Freud (1895, p. 296) calls the "flight from the stimulus". This simple principle also applies to a complex nervous system of interconnected neurons: "A [quantity] which breaks into a neurone from anywhere will proceed in the direction of the contact-barrier with the largest facilitation …." (Freud, 1895, p. 323). Primary processes, then, are those mental processes that are characterized by these functional principles of releasing received activations by the shortest pathways possible.

When the protoplasm evolves into a structured living organism, closure implies that a fundamental distinction is settled between two kinds of stimuli received at the level of the irritable surface: namely, those stimuli that can be stopped by simple flight reactions and those that cannot be stopped by fleeing. In other words, as soon as a living organism arises, a difference between inside and outside is constructed (Maturana and Varela, 1980). The endogenous stimuli have their origin in the cells of the body and give rise to the major needs, such as respiration, hunger, thirst, sexuality etc. Importantly, Freud (1895, p. 317–8) indicates: "The removal of the stimulus is only made possible by an intervention which calls for an alteration in the external world (supply of nourishment, proximity of the sexual object) which, as a specific action, can only be brought about in definite ways." Secondary processes, then, are those mental processes which bring about specific—or what Freud calls 'adequate'—actions that aim at producing specific alterations in the external world. Because of the human newborn child's fundamental helplessness, most of the first adequate actions require interaction with a fellow human being. When this fellow human helps the child, it will be "in a position, by means of reflex contrivances, immediately to carry out in the interior of his body the activity necessary for removing the endogenous stimulus." (Freud, 1895, p. 318). For example, if the mother, upon hearing her baby crying, has brought the child's mouth to her breast or to a bottle, reflex sucking movements will be enough for relief of the hunger signals.

The emergence of an organized memory structure

A successful adequate act has major consequences for the organization of the mental apparatus. First, it constitutes an *experience of satisfaction*, which has, according to Freud (1895, p. 318), three important consequences: (1) a lasting relief of the internal body tensions which had produced unpleasure; (2) an activation of the neurons which correspond to the perception of the object of satisfaction; and (3) feedback of the discharge of the released reflex movement which follows upon the specific action. In the case of the newborn drinking, there is a relief of the hunger excitation, an activation of a neuronal assembly corresponding to the perception of, for exmple, mother's breast and feedback of the sucking movement. Second, the experience of satisfaction reorganizes the neuronal pathways by facilitating the connection between these three neuronal events, i.e. between the activation indicating the internal tension or 'urgency' and the two memory images, namely the perceptual image of the object of satisfaction and the image of the satisfying movement (Freud, 1895, p. 319). These facilitations are the basis for an emerging organization in the mental apparatus during development, which gives rise to the 'ego' (Freud, 1895, p. 323). The ego is defined here as the total activation at a given time in a particular set of neurons which are also constantly excited by endogenous quantities and which have acquired an organization through facilitation.

However, in some cases it might happen that endogenous excitations signalling a need induce a wishful state in the ego and activate the two memory images, while the object of satisfaction is not actually present (Freud, 1895, p. 319). When hunger arises in a baby, for example, this will cause the baby to 'see' a breast or a bottle and to execute a sucking movement, even if there is no mother or bottle present. The wishful activation thus produces the same thing as a perception, namely a *hallucination*. When reflex action, such as the sucking movement, is thereupon started, the baby will be disappointed. Moreover, it might also happen that a reactivation of a hostile memory image is about to lead to the massive release of unpleasure and of defence, while the image comes from the inner mental life and not from the outside. For example, a stimulus such as a large shadow might lead to the activation of a memory image of an intruder and to the consecutive release of a defence reaction, such as running away. It is clear that these reactions become problematic as soon as they become automatic or reflexive, i.e. as soon as the flow of excitations follows the most facilitated pathway and therefore functions at the level of the primary process.

In other words, the first facilitations, brought about by satisfaction, produce an initial structure of the ego, which helps to deal with endogenous activations, but does so, in first instance, on a primary process mode. The primary process way of acting, however, assumes an unchanged world: perceived features of the stimulus activate previous pathways independent of the new context. For the external stimulations in a simple organism, this might be a successful strategy since it is often enough to fly to get rid of them. The first response of the system to the internal stimuli is to follow the same pattern, i.e. to get rid of them by following the fastest paths already present in memory. But it then quickly becomes clear that this primary process mode does not always seem to work, especially for the internal stimulations. On the contrary, quite often these actions do not bring relief from the tensions and result in disappointment, frustration or even damage. These new experiences add to the previous ones and produce novel pathways which further help to elaborate the complexity of the ego.

Structure interferes with primary processes

It is this increasing complexity which will provide means to interfere with the primary processes. Indeed, as a consequence of the fact that many different associations, or scenarios, are possible starting by the same (endogenous) stimulus, the processing of the stimulus is slowed down or, as Freud says, inhibited. Here Freud (1895, p. 319) gives a mechanical account: "[An intracellular quantity] in neurone *a* will go not only in the direction of the barrier which is best facilitated, but also in the direction of the barrier which is [excited] from the further side." The so-called 'side-cathexes' ('side-excitations'), or simultaneously active networks, are able to absorb the initial (endogenous) activations, and this is the mechanical principle for the inhibitory action of the ego (see Figure 15.1). Stated in modern terms, in a mature or heavily connected network of neurons, the progression of an activation is spread over multiple cortical areas such that the activation in original automatic or short-track pathways becomes dissolved or attenuated. It is this inhibition exerted by the ego which will make possible the use of a criterion for the discrimination between the inner mental and external real world.

Summary and consequences

A summary of the comparison between Freudian primary and secondary processes is proposed in Table 15.1.

In a phylogenetic perspective, primary process dynamics respond to an evolutionary pressure to get rid of external stimuli, while secondary process dynamics have developed under pressure to handle inner body stimuli; in a logical perspective, however, the aim of both processes is not fundamentally different, namely, to get rid of activations. While in a more primitive environment simple flight reactions are often sufficient to stop external excitation, internal activation urges the organism to undertake specific actions upon its environment, which requires a preliminary discrimination between between mental and real objects. In more complex environments, however, external stimulation often confronts the organism with the same challenges as internal activations and requires secondary process handling as well.

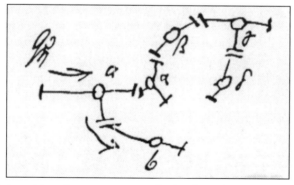

Figure 15.1 "Let us picture the ego as a network of cathected neurones well facilitated in relation to one another … . If we suppose that [an intracellular quantity] Qh enters a neurone *a* from outside …, then, if it were uninfluenced, it would pass to neurone *b*; but it is so much influenced by the side-cathexis [i.e. side-activation] a-α that it gives off only a quotient to *b* and may even perhaps not reach *b* at all. Therefore, if an ego exists, it must *inhibit* psychical primary processes." (Freud 1895, p. 324.)

Table 15.1 Comparison between primary and secondary processes according to Freud (1895)

	Primary process	**Secondary process**
Evolutionary pressure	Excitation of the external surface of the protoplasm	Emergence of an inner body in the organism
Aim	Relief of received (external) quantities	Relief of accumulating (endogenous) activations
Movement	Reflex-type reaction	Specific or adequate action
Mechanism	Flight from the stimulus	Interference and inhibition
Result	Inertia/wishful hallucination or massive defence	Experience of satisfaction/experience of frustration

Freud indicates that primary and secondary processes are not parallel but hierarchically dependent processes: specifically, for secondary processes to take place, primary processes have to be inhibited, i.e. their access to full, effective execution has to be prevented. This inhibition is brought about by the ego: it is its organization with multiple elaborate networks that allows flexible interference with more linear primary processes. Interference here means that instructions for actions do not solely depend on the incoming information, but that this incoming information is cross-checked with an already established internal organized structure; resulting decisions for action will then depend on this process of integration of new information in the existing structure (see also Merleau-Ponty 1963). Importantly, this internal organized structure reflects the history of how the subject's endogenous needs encountered satisfaction (or lack thereof) in the interaction with objects and with others.

Stated differently, the primary process functions with the stimulus information as the only reference point: starting from the stimulus, a causal chain, facilitated in memory, is activated which progresses linearly forward. In contrast, when the same stimulus is processed in a secondary process way, it is integrated in an already established organized structure, the ego, which is actualized on a moment-by-moment basis by the internal excitations signalling the current state of the body (e.g. hunger, thirst, temperature, fatigue, tensions etc.) and which enables identification of the source of the stimulus. In other words, while in the primary process there is no reference point for action besides the stimulus itself, the secondary process functions by relating the stimulus information to a reference point reflecting the current state of the body.

Indications of reality

As mentioned, for the secondary process to operate functionally, there must be a way to discriminate the origin of the activations in the wishful, respectively the hostile images. Indeed, in the case that these images are not originating from the actual real world, but have an internal origin, it is important to inhibit the primary process type reactions they elicit. Hence, for the secondary process to intervene, "it is a question of an indication to distinguish between a perception and a memory (idea)" (Freud, 1895, p. 325). Freud (1895, p. 325) formulates the hypothesis that "it is probably the ω neurones which furnish these indications of reality". These ω neurons have a particular status: even though they are "activated along with perception" and "behave like organs of perception" (Freud, 1895, p. 309), their discharge direction is efferent, i.e. in the direction of motility (Freud, 1895, p. 311). The ω neurons are thus a system of motor neurons which are engaged in the constitution of perception. Indeed, as is discussed further, Freud adhered to the neuro-anatomical views of a late-nineteenth century physiology school, chief among whom was Hermann von Helmholtz. Helmholtz (1867, 1878) proposed that the main contribution to perception is the motor command itself, rather than the sensations elicited by its execution; perception is then constituted as the systematicity which arises in the interaction between given motor commands and received sensations. This sensorimotor approach can also be found in Freud's thinking when he proposes: "it must be assumed that the ω neurons are originally linked anatomically with the paths of conduction from the various sense organs and that they direct their discharges back to the motor apparatuses belonging to those same sense organs." (Freud, 1895, p. 326). Moreover, Freud (1895, p. 325) indicates: "In the case of every external perception a qualitative excitation occurs in ω .... [this] ω excitation leads to w discharge, and information of this, as of every discharge, reaches Ψ." where Ψ is a system of cortical neurones with memory capacity responsible for psychical processes in general (Freud, 1895, p. 300). Freud (1895, p. 325) adds: "The information of this discharge from ω is thus the indication of quality or of reality for Ψ." Since information of the ω discharges is only produced when there is active perception through the ω neurons, this information then furnishes a criterion to distinguish external perceptions from internal images.

There is, however, one exception according to Freud (1895): namely, indications of reality will also be produced for internal mental images when these are massively activated, i.e. activated without attenuation from the ego. In other words, in the case of massive activation, a memory image acquires the same status as a perception, i.e. it becomes a hallucination. Therefore, only if there is inhibition by the ego do the indications of ω discharge become indications of reality for distinguishing between perception and memory (Freud, 1895, p. 326).

The fundamental difference between primary and secondary processes is that thanks to an operational ego, automatic activations of memory images are attenuated in the secondary process; the signs of reality under these conditions are indications of the real external presence of the object and the released action becomes an adequate action. Freud (1895, pp. 326–327) summarizes: "Wishful cathexis to the point of hallucination [and] complete generation of unpleasure which involves a complete expenditure of defence are described by us as psychical primary processes; by contrast, those processes which are only made possible by a good cathexis of the ego, and which represent a moderation of the foregoing, are described as psychical secondary processes."

Comparison with modern sensorimotor theories of action

The indications of reality and the efference copy model.

According to modern central monitor or internal forward models (e.g. Frith, 1992; Wolpert, 1997; Blakemore *et al.*, 1998), the sensory consequences of a self-produced movement can be accurately predicted on the basis of a copy of their original motor commands or efference copy. This model was first introduced by Helmholtz in the nineteenth century to explain the localization of visual objects. To calculate the localization of an object in reference to the head, the central nervous system has to take both the retinal location of the object and the gaze direction into account. Helmholtz's (1867) genial idea was that the brain predicts this position of the gaze on the basis of a copy of the motor command sent to the eyes, i.e. on the basis of what is now called the efference copy. In the modern efference copy models (e.g. Blakemore *et al.*, 1998), the predicted sensory feedback, calculated on the basis of the efference copy, is compared with the actual sensory feedback. This prediction can be used to attenuate the sensory effects of the movement and thereby to distinguish sensory events due to self-produced motion from the (unattenuated) sensory feedback caused by the environment, such as contact with objects.

At the time when Freud was writing 'The project', he was greatly influenced by the physicalist physiology of Helmholtz (1867). Helmholtz was is in fact the founder of the school of physiology in which Freud received his training—the so-called Helmholtz School of Physiology, involving Brücke, du Bois-Reymond, and others. In the earlier written monograph 'On aphasia', Freud (1891, p. 73) still uses the term 'innervation feeling' which was commonly known at that time (by, among others, Helmholtz, James, Bain, Wundt, and Mach—see James, 1890) to indicate the 'feeling of discharge into the motor nerves' upon which Helmholtz based his 'efference copy' model. Therefore, it appears through its writings that Freud was aware of Helmholtz' model and adhered to it. In 'The project' Freud (1895, p. 325) proposes that the 'indications of reality' are given by 'the informations of discharge', or, literally from Freud's text, the 'Abfuhr Nachrichte', or 'efference messages'. Moreover, he specifies that these efference messages 'as for every efference message' flow back to the central nervous system (Freud, 1895, p. 325). It is most likely, therefore, that Freud[1] here uses Helmholtz' model and, by extension, it does not seem far-fetched to suggest a parallel between the 'Abfuhr Nachricht' in Freud's model and the 'efference copy' in the recent forward models.

Importantly, the functions Freud assigns to the indications of reality bear similarities with those given to the efference copies. Indeed, the 'indications of reality' constitute the criterion which allows for the distinction between images generated upon external stimulation and those generated internally. When an image of an object is activated simultaneously with information of active perception in (the ω neurons of) the visual apparatus, there is reason to believe that the object is indeed present in reality, and action upon it can be released. In the modern forward models, the efference copy information constitutes a criterion to discriminate self from nonself. For example, efference copy information allows recognition that a movement of the body is generated upon a self-generated command, and is not imposed upon the subject by an external intervention (Frith, 1992). Because the sensory feedback of self-generated movements predicted on the basis

---

[1] A probable reason why Freud does not explicitly refer to von Helmholtz here is that 'The project' was a manuscript not destined for publication and published after his death in 1950.

of the efference copy is attenuated—a notion unknown in Freud's time—the forward model also allows discrimination of the sensory consequences of one's own movement and sensory input caused by the environment (e.g. Blakemore *et al.*, 1998). In summary, there are historical, neuroanatomical and functional arguments for a parallel between Freud's indications of reality and modern efference copies.

The secondary process and the dorsal pathway

If we accept this parallel, this has implications for Freud's model of primary and secondary processes. Freud (1895, p. 325) indicates that the secondary process can only operate if it can make use of the indications of reality. In other words, the secondary process can only be carried by a neuronal trajectory which implies the use of efference copies. Neuroanatomically, efference copies are generated at the level of the motor pathways from which they are derived; this is in the prefrontal cortex, especially the supplementary motor areas (Haggard and Whitford, 2004). They are consecutively used in the control and the planning of action at the level of the dorsal trajectory over the parietal area (Blakemore and Sirigu, 2003; Sirigu *et al.*, 2004). Hence, for this and other reasons, which will be developed, a similarity between the secondary process and the dorsal pathway is proposed.

Intentional action

The dorsal pathway is the 'vision for action' pathway in Milner and Goodale's (1995) model. The dorsal stream and associated pathways are responsible for the programming and for the visual control of goal-directed action. The dorsal stream also corresponds to the 'pragmatic' processing in Jeannerod's (1994) and in Jeannerod and Jacob's (2005) revised look at the two-visual systems model; the pragmatic processing allows the handling of complex representations of actions such as schemas for the use of cultural tools. This function of the dorsal pathway corresponds with the function of the secondary process in Freud's model. The secondary processes, indeed, carry the deployment of 'specific' or 'adequate' actions; these adequate actions are so called because they aim at producing a specific change in the external world which will adequately relieve a specific body tension. In other words, they are subject-centered actions which involve planning in function of an overarching subjective intention or goal.

Spatial localization

The dorsal pathway is also the pathway enabling spatial localization. In Ungerleider and Mishkin's (1982) model the dorsal stream is the 'space channel' for object discrimination on the basis of their location in space. In Milner and Goodale's (1995) model it is the pathway for visuo-motor transformation, i.e. the automatic conversion of visual information of hand commands for reaching and grasping objects. Central to the dorsal pathway is the parietal cortex which plays an important role in assessing the context in which movements take place. To this end, the parietal cortex receives somatosensory, proprioceptive, auditory and visual information and uses this to determine the position of the body and the target in space (Andersen *et al.*, 1997). Efference copies of motor commands also converge on the posterior parietal cortex and provide information about body movements.

All these signals are combined in the posterior parietal cortex to form a representation of space. This representation can then be used to construct frames of reference for the coding of appropriate movements (e.g. Jeannerod *et al.*, 1995).

Freud did not attribute to the secondary pathway the same spatial abilities as are described here for the dorsal pathway. However, his model should be read in the context of the physiological knowledge of his time. One of Freud's main distinctions between primary and secondary process is that the reaction carried by the primary process is a linear response—as a sort of mirror image—to the stimulus, while in the secondary process the ego interferes as a third point between the stimulus and the reactive tendency. This ego is defined as an activation in a set of neurons which is continuously updated by endogenous body information. These internal body stimulations (e.g. hunger) are not altered by moving the body (e.g. by fleeing) and can therefore actualize the function of the ego as a reference point independent from the stimulus. A simple illustration of this would be that a primary process reaction upon an image of a food item would be to initiate salivation, while a secondary process action would be to check the visual information for its locus of origin ('is it a mental or a real image?') and with the intentions of the organism given by the status of the inner body ('do I wish to eat it?') in function of the development of an action plan (e.g. to grasp the item). At this general level of spatiality, Freud's secondary process, as in contrast to his primary process, bears some similarities with the dorsal pathway.

The primary process and the ventral pathway

The ventral pathway is the 'object-channel' in Ungerleider and Mishkin's (1982) model, the perception pathway in Milner and Goodale's (1995) model or the pathway for the visual imagery of objects in Jeannerod and Jacob's (2005) model. The ventral stream extends from the striate cortex to the inferotemporal cortex and plays a major role in object recognition and identification: elementary visual percepts arise from the automatic stage of processing whereby basic visual attributes—such as contours, shape, texture, colour etc.—of an object are assembled and bound together. In the ventral stream the items of the visual scene are classified on the basis of representations stored in memory in the temporal lobe (Owen *et al.*, 1996; Ishai *et al.*, 1999). It is proposed that this ventral pathway, though at first sight quite different from the description of Freud's primary process, nevertheless bears remarkable points of similarity with it for reasons which will be developed.

Object-centered action

Primary processes are characterized by the type of treatment they carry, namely reflex-type reactions, which are qualified in function of their eliciting stimuli, i.e. their form can be more or less linearly derived from the form of the incoming stimuli. Freud (1895, pp. 319, 320) indicates that the primary process reacts in an immediate way on the perception of the stimulus which triggers the automatic activation of associated memory contents such as memory images of objects and actions. In other words, the primary process searches to establish an 'identity of perception' (Freud, 1900, p. 671) between the incoming stimulus and the stored representations by the shortest pathway possible, be it in a hallucinatory mode. This 'identity of perception' is achieved by the fact that the primary process will lead to the activation of the same content elements independently of the context of the stimulus. In these aspects the primary process bears similarities with the ventral pathway, which is oriented on the immediate physical aspects of the stimulus (Freedman *et al.*, 2003) and which is engaged in the identification of the stimulus independently of its spatial orientation (Milner and Goodale 1995) with the help of stored memory contents for objects or gestures (Owen *et al.*, 1996; Ishai *et al.*, 1999; Peigneux *et al.*, 2004).

The ventral pathway also corresponds to the pathway of 'actions of objects as goals' in Jeannerod's (1994) and to the semantic pathway in Jeannerod and Jacob's (2005) model. These authors (Jeannerod and Jacob, 2005, p. 303) describe this pathway as follows: "the goal of semantic processing of visual inputs is the recognition of objects which involves segregation of a scene into separable objects and binding to each object of its appropriate visual attributes". This quote resonates with clinical descriptions of primary process dynamics in, for example, free association or dreaming. Indeed, these involve the segregation of a scene into separable objects and the treatment of the isolated objects regardless of their mutual relationships (Freud, 1900). Clinical observations and empirical results (e.g. Brakel *et al.*, 2002) also indicate that the primary process involves a parsing of the stimulus in its features, whereupon each feature is the starting point for an associative chain. This leads to a profusion of memory contents associated with the stimulus, which is what Freud (1895, p. 338) calls the 'compulsion to associate'. Here, then, there seems to be some agreement between the ventral pathway and the primary process at the level of its psychological manifestation.

Inhibition and hierarchy

Classically, the ventral pathway is considered the vision pathway for the conscious identification of objects, while the dorsal pathway is the vision-for-action pathway, engaging in a large number of operations which are not necessarily conscious (Milner and Goodale, 1995). This dichotomy has been questioned (e.g. Jeannerod, 1999). For example, it appears that the ventral pathway can engage in an extremely rapid and largely automatized analysis of visual information (Thorpe and Fabre-Thorpe, 2001). Moreover, the ventral pathway is able to perform parallel complex analyses on several objects simultaneously during a small time-window; subsequently only one or a very few objects are explicitly selected and consciously perceived (Rousselet *et al.*, 2004). The ventral pathway is integrated in a network of cortical areas allowing goal-oriented behaviors. Both the prefrontal cortex and the parietal cortex are thought to provide high-level, top-down constraints on computations performed in the ventral pathway (Desimone and Duncan, 1995). The intervention of the parietal cortex, in particular, is needed to filter out the influence of distractors during object discrimination; areas V4 and the temporo-occipital cortex in the ventral pathway might receive top-down bias from parietal cortex, allowing a target to be explicitly reported (Friedman-Hill *et al.*, 2003). The complex interactions between the different levels of the ventral pathway and the parietal cortex might therefore constrain the number of objects that can be perceived simultaneously and consciously reported (Rousselet *et al.*, 2004). Similar conclusions might apply to the prefrontal cortex. For instance, a recent model has been suggested in which 'selection for action' in the frontal eye fields affects object representations in the ventral pathway (Hamker, 2003). Overall, mechanisms in the prefrontal and parietal cortices constrain computations in the ventral pathway.

These observations indicate a hierarchical relationship involving a constraining interference of the dorsal pathway and the prefrontal cortex on the ventral pathway. A hierarchical relationship of this kind at the behavioral level has also been shown. Glover (2004, p. 4), for example, states that "an integration of spatial characteristics with information about an object's identity is usually required to compute a nonspatial characteristic. However, the reverse is not also true: nonspatial characteristics are not required to compute spatial characteristics.". In Jeannerod and Jacob's (2005, p. 309) account, too, the level of awareness of the object's attributes depends on its spatial positioning: "Loss of awareness of the spatial relations between objects (provoked by a lesion in the right inferior parietal lobe) produces loss of awareness of other visual attributes." This, however, they argue, is not true the other way around. Indeed, clinical observations with lesion patients show that "Loss of awareness of such visual properties of objects as their colour, shapes, sizes or orientations does not seem to lead to unawareness of the relative locations of objects." (Jeannerod and Jacob, 2005, p. 309).

These hierarchical considerations are similar to the hierarchical approach of the secondary–primary dichotomy. For the sensorimotor model, data suggest both a prefrontal and a parietal inhibitory effect on the ventral pathway. In Freud's model, the deployment of secondary processes involves the inhibition of primary processes; Freud mentions both an inhibitory influence of the ego (1895, p. 324) as well as a moderation effect of the secondary process (1895, p. 327; 1900, p. 603) on the primary process. It is interesting that there seems to be a parallel in function here between the ego and the prefrontal cortex; such a possible equivalence between the Freudian ego and the (pre-)frontal cortex has been proposed before (e.g. Kaplan-Solms and Solms, 2000; Solms, 2004). These similarities in interaction and inhibition dynamics between both models, psychodynamic and sensorimotor, strengthen the parallel between the secondary process and the dorsal pathway and between the primary process and the ventral pathway respectively.

Conscious and unconscious processes

The proposed parallels might sound surprising given the classical view, in which the ventral pathway is the pathway for conscious identification, while the dorsal pathway is the action pathway, which does not necessarily operate consciously (Milner and Goodale, 1995). This seems to be a contradiction with the psychodynamic topology, in which the primary processes are characteristic for unconscious mental life—as become manifest in e.g. free association, dreams, slips of the tongues, hysterical symptoms and schizophrenia—while secondary processing is characteristic for conscious mentation. Both models, however, need to be articulated more precisely in this respect.

First, as indicated, the sensorimotor model should be nuanced: indeed, it appears that not all ventral processing is conscious; moreover the selection of those ventrally

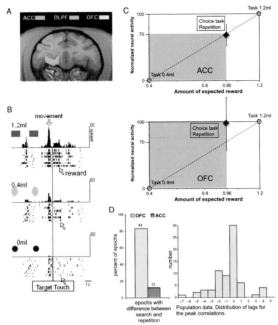

ate 1 (A) Localization of areas of interest on a magnetic resonance imaging frontal section in a monkey. (B) Unit activity of one neuron recorded the dorsal anterior cingulate cortex (dACC) in No-choice task. The firing rate of the neuron increases at the time of movement and is modulated e time of touch on a stimulus. (C) Normalized pre-reward activity in trials: 0, 0.4, 1.2 ml, and choice trials in ACC and orbitofrontal cortex (OFC). pulation data. Task values are in abscissa. Data points in ordinates are the normalized average activities of epochs (mean ± SD). (There is no error r for trial 1.2 ml and trial 0.4 ml, which following normalization are equal, in each epoch, to 100 and 0, respectively.) (D) Proportion of epochs th different activity in search and repetition in the Choice task for OFC and ACC (bar graph on the left). On the right: correlation analysis between rformance and activity. Population data. Distribution of lags for the peak correlations. Negative lags indicate performance in advance of neural tivity. When the cross-correlation was statistically significant at a time lag (trial), this lag—positive or negative—indicated a statistically significant ne shift between the two curves and an advance of one curve over the other. When significant correlations were observed at different lags, we bitrarily selected the time lag corresponding to the largest correlation.

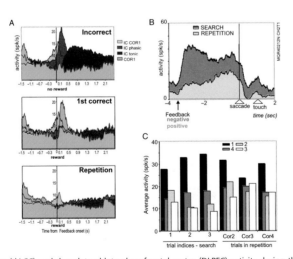

ate 2 Dorsal anterior cingulate cortex (dACC) and dorsolateral lateral prefrontal cortex (DLPFC) activity during the PS task. (A) the three histograms resent average activity of different neuronal population recorded in dACC. Activity is aligned on feedback for incorrect trials in search (upper histogram), st correct trials–reward (middle) and for correct trials during repetition—reward (bottom). Each population histogram is represented with a different lour: light orange: neurons with increased activity at the time of negative and positive feedback during search (incorrect first correct; n = 20 neurons). ark orange and red: neurons with increased discharge after errors. Phasic (in orange; n = 18 neurons) and tonic (in red; n = 39 neurons) activity are parated (see also Figure 2.3A). Blue: neurons that responded only after the first reward, i.e. the positive feedback terminating the search period = 13). (B) Average activity for one neuron recorded in the DLPFC. Activity is averaged separately for search trials and repetition trials, and aligned n the feedback (i.e. negative in search, positive in repetition). (C) Average activity for one neuron, measured in the delay before the saccade toward e target chosen during successive trials in search and repetition. The activity is measured for each target location (1 to 4). Note the change in firing mplitude and in selectivity (difference between the four locations) during search.

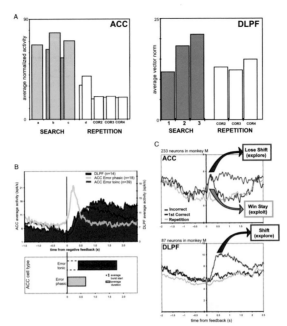

Plate 3 Dorsal anterior cingulate cortex (dACC) and dorsolateral lateral prefrontal cortex (DLPFC) activity during the Problem-solving (PS) task. (**A**) The two histograms present average measures on population activity recorded in ACC (left) and DLPFC (right) for the different trials of search and repetition periods of the PS task. ACC measures are based on normalized average activity at the around responses (from Procyk et al., 2000). For DLPFC activity the histogram shows average selectivity vector norm which amplitude reflects the spatial selectivity or discrimination between spatial positions (from Procyk and Goldman-Rakic, 2006). Note the clear transition on both areas between search and repetition, i.e. as soon as the animal discovers the correct response. (**B**) Average population activity for ACC error-related neurons (red and orange) and DLPFC delay (tonic) activity. PSTH are aligned on negative feedback (see text). Neurons are issued from separate recordings in the same monkey for both areas. The lower graph represents average start time and duration of significant firing for the two populations of error-related ACC neurons, i.e. phasic and tonic. Note that the two populations are overlapping in terms of duration. (**C**). Grand average of 233 ACC neurons and 87 DLPFC neurons that were task-related but were not discriminated according to their specific event-related properties. Average discharge rates are aligned on negative feedback, first correct/reward, and repetition reward. Note that whereas ACC shows detection of negative feedback, it is positive when those are relevant for behavior adaptation. DLPFC neurons show a tonic activation only during exploration and in parallel with tonic ACC activation

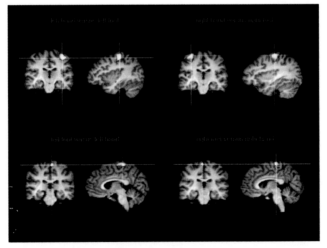

Plate 4 Cortical activation for the direct contrast of all left- and right-hand responses with all left- and right-foot responses (upper part). The lower part of the figure displays cortical activations for the direct contrast of all left- and right-foot trials with all left- and right-hand trials. The activation threshold was again set to $z > 3.1$.

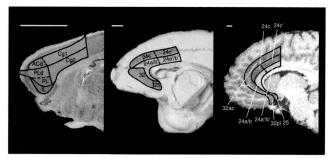

Plate 5 Comparative anatomy of the rodent (rat, left), and primate (macaque, centre and human, right) anterior cingulate cortex (ACC). In the macaque the ACC is divided into two broad regions: (i) ACC gyrus (blue) immediately dorsal and rostral to the corpus callosum and including area 24 (24a and 24b rostrally, 24a' and 24b' caudally), 32, and 25. (ii) ACC sulcus (red). A further cytoarchitectonic subdivision of area 24, 24c, occupies most of the sulcal ACC. Its caudal part, 24c', contains the rostral cingulate motor area (CMAr). Similarly, although further subdivision is possible, it is also useful to consider two broad subdivisions within the human ACC. Human ACC gyrus areas 32pl, 25, 24a and 24b resemble the macaque gyral areas 32, 25, 24a and 24b (Vogt et al., 1995; Ongur et al., 2003). Human areas 24c, 24c', and 32ac in the ACC sulcus and, when present, the second superior cingulate gyrus (CGs), bear similarities with the areas in the macaque ACC sulcus and include the cingulate motor areas (Vogt et al., 1995; Ongur et al., 2003). The identification of homologous structures in the rat is more controversial. There is a good case for thinking that parts of the rodent brain resemble the primate ACC gyrus [Cg1, posterior Cg1, infralimbic cortex (IL) and prelimbic cortex (PL)]. There is no equivalent of the primate ACC sulcus in the rat but it might tentatively be argued that rat rostral ACd bears some resemblance in its anatomical connexions.

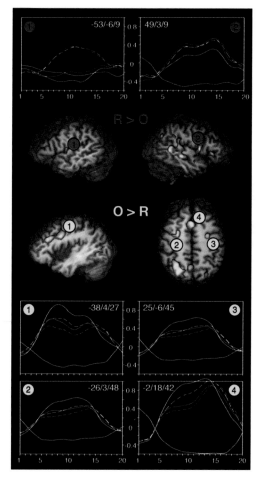

Plate 6 Middle panel shows group-averaged ($n = 20$) statistical maps of significantly activated areas for prediction based on objects as compared to rhythm (O > R) and vice versa (R > O), each collapsed across visually and acoustically presented stimulus sequences. z-Maps were thresholded at $z = 3.09$. Percentage signal changes are shown for all premotor activations (upper and lower panels) in order to demonstrate significant interactions of stimulus modality (visual = solid lines, auditory = dashed lines) and stimulus property (object = yellow lines, rhythm = red lines). In particular, left and right inferior ventral premotor cortex (tagged by red numbers 1 and 2, respectively) showed highest signals for RA and lowest for OV, with RV and OA in between. Although it has to be considered that left inferior ventral premotor cortex exposed a considerable preference for auditory as compared to visual stimuli, interaction was significant in both inferior ventral premotor areas. Left superior ventral as well as left and right dorsal premotor cortex and left presupplementary motor area (tagged by yellow numbers 1, 2, 3 and 4, respectively) showed the opposite pattern.

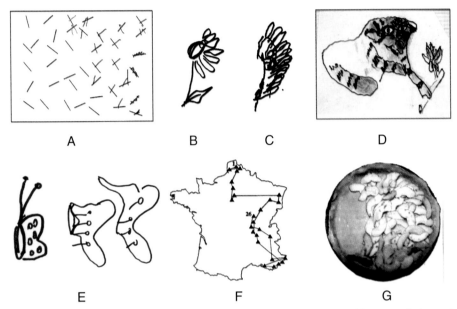

Plate 7 Neglect is a spatial cognition disorder. Left space-centered neglect assessed by a cancellation task (Albert, 1973) (**A**). Left object-centered neglect assessed by drawing from memory of a daisy or a tiger with three examples of performance: omission of left-sided petals (**B**). Ipsilateral perseverations (**C**). Lack of colour on the left part of the drawing (**D**). Left object-centered neglect with an 'allochiria' phenomenon: patients were asked to copy a butterfly. They were unable to draw a symmetrical object but the whole object was located on the right part of the drawing superimposed in one case, juxtaposed in another one (**E**). Left representational neglect evidenced by mental evocation of the map of France in a right-brain-damaged patient (**F**). An ecological consequence of neglect and visuo-spatial disorders, illustrated by an apple-tart made by a right-brain-damaged patient (**G**).

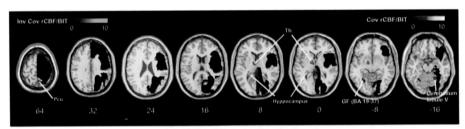

Plate 8. Functional imaging positron emission spectroscopy study: covariation analysis between modification of regional cerebral blood flow (rCBF) and behavioral inattention test (BIT) after prism. The overlay lesion mask of five patients with left neglect (in black), with activations mapped onto the horizontal slices corresponding to z-coordinates −16, −8; 0, 8, 16, 24, 32 and 64 in Talairach and Tournoux space, constructed by using the identical or the closest-matching horizontal slices of each individual. In red (Cov): areas of significant increase in neural activity (cluster level $p < 0.05$, corrected according to Gaussian random field theory) associated with the analysis of covariation between the increase of rCBF and the improvement of BIT after prism adaptation (PA). In blue (Inv Cov): areas of significant decrease in neural activity (cluster level probability, $p < 0.05$, corrected) associated with the analysis of covariation between the decrease of rCBF and the improvement of BIT after PA (from Luauté et al., 2006c). PCU, precuneus; Th, thalamus; GF, gyrus fusiform; BA, Brodmann area.

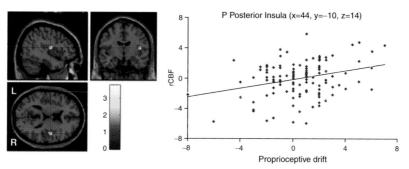

Plate 9 Activity in the right posterior insula (x = 44, y = −10, z = 14) was positively correlated (t = 3.41, p < 0.05) with the proprioceptive drift towards the rubber hand. Positive drifts indicate a drift towards the rubber hand, and negative drifts indicate a drift away from the rubber hand. Activations show averaged data over 10 participants. L, left; R, right; rCBF, regional cerebral blood flow. (Data from Tsakiris et al., 2006.)

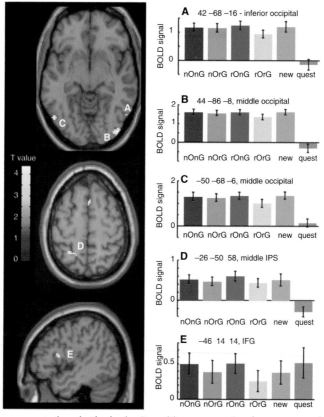

Plate 10 Grasp representations in the brain. Repetition suppression for grasp was found in occipital regions, middle intraparietal sulcus (IPS) and inferior frontal gyrus (IFG). All regions show stronger responses to novel grasps (red and dark blue) compared to repeated grasp (orange and light blue). n, novel; r, repeated; O, object goal; G, grasp; new, first stimulus of a block; quest, question trial.

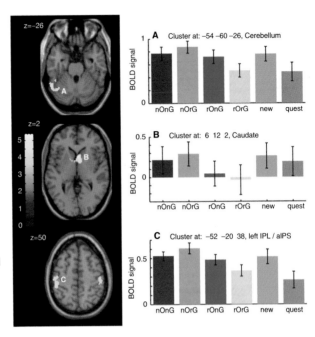

Plate 11 Goal representations in the brain. Repetition suppression (RS) for the goal object was found in the cerebellum, basal ganglia and left inferior parietal lobule (IPL)/anterior intraparietal sulcus (AIPS). All three regions show stronger responses to novel goals (red and orange) compared to repeated goals (blue). n, novel; r, repeated; O, object goal; G, grasp; new, first stimulus of a block; quest, question trial.

Plate 12 Cortical activation pattern during observation of animal hand shadows and real animals. Significantly activated voxels ($p < 0.001$, fixed effects analysis) in the moving animal shadow and moving real animal conditions after subtraction of the static controls. Activity related to animal shadows (red clusters) is superimposed on that from real animals (green clusters). Those brain regions activated during both tasks are shown in yellow. In the middle part of the figure, the experimental time-course for each contrast is shown (i.e. C1, moving; C2, static). Note the almost complete absence of frontal activation for real animals in comparison to animal shadows, which bilaterally activate the inferior frontal gyrus (arrows). (Modified from Fadiga et al., 2006a.)

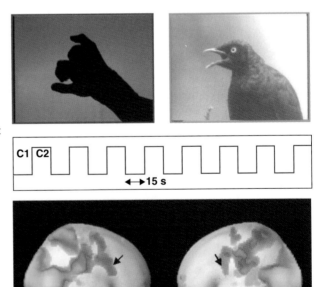

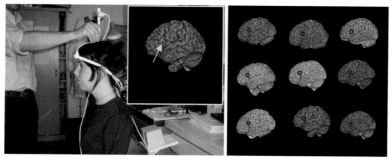

Plate 13 The procedure used in the phonological priming experiment to map individual Broca's areas. On the left, the electromagnetic tracking procedure is shown. For each subject, the center of *pars opercularis* of the inferior frontal gyrus was identified (yellow arrow). The panel on the right shows the three-dimensional reconstructed brain of nine subjects with a red circle superimposed indicating the location selected for administering transcranial magnetic stimulation during the experimental paradigm.

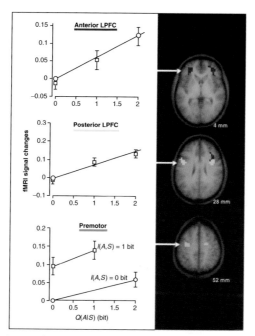

Plate 14 Frontal activations with respect to demands of sensory and cognitive control. Green: activations varying with sensory control [*I*(*S*,*A*)] (premotor cortex). Yellow and red: activations varying with cognitive control only [*Q*(*A*/*S*)]. Yellow: posterior lateral prefrontal cortex (LPFC) (BA 44/45). Red, anterior LPFC (BA 46). Numbers in the right panel are vertical Talairach coordinates of axial slices (neurological convention). Functional magnetic resonance imaging (fMRI) data are from Koechlin *et al.* (2003).

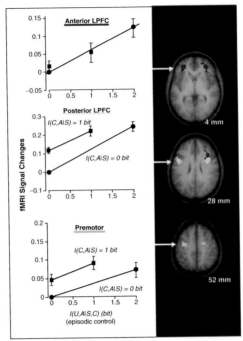

Plate 15 Frontal activations with respect to demands of contextual and episodic control. Green: premotor activations. Yellow: activations varying with contextual control [$I(C,A|S)$] [posterior lateral prefrontal cortex (LPFC), BA 44/45]. Red: activations varying with episodic control only {[$I(U,A|S,C)$], anterior LPFC, BA 46}. Numbers in the right panel are vertical Talairach coordinates of axial slices (neurological convention). Functional magnetic resonance imaging (fMRI) data are from Koechlin et al. (2003).

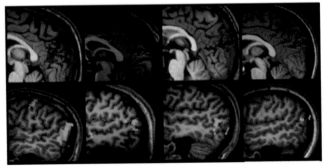

Plate 16 Two regions implicated in theory of mind, the medial precuneus (red) and the right temporo-parietal junction (green), in four individual subjects. Shown are medial and right lateral sagittal slices from the whole-brain contrast, False belief > False photo stories (e.g. Saxe and Kanwisher, 2003, Experiment 2), in each individual $p < 0.001$ uncorrected, $k > 10$.

processed contents which come to consciousness is likely operated by the dorsal pathway and the prefrontal cortex. In this understanding of the sensorimotor dichotomy, the dynamical interactions between ventral and dorsal pathways are quite similar to the interactions described by Freud. Indeed, primary processes are, in Freud's understanding, continuously operational, even when they are overridden by secondary processes: the interference of the secondary process is limited to the extent to which these primary processes have access to consciousness. When secondary processing is temporarily suspended, such as in dreams or in parapraxes, the primary process has an unrestrained access to consciousness. In conscious mental life this is mostly not the case, but even then, secondary processes are not to be equated with conscious experience itself. Instead, secondary processes *enable* mental operations which are typical for conscious mental life, such as the discrimination between mental and real images. These mental operations as such do not constitute the content of consciousness; instead, this content is given by those images that have not been prevented from access to consciousness by the ego. Moreover, once they have gone through this selection, the images—mental or real—are experienced together with an awareness of their origin, namely interior or exterior. This view is in agreement with Shevrin (1998), who proposes that the very function of consciousness for the mental apparatus is to enable the distinction of various mental contents in function of their origin, either external or internal, either percepts, memories, thoughts or fantasies.

In the sensorimotor approach for access to consciousness, Jeannerod and Jacob (2005) stress the primacy of spatial localization. Based on clinical observations with brain-lesioned patients, they contend that "visual processing in the dorsal pathway can build visual representations of the spatial relations among distinct proto-objects almost devoid of other visual attributes" (Jeannerod and Jacob, 2005, p. 309). On the other hand, Jeannerod and Jacob (2005, p. 309) remark that "in neglect patients, the visual attributes of objects in the neglected hemispace are still covertly processed by the relevant areas in the ventral pathway. But the patient remains unaware of the visual attributes of stimuli located in their neglected hemispace." In other words, the authors defend the idea that spatial access is a condition for access to conscious mental contents, but the absence of it would not prevent unconscious processing of these contents; on the other hand, an absence of processing in the ventral pathway does not prevent a form of schematic consciousness. There is some correspondence between this view and Freud's model, since it stresses the role of the spatial localization as an enabling condition for access to consciousness, the contents of which are then (also) given by the ventral pathway: in Freud's model, secondary processing is an enabling condition for access to consciousness while primary processing contributes to its contents.

If we do the hypothetical exercise of putting both models together, they seem to indicate that the enabling condition for consciousness of content—i.e. the access to *what something is*—is the primacy of establishing first *that something is there* which needs to be identified. This awareness of the fact that 'something is there' would be carried by the dorsal pathway in the sensorimotor model, because this is the pathway for spatial localization. In parallel, it would be carried by the secondary processing in the psychodynamic model, because this is the pathway that establishes the exteriority of a stimulus, i.e. the fact that something is there which is not me. Once this position or status of the stimulus is established, it can be given a content, either by the ventral pathway in the sensorimotor model or by the primary processing in the psychodynamic model. Moreover, it is most probably the prior localization of the stimulus which will constrain the selection of one identity amidst a range of possible identities. For the sensorimotor models, this is suggested by empirical results showing the selection effect of the dorsal pathway and the prefrontal cortex on the parallel processing in the ventral pathway (see 'The primary process and the ventral pathway' above). For the psychodynamic models, this is suggested by clinical observations, showing a profusion of possible interpretations of a same stimulus—including a great many that make no sense in the given context—in situations of (temporary) suspension of secondary processing, such as in free association or in dreaming.

This line of thought has the advantage of explaining paradigms used to establish unconscious processing. Subliminal priming paradigms establish unconscious processing on the basis of the so-called 'dissociation paradigm': though people are completely unable to *detect* stimuli in a subliminal forced-choice paradigm, they appear to perform significantly better on *identification* and *categorization* tasks presented at the same level of subliminality (Snodgrass *et al.*, 2004). This could be explained by the difference in status of detection on the one hand and identification or categorization on the other. Detection, indeed, by definition requires the ability to indicate that a mental content is coming from the outside world—and is therefore not merely a thought or a memory. For this reason, detection requires the ability to distinguish inside from outside, which is an ability of the secondary process. Identification and categorization tasks, in contrast, can be performed independently of the localization of mental contents. It does not matter if the stimuli are mental or real; as long as there is some access to the *content* of these stimuli, the identification and categorization tasks will not be performed randomly. Therefore, these tasks do not appeal to secondary processing but need only primary processing. If we venture to make a projection to the sensorimotor models along the lines of the paper, we would say that these tasks only require mobilization of the ventral 'What?' pathway, without need for information of the dorsal 'Where?' pathways.

Clinical illustration

In the Freudian model, positive psychotic symptoms, such as hallucinations and perceptual distortions, are due to a relative supremacy of primary processes versus a downplay of secondary processes (1900, p. 568; 1915, pp. 197, 199–204). Clinical observations of these psychotic experiences therefore inform us about what 'goes wrong' when there is a relative absence of secondary processing. This brief case description[2] is from a patient with an established *Diagnostic and Statistical Manual* diagnosis of schizophrenia. The patient has a delusional system, reports voices and produces neologisms. He takes neuroleptic medication.

---

2 Observations made by the author at the Psychiatric Centre Sint-Amandus in Beernem, Belgium, during the period September 2005–February 2006 (see also Van de Vijver *et al.*, 2006).

Brief description

RV is a 45-year-old man, whose major difficulty is that, often, when he directs a glance to the world, the perception of this world invades him. He complains of penetrating sensations, 'people and things sticking onto his skin', 'people walking through him', things 'penetrating him'. In other words, he has great difficulty in creating an experience of distance between him and his percepts. To restore a bearable relation to the world, he has to physically move back and forth around his visual targets: he frequently backs up on his steps, to move forward again; he opens doors by opening them partially, then closing them again partially, then reopening them, etc.; he does and undoes repeatedly, either completely or partially, some of his gestures, both in the forward and in the backward direction. Specifically, he details one chain of events which is painful to him: moving people or things in the world cause a 'fizz' or a 'pinching feeling' on his retina, which then constitutes the unique cause of an 'undesirable image'. These undesirable images are often of an incisive and penetrating content, such as 'a needle in the eye', 'the disintegration of my photo-apparatus', 'a penis through my knife', 'my pectoral muscle torn', 'my viscera extirpated', 'my balls unhooked', etc. To undo the image, the moving target that caused the pinch on his retina is asked to undo the movement: he asks people around him to back up, to undo in backward direction what they did in the first place. When they agree to do so, he watches the scene fixedly, leans his head somewhat forward, firmly closes his eye and holds this pose for a second, before looking up again. In case they do not accept to submit to his request, he remains pursued by the painful image. Places where he has been are thus occupied with an accumulation of as-yet-undone undesirable images.

Comments

Since in a psychodynamic perspective the secondary processing is thought to be relatively absent in psychosis, one hypothesis might be that the indications of reality corresponding with RV's visual perception are lacking or disturbed. Since the indications of reality have the function to distinguish interior from exterior or 'me' from 'not-me', the expected consequence of this disturbance would then be a difficulty in experiencing the exteriority of the visual percepts, which is exactly what RV complains about. If we apply to this case the proposed parallel between the indications of reality and the efference copies (see 'The indications of reality and the efference copy model' above), the hypothesis would be that RV's disturbance is situated at the level of the efference copies of his eye movements.

If this is true, a number of consequences are expected. First, the reflexive eye movement following a moving target would still occur, but would not be recognized as being under command of the self. In other words, it would feel as if the eyes were forced by some external agent to make small movements to follow the target, something one could tentatively describe as a 'pinching' on the retina, which is what RV reports about his experience. The supposedly missing efference copies would coincide with Frith's hypothesis (1992) for the voices heard by psychotic patients: these are thought to be due to self-generated subvocal movements of the articulatory system which are not recognized as being self-generated, possibly due to absence of the efference copies. In Blakemore *et al.*'s (1998) comparator model, the efference copies enable the anticipation of the sensory feedback of the activated movement such that this sensory feedback is pre-emptively attenuated. If the efference copies of the eye movements are supposedly missing or disturbed in RV, then the consecutive attenuation should also be lacking, which might explain RV's conscious experience of his eye movement upon a moving target. Second, in a sensorimotor approach of normal perception (e.g. Glover, 2004, pp. 6–7) the combined visual and proprioceptive feedback and efference copy information are fed to the dorsal pathway over the superior parietal lobe, which is responsible for establishing the spatial object properties model. If a disturbance at the level of the efference copies of the eye-movements is supposed, it makes sense that this would manifest itself at the level of the spatial experience of the percepts.

Moreover, in an enactive perspective (e.g. Noë, 2005), a perception is constituted by the implicit knowledge of the sensorimotor contingencies describing the way sensory stimulation varies with movement. Lenay (2006, pp. 39, 41, 43) proposes that the ability to create an experience of distance or an exterior space for the content of what is perceived, is precisely the ability to reversibly move back and forth around the visual target. This movement would normally be constituted by a structurally unconscious eye-movement around the target. The idea that RV's inability to create an impression of distance correlates with the impression that his eye-movements are at that moment not unconscious or not attenuated, might suggest that this attenuation is a necessary condition for the creation of an exterior perception space and of the experience of distance. In any case, if we suppose that RV's eye movements are at particular moments not able to create this experience of distance, he might be tempted to replace this back-and-forth eye movement by a back-and-forth body movement, which is what is observed. The hypothesis of a disturbance at the level of the efference copies of RV's eye movements may therefore explain some of his observed behaviors.

Finally, there is the problem of how to understand RV's profusion of undesirable images in this context. In a Freudian approach this could be understood as the consequence of the relative absence of the secondary processing: in an attempt to make sense of the experience of intrusion, RV produces in an associative way an unrestrained range of primary process (memory and fantasy) contents which then have a relatively easy access to consciousness. If the secondary processes were functional, they would verify that these images do not correspond with reality and refrain their access to consciousness; without the selective influence of the secondary process, a direct 'window into RV's unconscious' opens up.

In summary, the analysis of this brief clinical description is coherent with the Freudian hypothesis of a downplay of the secondary processes and of a problem at the level of the 'indications of reality'. In parallel, a sensorimotor disturbance in the dorsal pathway with a problem at the level of the efference copies would also coherently make sense of the observed symptoms. Several studies have indeed indicated a disturbance of the dorsal parietal pathway (e.g. O'Donnell et al., 1996; Danckert et al., 2002; Doniger et al., 2002; Maruff et al., 2003; Kim et al., 2006) in the pathophysiology of schizophrenia. These clinical observations, then, give further support to the suggestion of a similarity between the secondary process and the dorsal pathway.

Table 15.2 Comparison between the Freudian model of the mental apparatus (1895) and modern sensorimotor two-visual systems models

Model	Freud	Sensorimotor
	Primary process	*Ventral pathway*
Reacts	in an immediate way on the features of the stimulus	in an immediate way on the features of the stimulus
Aims at	'perceptual identity'	recognition and identification
Is insensitive to	contextual configuration of the stimulus	spatial configuration of the stimulus
Is characterized by	a profusion of associated memory contents	parallel processing
Is inhibited by	the ego	prefrontal fibres
Delivers after selection	contents of consciousness	contents of consciousness
	Secondary process	*Dorsal pathway*
Makes use of	indications of reality	efference copies
Aims at	specific or adequate actions	goal-directed, planned or intentional actions
Is able to take the locus of the stimulus into account thanks to	a reference point independent of the stimulus given by the inescapable internal activations	spatial localization
Constrains	primary processes	ventral pathway
Enables	access to consciousness	access to consciousness
In psychosis it is	downplayed	dysfunctional

Conclusions

To conclude this comparison between a psychodynamic concept of the mental apparatus and a sensorimotor brain concept, it is proposed (1) that Freud's concept of indications of reality parallels the modern concept of efference copies and (2) that the neurophysiological ventral–dorsal dichotomy allows a dissociation of mental processing compatible with the Freudian primary–secondary dichotomy. On this basis, the primary process is argued to involve the ventral pathway, and the secondary process to involve the dorsal pathway. The specific points of similarity between the Freudian and the sensorimotor model are summarized in Table 15.2.

Acknowledgments

The author thanks Gertrudis Van de Vijver and Yves Rossetti for critical comments and discussion. Support for this research was provided by Howard Shevrin, the Belgian American Educational Foundation and the International Neuro-Psychoanalysis Society.

References

Andersen, R. A., Snyder, L. H., Bradley, D. C. and Xing, J. (1997) Multimodal representation of space in the posterior parietal cortex and its use in planning movements. *Annual Review of Neuroscience*, **20**, 303–330.

Bazan, A. and Van Bunder, D. (2005) Some comments on the emotional and motor dynamics of language embodiment. A neurophysiological understanding of the Freudian Unconscious. In De Preester, H. and Knockaert, V. (eds), *Body Image & Body Schema, Interdisciplinary Perspectives*, pp. 49–107. John Benjamins, Amsterdam/Philadelphia.

Blakemore, S. J. and Sirigu, A. (2003) Action prediction in the cerebellum and in the parietal lobe. *Experimental Brain Research*, **153**, 239–245.

Blakemore, S. J., Wolpert, D. M. and Frith, C. D. (1998) Central cancellation of self-produced tickle sensation. *Nature Neuroscience*, **1**, 635–640.

Brakel, L. A.W., Shevrin, H. and Villa, K. K. (2002) The priority of primary process categorizing: experimental evidence supporting a psychoanalytic developmental hypothesis. *Journal of the American Psychoanalytic Association*, **50**, 483–505.

Danckert, J., Rossetti, Y., d'Amato, T., Daléry, J. and Saoud, M. (2002) Exploring imagined movements in patients with schizophrenia. *Neuroreport*, **13**, 605–609.

Desimone, R. and Duncan, J. (1995) Neural mechanisms of selective visual attention. *Annual Review of Neuroscience*, **18**, 193–222.

Doniger, G. M., Foxe, J. J., Murray, M. M., Higgins, B. A. and Javitt, D. C. (2002) Impaired visual object recognition and dorsal/ventral stream interaction in schizophrenia. *Archives of General Psychiatry*, **59**, 1011–1020.

Freedman, D. J., Riesenhuber, M., Poggio, T. and Miller, E. K. (2003) A comparison of primate prefrontal and inferior temporal cortices during visual categorization. *Journal of Neuroscience*, **23**, 5235–5246.

Freud, S. (1891/1978) *On Aphasia, A Critical Study* (Stengel, E., trans.). International Universities Press, New York.

Freud, S. (1895/1966) Project for a scientific psychology (Stratchey, J., trans.). In *Standard Edition I*, pp. 281–397/410. Hogarth Press, London. (Original publication in 1950.)

Freud, S. (1900/1958) The interpretation of dreams (Stratchey, J., trans.). In *Standard Edition IV–V*, pp. 339–627. Hogarth Press, London.

Freud, S. (1915/1957) The unconscious (Stratchey, J., trans.) In *Standard Edition XIV*, pp. 159–215. Hogarth Press, London.

Friedman-Hill, S. R., Robertson, L. C., Desimone, R. and Ungerleider, L. G. (2003) Posterior parietal cortex and the filtering of distractors. *Proceedings of the National Academy of Sciences of the USA*, **7**, 4263–4268.

Frith, C. D. (1992) *The Neuropsychology of Schizophrenia*. Erlbaum, Hove, UK.

Glover, S. (2004) Separate visual representations in the planning and control of action. *Behavioral and Brain Sciences*, **27**, 3–78.

Haggard, P. and Whitford, B. (2004) Supplementary motor area provides an efferent signal for sensory suppression. *Cognitive Brain Research*, **19**, 52–58.

Hamker, F. H. (2003) The reentry hypothesis: linking eye movements to visual perception. *Journal of Vision*, **3**, 808–816.

Helmholtz, H. (1867/1962) *Handbuch der physiologischen Optik*, 12th edn. Leopold Voss, Hamburg. [English translation: Southall, J. P. C., ed. and trans. (1962) *A Treatise on Physiological Optics*. Dover, New York.]

Helmholtz, H. (1878/1971) The facts of perception. In Kahl, R. (ed.), *Selected Writings of Hermann von Helmholtz*. Wesleyan University Press, Middletown, CT.

Ishai, A., Ungerleider, L. G., Martin, A., Schouten, J. L. and Haxby, J. V. (1999) Distributed representation of objects in the human ventral visual pathway. *Proceedings of the National Academy of Sciences of the USA*, **96**, 9379–9384.

James, W. (1890/1981) *The Principles of Psychology*. Dover, New York.

Jeannerod, M. (1994) The representing brain: neural correlates of motor intention and imagery. *Behavioral and Brain Sciences*, **17**, 187–245.

Jeannerod, M. and Jacob, P. (2005) Visual cognition: a new look at the two-visual systems model. *Neuropsychologia*, **43**, 301–312.

Jeannerod, M., Arbib, M. A., Rizzolatti, G. and Sakata, H. (1995) Grasping objects: the cortical mechanisms of visuomotor transformation. *Trends in Neurosciences*, **18**, 314–320.

Kaplan-Solms, K. and Solms, M. (2000) *Clinical Studies in Neuro-Psychoanalysis. Introduction to a Depth Neuropsychology*. International Universities Press, Madison, CT.

Kim, D., Wylie, G., Pasternak, R., Butler, P. D. and Javitt, D. C. (2006) Magnocellular contributions to impaired motion processing in schizophrenia. *Schizophrenia Research*, **82**, 1–8.

Lenay, C. (2006) Enaction, externalisme et suppléance perceptive. *Intellectica*, **43**, 27–52.

Maruff, P., Wilson, P. and Currie, J. (2003) Abnormalities of motor imagery associated with somatic passivity phenomena in schizophrenia. *Schizophrenia Research*, **60**, 229–238.

Maturana, H. R. and Varela, F. J. (1980) Autopoiesis and cognition: the realization of the living. *Boston Studies in the Philosophy of Science*, **42**. D. Reidel, Dordrecht.

Merleau-Ponty, M. (1963/1983) *The Structure of Behaviour*. Duquesne University Press, Pittsburgh.

Milner, A. D. and Goodale, M. A. (1995) *The Visual Brain in Action*. Oxford University Press, Oxford.

Noë, A. (2005) *Action in Perception*. MIT Press, Cambridge, MA.

O'Donnell, B. F., Swearer, J. M., Smith, L. T., Nestor, P. G., Shenton, M. E. and McCarley, R. W. (1996) Selective deficits in visual perception and recognition in schizophrenia. *American Journal of Psychiatry*, **153**, 687–692.

Owen, A. M., Milner, B., Petrides, M. and Evans, A. C. (1996) Memory for object features versus memory for object location: a positron-emission tomography study of encoding and retrieval processes. *Proceedings of the National Academy of Sciences of the USA*, **93**, 9212–9217.

Panksepp, J. (1999) Emotions as viewed by psychoanalysis and neuroscience: an exercise in consilience. *Neuropsychoanalysis*, **1**, 15–38.

Peigneux, P., Van der Linden, M., Garraux, G., Laureys, S., Degueldre, C., Aerts, J., Del Flore, G., Moonen, G., Luxen, A. and Salmon, E. (2004) Imaging a cognitive model of apraxia: the neural substrate of gesture-specific cognitive processes. *Human Brain Mapping*, **21**, 119–142.

Rossetti, Y. and Pisella, L. (2002) Several 'vision for action' systems: a guide to dissociating and integrating dorsal and ventral functions. In Prinz, W. and Hommel, B. (eds), *Common Mechanisms in Perception and Action, Attention and Performance*, Vol. XIX, pp. 62–119. Oxford University Press, Oxford.

Rousselet, G. A., Thorpe, S. J. and Fabre-Thorpe, M. (2004) How parallel is visual processing in the ventral pathway? *Trends in Cognitive Sciences*, **8**, 363–370.

Shevrin, H. (1998) Why do we need to be conscious? A psychoanalytic answer. In Barone, D. F. Hersen, M. and VanHasselt, V. B. (eds), *Advanced Personality*, Chapter 10. Plenum Press, New York.

Shevrin, H. (2001) Event-related markers of unconscious processes. *International Journal of Psychophysiology*, **42**, 209–218.

Sirigu, A., Daprati, E., Ciancia, S., Giraux, P., Nighoghossian, N., Posada, A. and Haggard, P. (2004) Altered awareness of voluntary action after damage to the parietal cortex. *Nature Neuroscience*, **7**, 80–84.

Snodgrass, M., Bernat, E. and Shevrin, H. (2004) Unconscious perception: a model-based approach to method and evidence. *Perception & Psychophysics*, **66**, 846–867.

Solms, M. (2004) Freud returns. *Scientific American*, **290**, 83–88.

Thorpe, S. J. and Fabre-Thorpe, M. (2001) Seeking categories in the brain. *Science*, **291**, 260–263.

Ungerleider, L. and Mishkin, M. (1982) Two cortical visual systems. In Ingle, D. J. Goodale, M. A. and Mansfield, R. J. W. (eds), *Analysis of Visual Behaviour*, pp. 549–586. MIT Press, Cambridge.

Van de Vijver, G. and Geerardyn, F. (2002) *The Pre-psychoanalytic Writings of Sigmund Freud*. Karnac, London.

Van de Vijver, G., Bazan, A., Rottiers, F. and Gilbert, J. (2006) Enactivisme et internalisme: de l'ontologie à la clinique. *Intellectica*, **43**, 93–103.

Wolpert, D. M. (1997) Computational approaches to motor control. *Trends in Cognitive Sciences*, **1**, 209–216.

16

Predictive attenuation in the perception of touch

Paul M. Bays and Daniel M. Wolpert

The ability to distinguish sensations resulting from our own actions from those with an external cause is a fundamental aspect of human behaviour. This distinction is in some cases reflected directly in perception: for example, tickling oneself produces a less intense sensation than being tickled by someone else. In this chapter we review the evidence for a general process of sensory filtering that attenuates self-generated tactile sensation. This process depends upon a temporally precise prediction of the sensory consequences of one's actions. We demonstrate experimentally that tactile attenuation specifically affects self-generated sensory input, leaving unchanged externally generated sensations in the same part of the body. The level of attenuation does not vary with stimulus intensity, but rather consists of a constant subtraction in the perceived intensity of the self-generated stimulus. However, the level of attenuation can be reduced by introducing a spatial separation between the active effector and the body part in which the touch is felt. This suggests that tactile attenuation is modulated by the degree to which the context of the action is consistent with self-generation. We discuss these findings with reference to the proposed purpose of sensory attenuation as a means of enhancing the salience of unexpected external events.

Discriminating between self- and externally generated sensation

Whenever we move, speak or otherwise perform an action the resulting changes to our body and the environment are detected by our sensory systems. Under normal circumstances we recognize these sensations as the consequences of our actions and are able to distinguish them from similar sensations that are generated externally. We are unlikely to mistake the sound of another person talking for our own voice, and we have no difficulty distinguishing between movements we make ourselves and movements that are passively applied to our body by external forces. This ability to perceive our own actions as distinct from other people's is an important part of our perception of ourselves as a single unified self, capable of willed action, and is probably crucial to our functioning as a social animal. The ability to discriminate between self- and externally generated sensory input is also thought to play a role in some of the more fundamental functions of our sensory and motor systems.

The earliest evidence for such a role came from the investigation of eye movements. When we move our eye the image of the world on our retina also moves, and yet we do not perceive the world to move. This is not simply because we have an expectation that the world will remain stable: as Descartes observed in his *Treatise of Man* (1664), tapping on the side of the eye with a fingertip generates an illusion of motion in the opposite direction, exactly as one would expect to occur during an eye movement. In the nineteenth century, inspired by Descartes' observations, Helmholtz (1867) proposed that during normal eye movements the expected shift in the retinal image is compensated for in perception according to the 'effort of will' required to generate the movement. A century later, two separate studies both published in the same year proposed a model for this compensation (Sperry, 1950; von Holst and Mittelstaedt, 1950). According to von Holst's 'principle of re-afference', when the motor areas of the brain generate a motor command signal to move the eyes they also send a copy of the command to the visual areas. This 'efference copy' is used to generate a prediction of the change to the visual input that will result from the eye movement (termed the 'corollary discharge' by Sperry). This predicted shift in the visual input is then reversed and applied to the actual visual input at an early stage of processing, cancelling the real shift in the retinal image with the result that a stable percept of the world is maintained.

The illusory movement observed by Descartes, Helmholtz and others when tapping on the side of the eye has a clear interpretation under von Holst's model: the pressure applied by the finger causes a movement of the eye, but because this movement is not generated by the motor areas controlling the eye muscles an appropriate efference copy is not sent to the visual areas and the resulting retinal shift is not compensated for. As a result the world appears to move in the opposite direction to the applied force.

Subsequent research has confirmed a role for efference copy in visual perception (e.g. Mach, 1885; Kornmuller, 1930; Mack and Bachant, 1969; Stevens *et al.*, 1976) although a number of findings suggest that it may be only one of several mechanisms involved in maintaining visual stability (Bridgeman *et al.*, 1975; Matin *et al.*, 1982; Grusser *et al.*, 1987; Pelz and Hayhoe, 1995). Nonetheless, the principle proposed by von Holst and Sperry of predicting the sensory consequences of action has been highly influential. Modern formulations of this theory (illustrated in Figure 16.1) include a forward model: an internal representation of the body and environment that is used to predict the consequences of a motor command (Jordan and Rumelhart, 1992; Miall and Wolpert, 1996).

The predictions generated by forward models also have a number of other proposed uses within sensory and motor systems. A prediction of the way in which a motor command will change the state of the body and the environment is thought to underlie anticipatory motor control: for example, maintaining posture (Gahery and Massion, 1981; Massion, 1992) and generating appropriate grip forces when manipulating objects (Johansson and Cole, 1992; Flanagan and Wing, 1997). A prediction of the sensory feedback resulting from a motor command may not only underlie perceptual stability as in Von Holst's model, but also be used in mental simulation (Sirigu *et al.*, 1996), in context estimation, and to compensate for inaccuracies and delays in sensory feedback (for a review see Davidson and Wolpert, 2005).

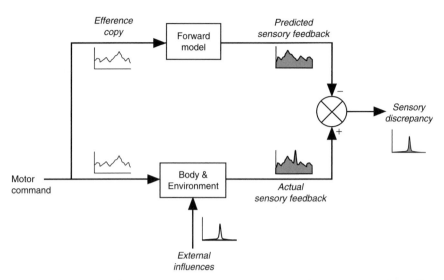

Figure 16.1 Distinguishing between one's own actions and external events. On the basis of efference copy, a forward model predicts the sensory feedback that will result from a planned action. The actual sensory feedback will reflect the sum of self- and externally generated changes to the body and environment. Subtracting the predicted from the actual sensory input reveals an estimate of the sensory feedback due to external influences.

Sensory cancellation of tactile sensation

As well as maintaining perceptual stability, it has been suggested that a cancellation mechanism of the kind illustrated in Figure 16.1 could also filter sensory input in order to help detect unexpected changes in our environment. By subtracting a proportion of the predicted sensory input from the actual input at an early stage of processing, self-generated sensations could be attenuated, thereby enhancing the salience of unexpected external events. An everyday example of such attenuation may be found in the perception of tickle. It is a common experience that it is hard to tickle oneself, and empirical studies have confirmed that a self-generated tickle is perceived as less intense than an identical stimulus imposed externally (Weiskrantz *et al.*, 1971; Claxton, 1975; Blakemore *et al.*, 1998b).

Several recent studies have shown that this phenomenon is not limited to tickling, but applies to the sense of touch in general. In a study by Shergill *et al.* (2003), a constant force was applied to a subject's finger by a torque motor; subjects were then instructed to reproduce the force they had just felt by pressing with a finger of the other hand. Subjects consistently overestimated the force required (Figure 16.2, filled circles), implying that the sensation of force in the passive finger was perceived as substantially weaker when it was self-generated than when it was externally applied.

This effect is not simply due to a failure of memory: the same subjects accurately reproduced the target force when they controlled the torque motor output with a joystick

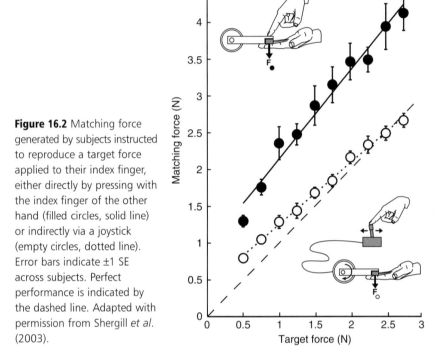

Figure 16.2 Matching force generated by subjects instructed to reproduce a target force applied to their index finger, either directly by pressing with the index finger of the other hand (filled circles, solid line) or indirectly via a joystick (empty circles, dotted line). Error bars indicate ±1 SE across subjects. Perfect performance is indicated by the dashed line. Adapted with permission from Shergill *et al.* (2003).

(Figure 16.2, empty circles). In this situation the active hand is not generating the force directly, but instead the movement of the hand is translated into a force via the torque motor. A study investigating the control of grip force (Blakemore *et al.*, 1998a) has shown that in this unusual situation predictive mechanisms are not employed. When one hand pushes on an object gripped in the other hand a precise anticipatory modulation of grip force is seen. However, when the force on the gripped object is instead controlled indirectly via a joystick, grip force modulation ceases to be predictive. In Shergill *et al.* (2003), the absence of attenuation when subjects reproduced the target force via the joystick is consistent with a similar failure of prediction.

Sensory prediction deficits in schizophrenia

The force-matching task described above has subsequently been used to test sensory prediction in patients with schizophrenia. As discussed, one role of sensory prediction may be to identify movements as either self- or externally generated. If the predicted sensory input associated with a movement matches the actual sensory input, the movement is labelled as one's own. However, if the predicted and actual sensory inputs are discordant, as when one's arm is passively moved by someone else, the movement is labelled as externally generated.

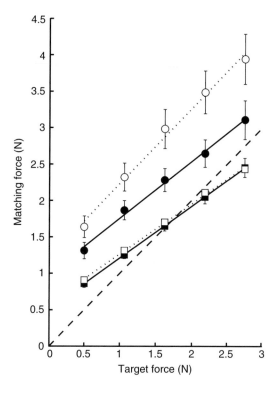

Figure 16.3 Matching force generated using the right index finger (circles) and joystick (squares) as a function of the externally generated target force, for patients (filled shapes) and healthy volunteers (empty shapes). Error bars indicate ±1 SE across subjects. Dashed line represents perfect performance. Adapted with permission from Shergill et al. (2005).

If the mechanism that predicts the sensory consequences of action was dysfunctional and produced inaccurate predictions, this could cause the misattribution of self-generated actions as externally-generated (Feinberg, 1978; Frith, 1992; Frith et al., 2000). Many patients with schizophrenia demonstrate just such a deficit, in which self-generated actions are experienced as being under outside control or self-generated speech is misperceived as an auditory hallucination (Schneider, 1959).

Shergill et al. (2005) used the force-matching task to directly test the hypothesis that patients with schizophrenia are defective in predicting the sensory consequences of their actions. Patients reproduced external forces substantially more accurately than age-matched control subjects (Figure 16.3), implying that the normal attenuation of the self-generated sensation was reduced in the schizophrenic patients. This study therefore provides strong evidence for a dysfunctional predictive mechanism in schizophrenia. As discussed above, efference copy signals can be used to generate both sensory and state predictions. State predictions are responsible for anticipatory motor control, which does not appear to be affected in schizophrenia (e.g. Delevoye-Turrell et al., 2003). The deficit therefore seems to be specific to the sensory prediction of the consequences of action, as it is this sensory prediction that is implicated in both sensory attenuation and identification of self-action.

Tactile attenuation is the result of a temporally tuned predictive mechanism

The mechanism of tactile attenuation has been further investigated by two studies which examined the perception of self-generated taps made by one finger on another. In Bays *et al.* (2005), subjects used their right index finger to tap a force sensor mounted above, but not in contact with, their left index finger. When a motor generated a tap on the left finger synchronous with the right tap, simulating contact between the fingers, the sensation of force in the left finger was attenuated compared to the same tap experienced during rest. By delaying or advancing the left tap relative to the active right tap, the time-course of this attenuation was mapped out, revealing a roughly symmetrical and relatively broad period of attenuation centered on the precise time at which the action would normally cause a tactile sensation (Figure 16.4A).

There are interesting parallels between the results of this study and the findings of a grip force study which also investigated force pulses (Johansson and Westling, 1988).

Figure 16.4 (A) Perceived magnitude of a tap made by the right index finger on the left as a function of the asynchrony between right finger contact and the tap on the left finger. Positive asynchrony indicates that right finger contact occurs first (i.e. the tap is delayed). Perceived magnitude was assessed by comparison with a reference tap delivered at rest. Adapted with permission from Bays *et al.* (2005). **(B)** Anticipatory modulation of grip force when dropping a ball into a grasped cup. Average load force (top) and grip force (bottom) on trials when the ball lands in the cup (dotted line) or is prevented from doing so (solid line). Abscissa shows time relative to the first peak in the mean load force due to impact (dashed line). Adapted with permission from Johansson and Westling (1988).

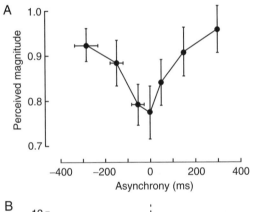

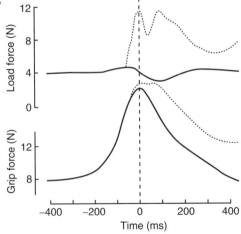

In this previous study, subjects dropped a ball from one hand into a cup supported in a precision grip by the other hand. The initial impact of the ball in the cup generated a brief force pulse similar to the taps used as test stimuli in the current study (dotted line, Figure 16.4B top). To prevent the cup from slipping out of their grasp as a result of the impact, subjects increased their grip force around the time of contact. Occasionally, the experimenter prevented the dropped ball from hitting the cup, revealing a purely antici-patory component of the grip force modulation. The time-course of this grip force increase (solid line, Figure 4B bottom) bears a number of similarities to the time-course of attenuation seen in the current study: it has a similar temporal width, is roughly symmet-rical, and is centered on the expected time of the initial force peak. These similarities are consistent with the hypothesis that tactile attenuation, like grip force modulation, depends on a prediction of the consequences of action generated by a forward model. In both cases the time profile is considerably broader than the actual duration of the force pulse. This could reflect inaccuracy or uncertainty of the internal model in predicting the time of the contact event, or a 'safety margin' built into the attenuation and grip force systems to allow for the possibility of a prediction error.

While the results of the psychophysical studies of attenuation described above are consistent with a predictive mechanism, they are equally consistent with a reconstructive or postdictive mechanism. A postdictive mechanism is one in which the percept of a sensory event is constructed from sensory information received around the time of the event (Dennett and Kinsbourne, 1992; Eagleman and Sejnowski, 2000; Rao *et al.*, 2001). In this mechanism the original sensory input is available for a period after the event and its processing can depend substantially on other events that occur in close temporal proximity. Bays *et al.* (2006) found strong evidence to suggest that attenuation of self-generated tactile sensation results from a predictive, not postdictive, mechanism. When one finger made a tapping movement above a finger of the other hand, sensation in the passive finger was attenuated only when contact was expected between the fingers. Furthermore, the level of attenuation observed when contact was expected was the same whether or not the contact actually occurred. These results are inconsistent with a post-dictive mechanism, which would have access to the actual sensory feedback in determin-ing the level of attenuation, and hence confirm that tactile attenuation results from a prediction of the sensory consequences of action.

Here we conduct two new experiments to examine in more detail the mechanism underlying tactile attenuation. In addition we perform a meta-analysis of data from a number of studies that have used the force-matching task.

Experiment 1: Spatial and magnitude influences on attenuation

A previous study of predictive motor control has shown that accurate prediction requires a natural correspondence between actions and their sensory consequences (Blakemore *et al.*, 1998a). Two robot arms were used to simulate holding an object between the hands. As with a real object, when subjects tried to move the object with their left hand it caused a force to be transmitted to the right hand. Subjects generated an anticipatory increase in grip force in the right hand to prevent the object from slipping. For the simulation of a real object to be complete, force feedback must in turn be transmitted back to the left hand, resisting its movement. When the experimenters changed the gain of this force feedback, making the context less consistent with a real object, the anticipatory grip-force response was diminished. This suggests that the motor prediction underlying grip-force modulation depends on a realistic relationship between force input and output. Similarly, predictive tactile attenuation may require a realistic correspondence between force-generation and sensation.

To investigate this possibility, we conducted an experiment in which subjects reproduced target forces applied to their finger by pressing through a virtual object, simulated by two torque motors. This allowed the force generated by the active right finger to be dissociated from the force delivered to the passive left finger. We used this dissociation firstly to manipulate the spatial co-alignment between active and passive fingers. If predictive attenuation requires a realistic spatial correspondence between force input and output, introducing a horizontal separation between the fingers should decrease the level of attenuation observed in the matching task. Secondly, we manipulated the gain: doubling or halving the force transmitted from the active finger to the passive finger. If predictive attenuation requires that the force generated by the active finger be equivalent to the force experienced in the passive finger, adjusting the gain will reduce the level of attenuation.

Methods

After providing written informed consent, 16 right-handed subjects (nine male, seven female, aged 18–40 years) participated in the experiment. The experimental protocol was approved by a local ethics committee. Each subject rested his or her left index finger in a moulded support. A force sensor (Nano-17 6-axis F/T sensor, ATI Inc.) rested on the tip of the finger at the end of a lever attached to a torque motor (Maxon Motors UK, Model RE35; geared in ratio 1:4.8). The motor was fitted with a rotary optical encoder (Incremental Encoders Direct Ltd, Model SA40). To start each trial the torque motor applied a constant target force to the tip of the subject's index finger for 3 s. Following an auditory go-signal, subjects were required to reproduce the force they had just felt by pressing with the index finger of the other hand. After 3 s an auditory stop-signal was given to end the trial. Each subject completed five consecutive experimental conditions in a pseudorandom order, each consisting of fifty trials: ten trials each of five target forces in the range 1–3 N.

Subjects generated the matching force on their left index finger indirectly, via a virtual link between two torque motors. Condition 1 was designed to simulate the direct generation of force as closely as possible. In order to produce the matching force, subjects pressed with their right index finger on a second force sensor situated directly above the first (Figure 16.5A). This force (recorded online at 1000 Hz and smoothed with a 15-point mean filter) was transmitted to the left index finger by the lower torque motor. Because the surface of the fingertip yields under pressure, applying a force led to a small downward deflection of the lower lever, which was recorded by the rotary encoder fitted

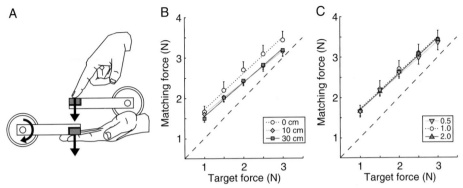

Figure 16.5 (A) Schematic of the experimental apparatus. Forces applied to the upper force sensor were transmitted with a variable gain to the left index finger via the lower torque motor. The upper torque motor could be moved in a direction lateral to the subject to introduce a spatial separation between the active and passive fingers. **(B)** Mean matching force generated by subjects with lateral separations between active and passive fingers of 0 cm (empty circles), 10 cm (diamonds) and 30 cm (squares). **(C)** Mean matching force generated by subjects with gains of 0.5 (downward triangles), 1.0 (empty circles), and 2.0 (upward triangles). Error bars indicate ± 1 SE across subjects. Dashed line represents perfect performance.

to the lower torque motor. In order to maintain an accurate simulation of a virtual object between the fingers, the upper torque motor adjusted the position of the upper force sensor online so as to maintain a constant vertical distance between the force sensors. It was previously explained to subjects that there would be no physical object between the fingers but that forces they produced would be transmitted to the other finger via the computer.

Conditions 2 and 3 were identical to condition 1 except that the upper torque motor was re-positioned, so that during force generation the left and right fingertips were separated laterally by a distance of 10 cm (condition 2) or 30 cm (condition 3). Conditions 4 and 5 were again identical to condition 1 except that now we adjusted the gain relationship between the fingers, such that a 1 N force applied by the right finger resulted in a 0.5 N (condition 5) or a 2 N (condition 6) force on the left finger.

The matching force level generated on the passive finger was calculated for each trial by taking the mean force recorded by the lower force sensor between 2000 and 2500 ms after the go-signal.

Results

In order to investigate some of the parameters that might affect sensory attenuation, in this experiment we created a dissociation between force input and output. The control condition (condition 1) simulated as closely as possible direct force-generation by the right index finger on the left, as in Shergill *et al.* (2003). As in the previous study, subjects applied substantially more force than was required to reproduce the target force

(Figure 16.5B, empty circles). This greater matching force was perceived by subjects as equal to the target force because a proportion of the self-generated sensation was attenuated.

Having created a dissociation between force input and output we were able to investigate the effect of spatial separation on attenuation. Introducing a 10 or 30 cm lateral separation between the active right and passive left fingers resulted in a reduction in the matching force level compared to the control condition, implying a reduced level of attenuation (Figure 16.5B, filled shapes). A two-way analysis of variance (ANOVA) (separation distance × target force) revealed a significant effect of separation on matching force level [$F(2,30) = 5.5, p = 0.009$]. *Post hoc* tests found no significant differences between the 10 and 30 cm separations [$t(15) = 0.17, p = 0.87$] but significant differences of both from the no separation condition [$t(15) > 2.5, p < 0.023$]. However, subjects still significantly overestimated the matching force required at both 10 and 30 cm separations [$t(15) > 3.66, p < 0.003$], implying that attenuation was not entirely abolished.

The effect on attenuation of varying the gain relationship between the fingers is shown in Figure 16.5C. In three conditions the gain was adjusted such that each newton of force applied by the right finger resulted in a 0.5, 1 or 2 N force on the left finger. A two-way ANOVA (gain × target force) revealed no significant effect of gain on matching force level [$F(2,30) = 0.23, p = 0.79$].

Discussion

It has been suggested that the attenuation of self-generated sensation described in this chapter may have evolved in order to increase the salience of externally generated sensation. To be effective therefore the underlying mechanism must be able to correctly identify when two parts of the body are interacting and apply attenuation only in such situations. This judgment is likely to be based on a range of factors, some of which we have attempted to identify in Experiment 1. In order to do this we simulated normal force-generation using a virtual link between two torque motors. Substantial attenuation was still observed even though subjects were made aware that there was no physical object between the fingers. However, when we introduced a lateral spatial separation between the fingers, the level of sensory attenuation was reduced. This suggests that a spatial co-alignment between force production and sensation may be one of the factors by which sensations are identified as self-generated. When force production and sensation are not aligned it reduces the confidence with which the sensation can be identified as self- rather than externally generated and so less attenuation is applied. Although infrequent, spatial misalignments in force of the size examined in this study can occur during manipulation of large objects, and this may explain why the attenuation is reduced but not abolished.

Probably the clearest evidence that two parts of the body are interacting is a precise correspondence between the force generated by one body part and the force felt in the other at the same moment. Consistent with this, it has been shown that introducing a temporal asynchrony between activity and tactile sensation reduces sensory attenuation (Blakemore *et al.*, 1999; Bays *et al.*, 2005). However, in this study we have demonstrated that altering the gain relationship between the fingers does not affect the level of attenuation. Specifically, doubling or halving the force transmitted from the active finger to the passive finger did not alter the extent to which sensation in the passive finger was attenuated. This result suggests that while temporal correlation between force generation and sensation may be required to elicit sensory attenuation, an equal magnitude of force does not appear to be important. This is perhaps to be expected: when one digit applies a force on another through an object, the relationship between the force applied and the resulting sensory input can vary substantially depending on the shape and consistency of the object, the surface area in contact with the passive digit, and the angle at which the active digit meets the surface.

The amount by which sensation in the passive finger was attenuated did not vary between the different gain conditions despite substantial differences in the force generated by the active finger. We have suggested that sensory attenuation may result from a cancellation process, in which a proportion of the predicted sensory input is removed from the actual input. If this is the case, the current finding suggests that the predictive mechanism must be capable of rapidly adapting to new gain relationships between motor output and sensory input in order to continue generating an accurate prediction. Alternatively it may be that sensory attenuation results from a gating process, in which sensory sites receiving self-generated input are identified and a fixed attenuation is applied to all sensory input from those sites.

Experiment 2: Is tactile attenuation the result of a gating or a cancellation mechanism?

During active movement of a digit or limb, the ability to detect small cutaneous stimuli is reduced in the moving body part (Angel and Malenka, 1982; Chapman et al., 1987) as is the perceived intensity of suprathreshold stimuli (Milne et al., 1988). This suppression or 'gating' of tactile input begins prior to movement onset and indeed prior to muscle activation as measured by electromyography (Williams et al., 1998), suggesting a mechanism based on efference copy (although see Williams and Chapman, 2002, for a discussion of the possible role of backward masking). The theory that sensory gating can be triggered by descending signals from motor planning areas is supported by a recent study by Voss et al. (2006). Pulses of transcranial magnetic stimulation (TMS) over primary motor cortex were used to delay planned finger movements at the motor output stage. Sensory suppression of cutaneous stimuli was observed at the intended time of movement, despite this being substantially prior to the actual onset of the movement.

While movement-related gating filters out sensations resulting from voluntary movement, it also removes externally generated sensations that are unrelated to the movement. By attenuating the sense of touch in parts of the body which expect self-input, this mechanism may enhance the relative salience of external stimuli elsewhere on the body. However, sensory gating cannot assist in detecting external tactile stimuli against a background of self-generated sensation. An example of a situation in which this is relevant is reading Braille, in which unpredictable tactile stimuli (the Braille dots) must be detected against a self-generated background stimulation caused by pressing one's finger to the paper and moving it across the page.

In order to assess whether the tactile attenuation demonstrated in the force-matching paradigm reflects a gating or a cancellation process, we examined the perception of an electrical cutaneous stimulus delivered to a finger receiving a self-applied pressure. If the attenuation of the self-generated force is the result of a nonspecific sensory suppression similar to movement-related gating then the perceived intensity of the electrical stimulus should also be attenuated. In contrast, a cancellation mechanism should affect only the self-generated force and not the externally generated electrical stimulus.

Methods

Ten right-handed subjects (four male, six female, aged 20–31 years) participated in the experiment. As in the force-matching experiments, each subject rested his or her left index finger in a support beneath a force sensor at the end of a lever attached to a torque motor. The perceived intensity of brief cutaneous stimuli delivered to the finger was assessed while constant forces were applied to it through the force sensor. On alternating trials forces were either externally applied by the torque motor or self-applied by the subject pressing with the index finger of the other hand. Each subject completed eight trials under each of these conditions at each of three levels of applied force (1, 2 and 3 N, in a pseudorandom order). In the self-generated condition the target force and the currently applied force were displayed as horizontal bars on a computer monitor: subjects were instructed to press on their finger through the force sensor so as to maintain the bars at the same vertical position on the screen.

During each trial, brief electrical cutaneous pulses were delivered simultaneously to the tip of the left index finger and to a second reference site on the body. The electrical stimuli were generated by an electrical nerve stimulator (Stanmore stimulator, research device designed and developed by the medical physics department, UCL, London, UK) using adhesive electrode pads (Red Dot, 3M Healthcare), with the anode at the fingertip. All subjects reported that the sensation of the cutaneous pulses in the left index finger was localized at the tip, beneath the force sensor. The reference site was either the tip of the ring finger of the left hand (five subjects) or the left ankle (five subjects). The magnitude of the reference pulse was fixed for each subject at a comfortable level between 150 and 200% of the detection threshold (determined prior to the experiment), whereas stimulus magnitude in the index finger was varied.

Following each stimulation, subjects verbally reported at which location the cutaneous pulse had felt stronger. The perceived intensity of the cutaneous stimuli in the index finger relative to the reference site was assessed by finding the point of subjective equality (PSE): the stimulus magnitude in the index finger that was perceived as equal to the reference stimulus. Prior to the experiment, a baseline PSE was obtained over 40 pulse pairs with no force applied to the finger. During the experiment, five pulse pairs were applied sequentially on each trial, giving a total of 40 responses for each condition and force level.

The PSE was obtained using an adaptive logistic regression procedure, as follows. After each response, the stimulus magnitude and subject's response were pooled with the data from all previous stimulations under the same condition and force level. The pooled data were fitted online with a logistic function, according to a maximum-likelihood procedure. The next stimulus intensity for that condition and force level was then chosen from a uniform random distribution bounded by the 1 and 99% points on the fitted logistic curve. This procedure limits the sampling range to stimulus intensities that will be most informative in estimating the PSE. The PSE is given by the 50% point on the logistic curve: the stimulus intensity at which the pulse in the left index finger is perceptually equal to the reference pulse and hence the subject is equally likely to make either response.

If attenuation of self-generated force is the result of a gating process then it will also attenuate externally generated sensations that occur in the same part of the body at the same time. The perceived intensity of the electrical stimuli in the left index finger will therefore be reduced when a self-generated force is applied to it. This will be observed as an increase in the PSE in the self-generated condition compared to the externally generated condition. In contrast, if attenuation results from a cancellation process it will affect only the self-generated force and not the externally generated electrical stimulus. In this case we will see no difference in PSE between conditions.

Results

Points of subjective equality estimated for each condition and force level are plotted in Figure 16.6, as a percentage of the baseline PSE for each subject. The perceived intensity of the cutaneous stimulation in the finger, as measured by the PSE, did not change significantly from baseline when forces were applied to the finger, either when the force was externally generated by the torque motor (empty circles) or self-generated by the subject

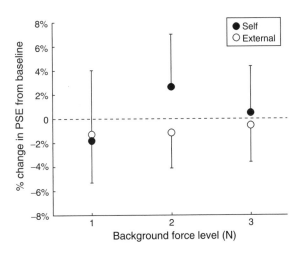

Figure 16.6 Perceived intensity of electrical stimuli in the index finger as a function of background force level, with an externally applied force (empty circles) or a self-generated force (filled circles). Perceived intensity is expressed as a percentage change in the point of subjective equality from a condition in which no force was applied.

[filled circles; paired *t*-tests: $t(9)$ <0.61, $p > 0.55$]. A mixed model ANOVA (condition × reference site × force level) of the normalized PSE revealed no significant effect of condition [$F(1,8) = 0.16$, $p = 0.70$], reference site [$F(1,8) = 0.19$, $p = 0.67$], or force level [$F(2,16) = 0.84$, $p = 0.45$], and no significant interactions ($p > 0.57$).

Discussion

The studies described in this chapter have shown that self-generated tactile stimulation is attenuated in comparison to identical external stimulation. This could result from a gating process similar to the mechanism that attenuates tactile sensation in a moving body part. Movement-related gating involves a general suppression of all tactile input from the active effector, with the result that stimuli unrelated to the movement, such as electrical cutaneous stimuli, are also attenuated. For example, a recent study by Voss *et al.* (2006), using an estimation technique identical to that described here, found that active movement of a stimulated finger increased PSE by 169% (SE 28).

In contrast, we observed no attenuation of electrical stimuli during application of a self-generated force: the mean increase in PSE when a self-generated force was applied to the stimulated finger was less than 1% (SE 3.5). This suggests that the tactile attenuation investigated in this chapter is not due to a nonspecific gating mechanism. Rather, these results are consistent with the action of a cancellation mechanism, which selectively attenuates only sensations that are predictable on the basis of the motor command signal.

A meta-analysis of results from the force-matching task

Since the force-matching task was first described in Shergill *et al.* (2003), we have conducted many experiments involving variations on that simple task. In the majority of these experiments at least one experimental condition was identical to the 'direct' condition in the original study, in that the subject reproduced a range of target forces applied to his or her resting left index finger by pressing directly with the finger of the other hand. A total of 107 subjects, consisting of participants in the studies described in this chapter and a number of unpublished pilot experiments, completed a block of 40 or more trials of this basic force-matching task, differing only in the range of target forces tested. This presents the opportunity to conduct a meta-analysis with enhanced statistical power, allowing us to accurately estimate the amount by which self-generated sensation is attenuated and to what extent attenuation varies between individuals.

Figure 16.7 shows the average matching force generated by all 107 subjects as a function of target force. As expected, subjects produced an exaggerated matching force at all levels of the target force tested, implying that the sensation of the self-generated matching force was attenuated so as to make it perceptually equal to the smaller target force. The results of the first force-matching study (Shergill *et al.*, 2003) suggested that the difference between matching and target forces might involve a change in slope as well as intercept. However, in this much larger data set (which includes the previous results) it appears that the amount by which the matched force exceeds the target force (the 'excess force') is approximately constant for all target forces. A linear regression analysis revealed a

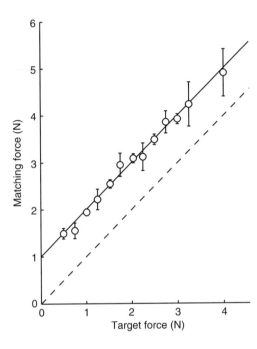

Figure 16.7 Mean performance of 107 subjects on the force-matching task described by Shergill et al. (2003). Subject-generated matching force as a function of externally generated target force (mean ± SE across subjects). Dashed line represents perfect performance. Solid line indicates the average line of best fit assuming a constant difference between matching and target force for each subject. Each subject was tested on five to 10 target forces over the course of 40–80 trials.

significant intercept [$t(106) = 12.0, p < 0.001$] but a slope parameter that did not differ significantly from unity [$t(106) = 1.32, p = 0.19$].

Figure 16.8 displays the variation in mean excess force across subjects. The data were well fitted by a normal distribution (Kolmogorov–Smirnoff test, $p = 0.12$) with a positive skew (skewness = 1.16). The mean excess force was 1.00 N (SD 0.87). Although a small number of subjects showed no or very weak attenuation (11% of sample produced mean excess force < 0.2 N), there does not appear to be any substantial bimodality to the distribution, and so the performance of these subjects is best explained by natural variation

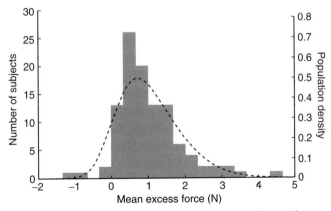

Figure 16.8 Histogram of the mean difference between matching and target forces across a sample of 107 subjects. Dotted line indicates the skew-normal distribution that best fits the data.

around the population mean. Only four subjects produced matching forces on average less than the target force.

In summary, the results of this meta-analysis suggest that the sensation of self-generated force is attenuated by a fixed amount, on average equivalent to a 1 N reduction in the perceived force. However, there is no a priori reason to believe that a constant difference in force measured on a newton scale corresponds to a constant subtraction in the perceived magnitude of the sensation. For example, it may be that the difference in perceived intensity between a 3 N and a 2 N force is smaller than the difference between a 2 N and a 1 N force. If this is the case, the fixed level of attenuation we have observed (1 N at all force levels) would actually reflect an attenuation in perceived intensity that varies with force level.

We therefore tested the perception of the constant forces used in the force-matching experiment in a group of 10 subjects (five male, five female, aged 22–32 years) using open magnitude scaling. Forces in the range 1–7 N were presented to subjects in the same way as target forces in the force-matching task. Subjects were instructed to rate the intensity of each stimulus with a number (no particular scale was specified). Each subject's responses were subsequently scaled to the range 0–1 so that means across subjects could be calculated. Results are shown in Figure 16.9.

Subjects' gave forces separated by 1 N significantly different intensity ratings throughout the tested range [$t(9) > 3.0$, $p < 0.02$] implying that the 1 N attenuation observed on average in the matching task is large enough to produce perceptible differences in the intensity of self- and externally generated forces. The magnitude rating was found to be approximately linearly related to the force in newtons over the range 1–5 N (dotted line in Figure 16.9), although the rated intensity began to saturate at higher force levels and a significantly better fit was achieved overall by a second-order polynomial [$t(9) = 7.9$, $p < 0.001$; solid line].

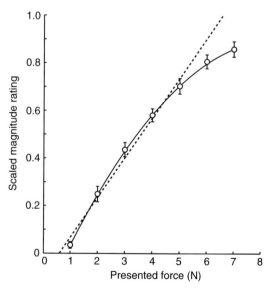

Figure 16.9 Perceived magnitude of constant forces applied to the fingertip. Mean ± SE rating shown, with a second-order polynomial fit for all forces (solid line) and a line of best fit for forces in the range 1–5 N (dotted line).

As the magnitude rating is roughly linearly related to force over the range tested in the force-matching task, we can conclude that the constant excess force observed in that task results from an approximately constant subtraction in the perceived intensity of the self-generated force.

General discussion

Self-generated tactile stimulation is perceived as weaker than the same stimulus applied by an external source. This phenomenon has been demonstrated, using a range of techniques, in the sensation of tickle (Weiskrantz *et al.*, 1971; Blakemore *et al.*, 1999), constant pressure (Shergill *et al.*, 2003), and brief taps (Bays *et al.*, 2005). The underlying mechanism may be similar to the cancellation model proposed by von Holst (1950) and Sperry (1950) to account for the stability of the visual scene during eye movements. According to this model, the expected sensory input is predicted on the basis of efference copy and subtracted from the actual sensory input at an early stage of processing. Our investigations have confirmed that tactile attenuation depends on a prediction of contact between parts of the body (Bays *et al.*, 2006) that is precise in terms of both time (Bays *et al.*, 2005) and location (Blakemore *et al.*, 1999).

Clearly in tactile attenuation the predicted input is not subtracted in its entirety; otherwise we would not be able to feel our own touch at all. In this chapter we have found evidence to suggest that the quantity of sensation subtracted from self-generated touch is constant, in the sense that it does not vary with the intensity of the self-generated input. This explains both the constant excess force produced at different target force levels in the force-matching task, and the fact that artificially changing the gain between force input and output does not affect performance in that task. Note that this result does not contradict our finding in Experiment 2 that tactile attenuation specifically affects self-generated forces. A gating mechanism, such as movement-related suppression, that does not discriminate between self- and externally generated sensation may nonetheless attenuate the sensory input in a way that varies with stimulus intensity. Similarly, a cancellation mechanism that specifically affects self-generated input may nonetheless attenuate all self-generated input equally, irrespective of intensity. This appears to be the case for tactile attenuation.

We have found that the level of attenuation can be altered by introducing a spatial misalignment between force production and sensation. This suggests that tactile attenuation is modulated by the degree to which the current context is consistent with self-generation. Spatial co-alignment of force is likely to be just one of many factors that interact in determining the level of attenuation. In Experiment 1, in order to limit our investigation to the single factor of spatial separation, we ensured that subjects were always aware (and could see) that there was no real object between their hands: only the tactile characteristics of an object were simulated. It is possible that the effects of spatial misalignment we observed might not have been found if the visual cues associated with a real object had also been present, or if the subjects had been blindfolded and led to believe they were interacting with a real object. A further question concerns adaptation: given sufficient interaction with the virtual object under a spatial misalignment, would the consistency of the relationship between force input and output eventually cause attenuation to return to normal levels? To date we have found no evidence for this kind of adaptation in tactile attenuation, although a comparable effect has been observed in grip-force modulation (Witney and Wolpert, 2003).

As discussed previously in this chapter, theoretical models of sensory prediction include a forward model, an internal representation of the body and environment that is used to transform planned motor commands into predicted sensory consequences. This forward model cannot be fixed, but rather its parameters must be updated whenever the environment in which we are operating changes. From this viewpoint, the modulation of tactile attenuation by a factor such as spatial co-alignment indicates that this factor is taken into account in determining the correct parameters of the forward model. Precisely how these parameters are updated is currently unknown, but according to one proposal, the MOSAIC model (Haruno et al., 2001), predictions made by multiple competing forward models are compared to sensory feedback, and the forward model with the smallest prediction error is selected to represent the current context. This model has the theoretical advantage that it can be extended to describe certain aspects of social interaction: a system of competing forward models that attempts to predict the observed behaviour of other people could potentially underlie action imitation and even theory of mind (Wolpert et al., 2003). However, if we are indeed able to predict the sensory consequences of another person's action, this does not appear to lead to sensory attenuation. Shergill et al. (2003) performed an experiment in which subjects took it in turns to press on each other's fingers, with the instruction to each reproduce the last force they had felt. The result was a rapid escalation of force, suggesting that while the forces subjects applied themselves were attenuated, the forces applied to them by the other participant were not.

It has been suggested that the purpose of sensory attenuation is to enhance the salience of unexpected external events. Consistent with this proposal, in this chapter we have shown that tactile attenuation specifically affects self-generated input, leaving unchanged externally generated sensations in the same part of the body. However, despite its theoretical appeal, there is currently no direct evidence to support the salience hypothesis. While it is clear that attenuation takes place, fundamental questions as to its purpose remain to be answered.

References

Angel, R. W. and Malenka, R. C. (1982) Velocity-dependent suppression of cutaneous sensitivity during movement. *Experimental Neurology*, 77, 266–274.

Bays, P. M., Wolpert, D. M. and Flanagan, J. R. (2005) Perception of the consequences of self-action is temporally tuned and event driven. *Current Biology*, 15, 1125–1128.

Bays, P. M., Flanagan, J. R. and Wolpert, D. M. (2006) Attenuation of self-generated tactile sensations is predictive, not postdictive. *PLoS Biology*, 4, e28.

Blakemore, S. J., Goodbody, S. J. and Wolpert, D. M. (1998a) Predicting the consequences of our own actions: the role of sensorimotor context estimation. *Journal of Neuroscience*, 18, 7511–7518.

Blakemore, S. J., Wolpert, D. M. and Frith, C. D. (1998b) Central cancellation of self-produced tickle sensation. *Nature Neuroscience*, 1, 635–640.

Blakemore, S. J., Frith, C. D. and Wolpert, D. M. (1999) Spatio-temporal prediction modulates the perception of self-produced stimuli. *Journal of Cognitive Neuroscience*, **11**, 551–559.

Bridgeman, B., Hendry, D. and Stark, L. (1975) Failure to detect displacement of the visual world during saccadic eye movements. *Vision Research*, **15**, 719–722.

Chapman, C. E., Bushnell, M. C., Miron, D., Duncan, G. H. and Lund, J. P. (1987) Sensory perception during movement in man. *Experimental Brain Research*, **68**, 516–524.

Claxton, G. (1975) Why can't we tickle ourselves? *Perception and Motor Skills*, **41**, 335–338.

Davidson, P. R. and Wolpert, D. M. (2005) Widespread access to predictive models in the motor system: a short review. *Journal of Neural Engineering*, **2**, S313–319.

Delevoye-Turrell, Y., Giersch, A. and Danion, J. M. (2003) Abnormal sequencing of motor actions in patients with schizophrenia: evidence from grip force adjustments during object manipulation. *American Journal of Psychiatry*, **160**, 134–141.

Dennett, D. and Kinsbourne, M. (1992) Time and the observer. *Behavioral and Brain Sciences*, **15**, 183–247.

Descartes, R. (1664) *Treatise of Man*. Prometheus Books, Amherst, NY.

Eagleman, D. M. and Sejnowski, T. J. (2000) Motion integration and postdiction in visual awareness. *Science*, **287**, 2036–2038.

Feinberg, I. (1978) Efference copy and corollary discharge: implications for thinking and its disorders. *Schizophrenia Bulletin*, **4**, 636–640.

Flanagan, J. R. and Wing, A. M. (1997) The role of internal models in motion planning and control: evidence from grip force adjustments during movements of hand-held loads. *Journal of Neuroscience*, **17**, 1519–1528.

Frith, C. D. (1992) *The Cognitive Neuropsychology of Schizophrenia*. Erlbaum, Hillsdale, NJ.

Frith, C. D., Blakemore, S. and Wolpert, D. M. (2000) Explaining the symptoms of schizophrenia: abnormalities in the awareness of action. *Brain Research, Brain Research Reviews*, **31**, 357–363.

Gahery, Y. and Massion, J. (1981) Co-ordination between posture and movement. *Trends in Neurosciences*, **4**, 199–202.

Grusser, O. J., Krizic, A. and Weiss, L. R. (1987) Afterimage movement during saccades in the dark. *Vision Research*, **27**, 215–226.

Haruno, M., Wolpert, D. M. and Kawato, M. (2001) Mosaic model for sensorimotor learning and control. *Neural Computation*, **13**, 2201–2220.

Helmholtz, H. (1867) *Handbuch der Physiologischen Optik*. Voss, Leipzig.

Johansson, R. S. and Westling, G. (1988) Programmed and triggered actions to rapid load changes during precision grip. *Experimental Brain Research*, **71**, 72–86.

Johansson, R. S. and Cole, K. J. (1992) Sensory-motor coordination during grasping and manipulative actions. *Current Opinion in Neurobiology*, **2**, 815–823.

Jordan, M. I. and Rumelhart, D. E. (1992) Forward models: supervised learning with a distal teacher. *Cognitive Science*, **16**, 307–354.

Kornmuller, A. E. (1930) Eine experimentalle Anesthesie der aussen Augenmuskeln am Menschen und ihre Auswirkungen. *Journal für Psychologie und Neurologie*, **41**, 354–366

Mach, E. (1885) *Analysis of Sensations*. New York, Dover

Mack, A. and Bachant, J. (1969) Perceived movement of the afterimage during eye movements. *Perception and Psychophysics*, **6**, 379–384.

Massion, J. (1992) Movement, posture and equilibrium: interaction and coordination. *Progress in Neurobiology*, **38**, 35–56.

Matin, L., Picoult, E., Stevens, J. K., Edwards, M. W., Jr., Young, D. and MacArthur, R. (1982) Oculoparalytic illusion: visual-field dependent spatial mislocalizations by humans partially paralyzed with curare. *Science*, **216**, 198–201.

Miall, R. C. and Wolpert, D. M. (1996) Forward models for physiological motor control. *Neural Networks*, **9**, 1265–1279.

Milne, R. J., Aniss, A. M., Kay, N. E. and Gandevia, S. C. (1988) Reduction in perceived intensity of cutaneous stimuli during movement: a quantitative study. *Experimental Brain Research*, **70**, 569–576.

Pelz, J. B. and Hayhoe, M. M. (1995) The role of exocentric reference frames in the perception of visual direction. *Vision Research*, **35**, 2267–2275.

Rao, R. P., Eagleman, D. M. and Sejnowski, T. J. (2001) Optimal smoothing in visual motion perception. *Neural Computation*, **13**, 1243–1253.

Schneider, K. (1959) *Clinical Psychopathology*. Grune & Stratton, New York.

Shergill, S. S., Bays, P. M., Frith, C. D. and Wolpert, D. M. (2003) Two eyes for an eye: the neuroscience of force escalation. *Science*, **301**, 187.

Shergill, S. S., Samson, G., Bays, P. M., Frith, C. D. and Wolpert, D. M. (2005) Evidence for sensory prediction deficits in schizophrenia. *American Journal of Psychiatry*, **162**, 2384–2386.

Sirigu, A., Duhamel, J. R., Cohen, L., Pillon, B., Dubois, B. and Agid, Y. (1996) The mental representation of hand movements after parietal cortex damage. *Science*, **273**, 1564–1568.

Sperry, R. W. (1950) Neural basis of the spontaneous optokinetic response produced by visual inversion. *Journal of Comparative Physiology and Psychology*, **32**, 482–489.

Stevens, J. K., Emerson, R. C., Gerstein, G. L., Kallos, T., Neufeld, G. R., Nichols, C. W. and Rosenquist, A. C. (1976) Paralysis of the awake human: visual perceptions. *Vision Research*, **16**, 93–98.

von Holst, E. and Mittelstaedt, H. (1950) Das Reafferenzprincip. *Naturwissenschaft*, **37**, 464–476.

Voss, M., Ingram, J. N., Haggard, P. and Wolpert, D. M. (2006) Sensorimotor attenuation by central motor command signals in the absence of movement. *Nature Neuroscience*, **9**, 26–27.

Weiskrantz, L., Elliott, J. and Darlington, C. (1971) Preliminary observations on tickling oneself. *Nature*, **230**, 598.

Williams, S. R. and Chapman, C. E. (2002) Time course and magnitude of movement-related gating of tactile detection in humans. III. Effect of motor tasks. *Journal of Neurophysiology*, **88**, 1968–1979.

Williams, S. R., Shenasa, J. and Chapman, C. E. (1998) Time course and magnitude of movement-related gating of tactile detection in humans. I. Importance of stimulus location. *Journal of Neurophysiology*, **79**, 947–963.

Witney, A. G. and Wolpert, D. M. (2003) Spatial representation of predictive motor learning. *Journal of Neurophysiology*, **89**, 1837–1843.

Wolpert, D. M., Doya, K. and Kawato, M. (2003) A unifying computational framework for motor control and social interaction. *Philosophical Transactions of the Royal Society of London, B*, **358**, 593–602.

17

The self and its body: functional and neural signatures of body ownership

Manos Tsakiris

'Body ownership' refers to the special perceptual status of one's own body, the sense that bodily sensations are unique to one's self. We studied the functional and neural signatures of body ownership by controlling whether an external object was accepted as part of the body or not. Watching a rubber hand being touched synchronously as one's own unseen hand gives the experience that the rubber hand is part of one's body. Asynchronous stimulation serves as a control. A behavioral proxy of the 'rubber hand illusion' (RHI) is a drift in the perceived position of one's own hand towards the rubber hand. A series of experiments suggests that body ownership during the RHI arises as an interaction between multisensory perception and top-down influences originating from representations of the body's permanent structure. The brain processes that produce incorporation depend both on current sensory integration and also on top-down processes reflecting a pre-existing reference of the postural and visual features of one's own body. The right temporo-parietal junction may underpin the assimilation of novel multisensory signals to this pre-existing reference representation of one's own body. The effect of multisensory integration and recalibration of hand position, namely the experience of body ownership of the rubber hand, is correlated with activity in the right posterior insula. These structures may form a network that plays a fundamental role in linking current sensory stimuli to one's own body, and thus also in self-consciousness.

Sensorimotor basis of the self: the sense of body ownership and the sense of agency

Recent advances in research methods and experimental designs have enabled cognitive neurosciences to study the neurocognitive functions that underpin selfhood. A novel approach in the study of selfhood that emphasizes its sensorimotor basis was triggered by a radical re-conceptualization of the role of sensory and motor processes within cognition as a whole. The sensorimotor functions of the brain are no longer considered as low-level processes that are independent from higher functions such as self-awareness, agency and social cognition. Within this framework, recent neuroscientific research has grounded the self in embodied action (Knoblich et al., 2003), and placed the body at the interface between the self and the world leading to the generation of new 'sensorimotor' theories of cognition (Prinz, 1997; Hommel *et al.*, 2001; O'Regan and Noë, 2001) and selfhood (Frith, 1992; Paillard, 1999; Gallese *et al.*, 2004; Tsakiris and Haggard, 2005a).

In the present chapter, we consider a particular sense of self defined as the minimal sense of owning a body and the actions originating from that body. This relationship between the self and the body is usually taken for granted in life (e.g. "this is my hand I see before me"). However, the neurocognitive processes by which the body is linked to the self are not fully understood (Gillihan and Farah, 2005). Cognitive neuroscience has to explain why and how percepts of action and bodily states are so clearly and inexorably "mine". A distinction proposed by Gallagher has advanced our understanding of the phenomenology of the minimal sense of self that is the focus of the present paper. Sensory events related to one's own body (e.g. touch, proprioception) are said to be characterized by a sense of body ownership, and motor events generated voluntarily by one's own body (e.g. actions) are said to be characterized by a sense of control or agency (Gallagher, 2000). The precise conditions for body ownership and agency, and their functional relationship, remain unknown. By definition, the sense of agency seems to accompany only voluntary actions, whereas the sense of body ownership is present during voluntary action (e.g. "I am moving my hand"), but also during involuntary or passive movement (e.g. "I feel my hand moving") or even sensory stimulation alone (e.g. "I see my hand"). Several important consequences follow from this distinction between agency and body ownership.

First, in the case of voluntary movement, it is particularly difficult to distinguish between the sense of agency and the sense of body ownership, because one could argue that we have a sense of agency of the action and a sense of ownership of the moving limb. However, it is unclear whether in the case of voluntary action, we are dealing with 'ownership of body part', rather than with 'ownership of movement' or even 'ownership of action' (see also Marcel, 2003). The simple fact that agency requires volition, or by necessity a motor command, whereas body ownership does not, suggests an asymmetry between these two senses. This asymmetry may be underpinned by differences in their phenomenology, in their functional properties (i.e. type of information processing involved), and in their respective neural signatures.

In addition, the fact that during agentic actions we can refer to both ownership of action/movement but also to ownership of body part may confound the interpretation of empirical evidence. Voluntary action always involves an inseparable combination of efferent and afferent information, and it is therefore difficult to experimentally isolate the specific contributions of efferent and afferent signals to body awareness during voluntary action (Tsakiris *et al.*, 2005, 2006a). Previous experimental studies have confounded agency and body ownership, by focusing exclusively on awareness of voluntary movement (Sirigu *et al.*, 1999; van den Bos and Jeannerod, 2002; Farrer *et al.*, 2003). For example, Farrer *et al.* (2003) presented subjects with visual feedback of their own actions. The feedback was distorted to varying degrees by an angular bias. Farrer and colleagues found that the activity in the right posterior insula was correlated with the match between the performed and viewed movement, suggesting, according to the authors, that the insular cortex is related to the sense of agency (see also Farrer and Frith, 2002). However, one could ask whether the observed neural activity in the right posterior insula reflects sensorimotor or intersensory matching alone. If activity in the right posterior insula was coding the intersensory match between proprioception and vision alone, it would be wrong to conclude that this area underpins the sense of agency. Instead, it could be argued that this area, by coding intersensory match alone, is critically linked to the sense of body ownership that does not require the presence of efferent signals. Thus, previous studies may have failed to isolate the additional component due to agency, over and above body ownership.

Whereas there are numerous behavioral and neuroimaging studies investigating the processing of sensor-motor interactions during voluntary movement, there are far fewer studies investigating the sensory awareness of one's own body in the absence of the motoric sense of agency. The scientific study of body ownership is particularly difficult and it raises important methodological problems. It is difficult to study experimentally the sense of body ownership, simply because the body is "always there" (James, 1890), present with me. Classical experimental designs cannot isolate the sense of body owner-ship by direct manipulations which make the body present in one experimental condition but absent in another. Moreover, it is not clear why and how one should experience a sense of ownership over one's own body. Certainly, we do not experience an explicit sense of ownership over our bodies, in the same way that we experience ownership of external objects that belong to us, such as our house or clothes. We do not acquire a body, we are rather born embodied. We cannot decide to disown our body, and in fact the main reason why the body is so intrinsically linked to a basic sense of self lies in the observa-tion that, unlike other objects, the body is always present. Contrary to the perception of an object, which can be perceived from different perspectives or even cease to be perceived, we experience "the feeling of the same old body always there" (James, 1890/1981, p. 242). When I decide to write something, I do not need to look for my hand, in the same way that I have to look for a pen or a piece of paper. Does this permanent presence make the body special? Merleau-Ponty (1962, p. 90) wrote: "It is particularly true that an object is an object in so far it can be moved away from me, and ultimately disappear from my field of vision. Its presence is such that it entails a possible absence. Now the permanence of my own body is entirely different in kind … Its permanence is not a permanence in the world, but a permanence on my part." The fact that the body is always present suggests that body awareness is not like any other form of object awareness, because the body is an 'object' that normally never leaves me. Thus body ownership, apart from being different from the feeling of controlling one's own body, is also different from ownership or awareness or perception of external objects.

The need for separate neuroscientific accounts of agency and body ownership is also supported by the clinical literature. The 'anarchic hand' syndrome is usually associated with damage to the supplementary motor area and/or the anterior corpus callosum (Della Sala et al., 1994). The main symptom is related to the behavior of the hand contralateral to the lesion; the contralateral hand performs simple, goal-directed move-ments which are not intended by the patient. In that sense, the behavior of the contralat-eral hand is thought to be anarchic. Despite the autonomous behavior of the affected hand, these patients retain a sense of ownership of the moving hand. In phenomenological terms, certain actions performed by the contralateral hand are experienced as disowned, not the hand *itself* (see also Marcel, 2003). Somatoparaphrenia is a neurological condition, which is usually related to anosognosia for hemiplegia, and occurs after predominantly right hemispheric lesions. Patients with somatoparaphrenia believe that their limb contralateral to the side of the lesion belongs to someone else (Nightingale, 1982; Bisiach *et al.*, 1991; Halligan *et al.*, 1995), and the disorder is often accompanied by the inability to feel tactile sensations in the 'nonbelonging' part of the body (Bottini *et al.*, 2002). Thus, whereas the anarchic hand syndrome is characterized by a failure to experience agency over the contralateral hand, somatoparaphrenia is characterized by a failure to experience ownership over one's own hand. These clinical paradigms aptly demonstrate the intrinsic difficulties encountered in the attempt to understand in neuroscientific terms the sense of agency and the sense of body ownership, and how these two senses contribute to a basic sense of selfhood. Even though the human body is above all an organ of action, the present chapter will consider the sense of body ownership that arises in the absence of action, that is, before the contribution of voluntary movement. Thus, the aim of the present chapter is to investigate the functional and neural processes that generate the sense of body ownership separately from the sense of agency.

The body in the brain

Recent neuroscientific research has focused on how multisensory percepts are processed by the brain to generate a coherent representation of the body. Multisensory integration gives rise to percepts that reflect not only the nature of environmental stimuli, but also the state of one's own body. Different sensory modalities are linked in distinct ways to both the representation and the experience of one's own body. For example, tactile information that we receive from our body is private and unique from an epistemological and a neurophysiological point of view. Conversely, visual information is not epistemologically private: I can see your hand or mine being touched, yet I can only feel touch on my own hand. Thus, multimodal sensory percepts need to be integrated in order to create a coherent representation of one's own body. Even though body ownership may arise from unimodal sensory input (e.g. touch, see Ehrsson *et al.*, 2005), interactions between different sensory modalities (e.g. touch, proprioception and vision) contribute to a better understanding of the body-related sensory processing that generates the unique experience of seeing, and at the same time feeling, one's own hand.

The representation of the body in the brain cannot be merely reduced to a registration of peripheral inputs. Lesions of the primary somatosensory cortex induce deficits in the tactile and proprioceptive sensations, but there is no evidence that they can cause alterations of higher-order body awareness (for a review see Berlucchi and Aglioti, 1997). Higher-order disorders of body awareness, such as anosognosia for hemiplegia (Pia *et al.*, 2004), somatoparaphrenia (Bisiach *et al.*, 1991), and autotopagnosia (Sirigu *et al.*, 1991) are frequently observed after lesions that involve the parietal lobes (for a review see Haggard and Wolpert, 2005). Body awareness relies upon a large neural network where somatosensory cortex, posterior parietal lobe and insular cortex play crucial and dissociable roles (Melzack, 1990). Thus, body awareness involves the perception of sensory inputs, the interpretation of these inputs in the context of a rich internal model of the body's structure, and the use of these inputs for an online representation of the body in space. In fact, neuropsychological research supports the idea that multiple representations contribute to body awareness that can be distinguished in a semantic or conceptual conscious representation of the body, a structural representation of the body, and an online, sensorimotor representation of the body in space (see Sirigu *et al.*, 1991; Suzuki *et al.*, 1997; Shelton *et al.*, 1998; Buxbaum and Coslett, 2001).

Overall, the review of the literature suggests that certain body representations refer to the conscious knowledge and perception of one's own body, while others refer to an internal model of the body that supports an implicit, subpersonal, knowledge that encodes the body's form, the constraints on how the body's parts can be configured, and the consequences of this configuration on touch, vision and movement (see also Gallagher and Cole, 1995; Gallagher, 2005; Graziano and Botvinick, 2001). One way to study this body model is in terms of the way it constrains multisensory interactions. Accumulating data suggest that the unimodal or multimodal sensory perceptions are neither raw nor immediate (for a review see Graziano and Botvnick, 2001). Instead, sensory stimuli seem to be processed and finally constructed with reference to an abstract body reference or scheme that guarantees the spatial coherence of the body. The process of weighting and integrating different sensory input into a cognitive body scheme is essential for the experience of a unified body (de Vignemont *et al.*, 2006). Recent research has taken a further step by looking into how sensory stimulation and perception generate a sense of ownership of the perceived body.

The rubber hand illusion (RHI): an experimental paradigm to study body ownership

The RHI is an experimental paradigm that allows the manipulation of body ownership and its study in the absence of movement and efferent information. In brief, watching a rubber hand being stroked synchronously with one's own unseen hand causes the rubber hand to be attributed to one's own body, to "feel like it's my hand" (Botvinick and Cohen, 1998). This illusion does not occur when the rubber hand is stroked asynchronously with respect to the subject's own hand. Thus, the RHI allows an external object to be treated as part of the body, or not, under experimental control, and for that reason it is one of the few viable ways of investigating body ownership scientifically.

One behavioral correlate of the RHI is an induced change in the perceived location of the participant's own hand towards the rubber hand. Botvinick and Cohen stimulated both the participants' hand and the rubber hand synchronously for 30 min, and they then asked the participants to make intermanual reaches with their unstimulated hand to the felt position of their stimulated unseen hand. The results showed that the intermanual reaches indicated a displacement of the felt position of the participant's own hand. Based on the pattern of intermanual reaching error, Botvinick and Cohen showed that participants perceived the position of their hand to be closer to the rubber hand than it really was, as if their hand had drifted toward the fake hand. In addition, the prevalence of illusion over time was positively correlated with a drift in the felt location of the subject's own hand towards the rubber hand. Similar patterns of proprioceptive drifts were obtained using different response methods.

In a recent experiment performed in collaboration with M. Costantini and P. Haggard, we asked participants ($n = 8$, six female, all right-handed, mean age 28.6 years, SD 4) to judge the felt location of their own unseen hand using two different ways. In some trials, subjects were asked to verbally report a number on a ruler presented at the same gaze depth as their own unseen hand and the rubber hand, and in some other trials they were asked to make a saccade to the location where they felt their stimulated unseen hand was. The experiment consisted of two conditions of synchronous or asynchronous visuo-tactile stimulation. Each condition was repeated twice, resulting in four blocks. Each block had 20 trials, 10 trials in which subjects were asked to make a saccade and 10 trials in which they were asked to make a judgment using the ruler. The order of judgments within blocks was pseudorandomized, and the order of blocks was counterbalanced across subjects.

The experimenter placed the participant's left hand at a fixed point inside a frame, whose top side was covered by one-way and two-way mirrors. The two-way mirror was used to make the rubber hand appear (during stimulation) and disappear (during judgment). At the beginning of each block, both the participant's left hand and the rubber hand were out of sight. A pre-test baseline estimate of finger position was obtained prior to stimulation. Participants saw a ruler reflected on the mirror. The ruler appeared at the same gaze depth as their own unseen hand and the rubber hand. Participants were asked "Where is your index finger?" and in response, they verbally reported a number on the ruler. They were instructed to judge the position of their finger by projecting a parasagittal line from the centre of their fingertip to the ruler. Next, the ruler was removed, subjects fixated at the centre of the mirror, and 5 s later they had to make a saccade at the location where they felt their index finger was. During the judgments, there was no tactile stimulation, and the lights under the two-way mirror were switched off to make the rubber hand invisible. The judgments were recorded and no feedback was given. After the judgments, the lights under the two-way mirror were turned on, and the rubber hand appeared in front of them, aligned with their midline. Participants were looking at the rubber hand in the same depth plane as their own hand. Visuo-tactile stimulation was delivered on the rubber hand and their hand either synchronously or asynchronously. Stimulation was delivered mechanically by two identical stepper motors to which identical paintbrushes were attached. The overall amount of stimulation was precisely matched across conditions. In order to avoid habituation effects, the speed and the direction of the paintbrushes were unpredictable. Participants were always stimulated horizontally on the index finger of their left hand, and the rubber hand was stimulated on the index finger in the same way. Visuo-tactile stimulation lasted for 12 s per trial. In the asynchronous conditions, the starting position of the paintbrush on the motor stimulating the rubber hand was offset by 90°, resulting in out-of-phase visuo-tactile stimulation. The total amount and spatial pattern of stimulation was the same across all conditions. Synchronous and asynchronous conditions differed only in the degree of temporal correlation of visual and tactile stimulation. After the stimulation period, the lights were automatically turned off for 8 s. In half of the trials, subjects were asked to make a judgment using the ruler, and in the other half they were asked to make a saccade at the location where they felt their hand was. The ruler was always presented with a random offset to ensure that participants judged finger position anew on each trial, and that they could not simply repeat previous responses. Participants were asked "Where is your index finger?" After their answer the ruler was removed, and a new trial of visuo-tactile stimulation started. The same process was followed for each condition.

Electro-oculogram (EOG) was recorded from electrodes at the outer canthi of both eyes connected to a DC amplifier. EOG raw data were filtered with a 0.1 Hz high-pass and a 40 Hz low-pass filter. The raw data of all trials per block were exported and further analyzed using LABVIEW. Saccade onset was determined as the starting point of continuously increasing amplitude, and saccade offset was determined as the endpoint of continuous EOG signal increase. EOG signal calibration that took place before and after the experiment allowed us to transform the EOG amplitude to physical units of centimeters.

A baseline pre-test judgment with both response types was obtained prior to visuo-tactile stimulation and a post-test judgment after stimulation in each trial. The pre-test judgment was subtracted from the post-test judgment. The term 'proprioceptive drift' refers to this change in perceived hand position as a result of visuo-tactile stimulation. A positive error represents a mislocalization toward the rubber hand. Figure 17.1, therefore, shows the change in the perceived position of the hand between the start and end of the stimulation period, across conditions. Large proprioceptive drifts towards the rubber hand were observed only after synchronous visuo-tactile stimulation. The proprioceptive drifts were submitted to 2 × 2 analysis of variance (ANOVA). The two factors were the mode of visuo-tactile stimulation (synchronous or asynchronous), and the second factor

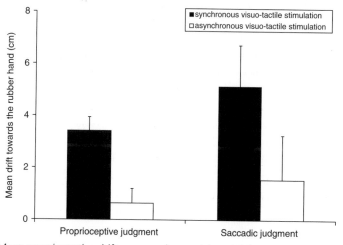

Figure 17.1 Mean proprioceptive drifts averaged over eight participants across conditions. Error bars indicate standard errors. Point 'zero' represents the felt position of the participant's hand prior to stimulation. Unpublished data collected with M. Costantini and P. Haggard.

was the response type (verbal–proprioceptive judgment or saccadic–proprioceptive judgment). Only the main effect of mode of stimulation was significant [$F(1,7) = 9.83$, $p < 0.05$], suggesting that both verbal and saccadic judgments are equally sensitive measures of RHI.

It seems that RHI reflects a three-way interaction between vision, touch, and proprioception: vision of tactile stimulation on the rubber hand captures the tactile sensation on the participant's own hand, and this visual capture results in a mislocalization of the felt location of one's own hand towards the spatial location of the visual percept. In addition, the presence of synchronized visual and tactile stimulation is a necessary condition for the inducement of the RHI, since RHI does not occur after asynchronous stimulation (Botvinick and Cohen, 1998; Ehrsson *et al.*, 2005; Tsakiris and Haggard, 2005b). Another experiment extends this view by suggesting that visuo-tactile correlation is both a necessary and sufficient condition for the RHI. Armel and Ramachandran (2003) stimulated the participant's hand and the rubber hand synchronously. After the stimulation period, the experimenter "injured' the rubber hand (e.g. the experimenter bent one of the rubber fingers backwards), and skin conductance responses (SCRs) were measured from the subject's unstimulated hand. As predicted, SCRs were significantly higher after synchronous stimulation than after the control condition. In a follow-up experiment, the rubber hand was replaced by a neutral object, in that case a table, and synchronous tactile stimulation was delivered on the table synchronously with tactile stimulation delivered on the participant's own hand. As in the previous experiment, after the stimulation, the table was 'injured'. Interestingly, SCRs were again higher after synchronous than after the control condition, suggesting, according to the authors, that both the fake hand and the table, and in principle any other object, can be self-attributed, provided that strong visuo-tactile correlations are present. It was argued that the illusion that "the fake hand/table is my hand" is the result of a purely bottom-up mechanism, which associates synchronous visuo-tactile events. In the strong version of this model, any object can become part of 'me', simply because strong statistical correlations between different sensory modalities are both necessary and sufficient conditions for self-attribution. Indeed, the possibility that the bodily self may in fact be built up by prior, repeated, bottom-up multisensory correlations cannot be excluded. Developmental studies suggest that intermodal matching is a prerequisite for self-identification (Rochat and Striano, 2000).

It is still debated whether current multisensory experience is assimilated to some representation, a form of a reference body model, possibly arising from prior experience and from cognitive but also innate body representations. The literature on body representation suggests that the body is a unique perceptual object, and thus, body-related percepts are not simply correlated, but they are integrated against a set of background conditions that preserve the coherence of the bodily experience. On this latter view, intermodal matching may not be sufficient for self-attribution. Contrary to the account according to which concurrent visual and tactile stimulation constructs a 'changed' body scheme (Armel and Ramachandran, 2003), concurrent visuo-tactile inputs may need to be integrated within a pre-existing reference of one's own body. Neurophysiological studies on monkeys support this view. Graziano *et al.* (2000) showed that bimodal neurons in parietal area 5 of the monkey brain were sensitive to the position of a fake arm when fake and real hands were stroked synchronously, but only when the fake arm was aligned with the monkey's body. Thus, it seems that these bimodal neurons do not simply integrate visual and tactile percepts, but they integrate them while preserving a coherent representation of the body. In fact, the results by Graziano *et al.* (2000) suggest that representations, at least in area 5, may even be detailed enough to incorporate visual discrimination between a left or right hand (see also Maravita *et al.*, 2003).

According to Armel and Ramachadran, the RHI "arises mainly from the 'Bayesian logic' of all perception; the brain's remarkable ability to detect statistical correlations in sensory inputs in constructing useful perceptual representations of the world—including one's body. It is especially intriguing that this bizarre perceptual representation (assimilating the table into one's body image) is so resistant to 'top-down' knowledge of the absurdity of the situation." (Armel and Ramachandran, 2003, pp. 1499–1500). However, it is hard to understand why it would be useful to assimilate external objects such as tables into our body. Moreover, what is implicitly suggested in this account of RHI is the idea that the experience of one's own body is basically a transitory internal construct that can be profoundly altered by stimulus contingencies and correlations that one encounters. On this view, any object could become part of the bodily self, and the experience of a lifetime of one's own body would be utterly irrelevant. However, there are several arguments that could be used to question that view. First, as the elegant study by Graziano *et al.* shows, bimodal neurons in parietal area 5 did not fire when the fake hand was replaced by a neutral object or by unrealistic substitutes of the arm. In addition, there is strong evidence pointing to several distinct kinds of body representations in the brain: there is a somatotopical organization in the sensory and motor cortices, a semantic knowledge of the body (Sirigu *et al.*, 1991), anatomical and structural representations coding for possible and impossible movements and postures (e.g. Costantini *et al.*, 2005), as well as body-schematic representations necessary for the online control of action and body-image representations that seem to be closely related to the conscious experience of one's own body. Given the existence of multiple representations of the body in the brain, it is necessary to investigate whether body representations modulate body ownership during the RHI.

"Is this *my* hand I see before me?"

Body ownership: interaction between multisensory integration and body representations

A series of behavioral experiments was performed to investigate the necessary and sufficient conditions for inducing the RHI. In particular, the experiments assessed the role of an abstract body reference and its interaction with multisensory (i.e. visuo-tactile) integration. We used the methods described above (for details see Tsakiris and Haggard, 2005b). Briefly, the subject's hand was placed out of view inside a frame covered by a mirror. The rubber hand appeared through the mirror, aligned with the subject's midline. Proprioceptive judgments were obtained using a ruler that appeared at the same gaze depth as the rubber hand, and participants judged the felt position of their own hand before and after each block.

The aim of the first experiment was to investigate the influence of the viewed stimulus content on the RHI by manipulating first the body configuration, and second, the identity of the viewed object. Thus, participants saw a rubber hand in a congruent posture with respect to their own hand, or a rubber hand in an incongruent posture with respect to their own hand (i.e. rotated by –90°), or a neutral object (i.e. a wooden stick of the same length as the rubber hand). In the experimental conditions, visuo-tactile stimulation between the rubber hand and the participant's hand was synchronous, whereas in the control conditions, stimulation was asynchronous. Figure 17.2 shows the mean proprioceptive drifts across conditions, i.e. the change in the perceived position of the hand between the start and end of the stimulation period across conditions. Proprioceptive drifts between synchronous and asynchronous conditions were significantly different only when subjects were looking at a rubber hand that was placed in a congruent posture with respect to their own unseen hand [$t(7) = 4.25$, $p < 0.006$, two-tailed]. Thus, the sense of body ownership as measured by proprioceptive drifts occurred only when the content of the viewed stimulus was congruent with the postural and visual representation of the participant's own hand.

Next, Tsakiris and Haggard manipulated the handedness identity of the viewed rubber hand. Participants were always stimulated on their left middle finger, and they saw a left or a right rubber hand being stimulated on its middle finger, either synchronously or asynchronously. Differences between synchronous and asynchronous conditions were significant only when participants were looking at a congruent rubber hand [$t(7) = 3.89$, $p < 0.04$, two-tailed], and they were not significant when subjects were looking at an

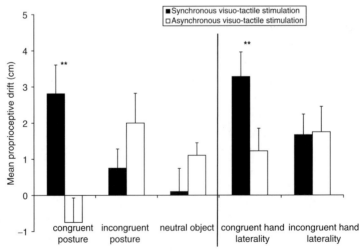

Figure 17.2 Mean proprioceptive drifts toward the viewed object. Error bars indicate standard errors. Asterisks indicate significant differences between synchronous and asynchronous stimulation. Point 'zero' represents the felt position of the participant's hand prior to stimulation. (Data from Tsakiris and Haggard, 2005b.)

incongruent rubber hand [$t(7) = 0.159, p > 0.05$]. Therefore, significant proprioceptive drifts occurred only when participants watched a rubber hand of congruent laterality (i.e. left).

These studies show that three factors originating from body representations seem to constrain the effects of intermodal matching: body specificity, anatomical constraints, and body part identity. The viewed object has to be a body part, and not a neutral object that has no functional connection with the body. The viewed body part has to be in a posture that is anatomically plausible and congruent with the posture of the subject's own body part, and of the same laterality as the subject's stimulated body part. These constraints on body-related multisensory perception suggest that body ownership is not a purely bottom-up process driven only by correlated afferent signals. Synchronized visuo-tactile stimulation is a necessary, but not a sufficient, condition for body ownership. In addition, body ownership cannot be simply a purely top-down process driven by abstract cognitive body representations, because that would not explain how an incorporation process of an external object is possible at all. Instead, body ownership seems to arise as an *interaction* between bottom-up processes linked to multisensory perception and top-down influences originating from a reference model of the body that is neurally represented.

Tsakiris and Haggard suggested that the brain processes that produce incorporation of the rubber hand depend both on current sensory integration (Botvnick and Cohen, 1998) and also on constraints driven by a pre-existing reference of the postural and visual features of one's own body (Tsakiris and Haggard, 2005b). The interaction between multisensory perception and the modulatory influence of a pre-existing reference body will cause the subjective feeling of body ownership of a rubber hand. On this view, three distinct processes underpin the generation of body ownership during the RHI. First, the object to be attributed to one's own body must fit with a pre-existing reference model of the body. Thus, it is necessary to identify the neural source of this general reference body that seems to be critical for the distinction between what may or may not become part of one's body. If the external object fits with that representation, multisensory stimulation will facilitate the assimilation of the external object in the updated body model. Second, when the criterion of body compatibility is satisfied, multisensory stimulation will cause the incorporation of the external object. It is therefore necessary to identify the neural processes that underpin this body-centered multisensory integration that drives the RHI. Finally, the very feeling of body ownership, that is, the subjective experience of body ownership, seems to be the phenomenal effect of multisensory integration, and it is therefore necessary to account for the neural processes that underpin the phenomenal experience of body ownership during the RHI.

Overall, we hypothesize that the functional interaction between multisensory integration and body representations should have identifiable neural signatures. In the following sections, we present a series of experiments investigating the distinct neural mechanisms that underpin the three processes involved in the generation of body ownership during RHI: (i) the distinction between what may or may not become part of one's body depending on a reference model of the body, (ii) the body-related multisensory integration and recalibration of hand position, and finally, (iii) the subjective feeling of body ownership.

The neural source of a reference model of the body

Recent studies suggest that the right temporal and parietal lobes may underpin a reference model of one's own body. Lesions in these regions may lead patients to deny ownership of their contralateral hand (Bottini *et al.*, 2002), to neglect the left side of their body (Mort *et al.*, 2003), or to deny paralysis of the left arm following stroke (Heilman *et al.*, 1998). Direct electrical stimulation of the right temporo-parietal junction (rTPJ) in a neurosurgical patient elicited experiences of seeing her body from an external perspective ('out-of-body experience'), and of illusory transformations of the arms and legs (Blanke *et al.*, 2002). Based on these results, Tsakiris *et al.* hypothesized that rTPJ may be the neural source of the reference model of the one's own body upon which novel multisensory stimuli are assimilated. To test this hypothesis, transcranial magnetic stimulation (TMS) was delivered immediately after synchronous visuo-tactile stimulation to investigate the role of this area in the processing of sensory events during RHI (Tsakiris M., Constantini M., and P. Haggard, unpublished study).

Ten participants watched a rubber hand being stroked by a brush, while their own unseen hand received identical and synchronous stimulation. Visuo-tactile stimulation lasted 2300 ms per trial. In half of the trials selected at random, a single TMS pulse was delivered over rTPJ 350 ms after the end of visuo-tactile stimulation, and just before participants judged the felt location of their own hand. To assess whether rTPJ activity was specifically involved in linking current sensory inputs to a mental reference body, the experimental design also included blocks in which subjects watched a neutral object (e.g. a spoon) being stroked in synchrony with their own hand. As before, the extent to which subjects incorporated the rubber hand or the neutral object was measured by asking the participants to judge the felt position of their own unseen hand at the beginning of each block, and then after each trial of multisensory stimulation. Finally, to control for non-specific effects of TMS, TMS was also applied over the vertex in separate control blocks while observing stimulation of either the rubber hand or of the neutral object. The same onset times and duration of events were followed in all conditions (i.e. rTPJ and Vertex stimulation).

A baseline pre-test proprioceptive judgment was obtained at the beginning of each block (Figure 17.3). The judgment error from the pre-test on each block was subtracted from each post-test judgment in that block. The term 'proprioceptive drift' refers to the change in the perceived position of the hand relative to baseline in each condition. A positive drift represents a mislocalization towards the rubber hand/neutral object location. The mean proprioceptive drifts (see Table 17.1) were analysed by $2 \times 2 \times 2$ repeated-measures ANOVA. The three factors were (i) the viewed object (rubber hand versus spoon), (ii) the site of stimulation (rTPJ versus vertex), and (iii) the presence of TMS (TMS versus No TMS). The main effect of viewed object was significant [$F(1,9) = 10.53, p < 0.05$]. None of the other main effects were significant. The interaction between the viewed object and the presence of TMS was significant [$F(1,9) = 9.34, p < 0.05$]. The interaction between the site of stimulation and the presence of TMS was also significant [$F(1,9) = 6.39, p < 0.05$]. Importantly, the three-way interaction was significant [$F(1,9) = 19.5, p < 0.005$]. Simple effects analysis showed that TMS over the vertex did not affect

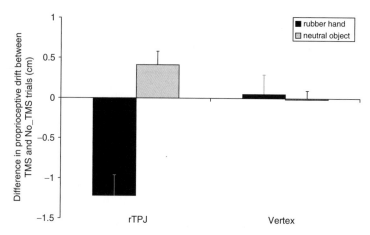

Figure 17.3 A baseline pre-test proprioceptive judgment was obtained at the beginning of each block, and post-test judgments were obtained after each trial. The pre-test judgment errors were subtracted from the post-test judgments prior to analysis. The term 'proprioceptive drift' refers to the change in the perceived position of the hand relative to baseline in each condition. The figure shows the effect of transcranial magnetic stimulation (TMS) as the difference in the proprioceptive drifts between TMS and No-TMS trials for each combination of viewed object and stimulated brain area. A positive drift represents a mislocalization towards the rubber hand/neutral object location. Error bars represent standard errors. (Data from M. Tsakiris, M. Constantini and P. Haggard, unpublished study.)

proprioceptive drift relative to No TMS trials [$t(9) = 0.23$, not significant, two-tailed, for the rubber hand, and $t(9) = 0.07$, not significant, two-tailed, for the object]. In contrast, TMS over the rTPJ, differences significantly reduced drifts when participants viewed the rubber hand [$t(9) = 4.67$, $p < 0.01$, two-tailed], and significantly increased drifts when participants viewed the neutral object [$t(9) = 2.55$, $p < 0.05$, two-tailed].

In a follow-up analysis, we investigated the correlation between the contribution of the mental body model to the RHI and the effect of TMS over rTPJ. The contribution of mental body model to the RHI was measured as the difference between proprioceptive drifts on No TMS trials when viewing a rubber hand, and when viewing a neutral object, in blocks where the TMS coil was held over the vertex. The contribution of the

Table 17.1 Mean (SE) proprioceptive drift towards the viewed object across conditions

	TMS coil over rTPJ		TMS coil over vertex	
	No TMS	TMS	No TMS	TMS
View rubber hand	5.3 (1.61)	4.08 (1.54)	3.93 (0.72)	3.99 (0.77)
View object	0.62 (0.75)	1.03 (0.89)	0.4 (0.50)	0.39 (0.46)

TMS, transcranial magnetic stimulation; rTPJ, right temporo-parietal junction.

rTPJ to the mental body model was measured as the difference between proprioceptive drifts when TMS was delivered over rTPJ while viewing the rubber hand, and No TMS trials in the same block. A robust regression fit showed a highly significant association between the two measures: $t(8) = 4.15$, $p = 0.003$. Thus, subjects who showed strong evidence of using a mental body model to process current sensory input, also showed greater reductions in RHI following TMS over rTPJ. This strong correlation suggests that the modulation of RHI by TMS over rTPJ is strongly related to the contribution of a mental body reference to the sense of body ownership.

Overall, TMS over rTPJ reduced the extent to which the rubber hand was incorporated into the mental representation of one's own body, and it also increased the incorporation of a neutral object. An object (i.e. a rubber hand) that would normally have been perceived as part of the subject's own body was no longer significantly distinguished from a clearly neutral object. Although the original prediction postulated a decrease in RHI after TMS over rTPJ while subjects were looking at a rubber hand, the results also showed an interesting pattern of increased incorporation of the external object after TMS. Tsakiris, Constantini and Haggard suggested that the disruption of neural activity over rTPJ blocked the contribution of the reference model of the body in the assimilation of current sensory input. As a result, any possible advantage of visual stimulation of a rubber hand over that of a neutral object was significantly diminished. In effect, when TPJ processing was disrupted by TMS, discrimination between what may or may not be 'self' became less definite, rendering the distinctions between external objects, own body parts and the self ambiguous. rTPJ may participate in the process of distinguishing between current sensory inputs that relate either to the self or to the external world. Thus, rTPJ may be necessary for the assimilation of novel multisensory signals to a pre-existing reference model of one's own body.

From multisensory integration to the feeling of body ownership

Introspective evidence from the original experiment (Botvinick and Cohen, 1998) showed that participants felt as if they were feeling the touch at the location where the rubber hand was seen to be touched, but also as if the rubber hand was their own hand. In a way, their tactile sensations were projected onto the rubber hand, which eventually felt like part of their own body. These observations might reflect the involvement of two separate components. First, there is a bottom-up process of integrating synchronized visual and tactile percepts, which is a necessary condition for producing the RHI. Second, this process produces persistent, vivid phenomenological changes in body representation, namely, the experience that the rubber hand is part of one's own body. The content of this changed body representation might be quite different from, and go beyond, the perception of correlated visual and tactile stimulation. In other words, the subjective feeling of ownership of the rubber hand may go beyond the correlation of a visual percept coming from vision of touch delivered on the rubber hand and of a tactile percept coming from tactile stimulation on one's own hand. The primary sensory events that 'cause' the rubber hand to be attributed to one's own body (e.g. multisensory correlation) may be different from the phenomenal 'effects' of ownership. Put another way, seeing the rubber hand and feeling tactile stimulation may cause the rubber hand to "feel like it is mine." This feeling is clearly distinct from the tactile and visual sensations themselves. Integrating synchronized visual and tactile percepts, then, is a necessary condition for producing the RHI. The result of this process is a persistent, vivid phenomenological change in body representation, namely, the experience that the rubber hand is part of one's own body. It may therefore be possible that the process of multisensory integration that drives the RHI and the subjective feeling of ownership over the rubber hand are linked to distinct neural processes that take place in different brain areas.

Ehrsson *et al.* (2004) showed bilateral neural activity in the ventral premotor cortex in the conditions that induced the RHI. Neural activity in the premotor cortex was related to the dynamic processes associated with the inducement of the illusion that occurs after a few seconds of visuo-tactile stimulation. Their study focused on the causes (i.e. congruent visual and tactile stimulation) of the RHI, but the RHI was not quantified behaviorally. As aforementioned, the synchronized visual and tactile stimulation causes the illusion, but the phenomenological effect within the illusion is a description of one's own body, and not a description of the sensory stimulation that causes the illusion. It is therefore possible that distinct neural processes underpin the *causes* that induce the RHI and the *effect* of RHI, i.e. the sense of ownership. This view is supported by the pattern of proprioceptive drifts induced during the RHI.

Data collected by Ehrsson *et al.* define the onset of RHI at approximately after 11.3 (±7) seconds of synchronous visuo-tactile stimulation. Data collected by Tsakiris and Haggard (2005b) show that the visuo-tactile correlation generates particularly strong proprioceptive drift towards the rubber hand during the first 60 s, after which the drift increases in a less exponential manner for up to 3 min (Figure 17.4). Based on these

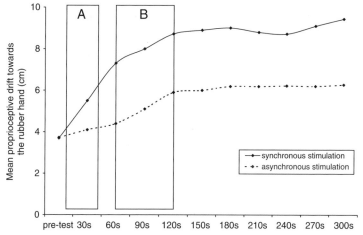

Figure 17.4 Proprioceptive drifts during the rubber hand illusion (RHI) as a function of time (data from Tsakiris and Haggard, 2005b). Data reported in the study by Ehrsson *et al.* (2004) were collected during time-window A. We hypothesized that neural responses during time-window B would reflect the steady state of incorporation, rather than the processes associated with the dynamic and rapid inducement of RHI.

observations, it seems that we can distinguish between an early process of multisensory integration and recalibration of hand position that would reflect the onset of the RHI, and the effect of this process that leads to the feeling of body ownership, i.e. the steady state of ownership of the rubber hand.

The distinction between the causes of the RHI and its phenomenal effect was used in a recent study to investigate the neural basis of the sense of body ownership (Tsakiris *et al.*, 2007). Participants were always stimulated on their unseen right hand, while they viewed a right or left rubber hand being stimulated either synchronously or asynchronously with respect to their own hand. Across all conditions participants judged the felt position of their own hand before and after visuo-tactile stimulation. The proprioceptive judgment was used as a behavioral measure of body ownership during the RHI. Tsakiris *et al.* (2007) used positron emission tomography (PET) to detect sustained neural activity that was specifically related to the stable state of ownership of the rubber hand, and not to the onset of the RHI *per se*. At the beginning of the trial, participants judged the felt location of their own middle finger. Then the rubber hand appeared and visuo-tactile stimulation was delivered for 125 s. Acquisition of the PET data began 60 s after the onset of visuo-tactile stimulation and lasted for 60 s (Figure 17.5). At the end of trial, participants judged anew the felt location of their own middle finger.

Based on these observations, it seems that by the onset of PET data acquisition (60 s after the onset of visuo-tactile stimulation), participants were already experiencing the illusion, and that the recalibration of their hand position associated with the onset of the illusion had already occurred. It is unclear whether sustained activity in the premotor cortex occurs during prolonged stimulation periods, or whether premotor activity reflects only the *onset* of the dynamic processes involved in ownership changes. The dynamic changes associated with the illusion onset were not emphasized in the present study due to the low temporal resolution of PET. Typically, epoch-related neural responses are assessed in PET because of the relatively long half-life of the radiotracers used. Thus, PET was used to detect sustained neural activity that was specifically related to the assimilation of visuo-tactile stimulation that leads to the feeling of ownership of the rubber hand, and not to the onset of the RHI *per se*.

To identify the neural correlates of the subjective experience of ownership, rather than the sensory conditions used to induce it, the analysis focused on the correlation between neural activity and a quantitative proxy of the RHI. SPM2 was used to identify brain areas where activity was associated with a behavioral measure of the illusion, namely the proprioceptive drift of the stimulated hand towards the rubber hand (Tsakiris and Haggard, 2005b). The proprioceptive drift for each trial was used as a covariate and regression with this covariate was calculated for every voxel in the whole brain. The significance of the regression was displayed in an SPM[t] map, which was then transformed into an SPM{z} and thresholded at $p < 0.0005$ uncorrected at the voxel level. The behavioral results showed a significant drift only in the congruent rubber hand/synchronous condition, confirming previous results (Tsakiris and Haggard, 2005b). In addition, introspective data showed that participants felt as if they were feeling

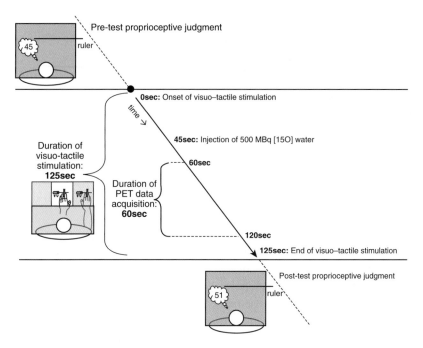

Figure 17.5 The experimental set-up and temporal sequence of events in Tsakiris *et al.* (in press). In the condition shown, the participant is looking at a congruent rubber hand identity with respect to her own stimulated hand. At the beginning of the trial, participants judged the felt location of their own middle finger. Then the rubber hand appeared and visuo-tactile stimulation was delivered for 125 s. Acquisition of the positron emission tomography (PET) data began 60 s after the onset of visuo-tactile stimulation and lasted for 60 s. At the end of trial, participant judged anew the felt location of her own middle finger.

the touch coming from the location where the congruent rubber hand was being touched, and that they felt as if the congruent rubber hand was their own hand. These introspective data replicate previous studies (Botvinick and Cohen, 1998; Ehrsson *et al.*, 2004), and corroborate the quantitative psychophysical data on the perceived position of the hand.

A negative correlation between the proprioceptive measure of the illusion and rCBF was observed in the contralateral parietal cortex, in particular in the left primary and secondary somatosensory cortices. A small or negative proprioceptive drift indicates that the rubber hand has not been attributed to one's own body, presumably because of a discrepancy between the proprioceptive and tactile experience of the subject's own hand, and the visual perception of the rubber hand. In these situations, the internal proprioceptive representation of the body is not captured by visual input. Thus, activity in the contralateral parietal cortex was strongest when subjects did not experience ownership of the rubber hand. Other studies have reported that the left parietal cortex is involved in distinguishing between self and other. For example, Ruby and Decety (2001) showed that the left inferior parietal and the somatosensory cortices were more activated for motor imagery of an action than for imagination of the same action realized by the experimenter. This result, among others, led the authors to propose that this area is critically involved in distinguishing self from other (see also Chapter 14). Other studies have also suggested that primary and secondary somatosensory cortices are associated with body awareness (Hari *et al.*, 1998; Schwartz *et al.*, 2005). Thus, a possible role of somatosensory cortex activation relates to the saliency of the representation of the subject's own hand when the pattern of multisensory stimulation does not support the incorporation of the rubber hand. Thus, somatosensory cortex activity would prevent the inducement of RHI by making the hand representation salient so that it becomes resistant to 'disturbing' stimulation.

The experience of ownership of the rubber hand as measured by the proprioceptive behavioral data was positively correlated with activity in the right posterior insula (Figure 17.6). Right insular activity is consistently implicated in self-attribution (Farrer and Frith, 2002; Farrer *et al.*, 2003), self-processing (Fink *et al.*, 1996; Vogeley *et al.*, 2004), and the representation of an egocentric reference frame (Fink *et al.*, 2003). The role of right posterior insula in integrating body signals related to egocentric representation, agency and possibly body ownership is supported by recent imaging studies. Farrer and Frith (2002) proposed that the sense of agency results from the integration of multiple body- and action-related signals. This integrating process was thought to involve the right insular cortex. Farrer *et al.* (2003) showed that activation in the right posterior insula decreased when subjects experienced a conflict between what they did and what they saw, suggesting that activity in the right posterior insula correlates with the degree of

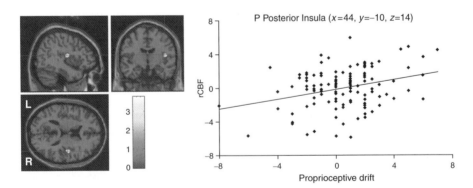

Figure 17.6 Activity in the right posterior insula ($x = 44$, $y = -10$, $z = 14$) was positively correlated ($t = 3.41$, $p < 0.05$) with the proprioceptive drift towards the rubber hand. Positive drifts indicate a drift towards the rubber hand, and negative drifts indicate a drift away from the rubber hand. Activations show averaged data over 10 participants. L, left; R, right; rCBF, regional cerebral blood flow. (Data from Tsakiris *et al.*, 2006.). See color plate section.

congruence between different signals used for attribution of actions to oneself. However, given that in the study by Farrer *et al.* (2003) afferent signals were not dissociated from efferent signals, it is not easy to interpret the insular activity, as it may either reflect sensorimotor congruency or simply intersensory congruency (e.g. proprioceptive and visual). If, for example, activity in the right posterior insula was coding the intersensory match between proprioception and vision, it would be wrong to conclude that this area underpins the sense of agency. Instead, one could argue that this area is linked to the sense of body ownership, which, as suggested above, can be generated during passive movements or somatosensation.

Interestingly, a recent lesion-mapping study suggests that the right posterior insula is commonly damaged in patients with anosognosia for hemiparesis, but is significantly less involved in hemiparetic patients without anosognosia (Karnath *et al.*, 2005; see also Cereda *et al.*, 2002; Berti *et al.*, 2005; see also the chapter by Berti and Pia). However, the extent to which these patients exhibited somatoparaphrenic symptoms was not formally assessed in these studies. Our results extend previous findings by showing a correlation between activity in the insula and sense of body ownership. In particular, activity in the right posterior insula was observed in the absence of efferent information, when participants experienced ownership over a body part as a result of multisensory stimulation alone.

Conclusion

A series of experiments suggests that body ownership during the RHI arises as an inter-action between multisensory perception and top-down influences originating from an abstract cognitive model of the body. The brain processes that produce ownership depend both on current sensory integration and also on top-down processes reflecting a pre-existing reference model of the postural and visual features of the body. The right temporo-parietal junction may underpin the assimilation of novel multisensory signals by maintaining a pre-existing reference representation of one's own body. Body-related sensory integration linked to the onset of body ownership during the RHI is related to bilateral premotor activity. The effect of multisensory integration and recalibration of hand position, namely the experience of body ownership of the rubber hand, is corre-lated with activity in the right posterior insula. These structures may form a network that plays a fundamental role in linking current sensory stimuli to one's own body, and thus also in self-consciousness.

Attribution of body ownership may be more fundamental than action attribution, since the latter involves an additional efferent component that the former lacks. Previous studies may have misidentified neural signatures of body ownership and signatures of motor agency, because they did not use designs that adequately disentangle afferent and efferent information. We suggest that a basic form of bodily self-consciousness is gener-ated in the brain by sensory stimulation and assimilation to a pre-existing body scheme. Agency would represent a special but important addition to this essentially sensory circuit for self-consciousness. Novel experimental designs should focus on how agency may modulate and interact with body ownership.

Acknowledgments

This work was supported by ESRC grant PTA-026-27-0889. The experiment described in the section on the 'rubber hand illusion' was performed in collaboration with Marcello Costantini and Patrick Haggard.

References

Armel, K. C. and Ramachandran, V. S. (2003) Projecting sensations to external objects: evidence from skin conductance response. *Proceedings of the Biological Society*, 270, 1499–1506.

Berlucchi, G. and Aglioti, S. (1997) The body in the brain: neural bases of corporeal awareness. *Trends in Neurosciences*, 20, 560–564.

Berti, A., Bottini, G., Gandola, M., Pia, L., Smania, N., Stracciari, A., Castiglioni, I., Vallar, G. and Paulesu, E. (2005) Shared cortical anatomy for motor awareness and motor control. *Science*, 15, 309(5733), 488–491.

Bisiach, E., Rusconi, M. L. and Vallar, G. (1991) Remission of somatoparaphrenic delusion through vestibular stimulation. *Neuropsychologia*, 29, 1029–1031.

Blakemore, S. J. and Frith, C. (2003) Self-awareness and action. *Current Opinion in Neurobiology*, 13, 219–224.

Blakemore, S. J., Bristow, D., Bird, G., Frith, C. and Ward, J. (2005) Somatosensory activations during the observation of touch and a case of vision–touch synaesthesia. *Brain*, 128, 1571–1583.

Blanke, O., Ortigue, S., Landis, T. and Seeck, M. (2002) Stimulating illusory own-body perceptions. *Nature*, 419, 269.

Bottini, G., Bisiach, E., Sterzi, R. and Vallarc, G. (2002) Feeling touches in someone else's hand. *Neuroreport*, 13, 249–252.

Botvinick, M. and Cohen, J. (1998) Rubber hands 'feel' touch that eyes see. *Nature*, 391, 756.

Buxbaum, L. J. and Coslett, H. B. (2001) Specialised structural descriptions for human body parts: evidence from autotopagnosia. *Cognitive Neuropsychology*, 18, 289–306.

Cereda, C., Ghika, J., Maeder, P. and Bogousslavsky, J. (2002). Strokes restricted to the insular cortex. *Neurology*, 59, 1950–1955.

Della, S. S., Marchetti, C. and Spinnler, H. (1994) The anarchic hand: a fronto-mesial sign. In Boller, F. and Grafman, J. (eds), *Handbook of Neuropsychology*. Elsevier, Amsterdam.

Ehrsson, H. H., Spence, C. and Passingham, R. E. (2004) That's my hand! Activity in premotor cortex reflects feeling of ownership of a limb. *Science*, 305, 875–877.

Ehrsson, H. H., Holmes, N. P. and Passingham, R. E. (2005) Touching a rubber hand: feeling of body-ownership is associated with activity in multisensory brain areas. *Journal of Neuroscience*, 25, 10564–10573.

Farrer, C. and Frith, C. D. (2002) Experiencing oneself vs another person as being the cause of an action: the neural correlates of the experience of agency. *Neuroimage*, 15, 596–603.

Farrer, C., Franck, N., Georgieff, N., Frith, C.D., Decety, J. and Jeannerod, M. (2003) Modulating the experience of agency: a positron emission tomography study. *Neuroimage*, 18, 324–333.

Fink, G. R., Markowitsch, H. J., Reinkemeier, M., Bruckbauer, T., Kessler, J. and Heiss, W. D. (1996) Cerebral representation of one's own past: neural networks involved in autobiographical memory. *Journal of Neuroscience*, 16, 4275–4282.

Fink, G. R., Marshall, J. C., Weiss, P. H., Stephan, T., Grefkes, C., Shah, N.J., Zilles, K. and Dieterich, M. (2003) Performing allocentric visuospatial judgments with induced distortion of the egocentric reference frame: an fMRI study with clinical implications. *Neuroimage*, 20, 1505–1517.

Frith, C. D. (1992) *The Cognitive Neuropsychology of Schizophrenia*. Erlbaum, London.

Gallagher, S. (2000) Philosophical concepts of the self: implications for cognitive sciences. *Trends in Cognitive Sciences*, **4**, 14–21.

Gallagher, S. (2005) *How the Body Shapes the Mind*. Oxford University Press, Oxford.

Gallagher, S. and Cole, J. (1995) Body schema and body image in a deafferented subject. *Journal of Mind and Behavior*, **16**, 369–390.

Gallese, V., Keysers, C. and Rizzolatti, G. (2004) A unifying view of the basis of social cognition. *Trends in Cognitive Sciences*, **8**, 396–403.

Gillihan, S. J. and Farah, M. J. (2005) Is self special? A critical review of evidence from experimental psychology and cognitive neuroscience. *Psychological Bulletin*, **131**, 76–97.

Graziano, M. S., Cooke, D. F. and Taylor, C. S. (2000) Coding the location of the arm by sight. *Science* **290**, 1782–1786.

Graziano, M. S. A. and Botvinik, M. M. (2001) How the brain represents the body: insights from neurophysiology and psychology. In Prinz, W. and Hommel, B. (eds), *Common Mechanisms in Perception and Action, Attention and Performance XIX*. Oxford University Press, Oxford/New York.

Haggard, P. and Wolpert, D. (2005) Disorders of body scheme. In Freund, Jeannerod, M., Hallett and Leiguarda (eds), *Higher-order Motor Disorders*. Oxford University Press, Oxford.

Halligan, P. W., Marshall, J. C. and Wade, D. T. (1995) Unilateral somatoparaphrenia after right hemisphere stroke: a case description. *Cortex*, **31**, 173–182.

Hari, R., Hanninen, R., Makinen, T., Jousmaki, V., Forss, N., Seppa, M. and Salonen, O. (1998) Three hands: fragmentation of human bodily awareness. *Neuroscience Letters*, **240**, 131–134.

Heilman, K. M., Barrett, A. M. and Adair, J. C. (1998) Possible mechanisms of anosognosia: a defect in self-awareness. *Philosophical Transactions Royal Society of London, B*, **353**(1377), 1903–1909.

Hommel, B., Musseler, J., Aschersleben, G. and Prinz, W. (2001) The Theory of Event Coding (TEC): a framework for perception and action planning. *Behavioural and Brain Sciences*, **24**, 849–878; discussion 878–937.

Karnath, H. O., Baier, B. and Nagele, T. (2005) Awareness of the functioning of one's own limbs mediated by the insular cortex? *Journal of Neuroscience*, **25**, 7134–7138.

Keysers, C., Wicker, B., Gazzola, V., Anton, J. L., Fogassi, L. and Gallese, V. (2004) A touching sight: SII/PV activation during the observation and experience of touch. *Neuron* **42**, 335–346.

Knoblich, G., Elsner, B., Aschersleben, G. and Metzinger, T. (2003) Grounding the self in action. *Consciousness and Cognition*, **12**, 487–494.

Maravita, A., Spence, C. and Driver, J. (2003) Multisensory integration and the body schema: close to hand and within reach. *Current Biology*, **13**, R531–R539.

Marcel, A. J. (2003) The sense of agency: awareness and ownership of actions and intentions. In Roessler, J. and Eilan, N. (eds), *Agency and Self-Awareness*, Oxford University Press, Oxford.

Melzack, R. (1990) Phantom limbs and the concept of a neuromatrix. *Trends in Neuroscience*, **13**, 88–92.

Merleau-Ponty, M. (1962) *The Phenomenology of Perception* (Smith, C., trans.). Routledge, London/New York.

Mort, D. J., Malhotra, P., Mannan, S. K., Rorden, C., Pambakian, A., Kennard, C. and Husain, M. (2003) The anatomy of visual neglect. *Brain*, **126**(Pt 9), 1986–1997.

Nightingale, S. (1982) Somatoparaphrenia: a case report. *Cortex*, **18**, 463–467.

O'Regan, J. K. and Noë, A. (2001) A sensorymotor account of vision and visual consciousness. *Behavioural and Brain Sciences* **24**, 883–975.

Paillard, J. (1999) Motor determinants of a unified world perception. In Aschersleben, G., Bachmann, T. and Müsseler, J. (eds), *Cognitive Contributions to the Perception of Spatial and Temporal Events, Advances in Psychology*, Vol. 129, pp. 95–111. Elsevier, Amsterdam.

Pia, L., Neppi-Modona, M., Ricci, R. and Berti, A. (2004) The anatomy of anosognosia for hemiplegia: a meta-analysis. *Cortex*, **40**, 367–377.

Prinz, W. (1997) Perception and action planning. *European Journal of Cognitive Psychology*, **9**, 129–154.

Rochat, P. and Striano, T. (2000) Perceived self in infancy. *Infant Behavior and Development*, **23**, 513–530.

Ruby, P. and Decety, J. (2001) Effect of subjective perspective taking during simulation of action: a PET investigation of agency. *Nature Neuroscience*, **4**, 546–550.

Schaefer, M., Flor, H., Heinze, H. J. and Rotte, M. (2006) Dynamic modulation of the primary somatosensory cortex during seeing and feeling a touched hand. *Neuroimage*, **29**, 587–592.

Schwartz, S., Assal, F., Valenza, N., Seghier, M. L. and Vuilleumier, P. (2005) Illusory persistence of touch after right parietal damage: neural correlates of tactile awareness. *Brain*, **128**, 277–290.

Shelton, J. R., Fouch, E. and Caramazza, A. (1998) The selective sparing of body part knowledge: a case study. *Neurocase*, **4**, 339–351.

Sirigu, A., Grafman, J., Bressler, K. and Sunderland, T. (1991) Multiple representations contribute to body knowledge processing. Evidence from a case of autotopagnosia. *Brain*, **114** (Pt 1B), 629–642.

Sirigu, A., Daprati, E., Pradat-Diehl, P., Franck, N. and Jeannerod, M. (1999) Perception of self-generated movement following left parietal lesion. *Brain*, **122**, 1867–1874.

Suzuki, K., Yamadori, A. and Fujii, T. (1997) Category-specific comprehension deficit restricted to body parts. *Neurocase*, **3**, 193–200.

Tsakiris, M., Costantini, M. and Haggard, P. "In-the-body" experiences: distinguishing the self from the world. Unpublished study.

Tsakiris, M. and Haggard, P. (2003) Awareness of somatic events associated with a voluntary action. *Experimental Brain Research*, **149**, 439–446.

Tsakiris, M. and Haggard, P. (2005a) Experimenting with the acting self. *Cognitive Neuropsychology*, **22**, 387–407.

Tsakiris, M. and Haggard, P. (2005b) The rubber hand illusion revisited: visuotactile integration and self-attribution. *Journal of Experimental Psychology, Human Perception and Performance*, **31**, 80–91.

Tsakiris, M., Haggard, P., Franck, N., Mainy, N. and Sirigu, A. (2005) A specific role for efferent information in self-recognition. *Cognition*, **96**, 215–231.

Tsakiris, M., Prabhu, G. and Haggard, P. (2006) Having a body versus moving your body: how agency structures body-ownership. *Consciousness and Cognition*, **15**, 423–432.

Tsakiris, M., Hesse, M., Boy, C., Haggard, P. and Fink, G. Neural signatures of body-ownership: a sensory network for bodily self-consciousness. *Cerebral Cortex*, 2007, doi:10.1093/cercor/bh1131.

van den Bos and Jeannerod, M. (2002) Sense of body and sense of action both contribute to self-recognition. *Cognition*, **85**, 177–187.

Vignemont de, F., Tsakiris, M. and Haggard, P. (2006) Body mereology. In Knoblich, G., Thornton, I., Grosjean, M. and Shiffrar, M. (eds), *Perception of the Human Body*. Oxford University Press, New York, in press.

Vogeley, K., May, M., Ritzl, A., Falkai, P., Zilles, K. and Fink, G. R. (2004) Neural correlates of first-person perspective as one constituent of human self-consciousness. *Journal of Cognitive Neuroscience*, **16**, 817–827.

18

The motor hierarchy: from kinematics to goals and intentions

Antonia F de C. Hamilton and Scott T. Grafton

The idea of hierarchical organization in the motor system has a long history, but the different components of the hierarchy have not been easy to localize in the human brain. We have recently developed a one-back paradigm for inducing repetition suppression in response to observed actions in functional magnetic resonance imaging (fMRI), which allows different levels of the motor hierarchy to be examined independently within the same stimulus set. Thirty-one participants viewed video clips of a hand taking a wine-bottle or a dumb-bell with either a precision or whole hand grip and performed one of four attentional tasks while fMRI images were acquired with a 3T scanner. We found suppression for repeated goals compared to novel goals in the anterior intraparietal sulcus (aIPS), cerebellum and basal ganglia, replicating previous results (Hamilton, A. F. and Grafton, S. T. (2006) *Journal of Neuroscience*, **26**, 1133–1137). Suppression for repeated grasps compared to novel grasps was found in the lateral occipital cortex (LOC), middle intraparietal sulcus and inferior frontal gyrus (IFG). An analysis of task revealed no main effects and no interactions between task and repetition suppression in any of the grasp or goal clusters. We suggest that these results are compatible with a model of the motor representational hierarchy in which aIPS represents goals or intentions and is placed at the top of the hierarchy. In this model, LOC provides a visual analysis of grasp, while IFG provides a motor analysis of grasp, both subsidiary to the goal representation in aIPS. We discuss this model in relation to other hierarchical control models, and in relation to the processing of actions for the self and others in the human mirror neuron system.

Introduction

An ordinary action such as pouring a glass of wine can be understood on many levels. The barman will reach for and grasp the bottle, then transport it and tilt it over the glass, carefully controlling the angle to avoid spilling. These kinematic components each require a precisely orchestrated pattern of muscle activity guided by proprioceptive and visual feedback. But a drinker waiting for the barman to finish pouring would likely consider only the goal of the action—to provide some refreshment. Three broad levels of description can be distinguished in this example—the goal level incorporates the intention of the actor and the outcome of the action; the kinematic level describes the shape of the hand and the movement of the arm in space and time; while the muscle level describes the patterns of activity in >30 hand and arm muscles which contribute to the action.

These three levels have a hierarchical relationship, and are relatively independent of one another. That is, the same goal may be accomplished with several different kinematic components, each of which could be accomplished by a variety of muscle activation sequences. Conversely, one particular pattern of muscle activity or one particular kinematic component may contribute to different goals in different contexts. The aim of the current paper is to determine if this descriptive hierarchy has a real cognitive counterpart, and if so, can the different levels of the hierarchy be localized in the human brain?

Background

The idea that the motor system is organized hierarchically to achieve particular goals has a long and broad history. Sherrington (1906) distinguished between upper and lower motor neurons, while Jackson (1889) referred to higher motor centers controlling simple movements. From a psychological point of view, William James suggested that voluntary movement is secondary to reflexive actions, and involves "an anticipatory image … of the sensorial consequences of a movement" (James, 1890). This image precedes the action and guides performance, acting as a goal or target state which the action should aim towards. These concepts came together in the work of Donald Hebb, who argued that our theories of different levels of description for behaviors, including abstract concepts such as goal, should also have a counterpart in different types of representation in the brain (Hebb, 1949).

More recently, theories of motor hierarchies have become more specific and have been applied to all levels of the motor system. For example, Keele et al. (1990) emphasized the ordered nature of high-level motor programs for feedforward control of movements, in particular in sequential tasks such as writing or typing. Hierarchical ordering is found implicitly in more detailed computational models of motor control, which always include some 'goal' parameters specifying the desired output of the system. This may be termed the 'desired trajectory' (Wolpert et al., 1998) or 'cost function' (Hamilton and Wolpert, 2002) or an 'instruction stimulus' (Arbib et al., 2000), but in every case, the goal is assumed to exist at a level of control above the detailed model.

Wohlschlager (2003) provides experimental evidence for a hierarchy of goals in children, showing that when a child imitates another person, he or she tends to copy goals rather than subgoals. In this model, objects and outcomes are considered to be higher goals than actions or movement paths, and goals are defined according to the ideomotor principles of William James. At an even more abstract level, Pacherie (2006) provides a philosophical analysis of action and intention which distinguishes motor intentions, present intentions and future intentions in a hierarchical scheme. All of these theories see motor control in terms of a refinement of information from an abstract goal ('to pour the wine') to a more detailed motor plan ('lift the bottle, tilt the bottle over the glass') to a precise specification of the reaching and grasping actions required to achieve each goal, and finally the activation of specific muscles in a coordinated sequence. The hierarchy for motor control parallels work on executive function which suggests a similar organization in terms of goals and subgoals in both problem-solving tasks (Norman and Shallice, 1986; Dehaene and Changeux, 1997) and in everyday life (Shallice and Burgess, 1991).

In addition to this linear planning, the majority of theories recognize the essential role of feedback loops in motor control. The role of spinal reflexes in eliciting and controlling action has been studied for over 100 years, and it is now clear that proprioceptive and motor systems are intimately linked in control loops at every level of the motor system. Though it has in the past been argued that the delays between a sensory event and a motor response severely limit the use of feedback control (Keele *et al.*, 1990), newer computational work reveals mechanisms which can largely mitigate these delays. In particular, forward models provide a mechanism for predicting and cancelling the sensory consequences of actions (Blakemore *et al.*, 1998; Wolpert and Flanagan, 2001). The idea of predictive forward models has recently been incorporated into a more sophisticated computational framework, where a system of multiple parallel forward—inverse model pairs is able to provide accurate control of action in a variety of contexts, in a model called MOSAIC (Wolpert and Kawato, 1998). Furthermore, it has been suggested that MOSAIC could be organized in a hierarchical fashion (Haruno *et al.*, 2003), and could even provide for understanding other people's actions (Wolpert *et al.*, 2003).

Thus, the idea emerges of a hierarchical system of loops, in which information flows in both directions between the different goal, kinematic and muscle levels. The cognitive structure of this system is illustrated in Figure 18.1, which presents a rough schema of a visual–motor loop for the control of hand actions. We distinguish the three major motor control levels—goal, kinematic and muscles, together with two levels of visual analysis— a general early analysis followed by more specific visual representations of moving body parts and the objects they interact with, and we assume that information flows in both directions between every level. This sketch is dramatically simplified and ignores the important role of proprioceptive feedback, as well as the more subtle distinctions within different levels, but it does set out the basic components we are interested in. Similar models have been proposed for both language (Geschwind, 1965) and hand actions (Tessari and Rumiati, 2004), but the localization of the different components in the human brain remains uncertain. In this chapter, we will focus on the visual analysis of action, the goal representation and the kinematic levels, and ask: can these three components of the visual–motor hierarchy be localized in the human brain?

The motor hierarchy in the brain

The inputs and outputs of the motor system ground the hierarchy in the brain. Thus, we should begin by assuming that the primary and secondary visual cortex provides the low-level visual analysis system, while primary motor cortex processes outputs to the spinal cord and thus the muscles (Lemon *et al.*, 1998). The higher levels of kinematics and goal representations are likely to be found within the neural systems involved in visually guided actions, which include the premotor cortex, supplementary motor areas, parietal cortex, cerebellum and the basal ganglia. Extensive electrophysiological recordings from these regions in awake, behaving primates give some clues to their functions.

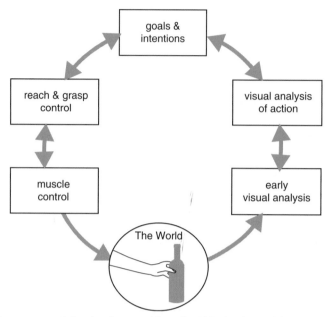

Figure 18.1 Components of the visual–motor hierarchy. This simple model assumes a control loop from visual analysis to an abstract goal representation and then to more detailed kinematic and muscle control.

Single-unit recordings in the inferior frontal cortex of the monkey have revealed neurons coding for grasp configuration and object shape (Rizzolatti *et al.*, 1988) and some of these are also responsive to the observation of actions (di Pellegrino *et al.*, 1992; Gallese *et al.*, 1996). In particular, it has been claimed that some cells in area F5 encode the goal of an action, because they respond when an action is inferred to have taken place out of sight (Umilta *et al.*, 2001). Similarly, single-unit recordings in the anterior intra-parietal sulcus (AIP) in the monkey have found neuronal coding of object shape and grasp (Sakata *et al.*, 1995), while it has been reported that neurons in monkey inferior parietal lobule (IPL) fire when a grasp and place action sequence is performed or observed (Fogassi *et al.*, 2005). These data have been interpreted in terms of neural coding for performed and observed intentions in the IPL. In contrast, studies of more abstract, symbolic goals implicate the frontal cortex in goal planning and control (Shima *et al.*, 1996; Saito *et al.*, 2005; Mushiake *et al.*, 2006). Thus, the monkey neurophysiological studies do not provide a consensus on the localization of goals or grasps in the brain.

Studies of the monkey brain are limited by the fact that in general, only one brain region, and often only one neuron, is tested at a time. This means that it is very difficult to obtain an overall picture of the motor hierarchy. Furthermore, the tasks used in different studies can be quite variable, and do not necessarily systematically separate the different levels of representation. In particular, studies of object grasping in monkeys have not systematically distinguished hand configuration from object identity (di Pellegrino *et al.*, 1992;

Sakata *et al.*, 1995). Finally, while there are homologies between the human and monkey brain, there are also major differences, which are matched by behavioral differences in planning, flexibility of action and the ability to infer other people's intentions, all of which are limited or absent in monkeys.

Human neuroimaging studies have the potential to examine the whole brain during more flexible and varied tasks than can be performed by monkeys, and have provided evidence for an extensive neural system for visual control of action, encompassing primary motor cortex, premotor cortex, inferior parietal cortex, supplementary motor area, cerebellum and basal ganglia (Grafton *et al.*, 1992, 1996). Many of these studies used simple finger tapping or tracking tasks, because the use of fMRI to examine more complex visually guided actions is severely limited by the scanner environment and the need to avoid movement artifacts. These environmental limitations can be avoided by studying imagined or observed actions rather than performed actions. There is increasing evidence that action observation activates brain structures similar to those involved in motor performance (Buccino *et al.*, 2001; Rizzolatti and Craighero, 2004), so observation can be taken, with caveats, as a proxy for performance.

Nevertheless, few human neuroimaging studies have even attempted to distinguish different levels of the motor hierarchy in either performance or observation. This is because any single task involving motor performance, imagined action or observation of action requires processing at all levels at once, which means that it is not easy to separate different components by means of a subtraction design. For example, if participants observe a video clip of a hand action during fMRI (e.g. Buccino *et al.*, 2001), brain regions involved in processing visual motion, hand kinematics, goals and intentions will all be activated, and a straightforward subtraction experiment cannot distinguish the different levels.

Some studies have attempted to segment these systems, for example, by showing videos of actions without an object and thus without a clear goal or intention, in comparison to videos of goal-directed actions (Pelphrey *et al.*, 2004). These authors report increased superior temporal sulcus (STS) activation for 'unintended' actions, but it remains unclear whether participants really see a movement towards empty space as a movement without an intention, or just as a movement with a more complex intention, e.g. communicating something to the observer. Similar problems would arise if 'accidental' actions were used as stimuli, because even children are able to perceive the true intention underlying the action (Meltzoff, 1995), so a subtraction between accidental and correct actions reveals brain regions involved in coding errors (Manthey *et al.*, 2003) but not those coding intentions. While subtraction designs have been used to separate reach and grasp within the kinematic level (Culham *et al.*, 2003), and to localize visual processing of human body parts (Downing *et al.*, 2001), it does not seem possible to examine goals, intentions or kinematics across levels in the motor hierarchy by a traditional subtraction design.

The aim of the current paper is to localize the different components of the motor hierarchy, using a repetition suppression (RS) design to examine each level independently, as detailed below. We use action observation rather than performance, and thus rely on the assumption that performed and observed actions involve the same neural systems (Rizzolatti and Craighero, 2004). Though this assumption restricts the conclusions we can draw about motor performance, the use of action observation allows us to address the question of the neural basis of action understanding and inferences about other people's intentions. This approach allows us to take a broader view of the motor hierarchy, examining several different levels of representation to obtain an overall model of action representation.

The current chapter has two specific aims. First, we plan to replicate our previous study (Hamilton and Grafton, 2006), which suggested that action goals are represented in the aIPS. This result is at odds with several previous studies which give frontal regions a role in goals (Koechlin and Jubault, 2006) and intentions (Iacoboni et al., 2005), and thus requires replication. As before, we focus specifically on object goals, where the goal of the action is to take a particular object and thus the goal is defined by the identity of the object taken. Second, we aim to localize the kinematic levels of the hierarchy, which have received less attention in the past. In particular, we will look for evidence of a dual representation of kinematics, in both visual and motor terms. Understanding these lower levels of the system will allow a more complete model of the visuo-motor control loop to be constructed, taking into account the known connectivity between brain regions as well as the fMRI activations.

The repetition suppression approach

Our experimental method measures a phenomenon known as repetition suppression (RS), which is not widely used in motor studies. However, RS has been extensively studied in the context of visual representations (Kourtzi and Kanwisher, 2000; Grill-Spector and Malach, 2001), where it is more commonly known as fMRI adaptation. The term repetition suppression will be used here as a more succinct and general descriptor, because reduced responses to repeated stimuli are not unique to fMRI. There are three major advantages to the RS approach. First, it allows us to look for changes within a class of stimuli or a level of the hierarchy rather than between classes. Thus, different levels of representation for the same stimulus can be analysed independently. Second, RS has been linked to reaction time priming (Maccotta and Buckner, 2004; Wig et al., 2005), though we do not make use of this link here. Third, RS data can be interpreted in terms of neuronal population coding, in accordance with two key principles:

1. Suppression from stimulus A to stimulus B occurs within a brain region *only* if some feature of both A and B is encoded in the same population of neurons in that region.

2. If stimulus B caused suppression in a region, release from suppression on presentation of stimulus C occurs *only* if some feature of B and C is encoded in different populations within that region.

Figure 18.2 gives a concrete example of these principles in a hypothetical brain area representing animals. In this region, one subpopulation of neurons encode 'dog', and a different population encode 'cat'. These two populations are interspersed and each

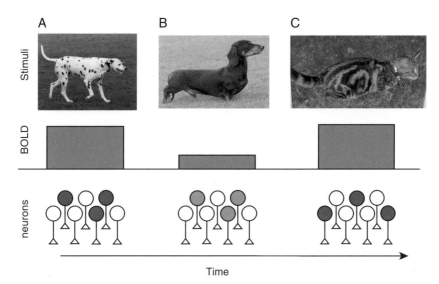

Figure 18.2 The likely mechanism of repetition suppression (RS). An example of RS is shown for a hypothetical brain area encoding animals in two populations of neurons, one for dogs and the other for cats. The top row illustrates the stimulus sequence. The bottom row illustrates hypothetical firing levels in intermixed populations of neurons representing 'dog' and 'cat' with the intensity of the colour indicating the level of firing.

contain the same total number of neurons, so they cannot be distinguished by a traditional fMRI subtraction design, but they can be discerned by measuring RS.

On seeing stimulus A, a Dalmatian, the neuronal population encoding 'dog' will fire vigorously and a robust BOLD response will be recorded. When a picture of a Daschund is shown next (B), the total activity in the 'dog' population is reduced and a suppressed BOLD response is recorded for the repeated stimulus. If the third stimulus (C) shows a tabby cat, the neuronal population encoding 'cat' will now respond robustly giving a strong BOLD signal. Thus, the presence of the predicted BOLD pattern in response to this stimulus sequence is evidence for distinct neuronal populations encoding 'dog' and 'cat' within a brain region. Note that this pattern of activation would not be seen if the brain area represented either a broader category (e.g. mammals), which would result in suppression over all stimuli, or a narrower category (e.g. each breed of dog in a different population), which would not give any suppression between breeds. Thus, RS can reveal the level of neural representation in different brain regions.

The validity of this interpretation depends on two simple assumptions. First is the assumption of population coding within brain regions, for which there is extensive evidence in many parts of the cortex (Georgopoulos *et al.*, 1982; Britten *et al.*, 1993). Second, the population response must be suppressed when the same stimulus feature is repeated. The precise pattern of suppression, which could be an overall reduction or a sharpening of neuronal tuning curves, remains a matter of debate (Grill-Spector *et al.*, 2006), as does the mechanism by which suppression might occur (Krekelberg *et al.*, 2006). However, the plausibility of population suppression to repeated stimuli is no longer in doubt, and thus the principle of measuring RS in order to infer neuronal population coding appears to be sound.

A final issue which must be addressed before employing RS in motor studies is the generality of the phenomena. The vast majority of studies have examined RS in visual regions such as the lateral occipital complex and fusiform face area (Henson, 2003). However, there is also evidence for RS in frontal (Buckner *et al.*, 1998) and parietal (Shmuelof and Zohary, 2005) regions, and RS studies have been used to examine for semantic (Thompson-Schill *et al.*, 1999), syntactic (Noppeney and Price, 2004) and numeric (Pinel *et al.*, 2001) representations in the brain. Thus, this phenomenon seems to be general to most of the cortex, and could plausibly apply to motor representations too. By measuring suppression in response to repeated features at different levels of the motor hierarchy, it should be possible to localize the representations involved in the human brain.

Applying RS to the motor hierarchy

To examine the motor hierarchy in the human brain, we used a sequence of stimuli designed to induce RS at three distinct levels: (1) the goal object of a reaching action, (2) the type of grasp used to reach the object, and (3) the weight of the object as revealed by lift velocity. Unlike many other RS studies (Grill-Spector and Malach, 2001), we use a one-back RS design (Figure 18.3), where each stimulus is defined as novel or repeated relative to the one stimulus before it. This approach is motivated by the fact that RS is largest on a single repeated trial immediately following the prime stimulus and amount of suppression does not increase after approximately eight stimuli (Grill-Spector *et al.*, 2006). Thus, a one-back design provides an efficient and flexible approach to inducing and measuring RS within a single set of stimuli. We measured RS for three stimulus characteristics: goal object, grasp and weight; independently in a $2 \times 2 \times 2$ factorial design where each factor can be either Novel or Repeated.

Based on previous work, we have predictions for RS at each level. The goal level was previously examined in an RS experiment (Hamilton and Grafton, 2006), which revealed that a region of the left aIPS encodes the goal of another person's action. Here we define a goal by the identity of the object which a person is reaching for, and note that our results do not necessarily generalize to all types of goal, such as tool use, or social goals. Nevertheless, the goal of reaching for an object is often a subgoal in other more complex tasks, and provides an ideal entry-point for the study of high-level action representation. The goal-object analysis here will be an attempt to replicate the previous study, in a more powerful scanner and with a more precisely controlled stimulus set. Thus, we predict that the same brain region, aIPS, will show RS for goal object.

The grasp level of representation could be localized to several regions, and in particular, we hope to distinguish visual analysis of grasp from a motor preparatory representation of grasp. Possible regions for motor grasp include aIPS which was traditionally considered a 'grasp area' (Sakata *et al.*, 1995) and IFG on the basis of the equivalence of this region to monkey F5, which has direct connections to primary motor cortex and neurons specializing for different grasp configurations (Rizzolatti *et al.*, 1988). Visual analysis of grasp could be carried out in a variety of extrastriate regions in the middle temporal gyrus, lateral occipital cortex (LOC) or STS, all of which have been associated with processing observed body parts (Downing *et al.*, 2001) and biological motion (Grossman *et al.*, 2000).

Object weight representations are likely to be similar to grasp representations, as both fall at the kinematic level of the hierarchy. Weight judgments are made based on the velocity of the actor's lifting action (Hamilton *et al.*, 2007), which could be expected to involve visual and biological motion regions, including middle temporal gyrus, LOC and STS. However, IFG is also required for accurate weight judgment (Pobric and Hamilton, 2006), and both this region and primary motor cortex show activity related to the biasing effect of box lifting on weight judgment (Hamilton *et al.*, 2006). Thus we predict that weight representations, like grasp, would be likely to be found in the extrastriate visual regions and premotor cortex.

The final factor we will examine is the effect of attention to different tasks on the level of RS in each region. That is, does top-down processing of one element of the scene influence the amount of RS for different elements in the scene? This is a critical question for the interpretation of RS studies, in particular those that report suppression in parietal or frontal regions, where the suppression could be interpreted in terms of attention rather than a specific neural population code for the stimulus characteristics. We examine task as a between-subjects factor to ensure that each participant focuses on only one task during the experiment, and predict no effects of task on RS.

Methods

Sixteen unique video clips were generated, each 4.5 s long, depicting a hand reaching for and taking either a dumb-bell or a wine bottle. Each of the objects could be grasped with either a precision grip on the neck of the bottle or middle of the dumb-bell, or with a power grip on the body of the bottle or the top of the dumb-bell. The object dimensions were precisely matched (neck/middle = 2.5 cm diameter; body/top = 7.7 cm diameter) so that the motor properties of each grip would be identical. Furthermore, each object could either be empty, weighing 0.5 kg, or filled with water/lead shot to a weight of 1 kg. These changes in weight did not alter the appearance of the object, so weight could only be judged by careful examination of the speed of the lifting action. Finally, each object could be placed on the far left of the table, or slightly behind and to the right, with the other object in the alternate location. Thus, the clips filled a 2 × 2 × 2 factorial design, with factors: Goal object (dumb-bell/wine), Grasp (power/precision), Weight (Heavy/Light), and clips were ordered to obtain RS for all of these factors simultaneously.

Thirty-one right-handed participants gave their informed consent to take part. In the scanner, the participants watched sets of video clips in a sequence determined by a one-back RS design as illustrated in Figure 18.3. In this design, each movie is defined as 'Novel' or

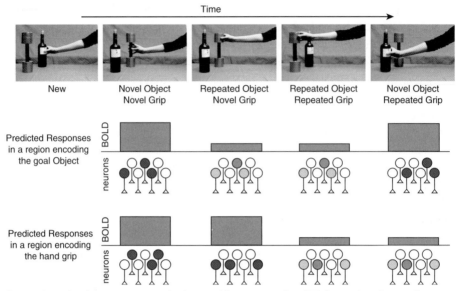

Figure 18.3 Stimulus sequence to obtain repetition suppression (RS) for goal and grasp in a one-back design. Top panel shows one frame from each video clip. Lower panels show predicted neural activity and BOLD in a region encoding goal object and a region encoding hand grasp.

'Repeated' on each of the three stimulus dimensions (goal, grasp and weight) relative to the one movie before. Thus, each movie contributes to the analysis on its own account, but also acts as a 'prime' for the next movie in the sequence. Movies were organized into sets, which each began with a new movie which primes the RS movie on the next trial but was not analysed. Each set contained between five and ten RS movies, and then ended with a question trial, followed by a short rest before the next set. All participants saw eight new movies, eight questions and 64 RS movies in a single functional run.

Different questions were assigned randomly to individual participants to assess the effects of task in a between-subjects design. Three participants were asked to determine the identity of the object taken on each trial (Object task), 11 were asked to determine the grip used on each trial (Grip task), 11 were asked to determine the object weight on each trial (Weight task) and the remaining six were asked to determine the location of the grasped object (Location task). These groups allow us to examine the influence of top-down control on RS at each level of the motor hierarchy. All participants were instructed to attend to every video and mentally perform the task for that clip. After a set of five to 10 videos, the task question appeared written on the screen and participants were required to answer as quickly and accurately as possible. These question trials ensured that participants were awake and on-task during the scanning but were not analysed further.

The experiment was carried out in a 3T Philips Intera scanner using an eight-channel phased array coil and 36 slices per TR (4 mm thickness, 0.5 mm gap); TR: 2000 ms; TE: 35 ms; flip angle: 90°; field of view: 24 cm; matrix: 80×80. The first two brain images of the functional run were discarded, then 233 images were collected and stored. Raw data for each participant were realigned, unwarped and normalized to the MNI template with a resolution of $2 \times 2 \times 2$ mm in SPM2. A design matrix was fitted for each subject, with each movie modeled as a boxcar convolved with the standard hemodynamic response function. The design matrix weighted each raw image according to its overall variability to reduce the impact of movement artifacts (Diedrichsen and Shadmehr, 2005). After estimation, 9 mm smoothing was applied to the beta images.

We calculated contrasts for novel object > repeated object, novel grip > repeated grip and novel weight > repeated weight. An exploratory analysis of interactions between object RS and grip RS was also conducted within a mask of the main effects. Results were analysed first over the whole group (regardless of task) and we report regions which survive a threshold of $P < 0.001$ uncorrected and 10 voxels over the whole brain in Table 18.1. However, we limit the discussion of results to clusters which fall within the predicted action representation network, or which survive the cluster level correction for multiple comparisons. To examine the effect of cognitive task on RS in the action representation system, a secondary analysis was carried out on the main clusters reported in Table 18.1. Mean BOLD signal over the cluster in each condition for each participant was extracted and subjected to a repeated measures ANOVA in SPSS with factors Grasp and Object (both novel or repeated), and a between-subjects factor of task (object, grasp, location or weight tasks). We looked for main effects of task or interactions of task with RS, and consider only effects which survive Bonferroni correction for the number of clusters tested to be significant, resulting in thresholds of $p < 0.0083$ for the object cluster set, and $p < 0.0063$ for the grasp cluster set.

Results

The neural representation of object weight

In the contrast of novel weight > repeated weight over all participants, no regions survived the $p < 0.001$ threshold. At a more liberal $p < 0.005$, cluster of 5 voxels was found in the left inferior occipital cortex (−38, −74, 4). This region is close to the lateral occipital location which is involved in the biasing effect of box lifting on weight judgment (Hamilton et al., 2006) and is within the predicted visual action regions. Thus, this result hints at a visual analysis of object weight. The effect may be weak because it was not easy to judge object weight in the clips used, and participants who were not alert to the different possible weights may not have discriminated object weight at all. More precisely controlled stimuli, for example from a high-speed video camera (Hamilton et al., 2007), might be needed to obtain a more robust localization of object weight. In particular, the question of IFG involvement in weight judgment, as suggested previously (Hamilton et al., 2006; Pobric and Hamilton, 2006), remains open.

The neural representation of hand grasp

Main effects of novel grasps compared to repeated grasps were found in three clusters in the inferior and middle occipital regions, a single cluster in the IFG, and a region of

Table 18.1 Coordinates of regions showing repetition suppression (RS) in the goal–object and grasp contrasts

Region	No. of voxels	t-value	Corrected p-values	MNI coordinates x	MNI coordinates y	MNI coordinates z	Uncorrected p-values
Goal–object contrast (wine bottle/ dumb-bell)							
Superior temporal gyrus	202	5.37	0.102	−50	4	−12	0.00000
Caudate	**255**	**5.24**	**0.049**	**6**	**12**	**2**	**0.00001**
L Inferior parietal lobule	**563**	**4.58**	**0.001**	**−52**	**−20**	**38**	**0.00004**
				−58	−24	30	
L Anterior intraparietal sulcus				**−46**	**−32**	**52**	
SMA	96	4.53	0.457	−10	20	46	0.000044
L Cerebellum	**303**	**4.37**	**0.027**	**−54**	**−60**	**−26**	**0.00007**
				−46	−64	−22	
				−46	−46	−22	
Lateral occipital cortex	15	4.19	0.985	−20	−56	10	0.000113
Inferior frontal gyrus	152	4.19	0.206	−58	10	34	0.000114
Intraparietal sulcus/cingulate	33	4.15	0.912	−24	−30	42	0.000125
Posterior superior temporal sulcus	26	4.09	0.948	−66	−40	6	0.000148
Cerebellum	25	4.00	0.953	−32	−50	−26	0.00019
Inferior temporal gyrus	38	3.82	0.882	52	−40	−26	0.000315
R Anterior intraparietal sulcus	127	3.79	0.296	54	−26	50	0.00034
Cerebellum	35	3.79	0.901	30	−42	−24	0.00034
Calcarine sulcus	10	3.79	0.994	−24	−64	20	0.00034
Caudate	11	3.78	0.992	−10	−12	18	0.00035

Table 18.1 (continued) Coordinates of regions showing repetition suppression (RS) in the goal–object and grasp contrasts

Region	No. of voxels	t-value	Corrected p-values	MNI coordinates			Uncorrected p-values
				x	y	z	
Middle occipital	13	3.77	0.989	48	-56	-6	0.000361
Superior precentral gyrus	13	3.72	0.989	60	6	36	0.00041
Cerebellum	34	3.70	0.907	46	-54	-30	0.00043
Thalamus	21	3.68	0.968	4	-22	2	0.00045
Cerebellum	10	3.66	0.994	-42	-86	-18	0.00048
Cerebellum	13	3.60	0.989	-14	-48	-26	0.00057
Inferior temporal gyrus	13	3.48	0.989	-32	10	-36	0.000769
Grip contrast (power/precision)							
Middle occipital	67	4.36	0.676	44	-86	-8	0.000071
SMA	51	4.09	0.794	2	14	62	0.00015
Middle occipital	40	4.05	0.870	-50	-68	-6	0.000165
Middle frontal gyrus	40	4.01	0.870	-40	30	30	0.000184
Middle occipital	12	3.91	0.989	36	-96	-14	0.000245
Frontal operculum	17	3.87	0.978	-46	14	14	0.000275
Middle intraparietal sulcus	16	3.70	0.981	-26	-50	58	0.000434
Inferior occipital	64	3.65	0.698	42	-68	-16	0.000494

Bold type indicates regions meeting the whole brain cluster corrected threshold.

the middle IPS. All these regions passed the $p < 0.001$ uncorrected threshold, and are listed in the top part of Table 18.1. Figure 18.4 illustrates the locations of the clusters and the RS effects. Weaker responses to repeated grasps (orange and pale blue bars) compared to novel grasps (red and dark blue bars) provide evidence for distinct neuronal populations encoding whole hand grips and precision grips in these regions. The RS effect

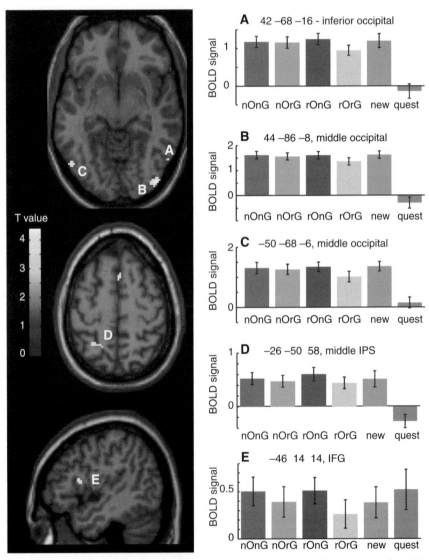

Figure 18.4 Grasp representations in the brain. Repetition suppression for grasp was found in occipital regions, middle intraparietal sulcus (IPS) and inferior frontal gyrus (IFG). All regions show stronger responses to novel grasps (red and dark blue) compared to repeated grasp (orange and light blue). n, novel; r, repeated; O, object goal; G, grasp; new, first stimulus of a block; quest, question trial. See color plate section.

appears weak in the plots due to individual differences in the absolute level of response, which do not have an impact on the repeated-measures analysis conducted in SPM. Outside the predicted network, RS for grasp was also seen in the SMA and middle frontal gyrus, but there was no evidence of RS for grasp in the more anterior portion of IPS or in IPL on either the left or right. These results are compatible with the idea of several grasp representations in the brain. In particular, the lateral occipital regions could contribute to a visual analysis of grasp, and the inferior frontal region to motor grasp representation, as hypothesized.

The neural representation of a goal object

The analysis of RS for goal object revealed a robust and extensive brain network (Figure 18.5 and Table 18.1). Three regions survived the whole brain cluster-corrected threshold in the grasp analysis, demonstrating stronger responses to novel goal objects compared to repeated goal objects. These were the left aIPS extending into the left IPL, a large cluster in the basal ganglia extending bilaterally through the caudate and putamen, and the left cerebellum. These findings provide a clear replication of the findings of Hamilton and Grafton (2006), where aIPS, basal ganglia and cerebellum were all reported. Additional regions showing RS for grasp over the $p < 0.001$ uncorrected threshold include SMA, IFG and STS, as listed in Table 18.1.

Interactions between goal object and hand grasp

An exploratory analysis of interactions between RS for goal and RS for grasp was carried out at a $p < 0.001$ uncorrected threshold and 10 voxel minimum cluster size within a mask of the main effects of Goal and Grasp. No brain regions showed a positive interaction between Goal and Grasp. A negative interaction was found in a small cluster of 32 voxels in the left aIPS (MNI coordinates −44, −34, 56). This region was located within the much larger cluster of 563 voxels, which spanned the IPL and aIPS and showed a strong main effect of RS for goal. The interaction cluster showed stronger activity in the novel Goal–repeated Grip and repeated Goal–novel Grip conditions compared to the novel Goal–novel Grip and repeated Goal–repeated Grip conditions. This pattern of activation implies that this region is sensitive to the association of a particular grasp with a particular object, and responds more robustly when that association changes. However, interactions in repetition suppression studies cannot easily be interpreted in terms of population coding, and further studies will be required to establish the robustness and meaning of RS interactions.

The effects of task

The effects of task were examined as a between-subjects factor in a repeated-measures ANOVA in each of eight grip clusters (those with more than 10 voxels) and six object clusters (those with more than 100 voxels). Within the grip clusters, there were no main effects of task (all $p > 0.1$) and no grip by task interactions (all $p > 0.1$). Similarly, analysis of the object clusters did not reveal any main effects of task (min $p = 0.097$) or object by task interactions (all $p > 0.1$). These results indicate that directing participant's attention

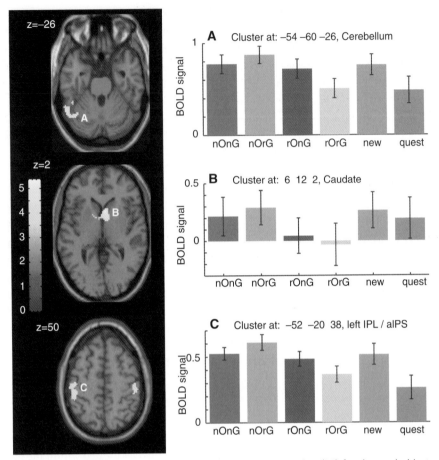

Figure 18.5 Goal representations in the brain. Repetition suppression (RS) for the goal object was found in the cerebellum, basal ganglia and left inferior parietal lobule (IPL)/anterior intraparietal sulcus (aIPS). All three regions show stronger responses to novel goals (red and orange) compared to repeated goals (blue). n, novel; r, repeated; O, object goal; G, grasp; new, first stimulus of a block; quest, question trial. See color plate section.

towards different aspects of the video clips does not influence the RS obtained to different motor components. This provides evidence that RS is unrelated to visual attention or cognitive factors, but is an obligatory part of processing action information.

Discussion

Using a repetition suppression experiment, we have been able to localize the different levels of the visuo-motor hierarchy in the human brain. We found evidence that LOC and IFG support a neural representation of hand grasp, while aIPS, basal ganglia and cerebellum contain a neural representation of the goal of an action. These clusters all fall within the predicted parietal–premotor action network, and are coherent with our previous data

(Hamilton and Grafton, 2006). In particular, we now have evidence for a dual representation of grasps in both occipital and premotor regions, which we can map onto the model of visual–motor processing (Figure 18.6), by assuming that LOC provides a visual analysis of grasp, while IFG provides a motor analysis of grasp. The representation of goal remains in the aIPS, as predicted by previous work (Hamilton and Grafton, 2006). Thus, we provide the first evidence of a functional dissociation between the IFG and aIPS regions of the visuo–motor hierarchy. These results allow us to propose a simple relationship between the motor hierarchy and the brain, illustrated in Figure 18.6. We now consider the evidence for the localization, function and connectivity of each level in turn.

Visual analysis of action

Our data indicate that a representation of observed grasps and observed kinematic patterns is found in a set of regions in the LOC. Similar regions have been reported in a variety of studies of action observation (Grezes and Decety, 2001), biological motion processing (Grossman et al., 2000), and viewing of parts of the human body (Downing et al., 2001). More recent data show that several regions in the human occipital and temporal cortex have selectivity for body parts, and that middle temporal regions which are selective for motion also have preferential responses to images of the human body (Spiridon et al., 2006). Similarly, a recent fMRI study of motion and body selectivity in the macaque reveals a patchwork of occipito-temporal regions with selectivity for observed motion

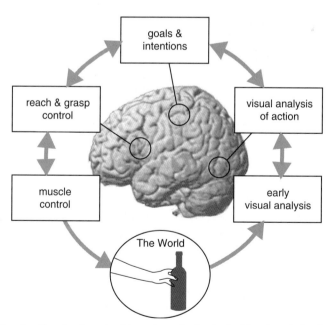

Figure 18.6 Mapping the visual–motor hierarchy onto the brain. Visual analysis of action takes place in the lateral occipital cortex, goals are represented in anterior intraparietal sulcus and kinematic control of grasp requires the inferior frontal gyrus.

and observed actions (Nelissen *et al.*, 2006). Our results also indicate a set of several lateral occipital regions which contain representations of observed grasps, rather than a single 'grasp' or 'visual kinematics' region. Based on the clear visual associations of these lateral occipital regions, we suggest that this network provides a visual analysis of the kinematic parameters of observed actions, as indicated on the right of Figure 18.6.

These data could be taken to imply that the kinematics of an observed action can be analysed purely by visual mechanisms (Jacob and Jeannerod, 2005), without the need for a motor simulation (Gallese and Goldman, 1998). However, there is increasing evidence for close links between visual and motor processing of kinematics. In particular, activity in EBA is modulated by the performance of a motor task (Astafiev *et al.*, 2004). Data from our own laboratory show that LOC has a prominent role in perceptual weight judgment and in the biasing effect of action on perception (Hamilton *et al.*, 2006). Together, these data implicate the lateral occipital network in visual processing of human actions with close links to the motor system. Our new results go further and demonstrate that these lateral occipital regions are able to perform a detailed analysis of the kinematic parameters of action, for both grasp configuration and object weight.

Somewhat surprisingly, we did not find any involvement of the posterior STS in the representation of grasp. A number of studies have emphasized the role of STS in detecting biological motion (Grossman *et al.*, 2000) and even detecting intentions (Pelphrey *et al.*, 2004), and STS has been proposed as the main visual input to the parietal action representation system (Keysers and Perrett, 2004). In contrast, the regions we report for grasp in this study, as well as for hand trajectory (Hamilton and Grafton, 2006) and box weight (Hamilton *et al.*, 2006) in previous studies, all lie below the STS in the middle or lateral occipital cortex, bordering the middle temporal gyrus. Some of these discrepancies may be due to lack of homologies between human and monkey brain and differences in nomenclature, especially in subtraction designs where large activation clusters can span several regions. The majority of human neuroimaging studies reporting STS activation use either whole-body motion, for example point-light figures (Grossman *et al.*, 2000) or eye-gaze stimuli (Pelphrey *et al.*, 2003), rather than hand actions. Further work will be needed to differentiate the roles of different occipito-temporal regions in representing action kinematics. Our own data point to a representation of hand grasp, hand velocity and hand trajectory in a patchwork of lateral occipital regions.

Action goals

Our analysis of RS for the goal of an action confirmed our previous results (Hamilton and Grafton, 2006) and demonstrated a central role for the left aIPS/IPL in the representation of object-goals. More specifically, we suggest that aIPS contains populations of neurons which encode different possible action goals, and these populations respond to the observation of a goal-directed action by another person. Thus, we place aIPS at the top of the motor hierarchy (Figure 18.6), with the most abstract action representation of those studied. The goal representation in the parietal cortex must also be qualified by the presence of an interaction with grasp in this region. The interpretation of this interaction in terms of neural population codes is not clear, and may have to await further research on the mechanism of RS. However, the presence of the interaction is indicative of the close links between the different regions of the visual–motor network, and the likelihood that information processing overlaps between these regions rather than being entirely segregated. It is also important to note that the goals we have studied were defined by the identity of the object taken by the actor, contrasting between a 'take wine bottle' goal and a 'take dumb-bell goal'. It remains to be seen if the same parietal regions encode other types of goal, for example manipulating the same object in different ways. Preliminary data from our own laboratory suggest that this is the case.

The idea that aIPS contains an abstract, goal representation is consistent with recent data showing that transcranial magnetic stimulation (TMS) over this region impairs the ability to reconfigure one's hand or arm to a novel action goal (Tunik et al., 2005). Recordings from the inferior parietal lobule in macaques, just below the monkey AIP, have provided evidence for neurons which encode both performed and observed action sequences (Fogassi et al., 2005), and are sensitive to the end state (goal) of a sequence rather than the initial action. However, there is also evidence that the anterior portion of the parietal sulcus has undergone an enlargement in the human relative to the macaque (Simon et al., 2002; Orban et al., 2006), suggesting that this region has taken on additional functions in the human brain. The ability to represent and interpret the goals of other people's actions might be one of these functions.

Our analysis of RS for goal also revealed robust goal representations in the basal ganglia and cerebellum. Similar regions were also found in our previous study (Hamilton and Grafton, 2006), but we did not discuss the result then, as it was not clear if the same type of repetition suppression behavior could be expected in subcortical regions compared to the cortex. However, given the strong replication we find in the present study, and the recent evidence of RS in the basal ganglia for language (Crinion et al., 2006), it seems likely that these results are important. There are also plausible reasons to believe that the cerebellum and basal ganglia might have a role to play in the control and monitoring of action goals. In particular, the cerebellum has a central role in the prediction of the sensory consequences of actions by means of forward models (Blakemore et al., 1998). As suggested in the Introduction, a hierarchical system of forward models (Wolpert et al., 2003) provides a plausible computational mechanism which could underlie the motor hierarchy. If the lowest level of this system, which deals with sensory prediction, were located in the cerebellum, it would be necessary for this system also to provide information to the higher levels, in the aIPS, and for these two regions to work together in the interpretation of goal-directed actions. Direct connectivity between the cerebellar nuclei and the aIPS has recently been demonstrated (Clower et al., 2005).

This connectivity study also revealed links between aIPS and the substantia nigra in the basal ganglia (Clower et al., 2005). The cluster showing RS for goal in the basal ganglia was located primarily in the right head of the caudate but extended to the left putamen. There is a variety of functions associated with the basal ganglia which might be relevant to the processing of goals. In particular, the basal ganglia have an important role in action sequencing (Graybiel, 1998; Lehericy et al., 2005) and in learning about the rewards associated with actions (Hollerman et al., 2000; Zink et al., 2004). Thus, the basal ganglia RS for goal might reflect a representation of an action goal as part of a sequence, or a representation of the value of the goal. Overall, our results imply a network for goal representation, where aIPS has a clear role at the top of the motor hierarchy, and BG and cerebellum provide a supporting function.

The motor representation of grasp

As well as the lateral occipital network for grasp, we found RS for grasp in a region of the IFG. We suggest that this is evidence of neuronal populations in this area encoding whole-hand and precision grips, which provide a motor representation of potential actions. The motor role of IFG has been demonstrated in both humans and monkeys. In particular, human IFG has been associated with the performance (Ehrsson *et al.*, 2000), imagination (Grafton *et al.*, 1996) and planning (Johnson-Frey *et al.*, 2005) of grasping actions in humans. In the macaque, region F5 in the inferior frontal cortex contains neurons which code for specific hand grasps (Rizzolatti *et al.*, 1988) but which also have mirror properties and respond to observed grasps (di Pellegrino *et al.*, 1992; Gallese *et al.*, 1996). The role of IFG in both kinematic control and the interpretation of observed kinematic patterns has also been demonstrated in humans. IFG is part of the network of regions active in motor tasks (Stephan *et al.*, 1995, Rizzolatti *et al.*, 1996), and is also required for judging the weight of a box lifted by another person (Pobric and Hamilton, 2006), a task which requires interpretation of kinematics (Hamilton *et al.*, 2007) rather than goals. This region is connected to both primary motor cortex and the spinal cord (Dum and Strick, 1991; Dum and Strick, 2002; Shimazu *et al.*, 2004), and thus is ideally placed to provide a motor grasp representation, closely linked to the performance of an action.

The localization of motor grasp representations to IFG places this region at a 'lower' stage of the motor hierarchy than aIPS, between the muscle output and the goal. This proposal is at odds with some studies which have attempted to link IFG to more abstract action understanding functions, such as the interpretation of goals (Umilta *et al.*, 2001) and intentions (Iacoboni *et al.*, 2005). A number of theoretical papers have also proposed links between the action representations in IFG and language (Rizzolatti and Arbib, 1998) or mentalizing (Gallese and Goldman, 1998) abilities. This proposal may have arisen partly from the historical accident that mirror neurons were explored in the IFG (di Pellegrino *et al.*, 1992) before they were studied in the inferior parietal cortex (Fogassi *et al.*, 2005). Furthermore, the studies which have linked IFG to abstract goals either did not distinguish between the configuration of the hand and the identity of the goal object (Umilta *et al.*, 2001), or did not control for context (Iacoboni *et al.*, 2005). Thus, we suggest that direct evidence for a goal representation in IFG is lacking. Instead, our own data clearly demonstrate a role for IFG in grasp and in representing the kinematics of hand actions.

Broader implications

Our model of the visual–motor hierarchy is a step towards defining the neural systems underlying motor control and action understanding in the human brain. As we make clear, the underlying cognitive structure we propose is based on previous models for language (Geschwind, 1965) and hand actions (Tessari and Rumiati, 2004). Our new data provide a grounding for these models in the brain, and thus allow us to make new predictions for fMRI, neuropsychological and neurophysiological experiments.

In particular, we provide the first evidence for distinct functions for the IFG and aIPS regions of the visual–motor loop, arguing that aIPS has more abstract goal representations whereas IFG has mainly lower level grasp representations. This conclusion conflicts with theories which place intention representations in the frontal cortex (Iacoboni et al., 2005) and which attempt to link sophisticated action understanding abilities in frontal cortex to language representations in Broca's area (Rizzolatti and Arbib, 1998). However, neither language nor action understanding depend on a single brain region, and it is quite possible that the production of language and hand actions are intertwined in the inferior frontal cortex, while the meaning of words (Spitsyna et al., 2006) and goals of actions are represented elsewhere.

There is one potential difference between our model in Figure 18.6 and the models previously proposed (Tessari and Rumiati, 2004), which include a direct connection between the visual analysis and motor grasp representations. Psychophysical evidence supports the existence of a direct connection, with both visual to motor (Kilner et al., 2003) and motor to visual (Hamilton et al., 2004) effects. However, we do not include this connection in the figure, because anatomical evidence is weak. Reviews of macaque neuroanatomy do not report a direct connection from superior and middle temporal regions to inferior frontal regions (Keysers and Perrett, 2004; Rozzi et al., 2006). However, a recent study using diffusion tensor imaging suggests that the human arcuate fasciculus, which is commonly considered to be a language pathway, extends from posterior middle temporal gyrus to IFG (Rilling et al., 2006). This fiber tract therefore has the potential to provide the direct connection between the visual and motor kinematic representations predicted by many psychophysical studies, and could easily be incorporated in our model. Further anatomical studies will be needed to confirm the result.

A second important issue for our model is that we have defined the visuo-motor hierarchy using action observation rather than motor execution, because this provides more precise stimulus control and avoids the limitations of the scanner environment. To draw conclusions about the organization of these brain systems for the control of one's own actions, we rely on the assumption of mirroring between performance and observation (Rizzolatti and Craighero, 2004). There is independent evidence for the involvement of aIPS in controlling goals (Tunik et al., 2005), and the localizations we propose do form a plausible model for the control of visually guided actions, but direct evidence that mirroring between self and other is specific to each level of the motor hierarchy remains to be discovered. In particular, it would be important to know if RS is seen for performed actions, both in the human and in the macaque brain.

Moving up the hierarchy

The model we present in Figure 18.6 describes the control and understanding of goal-directed hand actions, but does not itself explain the origin or selection of goals. The actions we have studied involve taking a single object, which is a very basic form of goal, but in real life, these actions would be likely to form one step towards achieving a more complex goal. For example, taking a wine bottle is just one component of pouring a glass of wine for a friend. Thus, we could postulate a continuing hierarchy of control for more complex action sequences, as suggested by studies of executive function (Koechlin *et al.*, 2003) and of planning goals in everyday tasks (Shallice and Burgess, 1991). However, there remains a gap between the simple action goals studied here and the long-range or abstract goals examined in motor planning tasks. Further studies of the cognitive and neural systems for complex actions will be needed to bridge the gap between motor and executive planning models. In terms of action understanding, there remains a similar gap between the understanding of action goals in the parietal cortex as described here, and the understanding of other people's beliefs, desires and other mental states in the 'theory of mind network' which includes the temporo-parietal junction and medial prefrontal cortex (Frith and Frith, 2003) but not the action understanding regions (Saxe, 2005).

Thus, hierarchical control above the goal level described here remains a complex and unresolved question. Furthermore, all hierarchical models of human cognition are vulnerable to the problem of a homunculus, who seems to be required at the top level to control the lower levels, but can neither be localized nor extinguished. A model composed of multiple overlapping control loops at a variety of levels, as implied here, has the potential to allow sophisticated motor control without a homunculus (Brooks, 1986), but evidence for such a system in the human brain remains to be found. We suggest that the RS approach to segmenting levels of representation, as outlined in this chapter, provides a useful method for interrogating and defining the higher and more abstract components of the motor hierarchy in future.

Conclusion

We have presented evidence for a hierarchical system for action understanding and visual–motor control in the human brain. This system is composed of a visual representation of action kinematics in the LOC, a goal/intention representation in the aIPS and a motor representation of kinematics in the IFG. The model is compatible with psychophysical and anatomical data, and provides a new framework for interpreting the computational processes underlying action understanding and simple social interactions.

References

Arbib, M. A., Billard, A., Iacoboni, M. and Oztop, E. (2000) Synthetic brain imaging: grasping, mirror neurons and imitation. *Neural Networks*, 13, 975–997.

Astafiev, S. V., Stanley, C. M., Shulman, G. L. and Corbetta, M. (2004) Extrastriate body area in human occipital cortex responds to the performance of motor actions. *Nature Neuroscience*, 7, 542–548.

Blakemore, S. J., Wolpert, D. M. and Frith, C. D. (1998) Central cancellation of self-produced tickle sensation. *Nature Neuroscience*, 1, 635–640.

Britten, K. H., Shadlen, M. N., Newsome, W. T. and Movshon, J. A. (1993) Responses of neurons in macaque MT to stochastic motion signals. *Visual Neuroscience*, 10, 1157–1169.

Brooks, R. A. (1986) A robust layered control system for a mobile robot. *IEEE Journal of Robotics and Automation*, **2**, 14–23.

Buccino, G., Binkofski, F., Fink, G. R., Fadiga, L., Fogassi, L., Gallese, V., Seitz, R. J., Zilles, K., Rizzolatti, G. and Freund, H. J. (2001) Action observation activates premotor and parietal areas in a somatotopic manner: an fMRI study. *European Journal of Neuroscience*, **13**, 400–404.

Buckner, R. L., Goodman, J., Burock, M., Rotte, M., Koutstaal., W, Schacter, D., Rosen, B. and Dale, A. M. (1998) Functional–anatomic correlates of object priming in humans revealed by rapid presentation event-related fMRI. *Neuron*, **20**, 285–296.

Clower, D. M., Dum, R. P. and Strick, P. L. (2005) Basal ganglia and cerebellar inputs to 'AIP'. *Cerebral Cortex*, **15**, 913–920.

Crinion, J., Turner, R., Grogan, A., Hanakawa, T., Noppeney, U., Devlin, J. T. *et al*. (2006) Language control in the bilingual brain. *Science*, **312**, 1537–1540.

Culham, J. C., Danckert, S. L., DeSouza, J. F., Gati, J. S., Menon, R. S. and Goodale, M. A. (2003) Visually guided grasping produces fMRI activation in dorsal but not ventral stream brain areas. *Experimental Brain Research*, **153**, 180–189.

Dehaene, S. and Changeux, J. P. (1997) A hierarchical neuronal network for planning behavior. *Proceedings of the National Academy of Sciences of the USA*, **94**, 13293–13298.

di Pellegrino, G., Fadiga, L., Fogassi, L., Gallese, V. and Rizzolatti, G. (1992) Understanding motor events: a neurophysiological study. *Experimental Brain Research*, **91**, 176–180.

Diedrichsen, J. and Shadmehr, R. (2005) Detecting and adjusting for artifacts in fMRI time series data. *Neuroimage*, **27**, 624–34

Downing, P. E., Jiang, Y., Shuman, M. and Kanwisher, N. (2001) A cortical area selective for visual processing of the human body. *Science*, **293**, 2470–2473.

Dum, R. P. and Strick, P. L. (1991) The origin of corticospinal projections from the premotor areas in the frontal lobe. *Journal of Neuroscience*, **11**, 667–689.

Dum, R. P. and Strick, P. L. (2002) Motor areas in the frontal lobe of the primate. *Physiology and Behavior*, **77**, 677–682.

Ehrsson, H. H., Fagergren, A., Jonsson, T., Westling, G., Johansson, R. S. and Forssberg, H. (2000) Cortical activity in precision- versus power-grip tasks: an fMRI study. *Journal of Neurophysiology*, **83**, 528–536.

Fogassi, L., Ferrari, P. F., Gesierich, B., Rozzi, S., Chersi, F. and Rizzolatti, G. (2005) Parietal lobe: from action organization to intention understanding. *Science*, **308**, 662–667.

Frith, U. and Frith, C. D. (2003) Development and neurophysiology of mentalizing. *Philosophical Transactions of the Royal Society of London, B*, **358**, 459–473.

Gallese, V. and Goldman, A. (1998) Mirror neurons and the simulation theory of mind-reading. *Trends in Cognitive Sciences*, **2**, 493–501.

Gallese, V., Fadiga, L., Fogassi, L. and Rizzolatti, G. (1996) Action recognition in the premotor cortex. *Brain*, **119**, 593–609.

Georgopoulos, A. P., Kalaska, J.F., Caminiti, R. and Massey, J. T. (1982) On the relations between the direction of two-dimensional arm movements and cell discharge in primate motor cortex. *Journal of Neuroscience*, **2**, 1527–1537.

Geschwind, N. (1965) Disconnexion syndromes in animals and man. I. *Brain*, **88**, 237–294.

Grafton, S. T., Mazziotta, J. C., Woods, R. P. and Phelps, M. E. (1992) Human functional anatomy of visually guided finger movements. *Brain*, **115** (Pt 2), 565–587.

Grafton, S. T., Arbib, M. A., Fadiga, L. and Rizzolatti, G. (1996) Localization of grasp representations in humans by positron emission tomography. 2. Observation compared with imagination. *Experimental Brain Research*, **112**, 103–111.

Graybiel, A. M. (1998) The basal ganglia and chunking of action repertoires. *Neurobiology of Learning and Memory*, **70**, 119–136.

Grezes, J. and Decety, J. (2001) Functional anatomy of execution, mental simulation, observation, and verb generation of actions: a meta-analysis. *Human Brain Mapping*, 12, 1–19.

Grill-Spector, K. and Malach, R. (2001) fMR-adaptation: a tool for studying the functional properties of human cortical neurons. *Acta Psychologica (Amst.)*, 107, 293–321.

Grill-Spector, K., Henson, R. and Martin, A. (2006) Repetition and the brain: neural models of stimulus-specific effects. *Trends in Cognitive Sciences*, 10, 14–23.

Grossman, E., Donnelly, M., Price, R., Pickens, D., Morgan, V., Neighbor, G. and Blake, R. (2000) Brain areas involved in perception of biological motion. *Journal of Cognitive Neuroscience*, 12, 711–720.

Hamilton, A. F. and Grafton, S. T. (2006) Goal representation in human anterior intraparietal sulcus. *Journal of Neuroscience*, 26, 1133–1137.

Hamilton, A. F. de C. and Wolpert, D. M. (2002) Controlling the statistics of action: obstacle avoidance. *Journal of Neurophysiology*, 87, 2434–2440.

Hamilton, A. F., Wolpert, D. M. and Frith, U. (2004) Your own action influences how you perceive another person's action. *Current Biology*, 14, 493–498.

Hamilton, A. F., Joyce, D. W., Flanagan, J. R., Frith, C. D. and Wolpert, D. M. (2007) Kinematic cues in perceptual weight judgement and their origins in box lifting. *Psychological Research*, 71, 13–21.

Hamilton, A. F., Wolpert, D. M., Frith, U. and Grafton, S. T. (2006) Where does your own action influence your perception of another person's action in the brain? *Neuroimage*, 29, 524–535.

Haruno, M., Wolpert, D. M. and Kawato, M. (2003) Hierarchical MOSAIC for movement generation. In Ono, T., Matsumoto, G., Llinas, R. R., Berthoz, A., Norgren, H. and Tamura, R. (eds), *Excepta Medica International Coungress Series*. Elsevier, Amsterdam.

Hebb, D. O. (1949) *The Organization of Behavior: A Neuropsychological Theory*. Wiley, New York.

Henson, R. N. (2003) Neuroimaging studies of priming. *Progress in Neurobiology*, 70, 53–81.

Hollerman, J. R., Tremblay, L. and Schultz, W. (2000) Involvement of basal ganglia and orbitofrontal cortex in goal-directed behavior. *Progress in Brain Research*, 126, 193–215.

Iacoboni, M., Molnar-Szakacs, I., Gallese, V., Buccino, G., Mazziotta, J. C. and Rizzolatti, G. (2005) Grasping the intentions of others with one's own mirror neuron system. *PLoS Biology*, 3, e79.

Jackson, J. H. (1889) On the comparative study of diseases of the nervous system. *British Medical Journal*, 2, 355–362.

Jacob, P. and Jeannerod, M. (2005) The motor theory of social cognition: a critique. *Trends in Cognitive Sciences*, 9, 21–25.

James, W. (1890) *Principles of Psychology*. Holt, New York.

Johnson-Frey, S. H., Newman-Norlund, R. and Grafton, S. T. (2005) A distributed left hemisphere network active during planning of everyday tool use skills. *Cerebral Cortex*, 15, 681–695.

Keele, S. W., Cohen, A. and Ivry, R. (1990) Motor programs: concepts and issues. In Jeannerod, M. (ed.), *Attention and Performance 13: Motor Representation and Control*, Chap. 3. Erlbaum, Hillsdale, NJ.

Keysers, C. and Perrett, D. I. (2004) Demystifying social cognition: a Hebbian perspective. *Trends in Cognitive Science*, 8, 501–507.

Kilner, J. M., Paulignan, Y. and Blakemore, S. J. (2003) An interference effect of observed biological movement on action. *Current Biology*, 13, 522–525.

Koechlin, E. and Jubault, T. (2006) Broca's area and the hierarchical organization of human behavior. *Neuron*, 50, 963–974.

Koechlin, E., Ody, C. and Kouneiher, F. (2003) The architecture of cognitive control in the human prefrontal cortex. *Science*, 302, 1181–1185.

Kourtzi, Z. and Kanwisher, N. (2000) Cortical regions involved in perceiving object shape. *Journal of Neuroscience*, 20, 3310–3318.

Krekelberg, B., Boynton, G. M. and van Wezel, R. J. (2006) Adaptation: from single cells to BOLD signals. *Trends in Neuroscience*, **29**, 250–256.

Lehericy, S., Benali, H., Van de Moortele, P. F., Pelegrini-Issac, M., Waechter, T., Ugurbil, K. and Doyon, J. (2005) Distinct basal ganglia territories are engaged in early and advanced motor sequence learning. *Proceedings of the National Academy of Science of the USA*, **102**, 12566–12571.

Lemon, R. N., Baker, S. N., Davis, J. A., Kirkwood, P. A., Maier, M. A. and Yang, H. S. (1998) The importance of the cortico-motoneuronal system for control of grasp. *Novartis Foundation Symposium*, **218**, 202–215.

Maccotta, L. and Buckner, R. L. (2004) Evidence for neural effects of repetition that directly correlate with behavioral priming. *Journal of Cognitive Neuroscience*, **16**, 1625–1632.

Manthey, S., Schubotz, R. I. and von Cramon, D. Y. (2003) Premotor cortex in observing erroneous action: an fMRI study. *Brain Research, Cognitive Brain Research*, **15**, 296–307.

Meltzoff, A. (1995) Understanding the intentions of others: re-enactment of intended acts by 18-month-old children. *Developmental Psychology*, **31**, 838–850.

Mushiake, H., Saito, N., Sakamoto, K., Itoyama, Y. and Tanji, J. (2006) Activity in the lateral prefrontal cortex reflects multiple steps of future events in action plans. *Neuron*, **50**, 631–641.

Nelissen, K., Vanduffel, W. and Orban, G. A. (2006) Charting the lower superior temporal region, a new motion-sensitive region in monkey superior temporal sulcus. *Journal of Neuroscience*, **26**, 5929–5947.

Noppeney, U. and Price, C. J. (2004) An FMRI study of syntactic adaptation. *Journal of Cognitive Neuroscience*, **16**, 702–713.

Norman, D. A. and Shallice, T. (1986) *Attention to Action: Willed and Automatic Control of Behaviour*. Plenum Press, New York.

Orban, G. A., Claeys, K., Nelissen, K., Smans, R., Sunaert, S., Todd, J. T., Wardak, C., Durand, J. B. and Vanduffel, W. (2006) Mapping the parietal cortex of human and non-human primates. *Neuropsychologia*, **44**, 2647–67.

Pacherie, E. (2006) Towards a dynamic theory of intentions. In Pocket, S., Banks, W. P. and Gallagher, S. (eds), *Does Consciousness Cause Behavior? An Investigation of the Nature of Volition*. MIT Press, Cambridge MA.

Pelphrey, K. A., Singerman, J. D., Allison, T. and McCarthy, G. (2003) Brain activation evoked by perception of gaze shifts: the influence of context. *Neuropsychologia*, **41**, 156–170.

Pelphrey, K. A., Morris, J. P and McCarthy, G. (2004) Grasping the intentions of others: the perceived intentionality of an action influences activity in the superior temporal sulcus during social perception. *Journal of Cognitive Neuroscience*, **16**, 1706–1716.

Pinel, P., Dehaene, S., Riviere, D. and LeBihan, D. (2001) Modulation of parietal activation by semantic distance in a number comparison task. *Neuroimage*, **14**, 1013–1026.

Pobric, G. and Hamilton, A. F. (2006) Action understanding requires the left inferior frontal cortex. *Current Biology*, **16**, 524–529.

Rilling, J. K., Glasser, M. F., Preuss, T. M., Ma, X., Zhang, X., Zhao, T., Hu, X. and Behrens, T. (2006) A comparative diffusion tensor imaging study of the arcuate fasiculus pathway in humans, chimpanzees and rhesus macaques. *Society of Neuroscience Abstracts*.

Rizzolatti, G. and Arbib, M. A. (1998) Language within our grasp. *Trends in Neurosciences*, **21**, 188–194.

Rizzolatti, G. and Craighero, L. (2004) The mirror-neuron system. *Annual Review of Neuroscience*, **27**, 169–192.

Rizzolatti, G., Camarda, R., Fogassi, L., Gentilucci, M., Luppino, G. and Matelli, M. (1988) Functional organization of inferior area 6 in the macaque monkey. II. Area F5 and the control of distal movements. *Experimental Brain Research*, **71**, 491–507.

Rizzolatti, G., Fadiga, L., Matelli, M., Bettinardi, V., Paulesu, E., Perani, D. and Fazio, F. (1996) Localization of grasp representations in humans by PET: 1. Observation versus execution. *Experimental Brain Research*, **111**, 246–252.

Rozzi, S., Calzavara, R., Belmalih, A., Borra, E., Gregoriou, G. G., Matelli, M. and Luppino, G. (2006) Cortical connections of the inferior parietal cortical convexity of the macaque monkey. *Cerebral Cortex*, **16**, 1389–1417.

Saito, N., Mushiake, H., Sakamoto, K., Itoyama, Y. and Tanji, J. (2005) Representation of immediate and final behavioral goals in the monkey prefrontal cortex during an instructed delay period. *Cerebral Cortex*, **15**, 1535–1546.

Sakata, H., Taira, M., Murata, A. and Mine, S. (1995) Neural mechanisms of visual guidance of hand action in the parietal cortex of the monkey. *Cerebral Cortex*, **5**, 429–438.

Saxe, R. (2005) Against simulation: the argument from error. *Trends in Cognitive Sciences*, **9**, 174–9.

Shallice, T. and Burgess, P. W. (1991) Deficits in strategy application following frontal lobe damage in man. *Brain*, **114** (Pt 2), 727–741.

Sherrington, C. S. (1906) *The Integrative Action of the Nervous System*. Yale University Press, New Haven, CT.

Shima, K., Mushiake, H., Saito, N. and Tanji, J. (1996) Role for cells in the presupplementary motor area in updating motor plans. *Proceedings of the National Academy of Science of the USA*, **93**, 8694–8698.

Shimazu, H., Maier, M. A., Cerri, G., Kirkwood, P. A. and Lemon, R. N. (2004) Macaque ventral premotor cortex exerts powerful facilitation of motor cortex outputs to upper limb motoneurons. *Journal of Neuroscience*, **24**, 1200–1211.

Shmuelof, L. and Zohary, E. (2005) Dissociation between ventral and dorsal fMRI activation during object and action recognition. *Neuron*, **47**, 457–470.

Simon, O., Mangin, J. F., Cohen, L., Le Bihan, D. and Dehaene, S. (2002) Topographical layout of hand, eye, calculation, and language-related areas in the human parietal lobe. *Neuron*, **33**, 475–487.

Spiridon, M., Fischl, B. and Kanwisher, N. (2006) Location and spatial profile of category-specific regions in human extrastriate cortex. *Human Brain Mapping*, **27**, 77–89.

Spitsyna, G., Warren, J. E., Scott, S. K., Turkheimer, F. E. and Wise, R. J. (2006) Converging language streams in the human temporal lobe. *Journal of Neuroscience*, **26**, 7328–7336.

Stephan, K. M., Fink, G. R., Passingham, R. E., Silbersweig, D., Ceballos-Baumann, A. O., Frith, C. D. and Frackowiak, R. S. (1995) Functional anatomy of the mental representation of upper extremity movements in healthy subjects. *Journal of Neurophysiology*, **73**, 373–386.

Tessari, A. and Rumiati, R. I. (2004) The strategic control of multiple routes in imitation of actions. *Journal of Experimental Psychology, Human Perception and Performance*, **30**, 1107–1116.

Thompson-Schill, S. L., D'Esposito, M. and Kan, I. P. (1999) Effects of repetition and competition on activity in left prefrontal cortex during word generation. *Neuron*, **23**, 513–522.

Tunik, E., Frey, S. H. and Grafton, S. T. (2005) Virtual lesions of the anterior intraparietal area disrupt goal-dependent on-line adjustments of grasp. *Nature Neuroscience*, **8**, 505–511.

Umilta, M. A., Kohler, E., Gallese, V., Fogassi, L., Fadiga, L., Keysers, C. and Rizzolatti, G. (2001) I know what you are doing. A neurophysiological study. *Neuron*, **31**, 155–165.

Wig, G. S., Grafton, S. T., Demos, K. E. and Kelley, W. M. (2005) Reductions in neural activity underlie behavioral components of repetition priming. *Nature Neuroscience*, **8**, 1228–33.

Wohlschlager, A., Gattis, M. and Bekkering, H. (2003) Action generation and action perception in imitation: an instance of the ideomotor principle. *Philosophical Transactions of the Royal Society of London, B*, **358**, 501–515.

Wolpert, D. M. and Flanagan, J. R. (2001) Motor prediction. *Current Biology*, **11**, R729–732.

Wolpert, D. M. and Kawato, M. (1998) Multiple paired forward and inverse models for motor control. *Neural Networks*, 11, 1317–1329.

Wolpert, D., Miall, C. and Kawato (1998) Internal models in the cerebellum. *Trends in Cognitive Sciences*, 2, 338–347.

Wolpert, D. M., Doya, K. and Kawato, M. (2003) A unifying computational framework for motor control and social interaction. *Philosophical Transactions of the Royal Society of London, B*, 358, 593–602.

Zink, C. F., Pagnoni, G., Martin-Skurski, M. E., Chappelow, J. C. and Berns, G. S. (2004) Human striatal responses to monetary reward depend on saliency. *Neuron*, 42, 509–517.

19

From hand actions to speech: evidence and speculations

Luciano Fadiga, Alice Catherine Roy, Patrik Fazio and Laila Craighero

This paper reviews experimental evidence and presents new data supporting the idea that human language may have evolved from hand/mouth action representation. In favor of this hypothesis are both anatomical and physiological findings. Among the anatomical ones is the fact that the monkey homologue of human Broca's area is a sector of ventral premotor cortex where goals are stored at representational level. In this region neurons have been found that respond to action-related visual stimuli such as graspable objects (canonical neurons) or actions of other individuals (mirror neurons). Among the physiological findings are some recent ones by our group showing that (i) during speech listening the listener's motor system becomes active as if she were pronouncing the listened words; (ii) the transcranial magnetic stimulation (TMS)-induced temporary inactivation of Broca's region has no effects on either phonological discrimination or on phonological priming tasks; (iii) hand gestures where the hand is not explicitly visible (i.e. animal hand shadows) activate the hand-related mirror neuron system, including Broca's region; (iv) frontal aphasic patients are impaired in their ability to correctly represent observed actions. On the basis of these data we strengthen the hypothesis that human language may have evolved from hand action representation. We conclude by speculating that the property of recursion, considered peculiar to human language, may have been introduced to hand actions by the fabrication of tools. The addition of this property to our action system may represent a critical intermediate step during the development of human language.

Introduction

"Organs develop to serve one purpose, and when they have reached a certain form in the evolutionary process, they became available for different purposes, at which point the processes of natural selection may refine them further for these purposes." This sentence comes from Noam Chomsky and it is taken from a letter in the *New York Review of Books* (Chomsky, 1996, p. 41) in which stresses that he believes "language is part of shared biological endowment" and can be studied in the manner of other biological systems "as a product of natural selection." He claims, however, that "evolutionary theory has little to say, as of now, about such matters as language."

In the present paper we will assume an evolutionary perspective in order to try to identify, by using Chomsky's words, the possible initial purpose at the basis of language evolution, and the organ which served that purpose.

The earliest attempts to localize the seat of language in the human brain were, perhaps not surprisingly, made by researchers in the field of phrenology, who located this faculty in the anterior part of the brain, bilaterally (Gall, 1822). This opinion would no doubt have disappeared along with the field of phrenology if it had not also found support in a series of experiments demonstrating that certain brain lesions abolish the ability of speech (aphasia), without destroying intelligence, and that these lesions are always located in the anterior lobes of the brain. It was Marc Dax who, during the early years of the nineteenth century, collected observations on aphasic patients and concluded that loss of language was preferentially associated with damage to the left half of the brain (see McManus, 2002). But it was Paul Broca who in 1861 began the study of the relationship between aphasia and the brain, by being the first to prove that aphasia was linked to specific lesions. The autopsy of his famous patient 'Tan' revealed that in his brain was present "a cavity with a capacity for holding a chicken's egg, located at the level of the fissure of Sylvius" (Broca, 1861). This area, a region that comprises the whole back part of the third frontal convolution, was later named Broca's area. Paul Broca made a very interesting remark regarding the deficits present in aphasics: "… which has perished in them, is therefore not the faculty of language, it is not the memory of words, it is not the actions of the nerves, … it is the faculty of coordinated movements, responsible for spoken language." Thus, he stressed the importance of the process at the basis of the capacity to coordinate meaningless articulatory movements in order to finally obtain a meaningful word. A few years after Broca's first studies, Wernicke proposed the first theory of language, which postulated an anterior, motor speech centre (Broca's region); a posterior, semantic language centre (Wernicke's region); and a fibres tract, the arcuate fascicle, connecting the two regions (Wernicke, 1874).

The neurosurgeon Wilder Penfield was the first to demonstrate experimentally the involvement of Broca's region in speech production by electrically stimulating the frontal lobe in awake patients undergoing brain surgery for intractable epilepsy. This method had been set up to help delimiting, during the course of the surgical procedure, regions whose excision would lead to severe language impairment. Penfield collected dozens of cases and was the first to report that the stimulation of the inferior frontal gyrus evoked the arrest of ongoing speech, although with some individual variability. The coincidence between the focus of the Penfield effect and the location of Broca's area was a strongly convincing argument in favor of the motor role of this region (Penfield and Roberts, 1959).

However, cortical stimulation gave also a different version of Broca's area role in language processing. A series of experiments demonstrated that both Broca's and Wernicke's areas are implicated in both the comprehension and production aspects of language (Ojemann et al., 1989; Burnstine et al., 1990; Luders et al., 1991; Ojemann, 1992; Schaffler et al., 1993). In particular, Schaffler et al. (1993) reported on three patients with intractable focal seizures arising from the language-dominant left hemisphere. Arrays of subdural electrodes were placed over the left temporal lobe and adjacent supra-sylvian region. Electrical stimulation of Broca's area produced marked interference with language output functions including speech arrest, slowing of oral reading, paraphasia and anomia. However, the authors reported that at some sites in this region cortical stimulation also produced language comprehension deficits, particularly in response to more complex auditory verbal instructions and visual semantic material.

Earlier, Luria (1966) had noted that Broca's area patients made comprehension errors in syntactically complex sentences such as passive constructions, but only when function words or knowledge of the syntactic structure were essential for comprehension. For instance, they had difficulty with the question "A lion was fatally attacked by a tiger. Which animal died?" Thus, again, the description of deficits caused by an interruption, either acute or chronic, of the activity in Broca's area underlines its involvement particularly when there is the necessity to combine single elements in order to extract a particular meaning. This description is in line with brain-imaging studies indicating that in language comprehension Broca's area is mainly activated during processing of syntactic aspects when higher levels of linguistic processing are required (see Bookheimer, 2002 for a review). For example, Stromswold (1995) compared right-branching sentences (e.g. "The child spilled the juice that stained the rug") to the more difficult centre-embedded structures ("The juice that the child spilled stained the rug"), finding increased activity in Brodmann's area 44 (BA 44) for the more complex constructions. Subsequently, Caplan et al. (1998) used the same stimuli as Stromswold (1995) and they again found that the focus of activity was in Broca's area. In a second experiment, they varied the number of propositions in sentences ("The magician performed the student that included the joke" versus "The magician performed the stunt and the joke"). In this experiment, differences were found only in temporal lobe regions, not in Broca's. Caplan et al. (1998) argue that in the latter experiment, the increased memory load is associated with the products of sentence comprehension, whereas in the former experiment, the load is with the "determination of the sentence's meaning", by stressing again the peculiar role of Broca's region in combining elements to obtain a final result.

The role of Broca's area in perception processing is not limited to the domain of speech. Since the early 1970s several groups have shown a strict correlation between frontal aphasia and impairment in gesture/pantomime recognition (Duffy and Duffy, 1975, 1981; Gainotti and Lemmo, 1976; Daniloff et al., 1982; Glosser et al., 1986; Bell, 1994). It is often unclear, however, whether this relationship between aphasia and gesture recognition deficits is due to Broca's area lesion only or if it depends on the damage of other, possibly parietal, areas. In fact, it is a common observation that aphasic patients are sometimes affected by ideomotor apraxia too (see Goldenberg, 1996) probably because of the large extension of the territory perfused by the middle cerebral artery.

However, the story becomes increasingly complicated if we review all the recent brain-imaging studies which report the activation of area 44/45 (see Fadiga et al., 2006b). One example is given by those studies that repeatedly observed activations of Broca's area (Mecklinger et al., 2002; Ranganath et al., 2003) while attempting to identify the neuronal substrate of the working memory. A series of papers by Ricarda Schubotz and

Yves von Cramon investigated nonmotor and nonlanguage functions of the premotor cortex (for review see Schubotz and von Cramon 2003) and showed that premotor cortex is also involved in prospective attention to sensory events and in processing serial prediction tasks. Gruber *et al.* (2001) compared a simple calculation task to a compound one and once again observed an activation of Broca's area. In an elegant study, Maess *et al.* (2001) have further investigated the possibility that area 44 is involved in playing with rules by studying musical syntax. By inserting unexpected harmonics, Maess *et al.* (2001) created a sort of musical syntactic violation. Using magnetoencephalography (MEG) they studied the neuronal counterpart of hearing harmonic incongruity and they found an early right anterior negativity, a parameter that has already been associated with harmonics violation (Koelsch *et al.*, 2000). The source of the activity pointed out BA 44, bilaterally.

The monkey homologue of human Broca's area

Thus, far from being exclusively involved in language-related processes, Broca's area seems to be involved in multiple tasks. At the same time it emerges from neuroanatomical studies that Broca's area, and in particular its *pars opercularis*, shares some cytoarchitectonic properties with the premotor cortices. Indeed, the granular cell layer (the IV cortical layer), which is clearly absent in BA 6, is only slightly present in BA 44. The frontal cortex becomes clearly granular only in area 45, the *pars triangularis* of the inferior frontal gyrus. So, what is the common functional aspect of its activation? Our approach to unravel the question of the role of Broca's area will be an evolutionary one: we will step down the evolutionary scale in order to examine the functional properties of the homologue of BA 44 in our 'progenitors'. From a cytoarchitectonic point of view (Petrides and Pandya, 1997), the monkey's frontal area which closely resembles human Broca's region is an agranular/dysgranular premotor area (area F5 as defined by Matelli *et al.*, 1985) (see Rizzolatti *et al.*, 2002) (see Figure 19.1). More recently, Nelissen *et al.* (2005) and Petrides (2006) have focused their attention on the parcelization of monkey area F5. Although with some differences, both studies agree on the fact that the caudal bank and the fundus of the arcuate sulcus differ from one another as far as cytoarchitectonics are concerned. While the bank is mainly agranular, the fundus is dysgranular. Moreover, this last sector of area F5 remains clearly distinct from the contiguous anterior bank region that both studies consider as pertaining to prefrontal cortex.

We will now examine the functional properties of this area by reporting the results of experiments aiming at finding the behavioral correlate of single neuron response.

Microstimulation (Hepp-Reymond *et al.*, 1994) and single neuron studies (see Rizzolatti *et al.*, 1988) showed that in area F5 are represented hand and mouth movements. Most of the hand neurons discharge in association with goal-directed actions such as grasping, manipulating, tearing, and holding, while they do not discharge during similar movements when made with other purposes (e.g. scratching, pushing away). Furthermore, many F5 neurons become active during movements that have an identical goal regardless of the effectors used for attaining it, suggesting that those neurons are able to generalize the goal, independently from the acting effector.

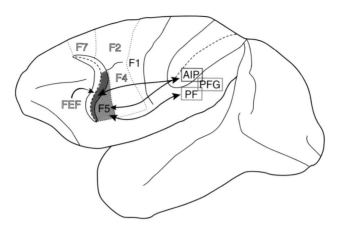

Figure 19.1 Lateral view of monkey left hemisphere. Area F5 is buried inside the arcuate sulcus (posterior bank, here in light blue) and emerges on the convexity immediately posterior to it (purple). Area F5 is bidirectionally connected with the inferior parietal lobule (areas AIP: anterior intraparietal, PF and PFG). Within the frontal lobe, area F5 is connected with hand/mouth representations of primary motor cortex (area F1), with sectors of area F2, with the mesial area F6 (not shown) and with prefrontal area 46. See colour plate section.

Using the action effective in triggering the neuron's discharge as classification criterion, F5 neurons can be subdivided into several classes: 'grasping', 'holding', 'tearing', and 'manipulating' neurons. Grasping neurons form the most represented class in area F5. Many of them are selective for a particular type of prehension such as precision grip, finger prehension, or whole hand prehension. By considering all the functional properties of neurons in this region, it appears that in area F5 there is a storage—a 'vocabulary'—of motor actions related to hand use. The 'words' of the vocabulary are represented by populations of neurons. Each indicates a particular motor action or an aspect of it. Some indicate a complete action in general terms (e.g. take, hold, and tear). Others specify how objects must be grasped, held or torn (e.g. precision grip, finger prehension, and whole hand prehension). Finally, some subdivide the action into smaller segments (e.g. finger flexion or extension).

All F5 neurons share similar motor properties. In addition to their motor discharge, however, several F5 neurons also discharge to the presentation of visual stimuli (visuo-motor neurons). Two radically different categories of visuo-motor neurons are present in area F5: neurons of the first category discharge when the monkey observes graspable objects ('canonical' neurons; Rizzolatti *et al.*, 1988; Rizzolatti and Fadiga, 1998). Neurons of the second category discharge when the monkey observes another individual making an action in front of it ('mirror' neurons; di Pellegrino *et al.*, 1992; Gallese *et al.*, 1996; Rizzolatti *et al.*, 1996a). The two categories of F5 neurons are located in two different subregions of area F5: canonical neurons are mainly found in that sector of area F5 buried inside the arcuate sulcus, whereas mirror neurons are almost exclusively located in the cortical convexity of F5.

When comparing visual and motor properties of canonical neurons it becomes clear that there is a strict congruence between the two types of responses. Neurons becoming active when the monkey observes small size objects, also discharge during precision grip. On the contrary, neurons selectively active when the monkey looks at a large object discharge also during actions directed towards large objects (e.g. whole hand prehension) (Murata et al., 1997). The most likely interpretation for visual discharge in these visuo-motor neurons is that, at least in adult individuals, there is a close link between the most common three-dimensional (3D) stimuli and the actions necessary to interact with them. Thus, every time a graspable object is visually presented, the related F5 neurons are addressed and the action is 'automatically' evoked. Under certain circumstances, it guides the execution of the movement; under others, it remains an unexecuted representation of it, that might be used also for semantic knowledge.

Mirror neurons, which become active when the monkey acts on an object and when it observes another monkey or the experimenter making a similar goal-directed action, appear to be identical to canonical neurons in terms of motor properties, but they radically differ from them as far as visual properties are concerned (Rizzolatti and Fadiga, 1998). In order to be triggered by visual stimuli, mirror neurons require an interaction between a biological effector (hand or mouth) and an object. The sights of an object alone, of an agent mimicking an action, or of an individual making intransitive (nonobject-directed) gestures are all ineffective. The object significance for the monkey has no obvious influence on mirror neuron response. Grasping a piece of food or a geometric solid produces responses of the same intensity. Typically, mirror neurons show congruence between the observed and executed action. This congruence can be extremely strict, that is the effective motor action (e.g. precision grip) coincides with the action that, when seen, triggers the neurons (e.g. precision grip). For other neurons the congruence is broader. For them the motor requirements (e.g. precision grip) are usually stricter than the visual ones (any type of hand grasping) (Gallese et al., 1996).

It seems plausible that the visual response of both canonical and mirror neurons addresses the same motor vocabulary, the words of which constitute the monkey motor repertoire. What is different is the way in which 'motor words' are selected: in the case of canonical neurons they are selected by object observation, in the case of mirror neurons by the sight of an action. Thus, in the case of canonical neurons, vision of graspable objects activates the motor representations more appropriate to interact with those objects. In the case of mirror neurons, objects alone are no longer sufficient to evoke a premotor discharge: what is necessary is a visual stimulus describing a goal-directed hand action in which both an acting hand and a target must be present.

Summarizing the evidence presented above, the behavioral conditions triggering the response of neurons recorded in the monkey area that is more closely related to human Broca's (ventral premotor area F5) are: (1) grasping with the hand and grasping with the mouth actions; (2) observation of graspable objects; (3) observation of hand/mouth actions performed by other individuals. Moreover, the experimental evidence suggests that, in order to activate F5 neurons, executed/observed actions must be goal-directed.

Does the cytoarchitectonic homology linking monkey area F5 with Broca's area correspond to some functional homology? Does human Broca's area discharge during hand/mouth action execution/observation too? Does it make difference, in terms of Broca's activation, if observed actions are meaningful (goal-directed) or meaningless? A positive answer to these questions may come from a series of brain-imaging experiments hereafter described.

The human mirror neuron system: brain imaging

Direct evidence of an activation of premotor areas during observation of graspable objects was provided by a positron emission tomography (PET) experiment (Grafton et al., 1997). Normal right-handed subjects were scanned during observation of 2D colored pictures (meaningless fractals) during observation of 3D objects (real tools attached to a panel) and during silent naming of the presented tools and of descriptions of their use. The most important result was that the premotor cortex became active during the simple observation of the tools. This premotor activation was further augmented when the subjects named the tool use. This result shows that, as is the case with canonical F5 monkey neurons, also in the absence of any overt motor response or instruction to use the observed stimuli, the presentation of graspable objects increases automatically the activity of premotor areas. A recent PET study conducted by Grèzes and Decety (2002) indicated that the perception of objects, irrespective of the task required to the subject (judgment of the vertical orientation, motor imagery, and silent generation of the noun or of the corresponding action verb), versus perception of nonobjects, was associated with activation of a common set of cortical regions. The occipito-temporal junction, the inferior parietal lobule, the supplementary motor area (SMA)-proper, the *pars triangularis* in the inferior frontal gyrus (Broca's area), the dorsal and ventral precentral gyrus, were engaged in the left hemisphere. The ipsilateral cerebellum was also involved. These activations are consistent with the idea that the mere perception of objects automatically activates representations of possible object affordances and the motor plans associated with their execution.

PET and functional magnetic resonance imaging (fMRI) experiments, carried out by various groups, demonstrated that when the participants observed actions made by human arms or hands, activations were present in the ventral premotor/inferior frontal cortex (Grafton et al., 1996; Rizzolatti et al., 1996b; Decety et al., 1997; Grèzes et al., 1998; Iacoboni et al., 1999; Decety and Chaminade, 2003; Grèzes et al., 2003). Grèzes et al. (1998) investigated whether the same areas became active during observation of both transitive (goal directed) and intransitive meaningless gestures. Normal human volunteers were instructed to observe meaningful or meaningless actions. The results confirmed that the observation of meaningful hand actions activates the left inferior frontal gyrus (Broca's region), the left inferior parietal lobule plus various occipital and inferotemporal areas. An activation of the left precentral gyrus was also found. During meaningless gesture observation there was no Broca's region activation. Furthermore, in comparison with meaningful action observations, an increase was found in activation of the right posterior parietal lobule. More recently, two further studies have shown that a meaningful hand–object interaction is more effective in triggering Broca's area activation than pure movement observation (Hamzei *et al.*, 2003; Johnson-Frey *et al.*, 2003). Similar conclusions have also been reached for mouth movement observation (Campbell *et al.*, 2001). For clarity reasons, it should be stressed here that the distinction meaningful/meaningless is just one possible interpretation. It is also possible that the differential involvement of the left/right inferior frontal gyri could be due to the effort made by participants in trying to find a meaning in the observed action.

Very recently (Fadiga *et al.*, 2006a), we investigated the possibility that Broca's area becomes specifically active during the observation of a particular category of hand gestures: hand shadows representing animals opening their mouths. Hand shadows only implicitly 'contain' the hand creating them (i.e. hands are not visible but subjects are aware of the fact that the animals presented are done by hand). Thus, they are interesting stimuli that might be used to answer the question of how detailed a hand gesture must be in order to activate the mirror neuron system. The results support the idea that Broca's area is specifically involved during meaningful action observation and that this activation is independent of any internal verbal description of the observed scene. Moreover, they demonstrate that the mirror neuron system becomes active even if the pictorial details of the moving hand are not explicitly visible: in the case of our stimuli, the brain also 'sees' the performing hand behind the appearance. During the fMRI scanning, healthy volunteers ($n = 10$) observed videos representing (i) the shadows of human hands depicting animals opening and closing their mouths, (ii) human hands executing sequences of meaningless finger movements, or (iii) real animals opening their mouths. Each condition was contrasted with a 'static' condition, in which the same stimuli presented in the movie were shown as static pictures (e.g. stills of animals presented for the same period of time as the corresponding videos). In addition, to emphasize the action component of the gesture, brain activations were further compared between pairs of conditions in a block design. Figure 19.2 shows, superimposed, the results of the moving versus static contrasts for animal hand shadows and real animal conditions (red and green spots, respectively). In addition to largely overlapping occipito-parietal activations, a specific differential activation emerged in the anterior part of the brain. Animal hand shadows strongly activated left parietal cortex, pre- and postcentral gyri (bilaterally), and bilateral inferior frontal gyrus (BA 44 and 45). Conversely, the only frontal activation reaching significance in the moving versus static contrast for real animals was located in bilateral BA 6, close to the premotor activation shown in an fMRI experiment by Buccino *et al.* (2004) when subjects observed mouth actions performed by monkeys and dogs. This location may therefore correspond to a premotor region where a mirror neuron system for mouth actions is present in humans.

The results shown in Figure 19.2 indicate that the shadows of animals opening their mouths, although clearly depicting animals and not hands, convey implicit information about the human being moving her hand in creating them. Indeed, they evoke an activation pattern superimposable on that evoked by hand action observation (Grafton *et al.*, 1996;

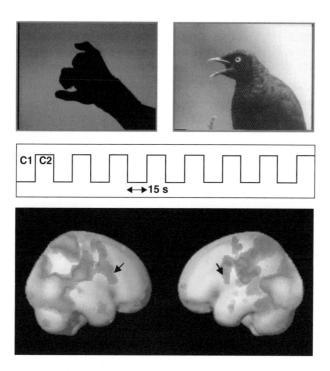

Figure 19.2 Cortical activation pattern during observation of animal hand shadows and real animals. Significantly activated voxels ($p < 0.001$, fixed effects analysis) in the moving animal shadow and moving real animal conditions after subtraction of the static controls. Activity related to animal shadows (red clusters) is superimposed on that from real animals (green clusters). Those brain regions activated during both tasks are shown in yellow. In the middle part of the figure, the experimental time-course for each contrast is shown (i.e. C1, moving; C2, static). Note the almost complete absence of frontal activation for real animals in comparison to animal shadows, which bilaterally activate the inferior frontal gyrus (arrows). (Modified from Fadiga et al., 2006a.). See color plate section.

Buccino *et al.*, 2001; Grèzes *et al.*, 2003). Consequently, the human mirror system (or at least part of it) can be seen more as an active interpreter than as a passive perceiver or resonator. Data from a recent monkey study (Umiltà *et al.*, 2001), in which the amount of visual information in observed actions was experimentally manipulated, led to similar conclusions. Here the experimental paradigm consisted of two basic conditions. In one, the monkey was shown a fully visible action directed toward an object ('full vision' condition). In the other, the monkey saw the same action but with its final critical part hidden ('hidden' condition). Before each trial the experimenter placed a piece of food behind the screen so that the monkey knew that there was an object behind it. The main result of the experiment was that more than half of the tested neurons discharged in the hidden condition (see Figure 19.3).

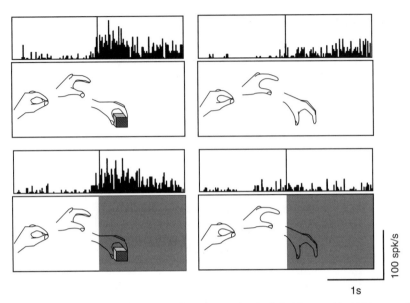

Figure 19.3 F5 neuron responding to grasping observation in full vision and in hidden condition (leftmost two panels) but not in mimed conditions (rightmost two panels). The lower part of each panel illustrates schematically the experimenter's action. The grey square inside the panel represents the opaque screen that prevented the monkey from seeing the action that the experimenter performed behind it. There were two basic conditions: full vision condition, and hidden condition. Grasping actions were either actually performed or mimed (without object). In each panel, histograms of neuron discharge (10 consecutive trials) are shown. (Modified from Umiltà *et al.*, 2001.)

From hand actions to 'speech actions'

Others' actions do not generate only visually perceivable signals. Action-generated sounds and noises are also very common in nature. One could also expect, therefore, that this sensory information, related to a particular action, could determine a motor activation specific for that same action. A recent neurophysiological experiment addressed this point. Kohler *et al.* (2002) investigated whether there are neurons in area F5 that discharge when the monkey makes a specific hand action and also when it *hears* the corresponding action-related sounds. The experimental hypothesis was based on the observation that a large number of object-related actions (e.g. breaking a peanut) can be recognized by a particular sound. The authors found that 13% of the investigated neurons discharge both when the monkey performed a hand action and when it heard the action-related sound. Moreover, most of these neurons discharge also when the monkey observed the same action demonstrating that these 'audio-visual mirror neurons' represent actions independently of whether they are *performed*, *heard* or *seen*.

Most recently, a brain-imaging study has revealed that perception of bilabial consonants (that recruited actively the lips to be pronounced) versus alveolar consonants (that, in contrast, recruited more actively the tongue) give rise to a somatotopic activation of the precentral gyrus (Pulvermuller *et al.*, 2006). Previously, Fadiga *et al.* (2002), by using transcranial magnetic stimulation, had shed light on the motor resonance occurring while listening to words. They revealed that the passive listening to words that would involve tongue mobilization (when pronounced) induces an automatic facilitation of the listener's motor cortex. Indeed, the tongue motor-evoked potentials (MEPs), evoked by transcranial magnetic stimulation (TMS) of left tongue motor representation, reached higher amplitudes when Italian subjects were listening to Italian words that recruited important tongue movements (/birra/) when compared to words recruiting less important tongue movements (/buffo/). Furthermore, the effect was stronger in the case of words than in the case of pseudowords (Figure 19.4, left).

These findings strengthen the idea that language and fine motor skills may share a common origin, and further suggest that recognizing a verbal stimulus to be a word or not might differentially influence the motor cortex excitability. In a more recent study (Roy *et al.*, unpublished data), we specifically addressed the hypothesis that the lexical status of a passively heard verbal item can selectively affect the excitability of the primary motor cortex of the tongue. Specifically, we aimed at answering two questions that were left unanswered by the previous study. On the one hand, the word versus orthographically regular pseudoword difference could be due to a familiarity effect, real words being more frequent than any pseudoword. On the other hand, one cannot exclude that, as words, pseudowords might yield to an effect analogous in amplitude, but delayed in time, on

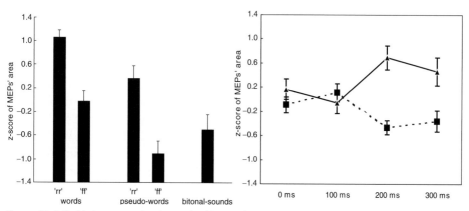

Figure 19.4 (Left) Average value (± SEM) of intrasubject normalized motor-evoked potential (MEP) total areas for each condition (modified from Fadiga *et al.*, 2002). Data from all subjects; 'rr' and 'ff' refer to verbal stimuli containing a double lingua-palatal fricative consonant /r/, and containing a double labio-dental fricative consonant /f/, respectively. (Right) Time-course of normalized MEP total area (± SEM), as evoked by transcranial magnetic stimulation (TMS) on tongue motor representation at different timings during listening of frequent (dotted line) and rare (continuous line) words (Roy *et al.*, unpublished data).

cortico-bulbar excitability. To shed further light onto these issues, we first sought to confirm and extend the phonological effect and then to disambiguate between the role of familiarity versus lexical status. To this aim, we recorded tongue MEPs by stimulating with TMS the left tongue motor representation, while subjects were passively listening to verbal stimuli (embedded with a double alveolar consonant i.e. /ll/) pertaining to three different classes: frequent words, rare words and pseudowords. During listening, we examined the time-course of motor cortex excitability by delivering single TMS pulses at four different time-intervals after the beginning of the double consonant (0, 100, 200, 300 ms). Electromyogram potentials evoked by TMS were recorded as in Fadiga *et al.* (2002). During the experimental session, subjects were required to listen carefully to the presented stimuli and, to maintain their attention, to perform a lexical decision on the last heard stimulus (word or pseudoword?) at the occurrence of an instructional signal randomly presented. Three main results were obtained. First, by stimulating the tongue motor area at 120% of the motor threshold, we further replicated the phonological effect previously reported by Fadiga *et al.* (2002), as listening to verbal stimuli embedded with consonant recruiting significant tongue movements induced higher MEPs (z-score for /ll/ = 0.187; for non /ll/ = −0.302; $p < 0.05$). Second, we found that, with respect to uncommon words, frequent words yield to the smallest tongue MEPs. Third, this pattern varied according to the timing of the magnetic pulse: when the TMS pulse was applied at the very beginning of the consonant or 100 ms afterwards, the evoked muscle activity did not differ across stimulus class. From 100 to 200 ms, the MEP area obtained for the rare words increased markedly (from −0.059 to 0.691). Then at 200 ms frequent words evoked the weakest tongue MEP while at 300 ms the difference between frequent and rare words was still present (Figure 19.4, right). Thus, the lexical status influenced the excitability of the primary motor cortex 200 ms after the beginning of the double consonant as rare words gave rise to the highest response.

Summarizing, these results indicate that the motor system is activated during speech listening. However, it is unclear if this activation could be interpreted in terms of an involvement of motor representations in speech processing and, perhaps, perception. This last possibility is in agreement with the idea originally proposed by Liberman (Liberman *et al.*, 1967; Liberman and Mattingly, 1985; Liberman and Wahlen, 2000) starting from the perspective that sounds at the basis of verbal communication could be a vehicle for motor representations (articulatory gestures) shared by both the speaker and the listener, on which speech perception could be based. In other terms, the listener understands the speaker when her articulatory gestures/representations are activated by verbal sounds (motor theory of speech perception). In the next section, we will discuss this issue and we will present the results of some new experiments performed both on normal subjects and patients, that may help to clarify the role of frontal motor cortices in speech processing.

Is Broca's region involved in speech perception?

Studies of cortical stimulation during neurosurgical operations and clinical data from frontal aphasics suggest that this is the case (see above). However, all these studies report that comprehension deficits become evident only in the case of complex sentence process-ing or complex command accomplishment. Single words (particularly if nouns) are almost always correctly understood. To verify this observation, we applied repetitive TMS (rTMS, that functionally blocks the stimulated area for hundreds of milliseconds) on speech-related premotor centers during single word listening (Fadiga *et al.*, 2006b). Data analysis indeed showed that rTMS was ineffective in perturbing subjects' performance. A possible objection could be, however, that words, because of their lexical content, acti-vate a complex network of areas, and thus the interruption of activity only in Broca's area is not sufficient to impair comprehension.

Does TMS perturb phonological discrimination?

On the basis of the previous results, we decided to use an experimental paradigm not involving words but meaningless pseudowords. Subjects were instructed to categorize a sequence of acoustically presented pseudowords according to their phonological char-acteristics, by pressing one among four different switches (L. Craighero, L. Fadiga and P. Haggard, unpublished data). Stimuli were subdivided into four different categories, according to the phonetic sequence of the middle part of the stimulus (/dada/, /data/, /tada/ or /tata/). Participants' left hemisphere was magnetically stimulated in three different regions by using rTMS: (a) the focus of the tongue motor representation, (b) a region 2 cm more anterior (ventral premotor/inferior frontal cortex), (c) a region 2 cm more posterior (somatosensory cortex). During the task, subjects had to listen to the presented stimulus and to press on a four-button keyboard (Figure 19.5c) the button identifying the middle part of the stimulus (e.g. /dada/). The correspondence between button and phonetic sequence was given by a four-picture display presented on a computer screen (Figure 19.5b) that was kept fixed for each subject but was counterbalanced across subjects. Repetitive

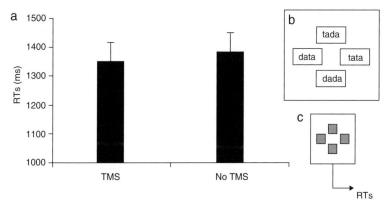

Figure 19.5 (a) Average value (± SEM) of subjects' reaction times (RTs) during the phonological discrimination task described in the text. Note the absence of RT modulation depending on the administration of transcranial magnetic stimulation (TMS) on a point roughly corresponding to BA 44 (2 cm in front of tongue primary motor representation). (**b** and **c**) The computer screen displayed to subjects and the keyboard for the response, respectively.

TMS (120% of individual motor threshold) was delivered at a frequency of 20 Hz in correspondence of the 2nd critical formant (200 ms), in correspondence of the 1st and of the 2nd critical formants (200 + 200 ms), and also during the whole critical portion of the presented word (600 ms). Results (Figure 19.5) showed no difference between the performances obtained during the different experimental conditions and for each stimulated site, neither in terms of errors nor for reaction times, demonstrating that rTMS was completely ineffective in perturbing phonological discrimination.

Does TMS perturb the phonological priming effect?

A possible interpretation of the absence of any effect of interference on phonologic discrimination might be that the discrimination task we used was either too simple or did not require a real phonologic processing because it might be accomplished by a simple acoustic discrimination of the serial order of two different (not necessarily phonologic) elements. For these reasons, we thus decided to use a 'phonological priming' task, a well-known experimental paradigm based on the observation that a target verbal stimulus is recognized faster when it is preceded by a prime sharing with the target its last syllable (rhyming effect, Emmorey, 1989). In a single-pulse TMS experiment we therefore stimulated participants' inferior frontal gyrus (BA 44) while they were performing a phonologic priming task. TMS was administered between the prime and the target. In this way, the noise produced by the TMS was not interfering with stimulus presentation. During the task, subjects were instructed to carefully listen to a sequence of acoustically presented pairs of verbal stimuli (disyllabic 'cvcv' or 'cvccv' words and pseudowords) in which final phonologic overlap was present (rhyme prime) or, conversely, not present. The pairs of presented stimuli pertained to four categories which differed for presence of lexical content in the prime and in the target (Table 19.1).

Subjects ($n = 8$) were requested to make a lexical decision on the target by pressing one of two buttons (word/pseudoword) with their index or middle finger. The association between fingers and lexical property was counterbalanced across subjects. Each category contained both rhyming and nonrhyming pairs. In some randomly selected trials, we administered single-pulse TMS in correspondence of left BA 44 (Broca's region) during the interval (20 ms) between prime and target stimuli. To avoid mislocalization of the target brain region, each subject underwent MRI scanning, and the position of subject's scalp covering the *pars opercularis* of the inferior frontal gyrus (BA 44) was assessed by using neuronavigation software developed in our laboratory (see Figure 19.6). In brief, a 6-DOF electromagnetic tracker (Flock of Birds, Ascension Technology) was attached to subject's forehead by an elastic band to compensate for head movements, and three *repere* points (bilateral *tragus* and *nasion*) were located by pointing on them using a stylus equipped with a second tracker. Then, the same *repere* locations were identified on the subject's MRI, and the two coordinate systems, that of subject's head and that of MRI, were put in register. Finally, for each point identified by the stylus on subject's scalp, the software gave in real time the corresponding three MRI sections passing from it (coronal, horizontal and sagittal).

Table 19.1 List of pairs of verbal stimuli used in the experiment. Stimuli pertained to four categories according to the presence of lexical content in the prime and in the target. Each category was subdivided into Rhyming and Non rhyming pairs according to the presence or absence of final phonologic overlap, respectively.

Prime trarget	Word–Word	Word–pseudoword	Pseudoword–word	Pseudoword–pseudoword
Rhyming	Tocca–Bocca	Corta–Zorta	Losse–Tosse	Cata–Zata
	Pera–Cera	Freno–Preno	Vanze–Stanze	Buota–Suota
	Tango–Fango	Tasca–Masca	Comba–Bomba	Cobia–Robia
	Bolla–Folla	Tizio–Cizio	Muga–Ruga	Nago–Sago
	Vita–Gita	Rana–Mana	Ciggia–Spiaggia	Tasna–Masna
	Fato–Lato	Caso–Zaso	Reta–Meta	Ciato–Viato
	Duna–Luna	Magno–Pagno	Paso–Vaso	Stoca–Ruoca
	Fare–Mare	Vecchio–Lecchio	Rento–Lento	Dano–Viano
	Zucca–Mucca	Colpe–Molpe	Vugno–Pugno	Tecra–Gecra
	Fido–Nido	Toro–Soro	Vesta–Testa	Polta–Solta
Non rhyming	Bomba–Zebra	Grugno–Buota	Lufo–Lesta	Zangra–Gispia
	Cesto–Sugo	Tana–Nago	Stali–Letto	Fazo–Rasuo
	Fiume–Scuola	Media–Tasna	Raga–Dopo	Diase–Noste
	Gara–Ritmo	Strada–Terto	Troli–Moro	Copa–Lafria
	Lago–Guancia	Vela–Marto	Neca–Tetro	Zasta–Guotra
	Mano–Granchio	Moro–Troli	Porpo–Tino	Piusca–Rieta
	Noia–Cielo	Freno–Tile	Gondo–Prato	Brona–Dasta
	Panno–Capra	Terme–Cagia	Revia–Piena	Zugra–Friepa
	Specchio–Stalla	Truppa–Giarti	Marto–Vela	Vutra–Ligri
	Topo–Patto	Ragno–Ligri	Zangra–Sedia	Tausa–Mifro

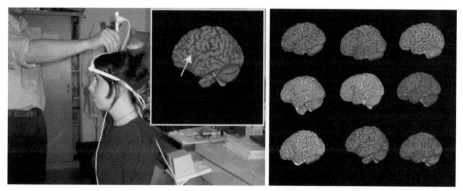

Figure 19.6 The procedure used in the phonological priming experiment to map individual Broca's areas. On the left, the electromagnetic tracking procedure is shown. For each subject, the center of *pars opercularis* of the inferior frontal gyrus was identified (yellow arrow). The panel on the right shows the three-dimensional reconstructed brain of nine subjects with a red circle superimposed indicating the location selected for administering transcranial magnetic stimulation during the experimental paradigm. See color plate section.

A three-way repeated-measures analysis of variance (ANOVA) on reaction times with TMS administration (present, absent), priming effect (rhyming, non-rhyming pairs) and type of pairs (W–W, W–PW, PW–W, PW–PW) as within-subject variables was performed. It showed that priming effect [$F(1,7) = 50,14, p < 0.001$] and type of pairs [$F(3,21) = 13,75, p < 0.001$] were significant factors. Moreover, it showed significant interactions between TMS administration and type of pairs [$F(3,21) = 5,98, p < 0.01$], between priming effect and type of pairs [$F(3,21) = 13,95, p < 0.001$], and between TMS administration, priming effect, and type of pairs [$F(3,21) = 3,37, p < 0.05$].

Newman–Keuls *post hoc* comparisons indicated that in trials without TMS (Figure 19.7, left panel), there are three main results: (i) strong and statistically significant facilitation (phonological priming effect) when W–W, W–PW, PW–W pairs are presented; (ii) no phonological priming effect when the PW–PW pair is presented; (iii) faster responses when the target is a word rather than a pseudoword (both in W–W and PW–W). An interesting finding emerges from the analysis of these results: the presence or absence of lexical content modulates the presence of the phonological priming effect. When neither the target nor the prime has the access to the lexicon (PW–PW pair), the presence of the rhyme does not facilitate the recognition of the target. In other words, in order to have a phonological effect it is necessary to have access to the lexicon.

In trials during which TMS was delivered (Figure 19.7, right panel), only W–PW pairs were affected by brain stimulation: the W–PW pair behaving exactly as the PW–PW one. This finding suggests that the stimulation of Broca's region might have affected the lexi-

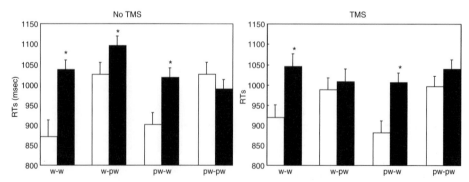

Figure 19.7 Reaction times (RTs ± SEM in milliseconds) during the phonological priming task for the lexical decision, without (left panel) and with (right panel) transcranial magnetic stimulation (TMS) administration. White bars: presence of rhyme between prime and target. Black bars: absence of rhyme. Asterisks above black bars indicate the presence ($p > 0.05$, Newman–Keuls test) of a phonological priming effect (response to rhyming target faster than response to non-rhyming target) in the relative condition. TMS administration did not influence the accuracy of the participants, which was almost always close to 100%. W–W, prime word/target word; W–PW, prime word/target pseudoword; PW–W, prime pseudoword/target word; PW–PW, prime pseudoword/target pseudoword.

cal property of the prime. As consequence, the lack of access to the lexicon determines the absence of the phonological effect. According to our interpretation, the TMS-related effect is absent in the W–W and PW–W pairs because of the presence of a meaningful (W) target. Being aware that a possible criticism of our result is that the task was implying a lexical decision, we replicated the experiment by asking six new subjects to detect whether the final vowel of the target stimulus was /a/ or /o/. Despite the absence of any lexicon-directed attention, the results (Figure 19.8) were exactly the same as in the case of the lexical decision paradigm, demonstrating that the absence of phonological priming in the pseudoword/pseudoword pairs was independent of subject's task.

Independently from the main aim of the present study, that of interfering on perception by administering TMS, the unexpected finding that in the pseudoword/pseudoword pair the phonological priming effect is abolished, provokes at least two necessary considerations. First, the classical view stating that before attributing a lexical content, the brain decodes the phonology (two-step processing), seems not to be substantiated by our data. Second, the phonological priming effect appears to be not purely 'phonological' because it disappears if at least one of the two members of the pair is not characterized by a meaningful lexical content.

Our interpretation of these results is that it is impossible to dissociate phonology from lexicon and particularly at Broca's level because there 'exist' only words. Thus, phonologically relevant stimuli are matched on a repertoire of words and not on individually meaningless 'phoneme assembly'. The original role played by the inferior fontal gyrus in generating/extracting action meanings might have been generalized during evolution, giving to this area the basics to build a new capability: a supramodal 'syntax' endowed with the ability to organize and comprehend hierarchical and sequential elements in meaningful structures. The motor resonance of tongue representation revealed by TMS

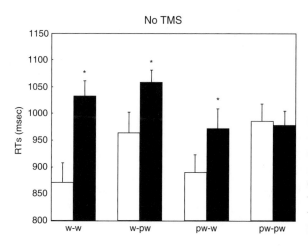

Figure 19.8 Reaction times (RTs ± SEM in milliseconds) during the phonological priming task for the vowel discrimination task (no transcranial magnetic stimulation). Convention as in Figure 19.7.

during speech listening (RR/FF) is probably a mixed phenomenon. Cortical regions others than area BA 44 (maybe BA 6) might be involved in the "acoustically evoked mirror effect" (Fadiga *et al.*, 2002) which is quite independent of the meaning of the presented stimuli. In this direction points the recent fMRI experiment by Wilson and colleagues (Wilson *et al.*, 2004) showing that the only cortical region constantly activated during both listening and production of meaningless syllables was bilaterally located in the superior part of ventral premotor cortex, dorsal to BA 44. However, it remains the fact that the lexical content of the listened words exerts a significant facilitation on primary motor cortex (M1) excitability (see Figure 19.4). It is likely that two distinct processes act on M1 at the same time: a meaning-independent one, which could be considered as the effect of a low-level motor resonance, and a lexical one, whose origin remains to be clarified by further experiments.

Do frontal aphasics show deficits in motor syntax?

What emerges from the temporary inactivation of Broca's area is that this area is not involved with purely phonological properties of the heard stimuli. The hypothesis we suggested in the previous section is that Broca's area, because of its premotor nature, could be involved in supramodal syntactic processing. If our hypothesis were true, we would expect that frontal aphasic patients suffering from lesion of Broca's region should, in addition to their classical symptoms in speech production and agrammatism, also show additional deficits in a more broadly 'motor' domain. In other words, people suffering from an inability to process syntax in the linguistic domain following frontal brain damage should be also impaired in another, motor, field, as long as supramodal syntactic skills are required. In particular, we hypothesized that the correlated defective domain would concern action. Tranel *et al.* (2003) also demonstrated that left frontal brain-damaged patients have difficulty in understanding action details when shown cards depicting various action phases. However, in their study, the authors asked patients to answer verbally to verbally posed questions. It is therefore possible that patients may have had more problems in understanding the intimate content of the action-related questions than in representing actions themselves.

To better verify the hypothesis that nonfluent aphasia may be accompanied by deficits in action understanding, we designed an experiment in which Broca's aphasic patients were presented with a simple scrambled 'motor sentence' which they had to reorganize (P. Fazio *et al.*, unpublished data). Patients were included in the study if they presented vascular lesions in the territory of the left middle cerebral artery, including the frontal inferior gyrus, and were diagnosed by a neuropsychologist as Broca's aphasics. Eleven patients met these initial enrolment criteria. All of them presented disorders of language production with agrammatic speech, while oral comprehension was largely preserved. Despite speech therapy, verbal fluency remained impaired at the time of the experimental investigation. Additionally, all 11 patients were screened to assess linguistic, praxic and general cognitive faculties and five patients suffering from apraxia have been successively excluded from the experimental testing. The experiment consisted of the presentation to each patient of 20 video clips, subdivided in two different classes: simple biological action (e.g. a hand grasping a bottle) and sequence of nonbiological moving object (e.g. a bicycle falling on the floor). After each video, patients were shown four snapshots taken from the video clip, randomly presented on a computer touch-screen; patients were then required to organize the frames so as to provide a meaningful order by touching the screen and by exchanging the position of the snapshot forming the sequence. As soon as they accomplished each trial, they had to press a validation button. We recorded and analyzed the accuracy and performance of the patient group and of a healthy control group, matching for age and instruction level.

A two-way repeated-measures ANOVA on reaction times, sequencing times, and accuracy, with Group (aphasics, controls) and Type of movement (biological, nonbiological) as within-subject variables was performed. It showed that Group was a significant factor for both reaction times [$t(1,5) = 15.174, p < 0.05$] and sequencing times [$t(1,5) = 17.025, p < 0.01$], indicating that aphasics were significantly slower than matched controls. The interaction between Group and Type of movement was not significant. As far as accuracy is concerned no main factors were significant but the interaction showed a tendency to significance [$t(1,5) = 5.85, p = 0.06$]. A two-tailed paired t-test ($a = 0.05$) indicated that controls showed no difference in accuracy between biological ($87 \pm 3\%$) and nonbiological movements ($77 \pm 6\%$), while aphasics performed significantly worse when they had to organize biological movements ($65 \pm 11\%$) with respect to nonbiological ones ($80 \pm 10\%$) (see Figure 19.9).

It is notable that this difference was specific for videos representing human actions since all patients were able to order other kinds of sequences, such as numbers. The difference in performance of patients between the two tasks is hardly compatible with a higher difficulty level of sequences representing human actions. Indeed, it took on average the same time for patients to perform the human and the nonbiological trials, whereas for healthy control subjects the opposite tendency prevails (more errors with nonbiological motion).

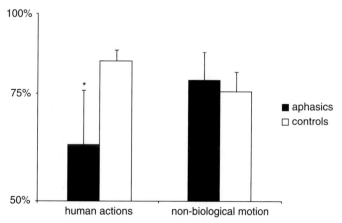

Figure 19.9 Percentages of correct trials (mean ± SEM) in frontal aphasic patients and in normal subjects matched for age, educational attainment and gender, during the sequencing task. Asterisk indicates the presence of a statistically significant difference in the performance of the sequencing task (see text).

Furthermore, the distribution of nonbiological motion trials in terms of sequencing time (i.e. difficulty) was coincident with that of human action trials.

Finally, as an additional control for the presence of syntactic deficits in a similar task but in the language domain, the patients were required to reorganize four tokens, each containing word pieces of a phrase, to compound a meaningful sentence (e.g. I turn – the key – and open – the door). They only reached 58% of accuracy in the latter task, thus confirming their profound agrammatism.

Although preliminary, these results are promising as they indicate a common impairment in syntactically organizing linguistic and motor material which, in the motor domain, is specific for biological motion, as a much better performance was observed with a sequential, nonbiological material. One could argue that this difference might depend on the biological versus nonbiological nature of the material. In this respect, brain-imaging studies have demonstrated that the observation of biological motion activates the premotor cortex, damaged in the tested population of patients, whereas nonbiological movement depends on a more posterior region (Grèzes et al., 2001; Saygin et al., 2004). However, the patients were presented with still frames that suggested, but never showed, real motion or movement. Moreover, our results are in accordance with previous studies showing that patients with lesions of Broca's area are impaired in learning the hierarchical, but not the temporal, structure of sequential tasks (Dominey et al., 2003, 2006). In the same vein, a study using event-related fMRI recently succeeded in disentangling hierarchical processes from temporal nested elements (Koechlin and Jubault, 2006). The authors reported that Broca's area and its right homologue control the selection and nesting of action segments integrated in hierarchical behavioral plans, regardless of their temporal structure. With respect to language, Broca's area is believed to process syntax, which is not a temporal sequence of words, but precisely a hierarchical structure defining the links between words. Therefore, our results add to the growing literature on the role of Broca's region. They strongly support Broca's role in processing a supramodal syntax which derives from the structure at the basis of action representation, which is embedded in the motor system. It is important to stress here that we are not dealing with the evocative capability of human language nor with its powerful capacity for generating/evoking abstract concepts. What we are interested in is the manner in which the verbal message is transmitted between the speaker and the listener, and in which syntax (at least in its canonical form) represents the set of rules allowing this transmission with efficacy.

Conclusions

At the beginning of this chapter we formulated the hypothesis that, in agreement with experimental findings on monkeys and humans, there should have been a common evolutionary pathway linking hand/mouth action representation and verbal communication. In general terms, this hypothesis is not new. For many years, several authors (Rizzolatti and Arbib, 1998; see Corballis, 2003) have proposed that human language may have been evolved from hand actions/gestures more than from the vocal call system, already present in inferior primates. Indeed, a gestural origin may account for some peculiarities of the human language (such as its combinatorial nature and the typically dyadic communicative process) that are absent in the directed-to-the-group and iconic vocal call system. Here, we have reviewed direct evidence in favor of an involvement of the motor system in speech processing, and have offered a reinterpretation of experimental evidence that may be summarized as follows.

Broca's area, the frontal region for speech production, is a premotor area, evolutionarily linked to a sector of monkey ventral premotor cortex (area F5a) where hand/mouth actions are represented. What characterizes these representations in the monkey cortex is (i) the presence of a goal, (ii) their organization in terms of vocabulary of actions, very often effector independent (e.g. grasping a small object with the right hand, with the left hand and with the mouth), (iii) their involvement in perception of similar actions performed by others, thanks to widely distributed visuo-motor properties.

Broca's area is involved in speech processing, not only during production but also during perception. This involvement is mainly at the sentence level (not at the word level) and it is positively correlated with the complexity of the sentences to be processed.

Broca's area becomes active in several nonspeech tasks having in common a syntactically organized structure (rhythms, music, mathematics, and complex sequences of actions). These domains share with speech the presence of rules that govern them in nonambiguous ways. In other words, they all deal with sequences organized according to a precise hierarchical structure.

This last point peculiarly emphasizes, in our view, the parallelism between speech and action representations. Indeed, both processes are organized in hierarchical structures hosting, when necessary, nested subroutines. Motor and speech sequences become significant because of the presence of the goal. Otherwise they remain meaningless assemblies of movements—in the case of actions, of words—in the case of sentences, or even of phonemes, in the case of single words. The glue linking the individual parts of a sequence in a meaningful way is in fact the goal of the action sequence.

In this light, the capacity of Broca's area to deal with sequences, not strictly speech-related, has been proposed by several investigators on the basis of the evidence that this region is constantly involved in processing rhythms, music, and complex actions (see the paradigmatic experiment by Gelfand and Bookheimer, 2003). In addition, the ventral part of BA 6 (vBA 6 or PMv, ventral premotor), bordering with Broca's region, is highly specialized in motor/abstract sequence processing, as shown by the seminal work by Schubotz and colleagues (Schubotz and von Cramon, 2003, 2004; Schubotz et al., 2004; Wolfensteller et al., 2004). Very recently, Fiebach and Schubotz (2006) have proposed a unifying theory that takes into account the experimental findings regarding ventral premotor cortex and Broca's area. Their belief is that the ensemble vBA 6–BA 44 may be considered "a highly flexible sequence processor, with the PMv mapping sequential events onto stored structural templates and Broca's area involved in more complex, hierarchical or hyper-sequential processing." Friederici (2006) approaches a similar conclusion: "While BA 44/45 is seen to be increasingly activated whenever the internal re-construction of a hierarchical structure from a sequential input is necessary, BA 6 is involved in the processing of local structural dependencies." Finally, Grewe et al. (2006) add new evidence to the hypothesis that linguistic functions of Broca's region, and more specifically of the *pars opercularis*, may depend on a 'suprasyntactic' role, as suggested by the fMRI evidence that the violation of a linearization principle that is purely semantic in nature (animate arguments should precede inanimate arguments) increases the activation of *pars opercularis*.

What we add to this theoretical framework here is the idea that speech is represented in Broca's region not because this part of the brain has developed for this specific purpose but because, in our progenitors, it was already the part of the brain where goals—and the hierarchically organized motor chains planned to achieve those goals—are represented (see Fogassi *et al.*, 2005). Therefore, the involvement of Broca's region in verbal communication could be provocatively considered an occasional 'epiphenomenon', motivated by its premotor origins. Consequently, forms of communication other than the verbal one, expressions of more ancient mechanisms, involve Broca's area because of its twofold involvement with motor goals: during execution of one's own actions and during perception of others' actions.

Several steps along this (putative) evolutionary pathway linking action representation (mainly hand actions) to linguistic syntax remain to be clarified, e.g. how object manipulation, introspectively driven, might have been transformed into communicative gestures. This passage has been considered a necessary prerequisite by several authors. It is possible, in our view, that the activity of the mirror neurons in the observer's brain, while looking at actions performed by another individual, may have contributed to the self–other distinction necessary to communicate. Moreover, as soon as our progenitors realized that their own actions were influencing the actions of others, the 'spark' may have appeared in their mind: the first nucleus of the dyadic, explicit communication.

Another issue, deserving particular consideration, is that raised by Fitch *et al.* (2005) in a recent paper on the origin of language. One of the points they make is that human language is exquisitely human because animal communication lacks the property of recursion, i.e. the ability to combine discrete elements (words) in an infinite variety of possible expressions. If one adopts this theoretical assumption, it follows that language may hardly have evolved from hand actions. Indeed actions are nonrecursive by definition: one cannot eat a piece of apple before grasping it.

There is, however, another possibility that may shed light on this intriguing puzzle which, as far as we know, has never been prompted before now. Linguists are familiar with the idea, originally proposed by Leroy-Gourhan (1964), that the appearance during evolution of the ability to make and use tools may have been the intermediate step linking action representation with human language. Here we propose the hypothesis that tool fabrication may have supplied action representation with the capability of recursion. Indeed, tool design and tool use expand the complexity of motor plans and project actions in temporal dimensions other than the present. This is particularly true in the case of tools fabricated to build other, new tools, which, in turn, would force the brain to postpone the ultimate goal following a complex, but quite flexible, hierarchy of subroutines/subgoals. These increased spatial–temporal degrees of freedom might have provided the brain with the first example of recursion of actions.

We believe that the discussion of this possibility could represent a fertile background for the interaction between linguistics and neuroscience, which represents an excellent approach to the study of language development in a multidisciplinary, convergent way.

Acknowledgments

This work has been supported by Italian MIUR, FCR and European Commission grants (Contact, Robot-cub and Neurobotics) to L.F. and L.C. and by the European Science Foundation OMLL Eurocores. We thank Rosario Canto for continuous support, Thierry Pozzo for providing us with the software for the experiment on aphasic subjects, Anna Cantagallo and Ferdinando Calzolari for their help with patients.

References

Bell, B. D. (1994) Pantomime recognition impairment in aphasia: an analysis of error types. *Brain and Language*, **47**, 269–278.

Bookheimer, S. (2002) Functional MRI of language: new approaches to understanding the cortical organization of semantic processing. *Annual Review of Neuroscience*, **25**, 151–188.

Broca, P. (1861) Remarques sur le Siége de la Faculté du Langage Articulé, Suivies d'une Observation d'aphemie (Perte de la Parole). *Bulletin de la Société Anatomique de Paris*, **6**, 330–357.

Buccino, G., Binkofski, F., Fink, G. R. *et al.* (2001) Action observation activates premotor and parietal areas in a somatotopic manner: an fMRI study. *European Journal of Neuroscience*, **13**, 400–404.

Buccino, G., Lui, F., Canessa, N. *et al.* (2004) Neural circuits involved in the recognition of actions performed by nonconspecifics: an FMRI study. *Journal of Cognitive Neuroscience*, **16**, 114–126.

Burnstine, T. H., Lesser, R. P., Hart Jr J. *et al.* (1990) Characterization of the basal temporal language area in patients with left temporal lobe epilepsy. *Neurology*, **40**, 966–970.

Campbell, R., MacSweeney, M., Surguladze, S. *et al.* (2001) Cortical substrates for the perception of face actions: an fMRI study of the specificity of activation for seen speech and for meaningless lower-face acts (gurning). *Cognitive Brain Research*, **12**, 233–243.

Caplan, D., Alpert, N. and Waters, G. (1998) Effects of syntactic structure and propositional number on patterns of regional cerebral blood flow. *Journal of Cognitive Neuroscience*, **10**, 541–552.

Chomsky, N. (1996) Language and evolution. (Letter.) *New York Review of Books*, 1 February, p. 41.

Corballis, M. C. (2003) From mouth to hand: gesture, speech, and the evolution of right-handedness. *Behavioral and Brain Sciences*, **26**, 198–208.

Daniloff, J. K., Noll, J. D., Fristoe, M. and Lloyd, L. L. (1982) Gesture recognition in patients with aphasia. *Journal of Speech and Hearing Disorders*, **47**, 43–49.

Decety, J. and Chaminade, T. (2003) Neural correlates of feeling sympathy. *Neuropsychologia*, **41**, 127–138.

Decety, J., Grèzes, J., Costes, N. *et al.* (1997) Brain activity during observation of actions: Influence of action content and subject's strategy. *Brain*, **120**, 1763–1777.

Di Pellegrino, G., Fadiga, L., Fogassi, L., Gallese, V. and Rizzolatti G (1992) Understanding motor events: a neurophysiological study. *Experimental Brain Research*, **91**, 176–180.

Dominey, P. F., Hoen, M., Blanc, J. M. and Lelekov-Boissard, T. (2003) Neurological basis of language and sequential cognition: evidence from simulation, aphasia, and ERP studies. *Brain and Language*, **86**, 207–225.

Dominey, P. F., Hoen, M. and Inui, T. (2006) A neurolinguistic model of grammatical construction processing. *Journal of Cognitive Neuroscience*, **18**, 2088–2107.

Duffy, R. J. and Duffy, J. R. (1975) Pantomime recognition in aphasics. *Journal of Speech and Hearing Research*, **18**, 115–132.

Duffy, R. J. and Duffy, J. R. (1981) Three studies of deficits in pantomimic expression and pantomimic recognition in aphasia. *Journal of Speech and Hearing Research*, **24**, 70–84.

Emmorey, K. D. (1989) Auditory morphological priming in the lexicon. *Language and Cognitive Processes*, **4**, 73–92.

Fadiga, L., Craighero, L., Buccino, G. and Rizzolatti, G. (2002) Speech listening specifically modulates the excitability of tongue muscles: a TMS study. *European Journal of Neuroscience*, **15**, 399–402.

Fadiga, L., Craighero, L., Fabbri Destro, M. *et al.* (2006a) Language in shadow. *Social Neuroscience*, **1**, 77–89.

Fadiga, L., Craighero, L. and Roy, A. C. (2006b) Broca's area: a speech area? In Grodzinsky Y and Amunts, K (eds), *Broca's Region*, pp. 137–52. Oxford University Press, New York.

Fiebach, C. J. and Schubotz, R. I. (2006) Dynamic anticipatory processing of hierarchical sequential events: a common role for Broca's area and ventral premotor cortex across domains? *Cortex*, **42**, 499–502.

Fitch, W. T., Hauser, M. D. and Chomsky, N. (2005) The evolution of the language faculty: clarifications and implications. *Cognition*, **97**, 179–210.

Fogassi, L., Ferrari, P. F., Gesierich, B., Rozzi, S., Chersi, F. and Rizzolatti, G. (2005) Parietal lobe: from action organization to intention understanding. *Science*, **308**, 662–667.

Friederici, A. D. (2006) Broca's area and the ventral premotor cortex in language: functional differentiation and specificity. *Cortex*, **42**, 472–475.

Gainotti, G. and Lemmo, M. S. (1976) Comprehension of symbolic gestures in aphasia. *Brain and Language*, **3**, 451–60.

Gall, F. J. (1822) *Sur les functions du cerveau et sur celle de chacune de ses parties*. Baillière, Paris.

Gallese, V., Fadiga, L., Fogassi, L. and Rizzolatti, G. (1996) Action recognition in the premotor cortex. *Brain*, **119**, 593–609.

Gelfand, J. R. and Bookheimer, S. Y. (2003) Dissociating neural mechanisms of temporal sequencing and processing phonemes. *Neuron*, **38**, 831–842.

Glosser, G., Wiener, M. and Kaplan, E. (1986) Communicative gestures in aphasia. *Brain and Language*, **27**, 345–359.

Goldenberg, G. (1996) Defective imitation of gestures in patients with damage in the left or right hemispheres. *Journal of Neurology, Neurosurgery and Psychiatry*, **61**, 176–80.

Grafton, S. T., Arbib, M. A., Fadiga, L. and Rizzolatti, G. (1996) Localization of grasp representations in humans by PET: 2. Observation compared with imagination. *Experimental Brain Research*, **112**, 103–111.

Grafton, S. T., Fadiga, L., Arbib, M. A. and Rizzolatti, G. (1997) Premotor cortex activation during observation and naming of familiar tools. *Neuroimage*, **6**, 231–236.

Grewe, T., Bornkessel, I., Zysset, S., Wiese, R., von Cramon, D. Y. and Schlesewsky, M. (2006) Linguistic prominence and Broca's area: the influence of animacy as a linearization principle. *Neuroimage*, **32**, 1395–1402.

Grèzes, J. and Decety, J. (2002) Does visual perception of object afford action? Evidence from a neuroimaging study. *Neuropsychologia*, **40**, 212–222.

Grèzes, J., Costes, N. and Decety, J. (1998) Top-down effect of strategy on the perception of human bioogical motion: a PET investigation. *Cognitive Neuropsychology*, **15**, 553–582.

Grèzes, J., Fonlupt, P., Bertenthal, B., Delon-Martin, C., Segebarth, C. and Decety, J. (2001) Does perception of biological motion rely on specific brain regions? *Neuroimage*, **13**, 775–785.

Grèzes, J., Armony, J. L., Rowe, J. and Passingham, R. E. (2003) Activations related to "mirror" and "canonical" neurones in the human brain: an fMRI study. *Neuroimage*, **18**, 928–937.

Gruber, O., Inderfey, P., Steinmeiz, H. and Kleinschmidt, A. (2001) Dissociating neural correlates of cognitive components in mental calculation. *Cerebral Cortex*, **11**, 350–359.

Hamzei, F., Rijntjes, M., Dettmers, C., Glauche, V., Weiller, C. and Buchel, C. (2003) The human action recognition system and its relationship to Broca's area: an fMRI study. *Neuroimage*, **19**, 637–644.

Hepp-Reymond, M. C., Husler, E. J., Maier, M. A. and Ql, H. X. (1994) Force-related neuronal activity in two regions of the primate ventral premotor cortex. *Canadian Journal of Physiology and Pharmacology*, **72**, 571–579.

Iacoboni, M., Woods, R., Brass, M., Bekkering, H., Mazziotta, J. C. and Rizzolatti, G. (1999) Cortical mechanisms of human imitation. *Science*, **286**, 2526–2528.

Johnson-Frey, S. H., Maloof, F. R., Newman-Norlund, R., Farrer, C., Inati, S. and Grafton, S. T. (2003) Actions or hand–object interactions? Human inferior frontal cortex and action observation. *Neuron*, **39**, 1053–1058.

Koechlin, E. and Jubault, T. (2006) Broca's area and the hierarchical organization of human behavior. *Neuron*, **50**, 963–974.

Koelsch, S., Gunter, T., Friederici, A. D. and Schroger, E. (2000) Brain indices of music processing: "non-musicians" are musical. *Journal of Cognitive Neuroscience*, **12**, 520–541.

Kohler, E., Keysers, C. M., Umiltà, A., Fogassi, L., Gallese, V. and Rizzolatti, G. (2002) Hearing sounds, understanding actions: action representation in mirror neurons. *Science*, **297**, 846–848.

Leroy-Gourhan, A. (1964) *Le geste et la parole*. Albin Michel, Paris.

Liberman, A. M. and Mattingly, I. G. (1985) The motor theory of speech perception revised. *Cognition*, **21**, 1–36.

Liberman, A. M. and Wahlen, D. H. (2000) On the relation of speech to language. *Trends in Cognitive Neuroscience*, **4**, 187–196.

Liberman, A. M., Cooper, F. S., Shankweiler, D. P. and Studdert-Kennedy, M. (1967) Perception of the speech code. *Psychological Review*, **74**, 431–461.

Luders, H., Lesser, R. P., Hahn, J. *et al.* (1991) Basal temporal language area. *Brain*, **114**, 743–754.

Luria, A. (1966) *The Higher Cortical Function in Man*. Basic Books, New York.

Maess, B., Koelsch, S., Gunter, T. C. and Friederici, A. D. (2001) Musical syntax is processed in Broca's area: an MEG study. *Nature Neuroscience*, **4**, 540–545.

Matelli, M., Luppino, G. and Rizzolatti, G. (1985) Patterns of cytochrome oxidase activity in the frontal agranular cortex of macaque monkey. *Behavioral Brain Research*, **18**, 125–137.

McManus, C. (2002) *Right Hand, Left Hand*. Harvard University Press, Cambridge, MA.

Mecklinger, A., Gruenewald, C., Besson, M., Magnié, M.-N. and Von Cramon, Y. (2002) Separable neuronal circuitries for manipulable and non-manipualble objects in working memory. *Cerebral Cortex*, **12**, 1115–1123.

Murata, A., Fadiga, L., Fogassi, L., Gallese, V., Raos, V. and Rizzolatti, G. (1997) Object representation in the ventral premotor cortex (area F5) of the monkey. *Journal of Neurophysiology*, **78**, 2226–2230.

Nelissen, K., Luppino, G., Vanduffel, W., Rizzolatti, G. and Orban, G. A. (2005) Observing others: multiple action representation in the frontal lobe. *Science*, **310**, 332–336.

Ojemann, G. (1992) Localization of language in frontal cortex. In Chauvel, P. and Delgado-Escueta, A. V. (eds), *Advances in Neurology*, Vol. 57, pp. 361–368. Raven Press, New York.

Ojemann, G., Ojemann, J., Lettich, E. and Berger, M. (1989) Cortical language localization in left, dominant hemisphere. An electrical stimulation mapping investigation in 117 patients. *Journal of Neurosurgery*, **71**, 316–326.

Penfield, W. and Roberts, L. (1959) *Speech and Brain Mechanisms*. Princeton University Press, Princeton, NJ.

Petrides, M. (2006) Broca's area in the human and the nonhuman primate brain. In Grodzinsky, Y. and Amunts, K. (eds), *Broca's Region*, pp. 31–46. Oxford University Press, New York.

Petrides, M. and Pandya, D. N. (1997) Comparative architectonic analysis of the human and the macaque frontal cortex. In Boller, F. and Grafman, J. (eds), *Handbook of Neuropsychology*, Vol. IX, pp. 17–58. Elsevier, New York.

Pulvermuller, F., Huss, M., Kherif, F., Moscoso del Prado Martin, F., Hauk, O. and Shtyrov, Y. (2006) Motor cortex maps articulatory features of speech sounds. *Proceedings of the National Academy of Sciences of the USA*, **103**, 7865–7870.

Ranganath, C., Johnson, M. and D'Esposito, M. (2003) Prefrontal activity associated with working memory and episodic long-term memory. *Neuropsychologia*, **41**, 378–89.

Rizzolatti, G. and Arbib, M. A. (1998) Language within our grasp. *Trends in Neurosciences*, **21**, 188–194.

Rizzolatti, G. and Fadiga, L. (1998) Grasping objects and grasping action meanings: the dual role of monkey rostroventral premotor cortex (area F5). In Bock G. R. and Goode, J A. (eds), *Sensory Guidance of Movement, Novartis Foundation Symposium*, pp. 81–103. Wiley, Chichester.

Rizzolatti, G., Camarda, R., Fogassi, L., Gentilucci, M., Luppino, G. and Matelli, M. (1988) Functional organization of inferior area 6 in the macaque monkey: II. Area F5 and the control of distal movements. *Experimental Brain Research*, **71**, 491–507.

Rizzolatti, G., Fadiga, L., Gallese, V. and Fogassi, L. (1996a) Premotor cortex and the recognition of motor actions. *Cognitive Brain Research*, **3**, 131–141.

Rizzolatti, G., Fadiga, L. and Matelli, M. (1996b) Localization of grasp representation in humans by PET: 1. Observation versus execution. *Experimental Brain Research*, **111**, 246–252.

Rizzolatti, G., Fogassi, L. and Gallese, V. (2002) Motor and cognitive functions of the ventral premotor cortex. *Current Opinion in Neurobiology*, **12**, 149–154.

Saygin, A. P., Wilson, S. M., Hagler, D. J. Jr, Bates E. and Sereno, M. I. (2004) Point-light biological motion perception activates human premotor cortex. *Journal of Neurosciences*, **24**, 6181–618.

Schaffler, L., Luders, H. O., Dinner, D. S., Lesser, R. P. and Chelune, G. J. (1993) Comprehension deficits elicited by electrical stimulation of Broca's area. *Brain*, **116**, 695–715.

Schubotz, R. I. and von Cramon, D. Y. (2003) Functional–anatomical concepts of human premotor cortex: evidence from fMRI and PET studies. *Neuroimage*, **20** (Suppl. 1), 120–131.

Schubotz, R. I. and von Cramon, D. Y. (2004) Sequences of abstract nonbiological stimuli share ventral premotor cortex with action observation and imagery. *Journal of Neuroscience*, **24**, 5467–5474.

Schubotz, R. I., Sakreida, K., Tittgemeyer, M. and von Cramon, D. Y. (2004) Motor areas beyond motor performance: deficits in serial prediction following ventrolateral premotor lesions. *Neuropsychology*, **18**, 638–645.

Stromswold, K. (1995) The cognitive and neural bases of language acquisition. In Gazzaniga, M. (ed.), *The Cognitive Neurosciences*, pp. 855–870. MIT Press, Cambridge, MA.

Tranel, D., Kemmerer, D., Damasio, H., Adolphs, R. and Damasio, A. R. (2003) Neural correlates of conceptual knowledge for actions. *Cognitive Neuropsychology*, **20**, 409–432.

Umiltà, M. A., Kohler, E., Gallese, V. *et al.* (2001) I know what you are doing: a neurophysiological study. *Neuron*, **31**, 155–165.

Wernicke, C. (1874) *Der aphasische Symptomencomplex. Eine psychologische Studie auf anatomischer Basis*. Springer-Verlag, Berlin.

Wilson, S. M., Saygin, A. P., Sereno, M. I. and Iacoboni, M. (2004) Listening to speech activates motor areas involved in speech production. *Nature Neuroscience*, **7**, 701–702.

Wolfensteller, U., Schubotz, R. I. and von Cramon, D. Y. (2004) "What" becoming "where": functional magnetic resonance imaging evidence for pragmatic relevance driving premotor cortex. *Journal of Neuroscience*, **24**, 10431–10439.

20

Action mirroring and action understanding: an alternative account

Gergely Csibra

Observed actions elicit covert motor activations in observers that, in case they were executed, would generate similar actions to the observed ones. I challenge the most popular explanation offered for these phenomena, according to which such action mirroring is generated by direct matching and serves the function of action understanding in terms of their goals. I propose that action mirroring is generated by action reconstruction via top-down emulation from action interpretation produced outside the motor system. Such action mirroring does not follow but anticipates ongoing actions and enables, beyond predictive tracking, action coordination with others. I argue that the available empirical evidence is more compatible with this alternative model than with the direct-matching account.

Action mirroring

Plenty of evidence shows that when human and non-human observers watch (or listen to) others' actions, their own motor system also tends to be activated. In addition, the motor activation induced by action observation[1] often roughly corresponds to the motor program that the observer would have to execute to perform the observed action. These phenomena, which I shall term collectively *action mirroring*, can be demonstrated in many ways. Behavioral methods reveal motor priming and motor interference effects (e.g. Brass *et al.*, 2001), neurophysiological measurements show covert muscle and motor neuron excitation (e.g. Fadiga *et al.*, 1995), and neuroimaging studies indicate automatic activation of motor and premotor areas of the cerebral cortex (e.g. Buccino *et al.*, 2001) upon action observation. But perhaps the clearest evidence of action mirroring comes from single-cell studies in monkeys demonstrating that a subset of premotor and parietal neurons, called *mirror neurons*, discharge both when the animal executes a certain motor act and when it perceives the same act performed by others (Rizzolatti and Craighero, 2004).

---

[1] Throughout this paper, I discuss only examples of *visual* observation of actions, but my argument can easily be extended to other modalities, such as audition.

To explain such a rich set of phenomena, one has to specify what functions they serve and what mechanisms these functions are achieved by. Action mirroring has been suggested to subserve imitation (Iacoboni *et al.*, 1999; Rizzolatti and Craighero, 2004; Iacoboni, 2005), intersubjectivity (Gallese, 2003), and empathy (Iacoboni, 2005). However, the more basic, and evolutionarily more ancient, function that action mirroring serves is thought to be simpler: it helps the observer to understand observed actions by extracting and representing the goal, or the meaning, of those actions (Rizzolatti *et al.*, 2001; Rizzolatti and Craighero, 2004; Blakemore and Frith, 2005). In fact, it seems to be "generally accepted that the fundamental role of mirror neurons is to allow the observing individual to understand the goal of the observed motor act" (Fogassi *et al.*, 2005, p. 665).

As for the mechanisms that allow action understanding by mirroring, the most popular proposal is known as the *direct-matching hypothesis* (Rizzolatti *et al.*, 2001). According to this hypothesis, "an action is understood when its observation causes the motor system of the observer to 'resonate'" (Rizzolatti *et al.*, 2001, p. 661), and this resonance allows the observer to figure out the outcome, and ultimately the goal, of the action because "he know[s] its outcomes when he does it" (Gallese *et al.*, 2004, p. 396). In other words, action mirroring provides a simulation device for goal understanding by automatically and mandatorily duplicating the observed action in the observer's motor system.

In this paper I challenge both of these claims. I shall propose that the primary function of action mirroring is not action understanding in terms of goals but *predictive action monitoring*. I shall also suggest that action mirroring in the observer is achieved not by direct matching but by *emulative action reconstruction*. Here is a brief outline of the argument I shall make in this paper. In the next section ('Visuo-motor translation during action mirroring') I shall argue that action mirroring cannot be direct but must be based on some kind of interpretation of the observed action. The section on 'Action mirroring and goal understanding' will review the empirical evidence regarding this interpretation and will conclude that it often includes assumptions about the goal of the observed action. This implies that action understanding may precede, rather than follow from, action mirroring. Then in 'Goal understanding without simulation' I shall illustrate by findings from human infants that this is possible: goals can be understood without simulation. Finally, I shall return to the question of what functions action mirroring serves. I shall suggest that by serving the primary function of predictive action monitoring, action mirroring will also support human-specific phenomena that are not less important than imitation and empathy: action coordination and engagement in joint actions.

Visuo-motor translation during action mirroring

Action mirroring requires activating the motor program that, if it were executed, would perform a similar action to the observed one. To achieve this, the brain has to perform a translation from the visual representation in which the observed action arrives at the neural system into motor code. In other words, just like the cortical mechanisms that transform the visual information about graspable objects into motor commands that guide grasping (Jeannerod *et al.*, 1995; Murata *et al.*, 1997), the mirror system also has to find a match for the visual representation of an action in terms of motor commands.

Direct matching versus reconstruction

The direct-matching hypothesis proposes that such a translation is performed by a resonance mechanism. This metaphor suggests that certain parts of the motor system, namely the mirror neurons (MNs), or more generally the mirror neuron system, are 'tuned' to visually represented information about actions, and become automatically activated whenever a match occurs. In other words, direct matching, which is defined as "mapping the visual representation of the observed action onto our motor representation of the same action" (Rizzolatti *et al.*, 2001, p. 661) refers to a cognitively unmediated matching process that *duplicates* the motor program of the observed action without interpreting it. The 'directness' of this process is also emphasized by the assertion that the result of the visual analysis of an action is "devoid of meaning" (ibid.), and so actions are interpreted and understood only after the visuo-motor transformation has been performed.

A full 'direct-matching' account of action-mirroring mechanisms will have to answer two questions about the nature of this matching process. First, one has to specify how the tuning of the MNs, which will determine the outcome of the direct-matching process, is established. This problem is analogous to the 'correspondence problem' known in theories of imitation (Heyes, 2001; Brass and Heyes, 2005), and it has been proposed that direct links between visual and motor representation of the same action are generated by general associative learning processes during ontogenesis (Keysers and Perrett, 2004; Brass and Heyes, 2005; Heyes and Bird, Chapter 21). The second question for a direct-matching process is to determine *what* exactly is to be reproduced from the observed act. Does the mirror system have to duplicate every minute detail of the observed act (including, for example, direction and speed of motion, angles between joints, etc.) in order to facilitate its understanding? If not, how to determine the appropriate level of visuo-motor transformation? I shall return to this question later, but first I introduce an alternative mechanism for action mirroring to be contrasted with direct matching.

An alternative mechanism to direct matching in action mirroring is *action reconstruction*. This mechanism reproduces the observed action through interpreting it at some level of visual analysis (see below) and feeding the result of this interpretation into the observer's own motor system. The idea of an action reconstruction mechanism comes from the recognition that visuo-motor translation is necessarily based on a visual analysis of the observed action, which must already have determined the decomposition of the action into relevant units, separated or merged its parts into smaller or larger segments, and disregarded some aspects of it (e.g. the position of the non-active hand in grasping) as irrelevant for reproduction. This kind of interpretation of actions is akin to the mid-level visual analysis of objects that determines the initial segmentation of a scene into relevant units to be analyzed further. Just like the mid-level scene analysis translates texture and motion information into objects (or object files, see Kahneman and Treisman, 1984), an analogous analysis can translate movements and body parts into actions to be mirrored. Visual analysis can go a long way in interpreting actions (and sequences of actions, see Subiaul *et al.*, 2004), as the activation of cells in the superior temporal sulcus (STS), which do not have motor properties, demonstrates (Perrett *et al.*, 1989; Pelphrey and Morris, 2006). Such interpretations may even include assumptions about the goal of the observed action. If observed actions receive mid- or high-level interpretation within the visual system before becoming transformed into motor code, the result of this analysis will provide the input to the motor system to be reproduced. What mirroring can then achieve is the reconstruction of the motor command needed to perform that action (cf. the 'ideomotor principle', James, 1890; Hommel *et al.*, 2001). In the last section of this paper I shall return to the question of what function such an action reconstruction could serve.

Imitation versus emulation

The distinction between direct matching and action reconstruction is analogous to the imitation versus emulation distinction used in the social learning literature. In this context, *imitation* refers to the overt reproduction of an observed action, while *emulation* (or at least one type of emulation, called goal emulation or end-state emulation) is the reproduction of the *outcome* of an action by the observer's own means (Tomasello, 1996; Whiten and Custance, 1996; Zentall, 1996; Custance *et al.*, 1999; Call *et al.*, 2005; Huang and Charman, 2005; Gergely and Csibra, 2006; Tennie *et al.*, 2006). While the distinction between these two types of overt action reproduction mechanisms can be conceptualized in many different ways, the crucial contrast between imitation and emulation lies in what information is copied over from the demonstrator to the observer: the means or the end (see also, Chaminade *et al.*, 2002). Suppose, for example, that you observe someone licking an envelope to seal it. When you want to seal an envelope next time, you may also lick it, imitating the action that you have observed. Alternatively, you may have learned from your observation that one has to apply moisture on the envelope in order to seal it. If you achieve this by a wet sponge, rather than by licking, you have attained the same end by alternative means, i.e. you have emulated the observed action.

Note that the reproduction of an observed action may be the same whether it is performed by imitation or emulation. Imitating an action will normally bring the action's outcome with itself, as long as it is a goal-directed means action (as opposed, for example, to a gesture). Likewise, if the observer has similar effectors and biological constraints to the model, it is likely that she will emulate the outcome of the model's behavior by the same means as it is achieved by the model, i.e. she will faithfully reconstruct the observed action. This is why, in studies of imitation, unusual or inefficient goal-directed actions are demonstrated to participants in order to test whether they tend to emulate the outcome by their own, more efficient way, or imitate the observed action faithfully (Meltzoff, 1988; Gergely *et al.*, 2002; Horner and Whiten, 2005). For example, to test whether infants are capable of deferred imitation, Meltzoff (1988) demonstrated an unusual action to them, in which the model switched on a box-light by pushing it with his forehead. If infants emulated the outcome, they would just use a simpler action to achieve the same goal: they could just push the box with their hands.

The distinction between imitation and emulation, or between action duplication and action reconstruction, however, is not absolute but relative. One way to characterize the relation between these concepts is to imagine imitation and emulation as two ends of a

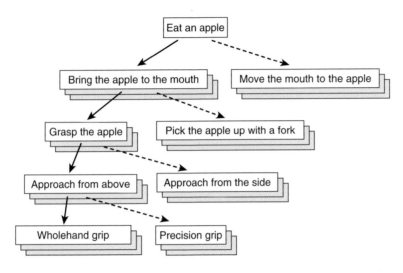

Figure 20.1 A simple action hierarchy.

continuum of decreasing fidelity of action reproduction (Whiten and Custance, 1996). Out of two copies of an action, the one that represents the less faithful reproduction would be considered an emulative response, while the other may be judged as an example of imitation. However, compared to a more accurate reproduction the latter response would be likely to be seen as emulation. Another, and perhaps better, way to characterize the relative nature of these concepts is describing them in relation to the action hierarchies of goal-directed actions. Specifically, whether a particular instance of action reproduction is considered to be imitation or emulation depends on what level the target action is defined in the action–goal hierarchy.

Action hierarchies

Actions are organized in a hierarchical manner (Jeannerod, 1994), which theories of imitation (Byrne and Russon, 1998) or action perception (Hamilton and Grafton, Chapter 18) cannot ignore. A simple action hierarchy is shown in Figure 20.1. In this scheme, the overarching goal of an action is the consumption of an apple, which requires a sequence of steps to achieve.[2] One of these steps could be to bring the apple to the mouth, which can be considered as a subgoal towards the higher-level goal of eating the apple. This subgoal, in turn, will also require a sequence of acts to complete; one of them will likely be 'grasping the apple'. To achieve this sub-subgoal, one has to perform a series of movements, which, in turn, can also be analyzed into smaller units down to the level of individual muscle activations.

---

[2] From a theoretical point of view, it would be better to characterize goals and subgoals as states of affairs than as actions. Thus, it would be more appropriate to separate out the goal state ('apple in the mouth') from the action that achieves this ('bringing the apple to the mouth'). For the sake of simplicity, however, I do not make this distinction in the text and in Figure 20.1.

Note, however, that often there are alternative means to achieve a certain goal or subgoal (see the right side of Figure 20.1). One can, for example, move one's mouth to the apple instead of the other way around (for many species this would be a more appropriate way of eating), or move the apple with a fork instead of by hand. These actions will also achieve the corresponding subgoals (apple in the mouth, getting hold of the apple to control its movement), but may involve different subactions and movements in the hierarchy below. When evaluating whether the reproduction of an action is an imitative or an emulative response, we have to judge whether it represents the same means as the model's action (compared to potential alternatives). If it does, it is considered to be an imitative response, if it does not (but achieves the same goal or subgoal), it is an emulative response. Note, however, that this evaluation requires us to specify which level of hierarchy is relevant for the reproduction of a given action.

Suppose, for example, that the model performed the apple-eating action and chose to perform it through the subgoals and subactions shown on the left side of Figure 20.1. In response, an imitator grasped an apple, brought it to her mouth and ate it. However, she took the apple by her thumb and index finger rather than using a whole-hand grip. Did she imitate the model's action? If action reproduction is evaluated at a low level where grip type is defined, she did not imitate but emulated the observed action. If, however, the model's action is defined at a higher level of the action hierarchy, the answer is affirmative; after all, she moved the apple to her mouth and not the other way around, and she grasped it by her hand instead of using a tool. At this level of analysis it is irrelevant whether minute details of her actions (like the grip type) matched to that of the model or not. For example, when infants imitate the head-touch action in variations of Meltzoff's (1988) experiment, they hardly ever copy exactly what the model has done. In fact, they frequently touch the light by their cheek, nose or chin, sometimes even kissing or biting the box (G. Gergely, personal communication). All these behaviors are considered to be imitative responses because the infants chose the same effector (their head) to perform the action as did the model. In other words, they imitated because they matched their action to the model's action at the appropriate level of description ('pushing the box by the head'). However, below that level they executed the action by their own means, i.e. they achieved this subgoal by emulation.

In fact, as we descend the action hierarchy, *any* action reproduction will at some point be seen as emulation rather than imitation because the differences between the imitator's and the model's body will not allow perfect matching in all movement parameters. This is, however, not a problem for imitation because, unless the imitator is a professional dancer or a mime artist, reproduction of perfect angles of joints, speed and acceleration of limb movement, etc. is irrelevant. My point here is not that imitation as such does not really exist, but rather that any instance of imitation is actually achieved by emulation. When someone imitates, she chooses a certain level of description of the observed action, and reproduces that level by reconstructing it in her own motor system.[3]

---

[3] In this respect, imitation is always goal-directed (Wohlschläger *et al.*, 2003), although the 'goal-directed emulation' term would express better the nature of action reproduction.

From this perspective, whether something is imitation or emulation is not a well-formulated question. Instead, one should ask how the imitator decides what is the relevant level in the action hierarchy on which an action is to be reproduced (see Williamson and Markman, 2006).

Bottom-up versus top-down

The analysis that I have applied to overt action reproduction (i.e. imitation) also applies to covert action reproduction (i.e. mirroring). Just as the *mechanism* of imitation is always emulation at a lower level, the *mechanism* of motor mirroring is always reconstruction. There is no mysterious mirroring process that directly transforms action observation into motor code. Rather, the observed action is analyzed at some level of precision and the result of this analysis is mapped onto the observer's motor system. One can call this mapping process 'direct matching' (Rizzolatti *et al.*, 2001) and such mappings may be established by 'direct' associations (see Chapter 21), but what is mapped during mirroring is not an uninterpreted signal but a description of the observed action at some level of the action hierarchy. The fine details of the resulting motor activation in the observer do not directly originate from the observation but are reconstructed from this description.

In this context, the crucial question about action mirroring and its relation to action understanding concerns the *level* of action interpretation where the mapping from visual to motor code takes place. The intuition behind the idea of 'direct matching' and the 'resonance' metaphor probably is that visuo-motor translation during mirroring occurs at a relatively low level (see the left side of Figure 20.2). Hierarchical models of motor control assume that higher and lower level motor modules are reciprocally connected to each other (Wolpert *et al.*, 2003). Thus, the low-level motor activation generated by mirroring could propagate upwards in the observer's own hierarchically organized motor system to estimate what higher level subgoals and goals might have generated the observed action (Wolpert *et al.*, 2003). This bottom-up activation may be the key to how the motor system contributes to goal understanding by mirroring, and it is the central idea behind simulative understanding of observed actions.

Alternatively, mirroring, just like imitation, can also be achieved at a higher level of action interpretation (when this is available). If the action interpretation system can construe the observed behavior in terms of higher-level or further goals, these can be mapped onto the observer's own action control system, within which it can propagate downwards to generate the corresponding motor code by covert emulation (see the right side of Figure 20.2). This top-down activation is also a kind of simulation, but it is predictive in nature, generating motor actions for goal conjectures (cf. Gallese and Goldman, 1998) rather than the other way around. This account of action mirroring proposes that observed actions are interpreted to the highest possible level before they are passed on to the motor system for reconstruction.

The relation between the two kinds of simulative exploitation of the observer's own motor system by action mirroring is illustrated in Figure 20.2. The difference between the two models lies in two factors: the action interpretation level at which visuo-motor translation is performed, and the propagation direction of activation within the

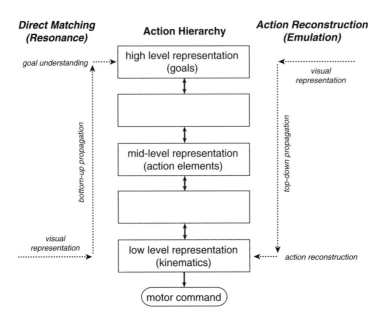

Figure 20.2 Contrasting 'direct matching' and 'action reconstruction' in a hierarchical action representation.

action control system following mirroring. Low-level mirroring (i.e. 'direct matching') and bottom-up propagation supports a simulation system that facilitates the understanding of the goals behind observed actions, while high-level mirroring and top-down propagation (i.e. 'action reconstruction') allows predictive emulation of observed actions on the basis of the high-level interpretation of the action achieved without low-level motor activation.

Action mirroring and goal understanding

In the previous section, I have provided a theoretical framework in which the relation between action mirroring, goal understanding, action hierarchy, simulation and emulation can be conceptualized. The question of what function action mirroring serves, however, is not a theoretical but an empirical question. In particular, the two alternative models of action mirroring (shown in Figure 20.2) are to be tested against the empirical findings accumulated in cognitive and neuroscientific research. Fortunately, the two models provide slightly different predictions for what kind of mirroring phenomena one would expect to find.

If action mirroring is achieved by visuo-motor translation at a low-level of action interpretation, we should find that low-level mirroring is always present and is matched well to the kinematics of the observed action. In contrast, if motor mirroring is produced by action reconstruction, we would expect to find that motor activation may not necessarily accompany action observation and, since it is produced by emulation, it may be different from the observed action. This section reviews some studies that are relevant for judging which of these predictions are confirmed by empirical findings.

Some aspects of basic mirroring phenomena are highly consistent with low-level action interpretation for mirroring. For example, observers seem to automatically imitate simple transitive and intransitive hand movements, measured by a facilitatory effect on performing compatible, and an inhibitory effect on executing incompatible, actions (Brass *et al.*, 2001; Press *et al.*, 2005; Bertenthal *et al.*, 2006). Observing someone making arm movements also interferes with executing different arm movements (Kilner *et al.*, 2003). These findings indicate a low-level mirroring process because the kinematic aspects of the observed action seem to have had an effect on the observer's kinematically similar or different movements. However, these phenomena are not relevant for judging between the two models of action mirroring because when higher-level action interpretation is not available, the emulator model also predicts low-level mirroring.

Low-level congruency between observed and mirrored actions also occurs in mirroring goal-directed actions. For example, a sizeable proportion (19–41%) of MNs in the monkey's ventral premotor and parietal cortex are classified as 'strictly congruent' (di Pellegrino *et al.*, 1992; Gallese *et al.*, 1996, 2002; Ferrari *et al.*, 2003). These neurons respond only to observed actions that are performed the same way (e.g. using the same grip type) as characterized by the motor properties of the same cell. Similarly, observation of goal-directed grasping actions tends to activate the same muscles that the observer should use for executing the same action (e.g. Fadiga *et al.*, 1995). These findings are indicative of low-level action mirroring but, since they involve observation of prototypical actions, they do not exclude the possibility that such mirroring phenomena are generated by emulative action reconstruction. Further findings, however, are more compatible with the predictions drawn from the emulative than from the direct-matching model of action mirroring.

Congruency in mirroring goal-directed actions

Monkeys' MNs do not respond to mimicked actions, for example, when they observe the experimenter pretending to grasp something in the absence of any objects (Gallese *et al.*, 1996). This finding is puzzling if action mirroring is performed by low-level direct matching because the low-level kinematics of a mimicked action is presumably similar to that of an object-directed action, and is available for mirroring. Similarly puzzling is the fact that observing a reaching act for an occluded target object elicits MN activation whereas the same movement does not trigger a MN response when the monkey knows that there is no food behind the occluder (Umiltà *et al.*, 2001). After all, the visual input is the same in the two conditions and low-level action mirroring is possible. These findings are often cited in support of the claim that MNs play a role in goal understanding, but what they really indicate is that MNs *reflect* action understanding rather than contribute to it. Consistent with the predictions drawn from the emulation model of action mirroring, MN activation in these studies seems to be conditional on action understanding and not the other way around.

Similar phenomena were also demonstrated in human neuroimaging studies. Action mirroring in humans is not restricted to transitive, object-direct actions (e.g. Bertenthal *et al.*, 2006), and the human ventral premotor cortex is sometimes activated by the observation of intransitive actions that do not involve any objects (Iacoboni *et al.*, 1999). Nevertheless, this activation is often higher for goal-directed actions than for actions whose goal is not evident (e.g. Nishitani and Hari, 2000; Chaminade *et al.*, 2001; Koski *et al.*, 2002; Johnson-Frey *et al.*, 2003).

It is not possible to measure the exact match of observation-induced motor activation in neuroimaging studies (though there is a good correspondence on the level of effectors, see Buccino *et al.*, 2001). However, such data are available from MN studies with monkeys. Although many MNs are 'strictly congruent', i.e. represent a good one-to-one correspondence between observed and executed actions, the majority of them (~60%, see Fogassi and Gallese, 2002) fall into the 'broadly congruent' category. Some of these neurons respond to two or even three types of observed actions (Gallese *et al.*, 1996), which are often related to each other in meaningful ways. A MN that is active during grasping by hand may also be activated by the observation of 'grasping with the mouth' (Gallese *et al.*, 1996). It is difficult to see how low-level motor mirroring could produce such a mismatch, but this kind of mirroring fits perfectly with the emulation model of mirroring. If the monkey has 'understood' the immediate goal of the action outside the motor system, from which the motor activation reconstructs the observed action, we would expect exactly this kind of correspondence between observation and execution: matching actions at a higher level with occasional mismatches at a lower level along the action hierarchy.

Even when a MN is activated only by the observation of a single action, it is not necessarily the same action as defined by the motor properties of the neuron. For example, di Pellegrino *et al.* (1992) reported that in many MNs, the effective observed and effective executed actions were *logically* related. "For example, the effective observed action was placing an object on the table, whereas the effective executed action was bringing food to the mouth or grasping the object" (di Pellegrino *et al.*, 1992, p. 179). It is hard to see how low-level action mirroring could result in such MN activation, while emulative mirroring, and especially predictive emulation, can easily explain such a phenomenon (see 'Action mirroring is anticipatory' below).

Further goals and intentions

The activation of MNs depends not only on the presence of target objects, but may also be tailored to the further, or higher level, goals of the observed individual. In a recent study, Fogassi *et al.* (2005) trained monkeys to perform two actions: grasping an object and putting it into their mouth (i.e. eating it), or grasping an object and putting it into a container (placing). Although the first part of these actions (grasping) was kinematically similar to each other, the researchers found separate sets of MNs in the inferior parietal lobule, which were preferentially activated before and during grasping according to the subsequent, to-be-executed action. In other words, some MNs showed higher activation when the monkey grasped the object to eat it, while others were more active when the monkey was about to place the object into the container. Crucially, these neurons responded similarly when the monkey observed the same actions performed by an experimenter. When the experimenter was about to eat the object, the 'grasping to eat' neurons were selectively activated; when he was about to place the object into the container, the other set of MNs fired. This is a clear demonstration that MNs take into account the further goal, and not just the perceived action, when responding to observed actions.

A neuroimaging study has recently concluded that the human inferior frontal cortex behaves the same way during action observation. Iacoboni *et al.* (2005) presented observers with actions (grasping a cup) either out of context, or in contexts that indicated one of two underlying intentions ('drinking tea' or 'cleaning up'). BOLD activation in the right inferior frontal cortex was higher when the context indicated the intention, i.e. the further goal, than when the action was presented alone, and the authors also found evidence for differential activation for the two intentions within the same region.

It is not clear how low-level mirroring would explain the differential motor activations in these studies, because these experiments were specifically designed to make it impossible for the observer to figure out the intention of the actor from observation of the action alone. The researchers in both studies made sure that, whatever the intention behind the observed action would have been, the perceptual and motor properties of the initial action (grasping) were as similar as possible. Thus, low-level action mirroring and prop-agating such activation upwards in the observer's action control system could not contribute to the understanding of distinct further goals or intentions for the observed actions.

In contrast, these results fit perfectly with the emulation model of action mirroring. Although the actions themselves did not carry information about the further goal of the actor in the studies cited above, the context did. For example, the monkey in the Fogassi *et al.* (2005) study could figure out the further goal of the observed action from the kind of object (food or non-food) involved, and whether or not a container was present. Such a goal attribution allowed them to emulate the action needed to achieve the goal by their own motor system, and this explains the differential activation of MNs during the observation of the initial action, which itself was not different between experimental conditions.

Mirroring non-executable actions

Action mirroring, almost by definition, requires the same or similar effectors and biological constraints between actor and observer. This may be the reason why mirroring phenom-ena cannot normally be elicited by nonhuman, robotic actions (Castiello *et al.*, 2002; Kilner *et al.*, 2003; Tai *et al.*, 2004; but see Press *et al.*, 2005), and this was the original explanation for why MNs did not appear to respond to actions performed by a tool, like grasping with a pincer (Gallese *et al.*, 1996). A recent study, however, casts doubt on the existence of such a constraint in action mirroring.

Ferrari *et al.* (2005) subjected monkeys to a long visual training of tool-using actions, like picking up food items by sticks. The monkeys passively observed as the experimenters manipulated these tools, and never learned themselves how to use them. In fact, when tested, one of the monkeys did not even make an attempt to use a stick to reach a desirable piece of food outside its cage. In spite of this, some MNs in their premotor cortex started to respond to the observation of tool use after 2 months of observational training.

When they saw the experimenter using a stick to pick up a piece of food, some MNs that were active while the monkeys themselves grasped food by hand, discharged. This is a clear example of mirroring activation for an action that the observer is unable to perform, which is incompatible with the idea of low-level motor mirroring. Nevertheless, the mirroring process was not random. As Ferrari *et al.* (2005) observed, "most tool-responding mirror neurons ... show a very good similarity between *the goal* of the observed and executed effective actions" (p. 216, italics added). In other words, MNs responded to the sight of a non-executable action with a different action that the monkey could have used to achieve the same goal. This is exactly what the emulation model of action mirroring predicts for observed actions whose goals are interpreted outside the motor system and then fed into the observer's action control system for reconstruction.

Action mirroring can even occur in response to biologically impossible actions. Costantini *et al.* (2005) measured observers' brain activation by functional magnetic resonance imaging while they were presented with finger movements that were within or outside the normal range of such actions. The impossible action depicted a hand with the little finger moving laterally for 90°. The results showed that the human ventral premotor cortex (part of the human 'mirror neuron system') was activated equally by the possible and impossible actions. Costantini *et al.* (2005) concluded that "the premotor system does not take into account the biomechanical constraints the observed movements would involve if they were actually executed" (p. 1765). Is it possible that such 'mirroring' of an impossible action is produced by 'direct matching'? As there is no matching action in the observer's repertoire, this is unlikely. However, it is conceivable that the visual system can provide an appropriate description of the end-state of such an action ('the little finger is perpendicular to the others'), which then the motor system attempts to approximate, albeit unsuccessfully, using the available motor programs. In other words, mirroring the observed action can be attempted by driving the motor system top-down from a mid-level interpretation of it.

Level of mirroring and goal understanding

While most findings that demonstrate action-mirroring phenomena fit both accounts of action mirroring, the ones I reviewed above appear to be incompatible with the direct-matching model. These findings show that low-level motor 'resonance' (i) is not mandatory (*pace* Gallese, 2006) but may depend on the interpretation of the observed action as goal-directed action, (ii) takes into account extra-motor, contextual information relevant to potential goals, and (iii) is evoked by non-executable actions when their goals can be estimated from visual information. These aspects of action mirroring suggest that goal understanding is not the output but the input of the mirroring process, and covert reproduction of the observed actions is generated by top-down emulation rather than by bottom-up propagation of activation from low-level motor resonance.

All these findings reflect a tension between two conflicting claims about action mirroring implied by the direct-matching hypothesis: the claim that action mirroring reflects low-level resonance mechanisms, and the claim that it reflects high-level action understanding. The tension arises from the fact that the more it seems that mirroring is nothing else but faithful duplication of observed actions, the less evidence it provides for action understanding; and the more mirroring represents high-level interpretation of the observed actions, the less evidence it provides that this interpretation is generated by low-level motor duplication.

Let me illustrate this point on the study of how MN activation reflects 'intention understanding' in monkeys (Fogassi *et al.*, 2005), discussed above in 'Further goals and intentions'. Marc Jeannerod (personal communication) suggested that the slight kinematic variation between the monkeys' 'grasping to eat' and 'grasping to place' actions might explain the activation difference across MNs. Fogassi *et al.* (2005) did not report the kinematic profile of the actions that the monkeys observed from the experimenter. If we assume, as Jeannerod suggested, that the observed actions included the same kinematic differences as in the monkeys' actions, and the monkeys' parietal MNs were sensitive to these parameters, then their activation represents a low-level mirroring phenomenon (in fact, it represents a lower-level mirroring than any of the earlier studies had demonstrated). However, nothing in this study would then suggest that the monkeys would have understood the 'intention' behind the observed actions. In contrast, if we accept Fogassi *et al.*'s (2005) argument that the selectivity of MNs was independent of the kinematic parameters and reflected 'intention' understanding based on contextual cues, then nothing in this study provided evidence that such an understanding is based on low-level mirroring (i.e. motor resonance). One cannot have one's cake and eat it too: the discharge of a set of MNs cannot represent the activation of the observer's motor system at low and high levels at the same time.

The emulation account of action mirroring, according to which mirroring is generated by action reconstruction from the highest available level of action interpretation, avoids this pitfall because it explains *both* why action mirroring may reflect the inferred goal of an action, *and* why it appears to provide a partial motor duplication for observed actions. However, such an account entails that the goal of an observed action can be estimated without the involvement of the low-level motor system.

Goal understanding without simulation

Understanding the goal of an observed action involves figuring out the content of the intention that generated the action.[4] Since there are always an infinite number of different intentions that may have produced any particular action (Jacob and Jeannerod, 2005), the extraction of the goal from an action is an *inverse problem* (Csibra and Gergely, 2007). Inverse problems (which usually attempt to infer causes from effects) do not have

---

[4] We have argued elsewhere that extracting the content of an intention (the goal) does not necessarily imply representing it *as* the content of a mental state (Csibra and Gergely, 1998; Gergely and Csibra, 2003). As this distinction is not relevant in the context of the present paper, I will not discuss it further.

analytical solutions, but their solution can be estimated by statistical methods. One way to describe the task of goal attribution is as a Bayesian problem (Baker *et al.*, 2006 see also Chapter 16). Under this description, the probability that a certain goal explains a certain action is estimated as

$$p(\text{goal} \mid \text{action}) = \frac{p(\text{action} \mid \text{goal}) \times p(\text{goal})}{p(\text{action})}$$

This equation says that this probability is proportional to the probability that this action is generated to achieve that particular goal state and to the probability of the goal state, and inversely proportional to the probability of the action. These last two terms [$p(\text{goal})$ and $p(\text{action})$] can be estimated by the accumulated experience with the frequencies of actions and outcomes (interpreted as goals). But where can the $p(\text{action} \mid \text{goal})$ term come from?

First, it can be estimated on purely statistical basis: the more times a certain outcome has been associated with a certain action, the more likely that they will go together again (Hommel *et al.*, 2001). A clear example of such associative learning is the study by Ferrari *et al.* (2005), in which monkeys learnt to associate goals with unfamiliar tool-assisted actions performed by experimenters (see 'Mirroring nonexecutable functions' above). This finding nicely demonstrates that such associative learning does not necessarily involve motor simulation. Second, the probability that a certain action is performed to achieve a certain goal can be estimated by motor simulation. The observer can feed the goal into her own motor system (switched to 'pretend' mode), and generate the action that she would be most likely to perform to achieve it (Gallese and Goldman, 1998). This is a powerful method for estimating the $p(\text{action} \mid \text{goal})$ term, with the obvious limitation that it can only be used for understanding known goals of individuals with similar motor constraints to the observer (Csibra and Gergely, 2007).

Finally, the likelihood that an action is performed to achieve a certain goal can also be estimated by *teleological reasoning* (Csibra and Gergely, 1998; Gergely and Csibra, 2003). Such reasoning[5] assumes that agents tend to conserve energy, and achieve their goals in the most efficient way available to them. In other words, teleological reasoning assumes that $p(\text{action} \mid \text{goal}) \approx$ (efficiency of action towards goal), and takes into account the situational constraints when evaluating efficiency. It has been demonstrated in several studies that human infants apply such teleological reasoning to interpret actions they observe. Here I shall briefly describe three studies showing that infants attribute goals (i) to non-human agents, (ii) to impossible actions, and (iii) to pretence actions. None of these goal attributions is based on motor simulation.

---

[5] The term 'reasoning' here does not imply conscious or deliberate cognitive processes. Just as certain operations within the visual (Scholl, 2005) and the motor (see Chapter 16) systems can be described as performing Bayesian inferences, the Bayesian reasoning process that applies teleological assumptions to infer goals can also operate automatically and without awareness.

Understanding goals of nonhuman agents

To investigate whether infants attribute goals to nonhuman agents, we presented 12-month-olds with computer animations, in which a circle repeatedly approached another one by jumping over an obstacle (Gergely *et al.*, 1995). Having habituated to this action, infants were then confronted with a modified situation, in which we removed the obstacle that had separated the agent from its goal, and we showed them two different events. One of them depicted the agent performing the same 'jumping' action as before, which was unnecessary and inefficient in the absence of the obstacle, and in the other event the agent approached its goal via the most efficient straight pathway. Looking-time measures indicated that, although it was perceptually more similar to the previously seen action, the infants found the 'jumping' action unexpected in this situation, suggesting that they predicted an efficient goal approach. A control condition, in which the infants were habituated to a non-necessary 'jumping' action, confirmed that this expectation was based on the goal attribution they had made when watching the efficient goal approach in the experimental condition.

Since the original report, this finding has been extended to younger infants (Csibra *et al.*, 1999; G. Csibra, unpublished data), different kinds of computer animations (Csibra *et al.*, 2003; Wagner and Carey, 2005), and different kinds of agents (Sodian *et al.*, 2004; Kamewari *et al.*, 2005). Studies with other paradigms also suggest that infants do not refrain from attributing goals (or, at least, preferences) to nonhuman objects (Luo and Baillargeon, 2005; Bíró and Leslie, 2007). None of these findings can be explained by motor simulation or resonance, because the goal-directed agents the infants observed in these studies did not have bodies or motor systems similar to the infants. Even the study that replicated the original results with human agents in 6-month-old infants (Kamewari *et al.*, 2005) involved motor actions (e.g. walking) that the participants were too young to be able to perform.

Understanding the goal of an impossible action

In a recent study, we tested whether 6–8-month-old infants were willing to extend goal attribution to a biologically impossible action (V. Southgate *et al.*, unpublished data). We reasoned that if young infants have not yet accumulated sufficient knowledge about the biological constraints of human bodies (Slaughter *et al.*, 2002), but expect that goal-directed actions take the most efficient course, they may erroneously predict a biologically impossible action if it were physically more efficient than a biologically possible goal approach. Briefly, we familiarized infants to a video clip in which a hand reached toward, grasped, and retrieved a ball from behind an obstacle. We then tested them with video clips showing a different situation, in which a second, new obstacle was introduced. Since the two obstacles together made it impossible for the hand to simply reach for the ball, we offered two new actions as solutions to the infants. In one of them, the hand pushed the second obstacle away and then retrieved the object the same way as during the familiarization, while the second action involved the hand snaking around the two obstacles forcing the forearm to take an S shape. While this second action is clearly impossible to perform by a human arm, were it biologically possible, it would represent a more efficient goal-directed action than the first one because it would get to the target object in a single step.

Our looking-time measures indicated that the infants found the efficient but impossible action more compatible with the original goal approach than the possible but less efficient action. In the control condition, in which the infants were familiarized to a nonefficient goal approach, we did not find such differential responses. This finding confirms that young human infants are willing to accept an objectively impossible action as a well-formed, goal-directed action if it appears to be more efficient than its alternatives. Note that this result suggests not only that infants, unlike adults, were not surprised to see a biologically impossible action, but also that they positively thought that this action was better in the given situation than the possible one. It is hard to see how a simulation-based goal understanding could explain such a finding.

Understanding pretence actions

Onishi *et al.* (2007) presented 15-month-old infants with the following sequence of actions. The actor turned two upside-down cups upright while demonstrating that they were empty. She then took an empty bottle, turned it over one of the cups as if she was pouring something into the cup, but no liquid left the bottle. She put down the bottle, and then took one of the cups and pretended to drink from it. Infants looked much longer at the 'drinking' action when it was performed with the cup that was not involved in the mimed pouring than when it was performed with the cup that should have contained some liquid, had the pouring been real (see Onishi *et al.*, 2007, for the control conditions). This demonstrates that infants expect that sequentially organized actions are directed towards a specific goal state: a pouring action is anticipated to result in an outcome state that provides the enabling condition (liquid in the cup) for a subsequent drinking action from the same cup. Crucially, infants recognized the causal and teleological relatedness of these actions even if no liquid was present and therefore neither the subgoal nor the final goal was ever achieved.

This finding is interesting in the context of this paper because infants at this age rarely drink from cups, are unable to pour from a bottle, and do not produce pretend actions themselves. Thus, even if they mirrored the observed action sequences faithfully, it would not have allowed them to understand these actions. In contrast, teleological reasoning, and their background knowledge about cups and bottles, did enable them to figure out the pretended goal of the pouring action and its relatedness to the subsequent drinking action. Goal understanding is possible without motor simulation.

The function of action mirroring

So far, I have argued that action mirroring must be based on some level of interpretation of the observed action, and tried to show that, when the action can be interpreted in terms of goals, such interpretation precedes, rather then follows from, action mirroring. Evidence from human infants demonstrates that goals of observed actions can be understood without the involvement of the motor system, and suggests that action mirroring can be achieved by top-down emulation. This conclusion, however, raises a question about the function of action mirroring: If actions can be understood without motor simulation, then why does the brain go on and reproduce them in the motor system?

One possible answer to this question is that the observer's motor system does not reproduce, but *pre*produces the observed action. In other words, the motor activation in the observer may not mirror but anticipate, may not shadow but foreshadow, what the other is doing. The perception of dynamic events, whether or not they involve social stimuli, is always predictive in nature (Wilson and Knoblich, 2005), and there are many benefits of being able to anticipate the immediate future in social interactions (see 'Why anticipate actions').

Action mirroring is anticipatory

Mirror neurons do not passively reflect observed actions but seem to anticipate them (see figures in Gallese *et al.*, 1996). 'Grasping mirror neurons', for example, start to discharge hundreds of milliseconds before the observed hand touches the target object, as if they mirrored the future. If the function of MNs is to anticipate impending actions, the existence of 'logically related' MNs (see 'Congruency in mirroring goal-directed actions' above) also makes sense. Logically related MNs (38% of all MNs in di Pellegrino *et al.*, 1992) respond to observed actions with a different action, but with one that could 'logically' follow the observed one. While it is not easy to see how 'direct matching' could result in such mirroring, this kind of motor response is expected if MNs anticipate both the course of the current action and the potential subsequent actions. Similar neurons have also been found in the parietal cortex in the study that reported intention-sensitive MNs (Fogassi *et al.*, 2005).

The temporal resolution of neuroimaging studies based on haemodynamic responses may not allow accurate measurement of timing relation between observation and motor activation, but other methods suggest that humans also anticipate the next move of an observed individual. This is evident in their eye movement patterns (Flanagan and Johansson, 2003; Falck-Ytter *et al.*, 2006), as well as in motor (Kilner *et al.*, 2004) and ventral premotor cortex (Nishitani and Hari, 2000; Chaminade *et al.*, 2001; Ramnani and Miall, 2004) activation.[6] In all these cases, the observer's own motor activation was triggered by their understanding of the goal, or immediate subgoal, of the observed action, and they seem to have simulated predictively what the other should do to achieve that goal. But goal understanding is not a necessary requirement for action prediction. If action mirroring generally serves a predictive function, it should use any information, and not just assumed goal states, that allows action anticipation.

---

[6] In fact, the premotor cortex seems to implement predictive procedures even in domains outside action perception (Chapter 7).

One such information is cyclic repetition of movement. Borroni *et al.* (2005) measured the modulation of muscle reflexes of people who watched an experimenter repeatedly performing wrist flexion and extension. They found that the excitability of the corresponding muscles in the observers was modulated with the same rate at which the action was performed. When the frequency of the demonstration was 1 Hz, the reflex modulation followed a 1 Hz cycle; when the demonstration was faster at 1.6 Hz, the excitability of the muscles also appeared to be modulated at 1.6 Hz. This is a clear demonstration of motor mirroring. However, the phase of the excitability cycle was advanced compared to that of the demonstration, i.e. the reflex modulation *preceded* rather than followed the demonstration by about 160 ms. Thus, motor mirroring in this study anticipated the movement of the observed hand, which was made possible not by goal understanding but by the cyclic repetition of the observed action.

Goal understanding and action prediction

Is the proposal that action mirroring serves a predictive function different from the one it is meant to replace, i.e. that it leads to goal understanding? One can say, after all, that the purpose of goal understanding is itself predictive: it tells the observer the likely outcome of an observed action. It is true that goal attribution enables two kinds of prediction to be made (Csibra and Gergely, 2007). The first one is the goal itself; goal attribution normally predicts the goal to be achieved. The present proposal, however, assigns an additional predictive function to action mirroring. While goal attribution itself allows us to jump ahead in time and predict a hypothesized future state, it also enables us to fill up the intervening time by action anticipation. In this kind of prediction, the hypothesized goal of the action is not the output, but serves as the input, of the prediction process (cf. Gallese and Goldman, 1998).

Others collected good arguments for why simulating an action is not sufficient for recovering the goal or the intention behind it (Jacob and Jeannerod, 2005; Saxe, 2005). However, there are equally good arguments for the role of simulation in action prediction (e.g. Wilson and Knoblich, 2005; Prinz, 2006; Csibra and Gergely, 2007). In fact, if the observer has a good guess about what the actor is trying to achieve (i.e. what the 'goal' is), and the actor is a conspecific with similar motor constraints to the observer, the most effective way to anticipate the actor's unfolding behavior is motor simulation by emulation. In this kind of predictive simulation, the observer feeds the hypothesized goal state into her own motor system, generates (but does not execute) the appropriate motor command, uses the corresponding forward model (Wolpert and Ghahramani, 2000; see also Chapter 16) to predict the visual consequences of this action, and attaches this prediction to the actor.

Thus, the present proposal is similar to other hypotheses (e.g. Gallese *et al.*, 2004) in that it interprets action mirroring as a simulation process. This simulation process, however, is not retrodictive, does not recover the intention that generated the action, but predictive, emulating the action needed to achieve a hypothesized goal.

Why anticipate actions?

What is the use of such online action anticipation of ongoing actions? First, it enables the observer to verify and revise goal attribution. In fact, in the first proposal for how action motor mirroring could support the understanding of intentions (Gallese and Goldman, 1998), the mirroring process was suggested to be exploited in this way (later to be abandoned for a 'direct-matching' approach). The only computational model that I am aware of and that attempts to model the understanding of intentions by MNs (Oztop *et al.*, 2005) follows the same strategy. In that model, the observer model 'knows' in advance the set of possible goals that the actor may try to achieve. When it observes a particular movement, it predictively simulates actions for these goal states sequentially until it finds one that matches the observed movement. The role of 'mirror neurons' here is to produce the expected sensory (visual) effects of the predicted action, which then can be compared to the observation. Note that what drives MNs in this model is not a 'direct-matching' mechanism but the goal conjectures generated outside the motor system. Yet, mirroring is a useful process to verify if these conjectures are valid.

Second, whether or not action anticipation is generated from goal conjectures, it is always beneficial to be ahead of events. For example, action anticipation gives the perceiver the opportunity in competitive situations to intervene in time if it becomes necessary, and allows for the quick recruitment of resources to deal with unexpected events. Perhaps this explains why MNs do not appear to respond to actions presented to the monkeys on a television screen (Ferrari *et al.*, 2003; Keysers and Perrett, 2004), and stop responding to actions performed on non-food objects "after a few or even the first presentation" (Gallese *et al.*, 1996). In these situations, the observed actions are irrelevant for the monkeys (they would not be able to get anything out of them), and hence they are not worth monitoring because intervention is either impossible (in case of actions seen on the television) or would be unrewarded (in case of nonfood objects).

Third, predictive tracking may also support learning about the physical environment in which the observed action takes place. For example, the motor system is involved in the weight estimation of objects from observation of lifting actions (Hamilton *et al.*, 2004; Pobric and Hamilton, 2007) though probably not through low-level mirroring of action kinematics (Hamilton *et al.*, 2005). If the kinematics of a perceived action differ considerably from what is anticipated by emulation, this allows us to revise the estimated weight or other invisible physical parameters of objects involved in the action.

Finally, action coordination between individuals is virtually impossible without action anticipation. Even the simplest task, like taking a walk with someone or handing over an object to someone, requires precise adjustment of the timing of movements to the other party. Humans, unlike other animals, are frequently engaged in cooperative and joint actions (Knoblich and Jordan, 2002; Pacherie and Dokic, 2006; Sebanz *et al.*, 2006). Perhaps this provides an explanation for why predictive action mirroring is so ubiquitous is humans.

Conclusions

This paper is concerned with the relation between mirroring and understanding of actions. The term 'understanding' has many different meanings. For example, Gallese (2006) assigns a role of mirroring in *experiential* understanding of others, which is "direct grasping of the *sense* of the actions performed by others" (p. 16). My analysis, however, was restricted to the question of whether action mirroring is involved in extracting the immediate or further goal (i.e. the potential content of the underlying intentions) of an action. The popular conception of the causal role of mirroring in understanding the 'meaning' of actions involves a direct, unmediated, automatic, mandatory, resonance-like transfer mechanism, which miraculously generates a copy of the motor command responsible for the observed action, and forms the basis of bottom-up identification of the goals (or intentions) that have guided that action. I showed that there is a theoretical alternative to this scenario, in which the motor activation during mirroring is generated in a top-down manner within the action control system from the level where the observer has been able to interpret the other's action. Beyond the fact that this alternative account has some theoretical advantages (e.g. it does not involve reversing the normal information flow in the motor system, as suggested by Blakemore and Decety, 2001), it is also more compatible with the empirical evidence.

On the other hand, the action–reconstruction account, just like 'direct matching', also asserts that action mirroring implements a simulation function in the motor system. This is, however, predictive, rather than retrodictive simulation mechanism. Such a simulation mechanism will, no doubt, also contribute to the 'understanding' of the observed action in a sense, though it may not supply the goal or the intention behind the action for free. Ironically, the function that I propose for such a simulation routine portrays the motor involvement in action observation as reflecting a perception-for-action procedure (allowing, for example, intervention or action coordination), while the direct-matching approach views it as a mechanism with a primarily epistemic purpose (i.e. 'understanding'). It is not action simulation that makes action understanding possible, but the other way around: it is action understanding that makes action emulation efficient.

This conclusion implies that the term 'mirroring' may be misleading because it does not capture the true nature of motor activation during action observation. Inevitably, many people will see my account of MN function as deflationary, but it is not necessarily so. If MNs are, in fact, *emulator neurons*, and they do not inform us about goals but enable us to be engaged in joint actions with others, they may play a more important role in social interactions than what is usually ascribed to them—a function that would be difficult to achieve without them.

Acknowledgments

This work was supported by the UK Medical Research Council (G9715587). I thank to Luciano Fadiga, György Gergely, Teodora Gliga, Antonia Hamilton, Kazuo Hiraki, Pierre Jacob, Mark Johnson, Magda Marton, Dan Sperber, Victoria Southgate, John S. Watson, Daniel Wolpert, and Jennifer Yoon for their valuable comments on earlier versions of this paper.

References

Baker, C. L., Tenenbaum, J. B. and Saxe, R. R. (2006) Bayesian models of human action understanding. *Advances in Neural Information Processing Systems*, 18.

Bertenthal, B. I., Longo, M. R. and Kosobud, A. (2006) Imitative response tendencies following observation of intransitive actions. *Journal of Experimental Psychology: Human Perception and Performance*, 32, 210–225.

Bíró, S. and Leslie, A. M. (2007) Infants' perception of goal-directed actions: development through cue-based bootstrapping. *Developmental Science*, 10, 379–398.

Blakemore, S-J. and Decety, J. (2001) From perception of action to the understanding of intention. *Nature Reviews Neuroscience*, 2, 561–567.

Blakemore, S-J. and Frith, C. (2005) The role of motor contagion in the prediction of action. *Neuropsychologia*, 43, 260–267.

Borroni, P., Montagna, M., Cerri, G. and Baldissera, F. (2005) Cyclic time course of motor excitability modulation during the observation of cyclic hand movement. *Brain Research*, 1065, 115–124.

Brass, M. and Heyes, C. (2005) Imitation; is cognitive neuroscience solving the correspondence problem? *Trends in Cognitive Sciences*, 9, 489–495.

Brass, M., Bekkering, H. and Prinz, W. (2001) Movement observation affects movement execution in a simple response task. *Acta Psychologica*, 106, 3–22.

Buccino, G., Binkofski, F., Fink, G.R., Fadiga, L., Fogassi, L., Gallese, V., Seitz, R.J., Zilles, K., Rizzolatti, G. and Freund, H-J. (2001) Action observation activates premotor and parietal areas in a somatotopic manner: an fMRI study. *European Journal of Neuroscience*, 13, 400–404.

Byrne, R. W. and Russon A. E. (1998) Learning by imitation: a hierarchical approach. *Behavioral and Brain Sciences*, 21, 667–721.

Call, J., Carpenter, M. and Tomasello, M. (2005) Copying results and copying actions in the process of social learning: chimpanzees (*Pan troglodytes*) and human children (*Homo sapiens*). *Animal Cognition*, 8, 151–163.

Castiello, U., Lusher, D., Mari, M., Edwards, M. and Humphreys, G. W. (2002) Observing a human or a robotic hand grasping an object: differential motor priming effects. In Prinz, W. and Hommel, B. (eds), *Common Mechanism in Perception and Action. Attention and Performance XIX*, pp. 315–333. Oxford University Press, Oxford.

Chaminade, T., Meary, D., Orliaguet, J-P. and Decety, J. (2001) Is perceptual anticipation a motor simulation? A PET study. *Neuroreport*, 12, 3669–3674.

Chaminade, T., Meltzoff, A. N. and Decety, J. (2002) Does the end justify the means? A PET exploration of the mechanisms involved in human imitation. *Neuroimage* 15, 318–328.

Costantini, M., Galati, G., Ferretti, A., Caulo, M., Tartaro, A., Romani, G.L. and Aglioti, S. M. (2005) Neural systems underlying observation of humanly impossible movements: an fMRI study. *Cerebral Cortex*, 15, 1761–1767.

Csibra, G. (unpublished) Goal attribution to inanimate agents by 6.5-month-old infants.

Csibra, G. and Gergely, G. (1998) The teleological origins of mentalistic action explanations: a developmental hypothesis. *Developmental Science*, 1, 255–259.

Csibra, G. and Gergely, G. (2007) 'Obsessed with goals': functions and mechanisms of teleological interpretation of actions in humans. *Acta Psychologica*, 124, 60–78.

Csibra, G., Gergely, G., Bíró, S., Koós, O. and Brockbank, M. (1999) Goal attribution without agency cues: the perception of 'pure reason' in infancy. *Cognition*, 72, 237–267.

Csibra, G., Bíró, S., Koós, S. and Gergely, G. (2003) One-year-old infants use teleological representations of actions productively. *Cognitive Science*, 27, 111–133.

Custance, D., Whiten, A. and Fredman, T. (1999) Social learning of an artificial fruit task in capuchin monkeys (*Cepus apella*). *Journal of Comparative Psychology*, 113, 13–23.

di Pellegrino, G., Fadiga, L., Fogassi, L., Gallese, V. and Rizzolatti, G. (1992) Understanding motor events: a neurophysiological study. *Experimental Brain Research*, **91**, 176–180.

Fadiga, L., Fogassi, L., Pavesi, G. and Rizzolatti, G. (1995) Motor facilitation during action observation: a magnetic stimulation study. *Journal of Neurophysiology*, **73**, 2608–2611.

Falck-Ytter, T., Gredebäck, G. and von Hofsten, C. (2006) Infants predict other people's action goals. *Nature Neuroscience*, **9**, 878–879.

Ferrari, P. F., Gallese, V., Rizzolatti, G. and Fogassi, L. (2003) Mirror neurons responding to the observation of ingestive and communicative mouth actions in the monkey ventral premotor cortex. *European Journal of Neuroscience*, **17**, 1703–1714.

Ferrari, P. F., Rozzi, S. and Fogassi, L. (2005) Mirror neurons responding to observation of actions made with tools in monkey ventral premotor cortex. *Journal of Cognitive Neuroscience*, **17**, 212–226.

Flanagan, J. R. and Johansson, R. S. (2003) Action plans used in action observation. *Nature*, **424**, 769–771.

Fogassi, L. and Gallese, V. (2002) The neural correlates of action understanding in non-human primates. In Stamenov, M. I. and Gallese, V. (eds), *Mirror Neurons and the Evolution of Brain and Language*, pp. 13–35. John Benjamins, Amsterdam.

Fogassi, L., Ferrari, P.F., Gesierich, B., Rozzi, S., Chersi, F. and Rizzolatti, G. (2005) Parietal lobe: from action organisation to intention understanding. *Science*, **308**, 662–667.

Gallese, V. (2006) Intentional attunement: a neurophysiological perspective on social cognition and its disruption in autism. *Brain Research*, **1079**, 15–24.

Gallese, V. and Goldman, A. (1998) Mirror neurons and the simulation theory of mind reading. *Trends in Cognitive Sciences*, **12**, 493–501.

Gallese, V., Fadiga, L., Fogassi, L. and Rizzolatti, G. (1996) Action recognition in the premotor cortex. *Brain*, **119**, 593–609.

Gallese, V., Fogassi, L., Fadiga, L. and Rizzolatti, G. (2002) Action representation and the inferior parietal lobule. In Prinz, W. and Hommel, B. (eds), *Attention and Performance XIX. Common Mechanisms in Perception and Action*, pp. 334–355. Oxford University Press, New York.

Gallese, V., Keysers, C. and Rizzolatti, G. (2004) A unifying view of the basis of social cognition. *Trends in Cognitive Sciences*, **8**, 396–403.

Gergely, G. and Csibra, G. (2003) Teleological reasoning about actions: the naïve theory of rational action. *Trends in Cognitive Sciences*, **7**, 287–292.

Gergely, G. and Csibra, G. (2006) Sylvia's recipe: The role of imitation and pedagogy in the transmisson of human culture. In Enfield N.I. and Levinson. S.L. (eds.), *Roots of Human Sociality: Culture, Cognition, and Human Interaction* pp. 229–255. Berg. Oxford.

Gergely, G., Nádasdy, Z., Csibra, G. and Bíró, S. (1995) Taking the intentional stance at 12 months of age. *Cognition*, **56**, 165–193.

Gergely, G., Bekkering, H. and Király, I. (2002) Rational imitation in preverbal infants. *Nature*, **415**, 755.

Hamilton, A., Wolpert, D. and Frith, U. (2004) Your own action influences how you perceive another person's action. *Current Biology*, **14**, 493–496.

Hamilton, A. F. de C., Joyce, D. W., Flanagan, J. R., Frith, C. D. and Wolpert, D. M. (2007) Kinematic cues in perceptual weight judgement and their origins in box lifting. *Psychological Research*, **71**, 13–21.

Hommel, B., Müsseler, J., Aschersleben, G. and Prinz, W. (2001) The Theory of Event Coding (TEC): a framework for perception and action planning. *Behavioral and Brain Sciences*, **24**, 849–937.

Horner, V. and Whiten, A. (2005) Causal knowledge and imitation/emulation switching in chimpanzees (*Pan troglodytes*) and children (*Homo sapiens*). *Animal Cognition*, **8**, 164–181.

Huang, C-T. and Charman, T. (2005) Gradations of emulation learning in infants' imitation of actions on objects. *Journal of Experimental Child Psychology*, **92**, 276–302.

Iacoboni, M. (2005) Understanding of others: imitation, language, empathy. In Hurley, S. and Chater, N. (eds), *Perspectives on Imitation: From Mirror Neurons to Memes*, Vol. 1, pp. 77–100. MIT Press, Cambridge, MA.

Iacoboni, M., Woods, R. P., Brass, M., Bekkering, H., Mazziotta, J. C. and Rizzolatti, G. (1999) Cortical mechanisms of human imitation. *Science*, **286**, 2526–2528.

Iacoboni, M., Molnar-Szakacs, I., Gallese, V., Buccino, G., Mazziotta, J.C. and Rizzolatti, G. (2005) Grasping the intentions of others with one's own mirror neuron system. *PLoS Biology*, **3**, 529–535.

Jacob, P. and Jeannerod, M. (2005) The motor theory of social cognition: a critique. *Trends in Cognitive Sciences*, **9**, 21–25.

James, W. (1890) *The Principles of Psychology*. Henry Holt, New York.

Jeannerod, M. (1994) The representing brain. Neural correlates of motor intention and imagery. *Behavioral and Brain Sciences*, **17**, 187–245.

Jeannerod, M., Arbib, M. A., Rizzolatti, G. and Sakata, H. (1995) Grasping objects: the cortical mechanisms of visuomotor transformation. *Trends in Neurosciences*, **18**, 314–320.

Johnson-Frey, S. H., Maloof, F., Newman-Norlund, R., Farrer, C., Inati, S. and Grafton, S. T. (2003) Actions or hand-object interactions? Human inferior frontal cortex and action observation. *Neuron*, **39**, 1053–1058.

Kahneman, D. and Treisman, A. (1984) Changing views of attention and automaticity. In Parasuraman, R. and Davies, D. R. (eds), *Varieties of Attention*, pp. 29–61. Academic Press. New York.

Kamewari, K., Kato, M., Kanda, T., Ishiguro, H. and Hiraki, K. (2005) Six-and-a-half-month-old children positively attribute goals to human action and to humanoid-robot motion. *Cognitive Development*, **20**, 303–320.

Keysers, C. and Perrett, D. I. (2004) Demystifying social cognition: a Hebbian perspective. *Trends in Cognitive Sciences*, **8**, 501–507.

Kilner, J. M., Paulignan, Y. and Blakemore, S. J. (2003) An interference effect of observed biological movement on action. *Current Biology*, **13**, 522–525.

Kilner, G., Vargas, C., Duval, S., Blakemore, S-J. and Sirigu, A. (2004) Motor activation prior to observation of predicted movement. *Nature Neuroscience*, **7**, 1299–1301.

Knoblich, G. and Jordan, J. S. (2002) The mirror system and joint action. In M. I. Stamenov and V. Gallese (eds), *Mirror Neurons and the Evolution of Brain and Language*, pp. 115–124. John Benjamins, Amsterdam.

Koski, L., Wohlsclager, A., Bekkering, H., Woods, R. P., Dubeau, M-C., Mazziotta, J. C. and Iacoboni, M. (2002) Modulation of motor and premotor activity during imitation of target-directed actions. *Cerebral Cortex*, **12**, 847–855.

Luo, Y. and Baillargeon, R. (2005) Can a self-propelled box have a goal? Psychological reasoning in 5-month-old infants. *Psychological Science*, **16**, 601–608.

Meltzoff, A. N. (1988) Infant imitation after a one week delay: long term memory for novel acts and multiple stimuli. *Developmental Psychology*, **24**, 470–476.

Murata, A., Fadiga, L., Figassi, L., Gallese, V., Raos, V. and Rizzolatti, G. (1997) Object representation in the ventral premotor cortex (area F5) of the monkey. *Journal of Neurophysiology*, **78**, 2226–2230.

Nishitani, N. and Hari, R. (2000) Temporal dynamics of cortical representation for action. *Proceedings of the National Academy of Sciences of the USA*, **97**, 913–918.

Onishi, K. H., Baillargeon, R. and Leslie, A. M. (2007) 15-month-old infants detect violations in pretend scenarios. *Acta Psychologica*, **124**, 106–128.

Oztop, E., Wolpert, D. and Kawato, M. (2005) Mental state inference using visual control parameters. *Cognitive Brain Research*, **22**, 129–151.

Pacherie, E. and Dokic, J. (2006) From mirror neurons to joint actions. *Cognitive Systems Research*, 7, 101–112.

Pelphrey, K. A. and Morris, J. P. (2006) Brain mechanisms for interpreting the actions of others from biological motion cues. *Current Directions in Psychological Science*, 15, 136–140.

Perrett, D.I., Harries, M.H., Bevan, R., Thomas, S., Benson, P.J., Mistlin, A.J., Chitty, A.J., Hietanen, J.K. and Ortega, J.E. (1989) Frameworks of analysis for the neural representation of animate objects and actions. *Journal of Experimental Biology*, 146, 87–113.

Pobric, G. and Hamilton, A. F. de C. (2006) Action understanding requires the left inferior frontal cortex. *Current Biology*, 16, 424–429.

Press, C., Bird, G., Flach, R. and Heyes, C. (2005) Robotic movement elicits automatic imitation. *Cognitive Brain Research*, 25, 632–640.

Prinz, W. (2006) What re-enacment earns us. *Cortex*, 42, 515–517.

Ramnani, N. and Miall, R. C. (2004) A system in the human brain for predicting the actions of others. *Nature Neuroscience*, 7, 85–90.

Rizzolatti, G. and Craighero, L. (2004) The mirror-neuron system. *Annual Review of Neuroscience*, 27, 169–192.

Rizzolatti, G., Fogassi, L. and Gallese, V. (2001) Neurophysiological mechanisms underlying the understanding and imitation of action. *Nature Review Neuroscience*, 2, 661–670.

Saxe, R. (2005) Against simulation: the argument from error. *Trends in Cognitive Sciences*, 9, 174–179.

Scholl, B. J. (2005) Innateness and (Bayesian) visual perception: reconciling nativism and development. In Carruthers, P., Laurence, S. and Stich, S. (eds), *The Innate Mind: Structure and Contents*, pp. 34–52. Oxford University Press, New York.

Sebanz, N., Bekkering, H. and Knoblich, G. (2006) Joint action: bodies and minds moving together. *Trends in Cognitive Sciences*, 10, 70–76.

Slaughter, V., Heron, M. and Sim, S. (2002) Development of preferences for the human body shape in infancy. *Cognition*, 85, B71–B81.

Sodian, B., Schoeppner, B. and Metz, U. (2004) Do infants apply the principle of rational action to human agents? *Infant Behavior and Development*, 27, 31–41.

Southgate, V., Johnson, M. H. and Csibra, G. (unpublished) Infants attribute goals to biologically impossible actions.

Subiaul, F., Cantlon, J. F., Holloway, R. L. and Terrace, H. S. (2004) Cognitive imitation in rhesus macaques. *Science*, 305, 407–410.

Tai, Y. F., Schefler, C., Brooks, D. J., Sawamoto, N. and Castiello, U. (2004) The human premotor cortex is 'mirror' only for biological actions. *Current Biology*, 14, 117–120.

Tennie, C., Call, J. and Tomasello, M. (2006) Push or pull: imitation versus emulation in human children and great apes. *Ethology*, 112, 1159–1169.

Tomasello, M. (1996) Do apes ape? In Heyes, C. M. and Galef, B. G. (eds), *Social Learning in Animals: The Roots of Culture*, pp. 319–346. Academic Press, New York.

Umiltà, M. A., Kohler, E., Gallese, V., Fogassi, L., Fadiga, L., Keysers, C. and Rizzolatti, G. (2001) I know what you are doing: a neurophysiological study. *Neuron*, 32, 91–101.

Wagner, L. and Carey, S. (2005) 12-month-old infants represent probable ending of motion events. *Infancy*, 7, 73–83.

Williamson, R. A. and Markman, E. M. (2006) Precision of imitation as a function of preschoolers' understanding of the goal of the demonstration. *Developmental Psychology*, 42, 723–731.

Wilson, M. and Knoblich, G. (2005) The case for motor involvement in perceiving conspecifics. *Psychological Bulletin*, 131, 460–473.

Whiten, A. and Custance, D. (1996) Studies of imitation in chimpanzees and children. In Heyes, C. M. and Galef, B. G. (eds), *Social Learning in Animals: The Roots of Culture*, pp. 347–370. Academic Press, New York.

Wohlschläger, A., Gattis, M. and Bekkering, H. (2003) Action generation and action perception in imitation: an instance of the ideomotor principle. *Philosophical Transactions of The Royal Society of London, B*, **358**, 501–515.

Wolpert, D. M. and Ghahramani, Z. (2000) Computational principles of movement neuroscience. *Nature Neuroscience*, **3** (Suppl.), 1212–1217.

Wolpert, D. M., Doya, K. and Kawato, M. (2003) A unifying computational framework for motor control and social interaction. *Philosophical Transactions of The Royal Society of London, B*, **358**, 593–602.

Zentall, T. R. (1996) An analysis of imitative learning in animals. In Heyes, C. M. and Galef, B. G. (eds), *Social Learning in Animals: The Roots of Culture*, pp. 221–243. Academic Press, New York.

21

Mirroring, association, and the correspondence problem

Cecilia Heyes and Geoffrey Bird

Introduction

Mirror phenomena are behavioral and neurophysiological reactions to social stimuli in which the stimulus and the response match or correspond; they share distinctive features. For example, observation of face-touching and foot-wagging elicit similar, overt behaviors from the observer (Chartrand and Bargh, 1999); observation of arm and hand movements selectively enhance motor-evoked potentials from the muscles involved in performing the same hand and arm movements (Strafella and Paus, 2000); facial expressions of disgust activate the insular cortex, which is also active during presentation of a disgusting smell (Wicker *et al.*, 2003); and the sight of a needle pricking a model's hand activates areas of the anterior cingulated cortex and anterior insula involved in pain processing (Morrison *et al.*, 2004; Avenanti *et al.*, 2005).

In this chapter we consider the extent to which mirror phenomena can be explained in terms of very simple associative processes. We will focus on motoric mirror phenomena, those in which action observation provokes the execution of similar overt or covert motor responses. The first section locates associative accounts of these phenomena among other 'mirror theories', and the second outlines one particular associative hypothesis, the associative sequence learning (ASL) model. The third section reviews evidence that the ASL model is applicable, not only to 'automatic' imitative responses, but also to cases of imitation learning and instructed imitation. In the final section we discuss extension of the ASL model to non-motoric mirror phenomena, and effects that may appear to be beyond its explanatory reach.

Thoughts about theories

Any hypothesis that purports to explain mirror phenomena (a 'mirror theory') needs to offer an account of their defining characteristic—the match or resemblance between stimulus and response. For example, it needs to explain why observation of hand movement typically elicits hand rather than foot movement, why facial expressions of disgust usually provoke disgust rather than merriment, and why a person who witnesses pain tends to react as if they were in pain rather than, for example, feeling angry. However, a satisfactory account of mirror phenomena must also explain why these relationships are not invariant; why expansive 'dominance' gestures sometimes elicit submissive responses (Tiedens and Fragale, 2003), and why witnessing another's pain sometimes produces a triumphal, rather than an empathetic, neural response (Singer *et al.*, 2004). Thus, the 'correspondence problem' (Brass and Heyes, 2006) has two faces. It challenges us to explain why mirroring happens and, under certain conditions, why it does not.

Two dimensions

Broadly speaking, mirror theories vary on two dimensions (see Figure 21.1). The first dimension relates to the ultimate source of the information that supports mirroring (Heyes, 2003). Nativist theories suggest that this information was acquired through natural selection and that it is stored in the genome. According to nativist theories, humans are born with a tendency to mirror certain stimuli, or with mechanisms that will support mirror reactions after minimal environmental input. Meltzoff and Moore's (1997) active intermodal matching hypothesis is a clear and explicit example of a nativist mirror theory. More commonly, nativist assumptions are implicit in statements about the evolutionary history or adaptive function of the mechanisms that mediate mirror phenomena (e.g. Rizzolatti, 2005). In contrast, empiricist theories suggest that the information that is crucial to solution of the correspondence problem comes from interaction between individuals and their environment, especially their social environment, during development. Thus, empiricist mirror theories, such as ideomotor theory, or the theory of event coding (Hommel *et al.*, 2001; Hommel, 2004) emphasize the importance of learning and experience in generating the potential for mirroring.

The second dimension relates to the mechanisms responsible for online mediation of mirror effects. We will refer to the two principal groups of theories that are distinguishable

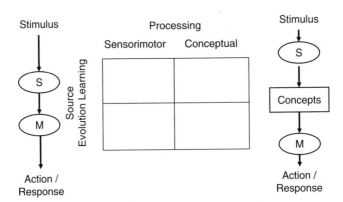

Figure 21.1 The dimensions used to classify mirror theories (centre), and schematic representations of the distinction between sensorimotor (left) and conceptual (right) models of mirroring. Sensorimotor models deny that conceptual or 'higher cognitive' processing intervenes between activation of sensory (or exteroceptive, S) and motor (or interoceptive, M) representations.

on this dimension as 'sensorimotor' and 'conceptual' theories. Sensorimotor theories propose that mirroring is mediated by direct excitatory and inhibitory connections between exteroceptive (e.g visual) sensory representations and motoric or, more broadly, interoceptive representations (see Figure 21.1). The 'associative sequence learning' model (Heyes and Ray, 2000; Heyes, 2001) and Keysers and Perrett's (2004) Hebbian hypothesis (cf. Hebb, 1949) provide clear examples of empiricist sensorimotor theories, and ideomotor theory is arguably another. There is no clearly identifiable example of a nativist sensorimotor theory, but the hypothesis discussed (and dismissed) by Meltzoff and Moore (1989), that imitation is mediated by innate releasing mechanisms, would fall into this category.

In contrast with sensorimotor theories, conceptual theories suggest that, when a mirroring response occurs, some kind of higher-level processing intervenes in a causal chain between stimulus processing and response activation (see Figure 21.1). The nature of this higher-level processing is seldom, if ever, specified. However, it is assumed to vary across categories of mirror phenomenon, and has been given a variety of names. For example, the higher-level processing has been described as 'semantic' (Tessari and Rumiati, 2004), 'symbolic' (Bandura, 1986), 'supramodal', 'amodal' (Meltzoff and Moore, 1997), and 'cognitive' (Goldenburg, 2006), and as involving 'appraisal' (de Vignemont and Singer, 2006). Many conceptual hypotheses are silent about the source of the information that makes higher-order processing possible, and therefore it is not clear whether they are broadly nativist or empiricist.

Building on models of apraxia (Rothi *et al.*, 1991), Rumiati and Tessari's (2002) two-route model suggests that overtly imitative behavior can be mediated by both sensorimotor and conceptual processing.

Associative sequence learning

Two empiricist sensorimotor models make explicit use of associative principles to explain motoric mirror phenomena: the associative sequence learning model (ASL) (Heyes and Ray, 2000; Heyes, 2001) and Keysers and Perrett's (2004) Hebbian hypothesis. The ASL model predates the Hebbian hypothesis and, although these theories are similar in spirit, they differ in two important respects. First, whereas both theories identify concurrent activation of sensory and motor components as an important condition for associative learning, the Hebbian model is, and the ASL model is not, purely correlative (Heyes, 2005). Within the Hebbian framework, correlated activation of sensory and motor components is sufficient for associative learning. In contrast, and in common with contemporary theories of associative learning in animals (see Pearce and Bouton, 2001, for a review), the ASL model assumes that learning depends on concurrent activation (contiguity) *and* on the extent to which activation of one component predicts activation of the other (contingency). Second, the two theories offer different levels of explanation. The ASL model is couched at a functional level; for example, it refers to sensory and motor representations, but does not make assumptions about their neural implementation. Consequently, although ASL was originally designed to explain overt behavioral imitation of observed body movement, it can readily be extended to account for other mirror phenomena (see 'Extending the ASL model to other mirror phenomena' below). In contrast, the Hebbian hypothesis is a neurobiological model; it seeks to explain motoric mirror phenomena with reference to the formation of connections between the superior temporal sulcus, inferior parietal cortex and area F5 of the monkey premotor cortex (where 'mirror neurons' have been located: Rizzolatti *et al.*, 1996). Given its anatomical and physiological specificity, Keysers and Perrett's Hebbin hypothesis cannot readily be applied to other mirror phenomena.

Ideomotor theory also appeals to associative learning, especially in its incarnation as the theory of event coding (Hommel *et al.*, 2001). The principal claim of this theory is that we are able to imitate the actions of others because our representation of another's action is similar to our representation of the same action performed by the self. Its weakness, as an account of imitation, is that it does not explain how we are able to imitate perceptually opaque actions, such as facial expressions and whole-body movements, that do not yield similar sensory input when instantiated by self and other. This limitation makes ideomotor theory unsuitable for extension from action mirroring (imitation) to sensation and emotion mirroring because many of these phenomena are opaque, i.e. the mirror stimulus and the mirror response are not perceived by the subject in the same modality or coordinate frame. Thus, although the ASL model, ideomotor theory and the Hebbian hypothesis are mutually compatible, and each has its own strengths and weaknesses, the ASL model is better able to encompass the full range of mirror phenomena.

The gist of the ASL model is very simple (see Figure 21.2). It suggests that motoric mirroring is mediated by excitatory links between sensory (primarily visual) and motor representations of the same behavior, and that these links, or 'matching vertical associations', are of two kinds. Direct vertical associations do not involve any intermediate representation, whereas indirect vertical associations link sensory and motor representations via a third representation. For example, a visual representation of a hand gesture (coding how the gesture looks) may be linked to a motor representation of the same gesture (coding what it feels like to perform the action), via another sensory representation (a sound). It is important to note two things about indirect vertical associations. First, by

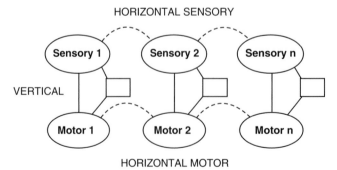

Figure 21.2 A schematic representation of the associative sequence learning (ASL) model of imitation.

hypothesis, the third representation either is not conceptual, or does not fulfill its function by virtue of any conceptual properties it may have. Second, indirect vertical associations are thought to function primarily as a means whereby direct vertical associations become established.

Where do vertical associations come from? The ASL model suggests that, whereas a few vertical associations may be innate, the majority are formed through experience that provokes concurrent activation of sensory and motor representations of the same movement. This experience may consist of concurrent observation and execution of the same movement, leading to a 'direct' vertical association, or it may involve exposure to a common stimulus in conjunction with, on some occasions, observation of the movement, and on other occasions with its execution. For example, an infant may hear a particular tapping sound, sometimes when she is hitting a table with her hand, and, at other times, when she sees a caregiver hitting a table in the same way (Jones, 2006). As a consequence of this 'acquired equivalence' experience (Hall, 1996), visual and motor representations of the hitting action will each become linked to a representation of the sound. This 'indirect vertical association' enables activation of the visual representation to be propagated to the motor representation via the sound representation, and, to the extent that it allows the sound concurrently to activate visual and motor representations of the hitting action, to the formation of a direct vertical association between them.

The ASL model addresses the second face of the correspondence problem, explains systematically counter-imitative behavior, with reference to nonmatching vertical associations. Thus, it assumes that links between a sensory representation of one movement and a motor representation of another can be formed in the same way as matching vertical associations, links between sensory and motor representations of the same movement. For example, matching vertical associations are formed when the learner simultaneously sees and executes the same action, whereas nonmatching vertical associations are formed when the sight of one action is regularly paired with the performance of another. The ASL model suggests that, if a system contains more matching than nonmatching vertical associations, and is therefore more prone to imitate than to counter-imitate, this discrepancy is due primarily to the environment in which the system has developed.

The human information-processing system typically develops in an environment that favors the formation of matching vertical associations in a number of ways. First, gross human anatomy is such that many movements of one's own distal appendages can be viewed in much the same way as those of another person. When we watch many of our own hand and finger movements, the appropriate motor representations are activated concurrently with sensory representations, arising from visual feedback, which are similar to the visual percepts that arise when we observe someone else performing the same movements. Second, the typical environment of human development contains optical mirrors and other reflecting surfaces—instruments that allow one's own facial and whole-body movements to be viewed from a third-party perspective—but not video playback devices which provide visual feedback from one movement during execution of another. Third, during early development, humans are surrounded by other humans who imitate them. Leaning over a cot, we coo when the baby is cooing, grimace when the baby is grimacing (Field *et al.*, 1985; Papousek and Papousek, 1989; Jones, 2006). We do not react to cooing with grimacing, and grimacing with cooing, in a way that would promote the formation of nonmatching vertical associations. Finally, there is language. Generally speaking, the range of movements constituting the referents of each action word look more alike, from a third-party perspective, than those of other action words. Only if natural languages contained words like 'grint', referring to you grinning and to me squinting, would the use of language promote formation of nonmatching vertical associations.

As it has been described so far, the ASL model could not explain imitation learning, i.e. imitation of actions that were not in the imitator's repertoire prior to model observation. To accommodate imitation learning, the ASL model assumes that a novel behavior consists of familiar elements or 'primitives' arranged in a novel sequence, and that two kinds of process are initiated when a novel behavior is observed (see Figure 21.2). First, sensory representations of the sequence components are activated and 'horizontal' links between them are formed. The model says little about these horizontal links because it assumes that they are not specific to imitation; that they are formed through the same sequence learning processes regardless of whether the novel behavior is imitated, counter-imitated, or merely stored allowing future recognition. However, to the extent that each sensory representation in the sequence is part of a matching vertical association, formation of the horizontal links between sensory representations will allow the second, imitation-specific process to occur. That is, successive activation of each sensory representation, by observation or recollection of the model's behavior, will provoke activation of matching motor representations in the same order, providing the potential for overt performance of a rough copy of the observed, novel movement. Furthermore, repetitive activation of this sequence of motor representations allows them to become horizontally linked. This horizontal linkage of motor representations constitutes motor learning, produces a new motor primitive, and improves the potential fluidity of imitative movement. Thus, according to the ASL model, imitation learning occurs when matching vertical associations allow sensory input from another's behavior, rather than feedback from one's own, to provide the input for motor learning (Heyes, 2003).

Evidence

Sources: natural selection versus learning

Evidence of facial gesture imitation in newborn infants (Meltzoff and Moore, 1977) motivated the original claim that imitation is innate, i.e. that natural selection is the source of the information that enables solution of the correspondence problem. This evidence is now undergoing a process of re-evaluation. Having examined all published experimental data on neonatal imitation, Anisfeld (1991, 1996) concluded that it is compelling for only one movement—tongue protrusion. For other candidates, such as mouth opening, lip protrusion, and hand waving, Anisfeld's analysis suggested that the data were inconclusive, either because too few infants had been tested, or because the reported effects could be artefacts produced by imitation of tongue protrusion. Supporting and extending this view, further experiments have indicated that neonatal imitation is confined to tongue protrusion (Couturier-Fagan, 1996), have failed to find imitation of tongue protrusion (Ullstadius, 1998), and have suggested that the tongue protrusion effect in early infancy is not sufficiently specific to constitute imitation. The latter studies show that the frequency of tongue protrusion in very young infants increases, not only when they have observed tongue protrusion, but also when they are exposed under comparable conditions to flashing lights (Jones, 1996) or rousing music (Jones, 2006).

In contrast, the results of a number of recent studies suggest that learning is important in relation to imitation. For example, two neuroimaging studies indicate that activation of cortical areas involved in imitation and movement observation depends on learned expertise in performing the observed movements. Using an elegant experimental design, Calvo-Merino et al. (2005) presented capoeira dancers, expert classical ballet dancers and nondancer control participants with video clips of closely matched capoeira and ballet movements. The capoeira experts showed stronger activation in the premotor, parietal and posterior STS regions when observing capoeira movements than when observing ballet movements, and the ballet experts showed stronger activation in the same areas when observing ballet movements than when observing capoeira movements. A later study by the same group found greater premotor, parietal and cerebellar activation when male and female ballet dancers viewed moves from their own motor repertoire, compared to opposite-gender moves that they saw frequently but did not perform (Calvo-Merino et al., 2006). This finding suggests that perceptual experience alone is not sufficient to support motor mirroring, and thereby implicates either practice, experience of performing the observed action, or sensorimotor training, experience of concurrently observing and executing the action, as the basis for mirror activation. Because ballet dancers train with optical mirrors, they not only practice same-gender moves more than opposite-gender moves, they also have more sensorimotor experience of the moves specific to their own gender.

Other evidence that learning is important for the development of imitative potential has been provided by studies of musicians. Haslinger et al. (2005) found that observation of piano playing was associated with stronger motor activation in pianists than in musically naïve controls, and that the two groups did not differ when observing control stimuli consisting of serial finger–thumb opposition movements. Buccino et al. (2004) scanned musically naïve participants while they were observing and reproducing guitar chords. They found activation in the lateral prefrontal cortex just before these novel actions were reproduced, and proposed a model of imitation learning in which the basic motor elements are activated via movement observation and are then selected and recombined, in prefrontal cortex, to match the models action. This hypothesis is highly compatible with the imitation learning mechanism assumed by the ASL model. Here matching vertical associations are automatically activated by movement observation and then combined via horizontal associations. The number and identity of the vertical associations which are activated depends on the motor repertoire of the imitator, while the ability to recombine such elements relies on another set of cognitive mechanisms concerned with serial order processing.

The recent discovery of 'tool-responding mirror neurons' in monkey ventral premotor cortex provides further evidence that mirroring depends on learning (Ferrari *et al.*, 2005). Each of these neurons fires when the monkey observes a human using a tool (stick and/or pliers) to secure food, and when the monkey grasps food with its own hand or mouth. Neurons with these properties were found in monkeys that had learned to grasp food and other objects offered to them using a tool, i.e. after numerous training trials in which the animals first observed tool use and then immediately directed a grasping action toward the object held by the tool.

The foregoing studies indicate that learning is an important determinant of mirroring potential, but they do not identify the kind of experience that is crucial. Mirroring potential could depend on repeated observation of actions (perceptual learning), repeated execution of actions (practise) or, as the ASL model predicts, on contiguous experience of action observation and execution, i.e. sensorimotor learning. We investigated this question using a behavioral, 'automatic imitation' procedure (Heyes *et al.*, 2005, Experiment 2). In the test phase of this experiment, participants completed a simple reaction time (RT) task in which they were required to open or to close their hand (blocked) as soon as they detected movement of a stimulus hand. In half of the trials the stimulus hand performed a compatible movement (e.g. opened when the required response was hand opening), and in the other half the stimulus hand performed an incompatible movement (e.g. closed when the required response was hand opening). Previous studies had shown that, under these conditions, responding is faster on compatible than on incompatible trials (Stürmer *et al.*, 2000), and that this effect is not due to spatial correspondence between the stimuli and responses (Heyes *et al.*, 2005, Experiment 1). Twenty-four hours prior to the test phase, participants were trained in one of two ways. In a choice RT procedure involving the open and the close hand movement stimuli, the compatible training group was instructed to match the observed actions (e.g. to respond to hand opening by opening their hand) and the incompatible training group was instructed to perform the opposite movement (e.g. to respond to hand opening by closing their hand). Although the training was not extensive (six blocks of 72 trials each), it had a substantial impact on test performance. Like untrained participants, the compatible training group responded faster in compatible than in incompatible trials, but the incompatible training group did not show this automatic imitation effect. Perceptual learning and practice were controlled in this study; the two groups observed and performed the hand movements with equal frequency in the course of training. Therefore, in accordance with the ASL model, the results suggest that automatic imitation depends on sensorimotor learning.

Mechanisms: sensorimotor versus conceptual

Effector effects

Recent research has begun to identify constraints on imitation—conditions in which healthy adult humans imitate less effectively—and the nature of these constraints is consistent with the view that imitation does not involve conceptual mediation. For example, Vogt *et al.* (2003) reported stronger automatic imitation effects when body movements were viewed from an 'own person' perspective (at the angle from which one views one's own movements) than from an 'other person' perspective (see also Maeda *et al.*, 2002). This is what one would expect if imitation depended on experience of ones own actions *and* on relatively low-level visual representations. If it depended on more conceptual representation, one would expect view independence to be the rule.

Behavioral experiments using the serial reaction time task suggest that conceptual mediation is unnecessary, not only for automatic imitation of familiar actions, but also for imitation learning. In these experiments (Bird and Heyes, 2005; Osman *et al.*, 2005), observers watched a model performing a complex sequence of finger movements in response to an asterisk moving between boxes arranged in a horizontal line on a computer screen. The observers were subsequently required to perform the task them-selves under three conditions: when the task was exactly the same as that performed by the model (basic transfer), when the screen stimuli were arranged vertically rather than horizontally (perceptual transfer), and when responses were made with the thumbs rather than the fingers (motor transfer). If the observers encoded what they saw concep-tually, if they acquired symbolically coded sequence knowledge by observation, they would be expected to perform well under each of these three conditions. In fact, when compared with controls who had not observed the model, the observers provided evidence of learning in the basic and perceptual transfer tests, but not in the motor transfer test. Similarly, when observational sequence training was followed by tests in which the observers' hands were crossed on the keyboard, there was evidence of imitation learning only when stimulus presentation was programmed such that observers performed the same sequence of finger movements as the model. There was no evidence of imitation learning when the stimulus sequence replicated that presented in the model, and required that response keys be struck in the modeled order, but using a novel sequence of finger movements (Bird and Heyes, 2005, Experiment 2). These findings imply that the observers' imitation learning was effector dependent, that it could not be transferred from fingers to thumbs, or from one anatomically defined sequence of finger movements to another. One would not expect conceptually mediated imitation learning to be effector dependent.

It is important to note that the ASL model, a sensorimotor theory, and conceptual theories do not make symmetrical predictions with respect to the effects of view and effector use on imitation. Conceptual theories predict that imitation will be view and effector independent because they postulate that high-level representations mediate imitation. However, the ASL model does not predict that view and effector dependence will be the norm. Rather, because it assumes that vertical associations can be formed at any level of representation where there is contiguity and contingency between the activation of sensory and motor representations, the ASL model is consistent with both view/effector dependence and independence. Therefore, the findings reported in this section are consistent with the ASL model but not with conceptual theories of imitation.

Animacy

A number of behavioral studies have reported a marked animacy effect on imitation, i.e. movements of mechanical devices, even when they are robotic (i.e. similar in appearance to human movements), do not support imitation as effectively as movements of the human body. For example, in a task involving the separation of two parts of an object, Meltzoff (1995) reported that 18-month-old infants completed the task after observing a demonstration by a human adult, but not after a demonstration performed by a mechanical device. In a series of experiments with healthy adults, Castiello *et al.* (2002) found that components of manual grasping movements, such as maximum grip aperture and time to reach peak velocity, were affected by prior observation of a human model grasping an object of the same or different size, and were not influenced by prior observation of a robotic hand/arm performing the same tasks. Similarly, Kilner *et al.* (2003) showed that performance of sinusoidal arm movements in a vertical or horizontal plane was subject to interference from simultaneous observation of another person performing incompatible arm movements, i.e. movement in the orthogonal plane. However, when the model was a full-size robot—with head, trunk, arms and legs—rather than a human, execution of the prespecified movements was unimpaired by simultaneous observation of incompatible responding.

Neurophysiological studies have also found stronger motoric mirror effects when participants observe human actions rather than movements of a mechanical device. Single-cell recording has shown that mirror neurons in area F5 of the monkey premotor cortex fire when the monkey grasps an object and when it observes a human hand grasping the same object, but not when the monkey sees the object grasped by a mechanical pincer (Gallese *et al.*, 1996). Similarly, PET has detected significant activation in the left premotor cortex when human participants observed manual grasping actions performed by a human model, but not when they were performed by a robotic hand/arm (Tai *et al.*, 2004).

Sensorimotor and conceptual models of imitation offer contrasting explanations for animacy effects. Postulating sensorimotor mechanisms, the ASL model suggests that human movements are more effective than mechanical movements as stimuli for imitation because, in humans, the potential to imitate is based on experience in which we concurrently observe human movement (our own, and that of others) and perform similar movements ourselves. According to this view, if a child was surrounded by sophisticated robots in the course of development, they would imitate robotic movement as effectively as human movement. In contrast, conceptual models would, presumably, explain animacy effects with reference to the different meanings of human and robotic stimuli. For example, a model of this kind might suggest that conceptual processing, after detection of a robotic movement stimulus, results in that stimulus being classified as inanimate, and blocks activation of a corresponding motor representation.

We have conducted a series of experiments testing the ASL model's sensorimotor account of animacy effects. These experiments used the hand opening and closing compatibility paradigm described above (see 'Sources: natural seletion versus learning' above; Heyes *et al.*, 2005). The first experiment showed that this example of automatic imitation is susceptible to an animacy effect, and that this effect is not due to low-level perceptual features of the stimuli (Press *et al.*, 2005). Participants were required to perform a prespecified movement (e.g. opening their hand) on presentation of a human or robotic hand in the terminal posture of a compatible movement (opened) or an incompatible movement (closed). Both the human and the robotic stimuli elicited automatic imitation; the prespecified action was initiated faster when it was cued by the compatible movement stimulus than when it was cued by the incompatible movement stimulus. However, even when the human and robotic stimuli were of comparable size, color and brightness, the human hand had a stronger effect on performance.

The second experiment used a training procedure, simulating the situation in which a child grows up among robots (C. Press, H. Gillmeister and C. M. Heyes, unpublished data). Participants completed the simple RT task described above before and after a period of compatible or incompatible training in which they responded to robotic stimuli in a choice RT task. The compatibly trained group responded to an open robotic stimulus by opening their hand and to a closed robotic stimulus by closing their hand, whereas the incompatibly trained group were instructed to use the reverse stimulus–response mappings. As predicted by the ASL model, compatible training eliminated the animacy effect (see Figure 21.3). Before compatible training with robotic stimuli, the compatibility effect was substantially larger for human than for robotic stimuli, but after compatible training the magnitude of this effect did not vary across stimulus categories. If compatible training eliminated the animacy effect solely by providing perceptual experience of the robotic stimuli, or practice in performing the response movements, one would expect incompatible training to have had a similar effect. In fact, incompatible training did not change the magnitude of the animacy effect, suggesting, in line with the ASL model, that it is contingent experience of observing and executing the same action that establishes the sensorimotor links which mediate imitation.

Empiricist conceptual models would allow that the meaning of robotic stimuli could change through experience; for example, that through interaction with a robot we could come to believe that it has mental states. However, the foregoing study did not give

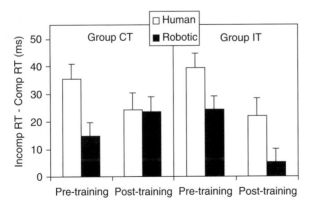

Figure 21.3 Mean compatibility effect (RT on compatible trials minus RT on incompatible trials) before and after training, when stimuli were human (white bars) or robotic (black bars) hands. In training, Group CT responded to open robotic hands by opening and to closed robotic hands by closing their own hands, whereas Group IT responded to open by closing, and to closed by opening.

subjects the kind of experience that one would expect to induce conceptual change, and there is no reason to believe that, after compatible training, participants had revised their beliefs about robots. Therefore, by examining the effects of learning on imitative performance, this study provides indirect but compelling evidence that animacy effects can be mediated solely by sensory and motor representations.

Goals

Potentially the strongest evidence in favour of conceptual models of imitation comes from studies suggesting that, when instructed to imitate, children and adults prioritize the reproduction of 'goals', the effects of actions on objects, over the reproduction of 'means', choice of effector and movement path. Several of these studies have used the pen-and-cups task. On each trial in this speeded response procedure the participant confronts a model as the latter moves a centrally located pen into one of two colored cups (object), using his right or his left hand (effector), while grasping the pen with his thumb pointing up or down (grip). Both when they are required to mirror imitate (e.g. to copy right-hand movements with the spatially compatible left hand) and to transpose (e.g. to copy right-hand movements with the spatially incompatible right hand), participants make fewer cup errors than hand errors, and fewer hand errors than grip errors (Wohlschläger and Bekkering, 2002; Avikainen *et al.*, 2003).

The goal-directed theory of imitation (GOADI; Gattis *et al.*, 2002; Wohlschläger *et al.*, 2003) explains the cup < hand < grip error pattern with reference to conceptual processes that intervene between stimulus processing and response activation. Specifically, GOADI suggests that 'the perceived act is cognitively decomposed into separate aspects', selected aspects or 'goals' are hierarchically organized, with ends taking priority over means, and then, through the ideomotor principle, selected goals elicit the motor programme with which they are most strongly associated (Wohlschläger *et al.*, 2003). This conceptual hypothesis appeals to the meaning, or functional significance, of stimulus components to explain why some are imitated more accurately than others. In contrast, the ASL hypothesis, a sensorimotor model, attributes biases in imitation to (1) input factors—variables affecting stimulus processing, (2) experience—the individual's history of learning, and (3) output factors—variables, such as task instructions, that influence whether activation of a motor representation is inhibited or expressed in overt behavior. In the case of the cup < hand < grip error pattern, input factors are the most plausible candidate. In all previous experiments involving the pen-and-cups task, the two cups were of different colors, whereas the hands and grips were, naturally, of the same color. Differential coloring of the cups could have reduced cup-errors by heightened the salience of the cups or by making them more discriminable than the hands or the grips.

To test this hypothesis, Bird, Brindley, Leighton and Heyes (in press, Experiment 2) gave two groups of participants the pen-and-cups task. For one group, the cups were colored red and blue, as in previous experiments. For the other group, the cups were of the same neutral color, but the model's hands were colored—she wore a blue glove on one hand and a red glove on the other. As predicted by the sensorimotor account, the cup < hand < grip error pattern was replicated in the cups-colored group but not in the hands-colored group. When the model wore gloves of different colors, participants made fewer errors in hand selection than in cup or grip selection.

Although predicted by the sensorimotor account, this result can also be explained by GOADI, a conceptual model. Shifting the color cue from the cups to the hands may have reduced hand errors (and increased cup errors), not by increasing the probability that participants would detect which cup had been moved in each trial, but by provoking them to revise their 'goal hierarchy'. For example, they may have inferred that the colored dimension was, in the context of the experiment, the most important stimulus dimension to imitate accurately, and this inference may have contributed to conceptual processing between stimulus detection and motor activation. Post-test questionnaire responses were inconsistent with this interpretation, showing that the colored dimension was judged to be the easiest to imitate but not the most important. However, to test the conceptual account more rigorously, J. Leighton, G. Bird and C. M. Heyes (unpublished data) used a 'geometric' version of the pen-and-cups task. Instead of watching a video in which a human model demonstrated each action to be performed, participants responded to a flashing array of geometric shapes on a computer screen. For example, when the trial began with successive flashing of (1) a square on the left of the screen, (2) the 'inside' rectangle attached to that square, and (3) the ellipse on the right of the screen, subjects were required to grip the pen between the index and middle fingers of their right hand, and to place it in the cup on their left. In terms of its low-level stimulus properties, the geometric array was matched with model demonstration, but the geometric stimuli could not be meaningfully parsed into 'means' and 'ends'. Therefore, the sensorimotor account predicted that the error patterns observed in previous pen-and-cups experiments would be replicated in the geometric version, whereas GOADI, which ascribes them to conceptual, goal-related processing, predicted that they would not. As Figure 21.4 indicates, the predictions of the sensorimotor model were correct. In the geometric task, there were minimal cup errors when the cups were colored, minimal hand errors when the hands were colored, and minimal grip errors when the grips were colored.

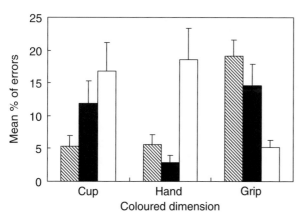

Figure 21.4 Mean percentage error (plus standard error of the mean) in the geometric pen-and-cups task, when the cups, hands or grips were of different colors. Cup selection errors are represented by hatched bars, hand selection errors by black bars, and grip selection errors by white bars.

How far can you go with associative learning?

Extending the ASL model to other mirror phenomena

The ASL model of action mirroring can be extended to account for a range of mirror phenomena reported in the literature. These phenomena are of three principal types: action mirroring (imitation), sensation mirroring, and emotion mirroring (emotional contagion/empathy). Because it has both sensory and affective components, empathetic pain straddles the boundary between the second and third categories. Using empirical examples of sensation and emotion mirroring, the following paragraphs indicate, in broad outline, how the ASL hypothesis can be extended to other mirror phenomena.

It has been shown that action mirroring can be explained with reference to 'vertical links', formed through associative learning, between 'sensory' (visual, auditory) representations of action, and the observer's internal 'motor' representations of a matching action. Once established, these vertical links allow activation of the sensory representation of an action (caused by action observation), to be propagated to the motor representation, which increases the probability that the observed action will be performed. In the basic ASL model, 'motor' representations were characterized as comprising both somatosensory information and motor commands (Heyes and Ray, 2000). To extend the model, it is necessary to emphasize their interoceptive sensory function. Thus, in an extended version of the model, the representation that mirrors would be characterized as an 'interoceptive' representation, coding what it 'feels like' to perform an action/to be touched/to be disgusted. The content of the representation initially activated by model observation would remain the same—it would code information about a social partner derived from the distal senses—but it would be described as an exteroceptive representation.

Evidence for sensation mirroring in the human brain has been provided by two recent studies investigating the neural response to observation of touch using fMRI (Keysers et al., 2004; Blakemore et al., 2005). Participants were either touched themselves, or observed another individual being touched. Both studies revealed overlapping activation of the secondary somatosensory cortex when participants were touched and when they observed another being touched. Furthermore, Blakemore et al. (2005) found somato-topic activation of the primary somatosensory cortex when participants were touched and observed another being touched. Thus, observation of touch causes the somatosensory cortex to become activated as if the individual had been touched. These effects can be explained by suggesting that an exteroceptive visual or auditory representation of touch is associated with the interoceptive sensory representation of what it feels like to be touched. This kind of association could be formed when the individual observes themselves being touched.

Emotional mirroring has been reported in a number of studies (e.g. Wicker et al., 2003; Morrison et al., 2004; Singer et al., 2004). In the study by Wicker et al. (2003), fMRI was used to study brain activity while participants either inhaled disgusting odorants, or viewed the facial expression of another individual who had inhaled the same odorants. As expected, participants who experienced disgust after inhaling the odorant showed activity in the insula (Zald and Pardo, 2000), but, interestingly, overlapping insula activity was also seen when participants viewed the disgusted facial expressions of another. Thus, observing indications of disgust in another (a disgusted facial expression) activated the same neural areas as when the participants experienced disgust themselves. This example of emotional mirroring can also be explained within the ASL framework if one supposes that vertical links can be formed between exteroceptive visual (a disgusted facial expression), or auditory (the 'yuck' sound in English), representations of disgust, and the interoceptive emotional representations of disgust. Associations between the exteroceptive and interoceptive representations of disgust may be formed when two individuals react to a common disgusting stimulus. In this example, each individual will have co-activation of their interoceptive emotional disgust response and of the exteroceptive visual and auditory disgust representations through observing the response of the other.

Challenges for the future

It is notoriously difficult to evaluate claims regarding the sources—natural selection versus learning—of information. To support their claims, nativist mirror theories concentrate on studies of very young infants, and empiricist mirror theories focus on the effects of training and expertise. However, neither the appearance of a phenomenon in early development, nor its susceptibility to change through learning, provide definitive evidence regarding the source(s) of the information that solves the correspondence problem. Research with very young infants is especially difficult to conduct and to interpret, and some innate tendencies are subject to change through learning. Therefore, it would be helpful to investigate the putative sources themselves; to know more about the selection pressures that have, according to nativist theories, shaped an innate capacity for mirroring, and about the developmental environments which, according to empiricist theories, support the learning that provides mirroring potential. The second of these challenges, to find out more about the environment of human development, is more tractable than the first, to find out about the environments of our evolutionary ancestors, but the developmental challenge is still formidable. Most research in psychology and neuroscience examines isolated systems, systems that have been pulled out of their natural environments and isolated, if not on a laboratory bench, then in a laboratory cubicle. In contrast, the kind of developmental research needed to sharpen the predictions and explanatory power of empiricist mirror theories requires observation of humans at all stages of development in their natural environments. Not just individuals, but their environments, need to be put 'on the bench'.

More familiar, but equally difficult, challenges must be met in order to test sensorimotor against conceptual accounts of mirroring. Some of these challenges are analytic, requiring the forging and maintenance of subtle distinctions, while others are empirical, requiring the development of ingenious experimental methods. On the analytic side, we need to distinguish conceptual mediation from other putative, higher-level effects on mirroring. 'Conceptual mediation' refers to the hypothesis that mirroring is achieved via a causal chain of processes in which some kind of higher-level processing is applied to the output of exteroceptive sensory processing, and it is the output from this higher-level analysis that causes activation of an interoceptive, or mirror, representation (see right side of Figure 21.1). There are at least two ways in which higher cognition could influence mirroring without constituting conceptual mediation thus defined. First, higher cognition could modulate activation of an exteroceptive representation. For example, when participants are told that a moving dot represents movement of a human arm, they may be more likely to imagine those movements, and therefore show a stronger automatic imitation effect, than when they are told that the dot movements were computer-generated (Stanley, Gowen and Miall, in press). Second, higher cognition could have an independent influence on activation of an interoceptive representation. In this case, higher cognition would have an impact on activation of the exteroceptive representation via a route distinct from the 'vertical link' connecting the exteroceptive and interoceptive representations. For example, when I see a friend waving at me through a window, my knowledge that I am in an interview situation may lead me to inhibit the interoceptive activation caused by the sight of the waving friend.

Research on mirroring is just getting underway. Many sensation- and emotion-mirroring phenomena were demonstrated for the first time in recent years, and, although imitation has been studied for more than a century, it has made substantial progress only in the last decade. It is likely to be difficult, but also rewarding, to find out exactly how the correspondence problem is solved.

Acknowledgments

This research was supported by the UK Economic and Social Research Council's research centre for Economic Learning and Social Evolution (ELSE), and by the European Community's Sixth Framework Programme under contract number: NEST 012929. We are grateful to Caroline Catmur, Helge Gillmeister, Jane Leighton and Clare Press for their contributions.

References

Anisfeld, M. (1991) Neonatal imitation. *Developmental Review*, 11, 60–97.

Anisfeld, M. (1996) Only tongue protrusion modeling is matched by neonates. *Developmental Review*, 16, 149–161.

Avenanti, A., Bueti, D., Galati, G. and Aglioti, S. (2005) Transcranial magnetic stimulation highlights the sensorimotor side of empathy for pain. *Nature Neuroscience*, 8, 955–960.

Avikainen, S., Wohlschläger, A., Liuhanen, S., Hanninen, R. and Hari, R. (2003) Impaired mirror-image imitation in Asperger and high-functioning autistic subjects. *Current Biology*, 13, 339–341.

Bandura, A. (1986) *Social Foundations of Thought and Action: A Social Cognitive Theory.* Prentice Hall, Englewood Cliffs, NJ.

Bird, G. and Heyes, C. (2005) Effector-dependent learning by observation of a finger movement sequence. *Journal of Experimental Psychology, Human Perception and Performance*, 31, 262–275.

Bird, G., Brindley, R., Leighton, J. and Heyes, C. (in press) General processes, rather than 'goals', explain imitation errors. *Journal of Experimental Psychology Human Perception and Performance.*

Blakemore, S. J., Bristow, D., Bird, G., Frith, C. and Ward, J. (2005) Somatosensory activations during the observation of touch and a case of vision-touch synaesthesia. *Brain*, 128, 1571–1583.

Brass, M. and Heyes, C. M. (2005) Imitation: is cognitive neuroscience solving the correspondence problem? *Trends in Cognitive Sciences*, 9, 489–495.

Buccino, G., Vogt, S., Ritzi, A., Fink, G. R., Zilles, K., Freund, H-J. and Rizzolatti, G. (2004) Neural circuits underlying imitation learning of hand actions: an event-related fMRI study. *Neuron*, **42**, 323–334.

Calvo-Merino, B., Glaser, D. E., Grezes, J., Passingham, R. E. and Haggard, P. (2005) Action observation and acquired motor skills: an fMRI study (cf. Hebb, 1949) with expert dancers. *Cerebral Cortex*, **15**, 1243–1249.

Calvo-Merino, B., Grezes, J., Glaser, D. E., Passingham, R. E. and Haggard, P. (2006) Seeing or doing? Influence of visual and motor familiarity in action observation. *Current Biology*, **16**, 1905–10.

Castiello, U., Lusher, D., Mari, M., Edwards, M. and Humphreys, G. W. (2002) Observing a human and a robotic hand grasping an object: differential motor priming effects. In Prinz, W. and Hommel, B. (eds), *Common Mechanisms in Perception and Action, Attention and Performance XIX*. Oxford University Press, New York.

Chartrand, T. L. and Bargh, J. A. (1999) The chameleon effect: the perception–behaviour link and social interaction. *Journal of Personality and Social Psychology*, **76**, 893–910.

Couturier-Fagan, D. A. (1996) Neonatal responses to tongue protrusion and mouth opening modeling. *Dissertation Abstracts International, Section B: The Sciences and Engineering*, **57** (3-B), 2173.

Ferrari, P. F., Rozzi, S. and Fogassi, L. (2005) Mirror neurons responding to observation of actions made with tools in monkey ventral premotor cortex. *Journal of Cognitive Neuroscience*, **17**, 212–226.

Field, T., Guy, L. and Umbel, V. (1985) Infants' responses to mothers' imitative behaviours. *Infant Mental Health Journal*, **6**, 40–44.

Gallese, V., Fadiga, L., Fogassi, L. and Rizzolatti, G. (1996) Action recognition in the premotor cortex. *Brain*, **119**, 593–609.

Gattis, M., Bekkering, H. and Wohlschläger, A. (2002) Goal-directed imitation. In Meltzoff, A. N. and Prinz, W. (eds), *The Imitative Mind*, pp. 183–205. Cambridge University Press, Cambridge.

Goldenburg, G. (2006) Imitation: is cognitive neuroscience neglecting apraxia. *Trends in Cognitive Sciences*, **10**, 94–95.

Hall, G. (1996) Learning about associatively activated stimulus representations: implications for acquired equivalence and perceptual learning. *Animal Learning and Behavior*, **24**, 233–255.

Haslinger, B., Erhard, P., Altenmüller, E., Schroeder, U., Boecker, H. and Ceballos-Baumann, A. O. (2005) Transmodal sensorimotor networks during action observation in professional pianists. *Journal of Cognitive Neuroscience*, **17**, 282–293.

Hebb, D. (1949) *The Organisation of Behaviour*. Wiley, New York.

Heyes, C. M. (2001) Causes and consequences of imitation. *Trends in Cognitive Sciences*, **5**, 253–261.

Heyes, C. M. (2003) Four routes of cognitive evolution. *Psychological Review*, **110**, 713–727.

Heyes, C. M. (2005) Imitation by association. In Hurley, S. and Chater, N. (eds), *Perspectives on Imitation: From Cognitive Neuroscience to Social Science*. MIT Press, Cambridge, MA.

Heyes, C. M. and Ray, E. (2000) What is the significance of imitation in animals? *Advances in the Study of Behaviour*, **29**, 215–245.

Heyes, C. M., Bird, G., Johnson, H. and Haggard, P. (2005) Experience modulates automatic imitation. *Cognitive Brain Research*, **22**, 233–240.

Hommel, B. (2004) Event files: feature binding in and across perception and action. *Trends in Cognitive Sciences*, **8**, 494–500.

Hommel, B., Musseler, J., Ascherschleben, G. and Prinz, W. (2001) The Theory of Event Coding (TEC): a framework for perception and action planning. *Behavioural and Brain Sciences*, **24**, 849–937.

Jones, S. S. (1996) Imitation or exploration? Young infants' matching of adults' oral gestures. *Child Development*, **67**, 1952–1969.

Jones, S. S. (2006) Newborn imitation or arousal? The effect of music on four-week-old infants' tongue protrusions. *Infant Behavior and Development*, **29**, 126–130.

Keysers, C. and Perrett, D. I. (2004) Demystifying social cognition: a Hebbian perspective. *Trends in Cognitive Sciences*, **8**, 501–507.

Keysers, C., Wicker, B., Gazzola, V., Anton, J.-L., Fogassi, L. and Gallese, V. (2004) A touching sight: SII/PV activation during the observation and experience of touch. *Neuron*, **42**, 335–346.

Kilner, J. M., Paulignan, Y. and Blakemore, S. J. (2003) An interference effect of observed biological movement on action. *Current Biology*, **13**, 522–525.

Maeda, F., Kleiner-Fisman, G. and Pascual-Leone, A. (2002) Motor facilitation while observing hand actions: specificity of the effect and role of observer's orientation. *Journal of Neurophysiology*, **87**, 1329–1335.

Meltzoff, A. N. (1995) Understanding the intentions of others: re-enactment of intended acts by 18-month-old children. *Developmental Psychology*, **31**, 838–850.

Meltzoff, A. N. and Moore, M. K. (1977) Imitation of facial and manual gestures by human neonates. *Science*, **198**, 75–78.

Meltzoff, A. N. and Moore, M. K. (1989) Imitation in newborn infants: exploring the range of gestures imitated and the underlying mechanisms. *Developmental Psychology*, **25**, 954–962.

Meltzoff, A. N. and Moore, M. K. (1997) Explaining facial imitation: a theoretical model. *Early Development and Parenting*, **6**, 179–192.

Morrison, I., Lloyd, D., di Pellegrino, G. and Roberts, N. (2004) Vicarious responses to pain in anterior cingulate cortex: is empathy a multisensory issue? *Cognitive Affective Behavioral Neuroscience*, **4**, 270–278.

Osman, M., Bird, G. and Heyes, C. M. (2005) Action observation supports effector-dependent learning of finger movement sequences. *Experimental Brain Research*, **165**, 19–27.

Papousek, M. and Papousek, H. (1989) Forms and functions of vocal matching in interactions between mothers and their precanonical infants. *First Language*, **9**, 137–157.

Pearce, J. M. and Bouton, M. E. (2001) Theories of associative learning in animals. *Annual Review of Psychology*, **52**, 111–139.

Press, C., Bird, G., Flach, R. and Heyes, C. M. (2005) Robotic movement elicits automatic imitation. *Cognitive Brain Research*, **25**, 632–640.

Rizzolatti, G. (2005) The mirror neuron system and imitation. In Hurley, S. and Chater, N. (eds), *Perspectives on Imitation: From Cognitive Neuroscience to Social Science*. MIT Press, Cambridge, MA.

Rizzolatti, G., Fadiga, L., Gallese, V. and Fogassi, L. (1996) Premotor cortex and the recognition of motor actions. *Cognitive Brain Research*, **3**, 131–141.

Rothi, L. F. G., Ochipa, C. and Heilman, K. M. (1991) A cognitive neuropsychological model of limb praxis. *Cognitive Neuropsychology*.

Rumiati, R. I. and Tessari, A. (2002) Imitation of novel and well-known actions: the role of short-term memory. *Experimental Brain Research*, **142**, 425–433.

Singer, T., Seymour, B., O'Doherty, J., Kaube, H., Dolan, R. J. and Frith, C. D. (2004) Empathy for pain involves the affective but not sensory components of pain. *Science*, **303**, 1157–1162.

Strafella, A. P. and Paus, T. (2000) Modulation of cortical excitability during action observation: a transcranial magnetic stimulation study. *Neuroreport*, **11**, 2289–2292.

Stanley, J., Gowan, E. and Miall, R.C. (in press) Effects of agency on movement interference during observation of a moving dot stimulus. *Journal of Experimental Psychology, Human Perception and Performance*.

Stürmer, B., Ascherschleben, G. and Prinz, W. (2000) Correspondence effects with manual gestures and postures: a study of imitation. *Journal of Experimental Psychology*, **26**, 1746–1759.

Tai, Y. F., Scherfler, C., Brooks, D. J., Sawamoto, N. and Castiello, U. (2004) The human premotor cortex is 'mirror' only for biological actions. *Current Biology*, **14**, 117–120.

Tessari, A. and Rumiati, R. I. (2004) The strategic control of multiple routes in imitation of actions. *Journal of Experimental Psychology, Human Perception and Performance*, **30**, 1107–1116.

Tiedens, L. Z. and Fragale, A. R. (2003) Power moves: complementarity in dominant and submissive nonverbal behaviour. *Journal of Personality and Social Psychology*, **84**, 558–568.

Ullstadius, E. (1998) Neonatal imitation in a mother-infant setting. *Early Development and Parenting*, **7**, 1–8.

Vignemont, F. de and Singer, T. (2006) The empathetic brain: how, when and why? *Trends in Cognitive Sciences*, **10**, 435–441.

Vogt, S., Taylor, P. and Hopkins, B. (2003) Visuomotor priming by pictures of hand postures: perspective matters. *Neuropsychologia*, **41**, 941–951.

Wicker, B., Keysers, C., Plailly, J., Royet, J. P., Gallese, V. and Rizzolatti, G. (2003) Both of us disgusted in My insula: the common neural basis of seeing and feeling disgust. *Neuron*, **40**, 655–664.

Wohlschläger, A. and Bekkering, H. (2002) Is human imitation based on a mirror-neurone system? Some behavioural evidence. *Experimental Brain Research*, **143**, 335–341.

Wohlschläger, A. Gattis and Bekkering, H. (2003) Action generation and action perception in imitation: an instance of the ideomotor principle. *Philosophical Transactions of the Royal Society of London, B*, **358**(1431), 501–515.

Zald, D. H. and Pardo, J. V. (2000) Functional neuroimaging of the olfactory system in humans. *International Journal of Psychophysiology*, **36**, 165–181.

Section 4

Conceptual and Symbolic Thought

cognitive architecture
human lateral prefrontal

In th... ...sed to describe the overall architecture of human lateral prefrontal ... n recent neuroimaging results. The theory elaborates on the view that the la... ...ontal cortex (LPFC) subserves cognitive control, i.e. the ability to select actions according to the context in which the agent is acting. We develop an information–theoretic approach to cognitive control that clarifies how cognitive control works as a unitary function though operating through multiple, interacting functional components implemented in distinct LPFC regions. We show that the LPFC implements three major temporal dimensions of control, namely the synchronic, diachronic and polychronic dimension, from posterior to polar LPFC regions. Furthermore, we show that within the synchronic dimension, the posterior LPFC regions, i.e. Broca's area and its right homologue, form a modular control system operating according to hierarchical structures of action plans. Thus, the theory especially suggests a basic segregation between two embedded prefrontal executive systems involved in the temporal and hierarchical organization of action and thought.

Introduction

Executive control is a brain function underlying the human faculty to act or think not only in reaction to external events but also in association with internal goals and states. Executive control participates in the voluntary production of goal-directed behaviors making humans feel as unitary and autonomous acting agents. In other words, executive control forms a central executive system that determines how humans decide to act. Executive control is considered as the cardinal function of the prefrontal cortex, a brain region forming the major part of the frontal lobes and comprising the set of cortical structures extending from the motor and premotor cortex to the most anterior prefrontal regions (Miller and Cohen, 2001). The prefrontal cortex is especially well developed in humans compared to other species, representing about one-third of the total cortical surface in humans (Fuster, 1989). Patients suffering from prefrontal lesions exhibit a dysexecutive syndrome that essentially takes two canonical forms (Mesulam, 2002). First, the abulic form is characterized by a lack of initiative, creativity with a propensity for passivity to external events, apathy and emotional blandness. The second form, usually referred to as the frontal disinhibition syndrome, has the opposite pattern characterized by impulsivity, distractibility and lack of foresight and judgments about actual and future outcomes of actions. Thus, frontal patients show a loss of capacity of self-regulating and controlling their actions and thoughts, although their perceptive, motor and memory abilities remain largely intact (Stuss and Levine, 2002).

Executive control is generally considered to operate through three basic dimensions that roughly correspond to the three main sectors of the prefrontal cortex. Briefly, the *emotional* dimension is subserved by the ventral, orbito-frontal sector involved in representing subjective values of stimuli and related actions learned from experience (e.g. O'Doherty *et al.*, 2001; Rolls, 2004). The *motivational* dimension is subserved by the medial prefrontal sector and corresponds to monitoring and evaluating ongoing actions or thoughts (e.g. Kennerley *et al.*, 2006, see also Chapter 6). Finally the *cognitive* dimension is subserved by the lateral prefrontal sector, which is involved in selecting and coordinating actions and thoughts (e.g. Miller and Cohen, 2001). In executive control, these three dimensions interact together, so that the phenomenological notion of 'goal' can viewed as a distributed representation over these three dimensions. For example the goal 'eating an apple' may be considered as the combination of 'I like apples' (emotional), 'I want an apple' (motivational) and 'I choose an apple' (cognitive) (Figure 22.1).

In this paper, I will focus on cognitive control and its implementation in the lateral prefrontal cortex (LPFC). The LPFC is the largest part of the prefrontal cortex extending from premotor to polar prefrontal regions and is reciprocally connected to posterior associative brain regions as well as to medial and orbital prefrontal regions. I will especially address the issue of the fractionation of cognitive control into multiple subprocessing, that is the issue of the architecture of cognitive control and the underlying functional

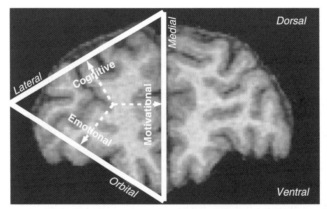

Figure 22.1 Executive control in the human prefrontal cortex. Executive control includes an emotional, motivational and cognitive dimension corresponding to the orbital, medial and lateral sector of the prefrontal cortex, respectively. These sectors are shown on a coronal section of the human prefrontal cortex.

organization of the LPFC. From a conceptual point of view, fractionating cognitive control is a challenging issue, given that this function is precisely involved in integrating and coordinating all kinds of available information for selecting appropriate actions/thoughts at each time in association with internal goals. Indeed, cognitive control has been conceptualized as a unitary, non-modular function (Fodor, 1982). As shown below, however, recent neuroimaging studies do not support this extreme view and provide consistent functional segregations in the LPFC underlying cognitive control. Conversely, the conceptualization of cognitive control as a unitary function highlights the fact that fractionating cognitive control into multiple functional components would be of little theoretical significance if at the same time no adequate theory accounted for functional integration and coordination across such segregated functional components. In this chapter, I propose a unified theory that describes the overall architecture of cognitive control and the underlying functional organization of the LPFC. The theory clarifies how cognitive control works as a unitary function though operating through multiple, interacting functional components implemented in distinct LPFC regions.

Multiple views of cognitive control in the LPFC

Before presenting the theory, I shall briefly review classical theories describing how cognitive control is implemented in the LPFC. These theories often present various, complementary rather than exclusive views of cognitive control, introducing several key functional concepts for understanding the implementation of cognitive control in the LPFC. I will show, however, that none of these theories alone provides an adequate or comprehensive framework for understanding the fractionation of cognitive control into multiple functional components. These theories can be grouped into two main categories, those that focus on processing cross-temporal contingencies and those focusing on top-down attentional modulation in cognitive control.

In the first group, the working-memory hypothesis proposed by (Goldman-Rakic, 1987, 1996) postulates that the LPFC implements working memory, i.e. the active maintenance of information over time until its subsequent use based on sustained, bi-stable neuronal activations. In this view the LPFC is organized in distinct, specialized cortical regions implementing working memory in the different cognitive domains including mainly spatial relations, object identity and linguistic domains. The theory accounts for the domain-specific projection system from posterior associative brain regions to posterior prefrontal regions (Pandya and Yeterian, 1996), the relative domain-specific prefrontal activations observed in several neuroimaging studies (Owen et al., 2005) and for the finding that neurons in the prefrontal cortex exhibit sustained activity (Wilson et al., 1993). However, the working-memory hypothesis faces several problems. First, active maintenance of information over time per se was found to be neither a sufficient nor a necessary component for activating prefrontal regions (D'Esposito et al., 1998; Pochon et al., 2001). Second, domain-specific activations were found only in posterior prefrontal regions (Sakai and Passingham, 2003, 2006) and even in the posterior prefrontal cortex such domain-based dissociations are not systematic (Rao et al., 1997; Nystrom et al., 2000).

Third, the working-memory hypothesis provides no conceptual framework explaining how functional integration and coordination occur across such specialized prefrontal regions. In sum, domain-specific prefrontal activations, when observed, appear to reflect more segregations of the input projection system from posterior brain regions to the LPFC than a basic functional feature of the LPFC function.

Similarly, Fuster (1989) proposed that the LPFC is critically involved in processing cross-temporal contingencies across events for action selection, i.e. in filling the temporal gap between perception and action. Fuster's hypothesis, however, does not assume a specific role of the LPFC in active maintenance of information over time- and domain-based functional segregations in the prefrontal cortex (Fuster *et al.*, 2000). Instead, his theory emphasizes the prominent role of the LPFC in representing multiple preparatory sets for action. The key assumption is that the LPFC is organized as a hierarchy of representations extending from premotor to polar prefrontal regions. In this hierarchy, more anterior regions are involved in processing gradually more complex and abstract action sets, ranging from single acts to programs and plans. Thus, in contrast to Goldman-Rakic's theory, Fuster proposed a principle of functional integration of multiple processes in the LPFC, namely a hierarchy of processing from premotor to polar prefrontal regions, which has received empirical support from recent neuroimaging studies (Braver *et al.*, 2003; Koechlin *et al.*, 2003; Velanova *et al.*, 2003). The key limitation of Fuster's theory, however, is its weak predictive power concerning functional segregations within the LPFC given that the theory provides no clear conceptual distinctions between the different levels of processing beyond the elusive notion of complexity and abstractness. A variant of Fuster's theory has been described by Grafman (1995, 2002) proposing that the LPFC stores in long-term memory and processes structured-event-complexes, i.e. action plans comprising series of perceptual-action events with more anterior regions involved in representing longer structured-event-complexes. Grafman's theory raises the important question about the exact nature of long-term representations in LPFC but still remains too elusive to make clear predictions about functional segregations in the LPFC.

The second group includes theories postulating that cognitive control modulates brain processing involved in action selection through top-down interactions originating from the LPFC, i.e. the LPFC is the source of top-down attentional modulation. Shallice (1988) and Shallice and Burgess (1996) proposed that the prefrontal function is a supervisory attentional system biasing competition between concurrent internal automatic routines represented in posterior cortices through top-down interaction from prefrontal to posterior brain regions. More recently, Shallice (2002) also described a possible fractionation of the supervisory attentional system into multiple cognitive processes based on an artificial intelligence framework. Shallice's theory, however, provides no theoretical framework describing and predicting the implementation of these multiple cognitive processes in the prefrontal cortex. Passingham proposes another hypothesis based on the notion of 'attention to action' stipulating that top-down attentional modulation exerts mainly from anterior to posterior frontal regions including the premotor cortex on various representations of action implemented in these regions (Passingham, 1993; Passingham and Sakai, 2004). Passingham's hypothesis emphasizes the prominent role of the LPFC in action preparation and selection at multiple representational levels, a hypothesis supported by experimental evidence (e.g. Sakai and Passingham, 2003; reviewed in Passingham and Sakai, 2004). The theory, however, does not specify the precise nature of these multiple representational levels. Finally, Miller and Cohen (2001) propose a theory emphasizing the notion of contextual processing in top-down attentional modulation. According to their theory, the LPFC is mainly involved in representing and processing contextual rules that will subsequently influence the selection of action in response to stimuli. The theory, however, provides no framework describing possible functional segregations within the LPFC.

In summary, the theories described above introduce several key concepts describing cognitive control and its implementation in the LPFC. Altogether, those theories suggest that the LPFC forms a top-down selection system as a hierarchy of representations extending from premotor to polar prefrontal regions processing cross-temporal contingencies and contextual rules of various complexity for selecting appropriate action at each time and in each context. Thus, the concepts introduced in those theories mainly appear as complementary rather than exclusive and I believe there is now an overall agreement about this general scheme. Beyond this general view, however, no theory seems to offer a clear theoretical and predictive framework describing the precise relations between these different functional concepts, the fractionation of cognitive control into multiple subcomponents implemented in different LPFC regions, and the organization of these subcomponents into an integrated cognitive architecture. A great part of these problems is likely to reflect the fact that cognitive control *per se* remains an underspecified psychological notion that was not clearly defined in an information-processing framework but only by default like a homunculus, i.e. a little person in the head who does all the tasks that are assumed not to be processed in peripheral systems (Baddeley, 2002).

An information–theoretic approach to cognitive control

To further understand the architecture of cognitive control and its implementation in the LPFC, we recently proposed an information-processing model of cognitive control. The basic idea is to clarify the psychological notion of cognitive control using mathematical concepts from Information Theory (Shannon, 1948; Berlyne, 1957; Deco and Obradovic, 1996) and to derive from such a formalization possible ways to fractionate cognitive control into subcomponents and to model integration between these subcomponents.

The basic model

Consider a set of independent actions $\{a\}$ that are selected with relative frequencies or probabilities $p(a)$. According to Information Theory (Berlyne, 1957), the total amount of information $H(a)$ required for *selecting* action a among the other alternative actions is given by:

$$H(a) = -\log_2 p(a)$$

Thus, if $p(a) = 1$, i.e. action a is the only possible action, so that selection requires no information to be processed, because there is no alternative action. Conversely, the closer to zero is $p(a)$, the smaller is the probability that action a is selected by chance and consequently, the larger is the amount of information that was processed for selecting action a. Consider now a set of stimuli $\{s\}$. Processing a stimulus s may provide some information for selecting action a, which is given by the *mutual information* $I(s,a)$ between s and a:

$$I(s,a) = \log_2 [p(a,s)/p(a)p(s)],$$

where $p(a,s)$ is the relative frequency that stimulus s occurs and action a is selected, $p(s)$ is the frequency of occurrence of stimulus s. Thus, if action a and stimulus s are unrelated, i.e. $p(a, s) = p(a)p(s)$, the mutual information $I(s,a)$ is equal to zero, so that stimulus s conveys no information for selecting action a. In contrast, if stimulus s invariably triggers action a, that is the probability to select a given the occurrence of s is equal to 1, i.e. $p(a|s) = 1$, then the mutual information $I(s,a)$ is equal to the total amount of information $H(a)$ required for selecting action a, so that stimulus s conveys all the information required for selecting action a. In psychological terms, this situation occurs when action a is an automatic response to stimulus s. Accordingly, we refer to the mutual information $I(s,a)$ as *sensory control* on action a.

Then, consider the following quantity usually referred to as the *conditional information*:

$$Q(a|s) = H(a) - I(s,a)$$

$$= -\log_2 p(a|s)$$

The quantity $Q(a|s)$ corresponds to the psychological notion of *cognitive control*, in the sense that it measures the remaining amount of information required for selecting action a which is not conveyed by stimulus s. As expected, this quantity is zero when action a is an automatic response to stimulus s [i.e. $p(a|s) = 1$] and increases as the probability of selecting action a following stimulus s decreases. In other words, the less action a is a prepotent response to stimulus s, the larger is the quantity $Q(a|s)$. Thus the quantity $Q(a|s)$ precisely measures the demand of cognitive control required for selecting action a in response to stimulus s. Furthermore, the total amount of information $H(a)$ required for selecting action a appears as the sum of sensory control $I(s,a)$ and cognitive control $Q(a|s)$.

To relate this model to behavioral performance, we can then compute the average demand of cognitive control $Q(A|S)$ over a series of trials corresponding to occurrences of stimuli $S = \{s\}$ and actual responses $A = \{a\}$, which is given by:

$$Q(A|S) = \Sigma_{a,s} \, p(a,s)Q(a|s)$$

$$= H(A) - I(S,A),$$

where $H(A) = \Sigma_a \, p(a)H(a)$ measures the average total amount of information involved in selecting responses A and $I(S,A) = \Sigma_{a,s} \, p(a,s)I(a,s)$ the average amount of information conveyed by stimuli S and related to responses A. With the minimal assumption that processing times or reaction times (RTs) vary as the total amount of information $H(A)$ to be processed for selecting responses A, the model then predicts that RTs vary as the sum of sensory and cognitive control:

$$\text{RTs} \sim I(S,A) + Q(A|S).$$

This prediction was explicitly tested in a recent study (Koechlin et al., 2003). The experiment required subjects to respond to successively presented, visual stimuli (colored squares) by pressing left or right response buttons. Series of stimuli were inter-mixed with instruction cues presented every 12 stimuli. Selecting a left or right response was either contingent upon both stimuli and instruction cues $[I(S,A) = 1; Q(A|S) = 1]$, or independent of stimuli and contingent upon instruction cues only $[I(S,A) = 0; Q(A|S) = 2]$, or contingent upon stimuli and independent of instruction cues $[I(S,A) = 1; Q(A|S) = 0]$. Finally, in other series, subjects had simply to repeatedly perform the same response with no selection $[I(S,A) = 0; Q(A|S) = 0]$. As shown in Figure 22.2, the experimental results confirmed the prediction. Subjects' RTs to series of visual stimuli were found to vary linearly as the sum of sensory and cognitive control, the two factors having additive effects on RTs. Furthermore, assuming that local brain activations as measured by functional magnetic resonance imaging (fMRI) vary as the amount of locally processed information, the model predicts that lateral prefrontal activations would vary as cognitive control $Q(A|S)$ only. In contrast, knowing that the premotor cortex is involved in selecting motor responses to stimuli, premotor activations are predicted to vary as the total amount of information $H(A)$ required for selecting responses, i.e. as the sum of sensory and cognitive control, with the former reflecting bottom-up information flows from posterior associative brains regions and the latter top-down information flows from lateral prefrontal regions to the premotor cortex. These predictions are in agreement with the network of anatomical connections previously described in the frontal lobes (Pandya and Yeterian, 1996). To test this additional prediction, Koechlin et al. (2003) analyzed fMRI activations in the frontal lobes in relation to action selection in response to series of stimuli. As predicted, lateral prefrontal activations were found to vary as the demand of cognitive control $Q(A|S)$ only, whereas activations in the premotor cortex

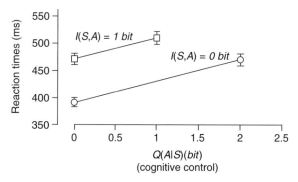

Figure 22.2 Additive effects of sensory and cognitive control on reaction times. Reaction times are for correct responses to stimuli according to sensory [$I(S,A)$] and cognitive [$Q(A/S)$] control. Data are from Koechlin et al. (2003). See text for details.

varied as the additive demand of sensory and cognitive control (Figure 22.3). Moreover, using functional connectivity analyses, Koechlin *et al.* (2003) provided evidence that the effect of cognitive control $Q(A|S)$ in the premotor cortex resulted from information flows between premotor regions and posterior LPFC regions contiguous to the premotor cortex.

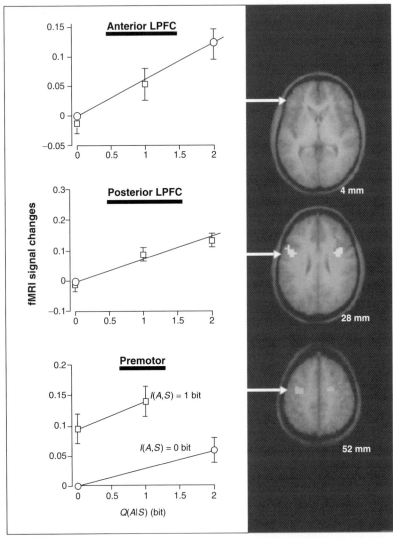

Figure 22.3 Frontal activations with respect to demands of sensory and cognitive control. Green: activations varying with sensory control [$I(S,A)$] (premotor cortex). Yellow and red: activations varying with cognitive control only [$Q(A/S)$]. Yellow: posterior lateral prefrontal cortex (LPFC) (BA 44/45). Red, anterior LPFC (BA 46). Numbers in the right panel are vertical Talairach coordinates of axial slices (neurological convention). Functional magnetic resonance imaging (fMRI) data are from Koechlin *et al.* (2003). See color plate section.

Thus, the present information–theoretic model of cognitive control quantitatively accounts for behavioral performances and the distinctive role of the premotor cortex and the LPFC in action selection. In particular, the model indicates that the LPFC is involved in processing and conveying to the premotor cortex through top-down interactions the remaining information $Q(A|S)$ that is unrelated to stimuli but required for selecting appropriate motor responses to those stimuli.

Fractionating cognitive control: the cascade model

The basic model described above shows that the total amount of information $H(A)$ required for selecting actions A is the sum of two components, namely sensory and cognitive control. In that sense, the model already includes a principle of fractionation, so that cognitive control appears as the fraction of information involved in action selection that is not conveyed by stimuli. On the basis of the same principle, cognitive control itself can be fractionated by considering additional signals conveying information about action selection. For instance, consider additional signals c in a set $\{C\}$. Cognitive control $Q(A|S)$ is then the sum of two components (see Figure 22.4):

$$Q(A|S) = I(C,A|S) + Q(A|S,C)$$

where $I(C,A|S)$ is the mutual information between signals C and actions A, which is not conveyed by stimuli S:

$$I(C,A|S) = \Sigma_{a,s,c}\, p(a,s,c)\, \log_2\, [p(a,c|s)/p(a|s)p(c|s)]$$

and $Q(A|S,C)$ is the fraction of information involved in action selection which is conveyed neither by stimuli S nor signals C:

$$Q(A|S,C) = \Sigma_{a,s,c}\, p(a,s,c)\, \log_2\, p(a|s,c).$$

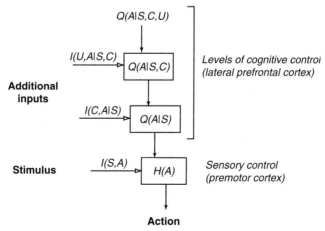

Figure 22.4 The cascade model of cognitive control. The figure shows the fractionation of cognitive control according to an information–theoretic approach. See text for notations.

Thus, $I(C,A|S)$ represents a level of control associated with signals C in the same way as sensory control is related to stimuli S, whereas $Q(A|S,C)$ represents a higher level of control which is unrelated to stimuli S and signals C. Furthermore, by analogy with the involvement of the premotor cortex in combining (1) sensory control through bottom-up information flows and (2) cognitive control through top-down information flows from posterior LPFC regions, the information–theoretic model suggests that posterior LPFC regions would be involved in combining (1) the control $I(C,A|S)$ associated with signals C through bottom-up information flows from posterior associative brain regions conveying signals C and (2) the higher level of control $Q(A|S,C)$ through top-down information flows from anterior LPFC regions involved in processing only this higher form of control. Thus, posterior LPFC activations would vary as the sum $Q(A|S)$ of the two forms of control, whereas anterior LPFC activations would vary only as the higher form of control $Q(A|S,C)$. Furthermore, as described above, the model also predicts that RTs vary as the additive demand of the two forms of cognitive control:

$$\text{RTs} \sim I(C,A|S) + Q(A|S,C)$$

Note that following exactly the same reasoning, the higher form of control $Q(A|S,C)$, in turn, can be broken down into two components by considering additional signals U (unrelated to signals C), so that

$$Q(A|S,C) = I(U,A|S,C) + Q(A|S,C,U)$$

with the prediction that the highest form of control $Q(A|S,C,U)$ involves even more anterior LPFC regions. At this point, of course, the model specifies only a formal functional architecture, given that the nature of control signals C and U (and possibly others) remains unspecified. However, this information–theoretic approach of cognitive control provides a quantitative and predictive model formalizing the idea that cognitive control is organized as a cascade of top-down control processes from anterior to posterior prefrontal to premotor regions (Fuster, 1989; Passingham, 1993; Grafman, 1995, 2002; Fuster et al., 2000; Passingham and Sakai, 2004). In this cascade model, each control level is engaged in action selection only when the information processed in lower levels is not sufficient for action selection, i.e. for resolving ambiguities, interferences or conflicts between concurrent actions. In such situations, higher levels are engaged and provide additional information that is not available to lower levels but required for selecting appropriate actions. Thus, the cascade model supports the principle of functional *subsidiarity*, so that higher control levels are engaged only when action selection cannot be effectively performed by lower levels. In relation to functional subsidiarity, the cascade model also contains a notion of functional *proximity*: higher control levels are involved in action selection by integrating information that is less directly linked to actions. In terms of anatomy, the principle of functional proximity is reflected by the fact that higher control levels are predicted to involve more anterior prefrontal regions (Fuster, 1989). Thus, the cascade model provides a theoretical functional architecture that may explain how cognitive control is fractionated into multiple control processes implemented in distinct prefrontal regions and how these multiple control processes are organized in an integrated cognitive architecture.

Fractionating cognitive control within the time domain

As mentioned above, the temporal theories of cognitive control indicate that time is a key dimension of cognitive control suggesting that cognitive control can be fractionated into multiple control levels depending upon cross-temporal contingencies between actions and events involved in selection. In the time domain, one can distinguish three major dimensions of cross-temporal contingencies along which cognitive control may operate. First, the *synchronic* dimension corresponds to the situation where the response to a stimulus depends upon the *immediate context* in which stimuli occur, i.e. upon contextual signals that are concomitant to stimulus occurrences. For example, picking up the phone in response to the phone ring (i.e. the stimulus) is the action you select if you are at home but not in a friend's house. In this example, the house represents the immediate context that may influence the action you perform in response to a stimulus. In other words, the immediate (perceptual) context in which a stimulus occurs may provide additional information that is not conveyed by stimuli and that may be required for selecting appropriate actions. Thus, the synchronic dimension is related to a component of control that differs from sensory control and that we refer to as *contextual* control (see also Miller and Cohen, 2001).

Second, the *diachronic* dimension corresponds to the situation where the response to a stimulus depends upon the *ongoing* temporal episode in which stimuli occur, i.e. upon occurrences of past events. In the example above, when the phone rings in your friend's house, you may answer provided that your friend previously asked you to respond to phone calls until she/he will be back. Your friend's instruction defines a new temporal episode during which appropriate actions may differ from previous ones. More generally, selecting appropriate actions may depend upon information conveyed by past events and that is not provided by the immediate context in which stimuli occur. Thus, the diachronic dimension is associated with another form of control that distinguishes from contextual control and that we refer to as *episodic* control (see also Fuster, 2001).

Third, the *polychronic* dimension is involved when the response to a stimulus depends upon a temporal episode that precedes the ongoing episode, i.e. upon events that occurred earlier than the events defining the ongoing temporal episode. In the phone example above, assume that your friends had asked you to respond to phone calls but later informed you that s/he wished to respond to the next phone call that s/he was expecting. Thus, this second instruction temporary puts the first instruction in a pending state until the next phone call occurs, so that you will not respond to the next call but you will respond to the following ones. Not responding to the first call depends upon the ongoing episode starting from the second instruction and therefore engages episodic control, whereas responding to the following ones is contingent upon the first pending instruction. Thus, selecting appropriate actions may depend upon information conveyed by past events but temporarily maintained in a pending state, while the subject is acting according to occurrences of more recent events. The polychronic dimension of behavior or thought involves an additional form of control referred to as *branching* control. Note that branching control appears as a key control process underlying multi-task performance, given that humans are known to be unable to control the execution of two tasks simultaneously (Pashler, 2000; Sigman and Dehaene, 2005). For instance, in dual-task performance, branching control is required for postponing execution of one task after completion of the other one.

The cascade model described in the previous section provides a framework to understand how these different forms of control processes may be implemented in different LPFC regions and interact together (see Figure 22.5). On the basis of the functional proximity principle and consistently with previous temporal theories of cognitive control (Fuster, 1989; Grafman, 1995), the cascade model suggests that the longer is the temporal

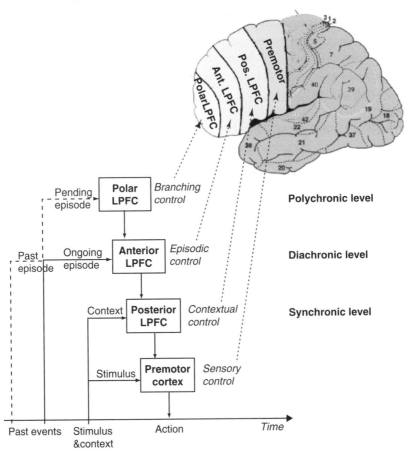

Figure 22.5 The fractionation of cognitive control within the temporal dimension. The figure indicates how the synchronic, diachronic and polychronic levels of cognitive control are implemented in the lateral prefrontal cortex (LPFC).

distance between actions and events involved in action selection, higher control levels and more anterior prefrontal regions are engaged. Thus, the cascade model states that contextual control represents the lowest level of cognitive control implemented in posterior LPFC regions and modeled by the information $I(C,A|S)$ related to actions A and conveyed only by immediate contextual signals C. The demand of contextual control increases when the occurrence of contextual signals C increasingly alters the responses to concomitant stimuli S. The next upper level corresponds to episodic control subserved by more anterior prefrontal regions and modeled by the information $I(U,A|S,C)$ related to actions A and conveyed only by the episodic signal U occurring in the past (e.g. instruction cues). The demand of episodic control increases after the occurrence of an event U, when selection rules in lower control levels increasingly deviate from those corresponding to the episode preceding event U. Finally, branching control corresponds to a higher control level implemented in even more anterior LPFC regions and modeled by the remaining amount of information $Q(A|S,C,U)$ involved in selecting actions A and which is conveyed only by events occurring earlier than the episodic signal U. The demand of branching control increases when episodic control has been engaged following the occurrence of an unpredicted event U and selection rules are again altered increasingly with respect to events preceding event U. For clarity in the following, we refer to the temporal episode that follows the occurrence of event U as the ongoing behavioral episode.

Contextual versus episodic control: empirical findings

Koechlin *et al.* (2003) tested the specific predictions of the cascade model in an fMRI study designed to variably engage contextual and episodic control only. Subjects were presented series of letter stimuli and had to make a left or right motor response to stimuli depending upon whether stimuli were vowel, consonant, lower-case or capital letters. Contextual signals were represented by the color of stimuli and indicated whether subjects had to select motor responses with respect to either the vowel/consonant categories or letter-cases. Episodic signals were instruction cues presented every 12-letter blocks and provided information about the contexts (i.e. the color) associated with each task-set (vowel/consonant versus letter-case discrimination tasks). The protocol was designed in order to separately vary across 12-letter blocks the demand of contextual and episodic control, that is the amounts of information $I(C,A|S)$ and $I(U,A|S,C)$ conveyed by color and instruction cues, respectively. Thus, selecting a left and right response was either contingent upon stimuli, contextual and instruction cues [$I(S,A) = 1$; $I(C,A|S) = 1$; $I(U,A|S,C) = 1$], or independent of contextual signals and contingent upon stimuli and instruction cues only [$I(S,A) = 1$; $I(C,A|S) = 0$; $I(U,A|S,C) = 2$], or contingent upon stimuli and contextual signals and independent of instruction cues [$I(S,A) = 1$; $I(C,A|S) = 1$; $I(U,A|S,C) = 0$], or contingent upon stimuli only [$I(S,A) = 1$; $I(C,A|S) = 0$; $I(U,A|S,C) = 0$].

The results confirm the model predictions. Behavioral RTs were found to vary as the additive demand of contextual and episodic controls, i.e. as the sum of amounts of information $I(C,A|S)$ and $I(U,A|S,C)$, respectively (Figure 22.6). Posterior LPFC regions (Broadman's area 44 and 45) showed activations varying as the additive demand of contextual and episodic controls [i.e. $Q(A|S) = I(C,A|S) + I(U,A|S,C)$], whereas more

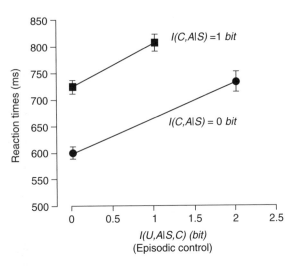

Figure 22.6 Additive effects of contextual and episodic control on reaction times. Reaction times are for correct responses to stimuli according to contextual [$I(C,A|S)$] and episodic [$I(U,A|S,C)$] control. Data are from Koechlin *et al.* (2003). See text for details.

anterior LPFC regions (BA 46) exhibited activations linearly varying as episodic control $I(U,A|S,C)$ only (Figure 22.7). Furthermore, effective connectivity analyses revealed that top-down information flows from anterior to posterior LPFC regions varied as the increasing demand of episodic control.

Overall, as noted by Koechlin *et al.* (2003), these findings as well as those reported in the previous section show that anterior LPFC activations were independent of relational complexity of action selection, i.e. of the number of independent relations to be processed for selecting appropriate actions or, equivalently, of the total amount of information $H(A)$ required for action selection, because anterior LPFC activations varied as episodic control only. Similarly, LPFC activations were independent of short-term memory load, because the increasing demand of cognitive control did not correspond to increasing short-term memory load. Instead, these findings support the information–theoretic cascade model of cognitive control: premotor regions are involved in processing contingencies between stimuli and actions and integrating additional information from posterior prefrontal regions for selecting appropriate actions. Posterior LPFC regions are involved in processing contingencies between contextual signals and premotor representations (i.e. sensorimotor associations) and integrating additional information from anterior LPFC regions for selecting appropriate sensorimotor associations according to the immediate context of action. And anterior LPFC regions are involved in processing contingencies between episodic signals and posterior LPFC representations (i.e. action-sets or consisted sets of sensorimotor associations evoked in the same context) for selecting appropriate action-sets according to the ongoing behavioral episodes. In particular, it is worth noting that the concept of episodic control is not reducible to the simple notion of active maintenance of information over time, because episodic control varies as the deviation between selection rules corresponding to the episodes preceding and following the occurrence of an episodic signal, regardless of the content and complexity of selection rules.

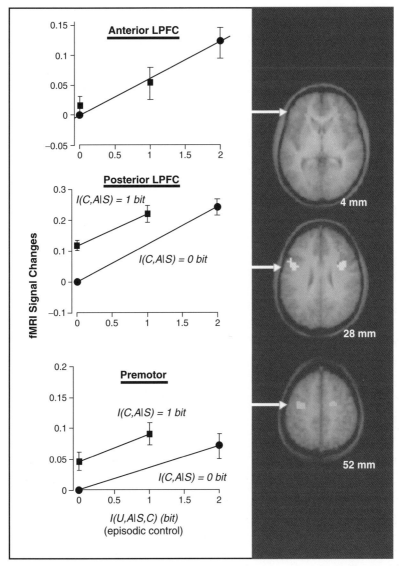

Figure 22.7 Frontal activations with respect to demands of contextual and episodic control. Green: premotor activations. Yellow: activations varying with contextual control [$I(C,A|S)$] [posterior lateral prefrontal cortex (LPFC), BA 44/45]. Red: activations varying with episodic control only {[$I(U,A|S,C)$], anterior LPFC, BA 46}. Numbers in the right panel are vertical Talairach coordinates of axial slices (neurological convention). Functional magnetic resonance imaging (fMRI) data are from Koechlin *et al.* (2003). See color plate section.

The cascade model fractionating cognitive control into contextual and episodic control subserved by posterior and anterior LPFC regions respectively is consistent with the pattern of prefrontal activations observed in various behavioral paradigms including learning, episodic memory, working memory and task-switching paradigms. For instance, in learning paradigms, anterior LPFC activations were reported when subjects were learning action sequences by trials and errors, that is when subjects received feedback signals altering behaviors in subsequent episodes (e.g. Jenkins *et al.*, 1994; Koechlin *et al.*, 2002). In episodic memory paradigms, anterior LPFC activations were especially observed in retrieval phases, when subjects selected actions based on the occurrence of previous events (review in Buckner and Koutstaal, 1998). In working-memory paradigms, posterior LPFC activations were reported, when subjects maintained task-sets in working memory, whereas anterior LPFC activations were observed when subjects had to select actions based on memorized information (Rowe *et al.*, 2000). In task-switching paradigms, posterior LPFC activations were observed when subjects switched between task-sets with respect to concomitant visual signals, whereas rostral LPFC activations were observed when subjects prepared task-sets for subsequent behaviors or when task-switching required additional control over several trials following switch signals (e.g. Dove *et al.*, 2000; Nagahama *et al.*, 2001). Moreover, Sakai *et al.* (2002), Velanova *et al.* (2003), Sakai and Passingham (2003) and Braver *et al.* (2003) examined time-courses of prefrontal activations in episodic memory, working memory and task-switching paradigms, respectively, and found that posterior LPFC exhibited phasic activations in association with action selection, whereas anterior LPFC showed sustained activations over behavioral episodes.

Episodic versus branching control: empirical findings

Empirical studies reported above show that episodic control is implemented in anterior LPFC regions and more specifically in BA 46. This finding suggests that higher levels of cognitive control in the cascade model, i.e. branching control, involve more anterior LPFC regions localized in the frontopolar cortex (BA 10). Accordingly, the cascade model states that the lateral frontopolar cortex is engaged, when action selection requires retrieval of additional information from the behavioral episode [i.e. $Q(A|S,C,U)$] that precedes the ongoing behavioral episode (i.e. preceding event U). For instance, the frontopolar cortex is engaged when execution of a first task is postponed after completion of a second task. Compared to more caudal LPFC regions, the lateral frontopolar cortex receives few direct projections from posterior brain regions conveying information from external events (see review in Ramnani and Owen, 2004). This distinguishing feature of polar LPFC regions is consistent with its putative role in branching control, because branching control consists of internally retrieving pending information rather than processing information from external events.

In an fMRI study, Koechlin *et al.* (1999) showed that polar LPFC regions are selectively engaged in branching control. They found that polar LPFC regions were engaged only when subjects had to postpone the execution of a primary task in order to first complete a secondary task. Neither switching between the two tasks nor simply delaying one task engaged polar LPFC regions. Moreover, in agreement with the cascade model predicting top-down control from anterior to posterior prefrontal regions, they found that polar LPFC activations in branching control were accompanied by increased anterior LPFC activations compared to those found in the task-switching and task-delaying conditions.

The involvement of polar LPFC regions in branching control is confirmed by several other studies on multi-tasking based on combining various cognitive tasks including semantic (Braver and Bongiolatti, 2002) and prospective memory tasks (Burgess *et al.*, 2001). Polar LPFC regions were also found to be robustly engaged in episodic retrieval tasks requiring subjects to retrieve events that occurred before the ongoing behavioral episode (Buckner, 2003), and in reasoning tasks requiring subjects to combine the outcome of multiple tasks for selecting appropriate responses to stimuli (Christoff *et al.*, 2001; review in Ramnani and Owen, 2004). Consistently, Hyafil and Koechlin (2005) recently showed using a computational model describing neuronal interactions between anterior and polar LPFC regions that branching control accounts for frontopolar activations in these behavioral paradigms, including episodic memory retrieval and relational integration paradigms.

A key theoretical distinction between episodic and branching control is that action selection in branching control is based on pending information unrelated to the ongoing behavioral episode, i.e. on information related to the behavioral episode preceding the ongoing one. Thus, branching control is involved provided that the ongoing and preceding episode are processed as distinct episodes. This situation occurs provided that the ongoing episode is not associated with the preceding one and starts contingently to unpredictable events. In the converse situation, the ongoing and preceding episode simply appear as parts of the same, longer, possibly more complex behavioral episode. Likewise, using a different terminology, branching control is involved in multi-task performance provided that the tasks are independent and are executed contingently to external events and are not organized as fixed elements of a single superordinate plan.

Thus, polar LPFC regions are predicted to be engaged when subjects postpone execution of a task in order to first respond to an unpredictable event, but to disengage when subjects plan to delay a task to first respond to an expected forthcoming event. Koechlin *et al.* (2000) tested this prediction in an fMRI study contrasting a random condition where subjects had to recurrently postpone execution of a primary task in order to perform a distinct task, when unpredictable events occurred and a fixed condition where subjects postponed execution of the primary task every three trials to recurrently perform the other task. As expected, the results showed a dramatic disengagement of polar LPFC activations in the fixed condition. Compared to a baseline condition, the random condition was associated with strong bilateral frontopolar activations, whereas virtually no lateral frontopolar activations were observed in the fixed condition. This result shows that the lateral frontopolar cortex is engaged only when the two tasks are unrelated and processed as two independent behavioral episodes. This important finding confirmed the functional and anatomical dissociation between the notion of episodic and branching control. More precisely, the distinction between these two levels of cognitive control is not based on increasing complexity of action selection or hierarchical structures of behavioral rules but on contingent retrieval of information associated with events corresponding to two distinct, unrelated episodes, i.e. the ongoing and preceding behavioral episode.

In summary, the cascade model based on Information Theory provides a conceptual and quantitative framework to understand the notion of cognitive compared to sensory control and its fractionation into multiple functional components. We briefly reviewed some experimental evidence supporting this model and showing that cognitive control in the LPFC is organized as a cascade of top-down selection processes extending from premotor to the most anterior lateral prefrontal regions and implementing the three basic *temporal* dimensions along which selection processes may operate, namely the synchronic, diachronic and polychronic dimension. The synchronic dimension is subserved by posterior LPFC regions and corresponds to contextual control involved in selecting premotor representations (sensorimotor associations) according to the immediate context in which stimuli occur. The diachronic dimension is implemented in anterior LPFC regions and corresponds to episodic control involved in selecting posterior LPFC representations (sensorimotor associations evoked in a given context) according to the temporal episode in which the subject is acting. Finally, the polychronic dimension is subserved by the polar LPFC regions and corresponds to branching control involved in retrieving/selecting an anterior LPFC representation, i.e. a past behavioral episode after it was interrupted by the ongoing behavioral episode.

Fractionating cognitive control within hierarchical structures

An important finding reported in the previous section is that anterior and polar LPFC regions were found to activate regardless of the complexity of behavioral episodes or, equivalently, of the hierarchical structure of action selection. Anterior and polar LPFC activations depended only on cross-temporal contingencies between actions and events involved in action selection. Thus, the functional segregation between posterior, anterior and polar LPFC regions appears to be restricted to the fractionation of cognitive control within the time domain into contextual, episodic and branching control respectively.

Cognitive control, however, is not restricted to the time domain. Action selection may also operate along the hierarchical structures of behavioral plans. For example, in response to an external signal, an action A may be selected because this signal triggers subjects to execute a motor sequence comprising action A as its initial state. In that case, action A is selected as the initial subordinate element of the motor sequence rather than as the response associated with the external signal. Thus, more generally, action selection may result from processing the hierarchical structure of action plans evoked by external signals rather than processing cross-temporal contingencies between events. This notion of cognitive control within hierarchical structures, referred to as *hierarchical* control, actually corresponds to the distinction between sensory and contextual control described above. In both sensory and contextual control, only immediate signals are involved in action selection with no processing of crosstemporal contingencies. Sensory control selects actions in response to stimuli, whereas contextual control selects sensorimotor associations in response to immediate contextual signals, so that the only difference between the two levels of control is the hierarchical level at which selection occurs: in response to immediate external signals, sensory control selects actions, whereas contextual control selects sensorimotor associations. For the cognitive control system, there is likely no difference between stimuli and contextual signals except the hierarchal level at which those signals participate to action selection. Thus, hierarchical control appears to be confined to the level of contextual control described above and subserved by posterior LPFC regions including Broca's area and its right homolog. This hypothesis is consistent with studies indicating that Broca's area plays a pivotal role in processing hierarchical structures in human language (Musso et al., 2003), in serial tasks (Dominey et al., 2003) and in visuo-spatial patterns (Bor et al., 2003).

An important remaining issue is whether, within the hierarchical dimension, cognitive control can be fractioned into several control levels. The most direct assumption is that different levels of control correspond to different hierarchical levels of action plans and that top-down interactions across control levels implement selection processes according to the hierarchical structure of action plans regardless of their temporal structures. As previously suggested (Dehaene and Changeux, 1997; Koechlin et al., 2002), action plans can be composed of at least three hierarchical levels: the level of *single motor acts* corresponding to sensory control; the level of *simple action chunks* including sequences of single motor acts or congruent sets of sensorimotor association (i.e. sensorimotor mappings); and the level of *superordinate action chunks* composed of simple action chunks, i.e. sequences or congruent sets of simple action chunks. For example, a sequence of categorization tasks like sorting a deck of playing cards first by suit, then by rank, then by color forms a superordinate chunk composed of three simple chunks (categorization tasks). Another everyday example is the preparation of a meal: preparing a whole meal that includes several courses forms a superordinate chunk composed of several chunks consisting of preparing every course, which in turn corresponds to performing a sequence of single motor acts.

Thus, according to this hypothesis, contextual control would be segregated into two levels of hierarchical control. Using the information–theoretic cascade model developed above, contextual control can be broken down as follows:

$$I(C,A|S) = I(C_s,A|S) + I(C_o,A|S,C_s),$$

where C_s and C_o denote external signals associated with simple and superordinate action chunks, respectively. As mentioned above, all external signals S, C_s and C_o differ only by the hierarchical control level with which they are associated. Those signals input any kind of information external to the control system including perceptual signals or internal sensorimotor feedback signals that typically occur in action sequences. The cascade model then makes two specific predictions (see Figure 22.8). First, according to the principle of functional proximity, the posterior part of Broca's area and its right homolog (i.e. pars opercularis, BA 44) would implement the first level of hierarchical control, so that activations in BA 44 would vary as the sum $I(C_s,A|S) + I(C_o,A|S,C_s)$, whereas the anterior part (i.e. pars triangularis, BA 45) would implement the higher level of hierarchical control and its activation would vary as the quantity $I(C_o,A|S,C_s)$ only. Second, according to the principle of functional subsidiarity, hierarchical control at the level of simple action chunks would be involved only when action selection is not reducible to sensory control. This situation occurs only at simple chunk boundaries, when subjects start or stop

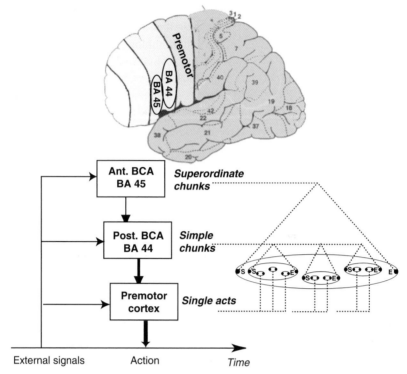

Figure 22.8 The fractionation of cognitive control within hierarchical structures of action plans. Approximate localizations of BA 44 and 45 in the prefrontal cortex are shown. The right diagram schematically represents how the hierarchical control levels are involved in processing start- (S) and end- (E) states of functional segments (i.e. chunks) that form the structure of action plans.

executing a sequence of single motor acts or a sensorimotor mapping. Indeed, at these boundaries, single motor acts or sensorimotor associations are selected or inhibited as start- or end-states of simple action chunks rather than as immediate successors of preceding actions or directly in response to external stimuli. Similarly, hierarchical control at the level of superordinate action chunks would be involved only at boundaries of superordinate chunks, e.g. when subjects initiate and terminate a sequence of categorization tasks. Thus, the cascade model predicts that selection of single motor acts would be associated with phasic activations in lateral premotor regions only (sensory control), while initiation and termination of simple chunks (possibly within a superordinate chunk) would be associated with phasic activations in premotor regions and BA 44, whereas initiation and termination of superordinate chunks would be associated with phasic activations in lateral premotor regions, BA 44 and 45.

These predictions fit exactly the pattern of activations reported in a recent experimental study examining prefrontal activations when subjects executed overlearned action plans (Koechlin and Jubault, 2006). In this experiment, superordinate chunks were overlearned sequences of letter categorization tasks performed on successively presented, visual letters. Subjects performed the first task of the sequence on a first letter, then moved on to the next task in the sequence to respond to the second presented letter and so on. Simple chunks were categorization tasks comprising superordinate chunks. In additional conditions, simple chunks were simply overlearned sequences of motor responses. In all conditions, Subjects started and stopped executing sequences, when contextual start and stop cues occurred. Koechlin and Jubault showed that BA 45 exhibited only phasic activations at boundaries of superordinate action chunks, whereas BA 44 exhibited phasic activations at boundaries of both simple and superordinate chunks, also including transitions between categorization tasks forming superordinate chunks. By contrast, lateral premotor regions were found to activate every time subjects selected a single motor act, i.e. in every trial comprising simple and superordinate chunks, including boundary and intermediate trials. Furthermore, in agreement with the notion of hierarchical control, activations in BA 44 and BA 45 were independent of the temporal structure of those action plans (simple chunks as categorization tasks or motor sequences) and BA 44 and 45 exhibited no significant sustained activations during execution of those action plans.

Koechlin and Jubault's study also showed no activations in LPFC regions anterior to BA 45, i.e. in BA 46 and 10 during execution of those overlearned action plans, suggesting the absence of episodic control during the performance of structured action plans. This result is consistent with the fact that in structured action plans, action selection is not contingent upon temporally distant events but depends only on sequential associations between successive single acts or action chunks. Conversely, in accordance with previous studies (Dronkers, 1996; Sakai et al., 1998; Tanji and Hoshi, 2001; Kennerley et al., 2004), Koechlin and Jubault found that processing sequential associations for planning subsequent motor acts and action chunks involved lateral inferior parietal regions, while planning subsequent motor acts additionally engaged the supplementary motor area complex. Altogether, these findings highlight functional dissociations between (1) planning/preparation based on processing sequential associations in action plans and implemented in the supplementary motor area complex and lateral inferior parietal regions, (2) hierarchical control based on processing hierarchical relations for action selection implemented in Broca's area and its right homolog, and (3) episodic control based on processing cross-temporal contingencies underlying action selection and subserved by anterior LPFC regions.

These empirical findings confirm that the hierarchical dimension of cognitive control is confined to Broca's area and its right homolog, which implement two cascading levels of hierarchical control in BA 44 and 45, respectively. Thus, Broca's area and its right homolog implement a specialized control system involved in selecting and nesting start- and end-states of functional segments that combine in structured action plans. This conclusion is consistent with the engagement of Broca's area in a variety of behaviors, including working-memory tasks based on chunking mental representations of action in memory (Bor et al., 2003), task-switching (Konishi et al., 1998; Dove et al., 2000) and task-sequence learning (Koechlin et al., 2002). Broca's area is also engaged when subjects observed movements performed by others provided that those movements are elements of action plans (Iacoboni, 2005; Iacoboni *et al.*, 2005) These behaviors are based on manipulating action chunks such as sensorimotor mappings, sequences of motor acts or sequences of sensorimotor mappings. For example, the system of hierarchical control may be involved in identifying action plans performed by others from their perceived movements, i.e. by identifying start- and end-states as well as the nesting of functional segments in sequences of observed movements.

The cascade model of hierarchical control is also compatible with recent theories of the role of Broca's area in human language. These theories suggest that Broca's area is involved in organizing linguistic segments that compose speech (Gelfand and Bookheimer, 2003; Indefrey and Levelt, 2004) and in chunking linguistic subordinate elements into superordinate representational structures within the phonological, syntactic and semantic dimensions of language (Hagoort, 2005). Moreover, posterior regions in Broca's area (i.e. BA 44/BA 6) were found to preferentially subserve phonological processing, whereas anterior regions (i.e. BA 45/BA 44) and anterior-ventral regions (i.e. BA 47/BA 45) preferentially subserve syntactic and semantic processing, respectively (see review in Bookheimer, 2002). Given that syntactic and semantic processing involve hierarchically higher linguistic representations (i.e. words and multi-word utterances) than those involved in phonological processing (phonemes/syllables within words), these findings are in agreement with the cascade model specifying that higher levels of hierarchical control are implemented in more anterior regions in Broca's area. Thus, the cascade model of hierarchical control in posterior LPFC regions appears also to account for the critical role of Broca's area in language, supporting the view that the different levels of cognitive control described herein are independent of cognitive domains (Thompson-Schill *et al.*, 2005).

Time, hierarchy and levels of cognitive control

In the previous sections, we have presented in detail a theory describing the functional organization of the LPFC and the related architecture of cognitive control. The theory makes a number of specific predictions about behavioral performances and prefrontal activations that were confirmed by experimental data and that explain the pattern of lateral prefrontal activations observed in a variety of behavioral paradigms. The theory outlines key principles of the lateral prefrontal function, which are summarized below.

Sensory versus cognitive control

Sensory control is involved in selecting a single act according to the stimulus or the preceding act. Sensory control is implemented in the lateral premotor cortex. By contrast, cognitive control is involved when action selection depends upon the context in which action takes place, i.e. upon any additional pieces of information unrelated to the stimulus or the previously executed act. Cognitive control is increasingly engaged when action selection becomes more contingent upon contextual information. Cognitive control is subserved by the LPFC and exerts by selecting premotor representations through top-down interactions from posterior LPFC to lateral premotor regions.

Levels of cognitive control

Cognitive control is organized as a cascade of top-down selection processes from the most anterior to posterior LPFC regions, so that higher control levels are subserved by more anterior LPFC regions. Sensory control simply appears as the final stage of the cascade. In this cascade, each level is involved in selecting lower-level representations by processing more remote contextual information that is not accessible to lower-level representations. A key principle—the subsidiarity principle—is that higher levels are engaged only when action selection cannot be effectively achieved by lower levels, i.e. when more remote contextual information is required for resolving indetermination occurring in lower-level processing. Additionally, every control level is increasingly engaged when action selection becomes more contingent upon contextual information related to this level. This means in particular that the engagement of higher control levels does not imply maximal involvement of lower control levels.

Hierarchical versus temporal control

The lower levels of cognitive control are implemented in Broca's area and its right homolog and correspond to the hierarchical levels forming the structure of hierarchically organized action sets/plans. Across these control levels, top-down selection operates according to this hierarchical structure and in association with the immediate perceptual context of action. The higher levels are implemented in more anterior prefrontal regions including BA 46 and 10 and correspond to the temporal context of action. Across these levels, top-down selection operates according to the temporal episodes in which action takes place, i.e. according to cross-temporal contingencies between events. Consistently with the subsidiarity principle, temporal control in higher levels is not engaged, while an action or an action set are subordinate elements of a superordinate structured action set that resolves any indetermination in action selection. In the converse case, temporal control is engaged, provided that actions or action sets are contingent upon occurrences of past events.

Episodic versus branching control

Temporal control includes two control levels, namely episodic and branching control. Episodic control is subserved by BA 46 and is engaged when selection rules in lower control levels (including sensory control) are altered after the occurrence of an event U compared to those corresponding to the episode preceding event U. Importantly, if the occurrence of this event is predicted, hierarchical rather than episodic control is engaged, because the novel selection rules following event U are also predicted and therefore are rather selected as a subordinate element of an ongoing superordinate action plan. Branching control is a higher control level implemented in the lateral frontopolar cortex (BA 10) and is involved when episodic control has been engaged following the occurrence of an unpredicted event U *and* selection rules are altered again with respect to events that occurred earlier than event U.

Conclusion

The present theory of the lateral prefrontal function is consistent with the previously proposed theories reviewed above. The present theory, however, offers a more comprehensive view and explains especially how cognitive control is segregated into multiple control processes subserved by distinct prefrontal regions and, at the same time, works as a unitary function for coordinating actions or thoughts. In particular, the theory provides a quantitative model describing the differential involvement of these control processes and their interactions. This model clarifies key conceptual distinctions between the notions of control levels, top-down selection, hierarchical and temporal control. All these features appear critical to understand the functional organization of the LPFC and the multiple patterns of prefrontal activations observed in a variety of behavioral paradigms.

The theory is based on an information–theoretic approach to cognitive control. An advantage of this approach is to provide precise quantitative predictions regarding behavioral performances and prefrontal activations that can be tested using neuroimaging techniques. This avoids reliance on various phenomenological terms, such as goals, intentions, tasks etc., or on specific behavioral protocols, which are certainly more intuitive but remain elusive or hardly predictive. Finally, the theory provides a possible framework to address a number of unresolved and delicate issues regarding the prefrontal cortex function, especially the interactions between cognitive control and motivational or emotional processes subserved by the medial and orbital sector of the prefrontal cortex, as well as the functional interactions between the LPFC, posterior associative brain regions and basal ganglia.

References

Baddeley, A. (2002) Fractionating the central executive. In Stuss, D. T. and Knight, R. T. (eds), *Principles of Frontal Lobe Function*, pp. 246–260. Oxford University Press, New York.

Berlyne, D. E. (1957) Uncertainty and conflict: a point of contact between information-theory and behavior-theory concepts. *Psychological Review*, 64, 329–339.

Bookheimer, S. (2002) Functional MRI of language: new approaches to understanding the cortical organization of semantic processing. *Annual Review of Neuroscience*, 25, 151–188.

Bor, D., Duncan, J., Wiseman, R. J. and Owen, A. M. (2003) Encoding strategies dissociate prefrontal activity from working memory demand. *Neuron*, 37, 361–367.

Braver, T. S. and Bongiolatti, S. R. (2002) The role of frontopolar cortex in subgoal processing during working memory. *Neuroimage*, 15, 523–536.

Braver, T. S., Reynolds, J. R. and Donaldson, D. I. (2003) Neural mechanisms of transient and sustained cognitive control during task switching. *Neuron*, 39, 713–726.

Buckner, R. L. (2003) Functional–anatomic correlates of control processes in memory. *Journal of Neuroscience* 23, 3999–4004.

Buckner, R. L. and Koutstaal, W. (1998) Functional neuroimaging studies of encoding, priming, and explicit memory retrieval. *Proceedings of the National Academy of Sciences of the USA*, 95, 891–898.

Burgess, P. W., Quayle, A. and Frith, C. D. (2001) Brain regions involved in prospective memory as determined by positron emission tomography. *Neuropsychologia*, 39, 545–555.

Christoff, K., Prabhakaran, V., Dorfman, J. *et al.* (2001) Rostrolateral prefrontal cortex involvement in relational integration during reasoning. *Neuroimage*, 14, 1136–1149.

D'Esposito, M., Ballard, D., Aguirre, G. K. and Zarahn, E. (1998) Human prefrontal cortex is not specific for working memory: a functional MRI study. *Neuroimage*, **8**, 274–282.

Deco, G. and Obradovic, D. (1996) *An Information–Theoretic Approach to Neural Computing*. Springer-Verlag, New York.

Dehaene, S. and Changeux, J. P. (1997) A hierarchical neuronal network for planning behavior. *Proceedings of the National Academy of Sciences of the USA*, **94**, 13293–13298.

Dominey, P. F., Hoen, M., Blanc, J. M. and Lelekov-Boissard, T. (2003) Neurological basis of language and sequential cognition: evidence from simulation, aphasia, and ERP studies. *Brain and Language*, **86**, 207–225.

Dove, A., Pollmann, S., Schubert, T., Wiggins, C. J. and von Cramon, D. Y. (2000) Prefrontal cortex activation in task switching: an event-related fMRI study. *Brain Research, Cognitive Brain Research*, **9**, 103–109.

Dronkers, N. F. (1996) A new brain region for coordinating speech articulation. *Nature*, **384**(6605), 159–161.

Fodor, J. (1982) *The Modularity of Mind*. MIT Press, Cambridge.

Fuster, J. M. (1989) *The Prefrontal Cortex*. Raven Press, New York.

Fuster, J. M. (2001) The prefrontal cortex—an update: time is of the essence. *Neuron*, **30**, 319–333.

Fuster, J. M., Bodner, M. and Kroger, J. K. (2000) Cross-modal and cross-temporal association in neurons of frontal cortex. *Nature*, **405**(6784), 347–351.

Gelfand, J. R. and Bookheimer, S. Y. (2003) Dissociating neural mechanisms of temporal sequencing and processing phonemes. *Neuron*, **38**, 831–842.

Goldman-Rakic, P. S. (1987) Circuitry of primate prefrontal cortex and the regulation of behavior by representational memory. In Plum, F. and Moutcastle, V. (eds), *Handbook of Physiology, The Nervous System*, Vol. 5, pp. 373–417. American Physiological Society, Bethesda, MD.

Goldman-Rakic, P. S. (1996) The prefrontal landscape: implications of functional architecture for understanding human mentation and the central executive. *Philosophical Transactions of the Royal Society of London, B*, **351**(1346), 1445–1453.

Grafman, J. (1995) Similarities and distinctions among models of prefrontal cortical functions. In Grafman, J., Holyoak, K. J. and Boller, F. (eds), *Structure and Function of the Human Prefrontal Cortex. Annals of the New York Academy of Sciences*, **769**, 337–368.

Grafman, J. (2002) The structured event complex and the human prefrontal cortex. In Stuss, D. T. and Knight, R. T. (eds), pp. 292–310. *Principles of Frontal Lobe Function*. Oxford University Press, New York.

Hagoort, P. (2005) On Broca, brain, and binding: a new framework. *Trends in Cognitive Sciences*, **9**, 416–423.

Hyafil, A. and Koechlin, E. (2005) *A Computational Model of Human Anterior Prefrontal Functions*. Computational and System Neuroscience International Conference, Salt Lake City, March 17–22, 2005.

Iacoboni, M. (2005) Neural mechanisms of imitation. *Current Opinion in Neurobiology*, **15**, 632–637.

Iacoboni, M., Molnar-Szakacs, I., Gallese, V., Buccino, G., Mazziotta, J. C. and Rizzolatti, G. (2005) Grasping the intentions of others with one's own mirror neuron system. *PLoS Biology*, **3**, e79.

Indefrey, P. and Levelt, W. J. (2004) The spatial and temporal signatures of word production components. *Cognition*, **92**(1–2), 101–144.

Jenkins, I. H., Brooks, D. J., Nixon, P. D., Frackowiak, R. S. and Passingham, R. E. (1994) Motor sequence learning: a study with positron emission tomography. *Journal of Neuroscience*, **14**, 3775–3790.

Kennerley, S. W., Sakai, K. and Rushworth, M. F. (2004) Organization of action sequences and the role of the pre-SMA. *Journal of Neurophysiology*, **91**, 978–993.

Kennerley, S. W., Walton, M. E., Behrens, T. E., Buckley, M. J. and Rushworth, M. F. (2006) Optimal decision making and the anterior cingulate cortex. *Nature Neuroscience*, **9**, 940–947.

Koechlin, E. and Jubault, T. (2006) Broca's area and the hierarchical organization of human behavior. *Neuron*, **50**, 963–974.

Koechlin, E., Basso, G., Pietrini, P., Panzer, S. and Grafman, J. (1999) The role of the anterior prefrontal cortex in human cognition. *Nature* **399**(6732), 148–151.

Koechlin, E., Corrado, G., Pietrini, P. and Grafman, J. (2000) Dissociating the role of the medial and lateral anterior prefrontal cortex in human planning. *Proceedings of the National Academy of Sciences of the USA*, **97**, 7651–7656.

Koechlin, E., Danek, A., Burnod, Y. and Grafman, J. (2002) Medial prefrontal and subcortical mechanisms underlying the acquisition of motor and cognitive action sequences in humans. *Neuron*, **35**, 371–381.

Koechlin, E., Ody, C. and Kouneiher, F. (2003) The architecture of cognitive control in the human prefrontal cortex. *Science*, **302**, 1181–1185.

Konishi, S., Nakajima, K., Uchida, I. *et al.* (1998) Transient activation of inferior prefrontal cortex during cognitive set shifting. *Nature Neuroscience*, **1**, 80–84.

Mesulam, M. M. (2002) The human frontal lobes: transcending the default mode through contingent encoding. In Stuss, D. T. and Knight, R. T. (eds), *Principle of Frontal Lobes Functions*. Oxford University Press, New York.

Miller, E. K. and Cohen, J. D. (2001) An integrative theory of prefrontal cortex function. *Annual Review of Neuroscience*, **24**, 167–202.

Musso, M., Moro, A., Glauche, V. *et al.* (2003) Broca's area and the language instinct. *Nature Neuroscience*, **6**, 774–781.

Nagahama, Y., Okada, T. Katsumi, Y. *et al.* (2001) Dissociable mechanisms of attentional control within the human prefrontal cortex. *Cerebral Cortex*, **11**, 85–92.

Nystrom, L. E., Braver, T. S., Sabb, F. W., Delgado, M. R., Noll, D. C. and Cohen, J. D. (2000) Working memory for letters, shapes, and locations: fMRI evidence against stimulus-based regional organization in human prefrontal cortex [see comments]. *Neuroimage*, **11** (5 Pt 1), 424–446.

O'Doherty, J., Kringelbach, M. L., Rolls, E. T., Hornak, J. and Andrews, C. (2001) Abstract reward and punishment representations in the human orbitofrontal cortex. *Nature Neuroscience*, **4**, 95–102.

Owen, A. M., McMillan, K. M., Laird, A. R. and Bullmore, E. (2005) N-back working memory paradigm: a meta-analysis of normative functional neuroimaging studies. *Human Brain Mapping*, **25**, 46–59.

Pandya, D. N. and Yeterian, E. H. (1996) Morphological correlations of the human and monkey frontal lobe. In Damasio, A. R., Damasio, H. and Christen, Y. (eds), *Neurobiology of Decision-making*, pp. 13–46. Springer-Verlag, Berlin.

Pashler, H. (2000) Task-switching and multitask performance. In Monsell, S. and Driver, J. (eds), *Attention and Performance XVIII: Control of Mental Processes*. MIT Press, Cambridge, MA.

Passingham, D. and Sakai, K. (2004) The prefrontal cortex and working memory: physiology and brain imaging. *Current Opinion in Neurobiology*, **14**, 163–168.

Passingham, R. E. (1993) *The Frontal Lobes and Voluntary Action*. Oxford University Press, Oxford.

Pochon, J. B., Levy, R., Poline, J. B. *et al.* (2001) The role of dorsolateral prefrontal cortex in the preparation of forthcoming actions: an fMRI study. *Cerebral Cortex*, **11**, 260–266.

Ramnani, N. and Owen, A. M. (2004) Anterior prefrontal cortex: insights into function from anatomy and neuroimaging. *Nature Reviews Neuroscience*, **5**, 184–194.

Rao, S. C., Rainer, G. and Miller, E. K. (1997) Integration of what and where in the primate prefrontal cortex. *Science*, **276**(5313), 821–824.

Rolls, E. T. (2004) The functions of the orbitofrontal cortex. *Brain Cognition*, **55**, 11–29.

Rowe, J. B., Toni, I., Josephs, O., Frackowiak, R. S. and Passingham, R. E. (2000) The prefrontal cortex: response selection or maintenance within working memory? *Science*, **288**(5471), 1656–1660.

Sakai, K., Hikosaka, O., Miyauchi, S., Takino, R., Sasaki, Y. and Putz, B. (1998) Transition of brain activation from frontal to parietal areas in visuomotor sequence learning. *Journal of Neuroscience*, 18, 1827–1840.

Sakai, K. and Passingham, R. E. (2003) Prefrontal interactions reflect future task operations. *Nature Neuroscience*, 6, 75–81.

Sakai, K. and Passingham, R. E. (2006) Prefrontal set activity predicts rule-specific neural processing during subsequent cognitive performance. *Journal of Neuroscience*, 26, 1211–1218.

Sakai, K., Rowe, J. B. and Passingham, R. E. (2002) Active maintenance in prefrontal area 46 creates distractor-resistant memory. *Nature Neuroscience*, 5, 479–484.

Shallice, T. (1988) *From Neuropsychology to Mental Structure*. Cambridge University Press, New York.

Shallice, T. (2002) Fractionation of the supervisory system. In Stuss, D. T. and Knight, R. T. (eds), *Principles of Frontal Lobe Function*, pp. 261–277. Oxford University Press, New York.

Shallice, T. and Burgess, P. (1996) The domain of supervisory processes and temporal organization of behaviour. *Philosophical Transactions of the Royal Society of London, B*, 351(1346), 1405–1411; discussion 1411–1412.

Shannon, C. E. (1948) A mathematical theory of communication. *Bell System Technical Journal*, 27, 379–423, 623–656.

Sigman, M. and Dehaene, S. (2005) Parsing a cognitive task: a characterization of the mind's bottleneck. *PLoS Biology*, 3, e37.

Stuss, D. T. and Levine, B. (2002) Adult clinical neuropsychology: lessons from studies of the frontal lobes. *Annual Review Psychology*, 53, 401–433.

Tanji, J. and Hoshi, E. (2001) Behavioral planning in the prefrontal cortex. *Current Opinion Neurobiology*, 11, 164–170.

Thompson-Schill, S. L., Bedny, M. and Goldberg, R. F. (2005) The frontal lobes and the regulation of mental activity. *Current Opinion in Neurobiology*, 15, 219–224.

Velanova, K., Jacoby, L. L., Wheeler, M. E., McAvoy, M. P., Petersen, S. E. and Buckner, R. L. (2003) Functional–anatomic correlates of sustained and transient processing components engaged during controlled retrieval. *Journal of Neuroscience*, 23, 8460–8470.

Wilson, F. A., Scalaidhe, S. P. and Goldman-Rakic, P. S. (1993) Dissociation of object and spatial processing domains in primate prefrontal cortex [see comments]. *Science*, 260(5116), 1955–1958.

23

Automatic and strategic effects in human imitation

Raffaella I. Rumiati and Alessia Tessari

Imitation is a very important ability that allows an agent to acquire efficiently a wide range of movements by observing a demonstrator performing them. The tendency to imitate has long been noted in normal and abnormal human behavior, and in the last decade there has also been an increase in the number of studies of imitation in children, monkeys and great apes. In this chapter we will review some main issues related to imitation, including whether imitation is innate or is the outcome of a learning process, whether it is uniquely human or is shared with other primates, as well as the most prominent accounts that have been put forward to explain how it works. We will then summarize the results from different sets of experiments which we have interpreted within a dual-route model. Normally, individuals use the sublexical, direct route to imitate novel, meaningless (ML) gestures and the lexical–semantic, indirect route (and possibly the sublexical route) to reproduce meaningful (MF) actions that are already in one's repertoire. We will show how a reduction in cognitive resources, caused either by experimental manipulations with healthy participants or brain damage, may end up affecting the route selection in imitation. In particular, when MF and ML actions are presented intermingled, participants selected the direct route because it is suitable for imitating both stimulus types. Moreover, in the new Experiments 1 and 2 we also demonstrated that the sublexical route is selected even when either ML (Experiment 1) or both ML and MF actions (Experiment 2) were presented for longer periods of time. Finally we will illustrate the cerebral correlates of imitation of different action types, derived from the lesion analysis of patients with a selective stimulus-specific apraxia, and from a positron emission tomography study with healthy participants performing an imitation task. Based on our results, we propose that imitation of MF and ML actions is supported by common as well by dedicated brain regions.

Imitation is an innate process that is not only human

The discoveries of Meltzoff and collaborators in developmental psychology have modified the view, generally accepted until then, that humans gradually learned to imitate during the first years of life. Meltzoff and Moore (1977) reported that 2–3-week-old infants were able to reproduce specific human gestures performed by the demonstrator, such as mouth opening, tongue protrusion, lip protrusion, and hand opening, suggesting that imitation is an innate ability. This interpretation was strengthened by the subsequent finding that infants can imitate gestures immediately after birth (Meltzoff and Moore, 1983, 1989). Other developmental studies with older children demonstrated that 3-year-olds are able to learn how to solve tool-use problems from imitation (Want and Harris, 2001), and that their imitation process is goal-directed (Bekkering *et al.*, 2000, for an extensive discussion of the goal-directed theory see later in this chapter).

In the last 10 years, several controlled studies with monkeys and great apes have used imitation as a tool for investigating continuities and discontinuities in the evolution of mind. Infant chimpanzees seem to imitate human facial gestures in the first week of life (Myowa, 1996; Bard and Russell, 1999; Myowa-Yamakoshi *et al.*, 2004), suggesting that in humans and chimpanzees neonatal imitation shares similar features both with respect to the type of gestures they perform, and to the time-window in which imitation is observed. But is imitation of facial gestures an evolutionary acquisition of apes and humans alone? According to Ferrari *et al.* (2006), who have recently reported that infant macaques imitate mouth gestures performed by humans on the first day of life, the answer is no. One difference between chimps and humans and the infant macaques studied by Ferrari *et al.* (2006) is that in the latter group imitation is seen only in the first days of life. This difference can be explained by the fact that motor and cognitive development is faster in the macaques than in both humans and chimpanzees.

Imitation is forever

Different research lines converge to support the argument that imitation is a contagious and automatic process. Social psychologists reported that we tend to whisper or speak louder when others do, scratch our head upon seeing someone else do it, walk slower in presence of elderly individuals, and cycle faster after seeing a cycling race on TV (Dijksterhuis and Bargh, 2001). This automaticity has been argued to be the 'social glue' that favours cooperation and affiliation among humans (Lakin *et al.*, 2003).

Using a stimulus–response (S-R) compatibility paradigm, Brass *et al.* (2000, 2005) showed how, in humans, the tendency to imitate seems to persist well into adulthood. The key finding of these studies is that observed finger movements, relative to symbolic or spatial cue, have a stronger influence on pre-instructed finger movement execution, and that the influence is even stronger (shorter reaction times) when observed and executed finger movements are compatible (i.e. observed and executed lifting; observed and executed tapping) compared with the incompatible mapping (lifting observed → tapping executed, and vice versa). These findings demonstrate that movement observation influences movement execution even in a task in which the response is predefined, thus supporting the assumption that this effect is automatic. Although in their experiments participants were not instructed to intentionally imitate the observed movements, Brass and colleagues argued that imitation of actions is a special case of S-R compatibility.

There are pathological conditions that alter dramatically the tendency to imitate observed behaviors of others, for instance after brain damage. On the one hand, there are patients with frontal lesions, who suffer from imitation behavior (IB) (Lhermitte *et al.*, 1986;

De Renzi *et al.*, 1996). Patients with this pathology imitate the examiner's gestures, although they have not been instructed and even been discouraged to do so. The authors proposed that IB is caused by an impairment of the inhibitory action of the mediobasal frontal cortex on the parietal lobe, thereby realizing parietal lobe activity. In this context, the behavior the patients imitate is not novel but belongs already to their motor repertoire. Brass *et al.* (2005) have clarified that the inhibition of prepotent imitative and general overlearned responses (as in the Stroop-like tasks) entails different functional mechanisms. Except for a common area related to the generation of the stop signal, inhibition of over-learned responses involves a fronto-parietal network, whereas the inhibition of imitative responses is sustained by areas that require distinguishing between self-generated and externally triggered motor representations.

On the other hand, patients with ideomotor apraxia (in short IMA) exhibit the oppo-site pattern, i.e. a dramatic reduction of their ability to imitate actions, following lesions typically, though not exclusively, of the left hemisphere (De Renzi *et al.*, 1981), and in particular of the inferior posterior parietal cortex (e.g. Goldenberg and Hagmann, 1997; Buxbaum *et al.*, 2005). A faulty imitation is not the only symptom of IMA for patients may also be impaired when they gesture on verbal command (Merians *et al.*, 1997). However, given that IMA patients often suffer from co-occurring aphasia, it is preferred to test them using an imitation task to circumvent possible poor comprehension.

'Direct' models of imitation

Different accounts have been submitted to explain how imitation works, ranging from the direct-mapping approach (e.g. Prinz, 1997) on the one end, to the active intermodal mapping (AIM) (Meltzoff and Moore 1977, 1997), in an intermediate level, to the dual-route (Rothi *et al.*, 1991; Rumiati and Tessari, 2002; Tessari and Rumiati, 2004) and the goal-directed theory (Bekkering, Wohlschläger and colleagues) on the opposite end.

The central tenet of the direct-mapping approach, as elaborated by Prinz and colleagues (Prinz, 1997; Hommel *et al.*, 2001), is that observing the effect of an action facilitates its execution because perception and action planning share a common repre-sentational code. Applying this concept to the brain, it follows that perception of an action activates the motor system directly. More specifically, it has been proposed that, in humans, the neural correlate of the direct mapping is the fronto-parietal mirror neuron system (MNS), engaged both in observation and execution of purposeful actions (e.g. Iacoboni *et al.*, 1999). The human direct matching–MNS seems to be tuned specifi-cally to biological actions. Tai *et al.* (2004), for instance, showed that when participants observed manual grasping actions performed by a human model, a significant neural response was elicited in the left premotor cortex. This activation was not evident for the observation of grasping actions, performed by a robot model, commanded by an experimenter.

The key concept of the AIM hypothesis, developed Meltzoff and Moore (1977) to explain early facial imitation, is that imitation is a matching-to-target process, based on the proprioceptive feedback loop that allows infants' motor performance to be evaluated against the perceived target. This is achieved because the seen and performed acts are coded within a common framework which enables newborns to detect equivalences between their own acts and ones they see. In 1997, the same authors have fleshed out the AIM hypothesis by adding three new theoretical concepts (Meltzoff and Moore, 1997). First, infants relate parts of their own bodies to corresponding ones of the adult's by means of an 'organ identification'. For instance, the child who sees a tongue protrusion, initially moves the tongue slightly in the oral cavity, as if the infant isolates the part of the body to move before processing how to move it. Second, infants need to learn through 'body babbling' what muscle movements achieve a particular body configuration, such as tongue protrusion, very much in the same way they learn the articulatory–auditory relation through vocal babbling. Thanks to this experiential process, infants learn to map movements and the organ-relation end-states. Third, 'organ relations', such as 'tongue-to-lips', serve as the cross-modal equivalence underlying imitation: infants attempt to match the organ relations they see exhibited by the adults with those they feel themselves make. Meltzoff and Moore (1997) argue that important aspects of later social cognition are rooted in this initial cross-modal equivalence between self and other.

There are, however, some facts that cannot be easily accounted for by a theoretical approach that directs all its emphasis towards a direct input–output correspondence. For instance, when asked to copy movements to a right or left ear (the object), using either the ipsilateral or the contralateral hand (the agent), performing a movement parallel to the body or one crossing the body line (the movement paths), or crossing their arms (the salient feature), children tended to select either the object or the agent correctly, but neglected the movement paths and the salient feature (Bekkering et al., 2000). If the mechanism underlying imitation were a direct matching, children should be able to imitate the action of the demonstrator as presented but they do not. By contrast, they seem to decompose the observed action into goals which can be the objects to which the actions are directed, the agents that perform actions, or the movement. Goals are hierarchically organized, with some of them being more important than others. The process of decomposing–recomposing the observed action depends critically on the cognitive resources available and this would explain why children, who have developmental limitations of their processing capacities, tend to reproduce the most relevant goals and ignore others. In Bekkering et al.'s (2000) study, objects and agents presumably were more important goals than movement paths.

In preverbal children, imitation of a goal-directed action seems to be an interpretative process rather than a simple re-enactment of the means used by the demonstrator (as in Meltzoff's view). Gergely et al. (2002) showed that 14-month-old infants imitated the action of lighting the lamp with the head in the condition in which the demonstrator had the hand occupied (pretending to be cold, she had a blanket wrapped around herself) more than when the demonstrator had her hands free (69 versus 21%). Finally, it appears that healthy adults too interpret the seen actions in terms of goals hierarchically ordered and end up performing the most important goals at the expense of the less important ones (Wohlschläger et al., 2003). This is achieved when the behavior to be imitated is made harder by increasing the number of potential goals.

Another set of findings not easily explained by the direct-mapping view relates to neuropsychology. There are patients with selective deficits for imitation of either ML or MF actions (Goldenberg and Hagmann, 1997; Peigneux *et al.*, 2000; Bartolo *et al.*, 2001). If there were a unique mechanism involved in imitation (i.e. direct matching), there should be no differences in imitation of different goals or types of movements.

In this chapter we will argue that a dual-process model for imitation can accommodate the latter findings better. One such model, analogous to those of language production (e.g. Patterson and Shevell, 1987), has been put forward first by Rothi *et al.* (1991), and subsequently modified by Goldenberg and Hagmann (1997), Cubelli *et al.* (2000), and Rumiati, Tessari, and colleagues (Rumiati and Tessari, 2002; Tessari and Rumiati, 2004; Rumiati *et al.*, 2005).

The dual-route model

Figure 23.1 reproduces a simplified and modified version of the model proposed by Rothi *et al.* (1991).

A key feature of this model is the presence of two distinct processing mechanisms for imitation: a sublexical, direct route for reproducing novel actions (but also those already known), and a lexical–semantic, indirect route for reproducing only overlearned actions. In this context, the term 'sublexical' refers to the conversion of the subunits in which

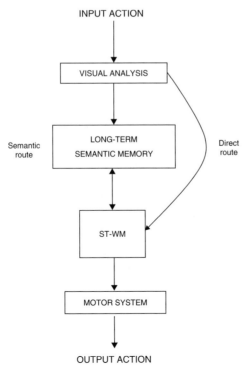

Figure 23.1 Two-route model of imitation from Tessari and Rumiati (2004). Following visual analysis, meaningful actions automatically activate the selection of the semantic long-term memory route. The sublexical, direct route is normally selected to imitate meaningless actions, but can also be used to reproduce both meaningful and meaningless actions when they are presented intermingled. ST/WM, short-term/working memory.

the seen action can be parsed, into a motor output, whilst the term 'lexical–semantic' refers to a process that applies to an action for which a lexical–semantic representation already exists.

Both known and novel actions are visually analyzed in a common stage; then, if the action to be imitated is already part of the repertoire of the person performing the imitation task, the action stimulus can be reproduced using the lexical–semantic route that comprises different processing stages, including the action input lexicon, the semantic system and the action output lexicon, before being held in a short-term/working-memory subsystem (see also Cubelli *et al.*, 2000, who refer to this latter processing stage as the 'buffer'). If, however, the action to be imitated is novel, then the subject has to use the sublexical, direct route, which allows the conversion of any input visually presented action into a motor output. The outcome of the visuo-motor transformation is then briefly kept in the short-term memory subsystem, a processing stage in common with the semantic route. At this point, known or novel actions held in memory can be generated by the imitators.

Observations of brain-damaged patients eventually provided support for some of the predictions derived from such a model. As far as imitation is concerned, four cases have so far been reported with selective imitation of ML actions (Goldenberg and Hagmann, 1997; Peigneux *et al.*, 2000; Bartolo *et al.*, 2001), and one with a selective imitation of MF actions (Bartolo *et al.*, 2001). In these studies, patients' ability to imitate has been assessed using separate lists of MF and ML actions so that they could, depending on the type of actions contained in the list, select either the sublexical or the lexical–semantic route, each of which could be damaged.

By contrast, in studies of large groups, patients showed no difference in their ability to imitate the two action types (De Renzi *et al.*, 1981; Cubelli *et al.*, 2000; Toraldo *et al.*, 2001). As patients were administered a test in which MF and ML actions were presented intermingled, they may have selected the sublexical route to perform the task because it allows imitation of both action types present in the list, and it reduces the costs of switching between processing routes. As this route was likely to be damaged in the patients examined, no difference in imitation of MF and ML actions was found.

Thus, the selection of the route that provides best imitation performance could depend not only on the type of action to be imitated (MF or ML) but also on other factors such as external (list) and internal (resources) conditions.

Evidence from healthy individuals

Tessari and Rumiati (2004) provided evidence in support of a dual-route model for action imitation by studying healthy participants. In three experiments, the authors imposed a deadline technique consisting of a fast presentation of the stimulus and a very limited time for the response. Tessari and Rumiati (2004) found that the deadline paradigm temporarily reduced the participants' abilities to imitate. To date, without time constraints, healthy observers imitate novel, ML and familiar, MF actions at ceiling, in either mixed or blocked conditions. The MF actions used in this study were pantomimes of object use, and the ML actions were similar in many respects to the MF ones except that they were not recognized. In Experiments 1 and 2, overall imitation was better with MF than with ML actions. More specifically, when ML and MF actions were presented in separate lists, participants selected the lexical–semantic route for MF actions and the sublexical route for ML actions, with MF actions being imitated better than ML actions (Experiments 1A and 2A). However, when MF and ML actions were presented intermingled, no difference in imitation of MF and ML actions was observed (Experiments 1B and 2B).

Tessari and Rumiati (2004) argued that participants selected the sublexical route in the mixed presentation (Experiments 1B, and 2B) and when there were more ML than MF actions in a list (Experiment 3B). Selecting the direct route allows imitation of both action types and reduces switching costs that would not easily be sustained by the subjects whose resources are limited by the deadline. Due to time constraints, healthy controls with reduced cognitive resources strategically select the imitation mechanism that is more convenient. Similar effects have been found in reading studies (e.g. Monsell *et al.*, 1992; Tabossi and Laghi, 1992): when non-words were inserted in a list of words, readers used the sublexical route to read regular words as well as nonwords, instead of selecting the lexical route.

After training, ML actions can be imitated even better than MF actions, perhaps because they have only one representation in episodic, long-term memory and therefore there is no competition among alternative representations prior to action selection (Tessari *et al.*, 2006).

Testing the strategic control in the mixed condition

In the study by Tessari and Rumiati (2004), the failure to report a difference in performance when subjects executed the imitation task in the mixed condition has an alternative explanation. We argued that, in this condition, MF and ML actions were imitated to the same extent because subjects selected a strategy (i.e. the sublexical, direct route) that allowed them to imitate both action types and to avoid switching costs. However, the inclusion of ML among MF actions might have lowered the overall performance. In order to overcome the resource limits, the cognitive system may build up motor hierarchies with the subunits of which the motor input is constituted. This must be particularly true for ML actions, as they have no underlying concept that may glue the motor units together. These operations are likely to require a little more than 1 s, which was the overall time we allowed subjects to watch the action to be imitated (Tessari and Rumiati, 2004). Had they been allowed more time to process the ML input, subjects would have been able to parse and transform it into a coherent motor output. Moreover, having reduced the time pressure, at least at the input end, subjects would have also been in the best position to select the imitative process according to the nature of the stimulus, i.e. lexical semantic for MF and direct for ML actions). This would lead to better imitation of MF relative to ML actions, as in the block presentation (see Tessari and Rumiati, 2004). To test this prediction, in Experiment 1 the presentation time of ML actions was increased in order to allow participants more time to visually analyze them. The ML actions used in this experiment were those from which the actions employed in Tessari and Rumiati (2004) had been 'extracted'. In other words, they were the same but more extended temporally.

Experiment 1: Longer presentation times for meaningless actions only

Seventeen right-handed individuals, all students of the University of Trieste, participated in the study. They had either normal or corrected-to-normal vision. Their handedness was tested with the Edinburgh Inventory (Oldfield, 1971). Except for the duration time of the ML actions, everything else was as in Experiment 2B from Tessari and Rumiati (2004), including the fact that participants were informed that there were two stimulus types presented intermingled. Each trial started with either a MF action which lasted for 1 s, or a ML action which lasted 2 s, followed by a 0.5 s blank interval at the end of which a beep sounded for 0.25 s.

Results are plotted in Figure 23.2. A paired-sampled t-test was performed on the accuracy results. No significant effect of Type of Action emerged [$t(16) = 1.012$, not significant]: mean MF = 63.71, SD = 7.34; mean ML = 65.71, SD = 5.50.

Experiment 2: Longer presentation time for both meaningful and meaningless actions

Participants did not seem to have selected the two processes depending on the stimulus type, as predicted, even though they were presented with ML actions for a longer time period than in the previous mixed presentation experiments (Tessari and Rumiati, 2004), and were aware of this manipulation. In contrast, participants may have allocated attentional resources to detect longer trials, leaving few resources for switching between mechanisms. We therefore carried out Experiment 2, in which both MF and ML actions were presented for a longer time period. With this manipulation we aimed to prevent participants from using the presentation time as a cue for identifying the stimulus type, and to allow them to apply the imitation route according to the stimulus type (direct route for ML and lexical-semantic route for MF actions).

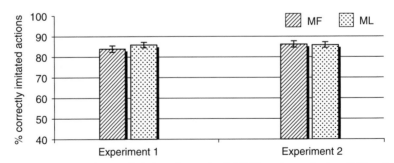

Figure 23.2 Percentages of correctly imitated meaningful (MF) and meaningless (ML) actions in Experiments 1 and 2 are plotted. Error bars represent standard errors.

Eighteen right-handed individuals, all students of the University of Trieste, participated in the study. They had either normal or corrected-to-normal vision. Their handedness was tested with the Edinburgh Inventory (Oldfield, 1971).

MF and ML actions, as well as the procedure were the same as in Experiment 1, except that both action types were now presented for 2 s. Both action types used in this experiment were those from which the actions employed in Tessari and Rumiati (2004) were extracted.

Correct responses were entered in a paired-sample t-test. No significant difference emerged between MF and ML actions [$t(17) = 1.45, P > 0.05$: mean MF = 66.37, SD = 5.74; mean ML = 68, SD = 4.81]. Results are plotted in Figure 23.2.

Further analysis

We compared the imitation performance in Experiments 1 and 2 of MF and ML actions, and found no difference for either type of action [independent sample t-test, $t(46) = 0.978$, $P > 0.05$, and $t(46) = 1.116, P > 0.05$, respectively]. In a second analysis, we compared Experiments 1 and 2 with Experiment 2B from Tessari and Rumiati (2004), and found a significant main effect of Experiment [$F(1,49) = 32.67, P < 0.001$]: performance in Experiment 2B was lower than that in Experiments 1 and 2 (mean Experiment 2B = 54.89, mean Experiments 1 and 2 = 68.36). The main effect of Type of Action and the Experiment × Type of Action interaction were not significant (all $P > 0.05$) (see Figure 23.3).

Discussion of Experiments 1 and 2

No significant difference emerged between imitation of MF and ML actions in either Experiment 1 or Experiment 2. Presenting ML actions (Experiment 1) or both ML and MF actions (Experiment 2) for a longer time than we did in a previous study (Tessari and Rumiati, 2004) does not seem to be sufficient for participants to switch between the two imitative processes. Compared with the results obtained in Experiment 2B (from Tessari and Rumiati, 2004), a decrease in processing demands on the cognitive system, made possible by the longer presentation time, improved overall subjects' performance in the

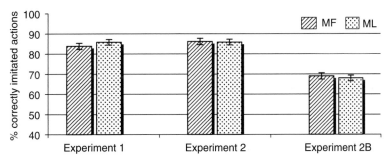

Figure 23.3 Percentages of correctly imitated meaningful (MF) and meaningless (ML) actions in Experiments 1, 2 and Experiment 2B (Tessari and Rumiati, 2004) are plotted. Error bars represent standard errors.

present Experiments 1 and 2, but it did not alter the strategy selection. The present results suggest that the lack of a difference in imitating MF and ML actions that we found in previous experiments in which the presentation was intermingled is unlikely to be due to ML actions lowering the overall performance.

Taken together, these studies suggest that, although there might be preferred mechanisms for imitating different action categories (the sublexical route for novel actions and the lexical–semantic route for familiar actions), there are circumstances in which the cognitive system overcomes this specialization. One such condition is offered by the mixed presentation. When it becomes apparent that there are new movements to be reproduced, mixed together with known ones, the sublexical route is selected because it permits us to imitate all possible movements. Here we presented a longer version of ML actions (Experiment 1) and MF and ML actions (Experiment 2) to free resources that in previous experiments (Tessari and Rumiati, 2004) might have been consumed in the attempt to process the visual input. Assuming that this interpretation is correct, we are tempted to conclude from the present results that the composition of the list is more critical and that resources may play an additional role when the imitation task is performed under time pressure and in brain-damaged patients.

Neuropsychological evidence

Brain-damaged patients, whose cognitive resources are reduced by the lesion, are expected to select the most convenient route for imitation according to the list composition, as healthy controls with limited time did (Tessari and Rumiati, 2004).

In a recent study (Tessari et al., 2007), 32 patients with either left- or right-brain damage (LBD and RBD) and 20 healthy age-matched controls were asked to imitate the same MF ($n = 20$) and ML ($n = 20$) actions which were presented either in separated blocks or intermingled. The stimuli were the same as in Tessari and Rumiati (2004). Behavioral results were analyzed at the group level and at the single-patient level. As a group, patients performed the imitation task worse than controls. Irrespective of the lesion side they showed a better performance in the blocked than in the mixed condition. However, altogether LBD patients' performed worse than RBD patients. No significant correlations were found between action recognition, object use and action imitation of all patients, suggesting that these three abilities do not entirely share the same representations or computations (see Buxbaum et al., 2005, for a different finding).

All patients in the study of Tessari et al. (2007) imitated MF and ML actions in the mixed presentation with the same accuracy. In contrast, eight patients showed a simple dissociation in imitation of MF and ML actions in the blocked presentation (see Figure 23.4).

The presence of single dissociations classical (cases 2, 6, 19, 31) suggests that sublexical and lexical–semantic routes involved in processing MF and ML actions in the context of imitation might be independent. However, in the case of patients (cases 13, 14, 23, 30) who showed only a *strong* dissociation (i.e. the performance on the task they do better on is worse than that of healthy controls), a damage to the second route cannot be excluded.

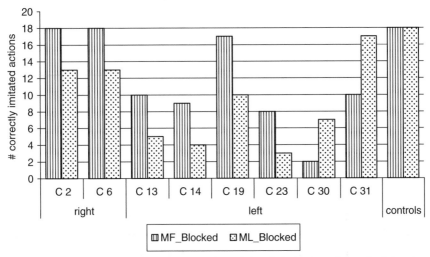

Figure 23.4 Performance of patients showing a dissociation in imitation of meaningful and meaningless actions in the blocked condition (see also Tessari *et al.* 2007); 'right' refers to patients with right-brain damage and 'left' to patients with left-brain damage.

It is the *classical* double dissociation (i.e. on the task on which patients are not impaired, they performed as accurately double as healthy controls) in imitation of MF and ML actions shown by two patients (cases 19 and 31) that allows us to argue for a functional independency of the two routes. Case 19, who imitated MF better than ML actions is likely to have a damaged sublexical route, whereas case 31 who imitated ML better than MF actions is likely to have a damaged lexical–semantic route.

The brain structures lesioned in the LBD patients who imitated MF actions better than ML actions overlapped in the superior temporal lobe and the ventral portion of the angular gyrus; and those lesioned in the RBD patients with the same behavioral deficit overlapped in the basal ganglia. On the other hand, the two patients who imitated ML better than MF actions had lesions involving the lateral and dorsal portion of the hippocampus, extending to the bordering white matter, and the dorsal angular gyrus.

Cerebral correlates of the two-route model

Overall, imaging studies carried out so far suggest that human imitation is sustained by a network of brain regions that include the inferior frontal gyrus, the dorsal and ventral premotor cortex, the inferior and the superior parietal cortex, and the posterior superior temporal cortex (see Brass and Heyes, 2005, for a review). To date, these areas have also been found activated during action perception.

Surprisingly few studies have investigated the cerebral correlates of the different processing mechanisms that may be involved in actual imitation. One such study is that performed by Peigneux *et al.* (2004) who, using positron emission tomography (PET), scanned subjects carrying out different tasks, including pantomime to command, imitation of novel and familiar gestures, and a functional–semantic association task. Among many interesting results, Peigneux *et al.* (2004) found that imitation of familiar (either symbolic or non symbolic) gestures was associated with activations in the left angular and middle frontal gyri, and the right supramarginal gyrus and inferior parietal lobule; whereas imitation of novel, ML gestures was associated with inferior and superior parietal lobes bilaterally.

In a further imaging study, Grèzes *et al.* (1999) required subjects to observe novel ML actions with or without the purpose of imitating them, in addition to observing stationary hands as a baseline. These authors showed that, irrespective of the subjects' intentions, the activations of some brain areas changed depending on the level of the subjects' familiarization with the perceived ML actions. In particular, as subjects became more familiar with ML, a reduction of the neural activity in the motion-related areas in the dorsal stream was observed, as well as an increase in activation within the inferior parietal and frontopolar cortices.

The issue of dedicated cerebral correlates for imitation of MF and ML actions was explored by Rumiati *et al.* (2005) in 10 healthy individuals (mean age = 26, SD = 1.9) using PET. Thirty MF and 30 ML actions were used to create the lists to be presented in five experimental conditions of a parametric design (100% MF–0% ML; 70% MF–30% ML; 50% MF–50% ML; 30% MF–70% ML; 0% MF–100% ML), and in the baseline condition (observation of mixed 50% MF and 50% ML actions). Imaging data were analyzed using SPM 99. Actions were comparable to those used in Tessari and Rumiati (2004) and in Tessari *et al.* (2007).

Three sets of analyses were carried out. First, relative to action observation (baseline), imitation of either MF or ML actions seems to be sustained by a network of brain regions including: the left primary sensorimotor cortex, the left supplementary motor area, the ventral premotor cortex, the primary visual cortex, the parieto-occipital junction bilaterally, the left insular cortex, the left thalamus and the right cerebellum. The second set comprises two correlations. During imitation, a significant positive correlation ($P < 0.05$, corrected) of regional cerebral blood flow with the number of MF actions was observed in the left inferior temporal gyrus only; in contrast, a significant positive correlation ($P < 0.05$, corrected) with the amount of ML movements was observed in the right parieto-occipital junction.

The third set of analyses includes two direct categorical comparisons. Imitating MF (100%) relative to ML (100%) actions showed differential increases in neural activity ($P < 0.001$, uncorrected) in the left inferior temporal gyrus, the left parahippocampal gyrus, and the left angular gyrus. In contrast, imitating ML (100%) relative to MF (100%) actions revealed differential increases in neural activity ($P < 0.001$, uncorrected) in the superior parietal cortex bilaterally, in the right parieto-occipital junction, in the right occipito-temporal junction (MT, V5), and in the left superior temporal gyrus. Increased neural activity, common to imitation of ML and MF actions, relative to action observation was observed in a network of areas known to be involved in imitation of actions including primary sensorimotor cortex, supplementary motor area, and ventral premotor cortex.

Conclusions

The studies reviewed in this chapter hopefully demonstrate that the two-route model can accommodate data from healthy and brain-damaged patients. It can account for stimulus-specific deficits shown by patients, and it can explain the strategic control exerted by individuals with reduced cognitive abilities on route selection. The ability to strategically select the most appropriate mechanism might be a general feature of the brain as it was found also in cognitive domains other than action.

Taken together, all these studies suggest that the lexical–semantic and sublexical mechanisms underlie action imitation, and, in addition to having in common some neural processes, also draw upon differential neural mechanisms.

In conclusion, a theory of *how* imitation is accomplished should include processes dealing with actions at input or at output, but should also consider the role of intermediate representational levels of actions and that of a strategic control.

Acknowledgments

We are grateful to all the people who collaborated to the studies reviewed in this chapter. We thank also Miriam Gade, Patrick Haggard, and an anonymous reviewer for their comments. This work was supported by a grant (PRIN) awarded by the Ministry of University and Research (MUR) and by the Bessel Prize awarded by the von Humboldt Stiftung.

References

Bard, K. A. and Russell, C. L. (1999) Evolutionary foundations of imitation: social cognitive and developmental aspects of imitative processes in non-human primates. In Nadel, J. and Butterworth, G. (eds), *Imitation in Infancy*, pp. 89–123. Cambridge University Press, Cambridge.

Bartolo, A. Cubelli, R., Della Sala, S., Drei, S. and Marchetti, C. (2001) Double dissociation between meaningful and meaningless gesture production in apraxia. *Cortex*, **37**, 696–699.

Bekkering, H. Wohlschäger, A. and Gattis, M. (2000) Imitation of gestures in children is goal-directed. *Quarterly Journal of Experimental Psychology*, **53**, 153–164.

Brass, M. and Heyes, C. M. (2005) Imitation: is cognitive neuroscience solving the correspondence problem? *Trends in Cognitive Sciences*, **9**, 489–495.

Brass, M. Bekkering, H. and Prinz, W. (2001) Movement observation affects movement execution in a simple response task. *Acta Psychologica*, **106**, 3–22.

Brass, M. Derrfuss, J. and von Cramon, D. Y. (2005) The inhibition of imitative and overlearned responses: a functional double dissociation. *Neuropsychologia*, **43**, 89–98.

Cubelli, R., Marchetti, C., Boscolo, G. and Della Sala, S. (2000) Cognition in action: testing a model of limb apraxia. *Brain and Cognition*, **44**, 144–165.

De Renzi, E., Motti, F. and Nichelli, P. (1981) Imitating gestures: a quantitative approach to ideomotor apraxia. *Archives of Neurology*, **37**, 6–10.

De Renzi, E., Cavalleri, F. and Facchini, S. (1996) Imitation and utilization behavior. *Journal of Neurology, Neurosurgery and Psychiatry*, **61**, 396–400.

Dijksterhuis, A. and Bargh, J. A. (2001) The perception–behaviour expressway: automatic effects of social perception on social behaviour. *Advances in Experimental Social Psychology*, 33, 1–39.

Ferrari, P. F., Visalberghi, E., Paukner, A., Fogassi, L., Ruggiero, A. and Suomi, S. J. (2006) Neonatal imitation in reshus macaques. *PLoS Biology*, 4, 1501–1508.

Gergely, G., Bekkering, H. and Kiraly, I. (2002) Rational imitation in preverbal infants. *Nature*, 14, 755.

Goldenberg, G. and Hagmann, S. (1997) The meaning of meaningless gestures: a study of visuo-imitative apraxia. *Neuropsychologia*, 35, 333–341.

Greenwald, A. G. (1970) Sensory feedback mechanisms in performance control. *Psychological Review*, 77, 73–99.

Grèzes, J., Costes, N. and Decety, J. (1999) The effects of learning and intention on the neural network involved in the perception of meaningless actions. *Brain*, 122, 1875–1887.

Iacoboni, M., Woods, R. P., Brass, M. *et al.* (1999) Cortical mechanisms of human imitation, *Science*, 286, 2526–2528.

Lakin, J. L., Jefferis, V. E., Cheng, C. M. and Chartrand, T. L. (2003) The chameleon effects social glue: evidence. *Journal of Nonverbal Behaviour*, 27, 145–162.

Lhermitte, F., Pillon, B. and Serdaru, M. (1986) Human autonomy and the frontal lobes. Part I: Imitation and utilization behavior: a neuropsychological study of 75 patients. *Annals of Neurology*, 19, 326–334.

Liepmann, H. (1908) *Drei Aufsätze aus dem Apraxiegebiet*. Kaeger, Berlin.

Meltzoff, A. N. and Moore, M. K. (1977) Imitation of facial and manual gestures by human neonates. *Science*, 198, 75–78.

Meltzoff, A. N. and Moore, M. K. (1983) Newborn infants' innate adult facial gestures. *Child Development*, 54, 702–709.

Meltzoff, A. N. and Moore, M. K. (1989) Imitation in newborn infants: exploring the range of gestures imitated and the underlying mechanisms. *Developmental Psychology*, 25, 954–962.

Meltzoff, A. N. and Moore, M. K. (1997) Explaining facial imitation: a theoretical model. *Early Development and Parenting*, 6, 179–192.

Merians, A. S., Clark, M., Poizner, H., Macauley, B., Gonzalez Rothi, L. J. and Heilman, K. L. (1997) Visual–imitative dissociation apraxia. *Neuropsychologia*, 35, 1485–1490.

Myowa, M. (1996) Imitation of facial gestures by an infant chimpanzee. *Primates*, 37, 207–213.

Myowa-Yamakoshi, M., Tomonaga, M., Tanaka, M. and Matsuzawa, T. (2004) Imitation in neonatal chimpanzees (Pan troglodytes). *Developmental Science*, 7, 437–442.

Nagell, K., Olguin, R. S. and Tomasello, M. (1993) Processes of social learning in the tool use of chimpanzees (Pan troglodytes) and human children (Homo sapiens). *Journal of Comparative Psychology*, 107, 174–186.

Patterson, K. E. and Shewell, C. (1987) Speak and spell: dissociations and word class effects. In Coltheart, M. Sartori, G. and Job, R. (eds), *The Cognitive Neuropsychology of Language*, pp. 273–294. Erlbaum, London.

Peigneux, P., Van der Linden, M., Andres-Benito, P., Sadzot, B., Franck, G. and Salmon, E. (2000) Exploration neuropsychologique et par imagerie fonctionelle cérébrale d'une apraxie visuo-imitative. *Review Neurologique*, 156, 459–472.

Peigneux, P., Van der Linden, M., Garraux, G. *et al.* (2004) Imaging a cognitive model of apraxia: the neural substrate of gesture-specific cognitive processes. *Human Brain Mapping*, 21, 119–142.

Prinz, W. (1997) Perception and action planning. *European Journal of Experimental Psychology*, 9, 129–154.

Rothi, L. J. G., Ochipa, C. and Heilman, K. M. (1991) A cognitive neuropsychological model of limb praxis. *Cognitive Neuropsychology*, 8, 443–458.

Rumiati, R. I. and Tessari, A. (2002) Imitation of novel and well-known actions: the role of short-term memory. *Experimental Brain Research*, **142**, 425–433.

Rumiati, R. I. Weiss, P. H. Tessari, A., Assmus, A., Zilles, K., Herzog, H. and Fink, R. G. (2005) Common and differential neural mechanisms supporting imitation of meaningful and meaningless actions. *Journal of Cognitive Neuroscience*, **17**, 1420–1431.

Tabossi, P. and Laghi, L. (1992) Semantic priming in the pronunciation of words in two writing systems: Italian and English. *Memory and Cognition*, **20**, 303–313.

Tai, Y. F., Scherfler, C., Brooks, D. J., Sawamoto, N. and Castiello, U. (2004) The human premotor cortex is 'mirror' only for biological actions. *Current Biology*, **14**, 117–120.

Tessari, A. and Rumiati, R. I. (2004) The strategic control of multiple routes in imitation of actions. *Journal of Experimental Psychology, Human Perception and Performance*, **30**, 1107–1116.

Tessari, A., Bosanac, D. and Rumiati, R. I. (2006) Effect of learning on imitation of new actions: implications for a memory model. *Experimental Brain Research* (ahead of print).

Tessari, A., Canessa, N., Ukmar, M. and Rumiati, R. I. (2007) Neuropsychological evidence for a strategic control of multiple routes in imitation. *Brain*, **130**, 1111–1126.

Toraldo, A., Reverberi, C. F. and Rumiati, R. I. (2001) Critical dimension affecting imitation performance of patients with ideomotor apraxia. *Cortex*, **37**, 737–740.

Wohlschläger, A., Gattis, M. and Bekkering, H. (2003) Action generation and action perception in imitation: an instantiation of the ideomotor principle. *Philosophical Transactions of the Royal Society of London, B*, **358**, 501–515.

24

Symbols and quantities in parietal cortex: elements of a mathematical theory of number representation and manipulation

Stanislas Dehaene

In this chapter, I put together the first elements of a mathematical theory relating neuro-biological observations to psychological laws in the domain of numerical cognition. The starting point is the postulate of a neuronal code whereby numerosity—the cardinal of a set of objects—is represented approximately by the firing of a population of numerosity detectors. Each of these neurons fires to a certain preferred numerosity, with a tuning curve which is a Gaussian function of the logarithm of numerosity. From this log-Gaussian code, decisions are taken using Bayesian mechanisms of log-likelihood computation and accumulation. The resulting equations for response times and errors in classical tasks of number comparison and same–different judgments are shown to tightly fit behavioral and neural data. Two more speculative issues are discussed. First, new chronometric evidence is presented supporting the hypothesis that the acquisition of number symbols changes the mental number line, both by increasing its precision and by changing its coding scheme from logarithmic to linear. Second, I examine how symbolic and nonsymbolic representations of numbers affect performance in arithmetic computations such as addition and subtraction.

Introduction

An ultimate goal of psychology is to provide lawful explanations of mental mechanisms in terms of a small set of rules, preferably framed in the language of mathematics, which capture the regularities present in human and animal behavior. Furthermore, those psychological laws should not remain stated solely at a descriptive level (although obtaining valid descriptive rules of behavior is usually an indispensable step on that road). Rather, they should be ultimately grounded in a neurobiological level of explanation, through a series of additional bridging laws linking the molecular, synaptic, cellular, and circuit levels with psychological representation and computations.

Are these ambitious goals out of reach? No. In the domain of perception and motor control, solid psychological and bridiging laws have been described, one of the most successful cases being signal detection theory. Furthermore, at a higher cognitive level, the work of Roger Shepard has suggested that internal cognitive processes of mental representation and transformation can be captured by elegant mathematical rules, including Bayesian principles of similarity and categorization (Shepard, 2001).

In the present chapter, I will suggest that a model inspired by those earlier successes can begin to capture the main regularities observed in a small domain of semantics: the representation of number. We now have a good mathematical theory of the format of representation by which numerical quantities are encoded mentally, as well as of the main laws by which these representations are used to generate behavior in simple identity judgments, comparisons and calculations. Furthermore, two spectacular advances in electrophysiology—the discovery of single neurons tuned to numerosity in the macaque monkey (Sawamura et al., 2002; Nieder et al., 2002; Nieder and Miller, 2003, 2004), and of neurons plausibly implementing random-walk accumulation models of decision (Gold and Shadlen, 2002)—have given us insight into the neuronal mechanisms from which those laws arise.

The mathematical principles which now constitute a sort of 'standard model' for numerical cognition have been described over the years by various people and in various publications (e.g. Shepard et al., 1975; Van Oeffelen and Vos, 1982; Link, 1990; Dehaene, 1992; Dehaene and Mehler, 1992; Gallistel and Gelman, 1992; Dehaene and Changeux, 1993; Cordes et al., 2001; Dehaene, 2002, 2003; Nieder and Miller, 2003; Piazza et al., 2004; Pica et al., 2004; Verguts et al., 2005; Barth et al., 2006; McCrink et al., 2006). One of the goals of this chapter is to present a single reference source for equations that are currently widely dispersed in the literature. Nevertheless, mathematically less sophisticated readers can skip all of these equations, because their main points are also explained in plain language in the text. The main purpose of this chapter, indeed, is to provide an accessible synthesis of this theory and to compare its predictions with reanalyses of a variety of data. I shall do so in a 'theory-first' manner, first presenting the mathematical principles and then some of the best evidence for or against them (although historically, of course, theory development occurred in reverse order).

As we shall see, our ability to capture a variety of findings with a small set of principles is impressive. Nevertheless, systematic integration of multiple data into a coherent framework also leads to the identification of two important unsolved problems: How does the coding of symbolic information differ from that of nonsymbolic information (e.g. representing the meaning of the word 'thirteen' versus the quantity represented by 13 dots)? And what are the mechanisms by which we compute operations of addition and subtraction?

Numerosity representation

We start by specifying how the cardinal of sets is represented mentally. The term *numerosity* is used to refer to the cardinal property of sets, and to distinguish it from culture-dependent *numerals* or *number symbols* such as the word 'three'. Many experiments indicate that humans and other animal species possess a refined mental representation of numerosity, even when the use of number symbols is not available (in animals, preverbal infants, or cultures with a reduced number lexicon) or is made impossible (e.g. by verbal interference in adults).

Mathematical theory: log-Gaussian model

The theory presented here (See Figure 24.1) postulates that each numerosity is represented internally by a noisy distribution of activation on an internal continuum or *mental number line*. Mathematically, the numerosity of a set of n dots is represented internally by a Gaussian random variable X (the *internal representative* of n) with mean $q(n)$ and with standard deviation $w(n)$. Those parameters altogether specify the nature and precision of the numerical code. In particular, the parameter $w(n)$ determines the internal variability or amount of noise in the coding scheme.

There are several possible choices for $q(n)$ and $w(n)$, but they are constrained by a strong empirical observation, the fact that *Weber's law* holds for numerosity stimuli. As further discussed below, Weber's law states that the minimal numerical change that can be discriminated increases in direct proportion to the magnitude of the numerosities involved. An alternative formulation is that numerosity discrimination depends only on the ratio of the numbers involved, not their absolute values.

The simplest theoretical postulate is that internal variability is the same for all of the represented numbers ($w(n) = w$). In order for Weber's law to hold, the internal variable then has to vary as the logarithm of the represented numerosity n ($q(n) = Log(n)$). In this case, the probability distribution which specifies the likelihood that a number n is represented, at a given moment, by a particular value x of the internal random variable X is given by:

$$p(X \in [x, x + dx]) = G\left(\frac{x - Log(n)}{w}\right) dx = \frac{e^{-\frac{(x - Log[n])^2}{2w^2}}}{\sqrt{2\pi w}} dx$$

(24.1)

where G is the normal curve. This equation simply means that a given input numerosity is represented, at different moments, by noisy values that tend to cluster around a location corresponding to $Log(n)$ on the number line. I will refer to this model as the *log-Gaussian model*. Note that the model has a single free parameter, w, the *internal Weber fraction* that specifies the degree of precision of the internal quantity representation.

An alternative model supposes that the internal variable scales linearly with n, but with a variability that also scales linearly with n ($w(n) = w \times n$, $q(n) = n$). This is called the *scalar variability model*. Both models make essentially identical predictions for discrimination and comparison behavior, differing only in subtle, second-order terms that relate to asymmetries in the response curves.[1] Thus, for purposes of computing error rates and response times, one may use one or the other model, depending on which is mathematically more tractable. More controversial, however, is whether the models are equivalent at

---

[1] When w is close to zero, as is true in human adults ($w \sim 0.15$–0.20), so that $log(1 + w) \sim w$, even the quantitative values of w obtained with the log-Gaussian model and with the scalar variability model are close to identical.

Stimulus of numerosity *n*

1. Coding by Log-Gaussian numerosity detectors

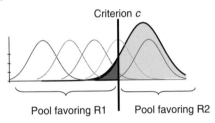

Internal logarithmic scale: log(*n*)

2. Application of a criterion and formation of two pools of units

Criterion *c*

Pool favoring R1   Pool favoring R2

3. Computation of log-likelihood ratio by differencing

Pool favoring R2   ⟶ LLR for R2 over R1
Pool favoring R1 ⟶

4. Accumulation of LLR, forming a random-walk process

Mean Response Time

Trial 1   Trial 2   Trial 3   Decision threshold for R2

Starting point of accumulation

Decision threshold for R1

Time

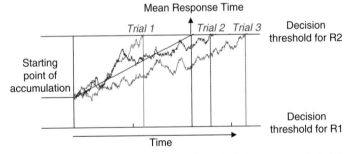

Figure 24.1 Overall outline of how the proposed mathematical theory accounts for elementary arithmetic decisions. Numerosity is coded by a fluctuating distribution of activation over log-Gaussian numerosity detectors. The decision is attained through to a random-walk process based on accumulation of estimates of the log-likelihood of the available responses. LLR, log-likelihood ratio.

all levels and, in particular, whether they can be distinguished at the neural level. Below, I will consider several subtle phenomena that seem to favor the logarithmic model.

Neuronal modeling

Jean-Pierre Changeux and I have presented a theoretical model of the neuronal implementation of the log-Gaussian hypothesis (Dehaene and Changeux, 1993), later elaborated by others (Verguts and Fias, 2004; Verguts *et al.*, 2005). Our model illustrates how approximate numerosity can be extracted from a retinotopic map through three successive stages: (1) retinotopic coding of object locations regardless of object identity and size; (2) representation of total activity by accumulation neurons which simply sum the activation on the object location map; (3) representation of each approximate numerosity by a distinct set of *numerosity detector neurons*, each tuned to a specific numerosity.

Because human and nonhuman animals can represent a large range of numbers (e.g. Cantlon and Brannon, 2006), we postulated a logarithmic spacing of neural thresholds, such that a decreasing number of neurons was allocated to increasingly larger numerosities (the alternative hypothesis of linear coding seemed implausible as it would imply that the vast majority of neurons encode large numerosities, although these numerosities are quite hard to discriminate). This principle of *compressive coding* was inspired by the known over-representation of species-relevant parameter ranges in sensory maps (e.g. fovea in retinotopic maps, hand and face in somatosensory maps, or even echo-locating frequencies in bat tonotopic maps). Simulations then showed that those neurons had approximately Gaussian tuning curves when plotted on a logarithmic axis—a neuronal implementation of the log-Gaussian hypothesis.

In the Dehaene–Changeux model, then, the firing rate of a numerosity detector neuron that responds preferentially to numerosity *p*, in response to a range of stimulus numerosities *n*, traces a bell-shaped curve which is Gaussian on a log scale and has a maximal firing peak at the location *p*. Mathematically, this tuning curve is given by:

$$f(n, p) = \alpha G\left(\frac{Log(n) - Log(p)}{w'} \right) = \alpha \frac{e^{-\frac{(Log(n) - Log(p))^2}{2w'^2}}}{\sqrt{2\pi}w'}$$

(24.2)

In this equation, *G* is the normal curve and *w'* is the *neural Weber fraction* which defines the degree of coarseness with which neurons encode numerosity. Note that *w'* can be quantitatively different from the psychologically defined internal Weber fraction *w*. This is because there is no simple relation between the single-neuron representation level (where tuning curves are characterized by parameter *w'*), and the psychological representation level (where the precision of a subject's representation is characterized by parameter *w*). Intuitively, it is easy to envisage cases in which these parameters are dissociated. For instance, even if single neurons had a very coarse tuning curve (high *w'*), it might still be possible to perform precise psychological judgment (low *w*) by averaging across an entire neural population. Conversely, even if some neurons had very precise codes (low *w'*), it might not be possible for decision mechanisms to separate their signals from those of other less informative neurons, thus resulting in a psychological level of performance lower than the best performance theoretical achievable (high *w*).

The neurophysiological literature contains many discussions of the bridging laws that relate single-neuron coding to psychophysical representation, particularly in the well-documented domain of movement perception (Shadlen *et al.*, 1996; Parker and Newsome, 1998; Shadlen and Newsome, 1998). There is no consensus yet on the best formulation of these bridging laws. Their determination requires careful analysis of the trial-to-trial firing rate variability, number of neurons contributing to behavior, structure of correlations between them, and pooling rule used to combine their responses into a single summary value. Nevertheless, some basic results are available. A simple analysis indicates that, if a bank of neurons with Gaussian tuning is used to encode a certain magnitude, then the best way to estimate which value is represented by this population is to compute their *population vector*, which is the mean of the preferred values of each neuron, weighted by their current firing rate [mathematically, this is the best estimator in the maximum likelihood sense (Dayan and Abbott, 2001, pp. 106–108)]. According to this population-vector model, a set of log-Gaussian neurons predicts a log-Gaussian psychophysical internal scale—but not necessarily with the same quantitative variability parameters w and w'.

Experimental evidence

Behaviorally, the main prediction of the log-Gaussian model concerns the metric of similarity between the representations of two numerosities n_1 and n_2 (with $n_1 < n_2$). The model predicts that the judged similarity between two numerosities should vary monotonically with the difference of their logarithms.

$$\text{Similarity } (n_1, n_2) = S(|Log(n_1) - Log(n_2)|) = S(Log(r)) \tag{24.3}$$

where S is monotonically decreasing and $r = n_2/n_1$ is the ratio of the two numbers.

Subjective similarity ratings conform to this rule (Shepard *et al.*, 1975). When subjects rated the conceptual similarity of two numbers, regardless of whether they were denoted by dot patterns, digits or words, a logarithmic similarity scale was recovered by nonmetric multidimensional scaling.

At the neural level, Dehaene and Changeux's (1993) model predicts the existence of a hierarchy of several types of neurons: object maps, accumulation neurons, and numerosity detector neurons. At present, strong evidence exists only for the latter type of cells (Nieder *et al.*, 2002; Nieder and Miller, 2003, 2004). Their properties conform in great detail to the proposed log-Gaussian model. Nieder and Miller trained macaque monkeys in a numerical match-to-sample task. On each trial, they attended to the numerosity of a sample set of visual dots and memorized it. After a delay, they were presented with a second numerosity and decided whether it was equal to the first. During both sample and delay periods, many neurons were tuned to a preferred numerosity, in the sense that they fired maximally to a given number of dots, and showed decreasing firing rates when the numerosity was smaller or larger than this preferred value. Collection of data from hundreds of trials led to a very precise characterization of each neuron's tuning curve. The hypothesis of a Gaussian curve on a *linear* axis (*scalar variability*) could be rejected. Rather, asymmetries in the tuning curves were compatible with the log-Gaussian hypothesis of a fixed-width Gaussian tuning curve once plotted as a function of log(*n*).

The numerosity-tuned neurons were initially found in prefrontal cortex, but later recordings in the depth of the intraparietal sulcus revealed another population of number neurons in, or close to, area VIP. The parietal cells differed from the prefrontal cells in two ways: they had a significantly faster latency, and they fired less strongly during the delay. Thus, the data are compatible with the hypothesis that numerosity is first computed and represented in intraparietal cortex, then transferred to prefrontal cortex for memory purposes. The object map and linear accumulation neurons postulated by the theory might then be tentatively associated with area LIP, which is retinotopic, monosynaptically connected to VIP, and thought to encode a saliency map of relevant object locations. Indeed very recently, neurons whose firing rate vary monotonically with number have been identified in area LIP (Roitman, Brannon and Platt, 2007).

The location where numerosity-sensitive neurons are found is a plausible homolog of the human intraparietal region found active during many mental arithmetic and numerical judgment tasks (Dehaene et al., 2003). Indeed its location in the depth of the macaque intraparietal sulcus could be roughly predicted from the finding of a homologous geometrical arrangement of surrounding sensorimotor regions in humans and macaques (Simon et al., 2002, 2004).

Following Nieder and Miller's finding, Manuela Piazza and I examined whether numerosity coding by log-Gaussian numerosity detectors could also be demonstrated in the human intraparietal sulcus (Piazza et al., 2004). Since we could not record from single human neurons, we took advantage of the functional magnetic resonance imaging (fMRI) adaptation method. While the subjects passively attended to the screen, we adapted them by repeatedly presenting, for several minutes, the same adaptation numerosity n_{hab}, which could be either 16 or 32 dots on different runs. We then presented occasional trials where the numerosity n_{dev} deviated by a variable amount from the reference value, up to twice smaller or twice larger. As in Nieder and Miller's study, stimuli were generated randomly by a Matlab program which provided precise control over non-numerical parameters (Dehaene et al., 2005). Based on past work, we expected *repetition suppression*, a decrease in the activity of the neurons coding for the adaptation numerosity. Using the above firing-rate function $f(n,p)$, we could predict mathematically the amount of activation expected to be elicited by a given deviant numerosity. Intuitively, this activation should reflect the combination of two Gaussians: one evoked by the adaptation numerosity, which created a Gaussian 'trough' in the neural population around the location of the adaptation value, and the second evoked by the deviant stimulus which is used to 'read out' the state of adaptation of the representation, and activates a Gaussian population of numerosity detectors which have been more or less adapted depending on their proximity to the adaptation value. Mathematically, the total activation which results from this combination is given by an operation called the convolution of the two Gaussians (see appendix of Piazza et al., 2004, for details). Thus, we expected the recovery from adaptation also to follow a Gaussian function of the difference of the logarithms of n_{hab} and n_{dev}, but with a width larger than the neural tuning curve by a factor of $\sqrt{2}$:

$$I(n_{hab},n_{dev}) = \lambda - \mu \frac{e^{-\frac{(Log(n_{hab})-Log(n_{dev}))^2}{4w'^2}}}{2\sqrt{\pi}w'}$$

(24.4)

The fMRI data conformed in great detail to this model. In a whole-brain search, only the left and right intraparietal regions showed an fMRI response which depended on the amount of numerical deviancy. The shape of this response was tightly fitted by a Gaussian once plotted on the appropriate logarithmic scale. Furthermore, in log scale the Gaussian had a similar width for adaptation values 16 and 32, thus showing that Weber's law holds. In the absence of direct single-neuron recordings in humans, those data, replicated by others in adults and 4-year-olds (Cantlon *et al.*, 2006; see also Temple and Posner, 1998), provide suggestive evidence that the same principle of log-Gaussian coding might be underlying numerosity perception in human adults, children, and nonhuman primates.

Recently, this method of numerosity adaptation has been extended to 2–3 month-old infants (V. Izard, G. Dehaene-Lambertz and S. Dehaene, unpublished data; V. Izard, PhD thesis, December 2005). We collected event-related potentials during adaptation–dishabituation with numerosities 2 versus 3, 4 versus 8, or 4 versus 12. Once babies were adapted to one of these numerosities, a right parietal negativity was evoked whenever the corresponding deviant was presented. Although lacking in precise localization, those results tentatively suggest that the parietal numerosity representation may be in place at a very early age in human development possibly with an early right hemisphere bias.

Open issues

A debated issue concerns whether behavioral and even neuroimaging or neurophysiological data may ever separate the log-Gaussian model from the linear scalar variability model. Randy Gallistel (personal communication) has repeatedly argued that they cannot. Behaviorally, indeed, I have demonstrated that both models predict an essential identical ratio dependence in a broad variety of judgments (S. Dehaene, unpublished work; see also below). At the neural level, Gallistel argues that a similar argument applies: the firing of the neurons can be considered as a sort of decision whose profile can be predicted from an underlying linear coding scheme with scalar variability. According to Gallistel, if each neuron were programmed as an ideal detector of numerosity on a linear continuum with scalar variability, it would show precisely the tuning curve asymmetries and ratio dependence that are thought to support the log-Gaussian model! If this argument is correct, then the models truly are inseparable, and are in fact mathematically equivalent. I would argue, however, that for fear of an infinite regress, it is not correct to postulate yet another, deeper level of linear representation on which the neurons act as optimal encoders. The presumption is that Nieder and Miller have recorded from what constitutes the brain's neuronal representation of number, and the log-Gaussian model appears to provide the most compact description of that code.

There may be other, less controversial ways to separate the models. The log-Gaussian model predicts a uniform distribution of preferred numerosities on a logarithmic scale, hence more neurons dedicated to small numerosities than to large ones. In Nieder and Miller's initial work, it was not possible to test this prediction, because only the numerosities 1–5 were tested. Nieder and Merten (2007) however extended this work to numerosities 1–30 and found that increasingly fewer neurons were tuned to larger numbers, compatible with the log-Gaussian model. It may not be entirely unrelated that, in all languages of the world, the frequency with which we *name* a given numerosity n is a sharply decreasing function of n (Dehaene and Mehler, 1992).

Against the log-Gaussian hypothesis, Brannon *et al.* (2001) have argued that, if numerosity were represented on a logarithmic internal scale, addition and subtraction operations would not be possible. Empirically, they showed that pigeons could be successfully trained to perform an approximate subtraction task. More generally, Gallistel and Gelman (1992) argued that a mental representation should be characterized by the type of operation it supports, and that competence for addition and subtraction provides incontrovertible evidence for a linear mental number line. In my opinion, however, this argument confounds the content of a representation with its form, *what* is being represented and *how* it is represented, or in Saussurian terms, the signified and the signifier. In the log-Gaussian model, *what* is being represented is a number n, although its internal representative is $q(n) = \log(n)$. It is equally absurd to state that when computing a subtraction $n_1 - n_2$, we should then subtract the logarithms of n_1 and n_2, than to say that, because a computer encodes numbers in binary format, it should always compute $1 + 1 = 10$! In brain and computer alike, the rules of transformation of the representatives $q(n_1)$ and $q(n_2)$ should be stated so that the result of the internal operation is isomorphic to the desired arithmetic operation. In the case of the subtracting pigeons, I showed that, whether the numbers were coded by a linear or a logarithmic scheme, a simple neural network could easily pass the behavioral test that Brannon *et al.* took as diagnostic of a linear subtraction operation (Dehaene, 2001). The issue of calculation algorithms is discussed further below.

A separate open issue concerns whether the proposed 'number line' representation constitutes the sole semantic representation of number. There is evidence, at least in human infants, for a distinct system of representation of small sets of objects (1, 2 or 3), thought to be based on object or event files, and not subject to Weber's law (for review, see Feigenson *et al.*, 2004). This system might be responsible for 'subitizing', the capacity to quickly and accurately name numerosities 1, 2 and 3 in adults. An alternative possibility, however, is that subitizing merely represents performance at the lower, most precise end of the number line continuum (Mandler and Shebo, 1982; Dehaene and Cohen, 1994; Cordes *et al.*, 2001; Piazza *et al.*, 2003). In animals, performance is quite often continuous over the whole range of numbers, with little or no evidence in favor of a distinct 'subitizing' system (Brannon and Terrace, 2000; Nieder *et al.*, 2002; Nieder and Miller, 2003, 2004; Cantlon and Brannon, 2006; but see Hauser and Carey, 2003). Thus, whether a distinct system exists, what are its neural mechanisms, and how they might be modeled mathematically remain open issues.

Numerosity discrimination, comparison and identification

I now turn to the utilization of the numerosity representation in simple cognitive tasks. Based on the postulated log-Gaussian representation, and assuming a certain form for the decision system, can one reconstruct animal and human performance in simple tasks?

I start with the prediction of performance (percentage correct) in various numerosity tasks, assuming that decision in this case is based on a single internal sample on the internal number line.

Theory

The theoretical principles applied here are identical to those used in signal detection theory to characterize psychophysical judgments. In turn, these principles can be derived from optimal Bayesian decision based on maximum likelihood or maximum a posteriori inference (Green and Swets, 1966; MacMillan and Creelman, 1991). In the most general terms, a behavioral experiment consists in presenting a set of numerical stimuli S_i, each of which is associated with one member of the set of responses R_j. On a given trial, the stimulus S is represented by a noisy random variable X on the internal continuum. The aim of the decision system is to select, among the set of possible responses R_j, the response R that has the greatest probability $P(R_j|x)$ of being correct, given the state x of the internal representation (the analysis can also be extended to the maximization of rewards associated with each response). Optimal responding can be achieved by finding the response R that maximizes this probability $P(R_j|x)$. By Bayes' rule,

$$P(R_j|x) = P(x|R_j)\, P(R_j)/P(x) \tag{24.5}$$

In this equation, only the first two terms vary with R_j. The first can be calculated: it consists in the mean of the Gaussian curves evoked by all the stimuli for which the correct response is R_j. The second term is often constant (all responses are equiprobable) or can be estimated over trials (possibly generating some bias).

The end result of this procedure is a family of *optimal response curves* $[g_j(x) = P(R_j|x)]$ which specify, for every possible value of the internal representation x, what is the probability that the response R_j is the correct one.[2] The optimal strategy, when observing an internal representation x, consists in selecting the response R_j for which $g_j(x)$ is the largest. This strategy defines a set of criteria that divide the internal number line into regions that should be responded to with different responses R_i. Once these criteria are set, it is easy to compute the probability of making a correct response to each stimulus S_i. One simply has to consider all of the possible internal encodings x of this stimulus, and to examine for which fraction of them the above decision rule leads to the correct answer. Mathematically, this is given by the integral of the internal Gaussian representation over the interval of response criteria that are associated with the desired response to that stimulus. In the same way, the entire stimulus–response matrix which defines the probability of making any given response to any given stimulus can be computed.

---

[2] In cases where a trial consists in the presence of two numerosities n_1 and n_2, those functions are defined over two internal variables x_1 and x_2 instead of one. Nevertheless the logic of finding which response has the highest probability of being correct remains the same. Furthermore, depending on the arrangement of the stimuli, one may frequently make the simplifying assumption that subjects base their decisions on a reduced variable such as the difference between x_1 and x_2. This approach has been adopted in what follows.

Application to experimental examples

To make this presentation more concrete, we now consider several simple examples.

Numerosity discrimination

The theory and experiments for this task have been presented by Van Oeffelen and Vos (1982). Briefly, in a block of trials, the subject is presented with one of two numerosities (e.g. 15 or 18 dots) and has to decide which numerosity is presented. Thus, the stimulus set comprises only two numbers n_1 and n_2 (with $n_1 < n_2$), and the response set is also limited to two responses: $R_1 = 'n_1'$ and $R_2 = 'n_2'$. Assuming equiprobable responses, the optimal response curves can be derived from the log-Gaussian representation curves according to:

$$g_j(x) = P(R_j \mid x) = \frac{G\left(\dfrac{x - Log(n_j)}{w}\right)}{G\left(\dfrac{x - Log(n_1)}{w}\right) + G\left(\dfrac{x - Log(n_2)}{w}\right)}$$

(24.6)

where G is the normal curve. It is easy to see that $g_2(x) > g_1(x)$ if and only if $x > c$, where $c = \frac{1}{2}\left[log(n_1) + log(n_2)\right] = log(\sqrt{n_1 n_2})$ is the response criterion. Hence, the optimal strategy, quite intuitively, consists in responding $R_1 = 'n_1'$ if the internal representation of the target falls closer to $log(n_1)$ than to $log(n_2)$, and to respond $R_2 = 'n_2'$ otherwise. The predicted performance is thus

$$P_{correct}(n_1, n_2) = \int_{-\infty}^{Log(\sqrt{n_1 n_2})} \frac{e^{-\frac{(x - Log[n_1])^2}{2w^2}}}{\sqrt{2\pi}w} dx = \int_{-\infty}^{+\infty} \frac{e^{-\frac{(x - \frac{1}{2}Log[r])^2}{2w^2}}}{\sqrt{2\pi}w} dx$$

(24.7)

Note that the latter form makes clear the dependence of performance on the ratio of the two numbers, $r = n_2/n_1$ (one version of Weber's law). Van Oeffelen and Vos (1982) tested this equation against human numerosity discrimination data, and found it to be quite accurate.

Ratio-dependent performance has also been observed during numerosity discrimination in human infants (Lipton and Spelke, 2003). Although the data are probably not quantitative enough for a formal fit of our equations, the Weber fraction appears to decrease with age: 6-month-old babies fail to discriminate numerosities in a 3:2 ratio, while 9-month-old babies can (Lipton and Spelke, 2003).

Numerosity comparison

In the nonsymbolic number comparison task, on each trial subjects are presented with a single set of dots and have to determine if its numerosity is larger or smaller than some fixed reference n_{ref}. Thus, the set of stimuli can be large, but the set of responses is reduced to two responses: larger or smaller. An analysis of the optimal strategy, along the above lines, shows that there is a single criterion c on the internal number line, and that subjects' response should be 'larger' if the internal representation exceeds this criterion, and 'smaller' otherwise. The optimal criterion c generally coincides with, or is close to, the internal representation of n_{ref}: $c = \log(n_{ref})$. For each target number, one can then predict the fraction of choices of the larger response as:

$$P_{larger}(n, n_{ref}) = \int_{-c}^{+\infty} \frac{e^{-\frac{(x-Log[n])^2}{2w^2}}}{\sqrt{2\pi}w} dx = \int_{-\infty}^{+\infty} \frac{e^{-\frac{(x-Log[r])^2}{2w^2}}}{\sqrt{2\pi}w} dx$$

(24.8)

Again, this equation makes apparent that performance should depend on the ratio of the stimulus and reference numbers, $r = n/n_{ref}$.

At least two successful tests of this equation have been published. First, Piazza et al. (2004) collected numerosity comparison judgments in adults. As shown in Figure 24.2, Equation 24.8 fitted the data very tightly. Ratio dependence was tested explicitly by testing two reference numbers, 16 and 32, and verifying that the slope of the psychophysical curves shifted by a factor of 2 on a linear scale (and was constant when plotted on a log scale). Second, Pica et al. (2004) used a slightly different version of the comparison task, where the subject sees two successive numerosities n_1 and n_2, and decides which is the larger. The theory is only slightly different here, and assumes that subjects respond '$n_1 > n_2$' if and only if the internal representatives are in the same order $x_1 > x_2$. It is easy to obtain analytic expressions for error rates, both under the log-Gaussian and under the scalar variability hypotheses:

Log-Gaussian model:[3]

$$P_{correct}(n_1, n_2) = \int_0^{+\infty} \frac{e^{-\frac{1}{2}\left(\frac{(x-(Log(n_2)-Log(n_1)))}{\sqrt{2}w}\right)^2}}{\sqrt{2\pi}\sqrt{2}w} dx = \int_0^{+\infty} \frac{e^{-\frac{1}{2}\left(\frac{x-Log(r)}{\sqrt{2}w}\right)^2}}{\sqrt{2\pi}\sqrt{2}w} dx$$

(24.9)

Linear, scalar variability model:

$$P_{correct}(n_1, n_2) = \int_0^{+\infty} \frac{e^{-\frac{1}{2}\left(\frac{x-(n_2-n_1)}{w\sqrt{n_1^2+n_2^2}}\right)^2}}{\sqrt{2\pi}w\sqrt{n_1^2+n_2^2}} dx = \int_0^{+\infty} \frac{e^{-\frac{1}{2}\left(\frac{x-(r-1)}{w\sqrt{1+r^2}}\right)^2}}{\sqrt{2\pi}w\sqrt{1+r^2}} dx$$

(24.10)

Both equations yield virtually identical predictions which, as made clear by the above equations, again depend solely on the ratio of the two numbers, $r = n_2/n_1$ (with $n_1 < n_2$). Pica et al. (2004) collected data from children and adult, both in French subjects and in Munduruku Indians from the Amazon. In all cases, performance conformed to the above equations, thus suggesting that numerosity judgments belong to a core set of arithmetic knowledge that is available independently of language, culture and education.

....

[3] Note that the sole difference with the equation characterizing performance in comparison with a fixed reference is a factor of 2 on the scaling of the parameter w. See MacMillan and Creelman (1991) for a cogent explanation of such subtle differences between psychophysical paradigms, particularly what they call two-choice tasks (where two stimuli n_1 and n_2 are presented) versus reminder tasks (where a single stimulus n is compared to a fixed reference).

Same–different judgments

Another simple task consists in asking subjects whether two numbers are the same or different. Piazza *et al.* (2004) used this task with a fixed reference. Subjects were presented on each trial with a single numerosity n and had to decide whether this numerosity was identical to, or different from, a fixed reference n_{ref} (this reference was fixed for an entire block, and subjects were reminded of it on each trial). If the different target numerosities are symmetrically distributed around the habituation numerosity on a logarithmic scale (which was the case in Piazza *et al.*'s stimulus set), then the subject's optimal criterion consists in responding 'same' whenever the internal representation of the stimulus numerosity n, x, falls within a symmetrical decision interval centered around the representation of the reference number. Thus, subjects should respond 'same' if and only if x belongs to $[\log(n_{ref}) - \delta, \log(n_{ref}) + \delta]$, where δ defines the width of the criterial region. Given this response strategy, the probability of responding 'same' to a stimulus numerosity n is given by:

$$P_{same}(n, n_{ref}) = \int_{Log(n_{same})-\delta}^{Log(n_{same})+\delta} \frac{e^{-\frac{(x-Log(n))^2}{2w^2}}}{\sqrt{2\pi}w}\,dx = \int_{-\delta}^{\delta} \frac{e^{-\frac{(x-Log(r))^2}{2w^2}}}{\sqrt{2\pi}w}\,dx \tag{24.11}$$

Again, performance should depend on the ratio of the stimulus and reference numbers, $r = n/n_{ref}$. As shown in Figure 24.2, an excellent fit with experimental data was observed, and ratio dependence was verified with two reference numbers, 16 and 32.

A related task was used by Nieder and Miller (2003) in macaque monkeys. As described earlier, on each trial, subjects were first presented with a sample number n_1, then after some delay with a second number n_2. They had to decide whether the first number matched the second, or differed from it. As shown in Figure 24.1, performance averaged across a very large number of trials was a remarkably regular function of the difference of logarithms of the two numbers (or, equivalently, of their log ratio), which Nieder and Miller (2003) showed to be well captured by a Gaussian curve.

According to the theory, a simplified though frequently close to optimal strategy for this task is to respond 'same' whenever the difference between the internal representatives x_1 and x_2 falls below a certain criterion δ. The probability of responding 'same' is then given by:

$$P_{same}(n_1, n_2) = \int_{-\delta}^{-\delta} \frac{e^{-\frac{1}{2}\left(\frac{x-(Log(n_2)-Log(n_1))}{\sqrt{2}w}\right)^2}}{\sqrt{2\pi}\sqrt{2}w}\,dx = \int_{-\delta}^{\delta} \frac{e^{-\frac{1}{2}\left(\frac{x-Log(r)}{\sqrt{2}w}\right)^2}}{\sqrt{2\pi}\sqrt{2}w}\,dx \tag{24.12}$$

where $r = n_2/n_1$ (with $n_1 < n_2$). Note that this equation, the integral of a Gaussian over a given interval, departs from the simple Gaussian used by Nieder and Miller (2003) to fit their data. Nevertheless, I have verified that the two fits are essentially indistinguishable and that the present equation thus provides an excellent account of the performance of Nieder and Miller's monkeys in numerical match-to-sample tasks.

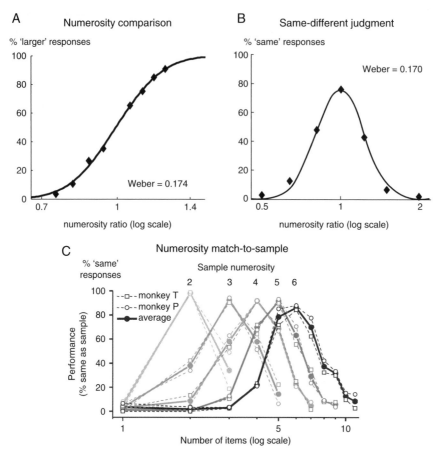

Figure 24.2 Human and macaque monkey performance in simple numerosity tasks is well-captured by the proposed psychophysical model. (**A**) Humans, larger–smaller comparison of large numerosities to a fixed reference (16 or 32). (**B**) Humans, same–difference judgment of large numerosities with a fixed reference (16 or 32). Both data sets are redrawn from Piazza *et al.* (2004). The dots are experimental data points, and the curve is the best fit by equations described in the text. The dependence of performance on the log numerosity ratio is evident. (**C**) Data from Nieder *et al.* (2002) for same–different judgment. The monkeys decide whether a sample numerosity (numeral appearing above each curve) matches a subsequently presented numerosity (abscissa, log scale). The curves appear as shifted versions of the curve in (**B**) again indicating that performance depends solely on log ratio.

Numerosity labeling

A final task consists in asking the subject to label numerosities using a set of verbal or nonverbal labels. For instance, one may ask human subjects to label sets of dots ranging from 10 to 100 with round numbers such as the decade names 'ten' to 'ninety' (Izard, 2005). Chimpanzees have also been trained to label numerosities using the Arabic digits 1–9 (Matsuzawa, 1985; Tomonaga and Matsuzawa, 2002). In humans, this task can be complicated by the use of slow but exact counting strategies, which fall beyond the scope of the present theory. In animals, however, and perhaps also in human cultures with few number words and no overt counting system, the proposal is that subjects do not count serially, but merely apply symbolic labels to their mental representations of approximate numerosity (Dehaene and Mehler, 1992; Tomonaga and Matsuzawa, 2002; Gordon, 2004; Pica *et al.*, 2004).

The theory for such numerosity-labeling tasks, developed by Izard (2005) assumes that, for each target numerosity *n*, subjects generate an internal representation *X* of the target numerosity, thus a Gaussian random variable centered on log(*n*), and respond with the verbal label *r* whose canonical representation on the number line log(*r*) falls closest to log(*n*). This strategy implies that the number line continuum is divided into distinct response domains according to a set of response criteria forming a *response grid* (Figure 24.3A). The response domain corresponding to response r_1 is separated from the domain corresponding to the next response r_2 by response criterion

$$c_+(r_1)=c_-(r_2)=Log\left(\sqrt{r_1 r_2}\right)$$

(24.13)

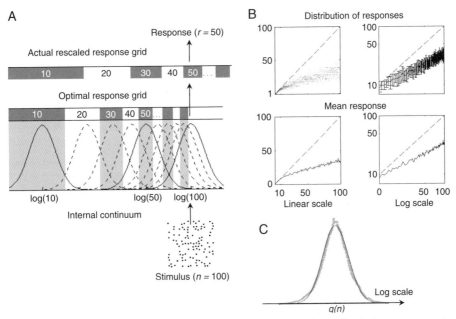

Figure 24.3 (**A**) Model of approximate numerosity naming (Izard, 2006). The input numerosity, once coded on the logarithmic number line, is categorized according to a response grid which is an affine rescaled version of the optimal logarithmically scaled grid. (**B**) Numerosity-naming responses of a representative subject, showing power-law responding with Weberian variability on a linear scale (left), and linear performance with fixed variability on a log–log scale (right). (**C**) Reconstructed distribution of the random variable leading to response choice [on a log scale, after centering on the modal value *q(n)* and averaging across all targets and subjects]. The observed distribution tightly fits the predicted Gaussian.

A complication is that subjects' responses are often poorly calibrated. For instance it is quite common for subjects to respond 'fifty' to a set of 100 or 200 dots (Minturn and Reese, 1951; Krueger, 1982). Véronique Izard showed that a simple assumption could still capture the subject's behavior. The assumption is that miscalibration is due to an affine scaling of the entire response grid. That is, instead of applying the optimal response criteria defined above, subjects actually use a linearly scaled grid of response criteria

$$c'_+ (r_1) = a\, c_-(r_1) + b = a\, Log\left(\sqrt{r_1\, r_2}\right) + b$$

(24.14)

where a is a stretch parameter and b a shift parameter, both of which typically differ from their optimal values (respectively 1 and 0).

Given this theory of the response selection process, the model predicts the frequency with which response r will be selected in response to numerosity n:

$$P(n,r) = \int_{ac_-(r)+b}^{ac_+(r)+b} \frac{e^{-\frac{(x-Log(n))^2}{2w^2}}}{\sqrt{2\pi w}}\, dx$$

(24.15)

In principle, this equation allows computation of any aspect of the subject's responses to any numerosity. In practice, it is difficult to obtain formal mathematical results. However, using plausible approximations, Izard (2005) was able to compute the subject's mean response to a given numerosity n. Interestingly, the response increases nonlinearly, as a power-law of the true numerosity n:

$$\overline{r(n)} = n^{\frac{1}{a}} e^{\frac{w^2}{2a^2} - \frac{b}{a}}$$

(24.16)

Izard (2005) showed that the above model provided a remarkably good fit to human subjects' numerosity naming data in the range 10–100. All subjects were initially miscalibrated and severely underestimated numerosity. In those cases, the predicted power-law relation was observed (see example in Figure 24.3B). A single example of a numerosity–name pairing was sufficient to recalibrate them to a quasi-linear relation. This recalibration process was well captured by a change in the parameters a and b. Furthermore, variability in the subjects' responses increased with stimulus numerosity on a linear scale, but became constant and with a linear stimulus–response relation once the data were plotted on a log–log scale (Figure 24.3B). Because a very large number of responses was collected for each subject, the data allowed for a reconstruction of the distribution of the internal random variable leading to response selection. On a logarithmic axis, this distribution traced an almost perfect Gaussian curve (Figure 24.3C).

In spite of these successes in modeling numerosity naming data, there are at least two directions where the theory will require extension. First, the theory assumes nonoverlapping response domains: each portion of the number line can be referred to by a single symbolic label. In natural speech, however, there are competing words or phrases for each numerosity. For instance the same quantity 13 can be truthfully named with variable degrees of precision as 'thirteen', 'a dozen' or 'ten–fifteen'. Dehaene and Mehler (1992) have proposed that each numeral has a defined response range, which is larger for round numbers such as 'fifteen' than for other numbers such as 'thirteen' (see also Pollmann and Jansen, 1996). Exactly how number word selection should be modeled in the presence of such competing responses and variable context remains to be determined.

A second area open to further research concerns tasks in which, instead of using a small set of discrete labels, the subject labels numerosity with a continuous or quasi-continuous response, for instance by tapping a key approximately as many times as the numerosity that was presented (Mechner, 1958; Whalen *et al.*, 1999; Cordes *et al.*, 2001). Such tasks probably do not involve the setting of a response grid, but rather a continuous monitoring of the numerosity being produced and a simple decision rule for stopping when that numerosity is thought to match or exceed the memorized one—a process which will not be further discussed here (but see for example Gibbon, 1977; Gibbon and Fairhurst, 1994).

Numerical response times

We now turn to the mental chronometry of arithmetic tasks. In many of the above tasks, response times vary systematically in parallel with the percentage of correct responses. Can arithmetic decision times also be accounted for by a simple mathematical model?

Theory

A simple idea concerning decisions under uncertainty was first introduced by Alan Turing in a cryptographic context, and a few years later by the statistician Abraham Wald (1947). In their view, the reason why decisions take a variable time which depends on the quality of the evidence, is because evidence must be accumulated until a pre-defined level of statistical certainty is achieved. The idea was imported into psychology by Stone (1960) and Laming (1968), then extended by Link (1975, 1990, 1992), Ratcliff (1988), Ratcliff and Rouder, 1998), and many others (e.g. Schwarz, 2001; Page *et al.*, 2004; Sigman and Dehaene, 2005). It plays a key role in modern models of decision making and response time distributions (for accessible syntheses, see Gold and Shadlen, 2001, 2002; Usher and McClelland, 2001; Smith and Ratcliff, 2004).

Here I shall explain this theory only in the case of a simple two-alternative decision (e.g. larger–smaller comparison; see Figure 24.1). Assume that the subject is presented with a target numerosity n, but instead of a single representative x, now has at its disposal a time series of independent samples x_t on the internal number line. According to Bayes' rule, each new sample allows updating of the posterior probability that the response R_j is the correct one, given all of the previous samples:

$$P(R_j|x_{1..t+1}) = P(x_{t+1}|R_j)\, P(R_j|x_{1...t}) / P(x_{t+1}) \qquad (24.17)$$

When only two responses are allowed, the mathematics can be simplified because a single quantity, the log-likelihood ratio (LLR), suffices to track how each additional sample changes the decision probabilities. This quantity is defined by the following equation:

$$LLR(t) = Log\left(\frac{P(R_2 \mid x_{1..t})}{P(R_1 \mid x_{1..t})}\right) \qquad (24.18)$$

Intuitively, the *LLR* measures the relative amount of support for response 2 over response 1. It is positive if the majority of the data supports response 2, and negative if it supports response 1. By Bayes' rule, one has

$$LLR(t+1) = LLR(t) + Log\left(\frac{P(x_{t+1} \mid R_2)}{P(x_{t+1} \mid R_1)}\right) = \sum_{i=1}^{t+1} Log\left(\frac{P(x_i \mid R_2)}{P(x_i \mid R_1)}\right) + Log\left(\frac{P(R_2)}{P(R_1)}\right)$$

(24.19)

This formula indicates that, by simple summation, one can add up the contributions of each random sample towards the decision (including a possible initial bias for one of the two responses). The successive bits of information contributed by each new sample should be added to produce an *internal random walk*. As time passes, the accumulated *LLR* will vary somewhat randomly up and down. However, if there is a consistent signal in the internal samples, it should progressively drift towards either positive or negative values. An optimal decision consists in waiting until the LLR has reached one of two fixed bounds $\pm\theta$, and then responding with response R_2 if LLR is positive, and with response R_1 if LLR is negative.

The value of θ, which is set by the subject, specifies the desired error rate. θ also determines how the subject deals with the speed–accuracy trade-off. Setting θ to a low value means that the decision threshold will be reached quickly, but with many errors (because internal noise will often lead the internal random walk to the wrong decision bound). Setting θ to a higher value means that decisions will be slower, but more accurate. A theory for the optimal choice of parameter θ, depending on the rewarding scheme and inter-trial interval, has been presented (Bogacz *et al.*, 2006).

Discrimination task

Although the formula that gives the increment to the LLR as a function of the observed internal sample x_i is complex, it becomes simpler in some particular cases such as the above-discussed numerosity discrimination task, where one must simply decide which of two possible numerosities n_1 or n_2 was presented. In this case, the formula becomes:

$$LLR(t+1) = \frac{Log(r)}{w^2} \sum_{i=1}^{t+1} (x_i - Log\sqrt{n_1 n_2}) + Log\left(\frac{P(R_2)}{P(R_1)}\right)$$

(24.20)

Since the samples x_i are Gaussian, this equation indicates that the random walk consists in a sum of Gaussian steps proportional to $x_i - c$, where $c = log(\sqrt{n_1 n_2})$. Quite intuitively, those steps are positive if the sample x_i is above the mid-point between $log(n_1)$ and $log(n_2)$, and negative otherwise. The mean and standard deviation of the step size are:

$$\mu = \pm\frac{Log(r)^2}{2w^2} \quad and \quad \sigma = \frac{Log(r)}{w}$$

(24.21)

Once again, they indicate that all aspects of performance (errors, mean RT, RT distribution) should depend solely on the log ratio r of the two numerosities n_1 and n_2.

Other tasks

In most other tasks, the mathematics becomes more complicated. According to the normative theory of optimal decision making outlined above, the step size should be

$$Log\left(\frac{P(x \mid R_2)}{P(x \mid R_1)}\right)$$

This function of x is usually rather complicated and need not be linear or even monotonic with x. Thus, the random-walk steps may have an unusual, mathematically intractable distribution. Nevertheless, in many cases the Gaussian random walk can be used as an analytically tractable approximation. It is also possible that the neural systems for decision making rely on such a Gaussian approximation because it is easier to compute neurally (Gold and Shadlen, 2001). Thus, in the literature, it is frequently assumed that each decision is based on a Gaussian random walk defined, for a given target numerosity n, by parameters μ and σ specifying the mean and standard deviation of the steps per unit of time. If needed, one may compare those analytic calculations with simulations of many random walks that behave according to the exact *LLR* equations.

Predictions of the model

In the Gaussian random-walk model, the decision time is defined as the first point at which the random walk crosses one of two absorbing barriers $+\theta$ and $-\theta$. Determining the distribution of decision time is a mathematically well-defined and physically well-known diffusion problem, for which much is known (see e.g. Wald, 1947; Link, 1992). Here I consider only the simplest case where there is no initial bias for either response.

First, performance and error rates can be computed. A generic formula for response rates (valid also for non-Gaussian steps) is:

$$P_{R=R_2} = \frac{1}{1+e^{-\lambda\theta}}$$

$$(24.22)$$

where λ depends on the distribution of the random walk steps

$$\left(\lambda = \frac{2\mu}{\sigma^2} \text{ for Gaussian steps}\right).$$

This equation shows that, in the random walk model, the dependence of errors on mean step size μ (hence on distance in a number comparison task, for instance) is a sigmoid function. Remember that, in the classical signal detection theory, the predicted function is the integral of a Gaussian. Although those functions differ in theory, they are sufficiently similar as to be empirically indistinguishable. However, the random walk model presents the advantage of capturing the well-known observation of a speed–accuracy trade-off: as shown by Equation 24.22, performance is not fixed, but increases in a predictable manner with θ, the response threshold.

The mean response times can also be predicted as:

$$RT = T_0 + \frac{\theta}{\mu}(2P_{R=R_2} - 1)$$

$$(24.23)$$

where T_0 is a constant additional time corresponding to the total duration of nondecision processes (e.g. perceptual and motor components). Note that RT decreases as an inverse function of step size, a function which is shallower than the above error curve. The sigmoid shape of errors and inverse shape of RTs as a function of log ratio constitute clear predictions of the random-walk model.

Finally, the variance and even the distribution of RTs can be calculated analytically (Smith and Ratcliff, 2004; Wagenmakers *et al.*, 2006). There is an exact formula for the probability density function of RT, but it is quite complex. A simpler formula can be obtained if one considers, as a first approximation, the problem of a random walk process hitting a *single* barrier (thus neglecting the effect of errors). Obviously this will be a good approximation only if the task and subject threshold afford relative error-free performance. In this case, the probability density function of RT is

$$p(RT \in [t, t+dt]) = \frac{\theta}{\sigma \sqrt{2\pi(t-T_0)^3}} \, e^{-\frac{(\theta - \mu(t-T_0))^2}{2\sigma^2(t-T_0)}} \, dt$$

(24.24)

A problem with the random-walk model, known at least since Laming (1968), is that it predicts an identical distribution of correct and error RTs. This problem, however, has been corrected in slightly more complicated versions of the model that assume trial-to-trial variability in the starting point of the random walk, the decision threshold, and/or the mean step size (Ratcliff and Rouder, 1998; Smith and Ratcliff, 2004). Naturally, those models have many additional free parameters.

Model identification

A specific difficulty with random-walk models is that their complexity often precludes easy identification of their parameters based on the available response time data. In the simplest model considered here, the minimum parameters that need to be fitted to each stimulus condition are: T_0 (nondecision time), θ (decision threshold), and μ (mean step size).[4] Here I consider two simple and effective strategies (for more sophisticated approaches, see e.g. Ratcliff and Tuerlinckx, 2002).[5]

Strategy 1

This strategy, which I derived from equations in Link (1992), requires only the mean RT and mean error rate in each cell of the experimental design (e.g. for each target number n).

---

[4] The standard deviation of step size, σ, is not independent of the other parameters once the time unit is fixed. It can thus be arbitrarily fixed (here, I took $\sigma = 1$).

[5] Both strategies will fail for cells of the experimental design which contain 0% or 100% errors. In such cases, it is possible to regularize the data by adding $1/2$ to the count of error trials.

From Equations 24.22 and 24.23, we first derive a simple relation between mean RT and errors:

$$RT(n) = T_0 + \frac{4\theta^2}{\sigma^2} \frac{P_{R=R_2}(n) - \frac{1}{2}}{Log\frac{P_{R=R_2}(n)}{1 - P_{R=R_2}(n)}}$$

(24.25)

This equation predicts that, across a range of stimulus conditions, there should be a linear relation between mean RT and a transformed function of the error rates. Thus, a first test of the random-walk model consists in checking, by linear regression, if this linear relation holds. If it does, then the intercept and the slope of the linear regression will provide estimates of T_0 and θ (assuming a fixed σ). Once these two parameters have been inferred, using Equation 24.23 μ can be estimated for each target n as

$$\mu(n) = \frac{\theta(2P_{R=R_2}(n) - 1)}{RT(n) - T_0}$$

(24.26)

The advantage of this procedure is that it includes an internal check of the validity of the random-walk model. The disadvantages include the assumption that T_0 and θ are identical across conditions, and that there is no response bias. The quality of the estimation is also highly dependent on the quality of the RT-error regression. If the data include errors due to another source, for instance guessing or inattention, then T_0 will be overestimated. For blocks of numerical comparison with a fixed notation, however, the assumption of fixed T_0 and θ is reasonable (the assumption is that perceptual and motor time are identical for all numbers, and that subjects set their criterion prior to seeing the target number). As we shall see, under these conditions the procedure recovers highly stable estimations of μ.

Strategy 2. Wagenmakers's EZ-diffusion model

This strategy is described in detail in (Wagenmakers *et al.*, 2006), so the equations will not be reproduced here. The strategy requires measurement of the mean RT, the variance of RT, and the mean error rate in each cell of the experimental design. From those three measures, an explicit formula recovers the parameters μ, T_0, and θ. Thus, an advantage of the EZ model is that it allows independent computation of all three parameters of the random-walk model separately for each cell of the experimental design. These parameters can then be submitted to an analysis of variance. Thus, unlike in strategy 1, one can explicitly test whether T_0 and θ remain fixed across experimental conditions. On the negative side, the strategy assumes that there is no response bias (see Wagenmakers, 2006, for more complicated alternatives) and is somewhat unstable numerically.

Experimental evidence

Number comparison

Number comparison is the numerical task that has received the most extensive treatment by the random-walk model (Link, 1975, 1990, 1992). I have verified that the model accounts for the performance and RTs in the data sets at my disposal (e.g. Dehaene, 1989; Dehaene et al., 1990, 1998; Piazza et al., 2004). Here I shall consider only a particularly dense set of data kindly provided to me by Cantlon and Brannon (2006), and which allows for a thorough test of the validity of the random-walk model in two species. In Cantlon and Brannon's experiment, two monkeys and 11 human subjects were presented with arrays of dots ranging from two to 30 dots. They had to select the smaller array or, in other blocks, the larger array. Here I have averaged across those two types of blocks.

Figure 24.4 shows the data and fits of the random-walk model obtained using strategy 1. The top graphs indicate that, in both species, the variations of RT and error rate with the distance between the compared numerosities (as measured by the logarithm of their ratio) are well captured by the functions predicted by the model. I verified that a much worse prediction is obtained if the numerical distance is measured by the difference between the two numerosities, rather than by the difference of their logarithms.

Note that the distance effect is steeper on error rates than on mean RTs, as predicted. In each species, the bottom left graph examines the linear relation between RT and transformed error rate predicted by Link (1975, 1992). This relation is verified in both humans and monkeys, and allows for an estimation of T_0 and θ. Interestingly, the response threshold θ is very similar across species (monkeys: 16.3; humans: 18.0), but the nondecision time appears slower in humans (monkeys: 342 ms; humans: 462 ms).

Most importantly, the mean step size of the random walk is an almost perfectly linear function of the log ratio of the two numbers (bottom right graphs in Figure 24.2). This linear function has a null intercept, i.e. the subjects appear not to be able to accumulate any information as the difference between the two numerosities becomes very small. The entire curve fits with the theory, which states that subjects accumulate a stochastic signal proportional to the difference of the log-Gaussian numerosity estimates provided by the two sets of dots. The slope of that function estimates, for a given numerical difference, the quantity of information that is accumulated per unit of time. Interestingly, this quantity, which plays a role similar to the internal Weber fraction in the simpler signal detection model, is somewhat smaller in monkeys (0.66) than in humans (0.99). This finding is in agreement with Cantlon and Brannon's conclusion that monkeys are somewhat less sensitive to numerosity information than (educated) humans.

Neuronal modeling

For a long time, the random-walk model was a purely psychological tool, and it was unclear whether it bore any relationship to actual neural network mechanisms. Recently, however, experiments and models on the neural mechanisms of decision making have flourished. Gold and Shadlen (2001, 2002) describe how neuronal populations might compute quantities relevant to the random-walk model. Furthermore, Mazurek et al. (2003)

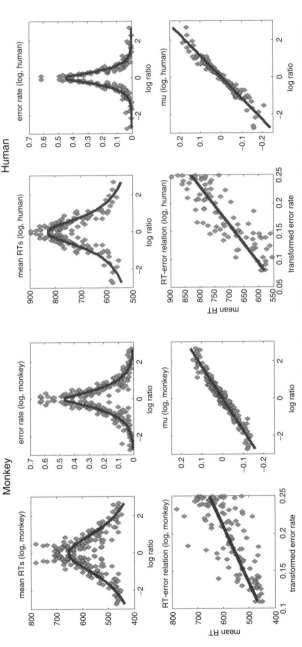

Figure 24.4 Analysis of numerosity comparison data using the random-walk model (reanalysis of data from Cantlon and Brannon, 2006). Two monkeys and 11 human subjects performed a larger–smaller comparison task on the same pairs of stimuli. Top panels show the mean reaction times (RTs) and mean error rates as a function of the log of the ratio of the two numbers, together with the best fits derived from the model. Note the different scales for monkeys and humans. The bottom left panel shows the predicted linear relation between RTs and transformed error rates (Equation 24.25 in the main text). Finally, the bottom right shows the most important 'hidden variable' recovered by the random-walk analysis, namely, μ, which characterizes the amount of information accumulated per unit of time. A different μ is estimated for each pair of numbers, and these μ-values are plotted as a function of log ratio. As predicted by the log-Gaussian model, μ increases linearly with the log ratio.

have proposed an explicit simulation model (see also Usher and McClelland, 2001), and Wong and Wang (2006) have described a neuro-realistic implementation of an accumulation-like neural decision process. Here, I briefly review these contributions.

Gold and Shadlen first note that the LLR, or a quantity monotonically related to it, can be quite easily computed as the difference of activity of two populations of neurons: those voting in favor of response R_1, and those voting in favor of response R_2. Thus, in the case of numerical tasks, a decision can be taken by selecting two relevant pools of numerosity-detecting neurons (e.g. those coding respectively for numbers smaller and larger than some reference), and computing the difference of their mean firing rates. The latter differencing operation can be accomplished either by a balance of excitatory and inhibitory feedforward connections, or by lateral competition between two competing populations of cells.

A second step consists in accumulating those difference signals. Mazurek *et al.* (2003) have shown how this can be accomplished by populations of decision neurons with a time delay and a self-connection. Intuitively, using those self-connections, the decision neurons can feed back onto themselves the neural activation that they received in the past, and hence maintain an accumulated record of the total amount. Wong and Wang (2006) have presented a realistic neuronal model of this process (see also Usher and McClelland, 2001; Machens *et al.*, 2005). Wong and Wang consider pools of selective and nonselective excitatory neurons connected to a pool of inhibitory inter-neurons. They explicitly calculate the mean field dynamics of this system in the presence of an input signal favoring one or the other populations. The bifurcation diagram shows how this dynamical system approximates the accumulator needed in the random-walk theory: the accumulated evidence progressively pushes the activity of the two competing neuronal pools away from a saddle point and towards one of two attractors corresponding to the two possible decisions, in a time directly related to the amount of input evidence.[6]

Thus, two key components of the random-walk model (LLR formation and accumulator mechanism) have received a plausible neuronal implementation. Still, it should be noted that there is currently no comprehensive model of an entire decision task at the neuronal level. Such a model would require specifying: (1) how task instructions lead to the selection of the appropriate pools of neurons; (2) how these neurons become transitorily linked to the appropriate decision units, with the appropriate excitatory or inhibitory weights; (3) how the decision threshold, leading to motor response initiation, is implemented. A model of tactile frequency comparison, which comes close to achieving these goals, has been recently presented by Machens *et al.* (2005; see also Lo and Wang, 2006).

Neurobiological and neuroimaging evidence

The plausibility of the random-walk model of simple response decisions was greatly strengthened when Michael Shadlen and colleagues discovered neuronal signals that

---

[6] Interestingly, in this neuronal model the evidence accrual process deviates from the neutral point at an exponential rate, a possibility that has rarely been considered in behavioral models, but may fit response time data better (see Page *et al.*, 2004).

appeared as plausible neural correlates of a stochastic accumulation process (Kim and Shadlen, 1999; Gold and Shadlen, 2001, 2002). Here I mention these data only briefly, because in spite of their intrinsic interest, they do not directly concern numerical tasks. During a motion judgment task, neurons whose firing appeared to constitute a plausible correlate of evidence accumulation were identified, first in prefrontal cortex (Kim and Shadlen, 1999), then in area LIP (Shadlen and Newsome, 2001) and other regions such as superior colliculus. The cells began deviating from baseline firing rates at a fixed latency of about 200 ms after the stimulus, and showed, on average, steadily increasing firing rates with a slope proportional to the amount of sensory evidence (here, the proportion of coherent motion in the display). Finally, they predicted the response of the animal, which appeared to be emitted once the neurons reached a fixed level of firing. All of these data have been captured in detail by the above-described neuronal models (Mazurek *et al.*, 2003; see also Smith and Ratcliff, 2004; Wong and Wang, 2006; Lo and Wang, 2006).

Other tasks have yielded similar data. In particular, Ranulfo Romo's team has characterized neuronal firing in many cortical areas during a tactile frequency comparison task (Romo and Salinas, 2003). Romo *et al.* have identified neurons, particularly in prefrontal cortex, whose activity initially increases with the evidence accrued from the first stimulus; they then subtract the evidence accrued from the second stimulus before converging to a decision as to which of these two quantities is the largest. This process seems to be highly similar to that postulated for numerical comparison, although for unknown reasons tactile frequency appears to be encoded by the monotonically increasing or decreasing firing of neurons rather than by Gaussian tuning to a specific value.

Decision processes based on differencing followed by accumulation have also been reported in humans using indirect neuroimaging methods. Most notably, when humans are asked to decide whether a noisy image depicts a face or a house, left dorsolateral prefrontal cortex activity is proportional to the difference between activation in the fusiform face area and in the parahippocampal place area and predicts behavioral performance (Heekeren *et al.*, 2004). Thus, this region, inscribed in a network of areas involving parietal and prefrontal regions, appears engaged in decision by evidence accumulation in humans. It seems likely that the same decision network would be involved in numerical tasks, but this has not been firmly demonstrated yet.

Symbolic and nonsymbolic numbers

Up to now, I have considered only the processing of nonsymbolic numerosities. I now turn to the processing of symbolic stimuli such as numbers presented as Arabic numerals or as written or spoken numerals.

Theory

How do written and spoken symbols come to have meaning? The *symbol grounding problem* consists in understanding how arbitrary shapes can ever acquire genuine meanings, over and above a mere network of relations to other symbols (Harnad, 1990). In the special case of numbers, I have proposed a simple solution to this grounding problem (Dehaene, 1997; see also Gelman and Gallistel, 1978). The nonsymbolic representation of numerosity is universally present in infants and adults of all cultures, and precedes the acquisition of linguistic symbols for numbers. When we learn number symbols, we simply learn to attach their arbitrary shapes to the relevant nonsymbolic quantity representations. Thus, the symbol '3' comes to evoke the very same representation that would be evoked by a set of three dots, namely a Gaussian distribution of activation over numerosity detector neurons. In neurophysiological terms, in the course of learning the meaning of numerals, neuronal assemblies involved in auditory and visual symbol analysis (respectively left superior temporal and bilateral ventral occipito-temporal cortices) must develop connections, direct or indirect, to neuronal assemblies in the depth of the intraparietal cortex.

According to an extreme version of this hypothesis, symbolic and nonsymbolic arithmetic tasks should then be captured by a single mathematical model with identical parameters including the internal weber fraction w. This hypothesis might be appropriate for certain experiments in which monkeys and apes are trained to recognize arabic digits and to attach them to the relevant numerosities by a pure process of association (Matsuzawa, 1985; Washburn and Rumbaugh, 1991; Tomonaga and Matsuzawa, 2002). Indeed, in those experiments, error rates are consistent with the use of estimation strategies comparable to those captured by the above mathematical model. However, there are reasons to believe that the situation might be more complex in humans. The acquisition of numerical symbols seems to provide access to a new level of competence for exact arithmetic. This conclusion is supported by several pieces of evidence. Cross-culturally, subjects whose culture has very few number words fail in exact arithmetic tasks that children in our culture easily perform (Gordon, 2004; Pica et al., 2004). Developmentally, the acquisition of counting is accompanied by a sudden emergence of precise responding, for instance in the 'give-a-number' task (Wynn, 1992b). Finally, neuroimaging and neuropsychological data indicate an association of exact arithmetic tasks with linguistic codes (Dehaene et al., 1999; Lemer et al., 2003).

To account for these unique consequences of acquiring symbolic information, a minimal assumption might be that the precision of the quantity code is modified by the acquisition of number symbols (Dehaene, 1997). Through interaction with a precise system, where each number n is distinguished categorically from its neighbours $n-1$ and $n+1$, the tuning curves of numerosity detector neurons would become narrower, and the number line representation would crystallize into categorically distinct domains (Pica et al., 2004). In keeping with Steven Kosslyn's hypothesis of hemispheric specialization for categorical versus coordinate relations (Kosslyn et al., 1989), one might expect this refinement of numerical precision to occur mostly in the left hemisphere, which is also in more direct connection to linguistic symbols. For mathematical modeling purposes, we would then assume that all of the above formulas, developed for nonsymbolic numerosities, continue to hold for symbolic number processing, merely with a smaller value of the Weber fraction w.

While this is a viable model, a recent neural network simulation suggests that exposure to symbols may induce even more changes to the numerosity network (Verguts and Fias, 2004) (see Figure 24.5). Verguts and Fias used nonsupervised learning in a network exposed either to numerosity information alone, or to numerosity paired with an approximate symbol (coarsely approximating a child's inputs during acquisition of number words). Each symbolic input was coded by an arbitrary discrete unit. When nonsymbolic information alone was presented, the network developed numerosity detectors similar to Nieder and Miller's neurons and possessing all of the key properties of the standard model (skewed tuning curves on a linear axis, which become Gaussian when plotted on a logarithmic axis). Crucially, after pairing with symbolic information, the same numerosity detector units became tuned to symbols as well. Yet, there were two key differences between the unit's responses to symbolic and nonsymbolic inputs (see Figure 24.5). First, the tuning curves for symbolic inputs were much sharper. The simulated neurons essentially have a discrete, all-or-none peak of firing for their preferred value (thus each neuron cares mostly about a single, precise number), but they also show a shallow surrounding area of local preference for neighbouring numbers. Second, the tuning curves no longer broaden as the numbers increase (Weber's law), rather they have a fixed width for all numbers tested (1–5). Thus, the network develops a new type of representation, *linear with fixed variability*.

What I find most interesting in Verguts and Fias's proposal is that the very same neurons are involved in coding the quantity meaning of symbolic and nonsymbolic numerical information. The predictions for neural recordings are clear. When tested with symbolic and nonsymbolic inputs, each neuron would show the same preferred quantity in both domains. Only the tuning curve would be narrower for symbolic than for nonsymbolic

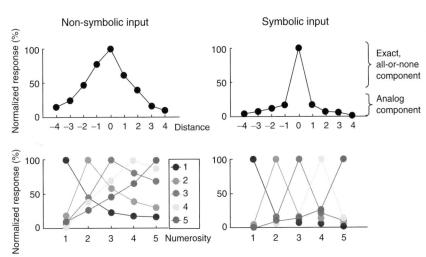

Figure 24.5 Numerical coding scheme emerging from Verguts and Fias's (2004) neuronal network after exposure to paired symbolic and nonsymbolic numerosities. When presented with nonsymbolic numerosities (left), the simulated neurons show broad distance-dependent tuning curves (top) that increase in width when plotted on a linear numerosity scale (bottom). When presented with symbolic numerals (right), the same neurons show sharp tuning curves (top) with fixed width as the number increases (bottom).

inputs, and this difference would increase as the numbers become larger. The fact that the same neurons are involved means that there should be partial transfer of learning: if we learned to perform exact arithmetic tasks, using quantities derived from symbolic inputs, the same circuits would then be capable of performing the same operations approximately when nonsymbolic inputs are presented. Verguts and Fias's model thus proposes a concrete implementation of how a single brain area can be involved in both approximate and exact calculation modes (Dehaene, 1992; Dehaene and Cohen, 1995).

Verguts and Fias's proposal can be further extended. It seems possible that only some of the numerosity detector neurons acquire this more precise 'numerical receptive field' as a result of being associated with symbols. Even in educated human adults, some numerosity detector neurons, particularly in the right hemisphere, might keep their approximate tuning curves. These neurons might then encode the approximate meanings of 'round numbers' such as ten, fifteen, or a dozen (Dehaene and Mehler, 1992). The existence of an intermediate range of such neurons, with variable tuning precision, might explain the linguistic universal of two-numeral constructions (e.g. 'ten twelve books', 'ten fifteen books', 'ten twenty books'), by which we can refer symbolically not only to a quantity, but also to its variable degree of precision (Pollmann and Jansen, 1996).

Do these possibilities exhaust the transformations induced to our semantic system by the acquisition of symbolic numerals? No. There is evidence that humans possess a rich semantic lexicon for numbers. This lexicon specifies at least the parity and divisibility properties of numbers (e.g. primes, powers of two, multiplication facts) (Dehaene et al., 1993), but also more anecdotal semantic information such as famous dates, brands, etc. (e.g. 1492, 747) (Cohen et al., 1994). At the moment, however, incorporating such complex semantic information is way beyond the scope of our simple mathematical model.

Experimental evidence

Distance effects with symbolic numerals

The hypothesis that symbolic numerals inherit many of the properties of the nonsymbolic numerosity representation has been validated in a large number of experiments. A first indication of its plausibility came from Moyer and Landauer's (1967) finding of a distance effect when subjects compared two arabic digits. Although there was no similarity between stimuli at the symbol level, the subjects' behavior indicated the use of a mental representation of quantity where conceptual similarity varies with quantity proximity. This observation was quickly extended to many tasks. Distance effects have been observed in two-digit numeral comparison (Hinrichs et al., 1981; Dehaene, 1989; Dehaene et al., 1990), with detailed characteristics that seemed largely compatible with the random-walk model (Link, 1990; Page et al., 2004; Sigman and Dehaene, 2005) (see below). Even when deciding whether two number symbols are the same or not, response times vary with numerical distance, suggesting a high automaticity of the symbol-to-quantity conversion pathway (Duncan and McFarland, 1980; Dehaene and Akhavein, 1995).

Stages of processing of symbolic numerals

The notion that symbolic numerals, regardless of their notation, pass through successive stages of symbol recognition followed by conversion to a nonverbal quantity code in parietal cortex was verified in several publications. I initially tested this issue using event-related potentials (ERPs) and the additive-factors method (Dehaene, 1996). During a comparison task with numbers presented as written words or as arabic numerals, response times showed additive effects of three factors: notation used (arabic or verbal), numerical distance, and motor effector (left or right hand). Additivity is consistent with serial stages of (1) numeral recognition, (2), notation-independent quantity comparison, and (3) response programming and execution. ERPs revealed signatures of all three stages, with a fast spread of activation first in left and right ventral occipito-temporal regions involved in numeral recognition, then in bilateral parietal cortices, where a distance effect was found, and finally in motor cortex. The separation between notation-dependent but distance-independent numeral processing in ventral occipito-temporal cortex, and notation-independent but distance-dependent quantity processing in intraparietal cortex, was later replicated in fMRI (Pinel *et al.*, 2001, 2004).

Recently, Mariano Sigman and I used another chronometric technique to examine the decomposition of the number comparison task into processing stages (Sigman and Dehaene, 2005, 2006). In a psychological refractory period (PRP) design, we asked subjects to perform the number comparison task together with another unrelated pitch categorization task with tones presented at variable SOAs relative to number onset. Using the locus of slack logic (Pashler, 1984), we showed that notation- and response-dependent stages of the task could be performed in parallel with stages of the tone task, but that the distance-dependent stage could not—it was performed strictly serially with the response decision stage of the tone task. We also showed that the response time distribution expected from the random-walk model (Equation 24.24) fitted the data superbly, and that this distribution was shifted accordingly when the numerical decision was delayed by the tone decision. This study thus confirms the parsing of the number comparison task into notation-dependent and quantity-dependent stages and suggests that only the latter involves a 'central system' or 'global workspace' that can only perform one operation at a time (Dehaene and Changeux, 2004).

Cerebral convergence of symbolic and nonsymbolic information

Manuela Piazza, Philippe Pinel and I recently used fMRI adaptation to test directly the hypothesis of common neural populations for symbolic numerals and nonsymbolic numerosities (Piazza *et al.*, 2006). During several minutes, subjects attended to the repeated presentation, every 1200 ms, of an approximate quantity presented either as a set of dots (e.g. 17, 18, or 19 dots) or as an arabic numeral (the numerals 17, 18 or 19). We verified that the BOLD fMRI signal adapted over the course of about 40 s in left and right intraparietal cortices, within regions isolated using an independent localizer scan (subtraction task). We then introduced sparse deviants which could be close or far quantities (e.g. 20 or 50), and could appear in the same or different notation. The results replicated our earlier finding that the intraparietal cortex signal shows a distance-dependent recovery from adaptation (Piazza *et al.*, 2004). Crucially, they also showed that this recovery holds even when the notation changes. This finding suggests, indirectly, that there must be populations of numerosity detector neurons jointly activated by symbolic and nonsymbolic notations, so that they can be habituated by one and transfer this habituation to the other.

Interestingly, in left parietal cortex, the effect was asymmetrical. When adaptation was to dots and the deviants were arabic numerals, there was recovery of adaptation to far but not to close quantities. However, when adaptation was to arabic numerals and the deviants were dots, there was recovery of adaptation to both close and far quantities (e.g. adaptation to 17–18–19, recovery to both 20 and 50). This finding suggests, in keeping with Verguts and Fias's (2004) model, that the quantities evoked by Arabic numerals may be more precise than those evoked by nonsymbolic sets of dots, at least in the left hemisphere, and hence the neuronal populations adapted by Arabic stimuli were narrower than those evoked by dot presentations. In the future, fMRI adaptation could be used to test more directly Verguts and Fias's (2004) model by plotting the profile of the adaptation curve as a function of numerical distance, and using this profile to infer the neuronal tuning curves for symbolic and nonsymbolic stimuli (Piazza *et al.*, 2004).

Acquisition of symbolic numerals

While several neuroimaging studies have observed nonsymbolic quantity representations in parietal cortex in young children (Temple and Posner, 1998; Cantlon *et al.*, 2006), very few studies have examined the acquisition of number symbols. The theory that I have outlined stipulates that, in the course of development, an increasingly automatized connection develops between ventral regions for symbol shape identification and intraparietal regions for quantity representation. Consistent with this idea, a recent fMRI study (Rivera *et al.*, 2005) has examined the evolution of brain activity with age (8–19 years) during a simple symbolic arithmetic task which was performed with equal accuracy at all ages. While most regions showed a decrease in brain activity, particularly in prefrontal cortex, suggesting a progressive automatization, only two regions showed an increase: left occipito-temporal cortex and left parietal cortex, exactly as predicted.

Log-to-linear shift during development

An interesting prediction unique to Verguts and Fias's model is that the acquisition of number symbols is accompanied by a change in the internal semantic representation. While the representation of nonsymbolic numerosity is logarithmically compressed, Verguts and Fias's model implies that the symbolic representation is linear. In their simulations, when activated by symbols, numerosity detector neurons have fixed tuning curves on a linear scale, suggesting that they encode a linear, fixed variability scale no longer subject to Weber's law. This prediction can be tentatively related to observations of a shift from a logarithmic to a linear mapping of number onto a spatial scale in the course of development (Siegler and Opfer, 2003). Siegler and Opfer asked their subjects (8-, 10- or 12-year-old children, plus an adult group) to point to the locations of numbers on a spatially extended segment labelled from 1 to 100 (or from 1 to 1000). Children of all ages performed this task well; both monotonically mapped number onto space, in agreement with the hypothesis that numerical quantities are represented internally on an internal continuum analogous to a mental 'number line' (Hubbard *et al.*, 2005). Furthermore, the older children (12-year-olds and adults) organized the numbers linearly, spreading them evenly on the spatial scale. However, the youngest children (8–10-year-olds) spontaneously implemented a compressive mapping which was well captured by a logarithmic function. For instance, they place 10 close to the middle of 1 and 100, and grouped all of the larger numbers towards the large end.

Siegler and Opfer's data cannot resolve whether this log-to-linear change occurs spontaneously in the course of development, or depends on exposure to language and education. However, we have recently obtained a similar logarithmic effect in *adult* Mundurukus, an Amazonian people with reduced number lexicon and access to education and tools (S. Dehaene, V. Izard, P. Pica and E. Spelke, unpublished data, see Pica *et al.*, 2004). On a segment marked with a single dot at one end and a set of ten dots at the other, we asked the Mundurukus to map the quantities 1 through 10 presented as sets of dots, series of tones, Munduruku numerals, or Portuguese numerals. In all of these modalities, the Munduruku performed logarithmically, similarly to Siegler and Opfer's younger children. Thus, although what triggers the conceptual shift from logarithmic to linear in children remains unknown, the fact that it is not observed in adult Mundurukus, who have very few spoken and no written numerals, suggests that mere maturation is not sufficient. Some experience with symbolic inputs seems necessary, but other factors such as explicit mathematical education and experience with measurement cannot be excluded.

Refined analyses of the symbolic comparison task

As noted above, the random-walk model, once fitted to RT and error data, provides a fine-grained estimation of the nature of representation and decision processes. To directly evaluate how these processes are organized for symbolic numerals, and to compare with the above nonsymbolic comparison task, I have reanalyzed the data for my studies of comparison of two-digit arabic numerals (Dehaene *et al.*, 1990). In this task, human subjects had to classify arabic numerals as larger or smaller than a fixed reference. Three experiments were performed: comparison with 55, with 65 or with 66.

Figure 24.6 shows the analysis of the data for comparison with 65, using analysis strategy 1. Both the RTs and error rates showed a distance effect which conformed well to the theory (errors showing a sharper decrease with distance than RTs). Furthermore, the expected relation between RT and transformed errors was always highly significant ($p \ll 0.001$), indicating that the random-walk model applies well to symbolic comparison. Finally, there was a highly significant increase in mean step size μ with numerical distance ($p \ll 0.001$). With respect to the above nonsymbolic comparison data, however, two distinctive features were observed. First, the variations of μ across the target numbers, were slightly better predicted by the linear model (i.e. by the difference between the target number and the standard 65) than by the logarithmic model (i.e. by the log ratio of the standard and target). Second, the μ were no longer strictly proportional to the numerical difference, as they were for nonsymbolic stimuli (Figure 24.4). There was a

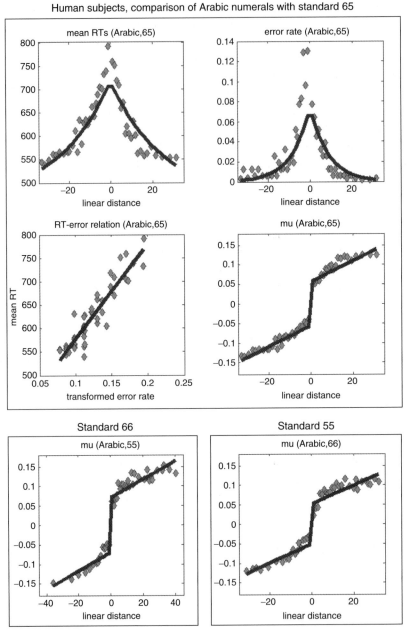

Figure 24.6 Symbolic comparison analyzed using the random-walk model (data reanalyzed from Dehaene *et al.*, 1990). Human subjects compared two-digit arabic numerals to a fixed standard of 65 (top), 66 (bottom left), or 55 (bottom right). The format is the same as Figure 24.4, with the exception of a linear scale for target numbers (abscissa). Relative to numerosity comparison (Figure 24.4), arabic numeral comparison is much more precise, with error rates peaking at only 13% (top right panel). Examination of the μ parameter indicates that the information accumulated per unit of time increases with the difference between numbers (rather than their log ratio), and shows a discontinuity at the origin (information is accumulated at a fast rate even when the numerical difference is minimal). RT, reaction time.

highly significant discontinuous offset as well ($p < 0.001$; compare Figures 24.4 and 24.6), indicating that as soon as the symbolic target was larger than the reference, even by one unit, a constant vote could be cast in favor of the 'larger' response.

These observations were replicated in analyses of two other symbolic comparison data sets (comparison with 55 and with 66; Dehaene et al., 1990; see Figure 24.6). Furthermore, in order to directly compare nonsymbolic and symbolic number processing within the same participants, Anna Wilson and I designed a new experiment in which, in different blocks, subjects had to compare numbers presented either as sets of dots or as two-digit arabic numerals (Dehaene and Wilson, unpublished data). In order to study Weber's law, on some blocks the numbers ranged from 11 to 39 and had to be compared to the reference 25, and in other blocks they ranged from 41 to 69 and had to be compared to the reference 55. In all cases, a highly regular distance effect was found, and the random-walk model provided an excellent fit of the data, including a highly significant RT-error relation. However, the recovered μ values showed that somewhat different numerical representations served as the basis for decision on symbolic and nonsymbolic trials (Figure 24.5). Two major differences were found. First, as above, on nonsymbolic trials the μ varied continuously with the numerical distance between the target and the standard (the range of targets was too small to tell whether this distance was better measured on a linear or log scale), but on symbolic trials there was again a clear discontinuous component. Second, when the magnitude of the numbers more than doubled (from standard 25 to standard 55), performance in the nonsymbolic block dropped, and the mean random-walk step size μ decreased by a factor of about two (Weber's law)—but no such decrease was observed for symbolic numerals, where it was just as easy to compare numbers around 25 as around 55.

What are the implications of these findings? The profile of mean step size μ suggests that two sources of information contribute to the decision-making process during symbolic number comparison. The first of these components grows, apparently linearly, with the difference between the target and the standard—this is a classical component of quantity-based evidence, similar to that found with nonsymbolic stimuli, except that the underlying continuum seems to be linear rather than logarithmic. The second component is all-or-none and provides a discrete vote for the larger response whenever the number is larger than the standard, or for the smaller response otherwise.

At first, the existence of this second component seems somewhat paradoxical. If such an accurate signal is available, why cannot the subject respond immediately, without being affected by the proximity of quantities? According to the random-walk model, the problem for the decision system is to extract the decision-relevant signals from other sources of noise. Assuming that numerosity detector neurons that have become very precise with symbolic exposure are intermixed with others that have remained imprecise, and that all are pooled together into the decision process, one would obtain precisely the observed summation of an exact, all-or-none signal and a distance-dependent analog signal. In Verguts and Fias's (2004) model, such exact and analog components are in fact present in the tuning curve of individual neurons (Figure 24.5). It would thus seem that this model can provide an excellent account of the data in Figures 24.6 and 24.7.

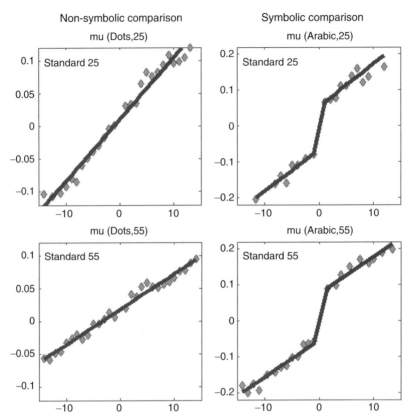

Figure 24.7 Replication of the differences between symbolic and nonsymbolic comparison within the same subjects (A. Wilson and S. Dehaene, unpublished data). The panels show the recovered μ for each of four distinct experimental blocks: comparison with standard 25 or 55, and with targets presented as sets of dots or as two-digit arabic numerals. Note that for simplicity, all data are plotted as a function of the linear distance between target and standard (although with nonsymbolic targets, a slightly better fit is obtained with log ratio). The key differences are (1) the amount of information per unit of time is subject to Weber's law for nonsymbolic targets, but not for nonsymbolic targets; (2) a discontinuity is present at the origin for symbolic, but not for nonsymbolic targets.

I also used strategy 2 to fit the EZ-diffusion model to the symbolic number comparison data. The findings for the mean random-walk step size μ were unchanged, but the EZ-diffusion also allowed for an estimation of the parameters T_0 (nondecision time) and θ (decision threshold) separately for each target. I did not observe any significant variation of the decision threshold θ, in keeping with the idea that this parameter is fixed prior to target presentation (however, see Botvinick *et al.* (2001) and Bogacz *et al.* (2006) for suggestions as to how this parameter may change from trial to trial). However, the nondecision time T_0 was systematically 70–100 ms slower for target numerals that fell within the decade of the standard (e.g. standard 65, targets between 60 and 69) compared to target numerals outside this decade. This aspect of the results resolves an older controversy concerning the origins of discontinuities in number comparison. The hypothesis of a digital-to-analog conversion during symbolic comparison suggested that RTs should be a smooth, continuous function of numerical distance. However, the results actually revealed small RT discontinuities at the boundaries of the decade of the standard (Hinrichs *et al.*, 1981; Dehaene *et al.*, 1990). The random-walk decomposition now shows clearly that these discontinuities arise outside of the decision system. In my analyses, the μ values that serve as inputs to the decision process never showed any discontinuity at decade boundaries, compatible with the hypothesis that decision is based on an analog quantity representation. However, the nondecision time showed a discontinuity, presumably imputable to a perceptual delay when the target number starts with the same decade digit as the standard and the subjects presumably have to orient more attention to the units digit.

In summary, the symbolic code for numbers appears to have both a perceptual cost (the need for longer perceptual analysis of the digital content of the stimulus) and a decision advantage (the decision is more precise and appears to be based, at least in part, on exact, all-or-none numerical information rather than solely on analog quantity information). All of the observed differences between symbolic and nonsymbolic number processing are compatible with Verguts and Fias's (2005) model of a narrowing and linearization of the tuning curves of numerosity detectors with exposure to symbolic inputs.[7]

Simple calculations

A final issue concerns how the number representation is used in simple arithmetic calculations such as addition or subtraction. Let it be clear from the outset that this part of the theory is much less developed. Here I focus exclusively on calculation with nonsymbolic numerosities, where some predictions can be made concerning error rates. Proposals as to how the theory might be extended to symbolic arithmetic will be briefly considered at the end.

A challenge to any theory of arithmetic is that a variety of tasks has been used to probe nonsymbolic calculation. Typically, subjects are shown two successive numerosities, either merely juxtaposed (Cordes *et al.*, 2003; Lemer *et al.*, 2003) or integrated into an animation that suggests an arithmetic operation of addition or subtraction (e.g. two sets of dots being added into a box) (Wynn, 1992a; McCrink and Wynn, 2004; Pica *et al.*, 2004; Barth *et al.*, 2005, 2006; McCrink *et al.*, 2006). Subjects mentally compute the corresponding result and respond using one of several modes. They may be presented with a third number, and asked to compare it explicitly with their result, either using

---

[7] Verguts and Fias further suggest that the symbolic number priming effect (Dehaene *et al.*, 1998; Koechlin *et al.*, 1999; Naccache and Dehaene, 2001) supports the model inasmuch as the size of the RT priming effect seems to vary with the linear distance between numbers rather than with their ratio (Reynvoet *et al.*, 2002).

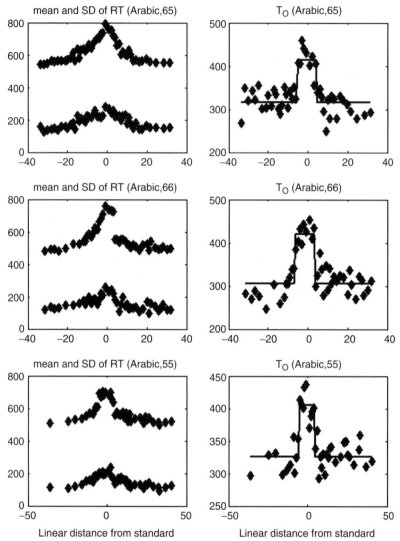

Figure 24.8 Mean and standard deviation (SD) of reaction time (RT) (left) and estimated nonde-cision time T_0 (right) in three experiments of two-digit number comparison analyzed with Wagenmakers' (2006) EZ-diffusion strategy for random-walk model identification. In all experiments, T_0 shows a clear discontinuity when the target crosses the decades boundary of the standard for comparison, suggesting an added perceptual cost of having to closely analyze the units digit. That this effect can be entirely attributed to nondecision processes is clearly visible in the graphs on the left, when the mean RT shows a sudden increase without any concomitant change in the standard deviation.

larger–smaller comparison (Pica *et al.*, 2004; Barth *et al.*, 2005, 2006) or same–different judgment (McCrink *et al.*, 2006). In preverbal infants, an implicit surprise reaction can be recorded when the outcome does not match the expected value (Wynn, 1992a; McCrink and Wynn, 2004). Educated subjects can also be asked to name the correct value or to point to it (Pica *et al.*, 2004).

Theory

My first postulate will be that the decision components of all of these tasks are performed according to above-described mechanisms of larger–smaller, same–different, and numerosity labelling judgments (see in particular Equations 24.8–12 and 24.15). The sole difference is that the basis for the subjects' response is no longer an externally given quantity n, but rather an internally computed quantity, the result of an internal transformation on external inputs n_1 and n_2 which approximates the requested operation $n_1 + n_2$ or $n_1 - n_2$.[8] Assuming that the outcome n is also represented internally by a Gaussian random variable X, the only remaining issue is how the mean and standard deviation of this variable vary as a function of the mean and standard deviation of the operands n_1 and n_2, separately for addition and for subtraction.

In the absence of any knowledge of the mechanisms of the internal transformation and their possible biases, the simplest normative model is one in which the subjects' mental estimations are unbiased, and thus the mental representation $q(n)$ of the result n of an addition or subtraction operation is, on average, placed at the appropriate location on the number line:

$$q_+(n) = q(n_1 + n_2) \text{ and } q_-(n) = q(n_1 - n_2) \tag{24.27}$$

where q is the *log* function. Note that the implementation of the internal transformations implied by Equation 24.27 is not trivial. It is not the logarithms of the operands themselves that must be added or subtracted, otherwise the result would be multiplication or division. Rather, the logarithmic compression of the number line must somehow be 'undone' before the addition or subtraction operation is computed. In spite of its apparent complexity, such a computation is clearly within reach of simple neural networks that learn to extract simple 'basis functions' and can function as arbitrary interpolators (Denève *et al.*, 2001). In fact, a computation formally similar to addition and subtraction is implemented by the parietal spatial updating mechanism (Duhamel *et al.*, 1992), which uses eye movement direction and amplitude to remap memories of saccade targets. The computation performed is analogous to vector addition, and is not impeded by the fact that the retinotopic map shows logarithmic foveal expansion. It is a highly intriguing anatomical fact that the areas involved in this vector addition process, VIP and LIP, overlap

---

[8] In its most general version, this hypothesis states that any number obtained as the output of some arithmetic calculation or decision can be re-used as the input into another. How such 'piping' of intermediate results occurs in the human brain remains highly unclear. My speculation is that it requires a central exchange system or global workspace, presumably involving prefrontal cortex, whose operation is necessarily serial and consciously controlled (see Dehaene and Changeux, 2004).

with those involved in number representation (Dehaene *et al.*, 2003; Nieder and Miller, 2004). This anatomical relation tentatively suggests a possible 'recycling' of the spatial remapping VIP–LIP circuitry for computationally similar arithmetic transformations (Dehaene, 2005; Hubbard *et al.*, 2005).

Can one make any predictions concerning the precision of such an addition or subtraction result? Clearly, the precision of the outcome should depend on the initial precision of the operands. Both the log-Gaussian model and the scalar variability model predict that number encoding is subject to Weber's law, i.e. variability proportional to the mean. If the random variables encoding the two numbers are stochastically independent, then their variances should add, leading to:

$$var_\varepsilon(n) = var(n_1) + var(n_2) \tag{24.28}$$

where, according to Weber's law, $var(n_1) = (w\,n_1)^2$ and $var(n_2) = (w\,n_2)^2$.

In this equation, ε is +1 for addition, and −1 for subtraction. The equation makes it clear that the precision of these operations should depend solely on the size of the operands. For instance, the same final precision is predicted for the operations $24 + 8$ and $24 - 8$, although the outcomes are centered on 32 and 16 respectively. An alternative equivalent formulation of this property states that, for equal results n, addition should always be more precise than subtraction.

Two refinements of Equation 24.28 have been proposed independently by Cordes *et al.* (2003) and by my collaborators and I (Barth *et al.*, 2006; McCrink *et al.*, 2006). First, there might be a covariance term if n_1 and n_2 are not estimated independently. For instance, subjects might compare n_2 with n_1, or in some subtraction displays with moving objects they might notice that some of the objects composing set n_1 appear to leave the display during presentation of n_2 (McCrink *et al.*, 2006). Such sources of covariance in the estimation of n_1 and n_2 would lead to a better precision on the outcome of $n_1 - n_2$ than expected based on the estimation of n_1 and n_2 in isolation—and to a *worse* precision on the outcome of $n_1 + n_2$.

A second source of variance might come from the operation itself and, in particular, the need to temporarily store the result n. In the absence of a more precise characterization of the arithmetic mechanism itself, both Cordes *et al.* (2003) and Barth *et al.* (2006) have proposed to subsume these effects under an additional term with Weberian variability on the outcome n.

With those two refinements, the variance of an operation result becomes:

$$var_\varepsilon(n) = var(n_1) + var(n_2) + 2\,\varepsilon\,cov(n_1, n_2) + \lambda\,var(n_1 + \varepsilon\,n_2) \tag{24.29}$$

where according to Weber's law, $var(n_1) = (w\,n_1)^2$, $var(n_2) = (w\,n_2)^2$, $var(n_1 + \varepsilon\,n_2) = w^2\,(n_1 + \varepsilon\,n_2)^2$, and λ is a scaling factor which indicates how much additional imprecision is due to calculation, over and above the intrinsic imprecision due to the internal representation. Yet, a difficulty with this equation is that, at present, no one has proposed a precise form for the covariance term, thus limiting its practical applicability.

Once precise hypotheses are made about the mean (24.27) and variance (24.28 or 24.29) of an arithmetic result, it is relatively easy to model specific tasks by modifying the above Equations 24.8–24.12, and 24.15. For instance, if the subject is asked to decide whether the arithmetic result $n_1 + n_2$ is larger or smaller than a third numerosity n, under the hypotheses of Equation 24.29 and assuming stochastic independence (no covariance term), Equation 24.10 then becomes:

$$P_{correct}(n_1, n_2, n_3) = \int_0^{+\infty} \frac{e^{-\frac{1}{2}\left(\frac{x-(n_1+\in n_2 - n_3)}{w\sqrt{n_1^2+n_2^2+n_3^2+\lambda^2(n_1+\in n_2)^2}}\right)^2}}{\sqrt{2\pi}w\sqrt{n_1^2 + n_2^2 + n_3^2 + \lambda^2(n_1 + \in n_2)^2}} \, dx$$

$$= \int_0^{+\infty} \frac{e^{-\frac{1}{2}\left(\frac{x-(r-1)}{w\sqrt{1+r^2+2\alpha(\alpha-1)+\lambda^2}}\right)^2}}{\sqrt{2\pi}w\sqrt{1 + r^2 + 2\alpha(\alpha - 1) + \lambda^2}} \, dx$$

with $r = \dfrac{n_3}{n_1 + \varepsilon n_2}$ and $\alpha = \dfrac{n_1}{n_1 + \varepsilon n_2}$

(24.30)

This equation was used by Barth et al. (2006) and, with the simplifying assumption $\lambda = 0$, by Pica et al. (2004) to model their numerosity addition and subtraction tasks.

Experimental evidence

The ability to combine two numerosities into simple addition and subtraction operations has been demonstrated in preverbal human infants using a surprise paradigm in which infants look longer when an arithmetically impossible outcome is presented (Wynn, 1992a; Koechlin et al., 1997). This competence was initially demonstrated for very small numerosities (1 + 1 or 2 – 1) around $4^{1/2}$ months of age, and it has recently been extended to large numerosities (5 + 5 and 10 – 5) in 9-month-old infants (McCrink and Wynn, 2004).

A simple prediction, common to all models, is that performance in such tasks should depend primarily on the ratio of the arithmetic result to the proposed result. This ratio dependence has not been tested in infants yet, but it has been observed in 5-year-olds (Barth et al., 2005) and adults (Pica et al., 2004; Barth et al., 2006). Barth et al. (2005) showed that 5-year-olds could perform a cross-modal addition combining visually and auditorily presented numerosities, thus confirming that the computation occurs at an abstract numerosity representation level rather than between visual images of sets.

Recently, a few studies have begun to generate quantitative data appropriate for testing the more precise predictions of the model (Cordes et al., 2003; Pica et al., 2004; Barth et al., 2006; McCrink et al., 2006). Pica et al. (2004) showed that Equation 24.28 (without covariance or λ terms) accurately fitted the data from Western and Amazonian subjects performing numerosity addition and subtraction tasks. Furthermore, a prediction of that equation, the fact that performance should be more precise for addition than for subtraction, was verified by Barth *et al.* (2006). However, Barth *et al.* (2006) also noted an important deviation which suggests rejection of this simple model. Somewhat counter-intuitively, Equation 24.28 predicts that the precision on the result n of an addition $n_1 + n_2$ can be better than if n had been presented directly to the subject. This is because, if the *variances* of n_1 and n_2 add, the *standard deviation* of the result can be proportionally smaller than the standard deviation of the initial values (by a factor which can be as large as 2). Barth *et al.* (2006), however, always observed worse performance in addition plus comparison (deciding whether $n_1 + n_2$ is larger or smaller than n_3) than in comparison alone. Similar observations were made by Cordes *et al.* (2003). Both authors suggest the need for an additional λ term reflecting the additional variance introduced by the arithmetic operation and the maintenance of the result n in memory. The Barth *et al.* (2006) data were accurately fitted by letting $λ = 1.3$.

Can one similarly prove the necessity of the covariance term? For subtractions involving large operands but a small result (e.g. $32 - 28$), the model without covariance predicts that final precision should be very poor, but this is not the case (Cordes *et al.*, 2003; McCrink *et al.*, 2006). McCrink *et al.* (2006) explicitly compared performance on matched pairs of operations such as $24 + 8$ and $24 - 8$. The model without covariance or λ term predicts equal final precision, but this was clearly false: in all cases subtraction was more precise, compatible with the covariance model. Unfortunately, the absence of a simple comparison baseline, without addition or subtraction, did not make it possible to further specify the parameters of the model.

Koleen McCrink and I also made a new observation that questions more deeply the above theoretical framework (McCrink *et al.*, 2006). In our experiments, over a large number of trials, we repeatedly presented subjects with the same operation (e.g. $24 + 8$), each time paired with a different outcome (e.g. 13, 16, 20, 24, 32, 40, 48). Subjects had to decide whether these outcomes were correct or not. In this way, we were able to trace a curve that indicated which numerosity subjects judged as the most likely outcome of a given operation. Surprisingly, although this value always fell close to the correct arithmetic outcome it presented a systematic bias. Additions were slightly overestimated, and subtractions were notably underestimated (in retrospect, a similar trend is perceptible in Cordes *et al.*, 2003). This observation tentatively suggests that the number line may be submitted to a 'representational momentum' effect similar to that found for physical motion (Freyd and Finke, 1984) or motion on the pitch continuum (Freyd *et al.*, 1990): during an addition operation, while moving towards larger numbers, the internal representation would 'move too far' towards the large end of the number line—and a converse shift towards small numbers would occur during subtraction. While the numerical momentum effect thus supports the hypothesis that arithmetic is analogous to motion on the number line, and that similar circuitry is recruited for both numerical and spatial updating (Hubbard *et al.*, 2005), this finding also complicates the search for a simple mathematical model of elementary arithmetic.

Open issues

A central question concerns the relation of these nonsymbolic arithmetic abilities to those deployed in calculation with arabic digits. The dominant view is that symbolic arithmetic is based on 'two calculation sytems' (Dehaene and Cohen, 1991), one based on quantity manipulations and used for nonsymbolic numerosities, and the other based on purely formal processes of symbol manipulation and explicit memory retrieval (Ashcraft, 1992). The hopes of capturing such a complex set of pathways by simple mathematical equations are dim. Nevertheless, it has been suggested that the simplest mathematical operations, particularly subtraction, may rely primarily on nonsymbolic quantity manipulations (Gallistel and Gelman, 1992; Cohen and Dehaene, 2000; Cohen *et al.*, 2000). The observation of highly regular effects of number size (Ashcraft, 1992), of clear distance effects when subjects are asked to evaluate the correctness of a proposed operation outcome (Ashcraft and Stazyk, 1981), and of joint impairments of symbolic and nonsymbolic addition after a small left parietal hemorrhage in a patient with dyscalculia and Gerstmann's syndrome (Lemer *et al.*, 2003) hint that elementary symbolic arithmetic relies heavily on quantity representations of the type described in this chapter. The emergence of new ideas concerning the encoding of symbolic and nonsymbolic quantities (Verguts and Fias, 2004) and of new possibilities to visualize the cerebral mechanisms of arithmetic, perhaps down to the single-neuron level (Nieder *et al.*, 2002; Nieder and Miller, 2003, 2004), invites new reflections on this topic.

Conclusion

I have presented a simple but powerful mathematical theory of number representation and manipulation. As mentioned in the introduction, although putting it all together has required some ingenuity, none of its elements are particularly original. The theory has been developed over the years by many groups, and it draws heavily on pre-existing developments in signal detection theory and random-walk models of decision making. Yet the virtue of such a theorizing effort is three-fold. First, it presents a homogeneous and formal description of behavior in simple numerical tasks, complete with detailed equations that can be quantitatively compared with human and animal performance. Second, it proposes bridging laws linking those behavioral approaches to the underlying neuronal mechanisms. With the emergence of single-neuron studies of arithmetic, those bridging laws will become increasingly testable. Third, the theory is simple enough that it can serve as a minimal 'standard model' on which to base further improvements.

An interesting issue is to what extent the present theory could be generalized outside the numerical domain. The coding principles outlined in 'Numerosity representation' are clearly not unique to numbers—in fact they make use of Gaussian tuning curves, population coding, and psychophysical decision mechanisms that have been used for years in coding of perceptual dimensions such as movement direction and spatial coordinates. Furthermore, mechanisms for combining two such values into simple arithmetic-like operations exist in many animal species which are known to compute vector sums, temporal differences or reward rates (Gallistel, 1990). It has been proposed that the general circuitry linking parietal areas VIP and LIP is jointly used for vector sums and differences in the domains of space, time and number (Hubbard *et al.*, 2005). Indeed, the coding and manipulation of spatial, temporal and numerical magnitudes might constitute an overarching function of the parietal lobes (Walsh, 2003). The present theory would readily extend to these domains. Still, one should remain aware that neuronal coding principles can also differ across domains, as exemplified by Gaussian tuning for number versus coding by monotonically varying firing rates for tactile frequency (Romo and Salinas, 2003). The range of solutions available to neuronal networks for solving arithmetic-like problems, as well as the reason for choosing one over the other, remain to be thoroughly theorized (see Verguts, 2006; Salinas 2006).

Even within the numerical domain, attempting to build an integrative theory has revealed at least four areas where our knowledge is insufficient: How do we encode symbolic numerals? What factors generate a switch from logarithmic to linear representations of quantity in the course of development? How do we compute simple arithmetic transformations? And what is the global architecture which permits flexible chaining of operations and feeding of the results of one operation into another ('piping')? I have no doubt that the present minimal propositions will serve as a useful target for experimenters, and hope that the advancement of numerical cognition will be such that they will have to be quickly replaced by more refined ideas.

Acknowledgements

This work was supported by INSERM, CEA, and a Centennial Fellowship from the James S. McDonnell Foundation. I gratefully acknowledge extensive discussions with many colleagues over the past twenty years, particularly J. Mehler, G. Dehaene-Lambertz, E. Dupoux, L. Cohen, J. P. Changeux, R. Shepard, R. Gallistel, R. Gelman, E. Koechlin, L. Naccache, P. Pinel, E. Spelke, H. Barth, A. Nieder, V. Izard, P. Pica, M. Piazza, M. Sigman, A. Wilson, and E. Hubbard. I am extremely grateful to Jessica Cantlon and Elizabeth Brannon for letting me analyze their raw data.

References

Ashcraft, M. H. (1992) Cognitive arithmetic: a review of data and theory. *Cognition*, **44**, 75–106.

Ashcraft, M. H. and Stazyk, E. H. (1981) Mental addition: a test of three verification models. *Memory and Cognition*, **9**, 185–196.

Barth, H., La Mont, K., Lipton, J. and Spelke, E. S. (2005) Abstract number and arithmetic in preschool children. *Proceedings of the National Academy of Sciences of the USA*, **102**, 14116–14121.

Barth, H., La Mont, K., Lipton, J., Dehaene, S., Kanwisher, N. and Spelke, E. (2006) Non-symbolic arithmetic in adults and young children. *Cognition*, **98**, 199–222.

Bogacz, R., Brown, E., Moehlis, J., Holmes, P. and Cohen, J. D. (2006) The physics of optimal decision making: a formal analysis of models of performance in two-alternative forced-choice tasks. *Psychological Review*, **113**, 700–765.

Botvinick, M. M., Braver, T. S., Barch, D. M., Carter, C. S. and Cohen, J. D. (2001) Conflict monitoring and cognitive control. *Psychological Review*, **108**, 624–652.

Brannon, E. M. and Terrace, H. S. (2000) Representation of the numerosities 1–9 by rhesus macaques (Macaca mulatta). *Journal of Experimental Psychology: Animal Behavior Processes*, **26**, 31–49.

Brannon, E. M., Wusthoff, C. J., Gallistel, C. R. and Gibbon, J. (2001) Numerical subtraction in the pigeon: evidence for a linear subjective number scale. *Psychological Science*, **12**, 238–243.

Cantlon, J. F. and Brannon, E. M. (2006) Shared system for ordering small and large numbers in monkeys and humans. *Psychological Science*, **17**, 401–406.

Cantlon, J. F., Brannon, E. M., Carter, E. J. and Pelphrey, K. A. (2006) Functional imaging of numerical processing in adults and 4-y-old children. *PLoS Biology*, **4**, e125.

Cohen, L. and Dehaene, S. (2000) Calculating without reading: unsuspected residual abilities in pure alexia. *Cognitive Neuropsychology*, **17**, 563–583.

Cohen, L., Dehaene, S. and Verstichel, P. (1994) Number words and number non-words: a case of deep dyslexia extending to arabic numerals. *Brain*, **117**, 267–279.

Cohen, L., Dehaene, S., Chochon, F., Lehéricy, S. and Naccache, L. (2000) Language and calculation within the parietal lobe: a combined cognitive, anatomical and fMRI study. *Neuropsychologia*, **38**, 1426–1440.

Cordes, S., Gelman, R., Gallistel, C. R. and Whalen, J. (2001) Variability signatures distinguish verbal from nonverbal counting for both large and small numbers. *Psychonomic Bulletin and Review*, **8**, 698–707.

Cordes, S., Gallistel, C. R., Gelman, R. and Latham, P. E. (2003) Nonverbal arithmetic in humans, Vancouver, BC. Paper presented at the Annual meeting of OPAM (Object Perception Attention and Memory), Vancouver, BC, November 2003.

Dayan, P. and Abbott, L. F. (2001) *Theoretical Neuroscience: Computational and Mathematical Modeling of Neural Systems*. MIT Press, Cambridge, MA.

Dehaene, S. (1989) The psychophysics of numerical comparison: a re-examination of apparently incompatible data. *Perception and Psychophysics*, **45**, 557–566.

Dehaene, S. (1992) Varieties of numerical abilities. *Cognition*, **44**, 1–42.

Dehaene, S. (1996) The organization of brain activations in number comparison: event-related potentials and the additive-factors methods. *Journal of Cognitive Neuroscience*, **8**, 47–68.

Dehaene, S. (1997) *The Number Sense*. Oxford University Press, New York.

Dehaene, S. (2001) Subtracting pigeons: logarithmic or linear? *Psychological Science*, **12**, 244–246.

Dehaene, S. (2002) Single-neuron arithmetic. *Science*, **297**(5587), 1652–1653.

Dehaene, S. (2003) The neural basis of the Weber–Fechner law: a logarithmic mental number line. *Trends in Cognitive Science*, **7**, 145–147.

Dehaene, S. (2005) Evolution of human cortical circuits for reading and arithmetic: the 'neuronal recycling' hypothesis. In Dehaene, S., Duhamel, J. R., Hauser, M. and Rizzolatti, G. (eds), *From Monkey Brain to Human Brain*, pp. 133–157. MIT Press, Cambridge, MA.

Dehaene, S. and Akhavein, R. (1995) Attention, automaticity and levels of representation in number processing. *Journal of Experimental Psychology: Learning, Memory and Cognition*, **21**, 314–326.

Dehaene, S. and Changeux, J. P. (1993) Development of elementary numerical abilities: a neuronal model. *Journal of Cognitive Neuroscience*, **5**, 390–407.

Dehaene, S. and Changeux, J. P. (2004) Neural mechanisms for access to consciousness. In Gazzaniga, M. (ed.), *The Cognitive Neurosciences*, 3rd edn, Vol. 82, pp. 1145–1157. Norton, New York.

Dehaene, S. and Cohen, L. (1991) Two mental calculation systems: a case study of severe acalculia with preserved approximation. *Neuropsychologia*, **29**, 1045–1074.

Dehaene, S. and Cohen, L. (1994) Dissociable mechanisms of subitizing and counting: neuropsychological evidence from simultanagnosic patients. *Journal of Experimental Psychology: Human Perception Performance*, **20**, 958–975.

Dehaene, S. and Cohen, L. (1995) Towards an anatomical and functional model of number processing. *Mathematical Cognition*, **1**, 83–120.

Dehaene, S. and Mehler, J. (1992) Cross-linguistic regularities in the frequency of number words. *Cognition*, **43**, 1–29.

Dehaene, S., Dupoux, E. and Mehler, J. (1990) Is numerical comparison digital: analogical and aymbolic effects in two-digit number comparison. *Journal of Experimental Psychology: Human Perception and Performance*, **16**, 626–641.

Dehaene, S., Bossini, S. and Giraux, P. (1993) The mental representation of parity and numerical magnitude. *Journal of Experimental Psychology: General*, **122**, 371–396.

Dehaene, S., Naccache, L., Le Clec'H, G., Koechlin, E., Mueller, M., Dehaene-Lambertz, G., van de Moortele, P. F. and Le Bihan, D. (1998) Imaging unconscious semantic priming. *Nature*, **395**, 597–600.

Dehaene, S., Spelke, E., Pinel, P., Stanescu, R. and Tsivkin, S. (1999) Sources of mathematical thinking: behavioral and brain-imaging evidence. *Science*, **284**(5416), 970–974.

Dehaene, S., Piazza, M., Pinel, P. and Cohen, L. (2003) Three parietal circuits for number processing. *Cognitive Neuropsychology*, **20**, 487–506.

Dehaene, S., Izard, V. and Piazza, M. (2005) Control over non-numerical parameters in numerosity experiments. Unpublished manuscript (available on www.unicog.org).

Deneve, S., Latham, P. E. and Pouget, A. (2001) Efficient computation and cue integration with noisy population codes. *Nature Neuroscience*, **4**, 826–831.

Duhamel, J. R., Colby, C. L. and Goldberg, M. E. (1992) The updating of the representation of visual space in parietal cortex by intended eye movements. *Science*, **255**, 90–92.

Duncan, E. M. and McFarland, C. E. (1980) Isolating the effects of symbolic distance and semantic congruity in comparative judgments: an additive-factors analysis. *Memory and Cognition*, **8**, 612–622.

Feigenson, L., Dehaene, S. and Spelke, E. (2004) Core systems of number. *Trends in Cognitive Sciences*, **8**, 307–314.

Freyd, J. J. and Finke, R. (1984) Representational momentum. *Journal of Experimental Psychology: Learning, Memory and Cognition*, **10**, 126–132.

Freyd, J. J., Kelly, M. H. and DeKay, M. L. (1990) Representational momentum in memory for pitch. *Journal of Experimental Psychology: Learning, Memory and Cognition*, **16**, 1107–1117.

Gallistel, C. R. (1990) *The Organization of Learning*. MIT Press, Cambridge, MA.

Gallistel, C. R. and Gelman, R. (1992) Preverbal and verbal counting and computation. *Cognition*, **44**, 43–74.

Gelman, R. and Gallistel, C. R. (1978) *The Child's Understanding of Number*. Harvard University Press, Cambridge, MA.

Gibbon, J. (1977) Scalar expectancy theory and Weber's law in animal timing. *Psychological Review*, **84**, 279–325.

Gibbon, J. and Fairhurst, S. (1994) Ratio versus difference comparators in choice. *Journal of the Experimental Analysis of Behavior*, **62**, 409–434.

Gold, J. I. and Shadlen, M. N. (2001) Neural computations that underlie decisions about sensory stimuli. *Trends in Cognitive Sciences*, **5**, 10–16.

Gold, J. I. and Shadlen, M. N. (2002) Banburismus and the brain: decoding the relationship between sensory stimuli, decisions and reward. *Neuron*, **36**, 299–308.

Gordon, P. (2004) Numerical cognition without words: evidence from Amazonia. *Science*, **306**, 496–499.

Green, D. and Swets, J. A. (1966) Signal detection theory and psychophysics. Krieger, New York.

Harnad, S. (1990) The symbol grounding problem. *Physica D*, **42**, 335–346.

Hauser, M. D. and Carey, S. (2003) Spontaneous representations of small numbers of objects by rhesus macaques: examinations of content and format. *Cognitive Psychology*, **47**, 367–401.

Heekeren, H. R., Marrett, S., Bandettini, P. A. and Ungerleider, L. G. (2004) A general mechanism for perceptual decision-making in the human brain. *Nature*, **431**(7010), 859–862.

Hinrichs, J. V., Yurko, D. S. and Hu, J. M. (1981) Two-digit number comparison: use of place information. *Journal of Experimental Psychology: Human Perception and Performance*, **7**, 890–901.

Hubbard, E. M., Piazza, M., Pinel, P. and Dehaene, S. (2005) Interactions between number and space in parietal cortex. *Nature Reviews Neuroscience*, **6**, 435–448.

Izard, V. (2005) Interactions between verbal and non-verbal numerical representations: theoretical and empirical approaches. PhD thesis, University of Paris VI, Paris.

Kim, J. N. and Shadlen, M. N. (1999) Neural correlates of a decision in the dorsolateral prefrontal cortex of the macaque. *Nature Neuroscience*, **2**, 176–185.

Koechlin, E., Dehaene, S. and Mehler, J. (1997) Numerical transformations in five month old human infants. *Mathematical Cognition*, **3**, 89–104.

Koechlin, E., Naccache, L., Block, E. and Dehaene, S. (1999) Primed numbers: exploring the modularity of numerical representations with masked and unmasked semantic priming. *Journal of Experimental Psychology: Human Perception and Performance*, **25**, 1882–1905.

Kosslyn, S. M., Koenig, O., Barrett, A., Cave, C. B., Tang, J. and Gabrieli, J. D. E. (1989) Evidence for two types of spatial representations: hemispheric specialization for categorical and coordinate relations. *Journal of Experimental Psychology: Human Perception and Performance*, **15**, 723–735.

Krueger, L. E. (1982) Single judgments of numerosity. *Perception and Psychophysics*, **31**, 175–182.

Laming, D. R. J. (1968) *Information Theory of Choice-reaction Times*. Academic Press, London.

Lemer, C., Dehaene, S., Spelke, E. and Cohen, L. (2003) Approximate quantities and exact number words: dissociable systems. *Neuropsychologia*, **41**, 1942–1958.

Link, S. W. (1975) The relative judgment theory of two choice response time. *Journal of Mathematical Psychology*, **12**, 114–135.

Link, S. W. (1990) Modelling imageless thought: the relative judgment theory of numerical comparisons. *Journal of Mathematical Psychology*, **34**, 2–41.

Link, S. W. (1992) *The Wave Theory of Difference and Similarity*. Erlbaum, Hillsdale, NJ

Lipton, J. and Spelke, E. (2003) Origins of number sense: large number discrimination in human infants. *Psychological Science*, **14**, 396–401.

Lo, C. C. and Wang, X. J. (2006). Cortico-basal ganglia circuit mechanism for a decision threshold in reaction time tasks. *Nat Neurosci*, 9(7), 956–963

Machens, C. K., Romo, R. and Brody, C. D. (2005) Flexible control of mutual inhibition: a neural model of two-interval discrimination. *Science*, **307**(5712), 1121–1124.

MacMillan, N. A. and Creelman, C. D. (1991) *Detection Theory: A User's Guide*. Cambridge University Press, Cambridge.

Mandler, G. and Shebo, B. J. (1982) Subitizing: an analysis of its component processes. *Journal of Experimental Psychology: General*, **111**, 1–21.

Matsuzawa, T. (1985) Use of numbers by a chimpanzee. *Nature*, **315**(6014), 57–59.

Mazurek, M. E., Roitman, J. D., Ditterich, J. and Shadlen, M. N. (2003) A role for neural integrators in perceptual decision making. *Cerebral Cortex*, **13**, 1257–1269.

McCrink, K. and Wynn, K. (2004) Large-number addition and subtraction by 9-month-old infants. *Psychological Science*, **15**, 776–781.

McCrink, K., Dehaene, S. and Dehaene-Lambertz, G. (2006) Moving along the number line: Operational momentum in non-symbolic arithmetic. manuscript submitted for publication.

Mechner, F. (1958) Probability relations within response sequences under ratio reinforcement. *Journal of the Experimental Analysis of Behavior*, **1**, 109–121.

Minturn, A. L. and Reese, T. W. (1951) The effect of differential reinforcement on the discrimination of visual number. *Journal of Psychology*, **31**, 201–231.

Moyer, R. S. and Landauer, T. K. (1967) Time required for judgements of numerical inequality. *Nature*, **215**, 1519–1520.

Naccache, L. and Dehaene, S. (2001) The priming method: imaging unconscious repetition priming reveals an abstract representation of number in the parietal lobes. *Cerebral Cortex*, **11**, 966–974.

Nieder, A. and Miller, E. K. (2003) Coding of cognitive magnitude. Compressed scaling of numerical information in the primate prefrontal cortex. *Neuron*, **37**, 149–157.

Nieder, A. and Miller, E. K. (2004) A parieto-frontal network for visual numerical information in the monkey. *Proceedings of the National Academy of Sciences of the USA*, **101**, 7457–7462.

Nieder, A., Freedman, D. J. and Miller, E. K. (2002) Representation of the quantity of visual items in the primate prefrontal cortex. *Science*, **297**(5587), 1708–1711.

Nieder, A. and Merten, K. (2007). A labeled-line code for small and large numerosities in the monkey prefrontal cortex. *J Neurosci, in press*

Page, R., Izquierdo, E., Saal, A., Codnia, J. and El Hasi, C. (2004) A response time model for judging order relationship between two symbolic stimuli. *Perception and Psychophysics*, **66**, 196–207.

Parker, A. J. and Newsome, W. T. (1998) Sense and the single neuron: probing the physiology of perception. *Annual Review of Neuroscience*, **21**, 227–277.

Pashler, H. (1984) Processing stages in overlapping tasks: evidence for a central bottleneck. *Journal of Experimental Psychology: Human Perception and Performance*, **10**, 358–377.

Piazza, M., Giacomini, E., Le Bihan, D. and Dehaene, S. (2003) Single-trial classification of parallel pre-attentive and serial attentive processes using functional magnetic resonance imaging. *Proceedings of the Royal Society of London, B*, **270**(1521), 1237–1245.

Piazza, M., Izard, V., Pinel, P., Le Bihan, D. and Dehaene, S. (2004) Tuning curves for approximate numerosity in the human intraparietal sulcus. *Neuron*, **44**, 547–555.

Piazza, M., Pinel, P. and Dehaene, S. (2006) A magnitude code common to numerosities and number symbols in human intraparietal cortex. *Neuron, in press*.

Pica, P., Lemer, C., Izard, V. and Dehaene, S. (2004) Exact and approximate arithmetic in an Amazonian indigene group. *Science*, **306**(5695), 499–503.

Pinel, P., Dehaene, S., Riviere, D. and LeBihan, D. (2001) Modulation of parietal activation by semantic distance in a number comparison task. *Neuroimage*, **14**, 1013–1026.

Pinel, P., Piazza, M., Le Bihan, D. and Dehaene, S. (2004) Distributed and overlapping cerebral representations of number, size and luminance during comparative judgments. *Neuron*, **41**, 983–993.

Pollmann, T. and Jansen, C. (1996) The language user as an arithmetician. *Cognition*, **59**, 219–237.

Ratcliff, R. (1988) Continuous versus discrete information processing: modeling the accumulation of partial information. *Psychological Review*, **95**, 238–255.

Ratcliff, R. and Rouder, J. (1998) Modelling response times for two-choice decisions. *Psychological Science*, **9**, 347–356.

Ratcliff, R. and Tuerlinckx, F. (2002) Estimating parameters of the diffusion model: approaches to dealing with contaminant reaction times and parameter variability. *Psychonomic Bulletin and Review*, **9**, 438–481.

Reynvoet, B., Brysbaert, M. and Fias, W. (2002) Semantic priming in number naming. *Quarterly Journal of Experimental Psychology A*, **55**, 1127–1139.

Rivera, S. M., Reiss, A. L., Eckert, M. A. and Menon, V. (2005) Developmental changes in mental arithmetic: evidence for increased functional specialization in the left inferior parietal cortex. *Cerebral Cortex*, **15**, 1779–1790.

Roitman, J. D., Brannon, E. M. and Platt, M. (2007). Graded Coding of Numerosity in Macaque Lateral Intraparietal Area. *PLoS Biol, in press*.

Romo, R. and Salinas, E. (2003) Flutter discrimination: neural codes, perception, memory and decision making. *Nature Reviews Neuroscience*, **4**, 203–218.

Salinas, E. (2006). How behavioral constraints may determine optimal sensory representations. *PLoS Biol*, **4**(12), e387.

Sawamura, H., Shima, K. and Tanji, J. (2002). Numerical representation for action in the parietal cortex of the monkey. *Nature*, **415**(6874), 918–922.

Schwarz, W. (2001) The ex-Wald distribution as a descriptive model of response times. *Behavioral Research Methods and Instruments in Computing*, 33, 457–469.

Shadlen, M. N. and Newsome, W. T. (1998) The variable discharge of cortical neurons: implications for connectivity, computation and information coding. *Journal of Neuroscience*, 18, 3870–3896.

Shadlen, M. N. and Newsome, W. T. (2001) Neural basis of a perceptual decision in the parietal cortex (area LIP) of the rhesus monkey. *Journal of Neurophysiology*, 86, 1916–1936.

Shadlen, M. N., Britten, K. H., Newsome, W. T. and Movshon, J. A. (1996) A computational analysis of the relationship between neuronal and behavioral responses to visual motion. *Journal of Neuroscience*, 16, 1486–1510.

Shepard, R. N. (2001) Perceptual–cognitive universals as reflections of the world. *Behavioral and Brain Sciences*, 24, 581–601; discussion 652–571.

Shepard, R. N., Kilpatrick, D. W. and Cunningham, J. P. (1975) The internal representation of numbers. *Cognitive Psychology*, 7, 82–138.

Siegler, R. S. and Opfer, J. E. (2003) The development of numerical estimation: evidence for multiple representations of numerical quantity. *Psychological Science*, 14, 237–243.

Sigman, M. and Dehaene, S. (2005) Parsing a cognitive task: a characterization of the mind's bottleneck. *PLoS Biology*, 3, e37.

Sigman, M. and Dehaene, S. (2006) Dynamics of the central bottleneck: dual-task and task uncertainty. *PLoS Biology*, 4, e220.

Simon, O., Mangin, J. F., Cohen, L., Le Bihan, D. and Dehaene, S. (2002) Topographical layout of hand, eye, calculation and language-related areas in the human parietal lobe. *Neuron*, 33, 475–487.

Simon, O., Kherif, F., Flandin, G., Poline, J. B., Riviere, D., Mangin, J. F., Le Bihan, D. and Dehaene, S. (2004) Automatized clustering and functional geometry of human parietofrontal networks for language, space and number. *Neuroimage*, 23, 1192–1202.

Smith, P. L. and Ratcliff, R. (2004) Psychology and neurobiology of simple decisions. *Trends in Neurosciences*, 27, 161–168.

Stone, M. (1960) Models for choice reaction time. *Psychometrika*, 25, 251–260.

Temple, E. and Posner, M. I. (1998) Brain mechanisms of quantity are similar in 5-year-olds and adults. *Proceedings of the National Academy of Sciences of the USA*, 95, 7836–7841.

Tomonaga, M. and Matsuzawa, T. (2002) Enumeration of briefly presented items by the chimpanzee (Pan troglodytes) and humans (Homo sapiens). *Animal Learning and Behaviour*, 30, 143–157.

Usher, M. and McClelland, J. L. (2001) The time course of perceptual choice: the leaky, competing accumulator model. *Psychological Review*, 108, 550–592.

Van Oeffelen, M. P. and Vos, P. G. (1982) A probabilistic model for the discrimination of visual number. *Perception and Psychophysics*, 32, 163–170.

Verguts, T. (2006) How to compare two quantities? A computational model of flutter discrimination. *Journal of Cognitive Neuroscience*, in press.

Verguts, T. and Fias, W. (2004) Representation of number in animals and humans: a neural model. *Journal of Cognitive Neuroscience*, 16, 1493–1504.

Verguts, T., Fias, W. and Stevens, M. (2005) A model of exact small-number representation. *Psychonomic Bulletin and Review*, 12, 66–80.

Wagenmakers, E.-J., van der Maas, H. L. J. and Grasman, R. P. P. P. (2006) An EZ-diffusion model for response time and accuracy. *Psychonomic Bulletin and Review*, in press.

Wald, A. (1947) *Sequential Analysis*. Wiley, New York.

Walsh, V. (2003) A theory of magnitude: common cortical metrics of time, space and quantity. *Trends in Cognitive Sciences*, 7, 483–488.

Washburn, D. A. and Rumbaugh, D. M. (1991) Ordinal judgments of numerical symbols by macaques (Macaca mulatta). *Psychological Science*, 2, 190–193.

Whalen, J., Gallistel, C. R. and Gelman, R. (1999) Non-verbal counting in humans: the psychophysics of number representation. *Psychological Science*, **10**, 130–137.

Wong, K. F. and Wang, X. J. (2006) A recurrent network mechanism of time integration in perceptual decisions. *Journal of Neuroscience*, **26**, 1314–1328.

Wynn, K. (1992a) Addition and subtraction by human infants. *Nature*, **358**, 749–750.

Wynn, K. (1992b) Children's acquisition of the number words and the counting system. *Cognitive Psychology*, **24**, 220–251.

25

Using conceptual knowledge in action and language

Michiel van Elk, Hein T. van Schie,
Oliver Lindemann and Harold Bekkering

Action semantics refer to the conceptual knowledge that is necessary to guide our actions and can be defined in terms of action goals and action means. The present chapter outlines the concept of action semantics and presents a review of the existing literature dealing with functional mechanisms underlying conceptual knowledge and goal-directed behavior. Recent empirical findings are presented which indicate that semantic information is selected in a flexible manner in accordance with the action intention of the actor, whereby long-term conceptual associations may be overruled by current behavioral goals. These results extend the *selection-for-action* principle beyond perception to include the selection of semantic information that is relevant for the upcoming action. Findings are interpreted within the light of contemporary models of conceptual knowledge in action.

Introduction

Within the booming field of cognitive neuroscience, a growing number of studies under-line the interrelatedness of perception, action and language. It is acknowledged that cognitive faculties do not operate in isolation, but rather share common neural mecha-nisms. This may come as no surprise, regarding the fact that the division of the mind in separate cognitive subsystems was originally inherited from intuitive folk-psychological concepts. The separate consideration of cognitive faculties has proven to be useful in acquiring a basic understanding of the workings of the brain. However, given the close interactions between different cognitive subsystems, it may be useful to think about adjusting our terminology to better cover the phenomena investigated. An exclusive focus on the uniqueness of each cognitive faculty may blind us for the elements that are common to different systems.

In the present chapter we introduce the concept of 'action semantics' as a useful tool to bring together the closely related fields of language, action and conceptual knowledge. In short, action semantics refer to the conceptual knowledge that is necessary to guide our actions. Both long-term and short-term action semantics are important for a successful interaction with the surrounding world. For example, although most of the time we use everyday objects in an appropriate manner, sometimes objects acquire a new function when used in a different context. Imagine yourself reading a newspaper while being disturbed by a mosquito. The folded newspaper will be an excellent device to get rid of the insect. Countless examples show that conceptual knowledge is selected and activated in a flexible way, according to the actor's current action goals (e.g. using a screwdriver to open a paint-bucket).

In the first part of this chapter we will discuss the nature of action semantics, the neural mechanisms supporting action semantics and its development over the course of life. It is suggested that action goals play a dominant role in understanding the behavior of others and in the selection of perceptual information for our own actions. In the second part we turn to the question of how conceptual knowledge might be represented within the brain. Different theories of conceptual knowledge in action will be discussed that disagree on the principles underlying the organization of conceptual knowledge. In the third section we will focus on the close relation between language and action. Whereas several studies report effects of language on action preparation, hardly any study investigated effects of action intention on the selection of semantic information. Recent experiments from our group show that semantics are automatically selected according to an actor's present action goal, even when actions are in conflict with long-term knowledge of object use (Lindemann *et al.*, 2006; M. Van Elk *et al.*, unpublished data). In the final part of this chapter we will discuss theoretical implications of the findings presented for theories about conceptual knowledge in action. We suggest that the study of action semantics brings together several closely related fields and provides insight into the functional mechanisms underlying goal-directed behavior.

Action semantics

We start this section by introducing the concept of action semantics. In subsequent paragraphs we will then focus on (i) the neural mechanisms that mediate the use of conceptual knowledge in action, (ii) the acquisition of action semantics in young children and (iii) the selection of perceptual and semantic information for action.

What are action semantics?

Action semantics refer to the conceptual knowledge that is necessary to guide our actions. More specifically, the conceptual knowledge used for actions consists of our knowledge about the function and the use of concrete objects. Whenever we encounter a well-known object, semantic information about object use will be retrieved automatically from memory. It is exactly this interplay between conceptual knowledge and action that is the topic of our investigation. The relation between action planning and conceptual knowledge has often been overlooked by theories in the domain of motor control. Likewise, theories of conceptual knowledge have paid little attention to the use of semantic knowledge for guiding behavior. For example, theoretical discussions on the modal or amodal nature of conceptual knowledge bypass the idea that our conceptual system in the first place evolved to enable us to cope with environmental demands. Being able to deal effectively with one's environment is essential to survival and a conceptual system that enables organisms to successfully manipulate the surrounding world surely has great evolutionary advantages.

Action semantics capitalizes on the idea that conceptual knowledge is closely related to the control of action.

Much of the information that is necessary to guide our actions is directly available to our senses. For example, we quickly pick up the natural object affordances that allow us to interact with categories of objects (e.g. seats) as well as specific instances of these categories (e.g. reclining chair, Gibson, 1986). However, not all information that is necessary to act successfully can be obtained directly through our senses. Within the first six months of their lives, children are able to grasp an object like a water faucet correctly, but the knowledge of how to turn a faucet is something that cannot be perceived directly upon mere observation of the object by itself. Most water faucets are round and can be acted upon in many ways in order to achieve the desired outcome. For most people, the knowledge that in most Western countries faucets are opened by means of a counter clockwise rotation will lead to the decision to grasp the tap with the thumb pointing upwards or away from the body allowing for a comfortable turning motion (Rosenbaum *et al.*, 1995). In other words, the stored conceptual knowledge about water faucets is used for guiding our actions.

Action semantics can be defined in terms of action goals (what to use an object for) and action means (how to use an object). With action means we typically denote the manner in which an object is handled (e.g. grasped), or more generally, the way in which we preferably interact with an object (e.g. a toothbrush is grasped at the handle, not at the brush). With action goals, on the other hand, we refer to the purpose or intent for which an object is used (e.g. a toothbrush is used for brushing teeth). Different levels of complexity can be discerned when describing action goals, ranging from high-level goal-representations to lower levels. For example, lessening one's thirst may be a general action goal, whereas lifting a cup and bringing it to the mouth represents a lower level of action goals. A useful taxonomy to distinguish between different levels of goal-representations includes: (1) physical goals that refer to concrete objects, (2) action goals that refer to the functional use of objects and (3) mental goals that reflect a desired state of affairs in the world (Bekkering and Wohlschläger, 2000). Both action and mental goals are closely related to the intention or purpose of the actor. Physical goals reflect a lower level description of action goals and can be defined in terms of a movement's goal-location.

Still little is known about the functional processes through which selection and coordination of action goals and action means come about. At the behavioral level, the selection of action means (e.g. the way in which an object is grasped) often seems to fulfill the requirements of the action goal (what one is intending to do with the object; Rosenbaum *et al.*, 1995), suggesting the possibility of a hierarchical organization supporting action semantics for goals and means. In accordance with this suggestion, previous research has implicated the importance of action goals for guiding the integrity and consistency of behavior over prolonged periods of time (Zalla *et al.*, 2003; H. T. Van Schie and H. Bekkering, 2007).

Neural mechanisms mediating action semantics

The division between semantics for action goals and means is supported by the study of neuropsychological patients with semantic dementia, who sometimes display selective loss of a particular category of semantic knowledge. Previous research has distinguished between different types of action deficits in patients with otherwise fully operational motor functions. Patients with ideational apraxia show a general loss of conceptual knowledge about the function of and the purpose for which they are used (Ochipa *et al.*, 1992). These patients are able to perform simple motor-acts and to retrieve tool names, but fail to use objects in an appropriate way (e.g. they can use a toothbrush as a spoon). In contrast, ideomotor apraxia refers to the inability to execute specific motor commands after damage to the left parietal or fronto-parietal cortex (Buxbaum, 2001). Ideomotor apraxic patients show spatio-temporal errors when pantomiming object use or may grasp an object in an inappropriate way to find themselves at a loss as to which movements to make with it (grasp a stylus with a full grip). The behavior displayed by both groups of patients suggests a dissociation between knowledge about the functional use of objects (action goals) and knowledge of the usual interaction (action means) associated with objects (cf. Leiguarda and Marsden, 2000).

Ideomotor deficits have been associated with damage to parietal cortex, which is involved in visuo-motor transformations necessary for grasping (e.g. Heilman *et al.*, 1981; Buxbaum *et al.*, 2003). In addition, damage to the left posterior parietal lobe is often associated with a deficit demonstrating the appropriate actions associated with particular objects (Ochipa *et al.*, 1989). Ideational apraxia on the other hand has been found in association with lesions in premotor and prefrontal areas (Sirigu *et al.*, 1998; Leiguarda and Marsden, 2000), consistent with recent evidence on the role of these areas in supporting goal-directed actions with objects after their prehension (H. T. Van Schie and H. Bekkering, 2007; Majdandzic *et al.*, in press).

Another important region that has been implicated in the retrieval of knowledge about actions is the posterior middle temporal region (MT) that is involved in the perception of motion (Tootell *et al.*, 1995). Damage to the middle temporal region in neuropsychological patients is associated with a deficit in the recognition of tools (Tranel *et al.*, 2003). The same area is also activated in association with verb generation reflecting actions to visually presented nouns (Fiez *et al.*, 1996) or objects (Martin *et al.*, 1995). Furthermore, Kable *et al.* (2002) found greater activity in bilateral MT to the presentation of action pictures than to pictures of objects, whereas words instead of pictures mainly activated left-sided MT. The reported activation of MT is consistent with the suggestion that accessing action knowledge involves incorporating motion features. In sum, these findings suggest that accessing action knowledge involves activating motor structures and areas supporting motor performance, consistent with the idea that action knowledge is stored or represented within the motor system (reviews in Martin and Chao, 2001; Tranel *et al.*, 2003). Thus, having discussed the neural mechanisms involved in action semantics, we now turn to the question of how we acquire action semantics over the course of our lives. Insight into the acquisition of conceptual knowledge for action is gained from developmental studies, which will be the focus of the next section.

Development of action semantics

Piaget was among the first to suggest that the central role of action experience in cognitive development should be addressed more broadly (Piaget, 1953). The production of goal-directed acts in the first year of life may not only refine the production of goal-directed acts in infants, it might also be crucial to the acquisition of conceptual knowledge about the world in general. Information gleaned from early action experiences may, for instance, facilitate sensitivity to the goal structure of infants' own and others' actions.

Even at a very young age, children extract the meaningful structure of the surrounding world at multiple levels of analysis. Moreover, developmental theorists have considered this capacity a prerequisite both for having intentions and for understanding the intentions of others (Gergely et al., 1995; Meltzoff and Moore, 1995). Indeed, the ability to construe actions in terms of goals can be observed in preschoolers. Eighteen-month-old infants infer the goal of uncompleted human action sequences and infants as young as 14 months tend to imitate intended but not accidental acts (Meltzoff, 1995; Carpenter et al., 1998). In addition, 14-month-old infants re-enact the final goal of a modeled action, but do not always reproduce the means. Gergely et al. (2002) convincingly showed that children will follow a given course of action to achieve the given goal only if they consider it to be the most rational alternative. Their results indicate that imitation of goal-directed action by preverbal infants is a selective, conceptual knowledge-based process, rather than a simple re-enactment of the means used by a demonstrator, as was previously thought. This action knowledge may subsequently be extended to allow infants to interpret a broad range of events with respect to their meaning and goal structure (Sommerville and Woodward, 2005). For instance, after watching an actor reach for and grasp a toy, infants show a stronger novelty response to a change in the actor's goal than to a change in the spatial location or trajectory of her reach (Woodward, 1998). Recent findings have stressed a correlation between the emergence of goal-directed behaviors and infants' ability to detect goals in the acts of others (Sommerville and Woodward, 2005). In addition, a measurable impact of action experience on action interpretation was demonstrated.

Developmental studies suggest that the ability to infer the intention of an observed actor is already present in children aged 12 months (e.g. Gergely et al., 1995). In a habituation study, 12-month-old infants were found to look longer at an object-directed action when an indirect reach-movement was made, but if no object was present no such preference was found (Phillips and Wellman, 2005). This suggests that children understand the observed action in terms of the actor's goal. However, recent findings suggest that children's understanding of actions is constrained by task context. While children tended automatically to imitate the observed action goal rather than the means by which it is performed (Bekkering and Wohlschläger, 2000), making the means more salient (e.g. putting an arrow on the movement-path) results in movement-related adjustments, although the goal of the action remains the same (Cox et al., unpublished data). Apparently, both goals and means play an important role in the acquisition of conceptual knowledge to interact with the surrounding world.

The mechanism underlying the acquisition of action semantics seems to be the ability to imitate, which is probably mediated by the human mirror system. The discovery of mirror neurons in primates that respond selectively to both the execution of an action and the observation of actions being performed by another actor, led to the idea of an observation–execution matching system that is crucial to the understanding of observed actions (Rizzolatti *et al.*, 1996). In humans a comparable mirror system was identified, encompassing such brain areas as the superior temporal sulcus, the inferior parietal lobule and the inferior frontal gyrus (e.g. Grafton *et al.*, 1996; Calvo-Merino *et al.*, 2005). Several possible functions regarding the activity in mirror neurons have been put forward, of which the most important include (1) supporting a goal representation of intended action, (2) providing a mechanism to understand observed behavior and (3) supporting the acquisition of new behavior by imitation (e.g. Iacoboni *et al.*, 1999; Umiltà *et al.*, 2001; Rizzolatti *et al.*, 2001). Mirror-related areas appear crucial to the understanding of observed actions and thereby provide the child with a mechanism to learn by observation. For example, recently it has been reported that the observation of errors performed by another subject led to an error-related brain response that was comparable to self-generated errors (Van Schie *et al.*, 2004). This suggests that similar mechanisms are recruited during monitoring of one's own or another's action.

Taken together, it seems that action understanding and acquisition of novel actions through observation are goal-directed activities, mediated by systems that support both the generation and observation of actions. The development of action semantics in young children enables them to make sense of observed actions and to perform goal-directed actions themselves. The acquisition and use of goal representations seems a critical aspect for the development of action semantics. In line with this suggestion are findings that underline the importance of action goals in dealing effectively with the enormous amount of information that enters our senses.

Action goals in perception and action

A guiding principle in perceptual processing is the ability to selectively attend to particular stimuli. According to the framework of selection-for-action (Allport, 1987) relevant information is selected in line with the action intention of the actor. For example, in the domain of visual perception it has repeatedly been found that specific visual information (e.g. orientation of an object) is selectively processed, depending on the action goal of the actor, e.g. grasping or pointing (Bekkering and Neggers, 2002; Hannus *et al.*, 2005). In a recent study we found a selective enhancement of early visual ERP components when subjects intended to grasp as compared to when they intended to point towards visually presented objects (H. T. Van Schie, M. Van Elk and H. Bekkering, unpublished data). Because processing of orientation is relevant for grasping but not for pointing, the orientation of the object needs to be processed more actively in visual areas. Craighero *et al.* (1999) instructed participants to grasp objects of a particular orientation in response to stimuli showing a final hand position that could be congruent or incongruent with respect to the intended grasp. Response latencies were fastest to pictures with the greatest similarity to the final hand posture of the intended grasping movement, suggesting a close link between action preparation and perceptual processing. Interestingly, enhancement of visual processing has also been reported in relation to language comprehension. Upon reading a description of a nail being pounded either into the wall or into the floor, participants were faster in processing visual stimuli congruent with the implied orientation (Stanfield and Zwaan, 2001).

These and other studies suggest that in addition to bottom-up information that is elicited by the perception of an object, top-down effects of the action context and intention of an actor may selectively modulate visual processing. A similar principle may also support the selection of object semantics in accordance with the action intention of an individual. One hypothesis that plays a central part in the current chapter is that the selection of conceptual knowledge for action is guided by the same principle that is proposed to underlie the selection of perceptual information for action.

Theories of motor control suggest that conceptual knowledge is involved in the selection of appropriate action plans (Rosenbaum *et al.*, 2001). Functional imaging studies confirm that conceptual knowledge about the appropriate manner of grasping an object becomes activated automatically upon object identification (Chao and Martin, 2000; Grèzes and Decety, 2002; Grèzes *et al.*, 2003). More specifically, it has been reported that action preparation and object perception are mutually dependent processes. For example, passive observation of tools has been reported to elicit motor activation in areas that are normally activated with tool use (e.g. Chao and Martin, 2000). In monkeys it has been found that neurons in grasping-related areas, namely the anterior intraparietal sulcus (AIP) and the ventral premotor cortex (F5), selectively respond to the passive observation of graspable objects (Murata *et al.*, 1997). These canonical neurons are selectively responsive to objects of a particular size and shape and probably play an important role in specifying the motor properties that are required for directing an action towards a particular object.

At the behavioral level it has been found that viewing an object automatically activates the appropriate hand shape for using it (Klatzky *et al.*, 1989). The same automatic effect of appropriate handgrip aperture has also been reported in response to reading words of graspable objects that afforded either a full or a precision grip (Glover *et al.*, 2004). Reading a word that represented a large object (e.g. 'apple') resulted in a larger grip aperture in the early part of the grasping movement as compared to reading a word that referred to a small object (e.g. 'grape'). In a similar fashion, Tucker and Ellis (2001) presented subjects with pictures for a categorical judgment and found a compatibility effect between response type (making a precision or full grip with the hand) and object size (e.g. faster responding to the presentation of car keys when making a precision grip).

Other studies suggest that action knowledge plays an important role in the retrieval of conceptual information. Chainay and Humphreys (2002) reported faster responding when making action decisions about the use of particular objects (e.g. do you perform a twisting or a pouring action with the object?) as compared to making contextual decisions (is the object typically found in the kitchen?). In addition, Yoon and Humphreys (2005) showed that activation of action knowledge plays a constitutive role in making functional judgments about object use. Participants observed objects either grasped with a congruent, an incongruent or without any handgrip and they verified the object name ('Is this the name of the object?') or the object action ('Is the object used for …?'). A congruency effect of the observed action on making action decisions was found, while no such effect was present for naming the object. Together these studies support the view that the action and motor systems are involved in object identification.

Thus, perception of an object is found to evoke activation of an appropriate motor-program that allows interaction with the object (e.g. facilitation of the appropriate hand-grip). These findings are consistent with the theoretical notion of Gibson (1986) that whenever an actor perceives an object, affordances will be inferred that inform the actor about the possible actions that can be directed towards the object. However, in addition to automatic (bottom-up) effects resulting from object perception, in many cases the manner of object interaction is determined by the intention of an actor or the action goal. That is, although chairs typically afford sitting down, in the context of a different action goal (e.g. getting something from a top shelf) a different manner of interaction may be selected. The flexible use of action semantics will be investigated in the third part of this chapter. Before doing so, however, we turn to different views on the organization of conceptual knowledge, in order to provide a theoretical background against which empirical findings may be evaluated.

Theories of conceptual knowledge

In general, theories on conceptual knowledge may be classified into two broad categories. According to amodal theories, concepts are abstract, amodal and arbitrary entities that operate independently from the sensorimotor systems (e.g. Fodor, 1983). Concepts are considered as part of symbolic representational structures that function in an analogous way to language, (e.g. 'language-of-thought' hypothesis). An important argument in favor of amodal theories of representation concerns the ease with which different tokens of a particular category (type) are recognized, independent of perceptual differences. However, amodal theories of concepts also face important difficulties such as a lack of empirical validation, giving a specification of the transduction process from perceptual states to symbols and the grounding problem. If all knowledge is only represented as a set of inter-related symbols, the meaning of a particular symbol can only be specified by its relation to, and in terms of, other symbols.

In contrast, modal theories of representation argue that concepts are grounded in modality-specific systems (e.g. Barsalou et al., 2003). Neuropsychological patients with damage to a particular sensory area and a specific deficit in categorical knowledge provide a powerful argument for the modal representation of concepts. Embodied cognition refers to different theories of conceptual representation that share the assumption of a multi-modal grounding of concepts across different sensorimotor areas (e.g. Clark, 1997; Gallese and Goldman, 1998; Lakoff and Johnson, 1999). However, embodied theories differ widely on the emphasis that is put on separate cognitive subsystems and on the way in which our conceptual knowledge is organized. It may be useful to think of modal theories on conceptual knowledge as differentiating along two different axes:

- the first axis covers whether conceptual knowledge is organized by principles internal to the organism or that it is rather determined by external, stimulus-driven processes;
- the second axis represents the theory's relative focus on perceptual or action-related processes.

Accordingly, theories of conceptual knowledge may be represented in a two-dimensional conceptual space, as represented in Figure 25.1. Of course, the division of theories along two axes provides us with a simplified picture that overlooks finer nuances of different theories. Nevertheless, we suggest that the proposed division provides us with a useful tool to think about different approaches in studying the acquisition and organization of conceptual knowledge. The different axes represent the relative emphasis that is put on top-down or bottom-up processes on the one hand and on action- or perception-related systems on the other hand. In the remainder of this section we will discuss different proposals for the retrieval of conceptual knowledge in relation to the domain of action and focus on the strengths and weaknesses of embodied accounts of conceptual representation.

Sensory functional hypothesis versus correlated structure principle

The sensory–functional hypothesis, put forward by Warrington and Shallice (1984), argues that conceptual knowledge is stored in modality-specific sensory and motor structures. Hence, identification of instances of different semantic categories depends critically upon activating particular modality-specific semantic subsystems in the brain. Category-specific semantic deficits are the result of damage to modality-specific semantic subsystems. For example, damage to the visual semantic subsystem probably impairs semantic knowledge of categories, for which visual features are a defining characteristic. Borgo and Shallice (2001) report a patient who had suffered from herpetic encephalitis, showing a severe deficit in category-specific knowledge for living things. Interestingly, this patient also was impaired when tested for knowledge of other sensory quality categories

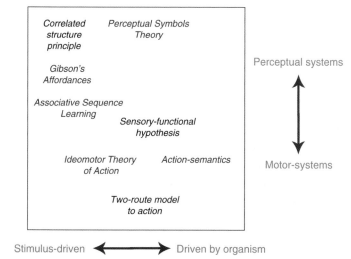

Figure 25.1 Theories of conceptual knowledge represented in conceptual space. Axes represent the relative emphasis that is put on bottom-up or top-down processing on the one hand, and on perceptual or motor systems on the other hand.

(substances, materials and liquids), while performance with man-made artifacts was relatively spared. This suggests that retrieval of specific conceptual categories may be highly dependent upon the processing of sensory qualities.

In contrast, Caramazza and Mahon (2003) propose that evolution favored domain-specific knowledge systems that resulted in a category-specific organization of semantic knowledge. According to the correlated structure principle, the organization of conceptual knowledge reflects the way in which different object properties are related to each other. Proponents of this alternative account usually point to the fine-graininess of the categories of category-specific deficits, e.g. independent impairment for the categories of fruits or animals (Caramazza and Shelton, 1998) and to the absence of a direct relation between severity of affected semantic modality and loss of category-specific semantic deficits. For example, Laiacona *et al.* (2003) report a patient with a good performance for 'sensory quality' categories, as assessed by verbal description compared to performance in a visual–verbal task, while showing a deficit in knowledge for living things. The assumption of a domain-specific organization of conceptual knowledge is consistent with the observation of fine-grained dissociations between different semantic categories.

Perceptual symbols theory

Perceptual symbols theory provides a perceptual theory of knowledge, according to which schematic representations are extracted from perceptual experience through a process of selective attention. A concept is represented by running a simulation of actual experiences with the concept and this process is referred to as re-enactment (Barsalou *et al.*, 2003). For example, when viewing a visual stimulus, neurons in sensory areas are activated and conjunctive neurons in association areas store the activated sensory features in memory. In the absence of the stimulus, the stored representation can be retrieved through re-enactment of the sensory areas by the association areas.

Perceptual symbols theory has received empirical support for example from property verification studies in which subjects are asked to decide whether a given property is related to a particular concept (Pecher *et al.*, 2004). Properties on subsequent trials could be either from the same or from a different modality. A modality-switching effect was found when a concept was previously presented with a property from a different modality. For example, reaction times were faster when verifying *loud* (auditory modality) for *blender* after previously verifying *rustling* (auditory) for *leaves* than after verifying *tart* (gustatory) for *cranberries*. These results suggest that subjects tend towards simulating a concept in a particular modality that was previously activated, thereby supporting a modal theory of conceptual representation. However, perceptual symbols theory focuses mainly on perceptual representations, leaving aside the organization of action knowledge, which is represented in Figure 25.1.

Ideomotor theory of action

We now turn to theories that explicitly focus on the representation of conceptual knowledge used in action. An intuitive and empirically validated idea dates back to William James, who stated that 'every representation of a movement awakens in some degree the actual movement which is its object' (James, 1890). Although ideomotor theory initially emphasized the intentional and private mental causes of action, it was hypothesized that goal representations are crucially important in action control. According to the ideomotor theory, actions are represented in terms of their effects and these effect-representations are helpful in the selection of actions, by predicting the consequences of one's actions (Hommel *et al.*, 2001). The acquisition of effect-representations depends strongly upon the formation of response–effect associations, in which a given response becomes paired with its associated sensory effects. A preschooler pressing a button of the television's remote control will soon find out the relation between a simple motor act and the switching on of the television. Consequently, this acquired response–effect association may guide future behavior.

In a typical experiment, it is shown that after training participants that a left key response elicits a high tone, a response facilitation occurs for left responses upon hearing the high tone (e.g. Hommel, 1996). According to the 'theory of event coding', actions and perceptual contents are coded in a common event-code (Hommel *et al.*, 2001). In principle, event-codes contain stored representations of contingent response–effect couplings. Thereby, the main focus of ideomotor theory of action is on the automatic processes by which arbitrary connections are established. The selection process, whereby an actor chooses a particular action on the basis of its stored effect-representations, remains largely out of focus.

Associative sequence learning

A closely related view that was specifically intended to account for imitation of observed actions is called associative sequence learning (ASL). Instead of focusing on response–effect couplings, ASL emphasizes the coupling between stimuli and particular responses. In principle, any association could develop between a stimulus and a particular response if they are co-activated repeatedly. Therefore, the way in which much of our knowledge is organized consists of contingent stimulus–response associations.

Heyes *et al.* (2005) have argued that imitation relies on learned associations between stimuli and actions. Participants had to respond to the observation of hand movements, by making a hand movement that was either congruent or incongruent to the observed movement (opening and closing). A stimulus–response compatibility effect was found for the observation of hand movements compatible with their own movement. However, when subjects were given a training 24 h prior to testing, in which they learned to close their hands in response to observed hand opening and vice versa, the stimulus–response compatibility of observed movement disappeared. Apparently, the automatic imitation of observed movements is mediated by experience and the authors suggest that imitation relies on processes of associative learning. According to this interpretation, neural connections involved in action observation and motor activation primarily reflect the learned association between observing and executing a particular action. Therefore, action representations consist of the learned association between stimuli and particular responses. Accordingly, ASL puts a big emphasis on bottom-up processing in the acquisition of conceptual knowledge for action.

Two-route model to action

Although many of our everyday actions rely on stored long-term representations—as is the case for bringing a cup to your mouth, which you have probably done countless times—we sometimes need to bypass this semantic knowledge, for example when you intend to catch a spider with a cup. Rumiati and Humphreys (1998) propose a two-route model to action, with a semantic route accessing stored action representations and a second route that runs directly from perception to action. This two-route model has been proposed, partly based on the study of neuropsychological patients showing a dissociation between semantic knowledge and the ability to manipulate objects (e.g. Buxbaum and Saffran, 2002). In a behavioral study with neuropsychologically healthy adults, participants performed either gesturing responses (gesturing the use of an object) or naming responses (verbally giving names) in response to pictures of objects (Rumiati and Humphreys, 1998). Responses for both speech and gestures were distinguished according to whether a visually related error (e.g. razor instead of hammer which have a similar shape but a different function) or a semantically related error (e.g. hammer instead of saw which differ in shape but are semantically related) was made. More visual errors relative to semantically related errors for gesturing object use as compared to naming objects were found, suggesting that naming and using tools relies on different processing routes. Furthermore Rumiati and Tessari (2002) found that healthy volunteers imitated meaningful actions better than meaningless actions and this enhanced performance contributed to the availability of stored action goals in long-term memory.

For meaningless actions, no long-term representation is available and imitation therefore relies on a direct route from vision to action, thereby placing more demands on action working memory. In a positron emission tomography study the neural mechanisms underlying imitation of both meaningful and meaningless actions were investigated (Rumiati et al., 2005). Imitation of meaningful actions activated the left inferior temporal gyrus, the angular gyrus and the parahippocampal gyrus (ventral stream), while the right parieto-occipital junction and superior parietal areas (dorsal stream) were mainly activated during imitation of meaningless actions, thereby supporting the view that both actions are mediated by different neural and functional systems. Imitation and execution of meaningful actions rely on accessing stored action semantic knowledge and online visual control, while the execution of meaningless actions in first instance relies on a dorsal perception–action system.

Overview

Theories discussed thus far disagree about the mechanisms underlying conceptual knowledge (e.g. perceptual simulation, learned association, direct or semantic routes to action). Each theory is based on specific neuropsychological findings and puts different emphasis on the importance of particular sensorimotor areas in the retrieval of conceptual knowledge.

As represented in Figure 25.1, we propose that a theory of action semantics should take into account the important role played by the actor's intentions. We argue that action goals play an important role in the acquisition and use of conceptual knowledge for action.

Furthermore, we agree that conceptual knowledge for action is represented in modality-specific brain areas, but that the organization and use of conceptual knowledge is guided by action goals. In the next section we will provide support for our position by presenting recent studies investigating effects of action on language processing. Before doing so, however, we will discuss the close relation between language and action in general. The topic of the organization of conceptual knowledge will be revisited in the final section, when we integrate empirical findings with contemporary theories of conceptual knowledge.

Semantics of action and language

Studies on the relation between language and action may give us more insight into the organization and selection of conceptual knowledge. Different experimental methods have established that action preparation can be affected by language and that action preparation involves accessing semantic knowledge. In the present section we will argue that action and language are highly dependent processes. Although the experiments that are discussed might seem to suggest unidirectional effects from one subsystem to the other, we would like to emphasize the common functional and neural mechanisms that underlie reported effects.

Links between language and action

In recent years a couple of studies have suggested that action planning and semantic processing are mutually dependent processes. For instance, Creem and Proffitt (2001) asked subjects to grasp common household objects while at the same time they either performed a visuo-spatial or a semantic task. Concurrent semantic processing resulted in more inappropriate grasping of the objects as compared to concurrent visuo-spatial processing, suggesting the involvement of the semantic system when preparing to grasp a meaningful object. Other studies showed that semantic properties of distracting words or objects influenced the planning and execution of grasping movements (e.g. Jervis et al., 1999; Glover and Dixon, 2002). Glover and Dixon (2002) had participants grasping objects, which resulted in an enlargement of maximum grip aperture for objects with the word 'large' printed on top of them as compared to objects with the word 'small'. In a similar way Gentilucci and Gangitano (1998) found that the words denoting 'far' and 'near' printed on objects affected movement kinematics similarly to the actual greater or shorter distances between hand position and object. These findings fit well with Glover's model of action control, according to which action preparation involves semantic processing, while action execution operates relatively independently from semantic processes (Glover, 2004).

Glenberg and Kaschak (2002) report the action sentence compatibility effect when participants judge the meaning of a sentence by making a movement towards or away from the own body. Participants showed difficulty when judging sentences that implied an action in the direction opposite to the response required for the sensibility judgment (e.g. responding 'yes' by making a movement towards the body while judging the sentence 'Close the drawer', which implies movement away from the body). Interestingly, the action sentence compatibility effect was found for imperative sentences (e.g. 'Close the drawer'), as well as for sentences describing the transfer of both concrete (e.g. 'Liz gave you the book') and abstract entities (e.g. 'Liz told you the story'). A similar effect was found by Zwaan and Taylor (2006) who had subjects judge the sensibility of sentences describing actions implying a particular direction by rotating a manual device (e.g. 'He turned down the volume' implies movement in a counter-clockwise orientation). A congruency effect was found for direction of manual responses and implied direction by the sentences, suggesting that understanding action sentences relies on motor resonance. These findings support the idea that understanding of meaning is grounded in bodily activity.

According to the principle of Hebbian learning, the efficacy of a neuronal ensemble onto another is strengthened whenever they become repeatedly co-activated (Hebb, 1949). This neuronal principle might underlie the close relation between language processing and action preparation. During language acquisition, for instance, children often develop specific links between a particular action and an associated word, probably resulting in a distributed functional network representing the meaning of words (Pulvermüller et al., 2005). Electrophysiological support for the involvement of the motor system in the understanding of action-related sentences comes from a study by Pulvermüller et al. (2005) that investigated the neural correlates of the processing of action verbs. Words that referred to specific body parts (e.g. 'kick' refers to foot, 'lick' to tongue etc.) elicited activity across the motor-strip close to the representation of the body parts to which the action words primarily referred. Tettamanti et al. (2005) identified a fronto-parietal circuit underlying listening to action-related sentences. This finding has been replicated several times and with different methods, including functional magnetic resonance imaging and transcranial magnetic stimulation (e.g. de Lafuente and Romo, 2004; Buccino et al., 2005) and suggests an underlying representation of action words, that consists of somatotopically organized neuronal assemblies.

Semantic information in action preparation

Taken together, recent findings suggest close relations between language and action systems. Although most studies discussed thus far investigated the influence of language on action, hardly any experiments have been conducted to explore the activation of semantic knowledge during action preparation. In a series of experiments we investigated whether the intention of an actor to use an object would involve selection of relevant semantic knowledge (Lindemann et al., 2006). Semantic activation in action preparation was investigated by using a language task in which priming effects of action context on the subsequent processing of words were measured. Semantic priming effects have reliably been reported when semantic context (e.g. a prime word or picture) facilitates processing of semantically related words, both for linguistic and nonlinguistic stimuli (e.g. Neely, 1991; Maxfield, 1997). For example, reading the word 'doctor' facilitates subsequent recognition of the word 'nurse', and no priming effect is expected if the subsequent word would be 'fireman'. Considering the importance of goals in stored representations for action, we hypothesized that the preparation of an action would provide a semantic context for the processing of a subsequently presented word, resulting in a priming effect for words consistent with the goal of the upcoming action. The experimental set-up is represented in Figure 25.2. In front of the subject two objects (a magnifying glass and a cup) were placed at a table. A picture of one of the two objects appeared on the screen, and subjects were instructed to prepare the action associated with the object. Subjects were prepared a particular motor action (e.g. drink from a cup), but waited for responding until a word appeared on the computer screen. When a pseudo-word was presented, no subsequent action was executed. Only if a valid Dutch word was recognized subjects performed the prepared movement.

In the first experiment, presented words could be either congruent or incongruent with the action goal (e.g. for the cup 'mouth' is congruent whereas 'eye' is incongruent). To control for the possibility of a simple picture-word priming effect, half of the subjects had to indicate by a simple finger-lifting response at which side of the table (left or right) the indicated object was present. If selection of semantic knowledge critically depends on the action intention of the actor, interactions between action planning and semantic processing were only expected in the grasping condition. Results are summarized in Figure 25.3 and, as can be seen, a word-congruency effect was found only when subjects intended to grasp the object and to bring it to the associated goal. That is, subjects responded faster when the presented word was congruent with their present action intention.

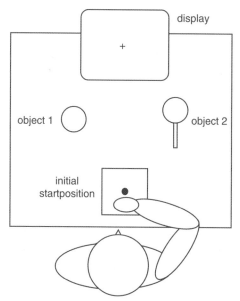

Figure 25.2 Schematic representation of the experimental set-up. A cup (Object 1), a magnifying glass (Object 2) and a computer screen were placed in front of the subject. Grasping of the objects was initiated by releasing the right hand from the starting position.

However, an alternative explanation for the absence of a congruency-effect in the finger-lifting condition might be that preparing a finger-lifting response is much easier than preparing a grasping movement. As a consequence, participants may have been better able to cognitively separate action preparation from word recognition, resulting in the absence of a behavioral interaction effect. In a second experiment this alternative explanation was ruled out by replacing words that represented the goal locations of the grasping movements by Dutch words denoting 'left' and 'right' that were more relevant to the finger-lifting task where subjects responded with left or right finger movements to indicate object position. Results showed a reversal of priming effects revealing priming for the finger-lifting condition but not for the grasping condition, confirming the hypothesis that action semantics are selectively activated in accordance with the action intended by the subject (see Figure 25.3).

In the third experiment a semantic categorization task was used instead of a lexical decision task, to ensure deep semantic processing of the words and to exclude the possibility that subjects' responses in the first two experiments only relied on visual word forms.

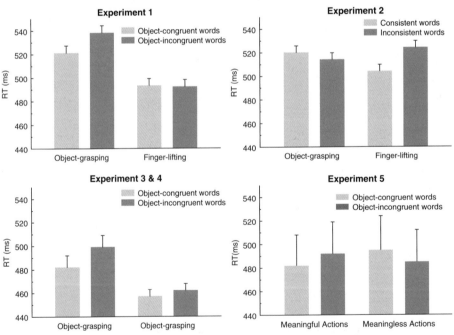

Figure 25.3 Mean response latencies arranged by action condition and word congruence. Subjects performed a lexical decision task with words representing goal locations in Experiment 1 and words representing spatial locations Experiment 2. Subjects performed a semantic categorization task in Experiment 3 and a final letter identification task in the Experiment 4. Error bars represent the 95% within-subject confidence intervals. RT, reaction time. In Experiment 5 subjects performed a semantic categorization task, while they prepared either meaningful or meaningless actions with the objects.

Target words again included body parts that represented the goal locations of the actions associated with either the cup or the magnifying glass. In addition, action-unrelated words that referred to body parts were used as filler items and words that referred to animals were chosen as no-go stimuli. Subjects were instructed to execute the action associated with the object, only when the word referred to a body part. If the word represented an animal no subsequent action was required. Again, a reduction in response latencies was found for words that were consistent with the action goal of the subject (e.g. 'eye' for grasping the magnifying glass). Finally it was hypothesized that if the interaction between words and action intention critically depended on deep semantic processing of the words, the effect should disappear if subjects attended to words only at a superficial level. As can be seen in Figure 25.3 the action-priming effect indeed disappeared if subjects performed a simple final letter-identification task instead of semantic categorization.

Together these experiments suggest that action goals form an integral part of the semantic representations that are activated during action preparation. Opposite to many of the automatic effects that were found in earlier studies investigating congruency effects between presented objects and required grips, when it comes to action goals, or functional knowledge of object use, action semantics (e.g. Tucker and Ellis, 2001) are not automatically activated upon observation of an object, as is shown by the absence of the word priming effect in the finger-lifting condition in the first experiment, but are selected in accordance with the action intention of the actor.

Semantic activation in preparing meaningful and meaningless actions

Although in everyday life many objects are normally associated with typical goal locations ('mouth' for cup), it is often the case that one object can be used in many different ways, depending on the context within which the object is perceived (e.g. using a knife to spread butter or to cut your meat). An important aspect in the evolution and selection of human behavior seems to be the ability to flexibly adjust one's strategies to environmental demands. Concerning the acquisition of action semantics, besides developing long-term representations of object use, it is equally important to be able to implement short-term action intentions (e.g. hitting a mosquito with a newspaper).

To investigate the effects of short-term action goals upon the activation of semantic information, we provided subjects with the instruction to perform meaningful and meaningless actions with a cup and a magnifying glass (M. Van Elk et al., unpublished data). In half of all blocks subjects were instructed to bring both objects to their mouth, while in the other half they were encouraged to bring both objects to their right eye. A semantic categorization task was used and subjects had to delay the execution of the action until they recognized a word that represented a body part (similar to the third experiment in Lindemann et al., 2006). It was hypothesized that if subjects prepared to execute a meaningful action that is normally associated with the use of the object (e.g. bringing the cup to their mouth) a similar word-congruency effect could be expected as in the previous experiments (e.g. faster responding to 'mouth' as compared to 'eye' for intending to use the cup). However, with the intention to perform a meaningless action (e.g. bringing the cup to the eye), long-term action knowledge has to be overruled in order to comply with the short-term action intention of the actor.

Results are represented in Figure 25.3, Experiment 5 and indicate that when subjects performed actions normally associated with the objects they were faster to respond to words that consistently described the goal-location of the action, replicating the results of Lindemann *et al.* (2006). Interestingly, when subjects intended to perform an incorrect action with an object, response latencies were sped up for words describing the short-term goal location of the intended action (e.g. faster responding to 'eye' compared to 'mouth', when intending to bring the cup to the eye).

These findings convincingly show that the intention to perform a meaningless action with an object can overrule priming effects from long-term conceptual knowledge associated with the object. Apparently, the present action goal of the actor determines the selection of semantic information in accordance with the intention of the actor. Theoretical implications of these findings will be discussed in the final part of this chapter.

Theoretical implications

As discussed in the section 'Theories of conceptual knowledge', a growing number of studies support the view that human cognition is deeply rooted in bodily activity (Gallese and Lakoff, 2005). Nowadays, discussion focuses on the way in which conceptual knowledge is organized and represented over different brain areas. In the present chapter we proposed the concept of action semantics as a useful way to think about conceptual knowledge for action. We argued that an important factor in the acquisition and use of action semantics is the action goal that is selected for a particular object. In the third section, two recent studies were discussed in more detail to support our view that semantics for action become activated selectively in accordance with the goal of the actor. When intending to grasp a cup, subjects responded faster if the target word consistently described the spatial goal of the intended action (Lindemann *et al.*, 2006). However, when subjects were instructed to perform meaningless actions with the objects, the word-congruency effects reversed according to the present action intention of the actor (M. Van Elk *et al.*, unpublished data). That is, subjects responded faster to the word 'eye' if they were intending to bring the cup to their eye, irrespective of the learned association in long-term memory to bring cups to the mouth.

In this final section we will compare different approaches to conceptual knowledge for action in relation to the presented findings. First, dissociations between functional knowledge ('what to use an object for') and pragmatic knowledge ('how to use an object') in neuropsychological patients are in line with our view that action goals and action means are two distinct aspects of action semantics (Leiguarda and Marsden, 2000). Exactly how action goals and means are represented in the brain is a matter of ongoing study. Different parts of the motor system appear to contribute to the retrieval of conceptual knowledge for action consistent with the sensory–functional hypothesis which argues for conceptual knowledge being organized according to modality (Warrington and Shallice, 1984).

A similar view is proposed by perceptual symbols theory (Barsalou, 1999) according to which conceptual knowledge is represented in modality-specific brain systems. Although perceptual symbols theory does not explicitly focus on conceptual knowledge used in action, the retrieval of conceptual knowledge about object use is believed to involve sensorimotor simulation that includes all necessary features of a previously encountered object. For example, a conceptual representation of 'cup' is acquired by countless interactions with cups and related actions directed towards them. Therefore the conceptual representation of cup would probably include a perceptual simulation of a prototypical 'cup' and a motor simulation of bringing the cup towards the mouth. Perceptual symbols theory could account for priming effects resulting from preparation of meaningful actions for which a perceptual simulation is available (Lindemann *et al.*, 2006). However, it is more difficult for the theory to explain the reversal of priming effects that were found with meaningless or unusual actions as presented in 'Semantic activation in preparing meaningful and meaningless actions' (M. Van Elk *et al.*, unpublished data).

Perceptual symbols theory takes the prototypical concept as the cornerstone around which our conceptual knowledge is built. It would be interesting to think about what kind of simulations might underlie the flexible use of conceptual knowledge. Given the short-term priming effects in congruence with the immediate action intention it might be that a perceptual simulation also includes the short-term goal. Whenever a person intends to bring a magnifying glass to the mouth, the goal-related concept 'mouth' might form part of the action representation. However, the way in which perceptual simulations are flexibly selected by combining different representations into new nonexisting concepts or by preparing novel actions would need to be clarified.

The two-route model to action proposes a direct route from vision to action that bypasses semantic information (Rumiati and Humphreys, 1998; Rumiati and Tessari, 2002). The two-route model accounts well for the failure of neuropsychological patients to imitate either meaningful or meaningless actions. Within this framework the findings of Van Elk *et al.* (unpublished data), in which participants performed either meaningful or meaningless actions with common objects, might be interpreted as reflecting the differential use of both pathways to action. When participants intend to perform meaningful actions with objects the semantic route is activated, in which long-term conceptual knowledge about the use of objects is represented. Thereby, the two-route model to action accounts nicely for the activation of semantic knowledge in the preparation of meaningful actions. In contrast, the indirect route from perception to action might be used when participants perform meaningless actions with objects. However, the priming effects of goal-relevant semantic information when preparing meaningless actions suggest that having a goal-representation is an important aspect that guides both our meaningful and meaningless actions.

According to ideomotor theory of action, stored effect-representations enable people to select the appropriate action. Event-codes consist of contingent response–effect couplings that have been shaped over the course of our lives. Accordingly, preparing to grasp a cup will be associated with the typical goal of bringing it to the mouth. In a similar way the principle of associative learning states that stimulus–response associations reflect the amount of experience of acting in a particular way towards visual stimuli. However, ideo-motor theory and associative learning face major difficulties when it comes to explaining short-term priming effects of action intention, as discussed in the present chapter. When subjects prepared meaningless actions with objects that they obviously had never conducted before, we found a selective activation of words that were congruent to the present short-term action goal. If priming-effects of action intention rely solely on asso-ciative learning we might have expected them to disappear when subjects prepared meaningless actions, just like automatic effects of imitation could be cancelled out by training participants to respond in a different way towards stimuli (Heyes *et al.*, 2005). In contrast, we have shown that priming of words that are congruent to normal object use could be reversed when subjects had an action intention different from normal object use (M. Van Elk *et al.*, unpublished data). This word-congruency effect reveals a counter-statistical association, as most participants probably will not have much experience bringing cups to their eye.

However, it might be argued that while participants repeatedly brought objects towards incongruent action goals, new short-term associations between grasping the object and the incongruent goal indeed were established. According to the associative learning approach (Heyes *et al.*, 2005), long-term stimulus–response associations were learned by practice and can be flexibly adjusted by training. Within the domain of imita-tion Heyes *et al.* (2005) convincingly showed that training participants to respond in an incongruent way to observed actions could cancel out the effects of automatic imitation. In a similar way, novel semantics for action might be established when subjects repeat-edly conducted unusual actions towards objects. By allowing the flexible acquisition of novel action semantics, both ideomotor theory and the principle of associative learning do a better job than other theories of conceptual knowledge in action. However, in contrast with both theories we suggest that the acquisition of novel action semantics depends heavily on the goal of the actor. It is not the case that associations are arbitrarily consolidated according to incoming bottom-up stimulus information. Typically, the action intention of a person determines what kind of information is selected and attended. For example, it does not seem plausible that the simple observation of a cup automati-cally elicits a complete motor program that subsequently needs to be inhibited. A much simpler view is that what you intend to do with a cup determines the kind of information that is selected.

To conclude, we propose that the selection of action semantics depends critically on the action intention of the actor. Whenever a usual action is conducted with an object, associated semantic information is being activated accordingly, whereas when an object is used in an inappropriate manner, the short-term behavioral goal temporarily overrules the long-term associations. The selection processes underlying action semantics there-fore bear resemblance to 'selection-for-action' in perception (Allport, 1987).

Conclusions

In sum, in the present chapter we sought to outline the concept of action semantics by presenting a review of existing literature on functional mechanisms underlying conceptual knowledge and goal-directed behavior supplied with recent empirical evidence supporting selection-for-action at the level of semantics. Our findings suggest a tight connection between semantic knowledge that is used in action and language, reflected by conceptual priming effects from action preparation to language processing. These findings suggest that the theory of selection-for-action (Allport, 1987) may be extended to include selection of semantic information that is relevant for the intended action and that the theory of selection-for-action may provide a useful framework for studying the associations between language, action and perception. We suggest that, comparable with the selection of perceptual information that is relevant to our current intentions and behavioral goals, the selection of action semantics may be equally important for smoothly moving throughout the world. Access to stored long-term conceptual action representations and acquisition of novel action semantics both enable us to adapt our behavior flexibly to continually changing environmental demands.

The study of action semantics provides important insight into the organization of our conceptual knowledge and supports the idea that action knowledge is represented in sensorimotor systems. In addition, mechanisms of action, perception and language should not be studied in isolation, since the retrieval of semantic information involves action, visual as well as lexical semantics. Developmental studies are expected to provide important insight into the acquisition of action semantics and neuroimaging studies may help to understand the neural organization underlying knowledge of action goals and action means. Behavioral and electrophysiological approaches may contribute to generate further insight into the timing of activation and the flexible selection of conceptual knowledge that guides our behavior, providing new and exciting directions for future research.

References

Allport, A. (1987) Attention and selection-for-action. In Heuer, H. and Sanders, A. F. (eds), *Perspectives on Perception and Action*, pp. 395–420. Erlbaum, Hillsdale, NJ.

Barsalou, L. W. (1999) Perceptual symbol systems. *Behavioral and Brain Sciences*, **22**, 577–660.

Barsalou, L. W., Simmons, W. K., Barbey, A. K. and Wilson C. D. (2003) Grounding conceptual knowledge in modality-specific systems. *Trends in Cognitive Sciences*, **7**, 84–91.

Bekkering, H. and Neggers, S. F.W. (2002) Visual search is modulated by action intentions. *Psychological Science*, **13**, 370–375.

Bekkering, H. and Wohlschläger, A. (2000) Action perception and imitation: a tutorial. In Prinz, W. and Hommel, B. (eds), *Attention and Performance XIX: Common Mechanisms in Perception and Action*, pp. 294–314. Oxford University Press, Oxford.

Bekkering, H., Wohlschläger, A. and Gattis, M. (2000) Imitation of gestures in children is goal-directed. *Quarterly Journal of Experimental Psychology*, **53**, 153–164.

Borgo, F. and Shallice, T. (2001) When living things and other 'sensory quality' categories behave in the same fashion: a novel category specificity effect. *Neurocase*, **7**, 201–220.

Buccino, G., Riggio, L., Melli, G., Binkofski, F., Gallese, V. and Rizzolatti, G. (2005) Listening to action-related sentences modulates the activity of the motor system: a combined TMS and behavioral study. *Cognitive Brain Research*, **24**, 355–363.

Buxbaum, L. J. (2001) Ideomotor apraxia: a call to action. *Neurocase*, **7**, 445–458.

Buxbaum, L. J. and Saffran, E. M. (2002) Knowledge of object manipulation and object function: dissociations in apraxic and nonapraxic subjects. *Brain and Language*, **82**, 179–199.

Calvo-Merino, B., Glaser, D. E., Grèzes, J., Passingham, R. E. and Haggard, P. (2005) Action observation and acquired motor skills: an FMRI study with expert dancers. *Cerebral Cortex*, **15**, 1243–1249.

Caramazza, A. and Mahon, B. Z. (2003) The organization of conceptual knowledge: the evidence from category-specific semantic deficits. *Trends in Cognitive Sciences*, **7**, 354–361.

Caramazza, A. and Shelton, J. R. (1998) Domain-specific knowledge systems in the brain: the animate–inanimate distinction. *Journal of Cognitive Neuroscience*, **10**, 1–34.

Carpenter, M., Akhtar, N. and Tomasello, M. (1998) Fourteen- through 18-month-old infants differentially imitate intentional and accidental actions. *Infant Behavior and Development*, **21**, 315–330.

Carpenter, M., Pennington, B. F. and Rogers, S. J. (2001) Understanding others' intentions in children with autism and children with developmental delays. *Journal of Autism and Developmental Disorders*, **31**, 589–599.

Chainay, H. and Humphreys, G. W. (2002) Privileged access to action for objects relative to words. *Psychonomic Bulletin and Review*, **9**, 348–355.

Chao, L. L. and Martin, A. (2000) Representation of manipulable man-made objects in the dorsal stream. *Neuroimage*, **153**, 260–265.

Clark, A. (1997) *Being There: Putting Brain, Body and World Together Again*. MIT Press, Cambridge, MA.

Craighero, L., Fadiga, L., Rizzolatti, G. and Umiltà, C. (1999) Action for perception: a motor-visual attentional effect. *Journal of Experimental Psychology: Human Perception and Performance*, **25**, 1673–1692.

Creem, S. H. and Proffitt, D. R. (2001) Grasping objects by their handles: a necessary interaction between cognition and action. *Journal of Experimental Psychology: Human Perception and Performance*, **27**, 218–228.

de Lafuente, V. and Romo, R. (2004) Language abilities of motor cortex. *Neuron*, **41**, 178–180.

Fiez, J. A., Raichle, M. E., Balota, D. A., Tallal, P. and Petersen, S. E. (1996) PET activation of posterior temporal regions during auditory word presentation and verb generation. *Cerebral Cortex*, **6**, 1–10.

Fodor, J. A. (1983) *Modularity of Mind: An essay on Faculty Psychology*. MIT Press, Cambridge, MA.

Gainotti, G., Silveri, M. C., Daniele, A. and Giustolisi, L. (1995) Neuroanatomical correlates of category-specific impairments: a critical survey. *Memory*, **3/4**, 247–264.

Gallese, V. and Goldman, A. (1998) Mirror neurons and the simulation theory of mind-reading. *Trends in Cognitive Sciences*, **2**, 493–501.

Gallese, V. and Lakoff, G. (2005) The brain's concepts: the role of the sensory-motor system in conceptual knowledge. *Cognitive Neuropsychology*, **22**, 455–479.

Gallese, V., Fadiga, L., Fogassi, L. and Rizzolatti, G. (1996) Action recognition in the premotor cortex. *Brain*, **119**, 593–609.

Gentilucci, M. and Gangitano, M. (1998) Influence of automatic word reading on motor control. *European Journal of Neuroscience*, **10**, 752–756.

Gergely, G., Nàdasdy, Z., Csibra, G. and Biró, S. (1995) Taking the intentional stance at 12 months of age. *Cognition*, **56**, 165–193.

Gergely, G., Bekkering, H. and Kir·ly, I. (2002) Rational imitation in preverbal infants. *Nature*, **415**, 755.

Gibson, J. J. (1986) *The Ecological Approach to Visual Perception*. Erlbaum, Hillsdale, NJ.

Glenberg, A. M. and Kaschak, M. P. (2002) Grounding language in action. *Psychonomic Bulletin and Review*, **9**, 558–565.

Glover, S. (2004) Separate visual representations in the planning and control of action. *Behavioral and Brain Sciences*, **27**, 3–24.

Glover, S. and Dixon, P. (2002) Semantics affect the planning but not control of grasping. *Experimental Brain Research*, **146**, 383–387.

Glover, S., Rosenbaum, D. A., Graham, J. and Dixon, P. (2004) Grasping the meaning of words. *Experimental Brain Research*, **154**, 103–108.

Grafton, S. T., Arbib, M. A., Fadiga, L. and Rizzolatti, G. (1996) Localization of grasp representations in humans by positron emission tomography. 2. Observation compared with imagination. *Experimental Brain Research*, **112**, 103–111.

Grafton, S. T., Fadiga, L., Arbib, M. A. and Rizzolatti, G. (1997) Premotor cortex activation during observation and naming of familiar tools. *Neuroimage*, **6**, 231–236.

Grèzes, J. and Decety, J. (2002) Does visual perception of object afford action? Evidence from a neuroimaging study. *Neuropsychologia*, **40**, 212–222.

Grèzes, J., Tucker, M., Ellis, R. and Passingham, R. E. (2003) Objects automatically potentiate action: an fMRI study of implicit processing. *European Journal of Neuroscience*, **17**, 2735–2740.

Hannus, A., Cornelissen, F. W., Lindemann, O. and Bekkering, H. (2005) Selection-for-action in visual search. *Acta Psychologica*, **118**, 171–191.

Hebb, D. O. (1949) *The Organization of Behaviour*. Wiley, New York.

Heilman, K. M., Rothi, L. J. and Valenstein, E. (1981) Two forms of ideomotor apraxia. *Neurology*, **32**, 342–346.

Heyes, C., Bird, G., Johnson, H. and Haggard, P. (2005) Experience modulates automatic imitation. *Cognitive Brain Research*, **22**, 233–240.

Hommel, B. (1996) The cognitive representation of action: automatic integration of perceived action effects. *Psychological Research*, **59**, 176–186.

Hommel, B., Müsseler, J., Aschersleben, G. and Prinz, W. (2001) The theory of event coding (TEC): a framework for perception and action planning. *Behavioral and Brain Sciences*, **24**, 849–937.

Iacoboni, M., Woods, R. P., Brass, M., Bekkering, H., Mazziotta, J. C. and Rizzolatti, G. (1999) Cortical mechanisms of human imitation. *Science*, **286**, 2526–2528.

James, W. (1890) *The Principles of Psychology*. Dover, New York.

Jervis, C., Bennett, K., Thomas, J., Lim, S. and Castiello, U. (1999) Semantic category interference effects upon the reach-to-grasp movement. *Neuropsychologia*, **37**, 857–868.

Kable, J. W., Lease-Spellmeyer, J. and Chatterjee, A. (2002) Neural substrates of action event knowledge. *Journal of Cognitive Neuroscience*, **14**, 795–805.

Klatzky, R. L., Pellegrino, J. W., McCloskey, B. P. and Doherty, S. (1989) Can you squeeze a tomato? The role of motor representations in semantic sensibility judgments. *Journal of Memory and Language*, **28**, 56–77.

Laiacona, M., Capitani, E. and Caramazza, A. (2003) Category-specific semantic deficits do not reflect the sensory/functional organization of the brain: a test of the 'sensory quality' hypothesis. *Neurocase*, **9**, 221–231.

Lakoff, G. and Johnson, M. (1999) *Philosophy in the Flesh*. Basic Books, New York.

Leiguarda, R. C. and Marsden, C. (2000) Limb apraxias: higher-order disorders of sensorimotor integration. *Brain*, **123**, 860–879.

Lindemann, O., Stenneken, P., Van Schie, H. T. and Bekkering, H. (2006) Semantic activation in action planning. *Journal of Experimental Psychology: Human Perception and Performance*, **32**, 633–643.

Majdanzic, J., Grol, M. J., Van Schie, H. T., Verhagen, L., Toni, I. and Bekkering, H. (in press). The role of immediate and final goals in action planning: an fMRI study.

Martin, A. and Chao, L. L. (2001) Semantic memory and the brain: structure and processes. *Current Opinion in Neurobiology*, **11**, 194–201.

Martin, A., Haxby, J. V., Lalonde, F. M., Wiggs, C. L. and Ungerleider, L. G. (1995) Discrete cortical regions associated with knowledge of color and knowledge of action. *Science*, **270**, 102–105.

Maxfield, L. (1997) Attention and semantic priming: A review of prime task effects. *Consciousness and Cognition*, **6**, 204–218.

Meltzoff, A. N. (1995) Understanding the intentions of others: Re-enactment of intended acts by 18-month-old children. *Developmental Psychology*, **31**, 1–16.

Meltzoff, A. N. and Moore, M. K. (1995) Infant's understanding of people and things: From body imitation to folk psychology. In Bermudez, J. L. Marcel, A. and Eilan, N. (eds), *The Body and the Self*, pp. 43–69. MIT Press, Cambridge, MA.

Murata, A., Fadiga, L., Fogassi, L., Gallese, V., Raos, V. and Rizzolatti, G. (1997) Object representation in the ventral premotor cortex (Area F5) of the monkey. *Journal of Neurophysiology*, 78, 2226–2230.

Neely, J. H. (1991) Semantic priming effects in visual word recognition: a selective review of current findings and theories. In Besner, D. and Humphreys, G. W. (eds), *Basic Progress in Reading: Visual Word Recognition*, pp. 264–333. Erlbaum, Hillsdale, NJ.

Ochipa, C., Rothi, L. J. G and Heilman, K. M. (1992) Conceptual apraxia in Alzheimer's disease. *Brain*, 115, 1061–1071.

Pecher, D., Zeelenberg, Z. and Barsalou, L. W. (2004) Sensorimotor simulations underlie conceptual representations: Modality-specific effects of prior activation. *Psychonomic Bulletin and Review*, 11, 164–167.

Phillips, A. T. and Wellman, H. M. (2005) Infants' understanding of object-directed action. *Cognition*, 98, 137–155.

Piaget, J. (1953) *The Origin of Intelligence in the Child* (trans. Cook, M.). Routledge & Kegan Paul. London

Pulvermüller, F., Shtyrov, Y. and Illmoniemi, R. (2005) Brain signatures of meaning access in action word recognition. *Journal of Cognitive Neuroscience*, 17, 884–892.

Rizzolatti, G., Fadiga, L., Fogassi, L. and Gallese, V. (1996) Premotor cortex and the recognition of motor actions. *Cognitive Brain Research*, 3, 131–141.

Rizzolatti, G., Fogassi, L. and Gallese, V. (2001) Neurophysiological mechanisms underlying the understanding and imitation of action. *Nature Reviews Neuroscience*, 2, 661–670.

Rosenbaum, D. A., Loukopoulos, L. D., Meulenbroek, R. G. J., Vaughan, J. and Englebrecht, S. E. (1995) Planning reaches by evaluating stored postures. *Psychological Review*, 102, 28–67.

Rosenbaum, D. A., Meulenbroek, R. J., Vaughan, J. and Jansen, C. (2001) Posture-based motion planning: applications to grasping. *Psychological Review*, 108, 709–734.

Rumiati, R. I. and Humphreys, G. W. (1998) Recognition by action: dissociating visual and semantic routes to action in normal observers. *Journal of Experimental Psychology: Human Perception and Performance*, 24, 631–647.

Rumiati, R. I. and Tessari, A. (2002) Imitation of novel and well-known actions: the role of short-term memory. *Experimental Brain Research*, 142, 425–433.

Rumiati, R. I. *et al.* (2005) Common and differential neural mechanisms supporting imitation of meaningful and meaningless actions. *Journal of Cognitive Neuroscience*, 17, 1420–1439.

Sirigu *et al.* (1998) Distinct frontal regions for processing sentence syntax and story grammar. *Cortex*, 34, 771–778.

Sommerville, J. A. and Woodward, A. L. (2005) Pulling out the intentional structure of action: the relation between action processing and action production in infancy. *Cognition*, 95, 1–30.

Stanfield, R. A. and Zwaan, R. A. (2001) The effect of implied orientation derived from verbal context on picture recognition. *Psychological Science*, 12, 153–156.

Tettamanti, M. *et al.* (2005) Listening to action-related sentences activates fronto-parietal motor circuits. *Journal of Cognitive Neuroscience*, 17, 273–281.

Tootell, R. B. *et al.* (1995) Functional analysis of human MT and related visual cortical areas using magnetic resonance imaging. *Journal of Neuroscience*, 15, 3215–3230.

Tranel, D., Kemmerer, D., Adolphs, R., Damasio, H. and Damasio, A. R. (2003) Neural correlates of conceptual knowledge for actions. *Cognitive Neuropsychology*, 20, 409–432.

Tucker, J. and Ellis, R. (2001) The potentiation of grasp types during visual object categorization. *Visual Cognition*, 8, 769–800.

Umiltà, M. A. *et al.* (2001) I know what you are doing. A neurophysiological study. *Neuron*, **31**, 155–165.

Van Schie, H.T. and Bekkering, H. (2007) Neural mechanisms underlying immediate and final action goals in object use reflected by slow-wave brain potentials. *Brain Research*, **1148**, 183–197.

Van Schie, H. T., Wijers, A. A., Kellenbach, M. L. and Stowe, L. A. (2003) An event-related potential investigation of the relationship between semantic and perceptual levels of representation. *Brain and Language*, **86**, 300–325.

Van Schie, H. T., Mars, R. B., Coles, M. G. H. and Bekkering, H. (2004) Modulation of activity in medial frontal and motor cortices during error observation. *Nature Neuroscience*, **7**, 549–554.

Warrington, E. K. and Shallice, T. (1984) Category specific semantic impairments. *Brain*, **107**, 829–854.

Woodward, A. L. (1998) Infants selectively encode the goal object of an actor's reach. *Cognition*, **69**, 1–34.

Yoon, E. Y. and Humphreys, G. W. (2005) Direct and indirect effects of action on object classification. *Memory and Cognition*, **33**, 1131–1146.

Zalla, T., Pradat-Diehl, P. and Sirigu, A. (2003) Perception of action boundaries in patients with frontal lobe damage. *Neuropsychologia*, **41**, 1619–1627.

Zwaan, R. A. and Taylor, L. J. (2006) Seeing, acting, understanding: motor resonance in language comprehension. *Journal of Experimental Psychology: General*, **135**, 1–11.

26

On the origin of intentions

Jan Peter de Ruiter, Matthijs L. Noordzij, Sarah Newman-Norlund, Peter Hagoort and Ivan Toni

Any model of motor control or sensorimotor transformations starts from an intention to trigger a cascade of neural computations, yet how intentions themselves are generated remains a mystery. Part of the difficulty in dealing with this mystery might be related to the received wisdom of studying sensorimotor processes and intentions in individual agents. Here we explore the use of an alternative approach, focused on understanding how we induce intentions in other people. Under the assumption that generating intentions in a third person relies on similar mechanisms to those involved in generating first-person intentions, this alternative approach might shed light on the origin of our own intentions. Therefore, we focus on the cognitive and cerebral operations supporting the generation of communicative actions, i.e. actions designed (by a Sender) to trigger (in a Receiver) the recognition of a given communicative intention. We present empirical findings indicating that communication requires the Sender to select his behavior on the basis of a prediction of how the Receiver will interpret this behavior; and that there is spatial overlap between the neural structures supporting the generation of communicative actions and the generation of first-person intentions. These results support the hypothesis that the generation of intentions might be a particular instance of our ability to induce and attribute mental states to an agent. We suggest that motor intentions are retrodictive with respect to the neurophysiological mechanisms that generate a given action, while being predictive with respect to the potential intention attribution evoked by a given action in other agents.

Introduction

Models of motor control or sensorimotor transformations presuppose the existence of an intention that is responsible for triggering a cascade of neural computations (Haggard, 2005; Wolpert and Ghahramani, 2000), yet it remains a mystery how or why motor intentions are generated. The concept of intention is somehow slippery, varying from a cognitive prediction of the immediate consequences of an action [i.e. 'intentions in action': Searle, 1983; 'proximal intentions': Bratman, 1987; 'motor intentions': Jeannerod, 2006] to a neurophysiological description of early preparatory processes (Snyder *et al.*, 1997; Calton *et al.*, 2002; Thoenissen *et al.*, 2002; Lau *et al.*, 2004)—see also Pacherie (2006) for a recent taxonomy of intention. Furthermore, the private nature of this phenomenon makes it difficult to investigate empirically, and several studies on motor intentions have followed the introspective approach of Libet *et al.* (1983). In this setting, subjects are asked to perform 'freely capricious' finger flexions, and the onset of their urge to move (W-judgments) is quantified by means of a cross-modal timing method. This seminal study reported that we become aware of our motor intentions ~200 ms before actually starting a movement, and ~150 ms before we think we have started to move (Libet *et al.*, 1983). Given that W-judgments occur much later than the first electrophysiological signs of movement preparation (Bereitschaftpotential: Kornhuber and Deecke, 1965), Libet's finding was the first empirical demonstration that, on a trial-by-trial basis, awareness of motor intentions cannot be causally related to action generation. Later studies have shown that W-judgments are related to a specific movement (Haggard and Eimer, 1999), and that parietal patients (but not cerebellar patients) are impaired in providing such judgments (Sirigu *et al.*, 2004), pointing to the possibility that W-judgments might be related to a perception of the motor preparatory process (Haggard, 2005). Accordingly, recent data have shown that the Libet's task is more appropriate to assess the effects of paying attention to the urge to move than to study motor intentions *per se* (Keller and Heckhausen, 1990; Lau *et al.*, 2006, in press). In particular Lau *et al.* (in press) have provided strong evidence in favor of the postdictive nature of W-judgments, by showing that the perceived onset of a motor intention can be shifted backward in time by applying transcranial magnetic stimulation at the level of the pre-supplementary motor area (SMA) up to 200 ms after the movement was executed. These results fit with the general thesis that motor intentions might represent confabulatory and postdictive phenomena (Wegner, 2002). However, the causal irrelevance of motor intentions for the performance of a movement raises the issue of their functional role. Why would natural selection preserve the use of neural resources for this confabulatory process?

In this chapter we argue that part of the difficulty that arises when dealing with motor intentions might be related to the received wisdom of studying sensorimotor and cognitive processes in individual agents. We suggest temporarily suspending the initial query concerning the origin of first-person intentions, and focusing first on the problem of how we induce intentions in other people. The rationale of this approach is to try to tackle the issue of third-person intentions, and then to use this knowledge to understand better how first-person intentions are generated.

At first glance, this approach sounds counter-intuitive, since it suggests that intention, a prototypically private phenomenon, might actually be better understood in a social context. Yet this approach simply relies on the assumption that generating intentions in a third person uses mechanisms that are similar to those involved in generating first-person intentions. This assumption is just a particular instance of the suggestion that understanding our own mental states might be related to our ability to understand the mental states of others (Frith and Frith, 2006b; Prinz, 2006), or more generally that apparently private cognitive phenomena might be better understood in a social perspective (Roepstorff and Frith, 2004; Smith and Semin, 2004; Knoblich and Sebanz, 2006).

In this social perspective, the issue of the origin of intentions can be re-phrased and operationalized as follows: How does an agent generate intentions in another person? Obviously, in order to alter the mental state of another person (we will call this person a 'Receiver'), the agent (a 'Sender') needs to generate an observable behavior (or refrain from generating it when the behavior is expected). The behavior of the Sender might then lead to the generation of intentions in the Receiver. With this approach, intentions have a clear starting point, defined by the behavior used to generate the intention. Furthermore, recognizing the intentions of a Sender from his overt behavior is one of the cornerstones of human–human communication: *communication is achieved when a recipient recognizes the intention with which a communicative act is produced* (Grice, 1957; Levinson, 1995; Sperber and Wilson, 2001). Therefore, the issue that we need to address first, before dealing with first-person intentions, is the issue of communication.

The generation of communicative intentions: encoding/decoding approaches

One might argue that communication is even less tractable than intention generation. However, the former issue enjoys the advantage of having been conceptualized in a few explanatory frameworks. For instance, several scholars take as a starting point the influential 'mathematical theory of communication' (Shannon, 1948). This theory identified the main elements of a communicative system, consisting of a Sender and a Receiver, using encoding and decoding mechanisms, respectively, to transfer a signal through a physical medium. We loosely use these elements in the analyses that follow, but this does not imply that we rely on the encoding/decoding framework of Shannon's theory. This theory was formulated to solve an engineering problem, namely to minimize the effect of noise on signal transfer, rather than a cognitive problem like the generation of communicative intentions. Even in a noiseless medium, a Sender would be left with the hard problem of selecting a particular behavior from his motor repertoire in order to evoke a specific intention in a Receiver.

Other authors have used Shannon's scheme and focused their analysis of human communication on the parity problem (Liberman and Mattingly, 1985). This is the problem of having a common code that counts for both Sender and Receiver, without any prior agreement. Liberman raised this issue in a phonetic context, trying to explain how the same phonetic unit can remain perceptually invariant despite dramatic changes in its acoustic properties as a function of the phonological context in which it was embedded. The solution he put forward, the 'motor theory of speech perception', consists in *the unique but lawful relationship between the gestures and the acoustic patterns* (Liberman and Mattingly, 1985). Recently, this theory has experienced renewed interest (Fadiga *et al.*, 2002; Pulvermuller *et al.*, 2006). However, it is not immediately obvious how the sensorimotor coupling between phonetic percepts and motor codes, postulated by this theory, could be applied to language, let alone communication in general. One is drawn to the suspicion that these approaches to the parity problem (Rizzolatti and Arbib, 1998) rely on a conceptual confusion between modality-specific sensorimotor regularities (phonetics), modality-independent linguistic constraints (language), and modality-independent inferential processes that depend on nonlinguistic information (communication).

This issue brings us to a more recent elaboration of the 'motor theory of speech perception' (Rizzolatti and Arbib, 1998; Arbib, 2005). The claim put forward in this elaboration is that sensorimotor couplings (motor resonance: Rizzolatti *et al.*, 1999) somehow allow for solving a semantic parity problem, not just the phonetic parity problem addressed by Liberman. The suggestion here is that Sender and Receiver can establish common ground by exploiting the dominant statistical regularities occurring in the interaction of their bodies with the environment: *actions done by other individuals become messages that are understood by an observer without any cognitive mediation* (Rizzolatti and Craighero, 2004). There is an obvious appeal in this perspective, given its simplicity and the potential for a solid neurobiological link between Sender and Receiver in the form of the mirror neuron system (Arbib, 2005). This position is further strengthened by the widespread use in animal communication systems of one-to-one mapping systems between physical and semantic properties of various behaviors, that is, mapping systems that in principle could be supported by the mirror neuron system. There are several examples, from the alarm calls of vervet monkeys (Cheney and Seyfarth, 1990), to bees' dances (Dyer, 2002), and cephalopod skin displays (Mather, 2004). These mapping systems work well for messages that need to be broadcast, rather than individually tailored, and in which the change in the environment generated by the Sender is unambiguously associated with a particular communicative effect. By the same token, this strength becomes a weakness when motor resonance mechanisms are invoked for solving the parity problem in nonconventional messages, i.e. messages in which there is not an *unequivocal* mapping between a sign and the signified. This is not a marginal problem. Studies on the pragmatics of language have shown that daily-life utterances are pervasively ambiguous: *as a rule, there is no 1:1 mapping between a communicative signal (gesture, speech, etc.) and its communicative intention* (Levinson, 1983). There are other important issues that are not immediately tackled by a motor resonance mechanism. For instance, it remains unclear how direct sensorimotor couplings between Sender and Receiver could float free from sensory or motor events that occur in the environment. This is crucial, since symbols used in communicative exchanges are different from perceptual or sensorimotor representations, insofar as symbols refer to mental representations of the Receiver (Hurford, 2004; Tomasello *et al.*, 2005). Finally, there is a third challenge for accounts of communicative abilities based on the mirror neuron system. Although mirror neurons are responsive to patently nonintentional communicative acts, like a monkey watching another grasping a fruit (Jacob and Jeannerod, 2005), it remains unclear whether and how motor resonance mechanisms can provide a comprehensive account of how Senders manage to generate communicative acts that can be understood by a recipient, acts whose communicative intention is *designed* to be interpretable for a specific Receiver. This particular selection process occurring in the Sender has been called *recipient design* (Sacks and Schegloff, 1979) or *audience design* (Clark and Carlson, 1982).

The generation of communicative intentions: inferential approaches

When the issue of the recognition of the intentions of a Sender is seen from the perspective of recipient design, the problem of parity requirement becomes subsumed in a larger and more fundamental problem. This is the problem of generating actions designed by taking into account that they will need to be interpreted by a specific Recipient. Therefore, the Sender generates a given behavior under the assumption that the Receiver will manage to infer the Sender's private intentions on the basis of his public behavior. From a formal computational viewpoint, the problem faced by the Receiver is intractable (Levinson, 1995; Sperber and Wilson, 2001). Therefore, its solution needs to rely on some heuristics that constrain a potentially infinite search-space. The nature of these heuristics constitutes the battleground between different current accounts of the distinctive human ability to interpret the behavior of conspecifics in terms of its underlying intentions. These accounts are 'theory theory' (Carruthers, 1996), 'theory of mind' (Leslie, 2000), and 'simulation theory' (Goldman, 1992; Heal, 1998). In a nutshell, we could think of constraining the search-space of the Sender by using a pre-existing database of psycho-logical laws ('theory theory') or people's mental states ('theory of mind'). This would allow one to predict and retrodict the relationships between people's actions and people's intentions. Conversely, simulation theory suggests that we infer the intentions underlying people's behavior by generating a simulation of the observed behavior, taking our own conceptual and sensorimotor machinery offline, and then reading the intentions generated by the simulation (Gallese and Goldman, 1998). Without going into the details of this ongoing debate (Gordon, 2005; Goldman and Sebanz, 2005; Saxe, 2005), it is evident that, in the context of communication, the Sender is facing an even more complex problem (i.e. a larger search-space) than the Receiver (empirical support for this claim can be found in J. P. De Ruiter *et al.*, unpublished data). Some authors have denied the existence of such a problem, arguing that the Sender does not normally engage in recipient design, but rather refines his communicative actions on the basis of corrective feedback from the Receiver in the course of multiple communicative exchanges (Keysar *et al.*, 2000). Yet this does not explain how a Sender could select a particular action (among an infinite set of possible actions) appropriate to communicate a particular intention to the Receiver. It might be argued that the communicative problem faced by Sender and Receiver can be solved by means of Bayesian inferential processes (Wolpert *et al.*, 2003), exploiting the commonalities of the priors instantiated in two agents sharing the same environment. However, this solution does not account for communicative actions selected against their dominant statistical priors (to express irony, for instance), and for the single-trial successful interpretation of signal-to-meaning mappings that a Receiver has never encountered before (as during fast learning of novel mappings).

Here, we advance the hypothesis that the heuristics used by the Sender to select a particular action to communicate his intentions is based on a prediction of the process of intention recognition that the Receiver could perform on such an action. The prediction exploits the intention recognition system of the Sender, and it is based on a conceptual model of the Receiver. This suggestion is an elaboration on previous theoretical suggestions that emphasized the inferential nature of communication (Grice, 1957; Levinson, 1983, 2000; Clark, 1985; Levelt, 1989; Sperber and Wilson, 2001). In the following sections, we will present the details of a novel experimental setting we have developed to test this hypothesis.

The tacit communication game (TCG)

In this game, there are two subjects (a Sender and a Receiver—for ease of exposition, we will consider a male Sender and a female Receiver). Sender and Receiver are seated behind separate screens, controlled by a single computer, displaying a 3 × 3 grid (the 'board': Figure 26.1) and two geometrical shapes (rectangles, circles, or triangles: in brief, the 'tokens'). The Sender can move (translate and rotate) the token below the board, the Receiver can move the other token. Translations and rotations were controlled by a hand-held controller, with four face buttons that moved the token to the left, right, up and down; two shoulder buttons rotated the token clockwise and counter-clockwise; a third shoulder button was used as a start button (see below). There were two more (target) tokens inside the game board (Figure 26.1). These target tokens indicated the position and orientation that Sender's and Receiver's (playing) tokens should have at the end of the trial. A trial was correct when the tokens of both Sender and Receiver were in the position and orientation indicated by their respective target tokens (goal configuration). On each trial of the game, Sender and Receiver are asked to overlay their tokens with the goal configuration. Crucially, in the 'communicative' trials, only the Sender has knowledge of the goal configuration. Therefore, in these trials, a Sender/Receiver pair can solve the game only if the Sender manages to convey his knowledge of the goal configuration

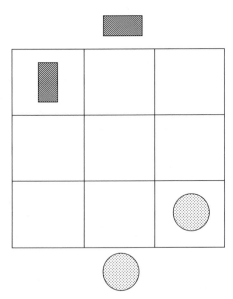

Figure 26.1 Example of workspace in the Tacit communication game, with the Sender's token (circle outside the grid) and his goal (circle within the grid), the Receiver's token (rectangle outside the grid) and her goal (rectangle within the grid).

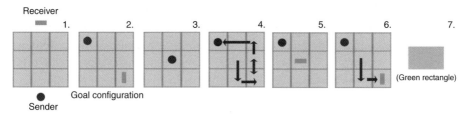

Figure 26.2 Sequence of events in a Communicative trial of the tacit communication game .

1. Sender and Receiver view their tokens (1.5 s)

2. The Sender, but not the Receiver, sees the goal configuration (unlimited time for inspection and planning).

3. The Sender signals his readiness to move by pressing the start button—his shape moves to the center of the board, and the goal configuration disappears.

4. The Sender moves his token on the game board by means of a multi-button controller (max. 5 s). The movements of the Sender's token are visible to the Receiver. The double arrow indicates that the Sender moved back and forth between those two positions.

5. The Receiver signals her readiness to move by pressing the start button—her shape moves to the center of the board.

6. The Receiver moves her token on the game board (max. 5 s). The movements of the Receiver's token are visible to the Sender.

7. Sender and Receiver receive feedback indicating whether they were correct (green box) or incorrect (red box) in matching their token to the goal configuration.

to the Receiver. The only way this could happen is by the Sender moving around his token on the board. Furthermore, participants (starting with the Sender) have unlimited time to prepare their movements and to signal their readiness to move by means of a button press. At this point, the token of the participant is automatically positioned at the centre of the board and the participant has 5 s to move around the board. Consider the problem illustrated in Figure 26.1. During communicative trials, the Sender has to decide not only how to move his token (the circle) to his goal location (down to the right), but also to communicate to the Receiver where *she* should place her token (the rectangle), and in which orientation. It is important to emphasize that the only way the Sender can convey this information to the Receiver is by translating and rotating his token in the board. Figure 26.2 provides a representative example of how the problem illustrated in Figure 26.1 was solved by our participants. Further details on the experimental set-up and on a validation of the TCG are provided by J. P. de Ruiter *et al.* (unpublished data).

There were two further types of trials, in which both Sender and Receiver could see the goal configuration. Therefore, in these trials, the Sender *did not* need to signal to the Receiver the position and orientation that her token should have taken by the end of the trial. In the 'control' trials, the Sender could move directly to his goal configuration, and the Receiver followed suit. In the 'noncommunicative' trials, the Sender was instructed first to overlay his token to the goal configuration of the Receiver, and then move to his goal configuration. The rationale of using these noncommunicative trials was to have trials that were matched to the communicative trials in terms of motor output, but without the need to engage in a communicative exchange (since both Sender and Receiver knew the goal configuration).

Within the communicative trials, the Sender was faced with a variety of communicative problems. The most difficult problems were related to the communication of orientation. If both the Sender and the Receiver had the same shape, or if the shape of the Receiver was not rotated, then the communicative task of the Sender was straightforward. In these trials, the Sender could apply a simple rule to solve the task (go first to the Receivers' goal, then to the Sender's goal). Accordingly, we called these 'conventional communicative' trials. In contrast, if the Sender and the Receiver had different shapes, or if the shape of the Receiver was rotated in such a way that its orientation could not be matched by the shape of the Sender, then the communicative task of the Sender was problematic. In these trials, the Sender could not apply a simple rule to solve the task. Accordingly, we called these 'unconventional communicative' trials.

Behavioral performance

We tested 24 Sender/Receiver pairs (aged 18–26 years, 24 male Senders, 24 female Receivers). Each Sender–Receiver pair performed 80 trials (40 control trials) in two sessions. The same stimuli (including shapes and goal configurations) were used in the communicative and the noncommunicative sessions. The Senders were successful in communicating the goal configuration to the Receivers (Figure 26.3A). In addition, the success rate of Senders and Receivers was much lower on these unconventional trials than on the conventional trials, but still well above chance levels (Figure 26.3B).

Cerebral activity

In the previous sections we have suggested that the communicative problem faced by the Sender might be solved by means of a prediction of intention recognition. Here, we test this hypothesis. If the generation of communicative actions (in the Sender) exploits his

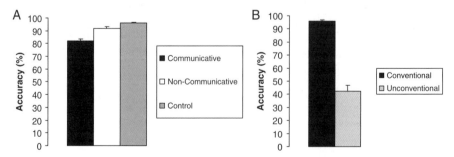

Figure 26.3 Tacit communication game performance. (**A**) Mean accuracy scores for Communicative, Noncommunicative and Control trials. Error bars indicate standard errors. (**B**) Mean accuracy scores for Conventional and Unconventional Communicative trials.

intention recognition system, then there should be a functional overlap between the intention recognition processes of Sender and Receiver. This functional overlap should give rise to a correspondingly cerebral overlap in the brain activity supporting these cognitive processes in the Sender and in the Receiver. Therefore, during performance of the TCG, we used functional magnetic resonance imaging (fMRI) to measure cerebral activity in Senders and Receivers. Given that during the TCG the Sender has an extremely limited time to move around the board (Figure 26.2), it is reasonable to assume that the bulk of simulation of intention recognition takes place after the Sender is presented with the goal configuration, and before he starts to move. Accordingly, the experimental design was organized to disambiguate cerebral activity evoked in the Senders during the planning phase (phase 3 in Figure 26.2) from the other trial events, and to compare the planning phase fMRI signal across the three experimental conditions (Communicative$_{Sender}$, Non-communicative$_{Sender}$, and Control$_{Sender}$ trials). It also appears reasonable to assume that, during the TCG, the Receivers need to engage in intention recognition mainly during the observation of the Senders' movements. Accordingly, we distinguished cerebral activity evoked in the Receivers during the observation of the Senders' movements (Communicative$_{Receiver}$) from the other trial events, and we compared this observation phase fMRI signal with the signal measured in a matched control condition. In this latter condition (Control$_{Receiver}$), the Receivers were asked to move their token to the last position on the board in which the Sender moved his token twice. Therefore, the Communicative$_{Receiver}$ and Control$_{Receiver}$ conditions were matched in terms of attentional load, movement planning, and movement execution, but differed with respect to the presence of intention recognition.

The results were clear-cut. In the Receivers, there was a cluster of significant activity along the posterior part of the superior temporal sulcus, in the right hemisphere (Figure 26.4A). This result confirms previous studies reporting activity in this region during intention

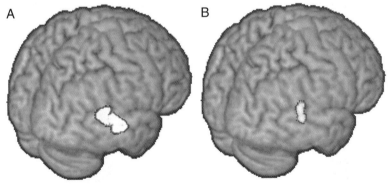

Figure 26.4 (A) Cerebral activity evoked in the Receivers during observation of the Senders' movements in the context of successful performance of the TCG. The cluster of differential activity covers the posterior part of the superior temporal sulcus. (**B**) Cerebral activity evoked in the Senders during planning of the Senders' movements in the context of successful performance of the TCG. This cluster of differential activity falls within the cluster described in panel A.

recognition (Castelli *et al.*, 2000; Saxe *et al.*, 2004; Zacks *et al.*, 2006), extending these inferences to the domain of human communication. Accordingly, the inferential process operating in Receivers (i.e. the recognition of communicative intentions) might rely on the posterior part of the superior temporal sulcus (pSTS) capacity to infer perceptual and/or conceptual scenarios different from those currently experienced by an observer, using learned priors to generate temporal predictions on different sensory materials (Frith and Frith, 2006a; Zilbovicius *et al.*, 2006). Crucially, we found that the same region, in the same hemisphere, was active in the Senders during the planning phase of the TCG (Figure 26.4B). We would like to emphasize that during this phase of the game there was no task-related change in sensory input or motor output (see phase 3 in Figure 26.2). Therefore the activity we measured in this region in the Senders cannot be related to visual motion or hand movements *per se*. This is further confirmed by a *post hoc* analysis of the activity of this region, in which it can be seen that the fMRI signal evoked in the Senders during the *performance* of the communicative movements (phase 4 in Figure 26.2) is not different from zero (Figure 26.5A, black bar).

We performed further controls. For instance, it could be argued that the differential activity we found in the Senders is related to differences in the complexity of the planned movements between Communicative and Noncommunicative trials. Therefore, we considered whether the number of moves performed in the subsequent trial phase

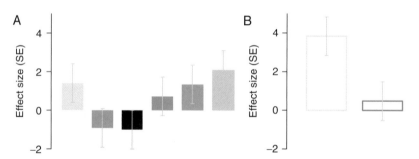

Figure 26.5 (A) Cerebral activity evoked in the right posterior superior temporal sulcus (MNI coordinates: 50, 42, −14, corresponding to the local maximum of the clusters described in Figure 4). The histograms represent the effect size (i.e. parameter estimates of a multiple regression analysis in standard error units) of different trial components. In yellow, activity evoked in the Sender during the planning phase of COMMUNICATIVE trials (corresponding to phase 2 of the TCG as described in Figure 2). In orange, activity evoked in the Sender during the planning phase of NON-COMMUNICATIVE trials. In black, activity evoked in the Sender during the execution phase of the TCG (phase 3 and 4, Figure 2). In grey, activity evoked in the Sender during the planning phase of communicative trials that was related to the number of moves performed in that trial. In cyan, activity evoked in the Receiver during the observation of the Sender's movements (phase 4, Figure 2). In pink, activity evoked in the Sender during the observation of the Receiver's movements (phase 6, Figure 2). **(B)** Differential cerebral activity (at 50, −42, 14) evoked in the Sender during the planning phase of communicative trials with either "unconventional" problems (yellow empty histogram) or "conventional" problems (magenta empty histogram).

(phase 4 in Figure 26.2) could explain the effect we observed—but this was not the case (Figure 26.5A, grey bar). Next, we explored whether this region was responsive during the observation of the Receiver's movements, a further indication that simulation of intention recognition and intention recognition share the same cerebral territory. It can be seen that there was a robust response during this phase (Figure 26.5A, cyan bar). Finally, we explored whether this region was differently engaged when the Sender needed to solve either conventional or nonconventional communicative problems (see behavioral experiment). It can be seen that this region is completely driven by the latter type of communicative problems (Figure 26.5B), an indication that simulation of intention recognition might be used parsimoniously, when it is not possible to solve a communicative problem by means of rule-based behavior.

Given that the processes involved in solving the TCG fall into the general category of making inferences about unobservable psychological states of other agents, we also explored whether we could isolate cerebral activity within the brain networks supporting the two main neurocognitive accounts of 'mind reading', i.e. theory of mind (ToM; Frith and Frith, 2005) and 'simulation theory' (as implemented in the mirror neuron system, MNS; Iacoboni, 2005). This enquiry was made possible by the fact that the cerebral structures supporting ToM and MNS have been mapped into relatively well-defined and largely segregated brain networks (Saxe, 2005; Frith and Frith, 2006b). Despite the increased sensitivity associated with using a-priori search regions (Friston, 1997), we did not find any statistically significant effect in either the ToM or the MNS networks.[1] Taken together, our findings support the hypothesis that Senders, in order to select an action that can convey their communicative intention, engage in a prediction of intention recognition. This prediction appears to be based on a conceptual model of the Receiver, since the intention recognition activity was independent of sensory inputs and motor outputs (Figure 26.5). This finding fits with the neurophysiology of the pSTS. This region is not a primary sensory or motor area, and it is not directly connected to sensory or motor areas (Boussaoud et al., 1990). In this respect, our results fall in the category of conceptual simulation mechanisms (as suggested by Nichols and Stich, 2003), and not in the domain of offline simulation mechanisms with the same inputs as those involved in motor control (as suggested by Gallese and Goldman, 1998 and Rizzolatti and Craighero, 2004). On a more neurobiological note, it can be noticed that the cerebral site involved in intention recognition and simulation of intention recognition (Figure 26.4) falls in a region that has been consistently implicated in the perception of biological motion (Allison et al., 2000; Pelphrey et al., 2005). Given the tight link between impairments in

---

[1] We used spherical volumes of interest, with radius = 10 mm, centered on the following stereotactical (MNI) coordinates: (a) ToM network: −48 −69 21; 54 −54 24; 0 60 12; 3 −60 24 (Saxe et al., 2004); MNS network: −50, 12, 14; 37, −44, 60; 59, −26, 33 (Iacoboni et al., 1999). We did not include the pSTS in the MNS network since pSTS neurons lack mirror properties, i.e. they respond during the observation of goal-directed actions, but not during the execution of similar actions (Perrett et al., 1989; Jellema et al., 2000; Iacoboni, 2005).

communicative abilities and perception of biological motion (Blake *et al.*, 2003; Dakin and Frith, 2005), it is conceivable that these two inferential processes might share a similar neuroanatomical and computational basis. Namely, this temporal region might be involved in evaluating the plausibility of current perceptual evidence given a series of biological priors (for instance: How likely is it that this collection of moving dots describes a person walking? How likely is it that 'can you tell me the time' is a question about my abilities?). One way to test this possibility is to assess whether inter-subjects variation in thresholds of biological motion detection predicts variation in communicative abilities.

On the origin of intentions

What does this tell us about the origin of intentions? In the Introduction, we asked the reader to suspend temporarily the initial query concerning the origin of first-person intentions, and to focus first on the problem of how we induce intentions in other people. We have argued that, in order to effectively induce intentions in other people, we need to select a particular behavior on the basis of a prediction of the intention that a Receiver will attribute to our behavior. In other words, when we are in a social context and we want to influence other people's mental states, we select our behavior on the basis of a preview of the effects of our actions on other people's mental states (Wolpert *et al.*, 2003; see Levelt, 1989 for a similar mechanism in the domain of speech production). This observation might be relevant for understanding the origin of our own intentions insofar as one could envisage that this social predictive mechanism is the same mechanism that generates our own intentions, even when we are in a private rather than in a social setting. The hypothesis we put forward is that what we perceive to be our own intentions are in fact predictions of the *potential* attribution of intentions triggered by our actions in others. In this perspective, the rules that govern the attribution process of first-person intentions might be the same rules that govern the induction of mental states in other agents for communicative purposes (the generation of communicative actions).

This hypothesis fits with the general notion that understanding our own mental states might be related to the ability to understand other people (Frith and Frith, 2006a); and that attributing causal intentions to our own independent minds appears to be a (modern) possibility among a series of historical trajectories, in which other agents (social and religious entities, for instance) were considered the source of intentionality supporting a given behavior (Prinz, 2006). However, it might be argued that our hypothesis is at odds with current models that link intention generation with awareness of the motor preparatory process (Haggard, 2005). These models are supported by empirical evidence pointing to a premotor region, the pre-SMA, as the region crucially involved in generating both actions and awareness of motor intentions (Fried *et al.*, 1991; Haggard and Magno, 1999; Lau *et al.*, 2004). In particular, Fried *et al.* (1991) directly stimulated the mesial frontal cortex of several patients with intractable seizures, evoking both the urge to move and, at higher stimulation currents, actual movements. Crucially, Fried *et al.* (1991) noted that the evoked movements were not necessarily the same movement for which an urge has been reported, and that movements were not invariably evoked when the stimulation current was raised. Therefore, Fried *et al.* (1991) actually provide strong evidence on the lack of a robust relationship, in the pre-SMA, between awareness of motor intentions (operationalized as an introspective 'urge to move') and actual movements. Accordingly, it is conceivable that activity found in the pre-SMA during performance of Libet's task might be related to paying attention to the motor preparatory process, rather than to the generation of motor intentions *per se* (Lau *et al.*, 2004, 2006, in press). By the same token, the hypothesis put forward in this paper predicts that other brain regions (like the pSTS), by virtue of their role in intention attribution, might in fact be responsible for intention generation. While this hypothesis remains to be tested, the available evidence already suggests that the same right pSTS region involved in the generation of third-person intentions might also be involved in the generation of first-person intentions (Toni *et al.*, 2001).

The hypothesis articulated in this paper might appear in conflict with previous suggestions that emphasize the reconstructive character of motor intentions (Wegner, 2002; Lau *et al.*, in press). In fact, it builds on those suggestions. Wegner (2002, 2004) suggested that conscious volitional experiences represent the 'emotion of authorship', a somatic marker important for building a sense of self, and possibly for tagging actions as open to future regulation. In this perspective, a currently experienced intention does not directly influence a currently selected action, but it might leave a cerebral trace that influences future instances of the same action. However, if motor intentions are *post hoc* narratives tuned to influence a future action, why would their phenomenological experience need to be shifted backward in time with respect to an ongoing action? Lau *et al.* (in press) have suggested that this backward shift might be a consequence of a general mechanism based on optimal Bayesian cue integration, in which the weight given to different sources of information is scaled on the variance of their estimate (Ma *et al.*, 2006). Our hypothesis is compatible with these considerations. Motor intentions can be retrodictive with respect to the neurophysiological mechanisms that generate a given action, while being predictive with respect to the potential intention attribution evoked by a given action in other agents.

Conclusions

This chapter has argued that intentions might not constitute a prototypical private phenomenon, as the intuitions of introspection would lead us to believe. Rather, intentions might be related to a need to account for the social consequences of our actions. Humans invariably try to account for the behavior of other agents in terms of underlying mental states. It is conceivable that this attitude might entail the attribution of a mental state to the very agent that generates this attribution. When it comes to intentions, we might interpret our own actions by using the same mechanisms devoted to evaluate other's actions.

This does not need to be a voluntary mechanism, as intention attribution appears to be a quite automatic phenomenon (Heider and Simmel, 1944; Michotte, 1954). On the other hand, a person usually does not elaborate on the intentions of each and every behavior produced, so we are not claiming that this mechanism is continually and necessarily at work. I can reflexively scratch my ear, computing all the necessary sensorimotor transformations necessary for bringing my fingernail to my earlobe without generating or recognizing an intention in this movement. But I can scratch my ear having the intention of doing so, and in this case we suggest that generating this intention relies on the same procedures that allow us to generate communicative actions.

There is some preliminary empirical support for this hypothesis. First, it appears that the generation of communicative actions is based on a prediction of the intention recognition of the Receiver. Second, there appears to be cerebral overlap between the structures supporting intention recognition, prediction of intention recognition, and first-person intention generation. These results point to the possibility of a cognitive overlap between the generation of communicative actions and the origin of first-person intentions, i.e. we hypothesize that the generation of our own intentions is essentially the same process as generating intentions in others. This hypothesis can be further tested, for instance by assessing whether alterations in the ability to generate communicative actions are associated with altered experiences of first-person intentions.

Acknowledgments

This work has been completed in the context of the European Union Integrated Project JAST (Joint Action Science and Technology), grant FP6-IST2-003747.

References

Allison, T., Puce, A. and McCarthy, G. (2000) Social perception from visual cues: role of the STS region. *Trends in Cognitive Sciences*, **4**, 267–278.

Arbib, M. A. (2005) From monkey-like action recognition to human language: an evolutionary framework for neurolinguistics. *Behavioral and Brain Sciences*, **28**, 105–124.

Blake, R., Turner, L. M., Smoski, M. J., Pozdol, S. L. and Stone, W. L. (2003) Visual recognition of biological motion is impaired in children with autism. *Psychological Science*, **14**, 151–157.

Boussaoud, D., Ungerleider, L. G. and Desimone, R. (1990) Pathways for motion analysis: cortical connections of the medial superior temporal and fundus of the superior temporal visual areas in the macaque. *Journal of Comparative Neurology*, **296**, 462–495.

Bratman, M. (1987) *Intention, Plans, and Practical Reason*. Harvard University Press, Cambridge, MA.

Calton, J. L., Dickinson, A. R. and Snyder, L. H. (2002) Non-spatial, motor-specific activation in posterior parietal cortex. *Nature Neuroscience*, **5**, 580–588.

Carruthers, P. (1996) Simulation and self-knowledge: a defence of theory-theory. In Carruthers, P. and Smith, P. K. (eds), *Theories of Theories of Mind*, pp. 22–38. Cambridge University Press, Cambridge.Castelli, F., Happe, F., Frith, U. and Frith, C. (2000) Movement and mind: a functional imaging study of perception and interpretation of complex intentional movement patterns. *Neuroimage*, **12**, 314–325.

Cheney, D. L. and Seyfarth, R. M. (1990) *How Monkeys See the World: Inside the Mind of Another Species*. University of Chicago Press, Chicago.

Clark, H. H. (1985) Language use and language users. In Lindsey, G. and Aronson, E. (eds), *The Handbook of Social Psychology*. Harper & Row, New York.

Dakin, S. and Frith, U. (2005) Vagaries of visual perception in autism. *Neuron*, **48**, 497–507.

De Ruiter, J. P., Noordzij, M. L., Newman-Norlund, S., Newman-Norlund, R., Hagoort, P., Levinson, S. C. and Toni, I. (submitted) Exploring human interactive intelligence.

Dyer, F. C. (2002) The biology of the dance language. *Annual Review of Entomology*, **47**, 917–949.

Fadiga, L., Craighero, L., Buccino, G. and Rizzolatti, G. (2002) Speech listening specifically modulates the excitability of tongue muscles: a TMS study. *European Journal of Neuroscience*, **15**, 399–402.

Fried, I., Katz, A., McCarthy, G., Sass, K. J., Williamson, P., Spencer, S. S. and Spencer, D. D. (1991) Functional organization of human supplementary motor cortex studied by electrical stimulation. *Journal of Neuroscience*, **11**, 3656–3666.

Friston, K. J. (1997) Testing for anatomically specified regional effects. *Human Brain Mapping*, **5**, 133–136.

Frith, C. and Frith, U. (2005) Theory of mind. *Current Biology*, **15**, R644–R645.

Frith, C. D. and Frith, U. (2006a) How we predict what other people are going to do. *Brain Research*, **1079**, 36–46.

Frith, C. D. and Frith, U. (2006b) The neural basis of mentalizing. *Neuron*, **50**, 531–534.

Gallese, V. and Goldman, A. (1998) Mirror neurons and the simulation theory of mind-reading. *Trends in Cognitive Sciences*, **2**, 493–501.

Goldman, A. (1992) In defense of the simulation theory. *Mind and Language*, **7**, 104–119.

Goldman, A. I. and Sebanz, N. (2005) Simulation, mirroring, and a different argument from error. *Trends in Cognitive Sciences*, **9**, 320.

Gordon, R. M. (2005) Simulation and systematic errors in prediction. *Trends in Cognitive Sciences*, **9**, 361–362.

Grice, H. P. (1957) Meaning. *Philosophical Review*, **66**, 377–388.

Haggard, P. (2005) Conscious intention and motor cognition. *Trends in Cognitive Sciences*, **9**, 290–295.

Haggard, P. and Eimer, M. (1999) On the relation between brain potentials and the awareness of voluntary movements. *Experimental Brain Research*, **126**, 128–133.

Haggard, P. and Magno, E. (1999) Localising awareness of action with transcranial magnetic stimulation. *Experimental Brain Research*, **127**, 102–107.

Heal, J. (1998) Co-cognition and off-line simulation: two ways of understanding the simulation approach. *Mind & Language*, **13**, 477–498.

Heider, F. and Simmel, M. (1944) An experimental study of apparent behavior. *The American Journal of Psychology*, **57**, 243–259.

Hurford, J. R. (2004) Language beyond our grasp: what mirror neurons can, and cannot, do for the evolution of language. In Oller, D. K. and Griebel, U. (eds), *Evolution of Communication Systems*, pp. 297–314. MIT Press, Cambridge, MA.

Iacoboni, M. (2005) Neural mechanisms of imitation. *Current Opinion in Neurobiology*, **15**, 632–637.

Iacoboni, M., Woods, R. P., Brass, M., Bekkering, H., Mazziotta, J. C. and Rizzolatti, G. (1999) Cortical mechanisms of human imitation. *Science*, **286**, 2526–2528.

Jacob, P. and Jeannerod, M. (2005) The motor theory of social cognition: a critique. *Trends in Cognitive Sciences*, **9**, 21–25.

Jeannerod, M. (2006) *Motor Cognition: What Actions Tell to the Self*. Oxford University Press, Oxford.

Jellema, T., Baker, C. I., Wicker, B. and Perrett, D. I. (2000) Neural representation for the perception of the intentionality of actions. *Brain Cognition*, **44**, 280–302.

Keller, I. and Heckhausen, H. (1990) Readiness potentials preceding spontaneous motor acts: voluntary vs. involuntary control. *Electroencephalography and Clinical Neurophysiology*, **76**, 351–361.

Keysar, B., Barr, D. J., Balin, J. A. and Brauner, J. S. (2000) Taking perspective in conversation: the role of mutual knowledge in comprehension. *Psychological Science*, **11**, 32–38.

Knoblich, G. and Sebanz, N. (2006) The social nature of perception and action. *Current Directions in Psychological Science*, **15**, 99–104.

Kornhuber, H. H. and Deecke, L. (1965) Hirnpotentialänderungen bei Willkürbewegungen und passiven Bewegungen des Menschen: Bereitschschaftspotential und reafferente Potentiale. *Pflügers Archiv*, **284**, 1–17.

Lau, H. C., Rogers, R. D., Haggard, P. and Passingham, R. E. (2004) Attention to intention. *Science*, **303**, 1208–1210.

Lau, H. C., Rogers, R. D. and Passingham, R. E. (2006) On measuring the perceived onsets of spontaneous actions. *Journal of Neuroscience*, **26**, 7265–7271.

Lau, H. C., Rogers, R. D. and Passingham, R. E. Manipulating the experienced onset of intention after action execution. *Journal of Cognitive Neuroscience*, in press.

Leslie, A. (2000) Theory of mind as a mechanism of selective attention. In Gazzaniga, M. (ed.), *The New Cognitive Neurosciences*, pp. 1235–1247. MIT Press, Cambridge, MA.

Levelt, W. J. M. (1989) *Speaking: From Intention to Articulation*. MIT Press, Cambridge, MA.

Levinson, S. C. (1983) *Pragmatics*. Cambridge University Press, Cambridge.

Levinson, S. C. (1995) Interactional biases in human thinking. In Goody, E. (ed.), *Social Intelligence and Interaction*, pp. 221–260. Cambridge University Press, Cambridge.

Levinson, S. C. (2000) *Presumptive Meanings: The Theory of Generalized Conversational Implicature*. MIT Press, Cambridge, MA.

Liberman, A. M. and Mattingly, I. G. (1985) The motor theory of speech perception revised. *Cognition*, **21**, 1–36.

Libet, B., Gleason, C. A., Wright, E. W. and Pearl, D. K. (1983) Time of conscious intention to act in relation to onset of cerebral activity (readiness-potential). The unconscious initiation of a freely voluntary act. *Brain*, **106** (Pt 3), 623–642.

Ma, W. J., Beck, J. M., Latham, P. E. and Pouget, A. (2006) Bayesian inference with probabilistic population codes. *Nature Neuroscience*, **9**, 1432–1438.

Mather, J. A. (2004) Cephalopod skin displays: from concealment to communication. In Oller, D. K. and Griebel, U. (eds), *Evolution of Communication Systems*, pp. 193–214. MIT Press, Cambridge, MA.

Michotte, A. (1954) *La perception de la causalite*, 2. ed. Publications universitaires de Louvain, Louvain.

Nichols, S. and Stich, S. P. (2003) *Mindreading: An Integrated Account of Pretence, Self-awareness, and Understanding Other Minds*. Clarendon Press, Oxford.

Pacherie, E. (2006) Toward a dynamic theory of intentions. In Pockett, S., Banks, W. P. and Gallagher, S. (eds), *Does Consciousness Cause Behavior?*, pp. 145–168. MIT Press, Cambridge, MA.

Pelphrey, K. A., Morris, J. P., Michelich, C. R., Allison, T. and McCarthy, G. (2005) Functional anatomy of biological motion perception in posterior temporal cortex: an FMRI study of eye, mouth and hand movements. *Cerebral Cortex*, **15**, 1866–1876.

Perrett, D. I., Harries, M. H., Bevan, R., Thomas, S., Benson, P. J., Mistlin, A. J., Chitty, A. J., Hietanen, J. K. and Ortega, J. E. (1989) Frameworks of analysis for the neural representation of animate objects and actions. *Journal of Experimental Biology*, **146**, 87–113.

Prinz, W. (2006) Free will as a social institution. In Pockett, S., Banks, W. P. and Gallagher, S. (eds), *Does Consciousness Cause Behavior?*, pp. 257–276. MIT Press, Cambridge, MA.

Pulvermuller, F., Huss, M., Kherif, F., Moscoso del Prado Martin, F., Hauk, O. and Shtyrov, Y. (2006) Motor cortex maps articulatory features of speech sounds. *Proceedings of the National Academy of Sciences of the USA*, **103**, 7865–7870.

Rizzolatti, G. and Arbib, M. A. (1998) Language within our grasp. *Trends Neuroscience*, **21**, 188–194.

Rizzolatti, G. and Craighero, L. (2004) The mirror-neuron system. *Annual Review of Neuroscience*, **27**, 169–192.

Rizzolatti, G., Fadiga, L., Fogassi, L. and Gallese, V. (1999) Resonance behaviors and mirror neurons. *Archives of Italian Biology*, **137**, 85–100.

Roepstorff, A. and Frith, C. (2004) What's at the top in the top-down control of action? Script-sharing and 'top-top' control of action in cognitive experiments. *Psychological Research*, **68**, 189–198.

Sacks, H. and Schegloff, E. A. (1979) Two preferences in the organization of reference to persons in conversation and their interaction. In Psathas, G. (ed.), *Everyday Language: Studies in Ethnomethodology*, pp. 15–21. Irvington, New York.

Saxe, R. (2005) Against simulation: the argument from error. *Trends in Cognitive Sciences*, **9**, 174–179.

Saxe, R., Xiao, D.-K., Kovacs, G., Perrett, D. I. and Kanwisher, N. (2004) A region of right posterior superior temporal sulcus responds to observed intentional actions. *Neuropsychologia*, **42**, 1435–1446.

Searle, J. R. (1983) *Intentionality. An Essay in the Philosophy of Mind*. Cambridge University Press, Cambridge.

Shannon, C. E. (1948) A mathematical theory of communication. *Bell System Technical Journal*, **27**, 379–423.

Sirigu, A., Daprati, E., Ciancia, S., Giraux, P., Nighoghossian, N., Posada, A. and Haggard, P. (2004) Altered awareness of voluntary action after damage to the parietal cortex. *Nature Neuroscience*, **7**, 80–84.

Smith, E. R. and Semin, G. R. (2004) Socially situated cognition: cognition in its social context. *Advances in Experimental Social Psychology*, **36**, 53–117.

Snyder, L. H., Batista, A. P. and Andersen, R. A. (1997) Coding of intention in the posterior parietal cortex. *Nature*, **386**, 167–170.

Sperber, D. and Wilson, D. (2001) *Relevance: Communication and Cognition*, 2nd edn. Blackwell, Oxford.

Thoenissen, D., Zilles, K. and Toni, I. (2002) Differential involvement of parietal and precentral regions in movement preparation and motor intention. *Journal of Neuroscience*, **22**, 9024–9034.

Tomasello, M., Carpenter, M., Call, J., Behne, T. and Moll, H. (2005) Understanding and sharing intentions: the origins of cultural cognition. *Behavioral and Brain Sciences*, **28**, 675–691.

Toni, I., Thoenissen, D. and Zilles, K. (2001) Movement preparation and motor intention. *Neuroimage*, **14**, S110–S117.

Wegner, D. M. (2002) *The Illusion of Conscious Will*. MIT Press, Cambridge, MA.

Wegner, D. M. (2004) Precis of the illusion of conscious will. *Behavioral and Brain Science*, **27**, 649–659.

Wolpert, D. M. and Ghahramani, Z. (2000) Computational principles of movement neuroscience. *Nature Neuroscience*, **3** (Suppl.), 1212–1217.

Wolpert, D. M., Doya, K. and Kawato, M. (2003) A unifying computational framework for motor control and social interaction. *Philosophical Transactions of the Royal Society of London, B*, **358**, 593–602.

Zacks, J. M., Swallow, K. M., Vettel, J. M. and McAvoy, M. P. (2006) Visual motion and the neural correlates of event perception. *Brain Research*, **1076**, 150–162.

Zilbovicius, M., Meresse, I., Chabane, N., Brunelle, F., Samson, Y. and Boddaert, N. (2006) Autism, the superior temporal sulcus and social perception. *Trends in Neurosciences*, **29**, 359–366.

27

"What was I thinking?"

Developmental and neural connections between theory of mind, memory and the self

Rebecca Saxe

Considerable attention has recently been paid to the idea that we use the same cognitive and neural resources for understanding others' actions and for understanding our own. Within the neuroscience literature, though, the focus has been almost exclusively on one version of this idea: that we have a system for acting, in which knowledge of our own actions is a given, and that we can use this system—through simulation, or 'resonance'—to 'automatically' understand the current actions of others. But a very different system for understanding action is also used for both others' actions and one's own: a theory (or set of concepts) for explaining why people act the way they do. This theory is used both for explaining others' actions ('theory of mind') and for producing justifications of one's own, particularly past, actions. Consistent with this proposal, a set of brain regions is implicated both in attributing mental states to others and to one's self: right and left temporo-parietal junctions and medial prefrontal and medial parietal cortices. This paper describes convergent evidence from developmental psychology and human neuroimaging for three claims: (1) there is a cognitive and neural system specifically for explaining actions (by attributing mental states), that is distinct from the motor system for acting; (2) this same system is used to generate explanations of our own (past or hypothetical) actions and of others' actions; and (3) this mechanism for mental state attribution is also a key component of recalling autobiographical episodic memories.

Introduction

There is a story about a professor emeritus at Columbia who met a student heading the other way on a sidewalk in Manhattan. The two stopped and a heated debate began. When they were finished, the professor said to the student, "Can you tell me, please, which way was I heading when you met me?" "You were heading downtown, Professor," said the student. "Oh good," said the professor, "That means I already ate my lunch."

In the domain of 'understanding human actions', there is an intuitive distinction between one's own actions, and actions executed by others. The neural mechanisms necessary for executing one's own goal-directed action are fairly concrete, including sensory perception of the local environment, motor planning and control. Understanding someone else's action may seem by contrast like a highly abstract—if not semi-miraculous—achievement. Recently, though, many researchers have proposed that this abstract higher cognitive function could have concrete sensorimotor foundations (Gallese and Goldman, 1998; Rizzolatti *et al.*, 2001; Gallese *et al.*, 2004). That is, an observer might understand someone else's action using the same cognitive and neural mechanisms that she uses to understand her own.

The idea is sometimes called the 'motor theory of social cognition' (Jacob and Jeannerod, 2005). We all possess a system for planning and executing our own goal-directed actions, and for doing so based on our perception of the world from our own perspective (e.g. I see the car keys on the table, I grasp the car keys and slide them into my pocket). With only a few adjustments, this system for acting could be used to predict others' actions. The necessary adjustments are (a) at the input, using the other person's (hypothesized) perceptual environment, rather than one's own and (b) at the output, generating a prediction rather than an action (Nichols and Stich, 2003). But the central mechanism—for formulating beliefs based on perceptual evidence, and combining beliefs and desires to generate action plans—would be the very same mechanism that the observer used for forming her own beliefs and planning her own actions. One presumed advantage of the motor theory of social cognition is its parsimony. Action prediction (and 'understanding') could be achieved with cognitive and neural mechanisms that the observer already needed for action planning and execution; we do not need to attribute to the observer a whole extra system for understanding others, a cumbersome and sophisticated conceptual 'theory of mind' (ToM). (For a broader discussion of motor theories of social cognition, and in particular the proposed roles of mirror neurons, see Chapter 20.)

The motor theory of social cognition may be correct for simple cases of observing someone's body motions through space. Nevertheless, there is a great deal of 'action understanding' that this view leaves out. In this chapter, I propose that in the domain of 'understanding human action', the cognitively relevant distinction is not between 'self' and 'other', but between action perception and execution on the one hand, and action explanation (by mental state attribution) on the other (Figure 25.1).

It may help to begin with an example. Imagine that you walk into the room just in time to see me slide your keys into my pocket. There may be motor knowledge (of grasping and placing, for example) that we share, and that that will help you to recognize and predict the dynamics of my action. But why am I taking your keys? Real understanding of my action, in this case, may require you to attribute to me a false belief: namely, I believe that the keys I'm taking are my own. What seems clear is that this explanation of my action does not rest on motor representations. Nothing about my motor plan for the grasp signals that it was caused by a false belief; at the time of grasping I had no experience that my belief was false. After the fact, though (perhaps after you have squawked in indignation), I can explain my action in exactly the same terms that you do. I can now apologize, explaining that I took your keys because I thought they were mine.

	Acting **(Motor Planning and** **Execution)**	**Action Explanation** **(Mental state** **attribution)**
Self	(1) Plan and execute goal directed actions	(4) Attribute mental states to self (usually past or hypothetical)
Other	(2) Perceive others' actions (as goal-directed)	(3) Attribute mental states to others

Figure 27.1 An 'action understanding' square. The traditional intuition divides this square horizontally, between 'self' and 'other'. Recently, neuroscientists and philosophers have argued that perceiving others' actions as goal-directed (2) relies on some of the same cognitive and neural mechanisms as planning and executing one's own actions (1). The transition in early childhood from just recognizing actions as goal-directed (2) to explaining action by attributing mental states to the actor (3) has been studied intensively by developmental psychologists. Furthermore, the ability to attribute mental states to oneself in order to explain past actions (4) develops simultaneously with the ability to attribute the same mental states to others (3). The current paper describes converging developmental and neural evidence, suggesting that the cognitively relevant distinction is the vertical one, between systems for acting and those for action explanation.

When we explain actions, we go beyond the observed motions and motor plans, to actively reconstruct the relevant contents of the actor's mind. That is, we use a ToM to explain others' actions, and also to explain and often to justify our own past and hypothetical actions (Gopnik and Wellman, 1992). Notably, while the motor theory of social cognition requires only that the observer be able to form beliefs based on perceptual evidence, the ToM mechanism requires that the observer have a concept of belief, and a causal theory of how people (including herself) form beliefs based on perceptual evidence.

In the current paper, I will describe convergent evidence from developmental psychology and human neuroimaging for three claims: (1) there is a cognitive and neural system for explaining actions (via mental state attribution), that is distinct from the motor system for acting; (2) this same system is used to generate explanations of our own (past or hypothetical) actions, as well as for others' actions; and (3) this mechanism for mental state attribution is a key component of recalling autobiographical episodic memories.

Theory of mind for others

As in my toy example of the stolen keys, it is when the actor has a false belief that the action explanation based on a mature ToM most obviously diverges from predictions based on motor planning and facts about the local environment (Dennett, 1978). For this reason, false beliefs figure heavily in the study of ToM development. In the basic design, a child watches while a puppet places an object in location A. The puppet leaves the scene and the object is transferred to location B. The puppet returns and the child is asked to predict where the puppet will look for the object. Three-year-olds think the puppet will look in location B, where the object actually is; older children think the puppet will look in location A, where the puppet last saw the object (Wimmer and Perner, 1983; Wellman *et al.*, 2001).

The false belief task is the most famous measure of the developing ToM, but the same change in children's understanding of mental states is evident in a range of tasks. Three-year-olds, for example, do not yet have differentiated concepts of 'not knowing' and 'getting it wrong', as illustrated elegantly by Ruffman (1996). A child and an adult observer ('A') are seated in front of two dishes of beads. The round dish contains red and green beads, while the square dish contains only yellow beads. Both A and the child watch while a bead from the round dish is moved under cover into an opaque bag. The child, but not A, knows that the chosen bead was green. Then the child is asked "What colour does A think the bead in the bag is?" The correct answer is that A does not know, or (even better) that A thinks it is red or green (but not yellow), Overwhelmingly, though, the children report that A thinks the bead is red. Note that this answer is not simply random: none of the children said A thinks that the bead is yellow. Rather, the actual result is best explained by an inaccurate generalization in the child's developing ToM: "Ignorance means you get it wrong" (Ruffman, 1996). Since A is ignorant of which bead was chosen from the round dish, A must think that it was the wrong colour, a red one.

Another example of young children's incomplete theory of beliefs concerns the sources of knowledge (Wimmer *et al.*, 1988; O'Neill *et al.*, 1992). One early notion of the relationship between mind and world is of a direct unmediated connection (Perner, 1991); on this conception, all features of an object are equally accessible to any mind that contacts that object. Thus, 3-year-olds expect that people can distinguish between a heavy and a light ball just as well by looking at the balls as by lifting them (Burr and Hofer, 2002). Note that this aspect of young children's ToM does not correspond at all to their own experience of gaining knowledge through acting. Rather, it again reflects a simplified heuristic that young children can use in action explanation: people learn about objects through (undifferentiated) perceptual contact.

It would certainly be misleading to claim that 5-year-olds 'have' a ToM whereas 3-year-olds do not have one (Bloom and German, 2000). Three-year-olds infer a character's desires from his behavior, and give systematic (albeit wrong) answers to false belief tasks, suggesting that these children do not hesitate to explain and predict people's actions based on inferred mental states. Moreover, even much younger children and infants make inferences about people's intentions, perceptions, and emotions, and the interrelations among these mental states and actions (e.g. Harris *et al.*, 1989; Repacholi and Gopnik, 1997; Phillips *et al.*, 2002). For example, 2-year-old children understand the basic relationship between desires and emotions. Given a story about a boy who wanted a puppy and then got one, 2-year-olds choose a happy face to show how the boy feels, but they choose a sad face if the boy who got a puppy had wanted a bunny (Wellman and Woolley, 1990; Wellman *et al.*, 1995).

Nor, obviously, could it be that 3-year-olds are incapable of having false beliefs, or be unfamiliar with the experience of ignorance themselves. Quite the contrary.

What, then, is the conceptual advance that distinguishes 5-year-olds from younger children and infants? The crucial difficulty for the younger children seems to lie in understanding how a belief or perception can represent a state of affairs that is different from the real one. They lack a clear distinction between what a person's mental state is about (the state of affairs to which the belief or perception refers) and how that state of the affairs is represented (what the person believes or perceives to be true of it; Perner and Ruffman, 1995). This distinction allows the older children to understand how people's mental representations of the world may differ from the way the world really is. As a result, 5-year-olds are sometimes said to have (and 3-year-olds to lack) a *representational* ToM.

In all, these results from developmental psychology suggest two broad conclusions about the cognitive systems that we use to understand actions. First, the system for action explanation is distinct from the system for acting. Second, this system for action explanation includes at least two distinct components: an early-developing component that allows children to explain actions based on simple perceptions, desires, and emotions, and a distinct, later-developing component that includes an understanding of representational mental states like belief. In the rest of this section, I will discuss recent results from functional imaging studies that strongly corroborate these two claims.

Following the tradition in developmental psychology, many of the early neuroimaging investigations of ToM required subjects to attribute false beliefs to people in stories or cartoons (Fletcher *et al.*, 1995; Goel *et al.*, 1995; Gallagher *et al.*, 2000; Saxe and Kanwisher, 2003; for a defense of verbal stories as stimuli in experiments on ToM, see Saxe, 2006a). A very reliable set of brain regions was implicated in the 'false belief' condition of each study (Figure 27.2), including right and left temporo-parietal junction, medial parietal cortex (including posterior cingulate and precuneus), and medial prefrontal cortex (not including anterior cingulate cortex). Note that none of these regions is implicated in the observer's own motor system (or in the so-called 'mirror system').

Before we conclude that these brain regions constitute a distinct neural system for ToM, of course, we must eliminate a whole range of alternative interpretations. There is more to solving a false belief task than a concept of belief, and there is more to a concept of belief than passing the false belief task (Bloom and German, 2000). In particular, attributing a false belief to another person depends heavily on two cognitive capacities that are not specific to ToM: inhibitory control and language (especially complement syntax).

In the classic false belief task, the subject must be able to juggle two competing representations of reality (the actual state of affairs and the reality represented in the protagonist's head) and to inhibit an incorrect but compelling answer (the true location of the object). In development, performance on false belief tasks is correlated with the child's overall ability to select among competing responses (Carlson and Moses, 2001; Carlson *et al.*, 2004). When the inhibitory demands of the task are reduced (e.g. if the object is destroyed instead of moved, or if the child does not herself know the new location

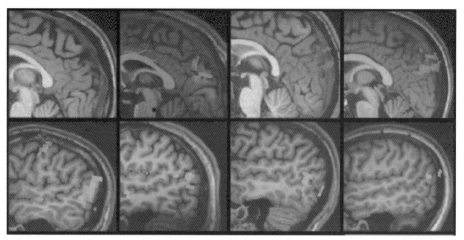

Figure 27.2 Two regions implicated in theory of mind, the medial precuneus (red) and the right temporo-parietal junction (green), in four individual subjects. Shown are medial and right lateral sagittal slices from the whole-brain contrast, False belief > False photo stories (e.g. Saxe and Kanwisher, 2003, Experiment 2), in each individual $p < 0.001$ uncorrected, $k > 10$. See color plate section.

of the object), children of all ages perform better (Wellman *et al.*, 2001). Finally, young children who fail the false belief task also fail control tasks that place comparable demands on executive function but do not include any reference to other minds or mental states (Zaitchik, 1990; Roth and Leslie, 1998). In a protocol closely matched to the false belief task, a photograph is taken of the object in location A, the object is moved to location B, and children are asked where the object will be in the photograph. No mental state understanding is required but 3-year-olds fail the task. In fact, typically developing children find the false photograph task harder than the false belief task (Zaitchik, 1990); by contrast, children with autism solve the false photograph task, but fail the false belief task (Leslie and Thaiss, 1992).

A brain region distinctly implicated in ToM must be specifically recruited for reasoning about beliefs, and must not show a high response during logically similar control conditions, like the false photograph task. Saxe and Kanwisher (2003, Experiment 2) therefore presented to subjects verbal stories modeled on the false belief and false photograph tasks. Twenty-eight subjects in the scanner read 24 short narratives about a representation (12 about a belief, 12 about a physical representation like a photo, drawing or map) that did not correspond to reality, usually because the content of the representation became outdated. Subjects then answered a fill-in-the-blank question either about the representation or about reality. None of the brain regions implicated in ToM showed a high response to the control condition, consistent with the hypothesis that these regions respond specifically during attribution of beliefs, and not to the inhibitory demands of the task *per se* (see also R. Saxe, L. Schulz and Y. Jiang, unpublished data; for a summary of story stimuli that do, and do not, elicit a robust response in the most selective ToM regions, see the Appendices).

Another capacity that is correlated with false belief task performance in development is language. In a striking example, deaf children of hearing parents (that is, whose parents are non-native signers) are selectively delayed in passing the false belief task (e.g. Peterson and Siegal, 1999). These children have similar difficulty even on nonverbal tests of false belief understanding, suggesting that the delay does not reflect the language demands of the tasks themsleves (e.g. Figueras-Costas and Harris, 2001). Moreover, even after accounting for the child's own skill with sign language, the child's performance on the false belief task is independently predicted by the *mother's* proficiency with sign language, and specifically her use of mental state signs (Moeller and Schick, 2006). Deaf children of deaf parents (native signers), by contrast, are not delayed (de Villiers, 2005). Clearly, linguistic exposure influences ToM development, but the mechanism underlying this influence remains controversial. One possibility is that this link specifically depends on syntactical development. Proficiency with particular grammatical structures (especially sentence complements, such as 'He knows that the cup is on the table' or 'The photograph shows that the chocolate was in the box') are necessary for forming sentences about some mental states, and therefore might be necessary for forming thoughts about other minds (de Villiers, 2000).

Given these results, we must eliminate the possibility that the brain regions implicated in ToM are instead involved in forming specific syntactic constructions, like sentence complements. To some degree, the false photograph control task answers this concern, since sentences about physical representations often use sentence complements. Another way to test this hypothesis is to present stimuli that imply the protagonists' false belief, but do not include any explicit statements of beliefs. Saxe and Kanwisher (2003, Experiment 1) did this by presenting to the subjects verbal stories that merely described a sequence of actions by a character. No mental states were explicitly mentioned, but the sequence of actions could most readily be explained in light of the protagonist's belief. The control stories were sequences of mechanical or physical events that similarly required subjects to infer an unstated physical causal process. As predicted, the right and left temporo-parietal junctions, medial parietal and medial prefrontal cortices showed a stronger BOLD response during the implied-belief stories than during the implied-physical stories. Seven subjects participated in both experiments in this study, so that we could directly compare the results of stimuli containing no sentence complement syntax (Experiment 1) versus complement syntax (Experiment 2), and mental states versus physical states. In individual subjects, only the contrast of mental versus physical content determined the recruitment of these 'ToM' brain regions. Gallagher *et al.* (2000) reached the same conclusion by comparing stories about false beliefs with nonverbal single-frame cartoons that required subjects to attribute beliefs to the characters. Again, the same brain regions were recruited when subjects attributed beliefs to the characters, independent of modality.

In all, these early fMRI investigations provide considerable convergent evidence for the first prediction derived from the trajectory of ToM development. There are brain regions specifically implicated in attributing mental states, and these brain regions are not part of the observer's own motor system. There is stronger evidence for a link between these brain regions and the development of ToM, though. As described above, the developmental evidence suggests that there are at least two components of ToM: an early-developing component that includes concepts of desires and perceptions, and a later-developing component that allows children to master the concept of a representational mental state. Of course, the most direct way to test this hypothesis would be to scan the brains of children; but even in the absence of pediatric neuroimaging, these developmental data do have implications for observations in the brains of adults. In our more recent studies, we have found that one of the brain regions implicated in ToM, the right temporo-parietal junction, reflects just the later-developing component.

To provide a more specific characterization of the brain regions implicated in ToM, Saxe and Powell (in press) gave subjects stories to read from three conditions, each highlighting a different aspect of reasoning about another person: (1) 'appearance' stories described representing socially relevant information about a person that is visible from the outside, like the person's clothing and hair colour; (2) 'bodily sensations' stories elicited attribution of early-developing ToM concepts: invisible, subjective, internal states that do not include a representational content, like hunger and tiredness; and (3) 'thoughts' stories described the contents of another person's thoughts or beliefs, specifically tapping the later-developing component of ToM. In the same experimental session, subjects also read the original false belief and false photograph stories as a baseline, and so that we could identify the regions implicated in ToM in each individual brain.

The three new conditions allowed us to contrast three different hypotheses about the functional profile of each region.

1. A region involved in any general aspect of social cognition, including detecting the presence of a person in the story, or tracking information about people, would show a high response in all three story conditions, since all included socially relevant information about a protagonist.

2. A region involved in the attribution of internal, subjective states that can be used to explain action (that is, in ToM as a whole, including both early- and late-developing components) would show a low response to the 'appearance' stories, which do not include any subjective states, and a high response to both 'thoughts' and 'bodily sensations'. The 'bodily sensations' stories elicited the highest ratings of 'empathy for or identification with' the protagonist in the story, so a high response specifically in that condition might also reflect feeling for, or with, the protagonist.

3. Only the 'thoughts' stories included representational mental states, so a brain region selectively reflecting the late-developing component of ToM should show a high response only in this condition.

Two other features of the experimental design are worth noting here. First, the beliefs described in the 'thoughts' stories were not necessarily false. Although false belief tasks provide a good behavioral measure of the development of ToM, the notion of a representational mental state applies equally to true and false beliefs. Indeed, in order for action explanation to function, we must assume that people possess (and we must attribute to them) mostly true beliefs, most of the time. Second, the hypotheses identified here can only be distinguished if subjects stick relatively closely to the actual content of the stories. If they so desired, subjects could of course attribute all sorts of beliefs and desires to the people mentioned in all three kinds of stories. These hypotheses assume that our ToM is relatively economical with its mental states attributions. One possible alternative is that all of the possible mental states of another person are automatically computed, with a separate, later mechanism selecting among these representations (Leslie, 2000; Leslie et al., 2005).

Saxe and Powell (in press) tested these three hypotheses in all four of the brain regions associated with ToM. In two brain regions, the results were unambiguous. The first was medial prefrontal cortex (MPFC, here divided into three subregions, see also German et al., 2004), which showed exactly the profile predicted by hypothesis 1: an equally high BOLD response to all story conditions that describe people. Thus, while MPFC is clearly implicated in some aspect of social cognition, its role is not restricted to the attribution of internal states in order to explain actions (that is, to ToM; for specific proposals about the role of MPFC see Frith and Amodio, 2005; Mitchell et al., 2006; Saxe, 2006b).

The other brain region with an unambiguous response profile was the right temporo-parietal junction (RTPJ), which showed the functional profile predicted by hypothesis 3: a high response when subjects read about either true or false beliefs, but a low response (no different from passive rest) when subjects read about false photographs, a person's physical appearance (see also Saxe and Kanwisher, 2003), or even a person's subjective, but nonrepresentational, mental state. (For a discussion of the contributions of the medial parietal region, see below.)

Further evidence for the selectivity of the RTPJ came from a second study, in which the kind of information provided was varied within each story, instead of across stories (Saxe and Wexler, 2005). Subjects read short verbal stories in three sections. The first section ('background') introduced the protagonist and described where s/he lived, or what job s/he had, or what classes s/he was taking. The second section ('mental state') described the protagonist's representational belief or desire. The third section described the 'outcome' for the protagonist. Since the background was presented alone for the first 6 s, the need to attribute mental states was delayed. Consequently, relative to false belief stories in which the mental state content was available immediately, the response in the RTPJ to the new stories was delayed 6 s.

Our data thus suggest a division in the neural system involved in making social judgments about others, with one component (the RTPJ) specifically recruited for the attribution of representational mental states, while a second component (the MPFC) is involved more generally in the consideration of the other person. Further support for this distinction comes from a series of studies of the attribution of personality traits (e.g. Schmitz et al., 2004; Ochsner et al., 2005; Mitchell et al., 2005). In one study, subjects read single words describing human personality traits like 'daring' or 'shy', and judged either (a) whether each word is semantically positive or negative, or (b) whether that trait applies to a specific well-known other (Schmitz et al., 2004). Importantly, personality trait words do not require subjects to attribute any specific mental states to the target. Consistent with the division described above, MPFC (and medial parietal cortex), but not RTPJ, is recruited significantly more for other-attribution than for semantic judgment.

The results described here again highlight a striking convergence between developmental psychology and functional neuroimaging of ToM. Both methods suggest the existence of a cognitive system, specifically for explaining actions in terms of the actor's mental states, that does not overlap with the observer's own system for acting. Furthermore, there is evidence in both cases that the concept of a representational mental state requires a distinct component of ToM that emerges later in development, and that recruits at least one distinct brain region, the RTPJ. All of the evidence described above concerns the attribution of mental states to other people; the next discussion will show that this same mechanism is used to attribute mental states to oneself.

Theory of mind for the self

Having a belief does not require attributing the belief to oneself, and acting because of a set of mental states does not depend on attributing those mental states to oneself. Nevertheless, there are contexts in which we do attribute beliefs to ourselves. Probably the most common context is when we feel called upon to justify actions that might otherwise seem morally dubious, as in the example of the stolen keys that I described at the beginning of the paper. In this example, the action to be justified is an action in the past, and the mental states that caused that action are also in the past. By the time I come to explain what I was thinking, I no longer believe that the keys are mine, or intend to pocket them. A past self is thus in a critical sense just like another person. The mental states that caused that person's action are not directly given in the current motor plan, and so they must be actively reconstructed.

Still, one might imagine that a person would have special privileged access to memories of her own past states, and that these memories could recreate directly the experience of acting sufficiently to obviate the need for reconstruction. For example, if I observed you taking my keys, I would need to infer your false belief from the perceptual context (e.g. room keys all look very similar) and other beliefs I have about how your mind works (e.g. a principle of charity). But if I was the unwitting thief, couldn't I just recall the moment of the theft, and directly re-experience the belief that the keys were mine without any attribution at all?

Results from developmental psychology suggest not (Gopnik, 1993). In a classic study, Gopnik and Astington (1988) gave children two different versions of the false belief task: one in which another person had a false belief, and another in which the child herself first experienced the false belief, and then was asked to report it a few minutes later after learning about the true state of affairs. Children were first shown a clearly identified candy box, and asked what they thought was inside. All children said that there would be candy inside. Next, the experimenter showed them that there were pencils inside. Then the box was closed up. The child was asked either (a) what another child would initially think was in the box, or (b) what they themselves initially thought was in the box. The result was that children showed no advantage for their own false belief, even though they had experienced it only minutes earlier. Moreover, performance on own and other false-belief question was correlated, independently of age (see also Moore *et al.*, 1990).

Similar results have been reported on a range of related tasks. For example, children are no better at reasoning about the sources of their own knowledge than they are at reasoning about the sources of others' knowledge (O'Neill *et al.*, 1992). Between 3 and 5 years old, children become able to distinguish between sources of their own knowledge, like visual perception versus verbal narratives about the same event (Wimmer *et al.*, 1988), and between their own newly learned versus old knowledge, like the meaning of 'maroon' versus 'red' (Taylor *et al.*, 1994).

The social psychologist Daryl Bem, in the late 1960s, reached the same conclusion about adult ToM. He observed that subjects who were asked to explain their own actions often made the same errors as observers who only read about the actions, and used this observation to argue against Cartesian first-person privilege: "If the reports of the observers are identical to those of the subjects themselves, then it is unnecessary to assume that the latter are drawing on "a font of private knowledge"" (Bem, 1967). Bem concluded instead that everyone uses a causal theory (i.e. a ToM) to explain behavior—both their own and other people's.

The absence of a first-person privilege in behavior explanation is particularly clear in the context of behavioral economics and decision making (Nisbett and Wilson, 1977). For example, Johanssen *et al.* (2005) showed subjects two pictures, and asked to pick the more attractive one. They were given the preferred photo, and immediately asked to explain why they chose that one. Through a sleight of hand, the experimenters some-times gave the subject their actual choice, but sometimes gave the unchosen picture. In all, subjects detected the swap very rarely. Remarkably, the justifications that subjects gave for choosing the swapped photograph (which they did *not* choose) were largely indistinguishable from justifications they gave for choosing the one that they did choose, in length, confidence, emotionality, detail, or number of embarrassed laughs. Subjects' own explanations appeared to operate much the way an external observer would, by finding the property of the outcome that could have justified choosing it, rather than by recalling the moment of the choice (seconds earlier) and directly re-experiencing those reasons.

These results make a straightforward prediction for neuroimaging studies of ToM: namely, subjects should not recruit the ToM brain regions when they are acting because of a (false) belief, but these regions should be robustly recruited if the subject is required to explain their action after the fact. Unfortunately, no study has directly tested this prediction. There is one experiment, though, that required subjects to attribute to them-selves not actual past mental states, but hypothetical mental states, in order to explain hypothetical actions (Vogeley *et al.*, 2001). As usual, subjects read short verbal stories about a protagonist. In this case, half of the stories included actions and thoughts described in the second person (e.g. "In the morning, when you leave the hotel, the sky is blue and the sun is shining. So you do not expect it to start raining.") Since these stories describe nonactual events and actions, the subjects cannot directly experience the action plans and mental states described in these stories; instead the subjects must interpret these stories as describing hypothetical actions, and so must actively infer and attribute the mental states that would cause those actions. To fit with the developmental data, these stories should recruit the same brain regions as are implicated in attributing mental states to others. Just as we would predict, Vogeley *et al.* (2001) reported that these second-person stories elicited a significant response (relative to a scrambled baseline) in the RTPJ. In fact, the stories in the second person elicited a significantly higher response in RTPJ than did false belief stories in the third person. Motor regions associated with action planning or execution were not recruited.

The distinction between the RTPJ and the MPFC described for attributions to others is also maintained for attributions to the self. When subjects are required to judge whether personality traits apply to themselves, the same medial prefrontal regions are recruited as when subjects judge whether those traits apply to a familiar other (Schmitz *et al.*, 2004; Ochsner *et al.*, 2005). By contrast, RTPJ response is not observed for personality trait attributions to the self or to another.

Data from developmental psychology and neuroimaging thus converge, to suggest that the very same mechanisms are used for attributing mental states to others and to oneself. Explaining and justifying one's own actions may even be a particularly natural use of this system. In order to attribute a representational mental state to themselves or to others, however, children must have the key insight that minds represent the world from a particular perspective, and that therefore people can form different (and even conflicting) mental representations of the same underlying state of affairs (Harris, 2005). The contrast between different perspectives on a single event may be particularly salient when the two perspectives occur in their own mind at different times. In fact, explaining one own's past action is just a special case; all autobiographical recall may require such attribution of mental states to oneself in the past. In the next section, I therefore turn to links between autobiographical memory and ToM.

Theory of mind and autobiographical memory

Autobiographical memory is more than just current knowledge based on past experience, because an autobiographical or episodic memory includes an identification of the source of the current experience (the recall) in a previous experience of the same person. Two aspects of a representational ToM might be therefore be necessary for episodic/ autobiographical memory. The first is the idea that it is possible to have different perspectives on, or experiences of, the same event. A memory inherently involves having two experiences of one event—the original experience of the event itself, and the later experience of recalling the event. More specifically, at the time of recall, the person must identify the source of the current experience of recall in the previously experienced event. To do so may depend on one dimension of a ToM: an understanding of the sources of knowledge.

Just such a link between the development of ToM and of episodic memory has been proposed by Perner (2001). Perner and Ruffman (1995) tested young children's free recall, along with two other measures: (a) a test of understanding the sources of knowledge, and (b) a test of memory capacity in cued recall, which depends more on familiarity or recognition than on identification of one's own past experiences as such. Children's scores on the ToM task and on free recall correlated with each other but not with performance on the cued recall task. That is, rather than a division between ToM and one cluster of all memory tasks, Perner and Ruffman propose a division between free recall and ToM tasks—both of which require understanding the sources of knowledge—and cued recall, which measures the information gained from past experience, but does not require the attribution of sources.

Understanding the sources of knowledge may help children to distinguish between real autobiographical memories and ideas derived from other sources. Between ages 3 and 5 years, children's memories become much less susceptible to suggestion, and this resistance to suggestion is correlated with performance on false belief tasks (Welch-Ross, 1999). Perner (2001) gave children the chance to learn about an event from one of two sources: direct experience, or indirect evidence. Children placed stickers in a box. In the direct condition, the child was allowed to study each sticker before placing the sticker. In the indirect condition, children wore a blindfold while doing the task, and then saw a video showing the stickers. The children were also assessed on multiple measures of understanding sources of knowledge. Children with poor understanding of sources of knowledge recalled more of the stickers from the indirect experience, while children with the best ToM recalled more of the stickers from the direct experience—presumably by using their autobiographical memories of the original event.

Also noteworthy, most adults' early autobiographical memories are from their fourth year, precisely around the time that children acquire a representational ToM (Wetzler and Sweeney, 1986: cited in Perner, 2001).

In all, developmental evidence suggests a strong relationship (possibly a necessary dependence) between episodic/autobiographical memory and ToM. The implication of this view is that recall of specific episodes should recruit the ToM brain regions even in adults. Just such a pattern of overlap appears to exist in medial parietal cortex, in the precuneus.

As described above, a region in the medial precuneus is reliably recruited in almost all fMRI studies of ToM (Fletcher et al., 1995; Gallagher et al., 2000), and in almost every individual subject in the contrast between false belief stories and false photograph stories (e.g. Saxe and Kanwisher, 2003; Saxe and Wexler, 2005). In the subsequent experiments, the functional profile of the medial parietal region was less selective than the RTPJ for representational mental state attribution. Saxe and Wexler (2005) found no significant delay in the response of the precuneus when 'background' information was presented for the first 6 s of the stories. On the other hand, Saxe and Powell (in press) did find that the response in the precuneus was higher during stories about 'thoughts' than during stories about 'bodily sensations' or about people's 'appearance', but this difference was smaller than that observed in the RTPJ and did not survive a correction for multiple comparisons. In all, there is strong evidence that the medial precuneus is recruited during ToM tasks.

Recently, evidence has also been mounting for a role for the medial precuneus in memory. Medial precuneus activation is associated with successful retrieval of both auditory and visual events (hits–correct rejections: Shannon and Buckner, 2004). There was also greater precuneus activation when the retrieved item was encoded using visual imagery or other deep encoding strategy, relative to shallow encoding (Fletcher *et al.*, 1995). Importantly, recruitment of the precuneus correlates with the same features of episodic memory retrieval that are most closely related to ToM in development. For example, Lundstrom *et al.* (2003, 2005) contrasted simple item recognition (which does not demand the attribution of a previous experience to the self) with recollection of the context of the original encoding event, including the spatial and temporal location of words and pictures during the original presentation. The source retrieval task selectively recruited a region in the medial precuneus. Precuneus activation is observed during retrieval of specific remote autobiographical memory, relative to retrieval of semantic knowledge for the same time period (Addis *et al.*, 2004; Gilboa *et al.*, 2004). Finally, Alzheimer's disease, which leads to impairments in autobiographical memory, also causes amyloid deposition, hypo-metabolism, hypo-activation and tissue atrophy in the medial precuneus (Greicius *et al.*, 2004; Shannon and Buckner, 2004; Buckner *et al.*, 2005; Rombouts *et al.*, 2005; Wang *et al.*, 2006).

Unfortunately, no study to date has directly compared within the same subjects the regions of the precuneus recruited during mental state attribution, and during recall of autobiographical events. But the group results are suggestive. There appears to be a single brain region, in the medial parietal cortex, implicated both in attribution of explicit mental states to others, and in the recall of events from one's own life—ranging from trivial recent events like a word-learning experience in the laboratory to meaningful remote personal events—but not in familiarity-based recognition. A similar pattern of correlations is observed in development. This convergence again supports the identification of a distinct cognitive and neural system involved in the attribution of mental states to the self and others, and that does not depend on the motor system for acting.

Conclusions

In the past few years, 'understanding others' actions' has seemed to some to be the paradigmatic case of a higher cognition function that is reducible to sensorimotor foundations. Observers understand others' actions in the same way that they understand their own. In this paper, I have argued that this formula, though plausible, conflates an important distinction between two distinct cognitive and neural mechanisms for 'understanding' action: the 'sensorimotor' mechanisms for planning, executing, and perceiving goal-directed actions, and distinct 'higher cognitive' mechanisms for explaining actions in terms of mental states. Both of these ways of understanding action can be applied to others' actions, and to one's own. The relevant distinction is therefore not between self and other, but between acting and action explanation.

Acknowledgments

Thanks especially to Nancy Kanwisher for wide-ranging discussions during the writing of this chapter. The fMRI resources used for the studies described here were supported by NCRR grant 41RR14075, the MIND Institute, and the Athinoula A. Martinos Center for Biomedical Imaging.

References

Addis, D. R., Moscovitch, M., Crawley, A. P. and McAndrews, M. P. (2004) Qualities of autobiographical memory modulate hippocampal activation during retrieval: preliminary findings of an fMRI study. *Brain Cognition*, **54**, 145–147.

Bem, D. J. (1967) Self-perception: an alternative interpretation of cognitive dissonance phenomena. *Psychological Review*, **74**, 183–2000.

Bloom, P. and German, T. P. (2000) Two reasons to abandon the false belief task as a test of theory of mind. *Cognition*, **77**, B25–31.

Buckner, R. L., Snyder, A. Z., Shannon, B. J., LaRossa, G., Sachs, R., Fotenos, A. F. *et al.* (2005) Molecular, structural, and functional characterization of Alzheimer's disease: evidence for a relationship between default activity, amyloid and memory. *Journal of Neuroscience*, **25**, 7709–7717.

Burr, J. E. and Hofer, B. K. (2002) Personal epistemology and theory of mind: deciphering young children's beliefs about knowledge and knowing. *New Ideas in Psychology*, **20**(2–3), 199–224.

Carlson, S. M. and Moses, L. J. (2001) Individual differences in inhibitory control and children's theory of mind. *Child Development*, **72**, 1032–1053.

Carlson, S. M., Moses, L. J. and Hix, H. R. (1998) The role of inhibitory processes in young children's difficulties with deception and false belief. *Child Development*, **69**, 672–691.

Carlson, S. M., Moses, L. J. and Claxton, L. J. (2004) Individual differences in executive functioning and theory of mind: an investigation of inhibitory control and planning ability. *Journal of Experimental Child Psychology*, **87**, 299–319.

de Villiers, J. (2000) Language and theory of mind: what are the developmental relationships? In Baron-Cohen, S., Tager-Flusberg, H. and Cohen, D. J. (eds), *Understanding Other Minds*. Oxford University Press, Oxford.

de Villiers, P. (2005) The role of language in theory-of-mind development: what deaf children tell us. In Astington J. W. and Baird, J. A. (eds), *Why Language Matters for Theory of Mind*, pp. 266–297. Oxford University Press, Oxford.

Dennett, D. (1978) Beliefs about beliefs. *Behavioural and Brain Sciences*, **1**, 568–567.

Figueras-Costa, B. and Harris, P. L. (2001) Theory of mind development in deaf children: a nonverbal test of false-belief understanding. *Journal of Deaf Students and Deaf Education*, **6**, 92–102.

Fletcher, P. C., Happé, F., Frith, U., Backer, S. C. and Dolan, R. J. (1995) Other minds in the brain: a functional imaging study of 'theory of mind' in story comprehension. *Cognition*, **57**, 109–128.

Gallagher, H. L. *et al.* (2000) Reading the mind in cartoons and stories: an fMRI study of 'theory of mind' in verbal and nonverbal tasks. *Neuropsychologia*, **38**, 11–21.

Gallese, V. and Goldman, A. (1998) Mirror neurons and the simulation theory of mind-reading. *Trends in Cognitive Sciences*, **2**, 493–501.

Gallese, V. *et al.* (2004) A unifying view of the basis of social cognition. *Trends in Cognitive Sciences*, **8**, 396–403.

Gilboa, A., Winocur, G., Grady, C. L., Hevenor, S. J. and Moscovitch, M. (2004) Remembering our past: functional neuroanatomy of recollection of recent and very remote personal events. *Cerebral Cortex*, **14**, 1214–1225.

Goel, V., Grafman, J., Sadato, N. and Hallett, M. (1995) Modeling other minds. *Neuroreport*, **6**, 1741–1746.

Gopnik, A. (1993) How we know our minds: the illusion of first-person knowledge of intentionality. *Behavioral and Brain Sciences*, **16**, 1–14.

Gopnik, A. and Astington, J. W. (1988) Children's understanding of representational change and its relation to the understanding of false belief and the appearance–reality distinction. *Child Development*, **59**, 26–37.

Gopnik, A. and Wellman, H. M. (1992) Why the child's theory of mind really is a theory. *Mind and Language*, **7**(1–2), 145–171.

Greicius, M. D., Srivastava, G., Reiss, A. L. and Menon, V. (2004) Default-mode network activity distinguishes Alzheimer's disease from healthy aging: evidence from functional MRI. *Proceedings of the National Academy of Sciences of the USA*, **101**, 4637–4642.

Harris, P. L. (2005) Conversation, pretense and theory of mind. In Astington, J. W. and Baird, J. A. P. (eds), *Why Language Matters for Theory of Mind*, pp. 70–83. Oxford University Press, Oxford.

Harris, P. L., Johnson, C., Hutton, D., Andrews, G. and Cooke, T. (1989) Young children's theory of mind and emotion. *Cognition and Emotion*, **3**, 379–400.

Jacob, P. and Jeannerod, M. (2005) The motor theory of social cognition: a critique. *Trends in Cognitive Science*, **9**, 21–25.

Leslie A. (2000) 'Theory of mind' as a mechanism of selective attention. In Gazzaniga, M. (ed.), *The New Cognitive Neurosciences*, pp. 1235–1247. MIT Press, Cambridge, MA.

Leslie, A. and Thaiss, L. (1992) Domain specificity in conceptual development. *Cognition*, **43**, 225–251.

Leslie, A. M., German, T. P. and Polizzi, P. (2005) Belief–desire reasoning as a process of selection. *Cognitive Psychology*, **50**, 45–85.

Lundstrom, B. N., Petersson, K. M., Andersson, J., Johansson, M., Fransson, P. and Ingvar, M. (2003) Isolating the retrieval of imagined pictures during episodic memory: activation of the left precuneus and left prefrontal cortex. *Neuroimage*, **20**, 1934–1943.

Lundstrom, B. N., Ingvar, M. and Petersson, K. M. (2005) The role of precuneus and left inferior frontal cortex during source memory episodic retrieval. *Neuroimage*, **27**, 824–834.

Mitchell, J. P., Macrae, C. N. and Banaji, M. R. (2005) Forming impressions of people versus inanimate objects: social-cognitive processing in the medial prefrontal cortex. *Neuroimage*, **15**, 251–257.

Mitchell, J. P., Banaji, M. R. and Macrae, C. N. (2006) The link between social cognition and self-referential thought in the medial prefrontal cortex. *Journal of Cognitive Neuroscience*, **17**, 1306–1315.

Moeller, M. P. and Schick, B. (2006) Relations between maternal input and theory of mind understanding in deaf children. *Child Development*, **77**, 751–766.

Nichols, S. and Stich, S. (2003) *Mindreading: An Integrated Account of Pretence, Self-awareness, and Understanding of Other Minds*. Oxford University Press, Oxford.

Ochsner, K. N., Beer, J. S., Robertson, E. R., Cooper, J. C., Gabrieli, J. D., Kihsltrom, J. F. and D'Esposito, M. (2005) The neural correlates of direct and reflected self-knowledge. *Neuroimage*, **28**, 797–814.

O'Neill, D. *et al.* (1992) Young children's understanding of the role that sensory experiences play in knowledge acquisition. *Child Development*, **63**, 474–491.

Perner, J. (1991) *Understanding the Representational Mind*. MIT Press, Cambridge, MA.

Perner, J. (2001) Episodic memory: essential distinctions and developmental implications. In Moore, C. and Lemmon, K. (ed.), *Self in Time: Developmental Perspectives*, pp. 181–202. Erlbaum, Hillsdale, NJ.

Perner, J. and Ruffman, T. (1995) Episodic memory an autonoetic consciousness: developmental evidence and a theory of childhood amnesia. *Journal of Experimental Child Psychology*, **59**, 516–548.

Peterson, C. C. and Siegal, M. (1999) Representing inner worlds: theory of mind in autistic, deaf and normal hearing children. *Psychological Science*, **10**, 126–129.

Phillips, A. T., Wellman, H. M. and Spelke, E. S. (2002) Infants' ability to connect gaze and emotional expression to intentional action. *Cognition*, **85**, 53–78.

Repacholi, B. M. and Gopnik, A. (1997) Early reasoning about desires: evidence from 14- and 18-montholds. *Developmental Psychology*, **33**, 12–21.

Rombouts, S. A., Barkhof, F., Goekoop, R., Stam, C. J. and Scheltens, P. (2005) Altered resting state networks in mild cognitive impairment and mild Alzheimer's disease: an fMRI study. *Human Brain Mapping*, **26**, 231–239.

Roth, D. and Leslie, A. M. (1998) Solving belief problems: toward a task analysis. *Cognition*, **66**, 1–31.

Ruffman, T. (1996) Do children understand the mind by means of simulation or a theory? Evidence from their understanding of inference. *Mind and Language*, **11**, 387–414.

Saxe, R. (2006a) Why and how to use fMRI to study theory of mind. *Brain Research*, **1079**, 57–65.

Saxe, R. (2006b) Uniquely human social cognition. *Current Opinion in Neurobiology*, **16**, 235–239.

Saxe, R. and Powell, L. It's the thought that counts: specific brain regions for one component of theory of mind. *Psychological Science*, in press.

Saxe, R. and Kanwisher, N. (2003) People thinking about thinking people: fMRI studies of theory of mind. *Neuroimage*, **19**, 1835–1842.

Saxe, R. and Wexler, A. (2005) Making sense of another mind: the role of the right temporo-parietal junction. *Neuropsychologia*, 43, 1391–1399.

Saxe, R., Schulz, L. and Jiang, Y. (submitted) Reading minds versus following rules: dissociating theory of mind and executive control in the brain.

Schmitz, T. W., Kawahara-Baccus, T. N. and Johnson, S. C. (2004) Metacognitive evaluation, self-relevance, and the right prefrontal cortex. *Neuroimage*, **22**, 941–947.

Shannon, B. J., Buckner, R. L. (2004) Functional–anatomic correlates of memory retrieval that suggest nontraditional processing roles for multiple distinct regions within posterior parietal cortex. *Journal of Neuroscience*, **24**, 10084–10092.

Taylor, M., Esbensen, B. M. and Bennett, R. T. (1994) Children's understanding of knowledge acquisition: the tendency for children to report that they have always known what they have just learned. *Child Development*, **65**, 1581–604.

Vogeley, K., Bussfeld, P., Newen, A., Herrmann, S., Happe, F. *et al.* (2001) Mind reading: neural mechanisms of theory of mind and self-perspective. *Neuroimage*, **14**, 170–181.

Wang, L., Zang, Y., He, Y., Liang, M., Zhang, X., Tian, L., Wu, T., Jiang, T. and Li, K. (2006) Changes in hippocampal connectivity in the early stages of Alzheimer's disease: evidence from resting state fMRI. *Neuroimage*, **31**, 496–504.

Welch-Ross, M. K. (1999). Preschoolers' understanding of mind: implications for suggestibility. *Cognitive Development*, **14**, 101–132.

Wellman, H. M. and Woolley, J. D. (1990) From simple desires to ordinary beliefs: the early development of everyday psychology. *Cognition*, **35**, 245–275.

Wellman, H. M., Harris, P. L., Banerjee, M. and Sinclair, A. (1995) Early understanding of emotion: evidence from natural language. *Cognition and Emotion*, **9**, 117–149.

Wellman, H. M., Cross, D. and Watson, J. (2001) Meta-analysis of theory-of-mind development: the truth about false belief. *Child Development*, **72**, 655–684.

Wimmer, H. and Perner, J. (1983) Beliefs about beliefs: representation and constraining function of wrong beliefs in young children's understanding of deception. *Cognition*, **13**, 103–128.

Wimmer, H. *et al.* (1988) Children's understanding of informational access as a source of knowledge. *Child Development*, **59**, 386–396.

Zaitchik, D. (1990) When representations conflict with reality: the preschooler's problem with false beliefs and "false" photographs. *Cognition*, **35**, 41–68.

Appendix A. Stimuli eliciting a robust response in the right temporo-parietal junction

1. (False beliefs.) Anne made lasagna in the blue dish. After Anne left, Ian came home and ate the lasagna. Then he filled the blue dish with spaghetti and replaced it in the fridge. Anne thinks the blue dish contains (choose one) spaghetti/lasagna. (Saxe and Kanwisher, 2003, Experiment 2.)

2. (Beliefs—not false.) Kate knew her colleague was very punctual and always came to work by 9:00. One day, he still wasn't in at 9:30. Since he was never late, Kate assumed he was home sick. (Saxe and Powell, 2006.)

3. (False beliefs—no mental state verbs.) A boy is making a papier maché project for his art class. He spends hours ripping newspaper into even strips. Then he goes out to buy flour. His mother comes home and throws all the newspaper strips away. (Saxe and Kanwisher, 2003, Experiment 1.)

4. (Mental states that are unexpected, given other information about the protagonist.) [Background: Your friend Carla lives in San Francisco. She has a top position at a large computer company there. She has been working at the same corporation for over 10 years.] Carla has always told you that she wants a husband who would expect her to stay at home as a housewife, instead of having her own career. (Saxe and Wexler, 2005.)

5. (Mental states described in the second person.) You went to London for a weekend trip and you would like to visit some museums and different parks around London. In the morning, when you leave the hotel, the sky is blue and the sun is shining. So you do not expect it to start raining. However, walking around in a big park later, the sky becomes grey and it starts to rain heavily. You forgot your umbrella. (Vogeley et al., 2001.)

Appendix B. Stimuli not eliciting a robust response in the right temporo-parietal junction

1. (False physical representations.) This map shows the ground floor plan. A photocopy was sent to the architect yesterday. The map initially had a flaw: the kitchen door was missing. It was added to the map this morning. The architect's photocopy (choose one) includes/doesn't include … the kitchen door. (Saxe and Kanwisher, 2003, Experiment 2.)

2. (Physical inferences.) The night was warm and dry. There had not been a cloud anywhere for days. The moisture was certainly not from rain. And yet, in the early morning, the long grasses were dripping with cool water. (Saxe and Kanwisher, 2003, Experiment 1.)

3a. (Descriptions of visible facts about people.) Harry looks just like a math professor. He wears dark old cardigans with holes in the elbows, corduroy trousers and brown loafers over green argyle socks. The shoes Harry wears are (choose one) brown/green. (Saxe and Kanwisher, 2003, Experiment 2.)

3b. (Visible facts that convey social information.) Joe was a heavy-set man, with a gut that fell over his belt. He was balding and combed his blonde hair over the top of his head. His face was pleasant, with large brown eyes. (Saxe and Powell, 2006.)

4. (Social background information about a person.) Your friend Carla lives in San Francisco. She has a top position at a large computer company there. She has been working at the same corporation for over 10 years. (Saxe and Wexler, 2005.)

5. (Bodily sensations—subjective but not representational states.) Marcus had been sick for three days. He had felt weak and had a high fever. On the fourth day his fever broke, and he woke up feeling cool and alert. (Saxe and Powell, 2006.)

Name Index

Subject Index

Please note that references to non-textual materials such as Figures will be in italic print.